Risk Management, Speculation, and Derivative Securities

Risk Management, Speculation, and Derivative Securities

Geoffrey Poitras

Faculty of Business Administration
Simon Fraser University
Burnaby, B.C., Canada

ACADEMIC PRESS
An imprint of Elsevier Science

Amsterdam   Boston   London   New York   Oxford   Paris
San Diego   San Francisco   Singapore   Sydney   Tokyo

Academic Press
An imprint of Elsevier Science.
525 B Street, Suite 1900, San Diego, California 92101-4495, USA
http://www.academicpress.com

Academic Press
84 Theobalds Road, London WC1X 8RR, UK
http://www.academicpress.com

Library of Congress Catalog Card Number: 2002104746

International Standard Book Number: 0-12-558822-4

PRINTED IN THE UNITED STATES OF AMERICA
02   03   04   05   06   07   MM   9   8   7   6   5   4   3   2   1

To my students: past, present, and future.

CONTENTS

PART II

Futures and Forward Contracts

5 The Mechanics of Spread Trading

6 Risk Management: Hedging and Diversification

PART **III**

Options Contracts

7 **Option Concepts**

8 **Option Valuation**

9 Application of Option Valuation Techniques

PREFACE

This book covers the following general topics: (1) the advanced application of risk management products; (2) assessment of methods for managing and evaluating risk; and (3) the use of derivative securities for maximizing firm value. Using selected chapters and sections, it is possible to use this book as a text in advanced courses on derivative securities, financial risk management, and international financial management. Yet, taken as a whole, this book goes beyond a textbook-level discussion. The primary focus of the book is pedagogical, to provide instruction on the important but often overlooked connection between risk management and speculation. A central theme is to demonstrate that effective risk management requires an in-depth understanding of speculative strategies.

To this end, this book aims to provide a unified treatment of important concepts and techniques useful in applying derivative securities in both risk management and speculative trading. Some of the techniques examined are well known, such as the Black-Scholes option pricing methodology. However, the extensions to specific situations, such as speculative trading strategies, are not. Other techniques examined in the book are either ignored or given too brief a treatment in conventional texts. This book is not intended to provide a comprehensive introduction to derivative securities. There are many excellent sources that contain the relevant background material. This book aims to proceed beyond an introductory treatment of derivative securities in order to have additional space and time to deal with more advanced topics. By design, this involves approaching the subject matter from a somewhat different perspective.

Much of the discussion revolves around the complementarity of the risk management decision problem and the speculative trader's decision problem. More precisely, it is demonstrated that optimal risk management decisions involve a speculative component; optimal risk management involves making speculative decisions. Hence, understanding of optimal strategies for speculative trading can assist in formulating appropriate risk management solutions. In turn, optimal speculation can be approached as a form of risk management decision problem, where the risk being managed arises from the speculative trading strategy. (As a practical illustration, this is the essence of the strategies employed by numerous hedge funds.) All this requires that careful attention be given to establishing a preliminary connection between risk management and speculation before proceeding to details of specific activities.

The book is divided into three parts. The first part deals with the general framework for risk management and speculation using derivative securities. The second and third parts deal with specific applications to forward contracts and options. Supplemented with components from the other two parts, each part is approximately equal to the material that can be contained in a one semester, senior undergraduate or Master's level course. A considerable amount of investments background is assumed at various points up to, say, the level of Alexander and Sharpe's book, *Investments* (1990). While at some point in the Options chapters (and associated Appendices) specialized mathematical knowledge is assumed, in general only basic algebra and calculus are needed to understand the discussion. Basic concepts are usually reviewed but without considerable explanation.

While this book is aimed at providing material relevant for academic presentations of derivative securities, the subject matter is also selected with the practitioner in mind. A substantial amount of the material covered is illustrated by practical applications involving what are, in many cases, complicated arbitrage-based trading strategies. Considerable discussion is given to designing derivative security trading strategies based on the underlying arbitrage relationships. Specific attention is given to covered interest arbitrage and cash-and-carry arbitrages for metals. In order to accurately understand the concepts, numerous price quotes are used to illustrate the main concepts.

RELATION TO OTHER BOOKS IN THE FIELD

The title of the book can be used to make a useful connection to where this book fits within the academic landscape. The subject of risk management spans a range of disciplines, including Management Science, Actuarial Studies, Strategic Management, Finance, Environmental Studies, and Medical Science. The inclusion of derivative securities in the title is intended to restrict the discussion to risk management situations where derivative securities can be used. This extends the scope beyond financial risk management to include strategic business risk management but would not include, say, industrial engineering and biomedical applications. This permits the complementarity in the various theoretical approaches used to model the risk management process to be examined. Yet, even by restricting comparisons to books on financial risk management, there is still a considerable number and variation of texts available for comparison. Within this range are books on managing credit risk, e.g., Shaeffer (2000); value at risk, e.g., Jorion (2001); financial engineering, e.g., Mason *et al.* (1995) and Stulz (2001); as well as the more general texts on derivative securities, e.g., Wilmott (1998) and Hull (2000).

Books on financial risk management can be roughly divided between those dealing with specific subjects in financial risk management, e.g., the value at risk books, and those dealing with financial risk management from a more general perspective, albeit motivated by specific examples. *Risk Management, Speculation, and Derivative Securities* aims to cover the subject from the general perspective. The benchmark text for the general approach to managing financial risk is, arguably, the book entitled *Managing Financial Risk* by Smithson, Smith, and Wilford (1995). This popular text is a combination of introductory theoretical analysis and practical illustration. However, the analytical treatment is relatively elementary. The strength of the presentation lies with the practical applications. This book can be contrasted with others, such as Doherty (1985), that have a strong theoretical motivation but give a somewhat artificial treatment of practical applications. Another benchmark text is *Cases in Financial Engineering* by Mason *et al.* (1995) which takes a case approach to the subject matter, dealing with practical issues in a sophisticated manner, but largely submerging the theoretical discussion in the case analysis.

In terms of these texts, this book has a theoretical treatment of corporate risk management at a level similar to Doherty, though without taking the same approach to the subject matter. The treatment of practical applications differs significantly from the case intensive approach of Mason *et al.* (1995). The approach of Smithson, Smith, and Wilford is a closer approximation. Yet, these texts all suffer from being too narrowly focused on financial risk management. Extending the field of view to include strategic business risk management, e.g., Oxelheim and Wihlborg (1997), is both natural and compelling. The advanced techniques of finance can be integrated with the strategic notion that business risks are interrelated and, in general, cannot be effectively analyzed in isolation from a range of other business risks. As a consequence, the market for this book will include both finance and strategic management.

In addition to texts dealing with financial and strategic risk management, this book also has substantial overlap with books on derivative securities. The number of excellent books on derivative securities is daunting. Starting in the early 1980's with Cox and Rubinstein (1985) and continuing to the present with Hull (2000), Jarrow and Turnbull (2000), and Wilmott (1998), the subject of derivative securities has produced efforts by many of the leading scholars in financial economics. It is difficult to carve a niche anywhere in this market. Yet, these texts are quite similar in content and approach: sophisticated treatments of derivative security valuation are the primary focus with risk management applications of secondary importance. To appeal to the academic textbook market for derivatives, these books devote considerable attention to describing the details of pricing various derivative securities. This leaves relatively little space to develop an advanced treatment of practical risk management applications.

An excellent example for comparison is the book entitled *Derivatives* by Wilmott (1998). This book is 739 pages long, an impressive effort. Yet, only pages 529–612 are dedicated to Risk Management and Measurement. A similar number of pages is dedicated to exotic options, a topic that is interesting mathematically but not of central importance to practical applications. Almost 20 pages of the risk management section are dedicated to the portfolio management problem, compared to 10 pages on value at risk. There is scattered treatment of practical issues elsewhere in *Derivatives* that also illustrates the comparison. Eighteen pages are dedicated to static hedging, which is approached from the viewpoint of an options market maker seeking to hedge an options book. Again, this is theoretically interesting but not of much direct use to those seeking guidance on implementing or improving financial risk management within the practical context of maximizing firm value.

Geoffrey Poitras
Burnaby, B.C., Canada

ACKNOWLEDGMENTS

The preparation of this book required permission to reproduce material from journal articles, newspapers, books, and magazines. The sources requiring permissions include the *Wall Street Journal, Toronto Globe and Mail, Management Science, Financial Management, Journal of Derivatives, Canadian Journal of Economics, Journal of Financial and Quantitative Analysis,* and *Journal of Portfolio Management.* Permission was also obtained from Pearson Educational to reprint material from Cox and Rubinstein's book entitled *Options Markets* (1985), Thompson Learning to reprint material from *Futures and Options* (1993) by Stoll and Whalley, and from Oxford University Press to reprint material from *Derivatives: Valuation and Risk Management* (2002) by Dubofsky and Miller. Though permission was not required, material from a number of government publications was used including the Bank of Canada *Review* and the Federal Reserve Bank of Atlanta, *Economic Review.* Useful information has also been obtained either directly or from the websites of the Bank for International Settlements, International Financing Corporation, International Swap and Derivatives Association, Chicago Board of Trade, Chicago Mercantile Exchange, Commodity Futures Trading Commission, Winnipeg Commodity Exchange, New York Board of Trade, and the Chicago Board Options Exchange.

Because this book is based on lecture notes prepared by the author starting around 1980 and continuing until the present, there have been numerous unnamed student contributions aimed at improving the exposition. Intellectual contributors I have been acquainted with either as a student or colleague include Phoebus Dhrymes, Bernard Dumas, Franklin Edwards, Howard Sosin, Marcus Hutchins, Frank Jones, Mark Powers, Suresh Sundaresan, David Modest, Don Chance, Lance Smith, Micheal Adler, and John Heaney. Among those I never had the opportunity to meet but whose writings had considerable influence include T. Hieronymous, H. Working, R. Leuthold, John Cox, Mark Rubinstein, Fischer Black, Philippe Jorion, Hans Gerber, and Hans Stoll. Finally the anonymous reviewers for the book also provided helpful insights and corrections. Last, but by far not least, are all the people at Academic Press who contributed many hours and much effort in getting the book into print, including Scott Bentley, Paul Gottehrer, and Debbie Bicher.

PART I

Derivative Securities, Risk Management, and Speculation

CHAPTER 1

Derivative Securities

I. DEFINITIONS AND OTHER BASIC CONCEPTS

A. WHAT ARE DERIVATIVE SECURITIES?

It is difficult to speak generally about derivative securities. It is possible to observe that a derivative security involves a contingent claim; it is a security that has some essential feature, typically the price, that is derived from some future event. This event is often, though not always, associated with a security or commodity delivery to take place at a future date. The contingent claim can be combined with other security features or traded in isolation. This definition is not too helpful because financial markets are riddled with contingent claims. Sometimes the contingent claim is left bundled with the spot commodity, in which case the derivative security is also the spot commodity (e.g., mortgage-backed securities). Yet, the term "derivative security" is usually restricted further to only include cases where the contingent claim is unbundled and traded as a separate security, effectively forwards, futures, options, and swaps. In what follows, this class of unbundled contingent claims will be referred to as *derivatives securities*.

Derivative securities trading is definitely not a modern development. The implicit and explicit embedding of derivative features was common in the types of securities traded in early markets. Early examples of securities with derivative features include claims on the 14th century Florentine *mons* that had a provision for redemption at 28% of par, though that provision was seldom exercised; 16th-century bills of exchange that combined a loan with a forward foreign exchange contract; and 18th century life annuities that featured terms to maturity dependent on specific life contingency provisions (Poitras, 2000). The "to arrive" contracts traded on the Antwerp bourse during the 16th century may be the first instance where a contingent claim was unbundled and traded as a separate security on an exchange. Previous to this time, such derivative security transactions had been limited to private deals between two signatories executed using *escripen* or notaries.

In addition to securities with embedded derivative features, early financial markets can be credited with beginning exchange trading in modern derivative security contracts.[1] Though the precise beginnings of option trading are difficult to trace, it is likely that there was trading in options, as well as "to arrive" contracts, on the Antwerp bourse during the early 16th century (Poitras, 2000). By the mid-17th century, trade in options and forward contracts was definitely an integral activity on the Amsterdam bourse (de la Vega, 1688). Trading in both options and forward contracts was an essential activity in London's Exchange Alley by the late 17th century (e.g., Houghton, 1694). The emergence of exchange trading of futures contracts can be traced to either 19th century Chicago (Hieronymous, 1977) or 18th century Japan (Schaede, 1989).

From these early beginnings, modern markets have achieved full securitization of a wide range of derivative securities. The modern Renaissance in derivative security trading has posed considerable problems for the accounting profession (e.g., Gastineau, 1995; Perry, 1997). In order to address the accounting problems raised by the use of derivative securities by firms for risk management and other purposes, the notion of "free standing derivatives" was introduced. This reference to free standing derivatives is precise accounting terminology borrowed from the financial accounting standard FAS 133 (FASB, 1998). Being "free standing", derivative securities pose fundamental problems for conventional methods of preparing accounts. This point has not been lost on the accounting profession, which has been engaged in ongoing attempts to

---

[1]Numerous historical sources—for example, Barbour (1950), Posthumus (1929), and Neal (1990)—make reference to trading "futures" contracts, instead of using the more correct reference to trading of "forward" contracts, for example, Hieronymous (1977, ch. 3). The term "futures contracts" has a precise modern meaning that the contracts of the 15th–18th centuries did not satisfy, though the Japanese rice market did come close to trading contracts that could qualify as futures contracts.

produce a set of standards that permit an accurate financial presentation of the accounts of the firm and do not permit substantial discretionary variation in the accounts. In a perfect world, two otherwise identical firms, both involved with using derivative securities, would not be able to present accounts that were substantively different, based on discretionary accounting choices, such as the method used to recognize gains or losses on the offsetting spot position.

The accounting profession is acutely aware of the question: What are derivative securities? The main difficulty for accountants is that the derivatives are free standing.[2] When the contingent claim is unbundled from the underlying transaction, it is difficult to attach that security back to the transaction that motivated the derivative security position. For obvious reasons, derivative securities require mark-to-market accounting. Yet, accounting for cash positions can be flexible: book value or market value, depending on the situation. Because of the potential for substantial discretionary manipulation of the accounts, accounting standards such as FAS 133 and 138 have been introduced. Under recent standards, the narrow class of unbundled contingent claims is now classified as free standing derivatives. As such, more flexible rules have been introduced to ensure that there is accurate hedge accounting for firms using these securities. This category excludes fixed income securities with embedded derivative features, such as mortgage-backed securities and callable or convertible bonds.[3] A key implication of all this for non-accounting professionals is that, due to the introduction of FAS 133, substantially enhanced information about derivatives positions is now available in annual reports and other sources of financial information for publicly traded companies (e.g., 10-Ks).

This approach to defining derivative securities is not without conceptual difficulties. An essential feature of the free standing derivative securities is the action of setting a price today for a transaction to take place at a date in the future. However, this feature is also present in other types of financial securities. A bond, for example, sets a price today for a sequence of fixed cash flows

---

[2]Another problem posed by derivatives is the ability to replicate a derivative payoff using dynamic trading in cash securities. For example, portfolio insurance replicates the payoff on a put option by actively trading a portfolio of stocks and bonds.

[3]There are numerous instances of explicit and implicit call or conversion provisions in historical security issues. For example, the Venetian *prestiti* had a call provision that allowed for principal value to be repaid at par, as finances permitted. Various 18th century government debt restructuring plans involved the introduction of conversion provisions. For example, there was the conversion of English government life annuities, issued under William III and Queen Anne, into long annuities, or John Law's Mississippi scheme which introduced conversion provisions for exchanging French government debt obligations into *Compagnie des Indes* stock.

that will be received in the future. Even a common stock sets a price today for a sequence of uncertain cash flows that will be received in the future. One element that distinguishes free standing derivative securities from financial securities such as bonds is the timing of the settlement. A forward contract involves settlement and delivery at maturity, while a bond involves settlement today with delivery in the form of payments at future maturity dates. Using this approach, an option contract is somewhat anomalous, requiring a payment today to acquire the right to make a settlement at a price that is set today. The distinction between the various cases actually lies with the respective cash flows.

B. Some Definitions

At this point, some of the jargon that characterizes derivatives trading will be introduced. For practical purposes, an attempt has been made to use the terminology of the marketplace. The occasionally colorful language is often transparent in intent but confusing in application. For example, in futures and forward markets it is conventional to use the following:

A *short* position involves the sale of a commodity for future delivery.
A *long* position involves the purchase of a commodity for future delivery.

However, in options markets a *long* position refers to the purchase of a call or put option, while a *short* position refers to the writing of a call or put option. This terminology applies even though purchasing a put option involves paying a premium for the right to sell for future delivery. In turn, a *short* position in the spot commodity market involves borrowing the commodity under a short sale agreement which is then sold in the spot market, generating a cash inflow. A *long* position in the spot commodity would involve a current cash outflow in exchange for possession of the physical commodity.

The use of analytical concepts such as profit functions requires introducing some notation that will be used throughout the book:

$F(t,T)$: The forward or futures price observed at time t for delivery at time T.
$S(t) \equiv S_t$: The *cash* or *spot* or *physical* price of the deliverable commodity observed at time t.

For consistency, it has to be that $T \geq N \geq t$. In much of what follows, the assumption, $F(T,T) = S(T)$ is made in order for the price of a futures contract observed on the delivery date $t = T$ to be equal to the price of the deliverable commodity. In effect, the spot commodity is taken to be the deliverable commodity. This condition is readily satisfied for forward contracts but requires assuming away the possibility of cross hedging if futures contracts are involved. Conventional time dates that will be used are $t = 0$ and $t = 1$ with N for contracts that are *nearby* or closer to delivery and T for contracts that are *deferred* or farther from delivery.

Using a strictly legal definition, it is possible to be reasonably precise about what constitutes a futures contract. However, differences in the legal definition of futures contracts across jurisdictions would create problems. For present purposes, a brief summary of a futures contract is all that is required:

> A *futures contract* is an exchange traded agreement between two parties, guaranteed by the clearinghouse, that commits one party to sell a standardized grade and standardized quantity of a commodity, asset, or security to the other party at a given price and specified location at a future point in time.

While useful, this brief summary disguises important features of futures trading. For example, one of the significant limitations of forward contracting is the requirement that precise specification of the grade and quantity of the commodity be determined by the parties to the contract. This procedure raises the problem of how to ascertain whether the commodity delivered meets the grade and quantity requirements. Because forward contracts typically require delivery of the commodity, this procedure is an essential feature of forward contracting. Because futures markets deal in a standardized commodity for which delivery can be avoided by taking an offsetting position prior to delivery, futures contracting avoids this problem.

Like futures, options have a specialized nomenclature. To understand this jargon, the essential notions of an option must be identified:

> An *option contract* is an agreement between two parties in which one party, the writer, grants the other party, the purchaser, the *right*, but not the obligation, to either buy or sell a given security, asset, or commodity at a future date under stated conditions.

Options almost always involve the purchaser making some type of premium payment to the writer. The timing and form of the premium payment depends on the specifics of the contract. For exchange-traded options and many over-the-counter (OTC) options, the premium is paid up front, when the option agreement is initiated. It is essential to recognize that an option does not represent an ownership claim. Rather, an option is a claim against ownership under prespecified conditions. While it is not necessary that options be exchange traded, many option contracts do originate on exchanges.

Given this, two types of options can identified:

- A *call* option gives the option buyer *the right to purchase* the underlying asset or commodity from the option seller at a given price.
- A *put* option gives the option buyer *the right to sell* the underlying asset or commodity to the option seller at a given price.

The seller of the option is often referred to as the option *writer*. An option purchaser makes a payment to the option writer referred to as the option *premium*. Once the premium has been paid, the purchaser has no further liability.

The following notation will be used for options:

$C[S,\tau,X]$ = price of a European call
$C_A[S,\tau,X]$ = price of an American call[4]
$P[S,\tau,X]$ = price of a European put
$P_A[S,\tau,X]$ = price of an American put
X is the exercise price
T is the expiration date
$\tau = T - t$, where $T \geq t$

The notation for time is handled in a somewhat nonstandard fashion, where t^* and τ are often used in preference to t and T. This is to specifically indicate that time is being counted backwards and the unit of measurement for t^* is fractions of a year. Hence:

$$t^* = (T - t)/365 = \tau/365$$

t^* is the fraction of the year remaining on the security, where $T - t$ is the number of days from settlement to expiration, with T being the expiration date and t the settlement date. The seemingly redundant use of the variable τ is to emphasize cases where time counts backward: At any time t, $\tau = T - t$ and, as t increases to T, τ is reduced to where, on the expiration date T, $\tau = 0$.

Various features for exchange traded option contracts can be identified. Some or all of these features may apply to other types of option transactions. In order to be accurately specified, option contracts require an *exercise* or *strike* price as well as an *expiration date* on which the right is terminated. The exercise price is the contractually specified price at which the purchaser is allowed to buy (for a call) or sell (for a put) the underlying asset or commodity. When the exercise price is below (above) the current underlying price, the call (put) option is said to be *in the money*. When the exercise price is above (below) the underlying price, the call (put) option is *out of the money*. An *at the money* option has the exercise price and underlying asset or commodity price approximately equal. Exercising an option involves completion of the relevant transaction specified in the option contract. Options that can be exercised prior to the stated expiration date are referred to as *American options*, in contrast to options that can only be exercised on the expiration

---

[4]The notation selected to designate Americans with the subscript A should not be confused with the general notational convention used to identify subscripts with partial derivatives.

date, commonly referred to as *European options*.[5] Depending on the type of option, either a spot delivery (physical settlement) or a net dollar value transaction (cash settlement) may be required to satisfy the conditions of exercise. Finally, the option contract will typically contain other adjustment provisions (e.g., handling of dividend payments, stock splits, and mergers for stock options).[6] Of particular importance, modern exchange-traded American stock options are *not dividend payout protected*; that is, the call option purchaser is not entitled to receive cash dividends paid on the underlying stock during the time between purchase and exercise.

In addition to exchange-traded options, there are numerous other examples of options. In corporate finance, important types of options arise with warrants, rights offerings, convertible bonds, preferred stock, and executive compensation packages.[7] It is even possible to interpret the firm's common stock or outstanding debt in terms of options. A *warrant* is an option issued by a corporation granting the purchaser the right to acquire a number of shares of its common stock at a given exercise price for a given time. When a warrant is exercised, the transaction results in a cash inflow to the corporation in exchange for a new issue of common shares, invariably resulting in a dilution of the outstanding common stock. Warrants are often exercisable prior to maturity, being "long term" at primary issue (e.g., 5 years or more). Occasionally, perpetual warrants with no fixed maturity date are offered. Given the long expiration dates, warrant exercise prices are usually set more than slightly above the current stock price. The precise conditions surrounding a warrant issue are contained in the *warrant agreement* that outlines the handling of stock splits, future new stock issues, and callability. Despite this, terms laid out in a warrant agreement are not always unambiguous. In effect, warrants are not as standardized as exchange-traded options.

Preemptive *rights issues*, sometimes called *subscription warrants*, are another form of option designed to facilitate sale of common stock.[8] However,

---

[5]This terminology can create confusions. For example, the bulk of options traded in Europe are actually American options. While European options are not as commonly traded, this form is often used for the analytical simplifications provided. Another confusion is the use of "cash settlement" to refer to satisfaction of the option exercise requirements with a net dollar value transaction. In effect, the use of "cash" here does not refer to the spot commodity, but rather to actual cash.

[6]While exchange traded stock options contain provisions for adjustment in the face of stock splits, mergers, and stock dividends, these options are not adjusted for cash dividends. In other words, exchange-traded stock options are *not* cash dividend payout protected.

[7]An important group of options is concerned with the various conversion features and callable features that are attached to a firm's debt issues. It is also possible to consider all the firm's securities as options, e.g., the common stock is an option on the unlevered portion of the firm's value while the outstanding debt is an option on the levered portion of firm assets.

[8]The specific procedures regarding rights issues vary across jurisdictions (e.g., Bae and Levy, 1994; Hietala, 1994; Poitras, 2001a).

unlike warrants that often support sales of stocks at a much later date, rights issues are short-dated; a 2- to 10-week duration period is typical.[9] In addition, rights issues are granted, on a *pro rata* basis to existing shareholders of record at the ex-rights date. In effect, shareholders receive the right to purchase a fraction of a new common stock issue equal to the fraction of the current outstanding common stock the shareholders of record own. Rights are valuable because the exercise price is usually set more than slightly below the current stock price, giving the right a definite market value.[10] Many rights issues are tradable, either on the OTC or centralized stock exchanges. Unlike rights issues and warrants, executive compensation options are usually not tradeable. These warrants are used to provide a bonus system to encourage senior management to pursue the interests of shareholders. Typically, these options are given (not sold) to the employee. The usefulness of this form of compensation in achieving its stated objective has been the subject of considerable debate and research.

From these basic types, there are numerous variations, both theoretical and practical. Options, for example, feature a bewildering array of possible theoretical variations, such as digital barrier options, knock-out Russian options, perpetual Bermuda options, and so on. One specialized derivative contract that possesses cash flows which can theoretically be replicated with a bundle of forward contracts is a swap. Such transactions can be defined in general terms as:

> A *swap* is an exchange of cash flows deemed to be of equal value at the time the swap is initiated.

While the future exchange of future cash flows is common to all swap transactions, certain types of swaps also include an exchange of current cash flows.

Swap transactions can be conceived as bundles of forward contracts. Early examples of such transactions occurred in foreign exchange (FX) markets, where the swap involved combining spot and forward FX transactions; for example, at $t = 0$ domestic funds are exchanged for foreign funds with an additional agreement that the foreign funds will be exchanged for domestic, at the current swap rate, at $t = 1$. While, in general, the cash flows involved in a swap can originate from any security, asset, or commodity, there are two

---

[9]The length of the period between the rights issue date and the exercise date is determined by a number of factors, including local stock exchange rules and firm preferences (e.g., Poitras, 2001a).

[10]This follows because of the value associated with immediate exercise of the right. The stock can be purchased and immediately sold at a higher price. The terminology *intrinsic value* is often used to refer to that component of an option's value that is associated with the immediate exercise value. However, even when the intrinsic value is zero, the option can still have a non-zero *time value* component.

important types of swaps: interest rate swaps and currency swaps. These swap types are a securitization of common underlying financial market transactions. In a "plain vanilla" interest rate swap (Abken, 1991), the cash flows involve fixed-to-floating interest rates. In a currency swap, the cash flows are cross currency. A plain vanilla interest rate swap does not involve an exchange of $t = 0$ cash flows, while a currency swap will exchange the $t = 0$ cash flows. There is a substantial number of variations for swap structures.

C. FUTURES VERSUS FORWARD CONTRACTS: BASIC ISSUES[11]

Futures and forward contracts both facilitate a fundamental market transaction: fixing a price today for a commodity transaction designated to take place at a later date. Unlike a futures contract, which is securitized and exchange traded, forward contracts come in a variety of forms. Some forward contracts, such as those traded on the foreign exchange markets, have many of the essential features of futures contracts. Other types of forward contracts are more complicated, such as the forward contracting provisions that were embedded in the Metallgesellschaft (MG) long-term oil delivery contracts. In some respects, futures contracts represent an evolution of forward trading.[12] Yet, much of the modern progress in derivatives contracting has come in OTC trading, the home of forward contracting.

Some of the practical differences between forward and futures contracting methods are illustrated in Table 1.1. Considerable variation is observed in the relative use of forward or futures contracting across commodity markets. For example, in currency markets, the large value and volume of individual trades have the bulk of transactions conducted in OTC forward and short-dated FX swap markets. Exchange-traded currency derivatives are an insignificant fraction of total trading volume. As trading in forwards is closely integrated with cash market transactions, direct trading in forward FX contracts is restricted to the significant spot market participants, effectively the large banks and financial institutions. Because currency forward and swap contracts do not have regular marking to market, restricting participation is needed to control default risk.

Currency forward and swap contracts have many features of futures contracts. For other commodities, forward contracts can take a variety of forms.

---

[11]Telser and Higinbotham (1977) provide a discussion of a number of the issues raised in this Section.

[12]The use of Eurodollar strips as a method of implementing or pricing interest rate swaps has received considerable attention. Dubofsky and Miller (2002) offers a textbook discussion of strips.

TABLE 1.1   Comparison of Futures and Forward Contracts

	Forwards	Futures
Contract amount	Depends on buyer and seller	Standardized
Price movement restrictions	No limit	Varies; can be restricted by the exchange with provisions for increase or decrease
Position limits	Market determined	Set by exchanges and regulators
Delivery date	Depends on buyer and seller	Standardized
Market location	Decentralized, often a telephone/computer network of dealers, brokers, and other members	Centralized exchange floor where trading is executed by open outcry between exchange participants
Clearing	No direct, separate clearing mechanism	The exchange clearinghouse
Settlement	By delivery of goods as specified in contract	Marking-to-market daily using a margin system; some deliveries by specialized traders
Regulation	Self-regulation, contract law, general securities law	Exchange rules, Commodity Exchange Act, CFTC, state regulators, specific legislation

Consider the industrial and precious metals for which active trading in both futures and forward contracts is observed. In the metals markets, the most important derivatives exchanges, the London Metals Exchange and the Commodity Exchange (COMEX), also play an important role in providing cash market supplies through the exchange delivery process. In other commodities, such as crude oil, due to the wide variation in deliverable grades, there are significant practical differences between the forward and futures contracts. Yet, despite requiring delivery of a standardized grade of oil, the New York Mercantile Exchange (NYMEX) crude oil futures contract still plays a key role in the cash market both as a pricing benchmark and as a delivery contract. For many agricultural commodities, such as grains and livestock, futures contracts are also the pricing benchmarks.

In general, forward trading is carried out in conjunction with cash market activity. This effectively excludes participation by traders not involved in the cash market. In some instances, the size of trades is so large that even smaller cash market traders are also excluded from directly participating in the forward market. These traders must access the cash market by placing and clearing trades with the larger market participants. This exclusivity is in keeping with the structure of cash deals that require an element of market recognition and implied creditworthiness in order to reduce riskiness. This feature of restricting direct access to forward trading has decided advantages, particularly in financial commodities such as currencies and debt instruments where large numbers of trades, involving millions of dollars per trade, are done each trading day. Much of this business is done through brokers, where credit lines in forward positions are imposed in order to further limit the intrinsic riskiness of forward contracting.

The intent of most forward trading is, ultimately, to deliver the spot commodity on the maturity date. As a rule, because forward contracts require settlement by spot delivery, it is somewhat difficult for purely speculative trading to occur. In addition, speculative interest is also deterred because forward contracts are not readily transferable. As a result, in order to offset a forward position for which the delivery is no longer desired, the trader must typically initiate another offsetting forward contract for the same grade, amount, delivery date, and delivery location.[13] The two offsetting positions are then settled by crossing the trade at delivery. For example, to offset a *long* forward position with Bank A for $10 million Canadian dollars delivered on June 12, the trader will enter a *short* forward contract with Bank B, also for $10 million Canadian dollars and delivery on June 12. On the delivery date, the trade will be crossed by taking delivery from Bank A on the long position and using the $10 million Canadian to make delivery on the short position with Bank B. The profit on the trade will be the difference in the price of the short and long positions. This process is decidedly different than in futures markets where trades are, effectively, done with the clearing-house and the futures position is canceled when a trader takes the offsetting position.

For some commodities, lack of liquidity in forward contracts makes it difficult for hedgers and other traders to find compatible grades, delivery dates, and delivery locations. In these situations, canceling the forward position by crossing in the cash market is difficult. Such complications will increase the attractiveness of using futures contracts. With the agreement of the counter-party, the forward agreement could be structured to have variation in the allowable grades and amounts or to be transferable under certain conditions. For forward agreements that do not contain such conditions, the best method of offsetting the forward position may be to engage in cash market transactions on the delivery date. For example, a metal refinery that has a forward contract to deliver copper cathodes but, for some reason, is unable to make delivery from current production, can enter the cash market for cathodes and purchase the copper necessary to settle the contract. The

---

[13]In certain cases, the forward position is transferable and the position can be sold to a third party that will be responsible for delivery. The risk to the seller of default by the third party illustrates the difficulties of forward contracting.

costs of engaging in such cash market transactions will vary according to the specifics of the situation.

The differences in the functioning of futures and forward markets impacts the specific method of contracting selected for conducting commodity trans-actions. For example, in contrast to forward trading, futures markets are designed to encourage participation by small speculative traders. The in-creased participation of speculators not directly involved in the spot market provides an important source of additional liquidity to futures markets not available in forward markets. In order to achieve this liquidity, certain restric-tions are imposed on trading, such as filing requirements and limits on position sizes. By restricting participation to large players in the spot market, many of the restrictions required for the functioning of futures markets are not present in forward markets. For hedgers, the underlying commodity for a futures contract does not, in many instances, have precisely the same charac-teristics as the hedger's spot commodity. Futures contracts are often entered into with the intention of closing out the position on the maturity date of the hedge and then covering the spot transaction in the cash market.

D. THE EXCHANGE

Another significant difference between futures and forward contracts arises because futures are exchange traded, while most forward contracts are created by individual parties operating in a less centralized market. Because a futures contract originates on an exchange, the traders originating the contract actu-ally use the exchange *clearinghouse* as the counter-party to their trade.[14] While both a short and a long trader are required to create a futures contract, both traders execute the trade with the clearinghouse. This allows a futures con-tract to be created without the problems associated with forward contracting which typically depends on the creditworthiness of the counter-party. By design, futures contracts are readily transferable via the trading mechanisms provided by the exchange. Because forward contracts depend on the perform-ance of the two original parties to the contract, these contracts are often difficult to transfer. One practical implication of this difference is that if a futures trader wants to close out a position, an equal number of offsetting

---

[14]Brinkman (1984) provides a useful overview of clearinghouse operations. While clearing-house members must also belong to the exchange, not all exchange members belong to the clearinghouse. There is a screening process to ensure that financial integrity and other require-ments are satisfied. In turn, clearinghouse membership can be profitable for a number of reasons. For example, on most exchanges clearing members post margin on the net clearing position, often using stock in the clearing corporation as collateral for part of the balance. This permits margin money from client accounts to be used for other purposes.

contracts for that commodity month is purchased and the original position is canceled. Forward contracts can be canceled by creating an offsetting forward contract with terms as close as possible to those in the original contract. Unless the forward contracts provide a method for cash settlement at delivery, this will potentially involve two deliveries having to be matched in the cash market.

Typically, trading on a futures exchange is conducted on an exchange floor with each commodity having a designated "pit" or trading area. The largest group of floor traders or *locals* in the pit are floor brokers, filling orders for speculators and hedgers acting through commission house accounts. Some brokers work for commission houses, some for their own account. The next type of pit traders are the speculators, usually trading for their own account. This group breaks down into one of three not mutually exclusive types of traders. These participants can be referred to by a number of possible names. Perhaps the most useful terminology is *scalpers, day traders*, and *position traders*. Scalpers attempt to profit from the bid/offer spread, sometimes called the *edge*, in effect playing the role of market maker. The scalper attempts to predict short-run, intra-day price movements. While scalpers typically hold positions for as short a period as possible, depending on the level of market activity, these traders and other speculators will take larger intra-day positions, holding them for a longer period. The skilled floor trader will be able to identify situations that arise both in the regular course of business (e.g., a large hedging order needs filling) and due to special circumstances (e.g., a rush of orders from an unexpected government report). These speculators are essential to the liquidity of futures markets.[15] Scalpers and day traders add substantially to the volume of trade, without having to post any margin, because trades are closed out prior to the last trade of the day. As a consequence, these traders do not have any direct impact on open interest.

Futures exchange market activity is more difficult to measure than, say, for stock exchanges, where transactions volume is sufficient. In order to provide a measure of trading activity that is independent of the activities of the market makers and day traders, the notion of *open interest* is used which indicates the number of contracts outstanding at the beginning of the trading day. Open interest represents the number of contracts that are being carried from one trading day to another. Because every futures contract that is created requires a long and a short position, open interest can only increase if both a new long and a new short position are created. If a new long (short) position is created

[15]Silber (1984) provides a useful analysis of the role of scalpers. The final group of speculators is the position traders, effectively professional speculators involved in taking large positions held for at least several days. These individuals provide a portion of the market for exchange seat rentals. The final group of pit traders is the employees of the large commercial firms using the futures market for hedging and speculation.

with a short (long) position that is closing out a previous position, open interest is unchanged. If both long and short positions are being closed out, open interest will decrease. This process is illustrated in Table 1.2. Because scalpers and day traders do not usually carry positions overnight, the activities of these traders only affect volume, not open interest. As a result, a more accurate indication of the participation of (position trader and other off-exchange) speculative activity would be to measure, say, the ratio of maximum open interest to contract deliveries.

E. The Futures Contract

To facilitate exchange trading, futures contracts possess a number of features; most important for present purposes are the features of *standardization* and *marking to market*. The essential elements of standardization have been recognized and emphasized for years. For example, Fowke (1957) identifies the essential elements involved in futures contract standardization:

> The elements of standardization provided by the futures contract and by the rules and regulations of the exchange governing such contracts may be identified under the following headings: (1) the commodity, (2) the quantity, (3) the range of quality within which delivery is permissible, (4) the month of delivery, (5) the nature of the option concerning specific grade and date of delivery, that is, whether it is a seller's or a buyer's option, and, finally, (7) the price.

Standardization is achieved by making each contract for a given commodity identical to all other contracts except for price and the delivery month, which is fixed according to a bi-monthly or quarterly schedule.[16] As a result, futures are a basis contract, with the actual price being for the commodity that is cheapest to deliver under the terms of the contract.

In order to be a viable instrument, futures contracts written for deliverable spot commodities require adequate supply of the commodity for delivery purposes. In order to ensure adequate supply, many contracts permit substantial variation in the commodity grade delivered or in the delivery location. The option for selecting the specific grade or delivery location is usually a *seller's option*. As a result, contracts that permit a range of deliverables will have one specific grade that is cheapest to deliver. Some contracts, such as the T-bond contract, have a number of different delivery options available (see Appendix II). Forward contracts differ widely in the degree of standardization. For example, forwards for financial commodities such as the major currencies or

---

[16]Commodities with bimonthly delivery dates (e.g., metals) usually require an active delivery month contract. In this case, a set number of months (3 for COMEX contracts) prior to the final delivery date for the alternative months a contract for delivery is initiated so that there is always a delivery contract for any given month.

TABLE 1.2 Open Interest, Futures Trading, and the Associated Cash Flows

Date	Trans. No.	Buyer	Seller	Volume	Contracts outstanding	Open interest	Price
1/1	1	A	B	1	1	0	3.00
	2	C	A	2	1		3.03
	3	C	D	3	2		2.96
	4	B	C	4	1		2.96
	5	D	C	5	0		3.00
	6	E	F	10	5		3.10
	7	G	H	15	10		3.10
	(Close) 8	F	E	18	7		3.00
2/1						7	

Profit (marking to market) from trading on 1/1

A	B	C	D	E	F	G	H
150	−200	−150	200	−2500	2500	−2500	2500

Margin account and marking to market cash flow for 1/1

Initial margin payment credit (receivable to clearinghouse)

A	B	C	D	E	F	G	H
750	750	750	750	3750	3750	3750	3750

Marking to market for 1/1

A	B	C	D	E	F	G	H
+150	+200	−150	−200	−2500	2500	−2500	+2500

Adjustment to margin balance from closing out the position

A	B	C	D	E	F	G	H
−900	−950	−600	−550				

Margin balance at end of trading 1/1

A	B	C	D	E	F	G	H
0	0	0	0	1250	6250	1250	6250

Assumptions: Contract is for 5000 units and initial margin deposit is $750 per contract, with a maintenance margin of $500. G is required to deposit an additional $1250 in order to satisfy the maintenance margin level of $(500)(5) = 2500; otherwise, the trade will be closed out at the open. G and H have 5 contracts O/S; E and F have 2 contracts O/S. Open interest on 2/1 = 7 contracts.

Government of Canada securities are *de facto* standardized,[17] indicating that the benefits associated with standardization are also important for some types of forward trading. In the absence of a clearinghouse, forward markets capture default risk efficiencies by excluding many of the potential, largely speculative participants who require standardization in order to participate effectively in the market. As with futures, standardization is an important support to market liquidity.

In addition to standardization, forwards and futures also differ in how changes in the value of the contract over time are handled. For futures, daily settlement, also known as *marking-to-market*, is required. In effect, a new futures contract is written at the start of every trading day with all gains or losses settled through a *margin* account at the end of trading for that day. This method of accounting also requires the posting of a "good faith" initial margin deposit combined with an understanding that, should the value in the account fall below a maintenance margin amount, funds will be transferred into the account to prevent the contract from being closed out. On the other hand, settlement on forward contracts occurs by delivery of the commodity at the maturity of the contract or, in certain cases, a cash settlement at maturity based on the difference between the forward price that was agreed upon and the prevailing spot price for the relevant commodity specification. Hence, futures have cash flow implications during the life of the contract while forwards do not.

Numerous studies on the difference between futures and forwards are available (e.g., Cox *et al.*, 1981; Richard and Sundaresan, 1981). Considerable interest has centered on the marking-to-market feature of futures. Assuming that the cost of commissions, good faith deposit, etc. are ignored, then the value of both futures and forwards contracts can be taken to be equal to zero upon creation. (This does mean that the price of the contracts is zero.) This follows from the derivative nature of contracting for future delivery; because no actual investment of funds is required to establish a position, only future changes in the value of the commodity will produce value. Absent marking to market, forwards involve settlement requiring one lump payment or delivery at maturity. In comparison, due to marking-to-market, futures contracts will involve a stream of payments over time. As a consequence, the value of the futures over its life will depend not only on the behavior of the price of the cash commodity but also on the covariance of the cash price with interest rates over the time path. In addition to theoretical analysis of this point, there are also numerous empirical papers which, for identical or nearly identical deliverable

---

[17]In contrast, many of the early interest rate swaps and forward (interest) rate agreements were not standardized. However, with the explosive growth of the swap market in the 1980s, the International Swap Dealers Association (ISDA) was formed by important market participants. The ISDA has contributed significantly to the standardization of swap agreements. (The ISDA has evolved into the International Swap and Derivatives Association.)

commodities, compare futures and forward price behavior. While, in some cases, there are some minor differences that cannot be explained by transactions costs, on balance futures and forward prices for the same commodity are more-or-less identical.

Due to the nature of futures and forwards, it is understandable that the mechanisms for delivery will also differ. Because forwards are usually initiated with the object of taking delivery in mind, participants in forward markets will invariably be capable of completing a delivery. This is definitely not the case in futures markets where the demands of delivery are compounded by the standardized grades and delivery locations that are required. As a result of the considerable cost in establishing and maintaining an operation capable of making deliveries, the futures delivery process is dominated by a relatively small number of specialist firms capable of capturing the sometimes significant profit opportunities that emerge during the delivery period. These firms are also often clearinghouse members. Because much of what follows will not be concerned with so-called delivery arbitrage activity, it will be convenient to assume that both futures and forward contracts obey the condition that the price of the contract on the delivery date is equal to the cash price of the deliverable commodity even though, in certain practical situations, this may not be precisely correct.

F. MARGINS[18]

An essential feature of the futures contract is the marking-to-market process inherent in margin system. The amount of margin deposited represents a "good faith deposit" that ensures a party to the futures contract meets his obligations. The margin deposit is *not* an investment in a commodity position. All that has been transacted is an agreement to buy or sell a given amount of the commodity at a future date for a prespecified price. This is decidedly different than margins for equity where the deposit is in partial payment for securities purchased in the cash market. Margin deposits for futures are only required to ensure sanctity of the contract in the face of fluctuations in its value. Given this, it is understandable that there are different types of margin requirements depending on the individual's position in the exchange process. The three general types of margin requirements are (1) clearinghouse margins, (2) exchange (but not

---

[18]The discussion of margins focuses on futures. There are numerous studies on the impact of changes in futures margin requirements on cash price volatility (e.g., Goldberg, Lawrence, and Hachey, 1992; Telser, 1981). For forward contracts, margins can appear in various guises, often as a "haircut" requirement that requires the posting of some fraction of the principal value of the contract. However, there is substantial variation of margining practices in the forward market, both across commodities and, in some cases, for forward contracts traded on the same commodity.

clearinghouse) member margins, and, (3) commission house margins. Specific details depend on the exchange and commodities involved and whether the trader is classified as a hedger or speculator. Acceptable collateral for deposit in a margin account also differs in much the same way.

In practice, clearinghouse members will typically receive the lowest margin requirements. Even though clearinghouse and other exchange members have the same stated requirements for each individual trading ticket generated, on almost all exchanges margin is assessed on a clearing member's net position, calculated by netting the number of short and long positions for a given commodity delivery month on the clearing member's books at the end of trading. While larger than effective clearinghouse margins, exchange member margins are small relative to the value of the underlying physical commodity being traded. For example, on August 31, 2001, the gold contract traded on the Commodity Exchange (COMEX) in New York had nonmember hedger, exchange member and clearing member margins of $1000, for both initial and maintenance margins. Nonmember margins for speculators were $1350 for initial and $1000 for maintenance margin. Margins are also given for calendar spreads, specific intercommodity spreads, and written options. Table 1.3 provides a summary list of speculator/nonexchange member margins for some of the important contracts as of November 1, 2001. Depending on the clearing member that is handling the trader's account, up to 25% of this margin must be met in cash. The remaining margin can be satisfied with a wide variety of acceptable collateral: warehouse receipts (with a "haircut" or markup), government securities, corporate and municipal bonds, equities, and, in the case of clearinghouse members, letters of credit. For one-to-one gold spreads, there is a decidedly lower, if somewhat more complicated, set of requirements. Specifically, there is a flat rate of $120 per spread up to 100 spreads and $200 per spread for all spreads above 100. There is also a per spread rate of $40 plus $20 per month of spread leg. Of these, the least expensive method is selected, depending on the type of trade involved.[19]

The highest margin requirements usually have to be satisfied by customers of commission houses who are not members of the exchange and have to use an exchange member to execute their trades. The actual margins vary from customer to customer and from commission house to commission house. For large active accounts, margin can typically be met with interest-bearing collateral such as treasury bills. Alternatively, margin balances may be deposited on behalf of the client in the dealer's money market account. Small, low-activity

---

[19]Spreads also receive favorable execution cost treatment. The commission cost structure parallels that for margins; that is, clearinghouse commissions are nominal or negligible, exchange member transactions fees are nominal, and commission house fees (brokerage) are highest and vary from customer to customer. Because scalpers and daytraders do not carry positions overnight, these traders do not usually have to worry about posting margin.

TABLE 1.3   Margins for Speculative/Non-Member Accounts: Selected Commodity
Futures Contracts[a]

Commodity	Outright Positions		Calendar Spreads[b]	
	Initial	Maintenance	Initial	Maintenance
Grains				
Corn	$405	$300	$65	$50
Oats	$675	$500	$135	$100
Soybeans	$945	$700	$338	$250
Soybean meal	$945	$700	$405	$300
Soybean oil	$405	$300	$135	$100
Wheat	$743	$550	$270	$200
Stock indexes				
S&P 500 Index	$21,563	$17,250	$188	$150
Nasdaq 100	$26,250	$21,000	$250	$200
Nikkei 225	$6,250	$5,000	$125	$100
Russell 2000	$21,750	$17,400	$157	$125
Currencies				
Canadian dollar	$608	$450	$34	$25
Euro FX	$2,025	$1,500	$68	$50
Japanese yen	$2,025	$1,500	$68	$50
British pound	$1,485	$1,100	$34	$25
Swiss franc	$1,350	$1,000	$34	$25
Agriculturals				
Live cattle	$810	$600	$270	$200
Feeder cattle	$979	$725	$709	$525
Pork bellies	$1,620	$1,200	$608	$450
Hogs	$1,080	$800	$486	$360
Butter	$5,400	$4,000	$3,240	$2,400
Interest Rates				
Eurodollar	$810	$600	$169	$125
Libor (1 month)	$608	$450	$135	$100
US Treasury bonds	$2,160	$1,600		
10 year Treasury note	$1,620	$1,200		

[a]Margins are exchange minimums for speculative accounts as calculated by the SPAN® (Standard
Portfolio Analysis of Risk) system which is used to calculate margins at the major futures
exchanges. Initial and maintenance margins for hedgers and exchange members are typical by
equal to the maintenance margin level for non-member speculative accounts.
[b]Many commodities feature a wide range of spread margins, depending on the type of trade being
executed. The calendar spread margins for grains are for old crop/new crop spreads, for pork
bellies are for new crop/new crop spreads; and for Eurodollar are for nearby spreads in consecutive delivery dates.
Source: Chicago Board of Trade and Chicago Mercantile Exchange websites.

accounts may be required to deposit cash. For example, to trade the COMEX
gold contract, small commission house accounts may be required to put up
$3000–$5000 cash in a money market account or deposit a $10,000 security

such as a treasury bill and meet cash-flow requirements on an ongoing basis. To understand the precise nature of the cash flows involved requires making a distinction between the two types of margin requirements: *initial margin* and *maintenance margin*. Up to this point, the discussion has implicitly focused on initial margin: the dollar value of the acceptable collateral that must be deposited in the margin account in order for the contract to be created. In turn, maintenance margin is the dollar value of the acceptable collateral that must be in the margin account at the beginning of a trading day. To avoid undue administrative hassles, for speculative traders this margin level is set at some fraction—usually between 70 and 85%—of the initial margin level.

Even though the implications of margin buying are well known, it is useful to review the implications of the leverage that futures trading provides. If the margin deposit is crudely treated as funds invested in the position, the leverage provided by futures is significantly greater than that provided by equities. To see this, assume that initial margin on a one-lot (or one contract) customer trade of the 100-oz COMEX gold contract has been assessed at $4000 with maintenance margin at $3000. If the price of August gold is taken to be, say, $400, then the underlying value of the gold being purchased is $40,000. If the trader goes long August gold at $400 and, in the next trading day, the price falls to $385, then the value of the position has fallen to $38,500—a loss of $1500. At the end of trading, this loss is debited from the margin account, leaving $2500, a value that is below the maintenance margin level. As this point, the commission house broker will call the customer with a "margin call," notifying the customer that if the margin account is not brought up above the maintenance margin level, the contract will be closed out. The payment that must be made to bring the margin account to an appropriate level is known as *variation margin*. At this point the customer must assess his position. A $15 move in the price of gold over one trading period has resulted in a 37.5% loss (i.e., $1500/$4000), in the value of the funds on margin deposit. Variation margin cash flows played a key role in a number of the recent debacles to be examined in Section III (e.g., for Metallgesellschaft and the Hunt brothers).

G. OTC Versus Exchange Trading: Policy Issues

The strategic direction of derivative security regulation, both in the United States and internationally, is almost incoherent. The difficulties associated with bringing greater clarity and direction are considerable. There are numerous unresolved theoretical issues that need to be identified and analyzed before practical implications can be drawn. One of the key theoretical issues to be addressed concerns the method of contracting (e.g., Abken, 1994). What is the best mix of OTC versus exchange trading for a particular commodity? It is possible to argue that OTC contracting needs to be legislatively discouraged in order to direct liquidity to futures and options exchanges where activity can be more closely monitored and the gains of concentrated liquidity and mark to market accounting can be captured. Others could argue that futures exchanges are little more than vestiges of an old transactions technology, extracting rents from a legislatively sanctioned monopoly.

The incoherence of strategic direction is apparent in the layering of regulation associated with the different methods of contracting. The resulting competition among the various regulatory bodies almost certainly imposes real economic costs. For example, a U.S. financial firm has a range of regulators concerned with monitoring and regulating derivative trading activity, from the Commodities and Futures Trading Commission (CFTC) to the Board of Governors to the Securities and Exchange Commission (SEC). There is also an array of less formal regulators, including the Bank for International Settlements (BIS), as well as the exchanges and trading associations.[20] Each of these regulatory entities requires resources, derived from the firm being monitored, in order to verify that there is compliance with the rules. Yet, a fragmented regulatory structure has only limited resources to dedicate for each individual regulator to verify that firms actually are in compliance with the particular part of the overall rules which that regulator is responsible for monitoring. All this is complicated by an extremely fluid market situation where new products and ideas are being introduced at a rapid pace.

To see the quandaries arising from this layering of regulation, consider the case of Barings Bank. This firm was an English merchant banking group. Though Barings had an impressive pedigree, in England the bank was mid-sized and considered relatively conservative. Faced with the competitive pressures surrounding the Big Bang in London's financial markets in 1986, the bank's strategy was to expand activities offshore in Asia, where Barings had a considerable market presence, with the Barings Securities affiliate being the top Western securities firm in Japan during the incredible runup in the Japanese equity market during the 1980s. Barings was acknowledged to have

---

[20]Examples of such associations include the International Swap and Derivatives Association (ISDA), the Counterparty Risk Management Policy (CRMP) Group, and the Derivaties Policy Group (DPG). The DPG "was formed by six major Wall Street firms in August 1994, to respond to the public policy issues raised by the OTC derivatives activities of unregulated affiliates of SEC-registered broker-dealers and CFTC-registered futures commission merchants. The DPG is a voluntary framework designed to provide the SEC and CFTC with information and analyses that would permit them to more systematically and rigorously evaluate the risks associated with OTC derivative products" (PWGFM, 1999, pp. 76–77). The CRMP is described in PWGFM (1999, Appendix F).

special status on a number of Asian exchanges, due to the sizable amount of business that Barings transacted. Barings was a clearing member of a number of Asian futures and options exchanges. Which regulatory body or individual was ultimately responsible for monitoring the activities that led to the bank's collapse? Possible candidates include English banking regulators, the Singapore International Monetary Exchange (SIMEX), the Monetary Authority of Singapore, and the internal banking auditors.

The explosion in derivatives trading has exhibited a number of trends toward increased trade using OTC contracting methods. These trends include the migration to international markets, the increasing growth of OTC derivative trading relative to exchange trading, and the emergence of sophisticated risk-management products. All this has been amplified by the revolution in information technology. Yet, little seems to have changed since Abken (1994, p. 19) summarized the regulatory *status quo* on OTC contracting:

> The central policy issue in derivatives regulation is whether further federal regulation is appropriate or whether the existing structure can oversee these markets. The six federal banking and securities regulators believe that the current regulatory structure is capable of supervising the OTC derivatives markets. Policy makers need to be cautious about changing regulatory structures because such alterations often bring unintended and unforeseen consequences.

As it turns out, regulatory denial conveniently sustains a *status quo* solution. It seems as though the desired regulatory outcome is whether the current regulatory structure is sufficient to prevent severe market disruptions. For pragmatic reasons, public deliberations about the optimal regulatory structure appear to be out of order.

Central issues in the debate over appropriate regulatory structure are not new. Increased regulation aimed at channeling market activity into one venue or the other runs the risk of imposing costs greater than the associated benefits, running the risk of inhibiting the innovation and development of new products and practices. A guiding assumption underlying the current regulatory structure seems to be that the self-interest of market participants, combined with benevolent regulatory oversight, is sufficient to contain the potential difficulties associated with the explosion in OTC derivatives trading. Consistent with this approach and spurred on by the Long-Term Capital Management (LTCM) collapse, major OTC market participants have recently banded together into self-regulatory groups motivated to develop rules-of-the-game aimed at heading off the potential interference of government regulators.

Through all this, there is an inherent tension between two views: One view strongly promotes the expanded use of OTC derivatives to achieve optimal risk management outcomes for firms operating in increasingly volatile and globalized markets. The OTC markets provide the flexibility and convenience needed to sustain progress in development of complicated risk management products. Limiting access to market makers and key players in the cash markets is an effective method of controlling both credit risk and system wide leveraging. The opposing view is seriously concerned about the increase in system-wide leveraging brought on by the increased use of derivatives. This increase in leverage is compounded by the increasing use of OTC products that are largely unregulated and for which there is only a patchwork of reporting standards. Channeling derivative activities through exchanges would make such activities more transparent. In addition, concentrating trading activity at specific exchange sites would enhance overall market liquidity, permitting a wider array of deferred delivery dates. Product innovation would not be stifled but, rather, would be designed to facilitate exchange trading.

To adherents of the first view, lack of regulatory oversight has hidden benefits associated with the reduced costs of making transactions and ability to tailor contracts to the specific needs of market participants. To adherents of the second view, exchange trading forces marking-to-market, leading to practical market value accounting and a systemwide failsafe mechanism to prevent excessive leveraging by individual market participants. The arguments supporting either side are persuasive, making it difficult to formulate and implement policy changes. Whether such policy changes are needed at all is debatable. Yet, warning signals abound; from the crash of 1987 to the collapse of LTCM to the high-tech stock bubble of 1999–2000, certain systemic and unexplained bouts of market volatility occur that seem out of proportion to the underlying fundamentals. As George Soros observed, this volatility could be exacerbated by the growth of financially engineered products that has increased the usage of dynamic delta hedging strategies that tend to amplify market movements.

II. HISTORY OF DERIVATIVES

Due to a significant number of high-profile and expensive losses, trading of derivative securities attracted considerable attention during the 1990s (see Table 1.4). The list of companies involved is striking, as is the size of the losses. From Barings Bank to Gibson's Greetings to Sumitomo Corporation, from Long-Term Capital Management to Proctor and Gamble to Orange County, losses ranging from hundreds of millions to billions of dollars have been reported. Such events induce a state of uneasiness among policymakers, corporate managers, investment professionals, even academics. While it is tempting to draw glib generalizations about the apparent misunderstanding of risk-management practices, closer inspection reveals a decidedly more complicated battlefield. In some cases, the relevant lessons that could be

TABLE 1.4   Recent Corporate Losses Arising from Derivatives Trading

Time	Company	Losses	Transactions
1979	Minpeco S.A., Peru	$100 million	Silver futures
1980	Hunt brothers' companies	$1.1 billion (est.)	Silver futures
1988	Hammersmith and Fulham	£500 million	Swaps
1993	Showa Shell Sheikyu	¥165 billion	Currency options and forwards
1993	Metallgesellschaft	$1.3 billion	Energy derivatives
1994	Codelco, Chile	$200 million	Copper futures
1994	Kashima Oil	$1.5 billion	Currency derivatives
1994	Proctor and Gamble	$157 million	Leveraged swaps
1994	Piper Jaffrey Companies	$700 million	Mortgage derivatives
1994	Sears	$237 million	Swaps
1994	Orange County, CA	$1.8 billion	Reverse repos
1995	Barings Bank, PLC	£900 million	Stock index futures and options
1996	Sumitomo Corporation	$1.8 billion	Copper futures
1998	Yokult Honsha, Japan	$523 million	Stock index futures and options
1998	Long-Term Capital Management	$4.4 billion	Numerous positions in various markets
1999	Ashanti, Ghana	$570 million	Gold exotic derivatives
2001	Enron	$1.2 billion	Energy derivatives

Source: Chance (1998), Jorion (2001), Williams (1995), McCarthy (2000).

learned cannot be convincingly determined, due to the veil of corporate secrecy surrounding specific events. In cases where the activities and motivations of the participants can be precisely determined, it seems that different debacles raise different types of quandaries. Upon closer inspection, it seems that some so-called debacles were not debacles at all.[21]

Large losses associated with derivative security trading are not unique to the 1990s. Even though the largest losses in absolute terms have happened more recently, this is consistent with the increasing use, availability, and complexity of derivative products. This has produced an evolution in the types of problems that are arising. Since the early 1970s, there has been a

---

[21]References to debacles, high profile failures, and great disasters abound (e.g., Kuprianov, 1995; Marshall and Siegel, 1996; Smith, 1997; Culp and Miller, 1998; Jorion, 2001). The various events have become part of conventional wisdom. Yet, the *Oxford Dictionary* (1986) defines a debacle to be a sudden disasterous collapse. This is a modern progression on earlier English usage, as in the *Oxford Dictionary* (1931), which defines a debacle to be a sudden deluge or violent rush of water, which carries before it blocks of stone and other debris. Figurative usage of debacle defines a debacle to be a sudden breaking up or a confused rout. In the 1990s, Barings Bank and LTCM both experienced a sudden disasterous collapse of a corporate entity. Though there were some tense moments, in the end there was only minimal disruption to other businesses. Other events, such as Sumitomo Corp., Procter and Gamble, and Orange County, were sudden but did not lead to a substantive collapse. Hence, there seems, at the outset, to be considerable overstatement surrounding the topics to be studied.

progressive relaxation in the United States of a range of restrictions on derivative security trading, many of which had originated in the antispeculation atmosphere of the post-Depression era. In conjunction with this relaxation, there has been an almost bewildering expansion in the variety of derivative securities being traded, both on the OTC markets and on the futures and options exchanges. From financial commodities to energy to equities to currencies, it is difficult to keep track of the rapid progress that has been and is being made in the development and application of derivative securities.

This modern Renaissance of derivative securities trading is somewhat anomalous. Historically, derivative security trading has been subject to prohibitions and restrictions, aimed largely at preventing the abuses that are at the root of many past derivative debacles. Such abuses have been present almost from the beginning of bourse trading in forward and option contracts in the early 16th century.[22] The early emergence of exchange trading is significant because the contracting process was securitized and, to a certain extent, transferable. This permitted the introduction of speculative trading to a degree that had not previously been possible. In turn, speculators enhanced market liquidity, facilitating the exchange process for a wide range of commodities. The importance of speculators in providing market liquidity has become even more important in modern derivative markets. However, the enhanced ability to use derivatives has meant that increased speculation in derivatives has been accompanied by ongoing attempts to use derivatives to manipulate markets.

Forward contracting, the process of setting a price today for a delivery that is to take place in the future, is inherent in the exchange process and can be traced to ancient times. Due to the difficulties of transport and communications, some form of forward contracting was essential to early markets. While there was some haphazard speculations, those involved in the process were usually direct producers and consumers of the goods being traded. Lack of transferability meant that speculations often involved delivery of goods. Aided by the enhanced liquidity of bourse trading, derivative security trading reached an almost modern state of development by the 17th century, when the Amsterdam bourse featured both forward and option contracts on commodities that included foreign stocks and shares. Gains and losses on these contracts could be settled by the payment of differences at a quarterly *rescontre*, much like the modern clearinghouse doing daily marking to market.

---

[22]The relevant early history can be found in Poitras (2000), together with the sources cited there. The beginning of bourse trading can be traced to early 16th-century Antwerp (van der Wee, 1977). The history of corners and other manipulative practices on the Antwerp bourse are well documented (e.g., de Roover, 1949). That such techniques would be known in late 16th-century Amsterdam is expected, if only due to the exodus from Antwerp in the last quarter of the 16th century.

With the growth and accessibility of derivative security trading came attempts at manipulation. An important early manipulation was a "bear raid" conducted around 1608 by Isaac le Maire and a group of eight other traders on the Amsterdam bourse (van Dillen 1930, 1935). The bear ring led by le Maire used short forward contracts as part of a larger strategy to depress the price of Dutch East India Company (VOC) shares. The trading activities of le Maire's group were apparently successful in holding down the price of VOC shares. The potential impact of the bear ring on share prices attracted the attention of the VOC directors and other politically connected investors. The result was a period of political debate that included some of the first writings on stock market structure and performance. The debate ended in February 1610 with the passing of the first substantive legislation designed to limit stock market manipulation. Selling of shares in blanco, also known as the "windhandel" or "wind trade", was prohibited. More precisely, short selling of securities, defined to mean the sale of securities not owned by the seller, was banned. This ban covered both cash sales and forward sales. In addition, it was required that shares which were sold had to be transferred no later than one month after the transaction. Private sanctions included the expulsion of le Maire as a VOC shareholder.

Unlike modern securities laws, many earlier prohibitions imposed on derivative security trading activities did not have criminal sanctions. Rather, edicts such as the 1610 prohibition on short selling removed the protection of the courts for the purpose of enforcing contracts. The inability of the edict to control the "wind trade" speculation in shares was evident with the establishment of the Dutch West India Company in 1621, when shares were sold on a "when-issued" basis, prior to the initial subscription. This prompted the issuance of another edict reinforcing the ban on selling shares not owned by the seller. Any trader seeking to repudiate a short sale could find refuge in the courts. Similar edicts in 1630 and 1636, during the time Frederick Henry held the office of Dutch Stadholder (Prime Minister), led to the use of the term "appeal to Frederick" to refer to a trader invoking the protection of the prohibition on short sales to avert payment on a losing position.

Around the time of the Glorious Revolution (1688), active trading in derivative securities appeared in London. The abuses of forward and options contracting soon became associated with stockjobbing. Almost from the beginning of English stock trading, attempts were made to severely restrict stockjobbing. Following the first English stock market debacle in the mid-1690s, the first important piece of English legislation was passed, the 1697 Act "To Restrain the number and ill Practice of Brokers and Stockjobbers." The following is from the preamble to the Act (Morgan and Thomas, 1962, p. 23):

BOX 1

Glossary of Some Early Security Market Terms

"To arrive" contracts: The development of exchange trading for future delivery in 16th-century Antwerp began with "to arrive" contracts that, typically, involved goods in transit and required cash settlement upon arrival of the goods.

Puts and Refusals: Common usage for options, starting in late 17th-century England (e.g., Houghton, 1694). Barnard's Act (1733) makes specific reference to puts and refusals when referring to option contracts. A refusal was a call option. Reference to option contracts as *privileges*, common in mid-19th-century America, was not common in 18th-century English security markets.

A deal for "ready money" or "money": a transaction for immediate delivery to be settled within no less than 2 days (e.g., Mortimer, 1761). Also called a deal for *cash*.

A deal for "time": A transaction for future settlement, effectively a forward contract in the security. Where a *rescontre* settlement system was in place, the transaction would typically have the next *rescontre* as the settlement date (e.g., Mortimer, 1761). Time contracts required delivery at a more deferred delivery date than to arrive contracts (e.g., Hieronymous, 1977, p. 74). Reference to "time bargains" was common in the 17th and 18th centuries, though this term could be used in a more general sense to describe trading in both option and forward contracts.

Stocks and shares: Though this term could apply to securities listed as stocks, that appeared with price quotes in the public newspapers and on brokers' lists, this general category included the government funds, joint stock of public companies, and the various debt securities issued by the public companies (Mortimer, 1761). Usage of the term evolved during the 18th century. Houghton (1694) still uses the European term *Actions*, a term that for Houghton lumps joint stocks and lottery tickets together with a range of commodities such as copper, coal, lead, and saltpeter. Following Mortimer, "shares" can refer to either "stocks of the public companies of England" or to shares in government debt issues, such as "shares in annuities." This usage was still conventional in the

(continues)

> *(continued)*
> late 19th century (e.g., Castelli, 1877). This interpretation of "shares"
> differs from Baskin (1988, p. 207, n. 29).
>
> *Heavy horse and light horse*: Subscriptions to 18th-century English
> government debt issues could be paid by installment, with the first
> deposit generally being 15% (Mortimer, 1761, p. 137), with further
> payments of 10 or 15% being required each month until the balance
> was paid. The full amount of the subscription could be paid in advance,
> with credit being given for the associated interest. During the period in
> which subscriptions were being paid, secondary market trading had to
> account for the unpaid balances on a specific security. *Heavy horse*
> referred to a security that was fully paid, while *light horse* had a balance
> remaining to be paid. Stockjobbers preferred to deal in the light horse,
> which required a smaller invested capital for the same notional princi-
> pal: "They have an opportunity for sporting with, and gaining profit on,
> a nominal thousand, for the same money, that it would cost to buy a
> hundred, heavy" (Mortimer, 1761, p. 138).

> whereas divers Brokers and Stock-Jobbers, or pretended Brokers, have lately set
> up and on most unjust Practices and Designs, in Selling and Discounting of Talleys,
> Bank Stock, Bank Bills, Shares and Interests in Joint Stocks, and other Matters and
> Things, and have, and do, unlawfully Combined and Confederated themselves
> together, to Raise or fall from time to time the Value of such Talleys, Bank Stock,
> and Bank Bills, as may be most Convenient for their own private Interest and
> Advantage: which is a very great abuse of the said Ancient Trade and Imployment,
> and is extremely prejudicial to the Public Credit of this Kingdom and to the Trade
> and Commerce thereof, and if not timely prevented, may Ruin the Credit of the
> Nation, and enndanger the Government itself.

Stockjobbers were seen as interlopers in the legitimate trade of brokerage. As a
consequence, the Act specifically restricted the trade of brokerage to those
brokers licensed by the City of London. The Act then limits the number of
licensed brokers to 100.

Options were a particularly onerous aspect of the early stock trading in
London. By the 1690s, an organized options market had emerged in London in
support of the increasing number of joint stock issues.[23] Morgan and Thomas
(1962, p. 24) observe:

[23]The early history of options trading in England can be found in Morgan and Thomas (1962)
and Dickson (1967). An early discussion can be found in Duguid (1901). Barnard's Act was
repealed in 1860.

> The complaints with which the (1697) Act was designed to deal cover three main points: promoters of companies were encouraged to sell their rights at a profit to inexperienced persons, so that the management of companies suffered, and they failed to fulfil the functions for which they had been granted privileges. Dealers "confederated themselves together" to raise or lower prices to their own profit and the injury of their clients. And options dealings were abused and became a means of fraud.

There was considerable disagreement in the broker community about whether options transactions were reputable. While potentially useful in some trading contexts, reputable brokers felt that options contributed to the speculative excesses common in the early financial markets. While trading in options and time bargains did contribute to the most important English financial collapse of the 18th Century, the South Sea Bubble of 1720, this event was due more to the cash market manipulations of "John Blunt and his friends" (Morgan and Thomas, 1962, ch. 2). In any event, dealing in time bargains and, options were singled out as practices that were central to "the infamous practice of stock-jobbing." In 1721, legislation aimed at preventing stockjobbing passed the Commons but was not able to pass the Lords. It was not until 1733 that Sir John Barnard was able to successfully introduce a bill under the title: "An Act to prevent the infamous Practice of Stock-jobbing." This Act is generally referred to as Barnard's Act.

The abuses associated with stockjobbing were due, at least partly, to the standard market practice of a significant settlement lag for some purchases of joint stock.[24] In effect, stock was sold but the short could have a considerable lead time to deliver the security. The separation of pricing from settlement and delivery leads to the immediate creation of time contracts or "time bargains." Similar settlement lags also applied to new stock issues. Initial trading involved establishing a price and paying a small deposit against the future delivery of stock. In cases where the selling broker did have possession of the underlying stock when the transaction was initiated, there was little or no speculative element in the time bargain. However, this was not the case when the seller did not possess the stock. In addition, the purchaser did not usually have to take possession of the stock at delivery but, rather, could settle the difference between the agreed selling price and the stock price on the delivery date.

Barnard's Act (1733) was designed to regulate those features of stock dealings associated with excessive speculation. The main provision of the Act was that:

---

[24]The process of purchasing joint stock was considerably different than the modern purchase of common stock (e.g., Dickson, 1967). Transfers had to be effected at the company offices. Deals could be and were made for cash at the company offices, with more or less immediate transfer. Deals made at venues such as Exchange Alley or the Royal Exchange usually had to involve final settlement and delivery at a later date.

> All contracts or agreements whatsoever by or between any person or persons whatsoever, upon which any premium or consideration in the nature of a premium shall be given or paid for liberty to put upon or deliver, receive, accept or refuse any public or joint-stock, or other public securities whatsoever, or any part, share or interest therein, and also all wagers and contracts in the nature of wagers, and all contracts in the nature of puts or refusals, relating to the then present or future price or value of any stock or securities, as aforesaid, shall be null and void.

There was a penalty of £500 on any person, including brokers, who undertook any such bargains. All bargains were to be "specifically performed and executed," stock being actually delivered and cash "actually and really given and paid," and anyone settling a contract by paying or receiving differences was liable to a £100 penalty (Morgan and Thomas, 1962, p. 62). It was further provided that "whereas it is a frequent and mischievous practice for persons to sell and dispose of stocks and securities of which they are not possessed," anyone doing so should incur a penalty of £500. However, despite the Act making options trading illegal, options trading continued to the point where, in 1820, a controversy over the trading of stock options nearly precipitated a split in the London Stock Exchange. A few members of the Exchange circulated a petition discouraging options trading. The petition passed, and members formally agreed to discourage options trading. However, when an 1823 committee of the Exchange followed up on this with a proposal to implement a rule forbidding Exchange members from dealing in options (which was already illegal under Barnard's Act), a substantial number of members voted against. A dissident group even began raising funds for a new exchange building. In the end, the trading ban rule was rejected because options trading was a significant source of profits for numerous Exchange members who did not want to see that business lost to outsiders.

A. The Development of U.S. Derivative Markets[25]

The use of contracts involving the purchase or sale of a commodity for future delivery was, almost certainly, carried over by the early European colonizers of North America. To arrive contracts, time bargains and options were all in use by the end of the 18th century. During the 19th century, derivative security trading experienced both revolution and counter-revolution. The revolution can be attributed to the subtle impact that American culture had on specific business practices. Writing in 1896, Emery (1896, p. 7) captures the main theme: "The American people are regarded by foreigners as the greatest of all

---

[25]There are a number of excellent older sources on this material, including Emery (1896) and Cowing (1965).

speculators." This drive to speculate facilitated American innovations in derivative securities: "It was not until the (19th) century... that the system [of dealings for time] became widely developed and not until the great expansion of foreign trade in the last fifty years that it became of great importance."

An important theme in progress of derivative security trading during the 19th century is the enhanced participation of speculators. Among other benefits, enhanced speculation increases market liquidity. Yet, speculative activity has decided disadvantages, such as the increased incentive and ability to manipulate markets. This and other pressures ultimately led to the introduction of futures contracts. Though time dealings were being conducted in a number of centres throughout the 19th century, the beginning of trade in futures contracts is usually traced to mid-19th-century Chicago, a city that was first incorporated as a village in 1833 and grew into a city of 4107 by 1837. In order to promote commerce, the Board of Trade of the City of Chicago was founded on April 3, 1848, with 82 members. This event, in itself, was not particularly noteworthy. The promotional usefulness of boards of trade had been recognized for quite some time. For example, around 1700, John Law of the infamous Mississipi scheme proposed the creation of a board of trade for the city of Edinburgh (Mackay, 1852, p. 4).

The Chicago Board of Trade initially served as a marketplace for members of the grain trade. A system of wheat standards was developed together with a system of inspecting and weighing grain. In 1859, the Board of Trade was authorized by Illinois state to engage in the measuring, weighing and inspecting of grain, effectively corn and wheat. As Hieronymous (1977, p. 73) observes: "The development of quality standards and an inspection process and the substitution of weighing for the measurement of grain greatly facilitated trade. The substitution of weight for volume measures made the development of grain handling machinery possible. Increase in physical efficiency was important in the development of Chicago as a great grain terminal." These developments facilitated the handling of grain in bulk, through the use of grain elevators. This permitted interchangeable warehouse receipts to be introduced, instead of having to deal in unstandardized, specific lots.

The grain trade of that time typically involved merchants at various points along major waterways, such as the Illinois–Michigan canal, purchasing grain from farmers that was then held in storage, often from fall or winter into spring. In this operation, the merchants' capital investment involved paying the farmers for their crops at delivery, costs of building and maintaining storage facilities, and providing funds for shipment of grain when required. In order to avoid the risk of price fluctuation and to satisfy bankers, merchants started to go to Chicago and make contracts for future, spring delivery of grain, at prices determined that day. The first such "time contract" was made on March 13, 1851, calling for delivery of 3000 bushels of corn in June at one cent below the March 13 cash price. The contracts called for delivery of a standardized grade at a later delivery date. Similar contracts for wheat appeared in 1852. However, while there were similarities to modern futures contracts, other terms and conditions were specific to the original parties to the transaction making the time contract similar to a forward transaction.

The development of futures markets in Chicago was significant because, in the years immediately following the introduction of time contracts, individuals not connected to the grain trade became interested in taking positions. The resulting contracts often changed hands numerous times before being purchased by a market participant actually interested in taking delivery of the grain. This marks the introduction of a fundamental feature of futures markets, the essential participation of speculators not directly concerned with the ownership of the underlying commodity. Exchange trading and purely speculative participants were characteristics not associated with trading in "to arrive" contracts and "privileges" that had characterized American commodities trading previously (Williams, 1982). This trade was concentrated primarily in flour and, in keeping with use of such contracts in Liverpool, in cotton. To arrive contracts in wheat, corn, rye, and pickled hams were also conducted with activity centering on New York. In contrast to time bargains, to arrive contracts typically featured short delivery dates and the expectation that delivery would be completed. While there is some evidence of limited speculative dealings in these "to arrive" contracts and "privileges" associated with the flour default of May 1847, participants to these transactions usually were merchants directly involved in the commodity business.

The increasing interest in time contracts led the Board of Trade to introduce a number of resolutions to curb abuses. Many of the abuses were consistent with speculative participation and longer delivery dates: "It seems that when time for settlement arrived some of the contracting parties were difficult to locate" (Hieronymous, 1977, p. 76) Out of this process came the beginnings of formal trading rules for futures contracts. In 1863, the Board adopted a rule that suspended the membership of anyone failing to comply with a contract, either written or verbal. On October 13, 1865, the General Rules of the Board of Trade explicitly acknowledged futures trading and adopted rules that included all the essential elements of a modern futures contract, including standardized contract terms, restriction of futures contract trading to exchange members, margin deposits to guarantee performance, and standardized delivery procedures. Prior to this date, individual traders had been responsible for establishment and enforcement of the terms of the contract. This development followed a similar move in 1864 by the Liverpool Cotton Brokers' Association introducing formal regulations for to arrive contracts in cotton.

Trade in futures and forward contracts has progressed dramatically since the first corn futures trade on the Chicago Board of Trade (CBOT) in 1865. Many other futures exchanges emerged in the period between the Civil War and World War I. In 1874, the Chicago Produce Exchange was formed by dealers trading in produce of various kinds. In 1898, a subgroup of the Produce Exchange known as the Produce Exchange Butter and Egg Board withdrew from the Produce Exchange and formed the Chicago Butter and Egg Board. This group is of interest because it established an active trade in time contracts for eggs, even though such trade was only a small proportion of the Butter and Egg Board's activity. When margin rules for time contracts were finally written in 1911 there was considerable controversy among the members. Finally, in 1919, a complete set of futures trading rules were written, and the mandate of the Butter and Egg Board was changed to include futures trading. The end product was the emergence of the Chicago Mercantile Exchange (CME), which started trading butter and eggs on December 1, 1919. (Currently, the CBOT and CME are still the two most important futures exchanges in the world.)

The period from the Civil War to the First World War also saw the emergence of other exchanges trading a range of different commodities. The New York Cotton Exchange was formed in 1870 and the New Orleans Cotton Exchange in 1871, though time contracts did not play an important role on the latter exchange for almost a decade. The Coffee, Sugar and Cocoa Exchange was initially founded in 1882 as the Coffee Exchange of New York City with the specific intent of trading in time contracts for coffee. Initially founded in 1872 to trade in butter, eggs, and cheese, a decade later the exchange acquired its current name, the New York Mercantile Exchange (NYMEX).[26] Other lesser exchanges such as the San Francisco Chamber of Commerce, Kansas City Board of Trade, and the Minneapolis Grain Exchange also have their origins in this period. Even the COMEX, which was formed in 1933, was the result of merging four small exchanges for raw hides, metals, raw silk, and rubber that had histories originating in that period.

Yet, this later 19th-century Renaissance for derivative securities trading was accompanied by a neo-Luddite attack from agrarians and Populists (e.g., Cowing, 1965; Hicks, 1961). The focus of the attacks was futures contracts. The antispeculation reasoning behind the attacks has been described by Cowing (1965, p. 5):

> The seemingly orthodox futures contract, occasionally used before the Civil War and an outgrowth of earlier "to arrive" and "forward delivery" agreements, began to receive unprecedented attention from speculators. Persons not previously connected with the commodities business had been attracted, and were buying and

---

[26]In 1999, the NYMEX merged with the COMEX.

selling futures contracts in the central markets, especially in Chicago and New York. The number of bushels and bales traded on the exchanges exceeded the annual production from 1872 on and in several years toward the end of the century amounted to sevenfold the annual crop. Prices had moved widely before the war because of weather, economic instability, and imperfect crop information, but it appeared that the new volatility was due to maneuvers by speculators with large purses. Thus "speculator" became more than ever a term of opprobrium; the physiocratic bias against those who produced no primary products was more bitterly asserted as the agrarian population shifted consciously to the defensive. The mysterious and remote commodity speculator seemed more of a parasite to the farmers than the local physician who was holding land for appreciation. Farmers identified the commodity speculator as the villian responsible for erratic price changes in Chicago, Minneapolis, and New York, especially around harvest time. The stage was set; the national crusade against the exchange speculator was about to begin.

The decline in agrarian conditions following the post-1886 droughts generated sufficient political will to produce the Hatch–Washburn bill of 1892. Instead of outlawing futures trading, this bill aimed to impose a prohibitive tax on speculative dealings in futures.

The Congressional debate on the issue surrounding the Hatch–Washburn bill is an essential primary source on 19th century views on derivative securities. The committee meetings leading up to votes on the bill included testimony from important agrarians, such as J.H. Brigham, Master of the National Grange, and C.W. Macune of the Farmers' Alliance and Industrial Union. Not only farmers were in favor of the bill; the testimony also included statements from millers, such as Charles Pillsbury, as well as grain and hog merchants. Pillsbury held that "neither grower nor miller had as much influence over prices as a few men around the wheat pit in Chicago. Short selling by these few made prices erratic and unstable; opinions based upon supply and demand were worthless in the face of this manipulation" (Cowing, 1965, p. 7). Pillsbury also maintained that the use of futures to hedge would not be necessary if price volatility due to speculation was eliminated.

In 1893, the Hatch–Washburn bill successfully passed the House, 167–40, and passed the Senate, 40–29, though there were some amendments that had to be returned to the House for approval.[27] which placed the bill too far down the calendar to be dealt with before the end of the session. A suspension of House rules was required for the bill to become law; however, suspension of rules requires a two thirds majority, and the vote, 172–124, fell short by 26

---

[27]The Senate debate included a vote on the George amendment which aimed to ban futures trading altogether. This amendment was prompted by the concern of Southern members about the use of tax-to-destroy as a method of dealing with the antispeculation arguments of the agrarians and Populists. This amendment was defeated by 51 to 19. However, as it turns out, the Southern supporters of the George amendment held the balance in the House vote to suspend rules that led to the defeat of the Hatch–Washburn bill.

votes. The gradual return of prosperity dampened, but did not eliminate, the drive of the antispeculator forces. However, it was not until after World War I that sufficient legislation, such as the Grain Futures Act (1922), was in place to curb the alleged abuses of the middlemen and speculators using the exchanges. By this time, the extreme antispeculator position of the agrarians had faded. Though the Act did contain provisions against manipulation, these were largely ineffective. The Act was successful in bringing the futures exchanges under federal supervision and in providing for "continuous fact-finding and supply of continuous trading information" (Hieronymous, 1977, p. 314).[28]

B. A CANADIAN PERSPECTIVE

In contrast to the development of organized commodity exchanges in the United States[29] the development of derivative securities trading in Canada has a different flavor. As expected, much of the agrarian discontent observed in the United States in the late 19th and early 20th centuries found similar expression in Canada. In some respects, the agrarian views were even more extreme in Canada, and the distrust of monopoly elements and speculators on the grain exchange even more deep rooted. Yet, despite this sympathetic undercurrent, the marketing solutions chosen in Canada differ dramatically from those in the United States. In the end, a government-sanctioned and controlled monopoly emerged to dominate the marketing of Canadian wheat.

After an initially unsuccessful attempt to establish a grain exchange in 1883, a group of local grain merchants and farmers successfully combined to form the Winnipeg Grain and Produce Exchange in 1887. While initially trade on the Winnipeg exchange was for cash market grain, by 1904 futures trading in wheat, oats, and flaxseed had begun. The exchange was reorganized in 1908 as the Winnipeg Grain Exchange. Not without sufficient reasons, this increasing sophistication of grain marketing was generally viewed with suspicion and contempt by farmers: "By the beginning of the ... century, disparities of bargaining power in the markets in which western farmers disposed of their produce served as the focus of agrarian protest in western Canada.... These disparities were attributed by the farmers to a deliberate and increasing

---

[28]Stassen (1981) is an excellent account on the restrictions that have been imposed on derivative security trading in the United States since the passage of the Grain Futures Act.

[29]The early history of derivative security trading in Canada is not well documented, though it is reasonable to assume that practices common in England and the United States would also be used in Canada. This implies the use of bills of exchange to extend credit in the early fur trading and fishing period. The use of "to arrive" contracts for various commodities, particularly in the 19th century in the flour trade, also is likely.

curtailment of competitive action among grain buyers and warehousemen at local market centres. . . . It was, moreover, clear from the start that the activities of local elevator operators and of most grain buyers were controlled by the head offices of their respective companies in distant places. These offices were centrally located in Winnipeg" (Fowke, 1957, p. 118).

The Canadian grain trade during this period was dominated by the production of wheat, primarily for export. This trade involved farmers transporting wheat to the local shipping point, at which there was typically more than one elevator. However, because the elevator and transportation activities were dominated by a small number of companies, there would be no price competition. One price would be quoted for a particular grade, based on the price on the Winnipeg exchange. In combination with a number of marketing practices such as the mixing and substitution of grains by local elevators, by World War I there had emerged in the farm community "the conviction that monopoly elements dominated the grain trade." This conviction "had become so deeply and so generally rooted in the minds of western grain growers that they pressed strongly for the socialization of the elevator system at both its local and terminal levels. For many farmers there was every readiness to replace private monopoly with public monopoly; for others it would be sufficient to provide an adequate network of government-owned country and terminal elevator companies" (Fowke, 1957, p. 123) Given that wheat had become the main source of income for the prairie provinces, considerable public and private efforts were expended to provide an alternative marketing system for grain.

The exigencies of the war effort provided the first opportunity for alternative marketing systems for Canadian grain. The Grain Export Company was created by the Allies in 1916 to provide North American wheat supplies for the War effort. In early 1917, the company's large wheat purchases led to a "corner" in the May time contract on the Winnipeg exchange (Ankli, 1982, pp. 273–274):

> This led to a panic situation and the closing of the futures market on 4 May. In June the Dominion government suspended all trading on the exchange and established the Board of Grain Supervisors. This board fixed the price of wheat and directed the marketing of all wheat from the elevators to the Allies' purchasing agents. The duties of this Board were suspended following the end of the war in 1919 and futures trading resumed. However, when it became evident that postwar conditions were far from normal, the first Canadian Wheat Board was established. It was to be the sole marketing agent of the entire 1919 crop. . . . Although the Wheat Board did not establish the final price, the farmers received the highest price they had ever received for wheat. They lauded the success of the Wheat Board and naturally saw cause and effect. The federal government declared the emergency at an end and dropped the Wheat Board in 1920; prices immediately fell. Farmers attributed this decline to the removal of government marketing and the reinstatement of open market systems.

The failure to reestablish the Wheat Board laid the foundation for the birth in 1923 of the cooperative Wheat Pools as a marketing alternative to the Exchange. Pooling was a system where "farmers voluntarily signed an agreement to deliver all their wheat to the pool for five years and would receive, in return, an initial payment per bushel and the remainder in interim and final payments based on the actual return for that grade."[30] In addition to providing an alternative marketing channel, the pools were also intended to implement a system of "orderly marketing" in which grain would be marketed more uniformly over the full year to adjust for typically lower prices in autumn when the crop is delivered. However, in practice, the orderly marketing strategy was not successful. Farmers did not, as a rule, receive a more favorable price from the pools than would have been paid by the Exchange. Despite this, from 1924 to 1929, the pools experienced incredible success, handling over 50% of Canadian grain during that period, as much as 70% in 1927. While attempting as much as possible to market grain outside the Exchange, the pools did use the Exchange for selling wheat. The pools also made considerable progress in the acquisition of local and terminal elevators. By 1929, the pools controlled almost half of the elevator capacity in western Canada.

The success of the pools ended abruptly in 1929 when the pool price for the initial payment was set too high. The collapse of wheat prices in 1930 had first the Prairie provincial governments and then the federal government intervening to prevent the collapse of the pools. In July 1931, the pools were restructured by separating the elevator operations from the marketing agency. Following this, the pools terminated the delivery contracts of their members and established voluntary pools that did not attract significant deliveries. The social and political need to fill the void in marketing services left by the pools led to the establishment of the Wheat Board. The Canadian Wheat Board Act of 1935 "empowered the Board to accept deliveries from producers at a minimum price. Excess receipts above this amount would be distributed to producers at the end of the crop year, and any losses would be assumed by the Dominion government. The Board was encouraged to make use of the open market system whenever possible" (Ankli, 1982, p. 275) In following years, when crops were short and prices were high, the Wheat Board accepted no deliveries. However, when supplies were plentiful, the Wheat Board price tended to be too high, and almost all wheat deliveries were made to the Board.

The demands of providing wheat for the Allied war effort proved incompatible with allowing farmers to market wheat through the Exchange when prices were favorable. In September 1943, the Wheat Board was made the sole buyer of Canadian wheat, and trading in wheat on the Winnipeg Grain Exchange

---

[30]The quote is from Friesen (1984, p. 337). A considerable amount of historical research has been done on the pools and related farmers movements (e.g., MacPherson, 1979).

was discontinued. The Wheat Board monopoly on the marketing of Canadian wheat for export continues to the present. This outcome is consistent with the historical resistance of Canadian wheat farmers, especially the representatives of farm organizations, to the open marketing system of the Winnipeg Exchange. The political importance of wheat producers was sufficient to produce pressures that led to the creation of the Canadian Wheat Board monopoly, which made the Canadian government a central part of the Canadian grain trade: "The existence of the Wheat Board has rendered inoperative traditional price discovery mechanisms such as futures and cash markets in Canada" (McCalla and Schmitz, 1979, p. 205). This left only the lesser grains, such oats and barley, for marketing by the Winnipeg Grain Exchange. It is ironic that the three interwar Royal Commissions that considered farmers' complaints all found that cash prices, as determined on the Exchange, were fair. As for futures trading, the *Report of the Commission to Enquire into Trading in Grain Futures* (1931, p. 72), concluded: "...futures trading, even with its disadvantages of numerous price fluctuations, is of distinct benefit to the producer in the price which he receives."

C. THE U.S. EXPERIENCE WITH OPTIONS

In considering the history of options trading in the United States, it is useful to make a distinction between stock and commodity options. Though there were instances of earlier trading, early U.S. trade in *commodity* options is usually associated with the beginnings of the Chicago Board of Trade (CBOT), where options were known as "privileges." Bid and offer privileges roughly corresponded to modern-day puts and calls. The similarity of privileges to gambling, as well as the prominent use of options in a number of market manipulations, led to numerous attempts to halt options trading. As early as 1865, the CBOT introduced a rule that denied the protection of the exchange to privilege traders. This rule was found to be both unpopular and ineffective and was withdrawn in 1869. Various legal challenges were launched to privilege trading, including an Illinois Supreme Court ruling that found privileges to be illegal. In 1890, the U.S. Congress attempted to ban commodity options but was unsuccessful in getting the legislation passed.

The social resistance to commodity option trading during this period was propelled by farm-based "populist" political movements that associated erratic price behavior with excessive speculation. These views were not without foundation. The limited amount of regulation of commodity and stock markets in the pre-World War I period permitted numerous corners and other market manipulations. Charles Taylor (1917) relates that one of the more "outstanding of these (corners) had to do with oats, and was operated by

Mr. Chandler, a prominent merchant. He peddled 'puts' about the city, inducing speculation on the part of a large number of people not ordinarily in the market. Chandler and his friends did not count on a large inrush of oats attracted to Chicago by the high prices and the corner failed. Many people lost money and there was much public indignation" (Hieronymus, 1977, p. 85). There was a prevailing belief among populists that brokers were using the exchange process to extract money from farmers. The social importance of many of the underlying commodities meant that commodity options received substantially more scrutiny than stock options.

Following the introduction of taxes on privilege earnings in 1921, the Grain Futures Act (1922) represented a significant step in curbing market abuses associated with derivative security trading. This Act required commodity exchanges and their members to maintain and file privilege trading reports. Combined with the authority of the Secretary of Agriculture to investigate exchange operations, this led to a substantial curtailment in commodity options abuses. However, some commodity options trading still continued and, following the collapse of agricultural prices associated with the Great Depression, pressure from farm lobbies led to the outright ban on commodity options trading, in selected commodities, legislated in the Commodity Exchange Act (1936). Included in the restricted list were wheat, cotton, rice,

---

BOX 2

The Sinclair Option Pool of 1929

One of the most profitable pools was the Sinclair Consolidated Oil option pool of 1929. While Sinclair stock was selling in the $28 to $32 range, a contract was obtained from Sinclair granting the pool an option to buy 1,130,000 shares at $30 per share. The pool then purchased 634,000 shares in the open market to bid up prices. The pool exercised its option, then liquidated all its holdings while the stock was selling in the $40 range. The pool also sold 200,000 shares short as the price fell. The pool's total profit was approximately $12.5 million from the following sources: $10 million profit from optioned shares purchased at $30 per share, $500,000 profit from shares purchased in the market, and $2 million profit from the short sales.

"Stock Exchange Practices," Senate Report 1455, 73rd Congress, 2nd Sess., p. 63; quoted in Teweles and Bradley (1982).

corn, oats, and barley. However, despite the restrictions, considerable trade continued in unlisted commodities such as coffee, silver, copper, and platinum, together with commodity options trading offshore, especially in London.

In the United States, trading in stock options began as early as 1790. Kairys and Varerio (1997) discuss the state of the options market during the 1870s when there was an "active market" among numerous brokerage firms in New York City. Much as with commodity options, stock option trading also played a significant role in market manipulations. As early as the 1890s, option pools were in operation (Teweles and Bradley, 1982, p. 269):

> A pool is a temporary association of two or more individuals to act jointly in a security operation of a manipulative character. There is no inherent reason why manipulation should be carried out through the use of pools; many such manipulations have been carried on with great financial success by single operators, such as Drew, Little, Vanderbilt, Gould and Keene. During the 1920s, however, the pool developed a high degree of popularity. The possibility of combining capital, trading skill, experience and corporate connections into one cooperative venture appeared so attractive that it became the typical organization procedure of manipulators of that era. There was no particular size of the pool of the 1920s and early 1930s. The Radio pool, one of the largest, had about 70 members, the first Fox pool had 32, and the second 42. The profitable alcohol pool of 1933 had only eight participants.

Two general types of pools were present in the 1920s: trading pools and option pools, with the latter being the most common. While trading pools acquired stock on the open market, option pools would acquire all or most of its securities by obtaining call options contracts to purchase stock at favorable prices. These options were acquired from various sources, such as the corporation, where the options took the form of warrants, as well as large stockholders, directors, officers, large speculators, and banks. While there was considerable diversity in the maturity of the options granted and the types of schemes involved, the primary objective of the option pool was to benefit through manipulation of the common stock price. The option pools were symptomatic of the types of abuses that contributed to the 1929 stock market collapse. The regulatory response implemented in the 1930s, culminating in the Securities Act (1934), was to prohibit all activities aimed at manipulating market prices and trading on insider information.

Franklin and Colberg (1958, pp. 29–30) illustrate the importance of options trading in the 1929 market collapse:

> Testimony before the Senate Committee on Banking and Currency in 1932 and 1933 disclosed that many of the financial abuses of the 1920s were related to the use of options. A favorite device of large stockholders was to grant options without cost to a pool which would then attempt to make these profitable by "churning" activities designed to bring the general public in as buyers of the stock. In addition, long-term and even unlimited-period option warrants were issued frequently in connection with new stock issues.

During the wave of securities market reform following the market collapse of 1929–33, considerable attention was given to terminating option trading all together.

BOX 3

Franklin and Colberg (1958) on the U.S. Stock Options Market in the 1950s

The Brokers
Practically all the Put and Call business in the United States is handled by about twenty-five option brokers and dealers located in New York City. These brokers operate through an association. All the contracts in which they deal are guaranteed or indorsed by member firms of the New York Stock Exchange. This indorsement guarantees the performance of the contract and makes options negotiable bearer instruments. The owner of the option may sell to anyone he chooses and the terms of the option remain unchanged. The purchaser of the option is not required to know anything about the maker of the option or about his financial standing because of this indorsement. Put and Call options can be bought and sold through a local broker, or one may place an order directly with a Put and Call broker.

The Seller of Options
Options can be, and sometimes are, sold by small investors. Most Puts and Calls originate, however, with large individual stockholders, particularly those who hold a "continuous portfolio." Such stockholders are in a position quickly to write most of the options for which a demand may arise because they are able to furnish stock which may be called for and to purchase stock which may be put to them. Institutional investors in stocks participate in writing options, but not to a large extent.

The Buyer of Options
Since no reports are required by, or rendered to, the Securities and Exchange Commission on this subject, and since brokers and dealers in Puts and Calls are likely to guard closely the source of their business, one may only speculate as to the geographic location, financial size, and other characteristics of the purchaser of options. However, an

(continues)

> (*continued*)
>
> examination of available information permits some inferences regarding the nature of the purchaser.
>
> The evidence indicates, therefore, that Puts and Calls are bought mainly for speculative purposes. Usually the options themselves are not the main vehicle in speculation; instead, actual purchases and sales of stocks ordinarily take place when options are worth exercising. Their use permits speculation with limited capital, with the potential loss restricted to the cost of the option plus commission and taxes. This inference is consistent with the remark of one veteran broker, as reported by *Barron's*, that speculation accounts for probably 80 percent of option trading. It appears that the emphasis usually placed by the Put and Call brokers on the "protection" which can be afforded by the use of such options is designed to secure for the trade the public acceptance generally enjoyed by commodity hedging and by many types of insurance.

In the process of developing a regulatory response to the market abuses that contributed to the financial market turbulence of 1929–33, it was accepted that the abuses associated with option pools would become illegal. However, in addition to the use of options in pool operations, there were other, more legitimate reasons for stock option trading. In the end, the brokerage industry was able to avoid the outright ban associated with commodity options. While initial legislation aimed at regulating the securities markets—the Fletcher–Rayburn bill (1934) called for a total ban on stock options—the brokerage industry was able to prevent this result. Instead, the Securities Act (1934) empowered the newly created Securities and Exchange Commission (SEC) to regulate the market and introduced the Put and Call Brokers and Dealers Association (PCBDA) that was designed to act as a self-policing agency, working closely with the SEC and other agencies to avoid further direct government regulation. Member firms of the PCBDA formed the basis for the OTC market trading of options that took place in the period leading up to the creation of the Chicago Board Options Exchange (CBOE) in 1973.

To appreciate the major advance that the CBOE represents, it is necessary to consider the state of equity option trading prior to the CBOE. Franklin and Colberg (1958) describe the general state of equity option trading at the end of the 1950s:

> Practically all of the Put and Call business in the US is handled by about twenty-five option brokers and dealers in New York City. The brokers operate through [the PCBDA]. All the contracts in which they deal are guaranteed or indorsed by

member firms of the New York Stock Exchange.... The Put and Call business is largely self-regulated, but a great deal of the aura of secrecy which surrounds this activity seems to stem from the early 1930s when the threat of strict regulation or even legislative extermination haunted the entire options trade. Testimony before the Senate Committee on Banking and Currency in 1932 and 1933 disclosed that many of the financial abuses of the 1920s were related to the use of options.

At this time, the options market was relatively small. Self-regulation, both by the exchanges and by the PCBDA, coupled with the ability of the SEC to require reporting of options trading was sufficient to prevent the abuses of previous years.

Among other significant regulatory changes introduced by the Securities Act, the SEC required all options sellers to post margins. Unscrupulous activities such as granting brokers options for touting a stock were banned together with the use of options to trade on inside information. In addition to the increased government regulation, self-regulation by the PCBDA also played on important role. Despite the success in reducing market abuses, the options traded in the OTC market were often illiquid, making it difficult to resell or transfer a given options contract to another party. In 1972, this started to change with creation of the Options Clearing Corporation, as a subsidiary of the CBOE. In following years, the American, Philadelphia, Pacific, and Midwest exchanges also introduced options trading. Trading on the CBOE commenced in April 1973 with 16 stock options. While initial interest in options trading was limited, by 1977 volume had increased substantially to the point where put options were introduced.

The implications and advantages associated with exchange trading of options are much the same as with futures. Strike prices and expiration dates of contracts are standardized to facilitate liquidity. The security of doing trades with the clearinghouse instead of a specific counterparty means positions are easier to unwind. Transactions and other costs are also lower. The present importance of stock option trading is reflected in the cost of exchange seats, for which the CBOE is always a leading contender for being most expensive. These successes with stock options were not, initially, matched by commodity options. After creation of the CFTC in 1974, a number of large commodity options frauds originating in London commodity options led, in 1978, to the CFTC banning all London options, dealer options, and domestic exchange-traded options, except under certain restrictive conditions.[31] These rules were

---

[31]Wolf (1982) provides background on the specific events that were associated with the CFTC options ban. Since the creation of the CFTC in 1974 to replace the Commodity Exchange Authority that had been part of the USDA, changes to commodity futures and options regulations have usually been associated with the regular 4-year reauthorization of the CFTC. For example, the 1982 reauthorization contained the Shad/Johnson accord Index Act that specifies the authority of the SEC and CFTC for stock-related products. This Act gave the CFTC exclusive jurisdiction over stock index futures and options while the SEC was given control over options on securities and currencies.

altered substantially in 1981 when new regulations on trading in commodity options were introduced. In 1982, trading began with options on futures for gold, heating oil, sugar, U.S. T-bonds, and certain stock indices. Over time, commodity option trading has been extended to currencies, Eurodollars, and a variety of other commodities. In this environment, the SEC has jurisdiction over options on physical securities, while the CFTC is responsible for options on futures.

III. RECENT DERIVATIVES DEBACLES

The modern Renaissance in derivative securities has, not surprisingly, been accompanied by a range of disasters associated with the use of derivatives (see Table 1.4). Some of the disasters tell stories that are all too familiar from past history, huge losses emerging from schemes to manipulate markets using the leverage inherent in derivatives contracts. Sometimes these schemes were motivated by personal or corporate greed, as in the Sumitomo copper corner or the Hunts' silver manipulation. Other disasters originated in another basic way: poor judgment about the business or operational risks being undertaken. This is arguably the source of the losses incurred by Metallge-sellschaft or Barings Bank. Yet, the modern period has also seen the emergence of a new type of event: "market completion and replication" disasters. In these disasters, seemingly new innovations originating from the financial engineering industry result in significant and unanticipated losses. In some of these disasters, strategies are pursued with the realistic objective of replicating an untraded derivative security but are ultimately defeated by liquidity and operational risks. The stock market crash of October 1987 and the collapse of Long-Term Capital Management (LTCM) fall into this group.

The Hunts' silver manipulation provides a useful starting point for illustrat-ing the derivative disasters of the modern period. Considered in isolation from the Hunts' other business interests, the silver dealings were purely speculative. Though the Hunts' did have ownership stakes in silver production (e.g., the Sunshine Mining Company), the purpose of those holdings seems to have been driven by the Hunts' activities in the silver futures markets, and not the other way around. The general business risk of these activities was determined exclusively by movements in the price of silver, a market risk. Yet, even though the risk management problem is quite simple, there does not seem to have been more than cursory attention given to evaluating the value at risk of the position. In the end, it seems that the losses that did emerge originated in a complex of legal risks, liquidity risks, and operational risks.

A. The Hunt Silver Manipulation (1979–1980)[32]

The impact of the activities of the Hunt brothers, Bunker and Herbert, on the silver market from June 1979 to March 1980 has been the subject of much legal wrangling and academic debate (e.g., Williams, 1995). At the center of the debate is the issue of market manipulation. Precisely what constitutes manipulation is not an easy concept to legally define. What constitutes legal activity in one situation may be illegal in other situations. These events in the silver market during 1979–80 also provide useful insight into the workings of futures markets. Playing fundamental roles in the incident were the exchange-oversight function, the crucial role of variation margin, and the details of the delivery process. The incident is also interesting because of the considerable economic analysis that was done on the event, arising from the lawsuits generated by specific events.

The central characters in the story are the Hunt brothers. Though the Hunts were not the only players in the arena, the social importance of their family focused attention on their role.[33] The Hunts started dabbling in the silver market in 1973, beginning with trading in silver futures. Being men of substantial wealth, it was not surprising that they soon expanded their silver activities to include the taking of delivery on futures contracts. From that point, until 1979, the Hunts became involved in an expanding attempt to dominate the global silver market. These activities included an attempt to gain control of the Sunshine Mine, the largest silver mine in the United States, from Sunshine Mining Company. As of January 1, 1979, the Hunts had accumulated approximately 37 million troy ounces of bullion, with an additional 25 million in futures positions, an amount equal to around $375 million at early 1979 prices (Williams, 1995, p. 20).

While interesting reading, the motives for the Hunts getting involved in the silver market have been told elsewhere (e.g., Fay, 1982). What is relevant here is that, as speculators, the Hunts were in a situation where business profitabil-

---

[32]Fay (1982) and Williams (1995) are excellent sources on this topic. The Sumitomo copper corner is similar in many ways to the Hunt silver dealings, though there were some significant differences, such as the Sumitomo losses were the result of a trading operation within a larger corporate entity.

[33]The Hunt family fortune was founded by the eccentric H.L. Hunt, who left three sets of children (Hurt, 1981). Bunker and Herbert were from the first of H.L. Hunt's families. This first family also includes Lamar Hunt, owner of the Kansas City Chiefs. Around 1980, the centerpieces of the Hunt family fortune were Penrod Drilling, an oil drilling company, and Placid Oil, the holder of large oil reserves and leases. The two companies, together with the family's other assets, were controlled through an elaborate network of over 200 companies and trust funds (Williams, 1995, p. 20).

ity depended almost exclusively on movement in the level of silver prices. Their business risk was almost exclusively a market risk. Given this large exposure to a specific commodity price, it is not surprising that the Hunts were involved in activities designed to control the price of silver. In the process of accumulating their large silver positions, the Hunts had also developed an intricate network of silver market players. Included in this network were two men from Saudi Arabia who, starting in the summer of 1979, combined with the Hunts to form the International Metals Investment Company (IMIC). This company was formed to engage in further trading in silver, especially silver futures. The Hunts also informally enlisted the participation of another group that traded primarily through ContiCommodity Services (Conti). Despite being an American company, Conti seems to have been fronting for offshore, primarily Middle Eastern, clients (e.g., Fay, 1982).

The relationship between the price of silver and the activities of the Hunts, IMIC, and the Conti group has been intensely examined in a 1988 civil court case, *Minpeco v. Hunt* (Williams, 1995). The plaintiff in the case, Minpeco, is a Peruvian government-owned metals marketing firm. The case against the Hunts was successful and $192 million in damages were awarded. The six-month trial produced what can only be characterized as remarkable evidence: "All the legal professionals involved with the Hunt silver litigation have remarked on its exceptional complexity in regard to both laws and facts. In addition to manipulation law, the Hunt case involved antitrust law, racketeering law and fraud-on-the-market doctrine" (Williams, 1995, p. xii). That the case went to trial is unusual, illustrating the complicated issues involved.[34] As the trial progressed, the various participants revealed information in detail that is not typically available.

The Hunt case illustrates the inherent vagueries determining what constitutes *illegal* manipulative activities. The timeline is important. Shortly after IMIC was formed, the price of silver began what is best described as a bubble (see Figure 1.1). At debate in the court case was the role of the Hunts in any market manipulation that took place (see Chapter 2, Section III, for further discussion of speculation and manipulation). The evidence is clear that, during the summer of 1979, the Conti group, in combination with IMIC, took large positions in COMEX silver futures; the Conti group targeted the December 1979 contracts, while the Hunts' focus was on February and March 1980. On August 31, 1979, the combined positions of the Hunts, IMIC, and the Conti group totalled 25% of December 1979 open interest on the COMEX and CBOT, with 32%, 47%, and 38% in the February, March, and May 1980 deliveries, respectively.

---

[34]Johnson (1981, p. 97) reports: "In fact, it's quite rare for there to be manipulation cases. There are, perhaps, not more than a half dozen manipulation cases of any true significance that have been reported in the courts."

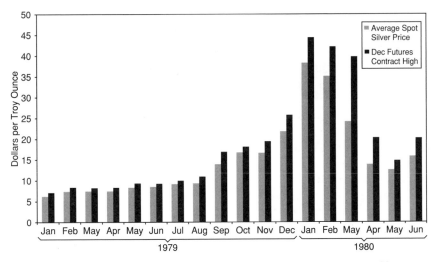

FIGURE 1.1 Monthly Silver Prices, January 1979 to June 1980. Spot price is the monthly average of the Handy and Harman daily closing price; COMEX December futures contract high is for the highest traded price for the December futures contract for that delivery year, e.g., the January 1980 (1979) value is for the December 1980 (1979) delivery.

Williams (1995, p.32) describes the extent of the Hunts' silver commitment:

> Manipulative schemers or not, Bunker and Herbert Hunt, in the summer of 1979, had doubled their already colossal bet on the price of silver. In just their personal accounts, including their half of IMIC and their existing holdings of bullion, they had positions approaching 140 million troy ounces (a level they kept more or less until the following March). At prevailing prices, the value of the silver they controlled exceeded $1.3 billion, a large fraction of their net worth. With every $1 movement in the price of silver, they gained or lost $140 million, an amount substantial even to them.

Given the size of these positions, the Hunts made considerable gains from the runup in prices that started around August 22 and continued to September 18, a rise from $9.537 to $15.90.

Not unlike the Cargill grain case over four decades previously, this abrupt price change surrounding a contract delivery triggered the oversight bodies within the futures exchanges. On September 4, the first of a number of initial margin increases was announced. In early October, the COMEX set up the Special Silver Committee to monitor the market and set rules as needed. Pressure was exerted on the visible longs, primarily Conti, to facilitate an orderly liquidation of the December contracts. However, until the December

1980 contract deliveries started to weigh on the market during the delivery month, the principal shorts were not having difficulty locating bullion for delivery. What did start occurring was a substantial decrease in market liquidity. The principal commercial shorts were exiting the market, many using an *exchange for physicals* (EFP) transaction.

An EFP is an off-exchange transaction in which the futures contract is settled by delivery of a nonstandard grade of the underlying commodity. An EFP is usually motivated by a commercial transaction; for example, a scrap copper producer can do an EFP with a scrap supplier where both are hedging using copper futures contracts. The futures contract offset is bundled with the commercial transaction. During October there were a number of large EFPs where major silver dealers (Mocatta Metals; Sharps, Pixley; J. Aron) seemed to be delivering a large portion of physical silver inventories to IMIC and others in exchange for cancellation of futures contracts with maturities covering December 1979 through April 1980 (Williams, 1995):

> IMIC's EFPs which supplanted most of its futures contracts, were perfectly consistent with its avowed business purpose of acquiring physical silver. Coupled with the deliveries already taken in September and October, IMIC had acquired 35.3 million troy ounces by mid-December, 27.8 million of that as bullion. Bunker and Herbert Hunt themselves took delivery of 6.425 million troy ounces during the fall of 1979. For the two Hunts, taking delivery afforded sizable tax advantages, given the increase in price since the summer. According to U.S. tax laws then applicable, a liquidation of a futures position, including a rollover into a later month, triggered a taxable event, upon which any gain would be taxed. In contrast, deliveries taken were not a taxable event; the gain, if it existed, would be taxed only when the silver was ultimately sold.

By November, the principal longs had accumulated a sufficiently large enough position in deliverable physical supply that the stage had been set for a squeeze on the shorts.

The price increases for spot silver during December and January were dramatic, from $20 on December 1 to $38.85 on January 1. The price increase was more than worrisome to COMEX officials. The December delivery had finished without failed deliveries but only with considerable exchange oversight. What transpired over the next three weeks was a remarkable series of COMEX decisions aimed at stabilizing the market. On January 7, position limits of 2000 contracts were imposed, with the proviso that those with current aggregate positions in excess of 2000 contracts be given a year to comply providing for at least a 10% reduction in position size per month. Deliveries were also limited to 500 contracts per month. Commercial firms making hedging decisions with transparent connection to physical stocks were exempted from the limits. The impact of this on the principal longs can be seen by recognizing that Bunker Hunt alone had long 13,055 contracts for

March 1980 delivery. The restrictions combined with the intense variation margin pressure being imposed on the commercial shorts triggered another round of EFPs with Engelhard Mineral and Chemical (Philipp Bros.), Bunker Hill Co., Swiss Bank Co., and others.

Faced with the bankruptcy of major commercial shorts, the end of the silver bubble came on Monday, January 21, 1980, when the COMEX announced that all trading in silver futures would be limited to liquidation only. This unprecedented step effectively closed the silver futures market. (The much smaller silver futures market on the CBOT followed suit the next day.) This action precipitated a drastic fall in the spot price of silver. Having traded briefly above $50/oz in the week prior, the close on Tuesday, January 22 was $34, a level that was maintained until mid-March when prices again fell precipitously to the $17 level. In the interim, the COMEX deemed that the pressure on the market had eased sufficiently, and the liquidation-only restriction on silver futures trading was lifted. The price behavior had reversed the pressures on the commercial shorts, placing the burden of variation margin squarely on the longs. The underlying strategy of taking profits in bullion, through EFPs and standing for deliveries, turned on the longs with a vengeance. The bullion, which could be used to secure financing, was declining in value and could only be partially leveraged. Considerable cash on hand had been expended to settle the EFPs.

Variation margin rules at the COMEX and on most exchanges provide for daily limits on the payments that have to be made to the account. This caps the daily cash-flow pressures, leaving a longer period of time for payment and the possibility that prices will recover. Nonetheless, given a long enough time frame, the payments will eventually be made. Englehard Mineral, an important commercial short, was reported to have paid $1.3 billion in variation margin on silver futures up to mid-January 1980. Though the notional variation margin was over $1 billion in mid-March 1980, the actual payments required from personal sources was some $60 million per day for the Hunts (Fig. 1.2). The cash flow pressure was such that on March 13 the Hunts and IMIC defaulted on variation margin payments to their brokers. After a brief period during which the brokerage houses covered unpaid variation margin balances, on March 27, 1980, the final phase of the bubble took place with brokers liquidating various cash and futures positions.

Under the selling pressure of the brokerage house liquidations, the price of silver dropped to $10.40/oz. The bubble had completely burst and new longs were entering the market. The Hunts were forced to mortgage key assets in the family portfolio, particularly Placid Oil, which secured a loan of $1.1 billion. By the end of April 1980, the outstanding balances for the Hunts at various brokerage houses had been paid. Though the court cases dragged on for years, the immediate crisis was over. The usual array of House and Senate

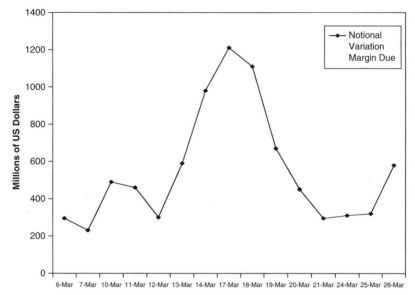

FIGURE 1.2   The price decline during March 1980 and the Hunts' and Conti group's national variation margin payments (*Source*: Adapted from Williams, 1995, p. 48.)

subcommittees, regulators' reports, and academic studies followed. One key finding of the regulators was that the key brokerage houses acting for the longs, Bache and Merrill Lynch, both acted imprudently by making large loans backed by bullion. The solvency of the firms could have been put in jeopardy. Yet, like the Cargill case, there is a strong case to be made regarding the lack of fairness from the exchanges regarding the Hunts.

B. Portfolio Insurance and the Stock Market Crash of October 1987

The Hunt silver market manipulation was a very old story being played in modern times. A group of traders, acting in concert, attempt to use a derivative contract delivery mechanism to allegedly manipulate prices for personal gain. As both the Hunts and Cargill discovered, a real risk in this type of activity is that the regulator may change the rules in midstream. Though the Hunt silver manipulation took place at the beginning of the modern Renaissance in derivatives trading, coming after the start of the CBOE and the beginning of trade in selected financial derivatives, the whole affair still has an old-world

---

BOX 4

An excerpt from the transcript of testimony given by George Soros to the United States House of Representatives Committee on Banking, Finance and Urban Affairs, April 13, 1994

The trouble with *derivative instruments* is that those who issue them usually protect themselves against losses by engaging in so-called delta, or dynamic, hedging. Dynamic hedging means, in effect, that if the market moves against the issuer, the issuer is forced to move in the same direction as the market, and thereby amplify the initial price disturbance. As long as price changes are continuous, no great harm is done, except perhaps to create higher volatility, which in turn increases the demand for derivative instruments. But if there is an overwhelming amount of dynamic hedging done in the same direction, price movements may become discontinuous. This raises the spectre of financial dislocation. Those who need to engage in dynamic hedging, but cannot execute their orders, may suffer catastrophic losses.

This is what happened in the stock market crash of 1987. The main culprit was the excessive use of portfolio insurance. Portfolio insurance was nothing but a method of dynamic hedging. The authorities have since introduced regulations, so-called "circuit breakers," which render portfolio insurance impractical, but other instruments which rely on dynamic hedging have mushroomed. They play a much bigger role in the interest rate market than in the stock market, and it is the role in the interest rate market which has been most turbulent in recent weeks.

---

flavor. By comparison, the role of delta hedging and portfolio insurance in the stock market crash of October 1987 is an identifiably modern event. This event was not generated by the desire for unwarranted gains but, rather, as fallout from the desire to innovate, to apply the techniques of financial engineering in pursuit of enhanced portfolio management outcomes.

The causes of the stock market crash of October 19–20, 1987, have been debated *ad nauseum*. The analysis includes reports by the exchanges (e.g., the CME and the NYSE), the regulators (e.g., the SEC, GAO, CFTC, and Brady Commission), and academic studies (e.g., Edwards and Ma, 1988; Tosini, 1988). For sheer attention and regulatory impact, the crash of 1987 could be the disaster of disasters. Incremental reforms were made to market practices, ranging from the introduction of trading circuit breakers triggered by large market moves to rules impacting the capitalization of specialists on the New York Stock Exchange (NYSE) trading floor to substantial increases in margin requirements for exchange traded stock index derivatives. Physical hardware changes were also made to the execution system for processing orders on the NYSE. As reflected in the comments of George Soros, another fallout from the crash was the drastically reduced use of stock markets for dynamic trading strategies designed to achieve replication of an untraded option payoff. Such schemes had been actively promoted to institutional investors by a number of the leading finance academics, including Fischer Black and Mark Rubinstein.[35]

In retrospect, the crash of 1987 still has many lessons for the present, if only these lessons could be adequately understood. Too often, it seems, analysis of the crash has the flavor of an apology for the current method of oversight. Tosini (1988, p. 35), a director at the CFTC at the time of the crash, is an excellent example: "There are many profound, complex and far-reaching issues before the CFTC, as well as other federal agencies and the Congress, concerning stock market and derivative market activities and performance during October...the call for 'further research' has hardly ever been more timely." The various reports made some key observations; for example, the Brady Report (1988) recognized that the markets for stocks, stock options, and stock index futures were actually one integrated market "linked by financial instruments, trading strategies, market participants and clearing and credit mechanisms." Despite this integration, the regulatory and institutional structure that was designed for separate markets was unable to deal with "inter-market" pressures. The Brady Commission recommended a number of reforms designed to provide for a more integrated approach to market oversight.

The crash of 1987 speaks directly to the problems raised by the systemic change in financial markets brought on by the modern Renaissance in derivative securities trading. Various events were replayed in the 1990s because some lessons were not fully understood. This happened because the analysis of the event, on the whole, focused on the specific events and did not adequately account for the singularity of the event. As measured by the Dow Jones Industrial Average (DJIA), the U.S. equity market had achieved a peak of 2722 in August of 1987. Price earnings (P/E) ratios for the Standard & Poors (S&P) 500 were averaging 23, relatively high considering the potential for

---

[35]A partial listing of key players implementing portfolio insurance strategies for large institutional investors includes: Leland O'Brien Rubinstein Associates, Aetna Life and Casualty, Putnam Adversary Co., Chase Investors Mgmt., JP Morgan Investment Mgmt., Wells Fargo Investment Advisors, and Bankers Trust Co. This list does not include the wannabes at Goldman Sachs, Salomon Bros., Nomura, and other firms seeking to gain status in this area. Goldman Sachs was the firm that employed Fischer Black at this time.

negative market sentiment. In modern parlance, the equity market was due for a correction. On Wednesday, October 15, 1987, a news release reported an unexpectedly large U.S. trade deficit, banks raised prime rates, and there was considerable downward pressure on equity prices. The S&P 500 fell from over 314 to below 306. Despite a calming statement by Treasury Secretary Baker on Thursday, the S&P 500 fell again to 298. When some negative Producer Price Index (PPI) and industrial production numbers hit the market at the open on Friday, the stage was set. Significantly, even though things were gloomy, none of this foreshadowed the events about to unfold. This leads to a key observation about the crash: It was a severe event that was not associated with a correspondingly severe negative information inflow to the market.

The crash actually started on Friday October 17, 1987. In the face of the somewhat negative sentiment, the DJIA fell a record 108 points. The S&P 500 started the day at 298 and fell to around 282. These were significant market moves that, all things considered, may have presented some buying opportunities. Over the weekend, there was some chatter about a dispute between the United States and Germany over interest rates, leading to speculation that the United States might let the dollar fall, an event that would be negative for U.S. equities. There was the usual carryover on foreign markets, such as Tokyo and Australia, though the wave of intense selling had not yet hit international markets. The New York market opening was confronted with news that the United States had attacked Iranian oil platforms in the Persian Gulf, which almost surely added to the rush of sell orders. At the open, the DJIA was down 67 points. The S&P 500 futures contract on the CME fell 18 points at the open. At a time when 100 million share volumes were uncommon events, the NYSE processed 50 million shares in the first half hour. Despite the market turbulence, a 10:00 a.m. meeting of NYSE officials and major brokerage houses did not feel a trading halt was needed.

The sequence of events that followed was structured around two institutional procedures. The first concerns the method of executing stock trades on the NYSE. Historically, stock trades on the NYSE required a floor broker for a member firm to walk the order to the NYSE trading post for that stock and execute the trade directly with the specialist or with another broker using open outcry. At the time of the 1987 crash, this was still the case for block trades involving 10,000 or more shares. This manual method of trading was inefficient and costly for trades involving large bundles of stocks that have to be sold at once. Such trades were being done not only by index arbitragers, but also by a wide range of market participants. To improve market performance for these and other traders, the NYSE introduced the designated-order turn-around (DOT) system in 1976. This system permitted the computerized execution of small trades. Effectively, brokers with member firms could enter trades into a computerized order system, permitting trades to be entered in brokers' offices. Upon receiving the order, the DOT system would automatically route the trade to the appropriate NYSE specialist, where it would be executed. The whole process takes a matter of minutes.

The success of the DOT system led to a new and improved version: the Super-DOT, implemented in 1984. This new system enhanced the execution times and access. This remarkable progress in information technology created its own demand from a growing legion of program traders. This category includes a range of trading strategies, including portfolio insurance and index arbitrage. Program traders could enter the exact weights for a portfolio of stocks that could be executed simultaneously by computer entry. Prior to DOT and Super-DOT, execution risk in such strategies was an important deterrent. Yet, the interactions between the progress in information technology and the ability to introduce new financial engineering products were not well understood at the time. Hints of the crash of October 1987 were observed on September 11–12, 1986 and on January 23, 1987, when "excessive" stock market volatility was observed. These preliminary tremors attracted some attention, and efforts were made to track the activities of program traders through the DOT system. A poll by NYSE of specialists and floor traders found that, almost without exception, program trading was done through the DOT. On average, in the year leading up to the crash, DOT orders from program traders were found to average around 18% of all DOT trades, with over 28% of all orders on October 19, 1987, being due to program traders.

In addition to the DOT, the other essential institutional feature to consider in evaluating the crash of 1987 is the short-sale rule. More precisely, the SEC Act prohibits short selling of securities, except when the short sale takes place either below the last sale price of that security or at the last price, if that price is above the preceding price. Like the SEC Act, this rule has origins in the antispeculator atmosphere of the post-Depression era. The idea is that the rule prevents excessive and accelerating downward pressure on prices during a market downturn; however, there is no such rule on futures markets. As such, dynamic portfolio insurance strategies could be implemented by shorting stock index futures instead of attempting to short the underlying stocks. In addition, the single-digit percentage margins on futures contracts were only a small fraction of the 50% margins on stocks. These substantive differences across markets can be attributed to the regulatory competition between the CFTC, which regulates futures, and the SEC, which regulates securities markets.

Portfolio insurance is a category that includes a range of trading strategies. One important strategy involves dynamically trading stock index futures in order to replicate the payoff on a portfolio composed of the underlying index and a put option. The reason that dynamic trading was used is associated with the relatively limited array of path-independent option products available.

Exchange-traded option maturities were a maximum 9 months, not all stocks had traded options, index options were relatively illiquid, and the OTC market lacked sufficient liquidity to provide options with the exercise price variation and longer term maturity dates that many institutional investors desired. Even though absence of arbitrage requires that cash-and-carry arbitrage conditions apply to the spot and futures markets, the sheer volume of trading on October 19 meant that a wide spread between the stock index futures and the stock index was seemingly inevitable. What emerged was much worse: an information technology breakdown. The rush of sell orders effectively crashed the DOT system. At 11:45 a.m. the ticker was approximately 1 hour behind and a number of stocks had yet to open because of the lack of an orderly market. By 2:00 p.m. volume had reached 400 million. The final numbers for October 19 were 603 million shares traded, with a drop of 508 points (23%) on the Dow and 80.75 points on the S&P 500, a loss of nearly 30%. At the bell, the ticker was approximately 130 minutes behind.

This slaughter on the stock exchanges led to a flurry of overnight activities. As the U.S. market collapse spread overseas, there was complete or almost complete trading halts on the Tokyo and Hong Kong exchanges. There was an unprecedented drop on the London Financial Times (FT) Index. The opening of the New York market was preceded by reassuring statements and actions from the Federal Reserve Board (FRB), major banks were lowering prime rates and the NYSE shut down the DOT system to prevent the execution of program trades. A temporary and partial trading halt was called just after 11:00 a.m. as the market approached 180 on the S&P futures, while the cash market was trading just below 220. This seemed to spell the end of the crash. Prices recovered and by 2:00 p.m. the spread between cash and futures narrowed close to normal levels, though the spread did widen as the close approached. At the end of the day, the DJIA was up 102 points on volume of 608 million shares. Due to actions taken to combat the crash, there was strong recovery of the dollar and a decline in interest rates. The low prices combined with the sudden brightening of the economic picture led to a buying spree, both in the United States and offshore. By the close Thursday, October 20, the market had recovered about half of what was lost on Monday.

The crash of 1987 was an unprecedented security market event. It exposed serious weaknesses in a regulatory system that was designed to fight the battles arising from old technology. Unlike the Hunt silver manipulation, this was not a story with good guys and bad guys. The problems originated from an inability to assess and structure the rapid changes in securities markets. This was a debacle that was created by a well-intentioned need to innovate, to improve portfolio management of large financial institutions. As it turns out, the portfolio insurance programs based on dynamic trading were generally unable to deliver the protection that was claimed *ex ante*. The situation for which the insurance was most important, the protection of losses in the event of a market collapse, led to preconditions that prevented the outcome from being achieved. The programs could only get so big and it was not possible for more than a small fraction of market participants to successfully pursue such strategies. In addition, there are numerous untold stories of other strategies, such as delta hedging by option traders, that also contributed to the crash. Undoubtedly, such traders also contributed to the selling via the DOT and on the floor that only added to the downward pressure on prices.

C. METALLGESELLSCHAFT AG AND ROLLING-STACK HEDGES (1993)

Circa 1994, Metallgesellschaft AG (MG) was the 14th largest corporation in Germany and was involved in a range of activities that included mining, engineering, and financial services. In December 1993, MG reported immense losses on positions in energy futures and swaps incurred by its U.S. affiliate, MG Refining and Marketing (MGRM). These losses were later determined to be around $1.3 billion, the largest derivatives losses by any firm up to that time. It took a $1.9 billion rescue package from 150 German and international banks to maintain the solvency of MG. While initial press reports attributed the losses to speculating in energy derivatives by MGRM, it turned out that MGRM was actually engaged in a sophisticated long-term marketing program for gasoline and heating oil. The saga of how a firm engaged in hedging activities could incur such losses has been told and retold, often brilliantly, by Culp and Miller (1994, 1995a,b,c), Mello and Parsons (1995a,b), Kuprianov (1995), and Edwards (1995). Culp and Miller (1999) have collected the relevant readings and provide an overview.

Mello and Parsons (1995a) outlined the background to the MGRM saga:

> Metallgesellschaft's U.S. subsidiary was reorganized in 1986 with equity capital of $50 million and net sales of $1.7 billion from trading in U.S. government bonds, foreign currency, emerging markets instruments, and various commodities. The U.S. subsidiary's oil business, organized under MG Refining and Marketing (MGRM), grew significantly between 1989 and 1993. In 1989 the company obtained a 49% stake in Castle Energy, a U.S. oil exploration company, whose transformation into a refiner MGRM helped finance. MGRM contracted Castle Energy to purchase their output of refined oil products—approximately 46 million bbl. per year—at guaranteed margins for up to 10 years, and assembled a large network of infrastructure necessary for the storage and transport of oil products. During 1992 and 1993, MGRM succeeded in signing a large number of long-term contracts for delivery of gasoline, heating oil, and jet fuel oil to independent retailers. By late 1993 MGRM had become an important supplier. In addition MGRM ran large trades in energy-related derivatives. Its portfolio included a wide

variety of over-the-counter forwards, swaps, and puts, and it did large amounts of trading in futures contracts on crude oil, heating oil, and gasoline on a number of exchanges and markets.

As stated, MGRM was involved in intermediating the spot market for oil products with the long-term forward market. For this business strategy to work, MGRM had to be directly involved in sophisticated risk management. Though some of the risk could be captured with longer dated OTC products, to accurately handle the risk it was assuming for customers MGRM also had to use oil complex futures contracts. Due to limited liquidity in longer dated delivery contracts, MGRM had to implement a rolling-stack hedging strategy, involving short-dated futures contracts.

As discussed in Chapter 6, Section I, and demonstrated in numerous sources (e.g., Culp and Miller, 1995a), a rolling-stack hedge can have a sizable basis risk. For the MGRM story, this basis risk was dramatically compounded by variation margin costs and certain peculiarities of German accounting principles. As a result, a promising business plan was destroyed by inadequate execution. That MGRM had a business plan is apparent. The plan commenced with the recruitment of a management team with a track record in implementing a similar plan at Louis Dreyfus Energy Corporation. The program was featured on the cover of the annual report of the parent corporation, MG. Under the forward supply or "flow delivery" contracts, MGRM had contracted to deliver approximately 160 million barrels of associated oil products, primarily heating oil and gasoline, at fixed prices under contracts stretching out 10 years. These contracts had a sell-back option clause, permitting the counterparty to terminate early if the market price was some threshold greater than the fixed price at which MGRM had contracted to deliver. The counterparties in these contracts were a mix of retail gasoline suppliers, large industrial corporations, and a few government bodies.

The fixed price contracts written by MGRM provided for a spread over current spot market prices of from $3 to $5 per barrel, with many of the contracts being written in the summer of 1993. This was the profit margin that MGRM had to design a hedging strategy to protect. The unhedged risk to MGRM was that prices would rise and MGRM would be obligated to deliver oil products at lower prices than market prices. To hedge this spot position, in late 1993 MGRM had a position of 100 to 110 million in energy swaps and 55 million barrels in heating oil and gasoline futures on the New York Mercantile Exchange (NYMEX). It seems that MGRM was pursuing a long one-to-one hedge. An important complication facing MGRM was the lack of liquidity in long-dated maturities for both futures and swaps. Instead of implementing a relatively riskless strip hedge (see Chapter 6, Section I), MGRM was obliged to use a rolling-stack hedge. Apparently, this was considered to be a benefit to

MGRM, due to rollover gains implied by a one-to-one hedge when futures prices are in backwardation.

Unfortunately for MGRM, in the later part of 1993 oil prices fell. While this would be an excellent outcome for an unhedged MGRM, the long hedge positions started losing significant amounts of variation margin. In addition, futures prices went into contango, dictating rollover losses instead of rollover gains. These negative-variation-margin cash flows were not matched by offsetting mark-to-market gains on the long-term forward delivery contracts. Such was the business risk that MGRM assumed. Prices fell from the $19 level to below $15; combined with the rollover losses, this decline in price meant cash flow requirements to the hedge of hundreds of millions of dollars. As it turns out, German accounting principles, which were applicable to the parent corporation, required the classification of these variation margin payments as losses. In what can only be described as a classic case study in strategic risk management, on December 17, 1993, the supervisory board of Metallgesellschaft fired the management board chairman and brought in new management with a mandate to liquidate both MGRM derivative security positions and its forward supply contracts.

The end result of the supervisory board decision can be estimated at $640–$800 million on the derivatives positions alone. The cancellation of the forward supply contracts was done without penalties, thereby releasing the counterparties from what was a positive cash-flow situation for MGRM, again losing value. The MGRM saga raises several key questions to examine. Among these points, one stands out: What were the members of the supervisory board thinking about when they pulled the plug on the operation? Unfortunately, the deliberations of the board, such as they were, are hidden behind the veil of corporate secrecy. It is apparent that the hedging strategy that was implemented was not well understood *ex ante* by the supervisory board. As such, Metallgesellschaft failed to follow a tenet of strategic risk management: The risk-management program is enterprise wide. Senior management needs to understand the stress test values for the various cash flows that could result from a particular risk-management operation.

D. Index Option Straddles and the Collapse of Barings Bank (1995)

Of all the derivatives debacles of the 1990s, the collapse of Barings Bank is the closest to being a *true* debacle. The Barings case is, arguably, also the most notorious, even inspiring a movie, *Rogue Trader*, in addition to numerous books and magazine articles. The general details are well known: In 1992, Barings Bank shipped a young clerk in its London office to its Barings Futures subsidiary in Singapore to handle settlement operations and back office accounting. The name of that clerk was Nicholas Leeson. Soon after getting settled into his job in Singapore, Leeson received permission to take the SIMEX exams, required for floor trading. He passed the exams and began activity as a floor trader on the SIMEX, while still holding responsibility for back office and settlement, a situation that persisted until, in late 1992, Leeson was named head trader and general manager for Barings Futures (Singapore) (BFS).

What transpired from the point of Leeson's assuming control of BFS is quite remarkable. Due to the veil of corporate secrecy, it is difficult to say precisely who knew what and when. Such points have been the subject matter of numerous media speculations. It is clear that Barings' senior management did approve Leeson to engage in proprietary trading for Barings' own account. The strategy that apparently was approved was interexchange arbitrage on two SIMEX contracts that are cross listed in Osaka. A trader follows prices on the two exchanges, seeking to purchase a lower priced contract on one exchange while "simultaneously" selling an otherwise identical higher priced contract on the other exchange. Actual profits will depend on a range of factors, including skill at executing trades quickly and at lowest cost. There were two contracts that Leeson could arbitrage: the Nikkei-225 stock index and the 10-year Japanese government bonds (JGBs). There is an element of speculation in such activities, but if the program is properly executed the operation is fully hedged, not unlike a specialized hedge fund.

What followed on Leeson's emergence was a BFS profit of £8.8 million for 1993, eight times the 1992 level. The first half of 1994, BFS reported profits of £20 million, a dramatic contribution to a bank with total pretax profit of £55 for the same period. These profits, occurred at the same time that profits at other investment banks were falling, due partially to a slump in global bond markets. While explainable in terms of the type of operation that was being run at BFS, the size of the profits did attract head office attention and an auditor was dispatched to Singapore in August 1994. What the auditor reported was significant: The auditor correctly identified that Leeson was in charge of both trading and settlement, a clear breach of sound operational management procedure. This finding was discussed by the Barings board and, for whatever reason, the decision was made not to tinker. This decision ultimately doomed the bank to failure (see Fig. 1.3).

It seems that, almost from the beginning, Leeson was hiding losses in the infamous Error Account #88888. Such accounts are usually used to capture settlement on floor trades that are disputed (e.g., due to an incorrect reading of hand signals). Information from such accounts is usually omitted until the dispute is resolved, as there is no ascertainable market value until that time. Using this blind, Leeson was able to instruct clerks at BFS to omit Account.

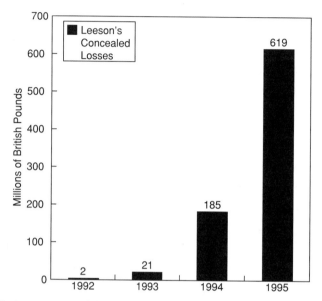

FIGURE 1.3   Leeson's Concealed Trading Losses at Baring's Bank (Singapore). (*Source*: Bank of England, Board of Banking Supervisors.)

#88888 when passing information along to the head office. An analysis of Leeson's activities reveals a range of oversight failures, such as a web of concealed trades, and trading on a proprietary account under the guise of trading for customer accounts. From an initial hidden loss of £2 million in 1992, Leeson was able to limit his trading losses until October 1993 when large losses reappeared. To avert the cash flow from variation margin calls that would likely have unraveled his schemes, Leeson was able to turn to the cash flow available from writing options.

The strategy for which Nick Leeson will be forever famous is the written straddle, though Leeson was also involved in related trades such as the written strangle. In Leeson's case, this strategy involved writing matched combinations of puts and calls on the Nikkei-225 futures contract (see Chapter 7, Section III). In order to maximize the time premium received, such options are usually written at-the-money. Such a strategy would generate substantial premium cash inflows, which Leeson could use to disguise the actual state of affairs at BFS. During 1994, actual (unreported) losses on trading activities were such that Leeson began pyramiding options positions. By January 1, 1995, the size of Leeson's position was short 37,925 Nikkei calls and 32,967 Nikkei puts, combined with a 1000+ long position in Nikkei stock index futures. The exposure of this position to large moves in the underlying security is a textbook illustration of the nonlinear impact of options on value at risk (VaR) (e.g., Jorion, 2001, pp. 215–219).

The Kobe earthquake of January 17, 1995, brought down the house of cards. How this particular house fell is a separate story in itself. In the face of a fall of 1500 points in the Nikkei, Leeson sustained a loss of £68 million. In reaction, Leeson began taking on increasingly larger positions in futures, both long Nikkei futures and short Japanese government bonds. The rationale for these trades was evident, Leeson was gambling in an attempt to recoup the losses. The next part of the story is that SIMEX permitted Leeson to execute this strategy. Kuprianov (1995, p. 24) relates the details:

> By Feb. 23, Leeson had bought over 61,000 Nikkei futures contracts represent-ing 49 percent of total open interest in the March 1995 Nikkei futures contract and 24 percent of the open interest in the June contract. His position in Japanese government bond futures totaled just over 26,000 contracts sold, representing 88 percent of the open interest in the June 1995 contract. Leeson also took positions in Euroyen futures. He began 1995 with long positions in Euroyen contracts...but then switched to selling the contracts.

The massive margin calls from SIMEX that hit Barings following the earth-quake generated meetings between the exchange and Barings officials. Under the mistaken impression that the SIMEX positions were being hedged with offsetting positions in Osaka, the Barings officials gave assurances that all obligations would be met.

In all of this, it is difficult to believe that someone somewhere did not step in to blow the whistle on this caper before Leeson was permitted to build up the staggering positions in futures. A firm with an equity capital of approxi-mately £440 million was exposed to variation margin losses more than double that amount. Apparently, no one was able to sit down and do some elementary calculations. In any event, the whole situation slowly unfolded. In mid-Feb-ruary, the head office dispatched a clerk who uncovered the inevitable irregu-larities, one particular item for $190 million being of especial interest. After having some difficulty tracking down an illusive Leeson, the clerk was finally able to set up a dinner meeting on February 23. Just after the start of the meeting, Leeson got up from the table to go to the washroom and did not return. He and his wife bolted that evening, Leeson faxing his resignation from a hotel in Kuala Lumpar. The fugitive couple was eventually taken off a plane in Germany, in a vein attempt to reach British justice. This plan, like so many others in Nick Leeson's life, was a failure. Leeson was returned to Singapore to face several years in jail.

Ultimately, Leeson's activities led to the demise of one of the most respected names in British banking, qualifying the event as a true debacle. Barings, founded in 1762, could boast that the Queen of England was a client. Yet, the default of Barings revealed serious cracks in the process by which futures exchanges operate. Competition between SIMEX and Osaka seems to have adversely impacted the end result. SIMEX was granting Leeson exemptions from speculative positions limits (see Section I) on the basis of offsetting positions in Osaka. This was done without accurate monitoring of whether there were positions in Osaka. There was little or no communication between the competing exchanges. Default of a major player, such as Barings, also triggered conflicts over margin rules and their implementation. Leeson's activities made it difficult for SIMEX to ascertain which margin deposits went with which client accounts. The whole question of legal claim to margin is complicated in the presence of a defaulting firm operating in so many jurisdictions.

E. THE COLLAPSE OF LONG-TERM CAPITAL MANAGEMENT (1998)

Long-Term Capital Management, LP (LTCM) was a Delaware limited partnership founded in early 1994, though the roots of the enterprise can be traced back to early 1993 when John Meriwether began to assemble of group of principles for the fund that was to become LTCM (Dunbar, 2000). Meriwether was at this time something of a Wall Street icon, having built the Salomon Bros. bond arbitrage group into an industry legend during the 1980s, only to be displaced in the aftermath of the Treasury auction scandal that hit Salomon in 1991.[36] By August 1993, seven "principals" had been assembled. In addition to previous members of the arbitrage team from Meriwether's time at Salomon, the group also included two of the most noteworthy individuals in modern finance: Robert Merton and Myron Scholes. It is reported that the collapse of LTCM in September 1998 was a serious financial hardship for Merton and Scholes.

LTCM was a hedge fund (see Chapter 3, Section IV). Yet, LTCM was much more than just a hedge fund, as the specifics of LTCM demonstrate (Presidential Working Group, 1999, p. 15):

> Overall, the distinguishing features of the LTCM Fund were the scale of its activities, the large size of its positions in certain markets, and the extent of its leverage, both in terms of balance-sheet measures and on the basis of more meaningful measures of risk exposure in relation to capital. The Fund reportedly had over 60,000 trades on its books, including long securities positions of over $50 billion and short positions of an equivalent magnitude. At the end of August, 1998, the gross notional amounts of the Fund's contracts on futures exchanges exceeded $500 billion, swap contracts more than $750 billion, and options and other OTC derivatives of over $150 billion.

[36]The Salomon Bros. Treasury auction scandal is delightfully examined in Lewis (1989).

With over 60,000 trades in place when the collapse came, the scope of LTCM activities was spread over a wide range of trading activities, concentrating primarily on bond market strategies. Not surprisingly given the background of the active principals, around 80% of the LTCM balance sheet was concentrated in government bonds of G-7 countries, though this disguises the use of substantial futures positions in interest rate futures and equity futures. These positions were spread over a dozen futures and options exchanges around the globe.

LTCM was initially a very profitable venture. In 1995 and 1996, LTCM averaged, net of fees, a 40% return per year, followed by slightly less than 20% in 1997. As an appeasement to certain fund investors, the decision was made to return approximately 36% of the fund's capital at the end of 1997, leaving $4.8 billion in capital to support the underlying positions. If Dunbar (2000, pp. 189–190) is correct, this releveraging was a conscious decision. To support his statement, Dunbar provides anecdotes from interviews with both Scholes and Miller in April 1998 as well as the following quote from Merton's December 1997 Nobel lecture:

> Non-financial firms currently use derivatives to hedge price risks. With improved lower-cost technology, this practice is likely to expand. Eventually, this alternative to equity capital as a cushion for risk could lead to a major change of corporate structures as more firms use hedging as a substitute for equity capital; thereby moving from publicly traded shares to closely held private shares.

This decision to return capital acted to releverage the fund, holding the size of the firm's positions constant. A similar result could have been accomplished by increasing the position sizes, without redistributing capital.

The first cracks in LTCM started to appear in May and June of 1998 when losses of $312 and $461 million hit the fund. Though not bound by the VaR-based capital rules applied to financial institutions (see Chapter 2, Section II), LTCM was an active user of the techniques and the fund operated with a monthly VaR constraint that was violated in both May and June. It was immediately apparent to LTCM management that position sizes had to be reduced in order to reduce the daily VaR from $45 million to $35 million. In a fund composed of so many different "money machines," this was a complicated task, especially as there was substantial differences in the liquidity of the various positions. The debate within LTCM over how this was to be accomplished was contentious. On one side were the wizards of Wall Street, traders with decades of combined experience running successful arbitrage operations. This group argued that the losses were an aberration, not likely to recur. Reducing volatility by selling off liquid positions would be sufficient to stem the tide.

In opposition to this view stood the giants of the academic world: Scholes and Merton. Dunbar (2000, p. 196) captures their position using a quote from the interview he had with Scholes two months prior to the deliberations about reducing LTCM position sizes:

> Suppose you have a hedged book, and then you have to reduce the size of your balance sheet due to adverse hits to your capital. There's always a tendency to reduce or sell your more liquid securities first. If things continue to go against you, then you're left with the more illiquid securities, and a very unhedged book. So that's a very bad strategy. You should reduce your book proportionately—liquid and illiquid together.

The difficulty with this position was that it would be painful, and it possessed a range of risks. For example, the process of unwinding some of the illiquid positions (e.g., market-maker positions in Russian bonds or long-dated equity options) could unsettle markets and generate further possible losses. In addition, the most liquid positions had nowhere near the profit potential of the least liquid. Ultimately, Meriweather sided with the traders and the decision was made to liquidate the most liquid positions.

Much as the Kobe earthquake decimated Nick Leeson, so did the Russian devaluation of the ruble and declaration of a debt moratorium on August 17, 1998, hit LTCM. Though LTCM did have some direct exposure to Russian debt, the impact of the Russian devaluation hit hardest through its impact on market liquidity and risk spreads in markets throughout the world. As the Report of the Presidential Working Group (1999, p. 15) points out:

> The size, persistence, and pervasiveness of the widening of risk spreads confounded the risk management models, estimated during more stable periods, suggested were probable. Moreover, the simultaneous shocks to many markets confounded expectations of relatively low correlations between market prices and revealed that global trading portfolios like LTCM's were less well diversified than assumed. Finally, the "flight to quality" (generated by the Russian devaluation) resulted in a substantial reduction in the liquidity of many markets, which, contrary to the assumptions implicit in their models, made it difficult to reduce exposures quickly without incurring further losses.

During the month of August 1998, LTCM lost $1.8 billion. This reduced capital to $2.3 billion and triggered a wide range of counterparty difficulties. Credit became difficult to obtain, haircuts were raised, OTC trades were difficult to execute...the list is endless. To add insult to injury, the fund became the source of intense media speculation during the early part of September 1998.

The end for LTCM came swiftly. On Monday September 21, it became apparent that there was a real likelihood of default on scheduled payments as early as Wednesday, September 23. Four principal counterparties for LTCM banded together on Tuesday and by Wednesday had put together a consortium of 14 firms able and willing to recapitalize LTCM with $3.6 billion in new equity in exchange for a 90% equity share in LTCM, along with operational control of the funds various positions. The claims of the original investors were thereby reduced to 10%, an indication of the size of the losses in September. As a result, the LTCM episode, which had the potential for creating considerable disturbance in financial markets, passed with only a few ripples. The burden of resolving the mess fell to those entities that had permitted LTCM to grow and flourish. The outcome is a credit to the integrity of those involved at LTCM who acted in the face of adversity and did not give in to the temptation to attempt to recover losses, *à la* Leeson.

F. LESSONS FROM THE RECENT DERIVATIVES DEBACLES

It is difficult to pick a "most important" lesson from the derivative debacles of the 1990s. There are the essential lessons for regulators. The growth of information technology, the globalization of trading, and the reliance on perceived creditworthiness in assessing complicated counterparties are all outstanding issues that threaten the *ad hoc* fabric of industry self-regulation and multiple national regulators. The debacles also provide lessons for corporate risk managers: Business plans that depend fundamentally on risk management using derivative securities need to be adequately stress tested and evaluated, and senior levels of management have to be an integral part of the risk-management decision process. These lessons apply for both financial firms, such as Barings, and nonfinancial firms such as MGRM. There are also lessons to be learned for end users: Risk management products can get so complicated that end users are unable to accurately price the derivative products being used, such as in the case of the leveraged swaps undertaken by Proctor and Gamble (Smith, 1997) or the tear-up and rollover swaps of Gibson Greetings (Overdahl and Schachter, 1997). Another lesson is that risk management products can be used as a guise to mask speculative activities (e.g., Orange County) (Jorion, 1997; Miller and Ross, 1997).

One of the most important lessons learned from the recent derivatives debacles is an old story: Strategic risk management is important. While the precise meaning of strategic management will be discussed in Chapter 2, Section IV, it can briefly be described as identifying, implementing, and monitoring the risk-management philosophy of the firm. Both MGRM and Barings had a risk-management philosophy that was fundamentally unsound. The process within which risk-management decisions were being made did not provide for adequate integration of senior management into the decision-making process. Communication between senior managers and line operators was corrupted. As the unnecessary losses sustained when unwinding the positions indicate, senior managers also did not have the analytical systems in place to fully appreciate the nuances of the decisions that had to be made when damage control was required.

In a corporate setting, risk management has to be approached in an integrated manner. Developing such an integrated approach is an essential feature of strategic risk management. Many, many firms are able to do this successfully. Yet, there are numerous cases where risk management has not been properly implemented. In some cases, the consequences are devastating. In the Barings case, giving Leeson line control for audit and trading was the result of not having systems in place to identify and rectify such situations. Strategic risk-management is a process. Sometimes the risk-management philosophy is well designed but the firm still fails due to misjudgment about the inputs to the risk-management process. LTCM had a sophisticated risk-management philosophy but was defeated by misjudgments about business and liquidity risks. In the end, it seems that strategic risk management is a necessary but not sufficient condition for a successful risk-management program.

Another essential, if often overlooked, lesson is also another old story: Accounting for derivatives is important. In some cases, accounting has played a direct role, such as in the MGRM case where German accounting rules for the variation margin payments on the rolling-stack hedges triggered decisions by senior management that, ultimately, cost over $1 billion. In other cases, accurate risk-management accounting was required. As discussed in Chapter 2, Section II, the need for such accounting systems in financial firms produced, during the 1990s, the value at risk (VaR) methodology for risk measurement. VaR is well suited to assessing market risk situations, and financial firms have embraced the technique; however, the extension of VaR to risk management for nonfinancial firms is, at best, exploratory (e.g., Godfrey and Espinosa, 1998). Even for financial firms, there are inherent difficulties with VaR. For example, it is not clear that VaR, which is associated with "normal reasonable loss", would have been much help to LTCM in assessing the risks that were being assumed.

There are also some new stories to be found in the debacles, including the bewildering array of risk-management products available. The immense risk-management industry now produces a vast range of products that end users have to assess and integrate, if needed, into risk-management planning. This creates the possibility of over-managing the risk. There are dangers as well as benefits in sophisticated risk management. Some products seem to be little more than gambling vehicles for risk managers (e.g., Orange County). Various debacles, such as MGRM, Proctor and Gamble (PG), Gibson's Greetings, and others, involved firms that undertook derivative positions or strategies that were not adequately understood. In the case of Gibson's and PG, the firms apparently fell victim to an aggressive investment banker that overpriced the products being marketed. In the MGRM case, the mechanics of the relatively sophisticated strategy of hedging a long-term forward oil delivery contract with a short-term rolling-stack hedge in oil futures was not well understood.

All lessons considered, it is possible to conclude that derivative debacles are not homogeneous events. A range of factors can contribute to a specific debacle, including attempted manipulation, fraud, and miscalculation. Through it all, the financial system has experienced some severe turbulence almost certainly associated with derivatives trading, such as the U.S. stock market crash of 1987 and the run up in silver and other metal prices in 1980. Fortunately, turbulence over the last decade has not been too significant, though the strength of the American economy during the 1990s could be masking fundamental weaknesses in the system within which risk-management activities are regulated. In the face of the explosion in products and usage, the regulation and oversight of derivatives markets still remain *ad hoc* and unstructured. How was LTCM, a hedge fund operating in the United States under exemptions in securities law, capable of leveraging capital of a few billion dollars into over a trillion dollars in principal value of derivative positions? The story, together with the cast of characters ranging from Meriweather to Merton and Scholes, is the stuff of market legends. Through it all, not a regulator is in sight.

Derivative securities pose real public policy problems. The LTCM collapse revealed many holes in the patchwork of U.S. regulators and regulation. That the event was contained is a tribute to the integrity of the players and speaks to the viability of the self-regulatory incentives inherent in the market system. However, a similar set of circumstances with different players may not have produced the same result. As the President's Working Group on the LTCM collapse concluded:

> The central public policy issue raised by the LTCM episode is how to constrain excess leverage more effectively. As events in the summer and fall of 1998 demonstrated, the amount of leverage in the financial system, combined with aggressive risk taking, can greatly magnify the negative effects of any event or series of events. By increasing the chance that problems at one financial institution can be transmitted to other institutions, leverage can increase the likelihood of a general breakdown in the functioning of financial markets.

The abuse of leverage in market meltdowns is a story stretching back to John Law and the Mississippi scheme. Leverage played a key role in the Great Depression of 1929–1933. The associated public policy lessons are also very, very old.

IV. CHARACTERISTICS OF USERS OF DERIVATIVE SECURITIES

A. SOURCES OF INFORMATION

Identifying users of derivative securities and their motivations presents some difficulties due to the lack of an organized system of collecting information about the relevant transactions. For the exchange-traded derivatives, which include futures, warrants, and some options, filing requirements for regulatory bodies such as the CFTC and the SEC, as well as the exchanges, provide some indication of the types of users, the size of trades, and so on. However, this information, such as that contained in the "Commitments of Traders" report issued by the CFTC (see Chapter 3, Section I), is cursory. In addition, a wide variety of derivative instruments are traded OTC, and trading activity in these markets is often considered proprietary information. Where the traders are financial institutions, reporting requirements for these institutions provide some additional information about OTC positions. As these firms are also market makers, some indication of market size can be determined. Where trading is done by publicly listed firms, some useful information can be obtained from annual reports. Though the methods of accounting for derivatives can make the balance sheet and income statements difficult to interpret (e.g., Gastineau, 1995), recent changes to accounting for derivatives, such as FAS 133, have improved this situation considerably. The annual reports of many financial institutions (e.g., the Bank of Montreal, the Royal Bank) are exemplary efforts at capturing the risk profile of the firm in the annual report.

Some data on derivative transactions is collected by dealer organizations, such as the International Swap and Derivatives Association (ISDA). This is consistent with the self-regulatory framework of the OTC markets. However, as the data originate from dealers, the classifications are in terms of types of contracts and do not address motives. A similar comment applies to data generated by the trade component of the financial press, such as the *International Financing Review*, *Risk* magazine, and *Euromoney*. These are sources for hard data on certain types of transactions. There is also a wealth of stories in these sources relating to motivations of particular end users as well as market makers. Though anecdotal, such reports are valuable insights into the past and current state of the market practices. In addition, these and other trade sources occasionally report surveys of both firms using derivatives and dealers in derivatives.

In addition to these sources, there are also academic surveys of both firms using derivatives and dealers in derivatives. Over the years, a number of such studies have been done. Some of the studies are aimed at specific types of risk, such as that of Batten, Mellor, and Wan (1993) on foreign exchange hedging by Australian firms or Tomek and Peterson (2001) on risk management in agricultural markets. Others are aimed at specific commodities, such as that of Gehr and Martell (1994) on use of derivatives in the gold market, or at specific types of derivatives (e.g., Abken, 1994). Finally, there are survey studies aimed at all derivative usage by nonfinancial firms—for example, Bodnar *et al.* (1995, 1996, 1998), Howtan and Perfect (1998), Berkman (1997), and Phillips (1995). In the following discussion, these studies provide an overview of the types of firms using derivatives and the instruments used to hedge (classified according to the type of commodity being hedged). Bodnar *et al.* (1995, p. 111) provide a useful conclusion about the general use of derivatives: "In marked contrast to the conclusions one would draw from reports in the press ... derivatives are not commonly used to 'speculate' on market movements. Indeed the survey indicates that derivatives are most commonly used to reduce the volatility of the firm's cash flows."

B. AVAILABLE INFORMATION ON DERIVATIVE USAGE BY FINANCIAL FIRMS

Derivative usage by financial firms is substantively different than for nonfinancial firms. Not only are certain financial firms the key market makers in the trading of derivatives, but the cash flows and balance sheets/market values of financial firms are directly exposed to market risks. Hence, financial firms are important end users of derivative products. This complementarity makes figures on derivative usage by financial firms particularly complicated to interpret. In addition, financial firms are subject to a wide range of regulations not applicable to nonfinancials. These regulations require a range of reporting requirements that do permit the derivative market activities of financial firms to be directly studied, in a way that is not possible for nonfinancial firms where derivative trading activities can be considered proprietary information. Various national and international government organizations, such as the BIS, the CFTC, and the Board of Governors, are useful sources of information.

For example, Abken (1994) reports information collected from government sources about the aggregate notional values of the derivative positions of the top ten U.S. financial institutions (see Table 1.5). The size of the derivatives positions appears staggering. Bankers Trust, for example, has a total derivatives position of $1.76 trillion on assets of only $84 billion. This one firm had almost $600 million in outstanding options positions. Recognizing precisely how notional principal relates to cash flow volatility is the subject of Chapter 9. These data make it apparent that the risk-management problems of financial institutions, particularly those involved in making markets in derivatives, are substantively different from those of nonfinancial firms. With the rapid growth

TABLE 1.5 Ten Holding Companies with the Most Derivatives Contracts (*June 30, 1993, Notional Amounts, in $ Millions*)

Rank	Holding company name	State	Assets	Total derivatives	Total futures and forwards	Total swaps	Total options
1	Chemical Banking Corporation	NY	145,522	2,117,385	1,245,500	554,257	317,628
2	Bankers Trust (NY) Corporation	NY	83,987	1,769,947	816,740	355,597	597,610
3	Citicorp	NY	216,285	1,762,478	1,207,132	264,811	290,535
4	J.P. Morgan & Co., Incorporated	NY	132,532	1,550,680	572,897	379,219	398,563
5	Chase Manhattan Corporation	NY	99,085	1,125,075	666,150	258,086	200,839
6	Bankamerica Corporation	CA	185,466	899,783	581,034	229,926	88,823
7	First Chicago Corporation	IL	49,936	452,780	276,790	100,666	75,324
8	Continental Bank Corporation	IL	22,352	170,052	61,058	52,953	36,041
9	Republic New York Corporation	NY	36,203	164,979	81,707	45,504	37,768
10	Bank of New York Company, Inc.	NY	41,045	91,434	63,128	12,200	14,106
	Top 10 Holding Companies			10,104,592	5,574,136	2,433,219	2,077,236
	Other 205 Holding Companies			617,374	247,461	227,276	142,574
	Total Notional Amount for All Holding Companies			10,721,965	5,821,597	2,680,497	2,219,811

Note: Table includes data for companies with total assets of $150 million or more or with more than one subsidiary bank.
Source: Abken (1994), compiled using data from the Board of Governors of the Federal Reserve System Consolidated Financial Statements for Bank Holding Companies (FR Y-9C).

in derivative trading, regulators of financial institutions reacted by making significant advances during the 1990s in determining the actual cash flow exposure of a financial institution to changes in market risk.

The Bank of Canada has for many years conducted a triennial survey of the foreign exchange business of Canadian banks. The survey is part of a coordinated effort by central banks in 43 countries to survey activity in the global foreign exchange and derivative markets. Tabulated results of the Canadian bank surveys appear every few years in the Bank of Canada's *Review* ("Survey of the Canadian foreign exchange and derivatives markets"). Using this source, the relative importance of foreign exchange swap trading relative to spot and outright forward trading in the Canadian foreign exchange market can be seen (Fig. 1.4). Virtually all participants in the Canadian foreign exchange market are surveyed. Examining Fig. 1.4 reveals that more than half of the dollar value of trading in foreign exchange is in the form of swaps,

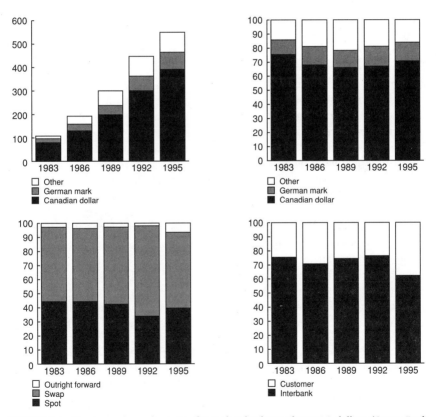

FIGURE 1.4 Foreign exchange business of Canadian banks involving U.S. dollars. (*Source*: Bank of Canada, *Review.*)

significantly more than outright spot transactions. Trading in outright forward exchange contracts is a relatively small part of foreign exchange trading. Swap trading is used for a range of banking activities and not just for covered interest arbitrage transactions. For example, banks will use swaps to balance the currency composition of deposits and investments.

C. THE WHARTON SURVEY OF NONFINANCIAL DERIVATIVE USERS

The Wharton surveys (Bodnar *et al.*, 1996, 1998) were motivated by a desire to create a database suitable for academic studies of risk management. Phillips (1995) is an earlier study along these lines. The Wharton survey is of particular value because of its initial motivation and its coverage. Only nonfinancial firms were surveyed, with an initial randomly sampled group of 2000 firms covering over 40 industries. In the initial survey, 530 firms responded, a 26.5% response rate. Of these 530 firms, 35% reported derivatives usage, with large firms having assets over $250 million being heavy users as 65% of firms in that category used derivatives. Only 12% of small firms, assets less than $50 million, used derivatives. Usage by type of firm and by industry group, as well as the distribution of the usage across type of instrument used, are given in Fig. 1.5. Of particular interest, nonfinancial firms are found to be big users of OTC forward contracts. This is in contrast to the reports for Canadian banks. This evidence is not contradictory; rather, it illustrates the real differences in derivative usage for financial and nonfinancial firms.

The Wharton survey also covers a range of other topics of interest. Regarding the motivations for derivatives transactions, of all firms reporting derivative usage 80% used derivatives to hedge a firm commitment, with 45% of firms frequently using derivatives for this reason. Hedging anticipated transactions was another important reason for using derivatives , with 76% hedging anticipated transactions with maturities less than 12 months (46% frequently) and 50% hedging transactions with maturities greater than 12 months (15% frequently). Other important reasons for using derivatives were hedging foreign dividends, 45% of total users (25% frequently); hedging an economic or competitive exposure, 40% of total users (16% frequently); reducing funding costs through new issue arbitrage, 33% of total users (5% frequently); reducing funding costs by taking a market view, 43% of total users (9% frequently); and hedging the balance sheet, 44% of total users (22% frequently). For 67% of nonfinancial firms reporting derivative usage, the most important reason for using derivatives was to minimize fluctuations in cash flow, a further 28% said the most important reason was to minimize fluctuations in accounting earnings.

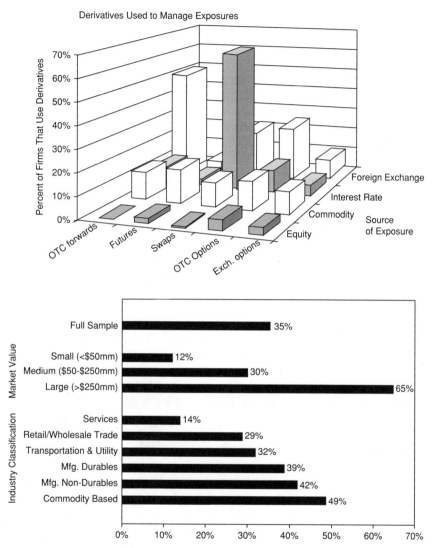

FIGURE 1.5 Derivatives usage by U.S. nonfinancial firms. (*Source*: Bodnar, G.M., Hayt, G.S., Marston, R.C., and Smithson, C.W. (1996). *Financial Management* 25: 113–133.)

Putting all this information together provides a snapshot of nonfinancial derivative security end users. The typical user is a large corporation in a commodity-based or manufacturing industry, utilizing predominately interest rate swaps and foreign exchange forward contracts to hedge firm commitments and anticipated transactions. Some typical users are also relying upon derivatives, such as interest rate and currency swaps, to lower or attempt to lower borrowing costs. All this points to the predominance of a transactions approach to hedging. Only 16% of all those firms reporting derivative usage identified frequently hedging an economic or competitive exposure. Though such patterns of usage may not always reflect best usage practices for derivatives, it is usually wise to presume that firms are using derivatives to manage their particular exposures in the best way possible.

In addition to information on usage, the Wharton surveys also offer information about market practices. For example, a question was asked about the lowest acceptable credit rating for a counterparty to a derivative transaction, and few firms allowed below an A rating. In regard to questions on the types of software used, there seems to be limited reliance on products developed by outside vendors. Finally, the Wharton surveys examined the extent of enterprise-wide or strategic risk management. A key step in strategic risk management is the integration of senior management into risk-management decisions. With this in mind, it was reported that more than half of the firms did not have a regular reporting schedule for relaying information about derivatives activity to the board of directors. This is a result from those firms reporting derivative usage. This disturbing result may simply reflect the low esteem with which the board of directors is held in large corporations. There may still be active, operational channels for risk-management reporting in place. However, it is more likely that the result is representative, signaling a need for nonfinancial corporations to pay attention to operational risks when implementing a program involving derivative securities.

D. OTHER SURVEYS AND STUDIES

Academic studies on derivatives usage abound, though the results are somewhat scattered, and limited by the data available and the tendency to focus on a particular theoretical framework (e.g., Gay and Nam, 1998; Berkman and Bradbury 1996; and Froot et al., 1993). Sometimes the studies are focused on specific issues that can readily be addressed with the data available. For example, the biweekly CFTC Commitments of Traders report divides open interest into positions held by large speculators, commercial hedgers, and small/unclassified traders. This data series stretches back to before World War II, when the series was collected by the Commodity Exchange Authority. At least since Houthakker (1957), studies have matched changes in positions for these three trader groups with changes in prices to determine which group of traders, on aggregate, earned what. Though results reported for different time periods and commodities do differ somewhat, Houthakker's (1957, p. 159) general conclusions are still useful:

> Large hedgers lost and the large speculators gained. The small traders lost in (some commodities) but did quite well in (other commodities).... Most conspicuous in these results is the consistent profitability of the large speculators' transactions ... the traditional picture of the small speculator as an incurable bull, too ignorant to understand shortselling, is incorrect. In fact, small traders do not appear to be less inclined to the short side than the large professional speculators.... On the other hand, the small traders are rather less successful when net short than the large speculators in similar circumstances.

In comparison with studies on motivations and activities of hedgers and risk managers, there are few studies examining speculators.

Many academic studies are motivated by the desire to provide an empirical basis for the different theories of hedging behavior (see Chapter 2, Section 4). For example, Géczy et al. (1997) explore notions advanced by Froot et al. (1993, 1994) that firms with greater growth opportunities and tighter financing constraints are more likely to engage in risk-management activities, particularly hedging. The rationale for this view is that by reducing cash flow variability firms are better able to access internal sources of funds to invest in growth opportunities. Examining the use of currency derivatives for a sample of 372 of the Fortune 500 nonfinancial firms, Géczy et al. (1997) find evidence in favor of the Froot et al. (1993) hypothesis. In addition, evidence was also provided that firms with either high levels of exchange rate exposure or economies of scale in hedging were also more like to use derivatives to manage currency risk. All this evidence is consistent with what is contained in the Wharton survey. Reducing cash flow variability is unambiguously the most important reason identified for using derivatives. Whether the benefits from this reduced variability are translated into a lower risk of bankruptcy or into more certain access to less expensive sources of internal financing or into enhanced profitability due to lower funding costs, or whatever, will depend on the specifics of the firms involved.

Tufano (1996) is an invaluable guide to sorting out the corporate motivations driving derivative usage. Tufano (p. 1097) explicitly recognizes the relative absence of information about derivative usage:

> Academics know remarkably little about corporate risk management practices, even though almost three-fourths of corporations have adopted at least some financial engineering techniques to control their exposures to interest rates, foreign exchange rates and commodity prices. While theorists continue to advance new rationales for corporate risk management, empiricists seeking to test if practice is consistent with these theories have been stymied by a lack of meaningful data. Corporations disclose only minimal details of their risk management programs and, as a result, most empirical analyses have to rely on surveys and relatively coarse data that at best discriminate between firms that do and do not use specific types of

derivative instruments. Case studies of individual firms, while providing greater detail on firm practices, typically lack cross-sectional variation to test whether existing theories explain behavior.

Why do firms use derivatives? The answer to this question is not easy to determine, if only because many firms view risk management practices as proprietary information and are reluctant to provide precise in-depth details about such activities. The recent implementation of FAS 133 imposes reporting requirements on publicly traded firms that will go part of the way to correcting this situation.

Tufano (1996) focuses on risk-management practices of over 50 publicly traded firms in the United States and Canada for which the exclusive primary line of business is gold mining. One advantage provided by the gold mines is the relatively transparent risk management: "Quarterly reporting provides investors with extensive information on firms' use of forward sales, swaps, gold loans, options and other explicit or embedded risk management activities" (p. 1098). Gold mining firms exhibit a wide range of risk management activities (p. 1098):

> The gold industry has embraced risk management: over 85 percent of the firms in this industry used at least some sort of gold price risk management in 1990–1993. Furthermore, mining firms have adopted very different risk management approaches, ranging from Homestake Mining, which sold all of its production at spot prices and made vigorous pronouncements against gold price management, to American Barrick, which featured its successful hedging program on the cover of its annual report.

The wide variation in risk-management practices and transparency in activities makes Tufano's sample particularly interesting.

Tufano tests for a range of theories that have been proposed to explain risk management activity and provides the following summary (1996, p. 1098–1099):

> I find that gold mining firms' risk management decisions are consistent with some of the extant theory. Managerial risk aversion seems particularly relevant; the data bear out Smith and Stulz's (1985) prediction that firms whose managers own more stock options manage less gold price risk, and those whose managers have more wealth invested in common stock manage more gold price risk. These results seem robust under a variety of econometric specifications, and using a number of proxy variables. In contrast, theories that explain risk management as a means to reduce the costs of financial distress, to break the firm's dependence on external financing, or to reduce expected taxes are not strongly supported. I also find that firm risk management levels appear to be higher for firms with smaller outside block holdings and lower cash balances, and whose senior financial managers have shorter job tenures.

This connection between a firm's usage of derivatives and managerial characteristics is not restricted to the gold industry. Schrand and Unal (1998) find similar evidence in the thrift industry. Examining a sample of thrift institutions that had converted from mutual to equity ownership, Schrand and Unal found that the level of risk management after conversion was related to the management compensation structure attained at conversion.

V. REGULATIONS, EXCHANGES, AND AVAILABLE CONTRACTS

A. INFORMATION ON THE INTERNET

The Internet is rapidly becoming an essential source for background information on derivative securities markets, especially for the options and futures exchanges. Information on government and self-regulatory agencies is also readily available on the Web. A number of sites provide a list of pointers to other sites. One such site is the web page for the author of this book, www.sfu.ca/~poitras; go to the links page, where many sites can be accessed, such as the National Futures Association (www.nfa.futures.org). There is also a link to a website for this book that contains a substantial amount of supplementary material relevant to, but not included in, the book. All those interested in finding out about derivatives trading are strongly recommended to browse the exchange websites, such as the CBT (www.cbot.com) and the CME (www.cme.com). Both of these websites are excellent. Typical information provided at an exchange website are contract specifications, margin requirements, recent exchange news, current and historical information on contract prices, volume and open interest, seat prices, and pointers to other sites. This information is so accessible that it will be reproduced here only if essential to the presentation.

A list of some relevant sites, grouped by categories, includes:

U.S. and Canadian Futures and Options Exchanges

Chicago Board of Trade	www.cbot.com
Chicago Board Options Exchange	www.cboe.com
Chicago Mercantile Exchange	www.cme.com
(includes International Monetary Market)	
Coffee, Sugar and Cocoa Exchange	www.csce.com
Kansas City Board of Trade	www.kcbt.com
New York Cotton Exchange	www.nyce.com
New York Mercantile Exchange	www.nymex.com
(includes COMEX)	
Mid-America Commodity Exchange	www.midam.com
Minneapolis Grain Exchange	www.mgex.com

Foreign Futures and Options Exchanges

Blagnova Borsa	www.eunet.si
EUREX Frankfurt	www.eurexchange.com

Hong Kong Futures Exchange   www.hkex.com.hk
London International Financial Futures Exchange   www.liffe.com
London Metal Exchange   www.lme.co.uk
Malaysia Monetary Exchange Bhd.   www.jaring.my
Marche des Options Negociables de Paris   www.monep.fr
Marche a Terme International de France   www.matif.fr
Rente Fija   www.meff.es
New Zealand Futures and Options Exchange   www.nzfoe.co.nz
Singapore International Monetary Exchange (SGX-DT)   www.simex.com.sg
The South African Futures Exchange   www.safex.com
The Sydney Futures Exchange   www.sfe.com.au
The Tokyo Grain Exchange   www.tge.or.jp
The Tokyo International Futures Exchange   www.tiffe.or.jp

Regulators

Commodity Futures Trading Commission   www.cftc.gov/cftc
NASD Regulation, Inc.   www.nasdr.com
Office of the Comptroller of the Currency   www.occ.treas.gov
Securities and Exchange Commission   www.sec.gov
Bank for International Settlements   www.bis.org

Organizations and Associations

Futures Industry Association   www.fiafii.org
International Organization of Security Commissions   www.iosco.org
International Swap and Derivative Association   www.isda.org
Managed Futures Association   www.mfahome.com

Other Exchanges (may trade some derivatives)

International Petroleum Exchange   www.ipe.uk.com
Korean Stock Exchange   www.kse.or.kre
NASDAQ   www.nasdaq.com
New York Stock Exchange   www.nyse.com
Philadelphia Stock Exchange   www.phlx.com
Singapore Stock Exchange   www.ses.com.sg
Tokyo Stock Exchange   www.tse.or.jp
Toronto Stock Exchange   www.tse.com

See also

Sourcebook   www.futuresmag.com

B. REGULATIONS

Much like information on contract specifications, margins, tick sizes, etc., the accessibility of information on the Internet makes redundant a detailed discussion of current rules and regulations governing derivative securities. Both the SEC and CFTC websites have a wealth of information. For example, the CFTC website has a link to "Law and Regulation" where the following information is available: a complete listing of the Commodity Exchange Act; a

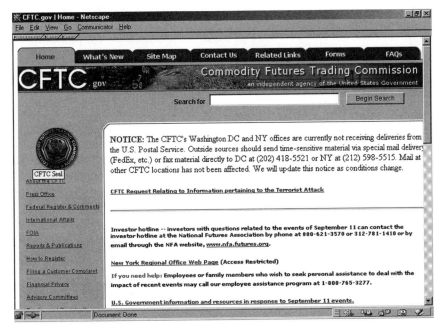

FIGURE 1.6   CFTC website.

downloadable copy of the most recent legislation, Commodity Futures Modernization Act of 2000 (H.R. 5660); drafts of proposed legislation; enforcement orders and complaints; and much more (see Fig. 1.6). Those interested in gaining familiarity with this material are strongly encouraged to visit the regulator websites. What is of immediate interest in this section is to overview the historical development of the regulatory framework.

In the derivative securities markets of the late 19th century, there were limited restrictions on market manipulation. "Cornering" the market was alleged on a regular basis.[37] The classic cornering strategy involved a *short squeeze*. In this case, the manipulating group acquires a controlling position in the deliverable commodity while simultaneously taking on all the nearby long positions the market will allow. The short squeeze occurs when the manipulators stand for delivery. The shorts cannot get enough of the deliverable commodity, and the spot price is bid up significantly to draw new (or

[37]Further background on the market manipulations that took place during this period can be found in Hieronymus (1977) who refers to the three-volume work by Charles Taylor, *History of the Board of Trade of the City of Chicago* (1917).

recycled) stocks into the market.[38] Recently, short squeezes have been associated with the market manipulations of the Hunt brothers leading to the silver price collapse of 1980 and those of the Sumitomo Corp. leading to the copper price collapse of 1996. In both of these cases, as in the Cargill case, exchange oversight played a key role in restraining questionable trading activity.

Historically, these types of abuses were compounded by the problem of contract defaults. Even though the early U.S. futures exchanges featured clearinghouses, membership was voluntary and firms cleared their own trades. In this system, the clearinghouse acted primarily to collect and disperse funds for firms marking to market at the end of the day. The weakness in the clearing mechanism was not corrected on the CBOT until 1925 when the CBOT Clearing Corporation was established. While the Clearing Corp. did not initially clear trades, it did provide a guarantee. This was provided by requiring that all members mark to market daily and post and maintain margin accounts. Since the establishment of the CBOT Clearing Corp., no money has been lost due to the default of a CBOT futures contract. Further complications were introduced by the presence of bucket shops, which did not actually make trades but only took on the other side, filling the order using prices quoted on the exchange. In effect, bucket shops were betting parlors where the bets were placed on commodity price movements.

Both futures and forward trading have always been governed by some combination of government and self-regulation. The restricted access typical of forward markets makes a large degree of self-regulation practical in those markets. The general public access applicable to futures has created a need for a greater degree of government regulation. While initial government intervention attempted to target futures contracts for abolition, by the early part of the 20th century it was generally recognized that improvements in the regulatory framework were more effective. In the United States, the Grain Futures Act, passed in 1922, contributed substantially to raising standards on exchanges and improving trading practices. The Act enabled the government to deal with grain exchanges directly, instead of targeting individual traders. By providing for licensing of futures exchanges, the Act put the onus on the exchanges to be more effective in self-regulation to prevent price manipulation by member firms (and their accounts). The requirement that all futures trading take place on futures exchanges effectively eliminated what remained of the bucket shops. The Grain Futures Act was amended in 1936 and renamed the Commodity Exchange Act (CEA), which is still the centerpiece of U.S. commod-

---

[38]A modern example of the short squeeze occurred in the late 1970s in the silver market when a group led by the Hunt brothers attempted to acquire a controlling interest in the spot silver market. Long futures and forward contracts were used to squeeze the shorts and force up the spot price of silver. Markham (1987) provides a more detailed discussion.

ities regulation. The CEA (1936) extended the government's control of futures trading considerably: Authority over speculative limits was established; registration requirements were imposed on floor brokers and futures commission merchants; cheating, fraud, and market manipulation were made specific criminal offenses; and restrictions were imposed on options trading.

By 1974, the growth in both volume of trade and the number of new contracts (over which the CEA had little effective control) brought a thorough reform. The CEA was amended to include the Commodity Futures Trading Act, which forms the basis of current U.S. government commodities regulation. The CEA (1974) empowers the Commodity Futures Trading Commission (CFTC), the futures industry counterpart to the Securities and Exchange Commission for equities (Fig. 1.6). The CFTC is an "independent," five-member commission appointed by the President, with authority to regulate all U.S. futures trading and exchange activity. Included in the CFTC's mandate was the right to approve both the introduction of new contracts and changes in exchange bylaws. Together with these powers, the CFTC also has considerable emergency authority, such as assessment of large civil fines and cease and desist orders. In 1978, several amendments were made to the Act dealing with the issue of jurisdiction. In opposition to the position of both the SEC and the U.S. Treasury, the CFTC was given exclusive jurisdiction over all futures contracts, including the newly emerging financial futures contracts. Subsequent and ongoing legislative action has focused on clarifying the jurisdiction over options on futures contracts, especially for stock index futures.

Regulatory agencies in all countries impose requirements on participants in futures trading. For example, regulations about the opening and management of individual client accounts at commodity brokerage houses are regulated provincially in Canada and federally in the United States, subject to relevant state statutes. The client deals with a registered futures representative of a securities firm. There are various categories of possible registration that can be satisfied. For example, in British Columbia, requirements are provided by the provincial Securities Commission (BCSC). In the Local Policy Statement 4–1, Sec. 1.1, concerning the Commodity Contract Act Registration Requirements, the BCSC states: "Commodity Contract Act section 13(1)(a) provides that no person shall trade in a commodity contract unless that person is registered as a commodity contracts dealer, as a commodity contracts salesman, as a commodity contracts trading partner or officer, or as a floor trader. Section 13(1)(b) provides that no person shall act as a commodity contracts adviser or as a commodity contracts advising partner or officer unless the person is registered as a commodity contracts adviser or as a commodity contracts advising partner or officer." The various, similar categories of registration in the United States are provided by the National Futures Association (NFA) at www.nfa.futures.org. The NFA is a self-regulatory organization approved by the CFTC to handle the registration of all futures professionals.

In Canada, the individuals typically involved in making trades for client accounts are commodity contracts salesmen, floor traders, and commodity contracts trading partners or officers. Registration for these designations involves satisfying proficiency requirements that, in Canada, include successful completion of the Canadian Futures Examination, given by the Canadian Securities Institute (CSI), and the National Commodities Futures Examination (NCFE) prepared by the Chicago Board of Trade for the National Association of Securities dealers (the NCFE is conducted in Canada by the CSI). Registration as a partner or officer also requires completion of the Partners/Directors/Officers Qualifying Examination. These individuals invariably work for securities firms that are registered to handle commodity accounts. Part of this registration process requires the preparation of a procedure manual that must describe "the policies relating to the acceptance of new accounts, including... a requirement that, prior to the opening of an account, the client is furnished with and signs copies of all applicable client information documents approved by the superintendent... [and] a requirement that the Designated Commodity Supervisor approve in writing all new accounts before they begin to trade... [as well as] the criteria used to review account applications" (Local Policy 4–1, p. 6)

In all locales, commodity futures trading regulations require that client information documents be completed. These items, which are identified legally, include the account application form, trading agreement, margin agreement, hedge letter, client authorization form/trading agreement for discretionary and managed accounts, and a client information/risk disclosure statement. Representative samples of the more significant forms that must be completed before a customer can commence trading futures contracts can be found by following the links at www.sfu.ca/~poitras. In British Columbia, commodity contract dealers are permitted to use their own agreements and statements, subject to the prior approval of a self-regulatory body or the Superintendent of Brokers. Once a client account has been correctly established, trading activity is subject to further regulation, such as position limits and filing requirements, associated with the exchange and legal jurisdiction in which the contract is being traded. In both the United States and Canada, dispute resolution is divided between the exchanges and the securities regulator: the CFTC in the U.S. and the provincial securities commission in Canada.[39]

---

[39]There are a range of other regulations associated with derivative security markets. For example, there are regulations governing the legal uses of derivative securities by pension plans, insurance companies, and other financial institutions.

C. The U.S. Exchanges, the OTC, and Foreign Markets

The derivative markets can initially be decomposed into the OTC markets and the exchanges. This is a useful distinction, if only to reflect the differences in reporting requirements and rights of access. Most equity exchanges offer options, such as warrants and rights issues, but the bulk of exchange trading of derivatives takes place on the various futures and options exchanges. Though not as formalized as the exchanges, the OTC derivatives market is centrally connected to a ring of specialized brokers and a core group of dealers. Restrictions placed on access to direct trading in the OTC markets serve to further define these markets.

From the early beginnings on the CBOT in the 19th century, trading in futures and options on futures has grown to global proportions. The number of contracts offered, volume, open interest, and all other measures of derivative trading have increased substantially over time. This growth has been dramatic since the introduction of financial futures. Trade in financial commodities started with currencies in 1972 on the International Monetary Market (IMM), a division of the Chicago Mercantile Exchange originally organized to trade foreign currencies and now offering a range of financial futures contracts. The next major step in the evolution of financial futures was the introduction of a fixed income futures contract, on Government National Mortgage Association bonds (GNMAs), in 1975 by the CBOT. Shortly thereafter, in 1976, the IMM introduced the Treasury bill futures contract. This was followed by the introduction of the Treasury bond contract on the CBOT. From this point, a wide range of financial futures contracts were introduced during the late 1970s and early 1980s.[40] These contracts included stock index futures, which were first introduced in the early 1980s starting with the Value Line Index on the Kansas City Board of Trade (KCBT) and the S&P 500 index at the CME. In conjunction with the emergence of financial futures, trading of oil complex futures on the NYMEX also experienced dramatic growth since being introduced in the early 1980s.

In the face of this surge of new futures products, traditional commodities, such as corn, sugar, and soybeans (introduced on the CBOT in 1936), have generally prospered. New contracts have also been offered in the traditional agricultural, industrial, and metallurgical commodity groups, such as the CME's introduction of frozen pork bellies in 1961, live cattle in 1964, live

---

[40]A considerable number of the new products were introduced on the International Monetary Market (IMM) division of the CME. With a few major exceptions such as the development of the T-bond contract, much of the CBOT's energy during the 1970s was dedicated to developing the CBOT Options Exchange.

hogs in 1966, and feeder cattle in 1971. A number of exchanges introduced plywood futures in the late 1960s. Other developments include the COMEX's introduction of gold and aluminum contracts and the NYMEX's palladium and platinum contracts during the 1970s and early 1980s. Table 1.6 provides a listing of the important U.S. exchanges, together with a summary of many important contracts currently traded. Because new futures contracts are being introduced on a regular basis, it is not feasible to present a listing of all

TABLE 1.6   US Futures Exchanges and Selected Contracts Traded

Exchange	Contract Commodities/Instruments
Chicago Board of Trade	Corn, oats, soybeans, soybean meal, soybean oil, wheat, rough rice, gold, silver, Treasury bonds, Treasury notes, municipal bond index, Dow Jones Industrials Average, 30-day federal funds, Agency notes
Chicago Mercantile Exchange (CME)	Feeder cattle, live cattle, live hogs, pork bellies, lumber, butter, milk
International Monetary Market Division of CME	Eurodollar time deposits, foreign exchange rates, overnight federal funds, Libor, Treasury bills, Agency notes
Index and Option Market Division of CME	Standard and Poor's stock indexes, Russell 2000 Index, Nikkei stock index, Goldman-Sachs commodity index, Nasdaq 100
MidAmerica Commodity Exchange	Wheat, corn, oats, hogs, cattle, soybeans, foreign exchange rates, Eurodollars, platinum, silver, gold, Treasury bills, notes and bonds.
New York Mercantile Exchange and Commodity Exchange Inc. (Two divisions, one marketplace)	Aluminum, copper, gold, silver, palladium, platinum, crude oil, heating oil, propane, unleaded gasoline, natural gas, electricity, Eurotop stock index
Kansas City Board of Trade	Wheat, Value Line stock index, Internet stock index, natural gas.
Minneapolis Grain Exchange	Wheat, oats, shrimp, cottonseed, electricity
New York Board of Trade, Includes as Divisions:	
New York Cotton Exchange, Coffee, Sugar and Cocoa Exchange Inc., New York Futures Exchange, Cantor Exchange	Cotton, orange juice, milk, European currency unit, foreign exchange rates, Treasury notes, Treasury bonds, U.S. dollar index, cocoa, coffee, sugar, consumer price index, CRB Futures Price Index, NYSE composite Stock Index

Source: CFTC *Annual Report, 2000*

available contracts or exchanges. For example, the currency futures contracts on the Philadelphia Board of Trade are not listed in Table 1.6. The wide variety of contracts available is evident; futures trading occurs in commodities ranging from orange juice to Eurodollar deposits. An essential feature of almost all the commodities traded is some element of storability. Historically important commodities such as butter and milk, which were not available for many years, have made a minor comeback in recent years.

Though the same commodity is sometimes offered on different exchanges, trading activity will tend to be attracted to the exchange where volume is highest making competing contracts unsuccessful. As a consequence, there tends to be only one exchange that features a specific commodity with exchanges tending to specialize in specific commodity groups. For example, the COMEX offers gold and silver contracts and the NYMEX offers the oil complex commodities. A notable exception to a specific commodity being traded at one exchange is provided by the Mid-America Commodity Exchange (MidAm), which offers a range of commodities listed on other exchanges but features contracts of smaller sizes. By conventional measures of contract activity, trading in MidAm contracts is not significant. While comparing contract significance is not obvious due to the substantive differences in commodity characteristics, Table 1.7 provides a listing of the most important U.S. futures contracts in terms of volume and open interest. This table reveals the leading role played by financial futures contracts, especially U.S. T-bonds, Eurodollars, and the S&P 500 index, as well as the oil complex commodities in the rankings. Traditional agricultural commodities are relatively less important, reflecting the substantial growth and development of financial futures markets in the last two decades.

The growth in derivative securities trading has not been confined to North America. A list of selected foreign futures exchanges is provided in Table 1.8. Many of the foreign exchanges trading futures contracts, such as the London Metal Exchange, have long histories, while others, such as the Hong Kong Futures Exchange, have been established only recently. Examining the types of contracts featured on these exchanges reveals that a number of contracts are traded globally, particularly soybeans, Eurodollars, and the currencies. A large number of contracts are also targeted at domestic market considerations, such as the Japanese government bond contracts on the Tokyo Stock Exchange and the All Ordinaries share price index on the Sydney Futures Exchange. In some cases contracts are denominated in local currency and, in others, US$ contracts are traded. This can introduce an element of currency risk for certain types of transactions, such as intermarket spreading strategies. Chapter 3, Section II, examines some of the technical issues behind this problem.

The success of derivative securities trading in the last two decades has created an environment where new contracts are being, almost continuously,

TABLE 1.7 Estimated Number of Futures Contracts Traded in U.S. Markets from Sept. 1998 through Sept. 2000

Exchange	Volume of Trading		Most (Number of Contracts) (1999–00 volume)
	1998–99	1999–00	
Chicago Board of Trade (CBT)	203,562,672	187,048,113	U.S. Treasury Bonds: 67,008,924 contracts 10 Year Treasury Notes: 42,769,912 contracts
Chicago Mercantile Exchange (CME) and International Monetary Market (IMM)	175,488,669	181,852,421	3 month Eurodollars: 100,452,601 contracts S&P Stock Index: 23,083,991 contracts
New York Mercantile Exchange (NYMEX) and Commodity Exchange Inc. (COMEX)	89,869,532	87,753,321	Crude Oil, Light 'Sweet': 37,526,778 contracts Natural Gas: 18,136,332 contracts
New York Board of Trade: includes Coffee, Sugar and Cocoa Exchange (CSCE), New York Cotton Exchange & Associates (NYCE) and New York Futures Exchange (NYFE)	16,070,698	15,954,369	Sugar, No. 11: 5,819,141 contracts Cotton No.2: 2,614,097 contracts Coffee C: 2,364,319 contracts
MidAmerica Commodity Exchange (MCE)	2,586,219	1,913,154	U.S. Treasury Bonds: 763,3354 contracts
Kansas City Board of Trade (KCBT)	2,378,920	2,345,727	Wheat: 2,324,744 contracts
Minneapolis Grain Exchange (MGE)	1,180,573	967,504	Wheat: 963,054 contracts
Total, All US Markets	491,137,790	477,834,609	
Average Month-End Open Interest (All U.S. Markets)	8,927,497	8,941,536	
Total Number of Contracts Settled by Delivery or Cash Settlement	3,631,916	2,871,972	

Source: CFTC *Annual Report 2000*

introduced. Recent examples are foreign stock indices, introduced on the CBOT, and interest rate swap futures, recently introduced on a number of foreign exchanges. Over time, in addition to the successful contracts, numerous unsuccessful contracts have also been introduced. Examples include the the commercial paper contract on the IMM and the GNMA I contract on the

TABLE 1.8   Selected Contracts Traded on Foreign Futures Exchanges

Country/exchange	Futures contracts/commodities
Australia	
Sydney Futures Exchange	Live cattle, wool, wheat, sorghum, Australian dollar, Australian 10-year bond, Australian 3-year bond, Eurodollar time deposit, 90-day bank-accepted bills, All Ordinaries share price index, electricity
Brazil	
Bolsa de Mercadorias & Futuros	Corn, cotton, soybeans, gold, coffee, U.S. Dollar, Brazilian Treasury bond, Sao Paulo stock exchange index, interest rate swaps
France	
Marché à Terme des International de France (MATIF)	2, 5 and 30 year Euro bonds, 90-day Euribor deposits, rapeseed, rapeseed meal, rapeseed oil, corn, milling wheat, CAC 40 stock index, Euro DJ stock index.
Great Britain	
International Petroleum Exchange of London	Gas oil, Brent crude oil, natural gas, electricity
London International Financial Futures Exchange (LIFFE)	British pound, Euro, 3 month Eurodollar Euribor, Euroswiss and Euroyen deposits, German government bond, Japanese government bond, long-, medium- and short-term gilts, sterling 3-month deposits, Financial Times stock exchange (FTSE) 100 and 250 Indexes, FTSE European stock index, MSCI European Index, swapnotes
London Metal Exchange	Aluminum, copper, lead, nickel, silver, zinc
Hong Kong	
Hong Kong Futures Exchange (now part of HKEx)	3 month HIBOR deposits, MSCI China Free stock index, Hang Seng stock index, selected foreign and domestic stocks
Japan	
Osaka Securities Exchange	Nikkei 225 and 300 stock indexes
Tokyo Commodity Exchange	Gold, platinum, silver, aluminum, rubber, gasoline, kerosene
Tokyo Grain Exchange	US soybeans, soybean meal, red beans, coffee, sugar, corn
Tokyo International Financial Futures Exchange	3 month Euroyen deposits, Yen, LIBOR-TIBOR spread
Tokyo Stock Exchange	Japanese 5, 10 and 20 year government bonds, Tokyo stock price index (TOPIX)

(*continues*)

TABLE 1.8 (*continued*)

Country/exchange	Futures contracts/commodities
New Zealand	
New Zealand Futures Exchange	New Zealand, 3, 5 and 10-year government bonds, 90-day bank-accepted bills, Barclays share price index, electricity
Singapore	
Singapore International Monetary Exchange (now part of SGX)	Singapore dollar, 10 year Japanese government bond, 3 month Eurodollar and Euroyen deposits, Nikkei 225 and 300 stock indexes, MSCI stock indexes for Taiwan, Singapore and Hong Kong, selected foreign and domestic stocks, Brent crude oil
Switzerland and Germany	
EUREX	Dow Jones Euro stock sector indexes

CBOT. Sometimes contracts are successful for a period and then stop being traded, one example being the gold futures contract on the IMM that at one time was almost as liquid as the COMEX gold contract. Another golden example is the gold contract traded on the Winnipeg Exchange prior to the lifting of U.S. gold trading restrictions. In addition to the failed contracts, many exchanges offer surrogates to successful contracts traded on other exchanges, such as the CBOT silver futures.

D. Available Contracts

For a number of reasons, the details of futures contract specifications for individual commodities will be of interest in later chapters. Summaries of the contract specifications for selected U.S. contracts are provided on the exchange websites. While some of this information, such as the delivery month and trading units, is available in the daily financial press, the information on daily price limits and, especially, the grade standards and delivery locations is not. The practical complications associated with actual delivery on futures contracts are reflected in the descriptions. For example, the CME feeder cattle futures contract requires delivery at approved livestock yards in Omaha, Sioux City, or Oklahoma City (or other approved locations with allowances). The Coffee, Sugar and Cocoa Exchange (CSCE) sugar contracts permit delivery of sugar from a number of countries to be delivered, f.o.b., at a

[41]In Canada, the Winnipeg Commodity Exchange features seven contracts: flaxseed, canola, domestic feed wheat, rye, oats, and two domestic feed barley contracts that depend on delivery points. Contract sizes are listed in tonnes, not bushels as for U.S. contracts. Prices are quoted in

port in the country of origin. Similar types of variation are permitted for the Winnipeg grain contracts.[41]

Because the delivery descriptions given are often brief summaries of the actual process, in some cases the description of the deliverable given is misleading. For example, the T-bond delivery requirements refer to bonds with at least 15 years to maturity, but there are a number of T-bonds, with a range of differing coupons, that satisfy this requirement (a similar situation prevails for T-notes). This requires a method for converting a given bond value into a comparable invoice amount of the par value of the "theoretical" 6%, 15-year bond that is now the conceptual deliverable commodity. For this purpose, conversion factors for each individual bond are provided based on a formula that takes account of the bond's coupon rate, the number of years/months/days to maturity, and the base 6% yield (formerly 8%). In practice, the formula is only an approximation that tends to favor one bond over another resulting in the concept of a cheapest deliverable bond (see Appendix II). The observed futures price for any commodity is always the price of the cheapest deliverable. Due to variations in market conditions, it is possible for the cheapest deliverable to change over the life of the contract.

There are numerous significant differences that occur across the range of available futures contracts. For example, Canadian and U.S. contracts are denominated in different currencies, with Canadian contracts using Canadian dollars. Another important difference is whether cash settlement or physical delivery is required when the futures contract matures. Cash settlement dictates that a payment of the gain or loss on the position is required at maturity, with no physical settlement. This feature is common on many financial futures contracts, such as the equity indices. Another significant difference can occur with the contract units, which can differ in size or in units of measurement. For example, the Mid-America Commodity Exchange typically features contracts that are some fraction of the contract size traded on the larger exchanges such as the CBOT. Differences in measurement units occur, with Winnipeg contracts being determined in tonnes and CBOT contracts being measured in bushels.

E. Specifically on Options

Since the commencement of exchange trading of stock options contracts on the CBOE in 1973, the growth of options trading has been staggering. Both

---

Canadian dollars. Variation in the deliverable grade and delivery location is permitted, consistent with contract delivery being used to facilitate cash market activity. A similar comment applies to delivery dates. For example, on the last business day of the contract, delivery is permitted at points other than Thunder Bay or Vancouver.

stock and commodity options have been involved in this growth. On the stock side, with the exception of the CBOE, which is the only major U.S. exchange devoted solely to options, the most important U.S. stock options exchanges are the relevant stock exchanges: the New York Stock Exchange, the American Stock Exchange (AMEX) the Philadelphia Stock Exchange, and the Pacific Stock Exchange.[42] Of these, the NYSE, AMEX, and Pacific Stock Exchange offer options only on individual stocks and stock indices. Philadelphia also trades options on spot currency, while the CBOE includes interest rate options on T-bonds and T-notes in addition to the agricultural commodities. As a rule, options on commodity futures are offered by the relevant futures exchange on which the underlying future is traded. Hence, in addition to the stock exchanges and OTC-based trading, the list of options exchanges is more-or-less the same as the list of U.S. and foreign futures exchanges given in Tables 1.7 and 1.8. For example, the COMEX offers options on silver and gold futures, while the IMM offers options on T-bill and currency futures.[43] Hence, options are available on the array of commodities that are traded in futures markets.

Exchange-traded stock options have certain characteristic features. Option prices are usually quoted on a per share basis while the contract calls for 100 shares to be delivered. Hence, the call premium to be paid per option contract (excluding commissions, margins, and other nonpremium costs) is 100 times the quoted price. Over the life of the option, this number may be adjusted to take account of factors such as stock splits. However, exchange-traded options are not protected against payments in cash dividends.[44] For exchange trading, American options are conventional. Both American and European options are common in OTC-traded options. In the U.S., available exercise prices are indirectly determined by the SEC, which has authority to approve stock option design features. While there is considerable diversity across exchanges, exercise prices are usually divisible by five and are offered over 5-point intervals for stock prices up to $100, and in $10 intervals thereafter. While trading in long-term stock options started on the relevant stock exchanges in the period following the crash of 1987, the traditional CBOE stock options still do not exceed 9 months to maturity.

For stock options traded in the United States, the last trading date is the third Friday of the expiration month. This date is sometimes colloquially referred to

---

[42]Because the CBOE trading floor is integrated with the CBOT futures trading floor, it is not completely accurate to refer to the CBOE as a purely options exchange.

[43]For the IMM and other exchanges, this statement is not technically correct because a different part of the exchange is responsible for trading options on commodities. In the IMM case, it is the Index and Options Market (IOM) Division of the Chicago Mercantile Exchange.

[44]Because exchange-traded stock options do not adjust options prices to account for cash dividends, this can create an early exercise trading opportunity. This point is discussed in later chapters.

as the "witching hour." At various times, this date also coincides with the expiration of associated index options and index futures, creating a "triple witching hour." For the S&P 500 futures and options, there are four triple witchings corresponding to the delivery months of March, June, September, and December. Since 1985, expiration dates for individual stock options are offered in cycles of four: January/April/July/October, February/May/August/November, and, March/June/September/December. In order to keep with the maximum 9-month maturity, only the most recent three expiration dates will be offered. Rules regarding margins, commissions, and execution are provided in the options contract specifications on the relevant exchange websites and will not be further examined.[45] (Margins are only required for written positions.) With this in mind, consider the October 6, 2001 futures option quotations given in Table 1.9. Using the S&P 500 option to illustrate the quoting procedure, the first column gives the available strike prices, the next three columns the call option prices for the October/November/December expiration dates, and the final three columns are the put prices for the same expiration dates.[46]

The contract specifications for options on futures contracts are closely aligned with the underlying commodity futures (see options contract specifications on the relevant exchange website) where the deliverable is typically one futures contract on the appropriate commodity. Examining options for specific commodities reveals that there are differences in the method by which the option expiration dates are determined. In some cases (e.g., currencies and stock indices), expiration takes place during the delivery month for the future. However, in most cases, option expiration is prior to the futures delivery month. As discussed in Chapter 8, Section IV, when there is a (positive or negative) carry cost relationship between the spot and the future (i.e., carry costs are not zero), then there will be a difference between the prices for options on spot and futures. With this in mind, consider the futures options prices given in Table 1.9. With the exception of information on the current commodity price which is included for common stock options, the quoting procedure is virtually identical to that for stock options. To calculate the premium to be paid for a futures option (excluding other costs), the information at the top of the quote section is used. For example, in Fig. 1.9, for a C$ call option with Dec. expiration and 6300 strike price: (US\$1.24/C\$100)(C\$100,000) = US\$1240. While

---

[45]Material on commission costs, trading rules, and so on can be obtained from various sources, such as the exchange websites or from the various introductory texts on derivative securities. In addition to material provided by the exchanges and commission houses, Cox and Rubinstein (1985) provide another useful, and more detailed, source for this material. In addition, Cox and Rubinstein (1985) offer relevant information about the U.S. tax implications and associated tax strategies for options trading.

[46]The letter "r" indicates that this particular option did not trade on this specific day. The letter "s" indicates that this specific option has not been opened for trading by the exchange.

TABLE 1.9   Price quotations for futures options, (*Source*: The Globe and Mail, Oct. 6, 2001. Reprinted with permission.)

CHICAGO MERCANTILE EXCHANGE

LIVE CATTLE 40,000 lbs, cents per lb

Price	Calls			Puts		
	Oct	Dec	Feb	Oct	Dec	Feb
6000.00	r	r	r	r	0.10	0.20
6200.00	r	8.475	r	r	0.15	0.30
6400.00	r	r	r	r	0.25	0.35
6600.00	3.60	r	r	r	0.50	0.60
6700.00	2.60	4.05	s	r	0.70	s
6800.00	1.60	3.25	r	r	0.90	0.95
6900.00	0.60	2.675	s	r	1.30	s
7000.00	r	2.075	4.275	0.40	1.70	1.35
7100.00	r	1.525	s	1.40	2.15	s
7200.00	r	1.125	3.10	2.40	2.75	2.10
7300.00	r	0.90	s	3.40	3.50	s
7400.00	r	0.65	2.00	4.40	4.25	3.05
7500.00	r	0.45	s	5.40	5.05	s
7600.00	r	0.35	1.125	6.40	5.95	4.15
7700.00	r	0.25	s	7.40	r	s
7800.00	r	.175	0.70	8.40	7.775	5.70
8000.00	r	0.10	0.45	r	r	r
8200.00	r	.025	0.25	r	r	r

Prev day call vol   2867   Open int.   29448
Prev day put vol   3056   Open int.   46698

LEAN HOGS 40,000 lbs, cents per lb

Price	Calls			Puts		
	Oct	Dec	Feb	Oct	Dec	Feb
4000.00	r	r	r	r	.025	.175
4200.00	r	r	r	r	.075	.225
4400.00	r	r	r	r	0.10	0.30
4600.00	r	r	r	r	0.15	.425
4800.00	11.95	7.50	r	r	.275	0.60
5000.00	r	5.75	6.55	r	0.50	0.90
5200.00	7.95	4.10	5.075	r	0.85	1.40
5300.00	6.95	r	s	r	1.15	s
5400.00	5.95	2.775	3.80	r	1.50	2.10
5500.00	r	2.025	s	r	1.75	s
5600.00	3.95	1.90	2.65	r	2.625	2.925
5700.00	2.95	1.40	s	r	3.125	s
5800.00	2.00	1.025	1.80	0.05	3.725	r
5900.00	1.15	.725	s	0.20	r	s
6000.00	0.50	0.50	1.15	0.55	r	r
6100.00	0.20	0.35	s	1.25	r	s
6200.00	0.05	.275	0.70	2.10	r	r

Prev day call vol   270   Open int.   13918
Prev day put vol   187   Open int.   10166

EURODOLLARS $1,000,000, pts of 100%

Price	Calls			Puts		
	Oct	Nov	Dec	Oct	Nov	Dec
9575.00	1.985	s	1.985	r	s	r
9600.00	1.735	s	1.735	r	s	r
9625.00	1.485	r	1.485	r	r	r
9650.00	1.235	r	1.235	r	r	r
9675.00	.985	.985	.985	r	r	.0025
9687.00	r	s	0.86	r	s	.0025
9700.00	.735	.735	.7375	r	r	.005
9712.00	r	s	.615	r	s	.0075
9725.00	.485	0.49	.495	r	.005	0.01
9737.00	0.36	r	0.38	r	r	0.02
9750.00	.235	.255	0.27	r	0.02	.035
9762.00	0.12	.155	0.18	.0125	.045	0.07
9775.00	.0325	.0825	0.11	0.05	0.10	.125
9787.00	0.01	r	.0625	r	s	0.20
9800.00	.005	.015	.0325	r	r	.295

Prev day call vol 238713   Open int. 3313868
Prev day put vol 174525   Open int. 3180182

S&P COMPOSITE $250 times index

Price	Calls			Puts		
	Oct	Nov	Dec	Oct	Nov	Dec
700.00	r	r	r	0.10	1.00	2.00
725.00	r	r	r	0.15	1.30	2.60
750.00	r	r	323.50	0.30	1.70	3.20
775.00	r	r	r	0.55	2.10	4.00
800.00	r	r	275.30	0.80	2.70	5.00
825.00	r	r	251.40	1.05	3.30	6.00
850.00	r	r	228.20	1.30	4.20	7.70

Price	Calls			Puts		
860.00	r	r	r	1.40	4.60	8.50
875.00	r	r	r	1.70	5.50	9.70
900.00	173.80	r	r	2.20	6.80	12.00
910.00	164.00	r	r	2.40	7.50	13.10
920.00	r	r	r	2.60	8.30	14.40
925.00	149.30	r	r	2.70	8.80	15.00
930.00	r	r	r	2.80	9.30	15.60
940.00	134.80	r	r	3.20	10.30	17.10
950.00	125.20	132.70	139.50	3.60	11.40	18.50
960.00	115.70	r	r	4.10	12.50	20.10
970.00	106.40	r	122.90	4.70	13.80	21.80
975.00	101.70	110.90	118.90	5.00	14.50	22.80
980.00	97.00	106.60	114.90	5.30	15.20	23.70
985.00	92.40	r	r	5.70	16.00	r
990.00	87.80	r	107.00	6.10	16.80	25.80
995.00	83.30	r	103.20	6.60	17.70	26.90
1000.00	78.80	90.10	99.30	7.10	18.60	28.00
1005.00	74.40	r	95.60	7.70	19.50	29.30
1010.00	70.10	82.10	91.90	8.40	20.60	30.50
1015.00	65.80	78.30	88.30	9.10	21.70	31.90
1020.00	61.60	74.50	84.70	9.90	22.90	33.30
1025.00	57.50	70.70	81.20	10.80	24.10	34.70
1030.00	53.40	67.00	77.70	11.70	25.40	36.20
1035.00	49.40	63.40	r	12.70	26.80	37.80
1040.00	45.70	60.00	71.10	13.90	28.30	39.50
1045.00	42.00	56.60	67.80	15.20	29.90	41.20
1050.00	38.40	53.30	64.60	16.60	31.60	43.00
1055.00	35.00	50.10	r	18.20	33.40	44.90
1060.00	31.70	47.10	58.50	19.90	35.30	46.80
1065.00	28.60	44.10	55.70	21.80	37.30	48.90
1070.00	25.70	41.20	52.80	23.90	39.40	51.00
1075.00	23.00	38.40	50.00	26.20	41.60	53.20
1080.00	20.30	35.70	47.30	28.50	43.90	55.40
1085.00	17.80	33.10	44.60	31.00	r	57.70
1090.00	15.50	30.60	42.10	33.70	48.70	60.20
1095.00	13.40	28.20	39.60	36.60	r	r
1100.00	11.50	25.90	37.20	39.70	54.00	65.20
1105.00	9.80	23.80	34.90	42.90	r	r
1110.00	8.30	21.80	32.70	46.40	r	70.60
1115.00	7.00	19.90	30.60	50.10	r	r
1120.00	5.90	18.10	28.60	54.00	r	76.50
1125.00	4.90	16.40	26.70	58.00	69.40	79.50
1130.00	4.10	14.80	24.90	62.20	r	82.70
1135.00	3.40	13.40	23.10	66.50	r	85.90
1140.00	2.80	12.10	21.40	70.90	80.00	89.10
1145.00	2.40	10.80	r	75.50	r	r
1150.00	2.00	9.70	18.40	80.10	87.60	96.10
1160.00	1.40	7.70	15.60	89.50	95.60	103.20
1165.00	1.10	6.90	14.40	94.20	r	r
1170.00	0.90	6.20	13.30	99.00	r	110.80
1175.00	0.75	5.50	12.20	103.80	108.30	114.70
1180.00	0.65	4.90	11.10	108.70	r	118.60
1185.00	0.55	4.40	r	113.60	r	r
1190.00	0.45	3.90	9.30	118.50	r	126.70
1195.00	0.40	3.50	8.50	r	r	130.90
1200.00	0.35	3.20	7.70	128.40	131.00	135.10
1205.00	0.30	2.80	7.00	r	r	139.40
1210.00	0.25	2.50	6.30	138.30	r	143.60
1220.00	0.20	2.00	5.10	148.30	r	152.40
1225.00	0.20	1.70	4.60	153.30	r	156.90
1230.00	0.15	r	4.20	158.20	r	161.50
1240.00	0.15	r	3.40	168.20	r	170.70
1250.00	0.10	1.00	2.80	r	r	180.10
1260.00	0.10	r	2.30	r	r	189.60
1270.00	0.10	r	1.90	r	r	199.20
1275.00	0.10	0.50	1.70	r	r	204.00
1280.00	r	s	1.55	r	s	208.80
1290.00	r	s	1.35	r	s	218.70
1300.00	r	0.35	1.10	r	r	228.40
1320.00	r	s	0.70	r	s	248.20
1325.00	r	s	0.65	r	s	253.20
1350.00	r	0.25	0.45	278.20	r	278.20
1375.00	r	0.20	0.35	r	r	303.20
1400.00	r	s	0.25	r	s	328.20
1500.00	r	s	r	r	s	428.20

Prev day call vol   4550   Open int.   76180
Prev day put vol   11746   Open int.   132909

BRITISH POUND 62,500 pounds, cents per pound

Price	Calls			Puts		
	Oct	Nov	Dec	Oct	Nov	Dec
1380.00	r	r	9.56	r	0.04	0.12
1400.00	r	r	7.66	r	0.08	0.22
1410.00	6.48	r	s	r	0.14	s
1420.00	5.48	r	5.86	r	0.20	0.40
1430.00	4.48	r	s	r	0.26	s
1440.00	3.48	r	4.14	r	0.34	0.68
1450.00	2.48	r	3.50	r	0.48	1.02
1460.00	1.48	2.28	2.88	r	0.80	1.40
1470.00	0.48	1.72	r	r	1.24	r
1480.00	r	1.26	1.70	0.52	1.78	2.22
1490.00	r	0.82	1.30	r	r	r
1500.00	r	0.54	0.96	r	r	3.48
1520.00	r	0.26	0.56	r	r	5.06
1540.00	r	0.14	0.28	r	r	6.78
1550.00	r	0.10	0.24	r	r	r
1560.00	r	0.06	0.20	r	r	8.68

Prev day call vol   627   Open int.   6264
Prev day put vol   254   Open int.   7874

CANADIAN DOLLAR $100K, cents/Cdn$

Price	Calls			Puts		
	Oct	Nov	Dec	Oct	Nov	Dec
6300.00	r	r	.124	r	.015	.028
6350.00	.047	.074	.089	r	r	.042
6400.00	r	.045	.061	.803	.048	.064
6450.00	r	.025	.041	.053	r	.094
6500.00	r	r	.026	.103	r	.128
6550.00	.r.	.r	.016	r	r	.168
6600.00	r	r	0.01	r	r	.212
6650.00	r	r	.007	r	r	.259
6750.00	r	s	.004	r	s	.355

Prev day call vol   67   Open int.   29767
Prev day put vol   110   Open int.   8826

GERMAN MARK 125,000 DM, cents/mark

Price	Calls			Puts		
			Dec			Dec
Prev day call vol			0	Open int.		0
Prev day put vol			0	Open int.		3

JAPANESE YEN 12.5M yen, cents/100 yen

Price	Calls			Puts		
	Oct	Nov	Dec	Oct	Nov	Dec
750.00	r	r	r	r	0.02	0.06
760.00	r	r	7.53	r	0.03	0.08
770.00	r	r	r	r	0.05	0.11
780.00	r	r	r	r	0.08	0.16
790.00	r	r	r	r	0.12	0.24
800.00	r	r	3.82	r	0.18	0.36
810.00	2.48	r	3.03	r	0.30	0.56
815.00	r	2.36	r	r	0.39	0.69
820.00	1.48	1.98	2.31	r	0.51	0.84
825.00	0.98	1.65	r	r	0.67	1.02
830.00	0.48	1.34	1.71	r	0.86	1.23
835.00	0.04	1.07	1.43	0.06	1.09	1.45
840.00	r	0.86	1.22	0.52	1.38	1.74
845.00	r	0.69	s	1.02	1.71	s
850.00	r	0.55	0.88	1.52	2.06	2.39
855.00	r	0.44	0.75	2.02	2.45	2.76
860.00	r	0.36	0.64	2.52	2.87	3.15
865.00	r	0.28	0.54	3.02	r	r
870.00	r	0.23	0.45	3.52	3.74	3.95
880.00	r	0.14	0.32	r	r	4.82
890.00	r	0.09	0.23	r	r	5.72
900.00	r	0.06	0.17	r	r	6.66
910.00	r	0.04	0.13	r	r	r
920.00	r	0.03	0.10	r	r	r
930.00	r	0.01	0.08	r	r	r
940.00	r	r	0.07	r	r	10.55

Prev day call vol   599   Open int.   43542
Prev day put vol   2004   Open int.   47267

margin requirements for written options positions are somewhat more complicated than for the associated future, a useful (if not fully accurate) rule of thumb is that the written option will have approximately the same margin as the associated future.

In the United States, the regulation of options is somewhat more complicated than for futures. Under the Shad/Johnson accord of 1982, options on futures are handled by the CFTC, while options on securities and spot currencies are under the SEC. Much as with futures, the regulatory authority is divided between the governmental agency, the relevant exchange on which the contract is traded, the Options Clearing Corporation, and the national associations, such as the National Association of Securities Dealers, the Put and Call Brokers and Dealers Association, the National Futures Association, and the Securities Investors Protection Corporation (which provides insurance against brokerage firm failure). In the case of options on futures, in addition to exchange requirements, options traders have to satisfy CFTC registration requirements. A similar situation exists in Canada, where regulation falls to a combination of the provincial Securities Commissions, the relevant exchanges, and the Investment Dealers Association. Further information on the historical development of regulatory issues can be found in Markham (1987), Edwards (1983), and Koppenhaver (1987).

BOX 5
_____

Becoming a Floor Trader

All Canadian and U.S. futures exchanges have procedures for individuals to become floor traders. These procedures differ from exchange to exchange. The following excerpts are taken from the Winnipeg Commodity Exchange publication, *Membership on the Winnipeg Commodity Exchange*:

In Winnipeg, floor traders are permitted to trade simultaneously as brokers and independents.... The initial start up costs of a new career as a floor trader are minimal.... For an annual fee of roughly $1750, The Winnipeg Commodity Exchange provides: a receptionist, a photocopier, a bank of telephones, and live quotations from Chicago and other major markets.... The opportunities for profit come from several different sources. First, the floor trader may trade for his own account, providing his own margin money.... Secondly, the floor trader may also

(continues)

(*continued*)

be registered as a "futures broker" by the Exchange. This allows the trader to trade for other members' accounts for a brokerage fee. These other members are often grain companies, brokerage houses, shippers and exporters.

...As a floor trader, you will find several avenues to pursue market information often unavailable to non-members. The state of the art news services located on the trading floor supply data from several of the most renowned and respected information suppliers in the world. Tick-by-tick, updating of price information from all of the major futures exchanges is at your fingertips including three major quote vendors, news wires and a weather channel, along with supporting technical and fundamental analysis.

...Individuals interested in Membership on the Exchange must complete the Application for Membership form. The Application for Membership includes such items as: references...and a business history section. The Exchange staff will verify the information included in the form and invite the applicant to complete a questionnaire on the operations of the Exchange and the commodities market. The application is then forwarded to the financial review committee and the membership committee.

The financial review committee will determine the financial eligibility of the applicant based on the Exchange By-Laws and Regulations. The membership committee will assess the details of the potential member's application during a brief interview. Upon approval by the financial review committee and the membership committee, the applicant is then eligible to purchase a seat on the Exchange.

Individuals will become eligible to trade their own account after completion of the Floor Traders Qualification Course. This course is run by a committee of several full time traders who will evaluate the applicants' trading ability in a series of pit simulations. Once the floor trader's qualification committee is satisfied with the trading ability of the applicant, he will be allowed to trade.

VI. QUESTIONS

1. Define the following: (a) futures contract; (b) forward contract; (c) open interest; (d) clearinghouse; (e) calendar spread; (f) initial, maintenance, and variation margin; (g) deliverable commodity.

2. What are the fundamental differences between "time bargains" and "to arrive" contracts? What historical preconditions were necessary for the emergence of futures trading in 19th-century Chicago?
3. What are the implications of having different regulatory authorities responsible for cash and futures markets? Give some specific examples of how having different regulatory authorities led to problems in cash markets.
4. What is a short squeeze? What is a corner? What are the institutional and trading requirements needed for a short squeeze to be effective? Discuss at least two actual instances where short squeezes were used to manipulate the cash market.
5. Using Schaede (1989), discuss what features of the Osaka rice market support the claim that this was the first functioning futures market, as opposed to similar trading in joint-stocks and other commodities on the Amsterdam bourse?

VII. SUGGESTIONS FOR ESSAY TOPICS

In a senior level, one-semester, three-credit-hour course, the expectations are for a paper of not less than 10 pages, double spaced, excluding bibliography and title page. Allowing for the wide diversity among topics, a paper of more than 25 pages is probably beyond the requirement. Papers are marked equally on research content, difficulty of analysis and formatting, grammar, spelling, and organization. All papers are expected to contain a bibliography that reflects the available literature on the subject under consideration. For papers of topical interest, it is essential that recent sources be included. For more analytical papers, referencing and discussion of important theoretical contributions are required.

Topics on the historical development of futures/forward or options trading: Tulipmania; The 19th-century History of U.S. Market Manipulations Using Derivative Contracts; The Role of Government in the Development of Derivative Securities Markets Since 1972; A specific instance of market manipulation using derivatives such as the Sumitomo Copper Scandal or the Hunt Silver Debacle

Portfolio insurance: The Role of Portfolio Insurance in the October 1987 Market Break; Comparison of the Different Types of Portfolio Insurance

Covered interest parity: Divergences from CIP; Using CIP Bounds To Formulate Trading Strategies

Valuation of implicit call or put options: Conversion Feature for Bonds; Mortgage Prepayment Option in Mortgage-Backed Securities; Shareholders' Equity as a Call on the Residual Value of the Firm; Pricing of the Unbundled

Options Embedded in Various Securities such as CMOs and REMICs; The Wild-Card Option and Other Options Associated with CBOT T-bond Futures of Other Contracts; Option Adjusted Spread Analysis of Fixed Income Securities

Valuation of real options in physical assets: The Waiting or Mothball Option in Capital Investment Decisions; The Option Component of Real Estate Prices; Scheduling of Freighter Traffic

Other practical topics: Hedging Strategy for a specific type of entity such as a financial institution, Global Airline, Oil producer, or Metal Refinery; The Clearinghouse; Interest Rate Swaps and/or Currency Swaps: Motivations for Engaging in Trade (e.g., Are Swaps a Zero-Sum Game?); Swap Pricing

Accounting issues for derivative securities: Tax Treatment of Futures and/or Options; Marking to Market Versus Book Value in Hedge Accounting; The Implications of FAS 133 (FASB 1998) and FAS 138 (FASB 2000); Currency Translations Rules—FASb 8 versus FASb 52

Comparison of specific types of options pricing formulae: Roll–Geske versus Black–Scholes; Cox's CEV versus Merton's Jump Diffusion; Restricted and Unrestricted Arithmetic Brownian Motion; Exotic Options—Pricing, Application, and Types Available

Study of a specific speculative futures or options trading strategy: Turtles; Tandems, Such as the TED; Soy Crush; The Crack Spread; The Spark Spread; The Box Spread; Creating Interest Rates Caps (and/or Floors) with Options

Other theoretical topics: Optimal Hedging; How Unbiased Are Futures Price Forecasts; Distributional Properties of Futures or Options

An issue of current topical interest: The Crackdown on Illegal Trading Activities on the CBOT; The Development of New Trading Instruments; Regulatory Issues Associated with Futures and/or Options; The Collapse of Long-Term Capital Management; Derivative Debacles of the 1990s.

CHAPTER 2

Risk-Management Concepts

I. PROFIT FUNCTIONS AND EXPECTED UTILITY MAXIMIZATION

The profit function is an essential tool in the analysis of derivative security trading strategies, for both risk-management and speculative purposes. The procedure for specifying the profit function proceeds by first writing down the relevant transactions in a trading schematic. The basic profit function is then specified from the schematic. For simple trading strategies, such as a naked speculation, the profit function and schematic are not too useful, as the basic insights can be obtained without much analysis. However, for more complicated trades, the profit function can be an invaluable aid. Once the basic profit function is specified, it is possible to do manipulations and substitutions that can be used to identify relevant features of the trading strategy. One important substitution that is often used is to replace the deferred contract prices with the cash and carry arbitrage conditions.

To complete the illustration of what determines the profitability of long and short positions, let Q be the number of units of the commodity purchased. At $t = 0$, the two parties to the futures contract for delivery of Q units at $t = T$

agree to a price of $F(0,T)$. Consider what happens if $F(1,T) > F(0,T)$ (i.e., futures prices for the commodity rise). The short position who agreed to sell Q units at $F(0,T)$ now is faced with a situation where the value of the commodity to be delivered is $QF(1,T)$ versus $QF(0,T)$ for the previous period. Pretending for the moment that $t = 1$ was actually the delivery date T, then the short would have to cover by going into the cash market, purchasing the appropriate number of units of the commodity, and delivering. This would require a larger outlay of funds, $QF(1,1) = QS(1)$, than would be received from the sale of the commodity through the futures markets, $QF(0,T)$. The opposite type of example would hold for the long position. Hence, it can be concluded that *short positions benefit from price falls while long positions benefit from price rises.*

While it is straightforward to illustrate the conditions under which long and short positions are profitable, the analysis is decidedly more complex when more involved positions are being considered. For this reason, it is instructive to illustrate how to convert the previous discussion into algebraic terms. Table 2.1 demonstrates that the profit function for the long futures position is $\pi(1,T) = Q\{F(1,T) - F(0,T)\}$. It follows that $\pi > 0$ when futures prices rise between $t = 0$ and $t = 1$. A similar profit function can be defined for *short* positions:

$$\pi(1,T) = Q\{F(0,T) - F(1,T)\}$$

In this case, $\pi > 0$ occurs when prices fall.

It is useful to recognize that the form of the profit function will depend on how the units, Q, are specified. Some presentations will vary the sign of Q such that when a long position is indicated then $Q > 0$ and, for a short position, $Q < 0$. In this case, what is referred to above as the long profit function will apply in both cases. If prices fall, and $Q < 0$ for a short, then profit will be positive. While this approach is somewhat tidier to use in presenting basic concepts, in the analysis of more complicated trading strategies this convention

TABLE 2.1   Profit Function for a Long Futures Position

Date	Cash position	Futures position
$t = 0$	None	Long Q units @ $F(0,T)$
$t = 1$	None	Close out position by going short Q units @ $F(1,T)$

Note: The profit function $\pi(1,T)$ can now be defined by observing that a change in value of the futures position is calculated by subtracting the purchase price from the sales price: $\pi(1,T) = Q\{F(1,T) - F(0,T)\}$. The position is profitable, $\pi > 0$, when prices rise.

will lead to variations in the signs of some terms when compared to derivations based on $Q > 0$ everywhere. Assuming $Q > 0$ throughout facilitates use of the rule for calculating profit: "What you sold it for minus what you bought it for." While in many cases the difference between using $Q > 0$ and Q of varying sign is transparent, there are instances where some care is required when comparing results given using the different specifications of Q.

The speculative profit function for a long or short position is relatively simple when compared to the profit function for a hedger, where both the futures and cash positions have to be taken into account. In addition, details for the hedge will vary depending on the specific hedge under consideration. To illustrate the hedger's profit function, consider the hedging problem confronting the stylized grain elevator operator of the 19th century. Grain was hauled by land to the riverside where the grain elevator was situated. The elevator operator paid the farmer the prevailing cash price and, in the case at hand, stored the grain through the winter until the river thawed in the spring. The elevator operator was concerned that grain prices would move adversely between the harvest and springtime. To offset this risk, the farmer engaged in a futures hedge with the traders at the Chicago Board of Trade (CBOT). The relevant transactions are described in Table 2.2. This profit function applies only to the hedge transaction; it does not account for other profits associated with the actual business. For example, there may be spoilage or loss of grain to vermin such that $Q_A(0) \neq Q_A(1)$, or the grain may be processed and sold in a different form.

The intricacies of hedging can be illustrated by extending the grain elevator hedge example in Table 2.2. The futures position in the example implicitly assumes that the elevator operator has grain for sale that is not deliverable against the futures position because it does not conform to the standarized grade. The possibility that the relationship between prices for different grades will change over the life of the hedge is a source of risk in the hedge. If the elevator operator has a deliverable grade of grain, then the futures hedge can

TABLE 2.2   Profit Function for a Grain Elevator Hedge Using Futures Contracts

Date	Cash position	Futures position
$t = 0$	Buy Q_A units of grain at $S(0)$ for storage in grain elevator	Short Q_H units at $F(0,T)$
$t = 1$	Q_A units are sold at $S(1)$ and loaded for shipment	Close out position with long Q_H units at $F(1,T)$

Note: If costs associated with carrying the commodity are ignored, the profit function for this type of hedge can be specified: $\pi(1,T) = \{S(1) - S(0)\}Q_A + \{F(0,T) - F(1,T)\}Q_H$.

be completed by making delivery. In this case, the futures hedge profit function takes the form of a profit function for a forward sale, a delivery hedge that is done using forward contracts, where the profit function is

$$\pi(1) = Q_A\{F(0,1) - S(0)\}$$

In this case, the costs of financing, storing the commodity, and making the delivery at maturity are ignored.

The profit function for the grain elevator hedge using futures explicitly recognizes that the size of the hedge position in futures may be different than the size of the cash position. As discussed in Chapter 6, the precise relationship between the size of the cash and futures positions can be formulated as an optimization problem from which an *optimal hedge ratio* can be determined. However, it is still revealing to assume that the hedge is one-to-one; that is, let $Q_A = Q_H = Q$, which, after some manipulation, gives:

$$\pi/Q = \{F(0,T) - S(0)\} - \{F(1,T) - S(1)\}$$

The profitability of the hedged position depends on the change in the difference between the spot and futures prices. If this difference narrows, the hedge will have $\pi > 0$.

The analytical usefulness of the profit function is also apparent when futures spread trades are considered. For example, the basic *intracommodity spread* trade, also called a *calendar spread*, involves offsetting, long and short, positions in different contract delivery months for the same commodity. If the spread is in different commodities, an *intercommodity* spread, the delivery months involved are less important. Intracommodity trades can be done for different reasons that will be discussed in later chapters. Recalling the use of N and T for the nearby and deferred deliveries of amount Q_N and Q_T, this trade is depicted in Table 2.3. One immediate interpretation of spread behavior from this profit function is to assume that the spread is one-to-one and intracommodity; that is, let $Q_N = Q_T = Q$, which, after some manipulation, gives:

$$\pi/Q = \{F(1,T) - F(1,N)\} - \{F(0,T) - F(0,N)\}$$

The one-to-one intracommodity spread that is short the nearby and long the deferred will be profitable if the (positive) difference between the deferred and nearby prices widens. The opposite would be true for the alternative spread: long the nearby and short the deferred.[1]

---

[1]There are a number of pitfalls in the practical interpretation of the spread trade profit function. For example, if the $t = 0$ difference between the deferred and nearby prices were negative, then profitability for the short nearby/long deferred spread would require that the absolute value of the difference between the prices narrow.

TABLE 2.3   Profit Function for an Intracommodity Futures Spread Position

Date	Nearby position	Deferred position
$t = 0$	Short Q_N units at $F(0,N)$	Long Q_T units at $F(0,T)$
$t = 1$	Close out position with long Q_N units at $F(1,N)$	Close out position with short Q_T units at $F(1,N)$

Note: In this case, the profit function can be specified: $\pi(1,T) = \{F(0,N) - F(1,N)\}Q_N + \{F(1,T) - F(0,T)\}Q_T$.

A. THE WEALTH PROCESS

In order to obtain applicability to a range of decision-making situations, the approach taken is to specify the wealth process, admitting the possibility of two random variables: price and yield uncertainty at the decision horizon date. The representative decision maker purchases an asset at time t and sells it at time $t + 1$ and purchases derivative securities to provide protection against down-side movements, either in price or yield, or both. The price and the yield at $t + 1$, the end of the investment horizon, can both be unknown at time t, the date the relevant risk-management decision is initiated. In some types of decision problems, such as the typical problem of investment in domestic assets, this level of generality is more than is required because there is only one random variable in this problem: the yield on domestic assets. However, where the problem involves investment in foreign assets, there are two random variables involved: the exchange rate and the yield on foreign assets (denominated in foreign currency terms). In other problems, such as a farmer subject to random crop yield or a mine subject to random ore quality, both price and quantity are uncertain. Given that price and yield can be uncertain, the optimization problem does not permit the amount of initial wealth invested in the asset to vary.[2] Starting from the given initial level of wealth, the investor's objective is to maximize a moment preference function for the value of terminal wealth assuming that the balance (possibly negative) of initial wealth that is not allocated to the risky asset will earn (pay) the risk-free rate of interest.

[2]In addition to the practical situations already listed, there are numerous other situations where the size of the risky asset position is fixed. Insurance decisions provide many cases, such as those involving fire or earthquake insurance on a house or how much crop insurance to purchase for an apple orchard. Other examples include the purchase of currency put options to protect against changes in exchange rates by a company bidding on a contract denominated in a foreign currency or a metals refinery concerned about declining prices for scrap already in inventory. In most practical situations, the decision about how many put options to purchase is unbundled from the real asset decision. In other words, the hedging decision is separated from the production decision (e.g., Feder *et al.*, 1980).

Initially, consider the wealth process for a decision maker not having access to any derivative securities. Once the initial structure of the terminal wealth function is specified, usage of derivative securities will be introduced. Following Poitras (1993) and others, allowing for *both* the quantity and the price to be random leads to the underlying wealth process:

$$W_{t+1} = AY_{t+1}P_{t+1} + [W_t - C(A)](1 + r)$$

where W_{t+1} is wealth at time $t + 1$; W_t is the known level of initial wealth; A is the fixed initial size of the asset (e.g., acres planted for a farmer); Y_{t+1} is the possibly random quantity per unit or yield per unit of the asset observed at $t + 1$; P_{t+1} is the random spot price at $t + 1$; $C(A)$ is the given cost function associated with purchasing A; and r is the risk-free interest rate.[3] Manipulation of the underlying wealth process gives the more conventional form of the wealth process for a single risky asset:

$$W_{t+1} = W_t(x(1 + R) + (1 - x)(1 + r)) = W_t((1 + r) + x(R - r)) = W_t + \pi_{t+1}$$

where π_{t+1} is the profit defined by the wealth process realized at time $t + 1$; x is $(C(A)/W_t)$ the given fraction of initial wealth invested in the risky asset; and $(1 + R)$ one plus $[(AY_{t+1}P_{t+1})/C(A)]$ one plus the rate of return on the risky asset. For simplicity of exposition, it will be assumed that $x > 0$ in what follows.[4]

The basic specification for the decision maker's terminal wealth function requires some additional terms if there is a need to capture the payoffs associated with, say, introducing a put option. While the terminal wealth function derived from the wealth process, with put options included, follows appropriately, some motivation is required. In particular, in the absence of some form of put option to provide asset insurance, there is a natural minimum on R, the rate of return on the investment. Either a complete catastrophic loss occurs where $Y_{t+1} = 0$ or a spot price of zero occurs at time $t + 1$, both cases corresponding to the result $(1 + R) = 0$. Significantly, three possible variants of put option payout are possible, each aimed at dealing with the different types of risks faced by the risk manager. More precisely, put option payouts can depend on the deviation of *price, yield,* or *revenue* from a stated exercise value. Payouts based on revenue provide protection against $Y_{t+1}P_{t+1}$

---

[3]In the domestic asset investment problem, it is typical to assume that $AP_t = AP_{t+1}$ is the initial value of asset units (e.g., shares of stock in the initial investment), making the problem somewhat simpler.

[4]Extending the analysis to situations where $x < 0$ does change the underlying conditions of the decision problem somewhat. For example, optimal solutions would involve the sale of put options. In many practical situations (e.g., crop insurance) this would not be possible. In some situations, the purchase of call options could be a feasible alternative. In addition, when the shape of the return distribution is negatively skewed and $x > 0$, this leads immediately to a negatively skewed distribution for terminal wealth. This situation changes when $x < 0$.

falling below a given floor. In contrast, payouts based on yield or price cannot guarantee a minimum return higher than $(1 + R) = 0$. For the farmer example of Chapter 6, Section I, put payouts based on revenue set a lower level for farm income but put option payouts guaranteeing a price of $\$K$ per bushel cannot prevent a 100% loss due to crop failure nor can a put payout based on yield providing for, say, $\underline{Y}$ bushels an acre prevent the future spot price falling to zero. However, put payouts based on either price and yield do reduce the probability of the total return attaining low values and, as a result, do alter the distribution for terminal wealth.

In practice, conventional exchange-traded put options are structured with payouts based on price. Other types of put options, such as multiple peril crop insurance schemes, are a type of yield insurance. Still other types of put options, such as some types of real options, provide revenue or income protection. The case where the put payout is based on revenue insurance produces a wealth process similar to the yield insurance case. Introduction of a put option based on price produces:

$$W^z_{t+1} = AY_{t+1}P_{t+1} + (W_t - C(A))(1 + r) + Q_z(\max[0, K - P_{t+1}] - z)$$

$$= W_t \left\{ x(1 + R) + (1 - x)(1 + r) + \frac{Q_z P_t}{W_t} \left[\max\left[0, \frac{K - P_{t+1}}{P_t}\right] - \frac{z}{P_t} \right] \right\}$$

$$= W_t \left\{ (1 + r) + x(R - r) + \gamma \left(\max[0, -R_P] - \frac{z}{P_t} \right) \right\}$$

where K is the exercise price on the put option that is assumed to be "at the money" (where $K = P_t$); z is the price per unit of output of the put; and Q_z is the number (in output units) of puts purchased, with the ratio γ being the asset value covered by the option position divided by initial wealth.[5]

This specification can be contrasted with that for put option payouts based on yield where, instead of the number of options to purchase, it is the fraction of A to insure that is the decision variable:

$$W^y_{t+1} = AY_{t+1}P_{t+1} + (W_t - C(A))(1 + r) + Q_y(P_{t+1} \max[0, \underline{Y} - Y_{t+1}] - L)$$

where L is the price (put premium) per unit of A for the yield put option; Q_y is the number of units covered by the yield put option; and $\underline{Y}$ is the yield floor provided by the put option or insurance plan. Defining the optimization problem by allowing the risk manager to choose the fraction of A to insure leads to:

[5]It is also possible to specify the put option using futures prices. However, because this involves the introduction of basis considerations, doing so complicates the analysis. Because exchange-traded options are often written using futures prices, construction using futures prices is in some cases potentially more realistic. The assumption that the option is at the money is not restrictive and is used only for notational convenience.

$$W_{t+1}^y = W_t\{(1 + r) + x[R - r] + x\lambda[\max[0,\underline{RR} - R] - l]\}$$

where l equals $(LA/C(A))$; $\lambda = (Q_y/A)$ is the fraction of A (e.g., the total planted acreage, covered or insured with the physical yield put option); and $\underline{RR} = \{P_{t+1}\underline{Y}A\}/C(A)$.[6] Assuming actuarially fair pricing requires insurance to impact the decision problem through its effect on downside risk and skewness.

This basic structure can be readily adjusted to account for other derivatives, such as futures or forward contracts. For example, if it is assumed that the only hedging instrument available is futures contracts, then the underlying wealth dynamics can be specified:

$$W_{t+1} = AY_{t+1}P_{t+1} + [W_t - C(A)](1 + r) + Q_f(f_{t+1} - f_t)$$

where Q_f is the quantity of futures contracts sold $(-)$ or bought $(+)$, and f_{t+1} and f_t are the futures prices observed at $t + 1$ and t respectively. Manipulation gives:

$$\begin{aligned}W_{t+1} &= W_t(x(1 + R) + (1 - x)(1 + r) + HR_f)\\ &= W_t((1 + r) + x(R - r) + HR_f)\\ &= W_t + \pi_{t+1}\end{aligned}$$

where H is the value $(f_t$ times $Q_f)$ of the hedge position divided by initial wealth (not the value of the spot position); R_f is $(f_{t+1} - f_t)/f_t$; and $(1 + R)$ is, again, $[(AY_{t+1}P_{t+1})/C(A)]$ one plus the rate of return on planting for a farmer.

B. THE EXPECTED UTILITY FUNCTION

The study of decision making under uncertainty is a vast subject. Financial applications almost invariably proceed under the guise of the expected utility hypothesis: people rank random prospects according to the expected utility of those prospects. Analytically, this involves solving problems requiring selecting choice variables to maximize an expected utility function. In some cases, such as the basic optimal hedging problem, the associated budget constraint is embedded in the argument of the utility function. In other cases, such as in optimal portfolio diversification models, the budget constraint appears as the

---

[6]It is simple to extend the profit function for the yield insurance case to cover revenue insurance. For revenue insurance, instead of two random variables associated with price and yield interacting to determine revenue (PY), there is only one random variable for revenue. The put option decision problem involves determining (Q_R/A), the fraction of A covered or insured with the revenue put option.

restriction that the sum of the value weights equals one. In either event, the central concern is expected utility, an essentially subjective construct that cannot be directly observed. A key step in the optimization problem is to specify an expected utility function that captures the true expected utility mapping.

The central tool in analyzing preferences over random outcomes is the expected utility function. Expected utility calculations involve taking expectations, which are conventionally modeled using statistical properties of random variables. This may involve the explicit introduction of probability densities. There is a profound connection between the choice of a specific probability distribution and the risk-aversion properties required of the expected utility function (e.g., Heaney and Poitras, 1994). As for the utility component of the expected utility function, even before von Neumann and Morgenstern (1947), it has been recognized that choosing over risky prospects is decidedly different than the textbook model of economic choice. As is well known, von Neumann and Morgenstern made a seminal contribution by proposing a set of axioms governing choice under uncertainty. Observing that the axioms are difficult to reject lends strong support to the von Neumann and Morgenstern approach.[7]

A key construct of the axiomatic approach is the linear choice function over risky prospects, better known as the expected utility function:

$$EU[x] = \sum_{j=1}^{S} \theta_j U[x_j]$$

where: $EU[x]$ is the expected utility of x; S is the number of possible future states of the world; θ_j is the probability that state j will occur; and $U[x_j]$ is the utility associated with the amount of x received in state j. The EU function ranks risky prospects with an ordering that is unique up to a linear transformation. While there are a number of possible selections for x, in what follows either terminal wealth or terminal profit will typically be used.

Beyond this foundation, developing various arguments can be tricky. For example, it is not apparent how to determine the θ_j. The axiomatic foundation cannot say much more than that the probabilities are subjective. General equilibrium models often proceed by assuming that expectations are homogeneous or that individual agents are homogeneous. Such assumptions permit the derivation of market equilibrium conditions, such as the capital asset pricing model (CAPM). However, general equilibrium concerns are of little use here. The decision problems encountered are partial equilibrium. The

---

[7]The axiomatic approach to choice under uncertainty has produced a considerable number of studies. Accessible and brief overviews are available in various sources (e.g., Henderson and Quandt, 1980, sec. 3.8; Layard and Walters, 1979, ch.13).

theoretical results apply to speculators and hedgers confronted with a parametric world of atomistic competition where their activities will not impact prices. In this process, the expected utility function can be an invaluable analytical tools. This can be readily demonstrated by applying an essential tool from functional analysis: the Taylor series expansion (see Appendix I).

To see this, consider the problem of determining the cost of risk. The solution to this problem would be useful in analyzing whether to buy insurance or to invest in a risky capital project. While there are a number of possible methods to extract the cost of risk, consider the following solution. Let the expected value of terminal wealth be $E[W_{t+1}] = \Omega$. Observe that Ω is a parameter that permits the *certainty equivalent* income of a risky prospect to be defined as $\Omega - C$, where C is the cost of risk. It follows from the expected utility axioms that the cost of risk, C, can be calculated as the difference between the expected value of the risky prospect and the associated certainty equivalent income:

$$U[\Omega - C] = \sum_{i=1}^{S} \theta_i U[W_i] = EU[W_{t+1}]$$

It is now possible to expand $U[\Omega - C]$ in a Taylor series and estimate the cost of risk by manipulating the first- and second-order approximations.

More precisely, expanding the function $U[\Omega - C]$ around Ω the first order approximation is

$$U[\Omega - C] = U[\Omega] + U'[\Omega](\Omega - C - \Omega) = U[\Omega] - U'[\Omega]C$$

Similarly, a second-order approximation for the function $U[W_{t+1}]$ can provide:

$$U[W_{t+1}] = U[\Omega] - U'[\Omega](W_{t+1} - \Omega) + \frac{1}{2}U''[\Omega](W_{t+1} - \Omega)^2$$

$$\rightarrow EU[W_{t+1}] = U[\Omega] + \frac{1}{2}U''[\Omega]\text{var}[W_{t+1}]$$

Using $U[\Omega - C] = EU[W_{t+1}]$ and manipulating gives:

$$C = -\frac{U''[\Omega]}{2U'[\Omega]}\text{var}[W_{t+1}] \quad \rightarrow \quad \frac{C}{W_t} = -\frac{U''[\Omega]W_t}{U'[\Omega]}\text{var}[1 + R]$$

This demonstrates theoretically that the cost of risk will vary across utility functions. This result also provides theoretical measures of the cost of risk. The measures of absolute risk aversion, $-\{U''/U'\}$, and relative risk aversion, $-\{U''W_t\}/U'$ are now textbook concepts (e.g., Elton and Gruber, 1995).

C. EXPECTED UTILITY AND MOMENT PREFERENCE

The relationship between moment preference and expected utility has received considerable attention. Important topics have included the conditions under which mean-variance analysis is consistent with maximizing expected utility (e.g., Kroll et al., 1984; Ormiston and Quiggin, 1994; Bell, 1995) and the implications of introducing skewness preference into the mean-variance framework (e.g., Kraus and Litzenberger, 1976; Hassett et al., 1985; Lim, 1989; Diacogiannis, 1994; Poitras and Heaney, 1999). Brockett and Kahane (1992), among others, have shown that there is not a direct correspondence between the derivatives of the expected utility function and moments of the return distribution. The implication is that maximization of a function defined over moments, such as mean-variance or mean-variance-skewness, may not give the same solution as directly maximizing expected utility. Yet, Meyer (1987), Ormiston and Quiggin (1994), and others demonstrate that the conditions on the random variables sufficient for mean-variance rankings to provide solutions consistent with expected utility rankings are relatively weak. Extensions providing the conditions on random variables required for mean-variance-skewness ranking to be consistent with expected utility ranking are currently unavailable.

As discussed in numerous sources (e.g., Loistl, 1976; Levy and Markowitz, 1979; Poitras and Heaney, 1999), the relationship between expected utility and moment preference objective functions can be motivated using a Taylor series expansion of $U[W]$, the decision maker's utility function (U) for wealth (W) evaluated at the expected value for terminal wealth $[\Omega](E[W_{t+1}] = \Omega)$:

$$U[W_{t+1}] = U[\Omega] + U'[\Omega](W_{t+1} - \Omega) + \frac{U''[\Omega]}{2!}(W_{t+1} - \Omega)^2$$
$$+ \frac{U'''[\Omega]}{3!}(W_{t+1} - \Omega)^3 + \ldots$$

Exploiting this type of expansion requires that certain technical conditions be satisfied. For example, convergence of the power series within the interval of interest is needed.[8] In addition, desirable properties for utility functions require: $U'[W] > 0$, nonsatiation; $U''[W] < 0$, risk aversion; and, $U'''[W] > 0$, preference for positive skewness.

---

[8]Further discussion of issues related to the general properties of a Taylor series expansion for approximating a general expected utility function can be found in Loistl (1976). Hassett et al. (1985) examine specific types of problems with the Taylor series that arise where skewness is involved. Brockett and Kahane (1992) discuss the connection between preference for moments and expected utility rankings of risky prospects, arguing that "$U'' < 0$ and $U''' > 0$ are not related to variance avoidance or skewness preference."

With relatively weak distributional restrictions (e.g., Hassett et al., 1985), the Taylor series representation of $U[W]$ can be transformed into an approximation for a general expected utility function based on the moments of the conditional distribution for W_{t+1}. The relevant approximation is derived by taking conditional expectations at time t and ignoring terms associated with moments higher than the second, for a mean-variance approximation, and moments higher than the third, for a mean-variance-skewness approximation. The general notation $EU[\cdot]$ will be used to denote such a moment preference functional. Taking expectations for the mean-variance-skewness case gives:

$$EU_{MVS}[W_{t+1}] \equiv EU_{MVS} = U[\Omega] + 0 + \frac{U''[\Omega]}{2!} \text{var}[W_{t+1}] + \frac{U'''[\Omega]}{3!} \text{skew}[W_{t+1}]$$
$$= U[\Omega] - b \, \text{var}[W_{t+1}] + c \, \text{skew}[W_{t+1}]$$

where $\text{var}[W_{t+1}]$ is the variance of terminal wealth, and $\text{skew}[W_{t+1}]$ is the skewness or centralized third moment for terminal wealth. Restrictions imposed by assuming risk aversion and positive skewness preference permit the coefficients in EU_{MVS} to be immediately signed as b, $c > 0$. Further restrictions on b and c, as well as the admissible range of W, can be derived by taking further derivatives of the Taylor series expansion and invoking Jensen's inequality. Setting $c = 0$ permits the mean-variance-skewness moment preference function to be reduced to the mean-variance function, EU_{MV}.

What are the implications of introducing this additional skewness term into the moment preference objective function? Currently, little information is available comparing solutions from mean-variance and mean-variance-skewness approximations. Information about such comparisons would be relevant for a range of decision-making situations, especially those involving skewness-altering securities such as options and insurance. The few studies that do compare the mean-variance and mean-variance-skewness objective functions illustrate some confusion as to the implications of introducing skewness. In particular, Prakash et al. (1996, p. 240) claim to "show how a risk-averse manager with sufficient preference for positive skewness may undertake projects with skewed payoff distributions that appear to be unfair gambles." Horowitz (1998) correctly takes exception to the Prakash et al. claim, arguing that there is no underlying utility function that is consistent with the central theoretical condition that Prakash et al. use: $3U'''/U'''' > \text{skew}[W_1]/\text{var}[W_1]$. Horowitz refutes the Prakash et al. claim by demonstrating that it is not possible for an expected utility function to conform to the Prakash et al. restrictions.

Studies examining the impact of skewness have been largely concerned with asset pricing and portfolio theory (e.g., Kraus and Litzenberger, 1976;

Sears and Trennepohl, 1983; Lim, 1989; Simaan, 1993). However, combining of securities into portfolios almost certainly reduces the skewness of the portfolio relative to the value-weighted sum of the individual asset skewness values. The structure of the decision problem under consideration here is more stylized, being concerned only with transforming the return distribution for an exogenously determined amount of a single asset into a "more desirable" distribution using a derivative security. This type of problem is typical of many risk-management situations (e.g., farming or mining), where the size of the spot position is predetermined by production considerations and the decision problem is to solve for the size of the hedge position. Allowing both the quantity of the risky asset and the size of the derivative security position to be endogenous substantively complicates the analysis without adding significantly to the usefulness of the solutions (e.g., Poitras, 1993). More importantly, practical situations where derivative securities would be used to manage risk often involve having the level of the risky asset fixed prior to assessing the size of the derivative security position.

Finally, while one obvious potential benefit of introducing skewness preference into the objective function is enhanced ability to model certain types of decisions problems, this gain is not without some costs. Compared to the mean-variance approach, the introduction of skewness significantly increases complexity of the solutions, permitting only complicated preference-dependent, closed-form solutions to be derived. This is due to the presence of quadratic terms in the first-order conditions arising from skew[W]. Though intuitive results can still be obtained by fully solving for the mean-variance part of the solution, this leaves an additional unresolved co-skewness term that is associated with the quadratic terms in the first-order conditions. This unresolved term will be utility function dependent, as it will contain the parameters b and c. Hence, solving for the mean-variance-skewness optimal demand requires b and c to be specified before an optimal solution can be obtained. In this process, the mean-variance optimal solution acts as a control variate against which the mean-variance-skewness optimal solution can be compared. Properties of this comparison can be developed in detail (e.g., Poitras and Heaney, 1999).

D. A Stylized Risk-Management Decision Problem

Firms and individuals face an array of risks that have to be managed. Some of these risks, such as those associated with loss from fire or theft, can be safely unbundled from decisions involving other types of risk. In formulating a general risk-management strategy for business enterprises, it is conventional to ignore these unrelated risks and restrict attention to the following categories of risk (Dowd, 1998 and Culp, 2001):

- *General business risks*: Risks specific to the industry or market of interest (e.g., yield uncertainty in farming, sales uncertainty for a retailer, production uncertainty for a mine); also referred to as *commercial risk*.
- *Financial and commodity market risks*: Risks associated with changes in prices for equities, exchange rates, interest rates, and commodities.
- *Credit and liquidity risks*: Risks associated with factors such as counterparty failure, costs associated with having to unwind a position, and the possibility that credit lines may be restricted.
- *Operational risks*: Risks that can include inadequate management control systems or incorrect pricing models.
- *Legal risks*: Risks associated with contract enforcement and variation.

The presence of these various types of risks begs an obvious question: Under what conditions can each of these risks be managed independently of the other types of risks? Some attention has been given to identifying *theoretical* conditions under which it is possible to separate the production decision from the risk-management decision (e.g., Danthine, 1978; Feder *et al.*, 1980). If there is separability, this implies that it is possible to use a risk-management process that considers the problem of managing, say, market risks independently of general business risks.

A common theme running through various so-called derivatives debacles is the apparent inability to understand the speculative component of the risk-management strategies that were being used. Under reasonable conditions, optimal risk-management decisions can be decomposed into the sum of two parts: the solution to a risk-minimizing problem and the solution to a speculative profit maximization problem. In effect, as demonstrated in various derivative debacles, implementing optimal risk management requires an understanding of speculation.

Textbook presentations often portray risk-management activities, such as hedging, as eliminating the risk of price fluctuations, leaving firm profit to be dependent solely on underlying productive activities. For example, by hedging the farmer is able to lock in the price that is received for the crop at harvest. This leaves profit to be determined by factors influencing the yield per acre. In practice, the hedging problem is much more complicated. Because hedge positions can lose money as well as make money, the hedging decision has speculative features. If the hedge loses money, then profits will be increased by not hedging. In the farmer example, this would occur when the price at harvest was higher than the price that was locked in using the hedge. If prices move adversely, then hedges will make money. Hence, unless the hedger is completely risk averse, the optimal hedge must take expected future prices into account. Is it optimal to hedge when prices are expected to move favorably?

In order to understand the optimal hedging problem, it is expedient to first consider the optimization problem for a speculator. Because speculators, by definition, do not have any cash market position, these traders are concerned solely with making profits from changing prices. Analytically, this problem can be structured as a question about *optimizing* some appropriately specified objective function. The convention in modern finance is to model the optimization problem using the maximization of expected utility. While a number of slightly different variables could be selected to determine expected utility, for our purposes an appropriately defined π will be used as the sole argument. Because it is difficult to interpret the optimal solutions when a general form is used for the expected utility function, this leaves the specific functional form to be selected. Following the convention in modern finance, (e.g., Elton and Gruber, 1995; Alexander and Sharpe, 1990; Ingersoll, 1987), the mean-variance expected utility function (EU) will be used:

$$EU[\pi] = E[\pi] - b \operatorname{var}[\pi]$$

where $b(> 0)$ is a parameter that measures the sensitivity of expected utility to changes in risk. The optimal speculative position for this objective function can now be identified.

To construct a mean-variance solution for the optimal speculative position, consider the profit function for a futures speculator who is either long the actual ($Q > 0$) or short the actual ($Q < 0$):

$$\pi(1) = Q\{F(1,T) - F(0,T)\}$$

The resulting expectation and variance of profit lead to the following (see Appendix I):

$$\max_{Q} \; Q\{E[F(1,T)] - F(0,T)\} - b Q^2 \sigma_f^2$$

$$\frac{\partial EU}{\partial Q} = \{E[F(1,T)] - F(0,T)\} - 2b \, Q\sigma_f^2 = 0$$

$$\Rightarrow \quad Q^* = \frac{E[F(1,T)] - F(0,T)}{2b \, \sigma_f^2}$$

The optimal speculative position size is seen to depend on three elements: the expected change in the futures price, the conditional variance of futures prices, and the speculator's sensitivity to risk. It is instructive to consider the different solutions that are associated with varying these elements.

The solution depends on a combination of the trader's attributes: subjective probability assessments of the trader about future states of the world, the trader's degree of risk aversion, and, the trader's ability to forecast. Under analytically restrictive conditions (that possibly could be loosened), the solution to the speculative trader's optimization problem can be aggregated to get implicit indications about the nature of market equilibrium. Given this, if, in aggregate, speculators behave as though they were risk neutral, then the speculators' offer curve for Q in terms of $\{F(1,T) - F(0,T)\}$ would be (theoretically) infinite at $E[F(1,T)] = F(0,T)$. To see this, observe what conditions the numerator of the optimal speculative position must satisfy for Q to be finite (required for markets to clear) and b goes to zero. If this were the case, hedgers would not pay a risk premium to speculators in the form of a systematic bias in the forecasting accuracy of the futures price. This is because speculators are already willing to participate when the futures price is an unbiased forecast. Given that the futures markets are designed to facilitate the participation of a wide range of traders, it is possible that b may vary across market environments, from risk loving to risk neutral to risk averse. Analysis of this situation could be explored by appropriate differentiation of the optimal speculative solution.

Given the solution to the optimal speculative position, it is now possible to develop a solution to the optimal hedging problem. In most practical situations, the hedger is faced with the question of what ratio of cash to futures positions should be selected. This can be translated into questions about *optimizing behavior*. As for the speculator, optimality has to be defined using the maximization of expected utility. This objective includes minimizing the variance (risk) of the hedged position as an important special case of the more general mean-variance expected utility function (EU): $EU[\pi] = a(E[\pi]) - b\mathrm{var}[\pi]$ where π is defined for the appropriate hedger profit function and a and $b(> 0)$ are appropriately defined parameters. If risk is taken to be variance, then the objective of minimizing risk can be reformulated in expected utility form as:

$$EU[\pi] = -\mathrm{var}[\pi]$$

which is the general mean-variance objective function with $a = 0$ and $b = 1$. These variations of the mean-variance objective function can be used to address the issue of whether hedgers are minimizers of risk or maximizers of expected utility (or both).

Over time, considerable academic attention has been given to the solution of the fundamental question: What ratio of spot to futures positions is most appropriate to maximize the expected utility of end-of-period profit? (See, e.g., Johnson, 1960; Ederington, 1979, Hill and Schneeweis, 1982; Stulz, 1984; Toevs and Jacob, 1986; Herbst *et al.*, 1989; Heaney and Poitras, 1991.) Much of this research has focused on estimating hedge ratios using an ordinary least squares (OLS) regression of spot prices on futures prices, the "optimal" hedge

TABLE 2.4   Stylized Short (Long) Hedge Profit Function

Date	Cash position	Futures position
$t = 0$	Buy (sell) Q_S at $S(0)$	Short (long) Q_F at $F(0,T)$
$t = 1$	Sell (repurchase) Q_S at $S(1)$	Close out with long (short) at $F(1,T)$

Note: This leads to the associated profit function for the short (long) hedger:

$$\pi(1) = Q_S\{S(1) - S(0)\} + Q_H\{F(0,T) - F(1,T)\}$$
$$(= Q_S\{S(0) - S(1)\} + Q_H\{F(1,T) - F(0,T)\})$$

The profit function can now be used to derive var$[\pi]$, which is the same for both the long and short profit functions:

$$\text{var}[\pi] = Q_S^2\sigma_S^2 + Q_H^2\sigma_f^2 - 2Q_SQ_H\sigma_{Sf}$$

where $\sigma_{Sf} = \text{cov}[S(1), F(1,T)]$, the conditional covariance of spot and futures prices with σ_f^2 and σ_s^2.

ratio being the estimated slope coefficient. This result can be derived from the stylized short (long) hedger trading profile in Table 2.4, where short refers to the hedger's position in futures.

Given the variance of trade profit, the optimal hedge ratio follows by solving the first-order conditions for max EU (with $EU = -\text{var}[\pi]$) using Q_H as the choice variable:

$$\frac{\partial EU}{\partial Q_H} = 2Q_H\sigma_f^2 - 2Q_S\sigma_{Sf} = 0 \quad \Rightarrow \quad \left(\frac{Q_H}{Q_S}\right)^* = \frac{\sigma_{Sf}}{\sigma_f^2} = \frac{\sigma_S}{\sigma_f}\rho_{Sf}$$

where ρ_{sf} is the correlation coefficient between the spot price, S and the futures price, F. A number of observations can be made about this solution. Most importantly, it identifies the minimum variance hedge ratio as the OLS slope coefficient in a bivariate regression of spot on futures prices.[9] This is the operational result that makes the minimum variance hedge ratio empirically attractive and accounts for its widespread use among practitioners. However, despite the widespread popularity of the approach, there are significant analytical limitations on its use and unanswered questions about its validity. For example, one important limitation is the dependence of the optimal solution on one choice variable: the size of the futures position. The size of the cash

---

[9]This follows from the equivalence of the OLS estimator and the *sample* estimators for the minimum variance hedge ratio. In terms of population parameters, the minimum variance hedge ratio is equivalent to the slope coefficient in a bivariate normal regression of spot on futures prices. Much discussion of the OLS result focuses on whether the price variables should be expressed in levels, changes, or rates of return (e.g., Myers and Thompson, 1989; Toevs and Jacob, 1986; Witt *et al.*, 1987).

position is taken as fixed and certain. No allowance is made for leveraging to purchase the spot commodity or for hedging situations where the size of the cash position is uncertain (e.g., the farmer who faces stochastic output). Before addressing these issues, it is important to address unanswered questions about its validity: Does $EU = -\text{var}[\pi]$ correspond to optimal solutions for other, more theoretically plausible, expected utility functions?

To see this, consider the optimal hedge ratio associated with maximizing $EU = E[\pi] - b\,\text{var}[\pi]$, the mean variance expected utility function. Observing that for the short hedge $E[\pi] = Q_S\{E[S(1)] - S(0)\} + Q_H\{F(0,T) - E[F(1,T)]\}$, the following problem and solution can be posed:

$$\max_{Q_H} EU[\pi] = E[\pi] - b\,\text{var}[\pi]$$

$$\frac{\partial EU}{\partial Q_H} = (F(0,T) - E[F(1,T)]) - b(2Q_H\,\sigma_f^2 - 2\overline{Q}_S\,\sigma_{Sf}) = 0$$

$$\Rightarrow \frac{Q_H^*}{Q_S} = \frac{\sigma_{Sf}}{\sigma_f^2} + \frac{F(0,T) - E[F(1,T)]}{2b\,\overline{Q}_S\,\sigma_f^2}$$

The optimal solution demonstrates that the mean-variance solution is composed of two parts: the minimum variance hedge ratio and the optimal speculative position. While the minimum variance component depends on the ratio of statistical parameters, the speculative component depends on the hedger's risk attitudes as reflected in b. Hedgers who are less risk averse will have lower b (*ceteris paribus*) and, as a result, will be more willing to take speculative positions in the form of over or under hedges. In addition, because the futures price variance enters in the numerator of the "speculative" term, as the *perceived* volatility increases the hedger will be less willing to take positions over or under the minimum variance hedge. More precisely, variances as well as expectations are conditional on the information available on the hedge date. These values are derived from the subjective probability assessments of the hedger. Hence, the less capable or willing the hedger is to make forecasts, the less important is the speculative component of the hedge.

II. MEASURING RISK AND EXPOSURE

A. RISK AND UNCERTAINTY

To be practical, the moment preference approach to modeling the optimal risk-management problem requires values for the relevant statistical parameters. The optimal solution to the stylized risk-management problem of Section I requires the variance and expected value for the distribution of futures prices as well as the covariance between the futures price and spot price. These parameters are all from the conditional distribution. Precisely how the conditional distribution is to be modeled raises deep philosophical questions, variants of which have been debated for centuries. For example, Thomas Bayes (1701–1761) suggested that the conditional (posterior) distribution is determined by combining prior beliefs with available empirical evidence. In the 20th century, both J.M. Keynes (1883–1946) and Frank Knight (1885–1972) advanced the notion that the variation in future outcomes is a combination of a measurable component, risk, and an unmeasurable component, uncertainty. At the time, this was an intellectual step forward, a reaction to the 19th-century belief of Stanley Jevons, Francis Galton, and others that future outcomes were ultimately measurable.

Knight and Keynes were both struggling with different facets of the impact of randomness on economic activity. When put within the context of the problems at hand, their seemingly arcane ideas still have considerable relevance. Knight worked within the tradition of classical economics, seeking to explain how economic profits can arise from uncertainty in the process of production and distribution. Classical economic theory depends on the assumption that outcomes are certain; if there is randomness, then the probabilities of the possible outcomes are known with certainty. In the absence of market imperfections, such as monopoly, classical economic theory argues that economic profits will dissipate to zero and each of the factors of production will earn their value of marginal product. Knight questioned this view, arguing that economic profits could still arise from the ability of entrepreneurs to resolve the uncertainty facing factors of production.

Knight still has relevance, not because of his theoretical musings, but because of his interpretation of the randomness arising from commercial risks. Part Three of *Risk, Uncertainty and Profit* (1921), especially the chapters on "The Meaning of Risk and Uncertainty" and "Structures and Methods for Meeting Uncertainty," contain many insights. For example, Knight discusses the application of "the principle of insurance" to "business hazards." After recognizing the wide divergence of insurable risks, from life to fire to marine to theft and burglary, Knight concludes (p. 252): "The possibility of ... reducing uncertainty by transforming it into a measurable risk ... constitutes a strong incentive to extend the scale of operations of a business establishment. This fact must constitute one of the important causes of the phenomenal growth in the average size of industrial establishments which is a familiar characteristic of modern life." Knight also clearly recognizes "specialization" in activities that isolate the "true uncertainty" in business risk including "organized speculation as carried on in connection with produce and security exchanges" (p. 257).

Perhaps the most important point involves Knight's interpretation of commercial risks, for example (p. 226):

> A manufacturer is considering the advisability of making a large commitment in increasing the capacity of his works. He "figures" more or less on the proposition, taking account as well as possible of the various factors more or less susceptible of measurement, but the final result is an "estimate" of the probable outcome of any proposed course of action. What is the "probability" or error (strictly, of any assigned degree of error) in the judgment? It is manifestly meaningless to speak of either calculating such a probability *a priori* or of determining it empirically by studying a large number of instances. The essential and outstanding fact is that the "instance" in question is so entirely unique that there are no others or not a sufficient number to make it possible to tabulate enough like it to form a basis for any inference of value about any real probability in the case we are interested in.

Risk is associated with objectively measured probabilities, while uncertainty requires subjective probability assessments. The economic rents to business ownership arise from correctly anticipating uncertain outcomes. While recognizing that "real uncertainty" can be reduced through consolidation, Knight (p. 234) recognizes "that it *is possible* does not necessarily mean that it *will be done*."

As for methods of dealing with uncertainty, Knight (p. 239) recognizes four general approaches:

> We may call the two fundamental methods of dealing with uncertainty, based respectively upon reduction by grouping and upon selection of men to "bear" it, "consolidation" and "specialization," respectively. To these two methods we must add two others... (3) control of the future, (4) increased power of prediction.

Knight recognizes the complementarity of the different approaches of dealing with uncertainty. For example, increased specialization permits more firm resources to be devoted to data collection and analysis, which improve the power of prediction. Writing in 1921, Knight has little to say about the use of derivative securities to "control the future." Other than occasional references, Knight also does not deal with specific aspects of financial risk and uncertainty. What Knight does says very clearly is that the randomness associated with economic risks, such as business risk, is composed of "risk," which is measurable in an objective sense, and "uncertainty," which is only measurable subjectively. It is in dealing correctly with uncertainty that "entrepreneurs" earn value. In terms of the stylized risk-management solution given in Section I, risk can be associated with variance minimization and uncertainty with speculation.

In contrast to Knight, Keynes provides little guidance on general methods of managing risks. Whereas Knight's *Risk, Uncertainty and Profit* wanders toward an endpoint, in *The General Theory of Employment, Interest and Money* (1936) Keynes proposes "not one, or two, but three or four 'models' of the workings of a modern economy" (Blaug, 1978, p. 682). Chapter 12 of *The General Theory* is a largely self-contained essay on "The State of Long Term Expectation." In this chapter, Keynes is concerned with the social consequences of instability in stock markets, arguing for government intervention to offset inherent deficiencies. The core of the argument revolves around an examination of the process by which expectations are formed in financial markets. Due to an excess bias towards maintaining liquidity, expectations in financial markets are focused on near-term prospects (p. 157): "Investment based on genuine long-term expectation is so difficult today as to be scarcely practicable."

The General Theory is a difficult book to read, quite untidy and poorly written. The importance of the book lies in the substance of certain arguments, who was making those arguments, and when the book was presented (i.e., during the stagnation following the economic collapse of the early 1930s). Many ideas are presented, some seemingly off-the-cuff. Such is the case with Chapter 12, where some of the observations are insightful; for example (pp. 154–155):

> It might be supposed that competition between expert professionals, possessing judgment and knowledge beyond that of the average private investor, would correct the vagaries of the ignorant individual left to himself. It happens, however, that the energies and skill of the professional investor and speculator are mainly occupied otherwise. For most of those persons are, in fact, largely concerned, not with making superior long-term forecasts of the probable yield of an investment over its whole life, but with forecasting changes in the conventional basis of valuation a short time ahead of the general public. They are concerned, not with what an investment is really worth to a man who buys it "for keeps," but with what the market will value it at, under the influence of mass psychology, three months or a year hence. Moreover, this behaviour is not the outcome of a wrong-headed propensity. It is an inevitable result of an investment market organized (to concentrate resources upon the holding of "liquid" securities). For it is not sensible to pay 25 for an investment of which you believe the prospective yield to justify a value of 30, if you also believe that the market will value it at 20 three months hence.

In true Keynesian fashion, this discussion is shortly followed with a not particularly erudite statement (p. 155): "The social objective of skilled investment should be to defeat the dark forces of time and ignorance which envelop our future." The modern reader is left glancing about for a Wall Street investment banker dressed as Luke Skywalker or Hans Solo.

What Keynes develops in Chapter 12 is a model where the heterogenous, subjective expectations of market participants leads to a financial market equilibrium in which prices are "subject to waves of optimistic and pessimistic sentiment, which are unreasoning and yet in a sense legitimate where no solid basis exists for a reasonable calculation" (p. 154). The implication is that prices can change "violently as the result of a sudden fluctuation of opinion due to factors which do not really make much difference to the prospective yield" (p. 154). Not only will prices be considerably more volatile than is justified by the long-term expectation, but prices will also typically depend more on "what average opinion expects average opinion to be" rather than on valuations that capture "the prospective yield of an investment over a long term of years" (p. 155). Prices are determined more by "*speculation*... the activity of forecasting the psychology of the market" than by "*enterprise*... the activity of forecasting the prospective yield of assets over their whole life" (p. 158).

Keynes was concerned about the potentially negative impact that price formation in capital markets can have on the macroeconomy: "When the capital development of a country becomes a by-product of the activities of a casino, the job is likely to be ill-done" (p. 159). As evidenced by the technology stock price bubble of 1999–2000, such observations still have relevance. However, this is not a book on macroeconomics. While Keynes has little to say about risk-management practices and the use of derivative securities, there is considerable insight about the stochastic properties of financial prices and the role of speculation in determining financial prices. Modern corporate risk management is largely concerned with managing commercial (enterprise) risks and financial risks to achieve the objective of shareholder wealth maximization. Keynes warns about the possibility that financial prices may not reflect long-term expectations of prospective yields and will likely be subject to inexplicable volatility. If so, this substantially complicates the problem of formulating optimal risk management strategies.

B. TYPES OF RISKS TO BE MANAGED

Following Merton (1993), Tufano (1996), Scholes (2001), and others, risk-management objectives of the type considered in this book can be achieved through diversification, hedging, and insurance. This classification is somewhat misleading, as it disguises the problem of specifying the hedging situation and gives the appearance that the risk being managed can, somehow, be managed in a systematic and unambiguous fashion. In emphasizing pro-active management techniques, methods needed for risk avoidance and risk absorption are not examined. The various risk-management approaches also differ in applicability to specific cases. In some situations, such as Tufano's gold-mining sample, the firms involved have little opportunity to exploit diversification opportunities to manage risk. In other cases, such as globally diversified investment funds, diversification is an integral part of risk management. Hedging situations vary, and the identification of an optimal risk-management strategy depends on the objective function specified. Similarly, the management of "risks" disguises the importance of the "uncertainty" contained in random future events. It is difficult to formulate general rules. Even if general rules can be derived, such rules rely crucially on information about the properties of the relevant random variables (i.e., the types of risks being managed).

Continuing with the "insurance principle" approach provided by Knight, actuarial science can provide an excellent source of general insights into the risk-management problems of interest (e.g., Vaughan, 1982). By design, actuarial science examines situations where only the chance of loss or no loss is considered. This is a restriction on the properties of the random variables being modeled. As such, there is only partial overlap with the situations of current interest, where the random variables, such as profits or wealth, can take both positive and negative values. Whereas insurance problems seek to reduce risk, it may be desirable to increase certain commercial risks if the potential gains significantly outweigh the possibility and size of loss. Given these qualifications, Vaughan (1982) suggests the following methods for handling the risks faced in actuarial science: *risk can be avoided* (e.g., by foregoing the writing of a policy); *risk may be retained* (e.g., by self-insuring); *risk may be transferred* (e.g., through hedging); *risk may be shared* (e.g., through the purchase of reinsurance); and *risk may be reduced* (e.g., by increasing audit surveillance).

The contrast between the actuarial science approach and that suggested by Merton (1993) is revealing. There are some close correspondences. Risk reduction can be equated to diversification, risk transference to hedging, and risk sharing to insurance. This leaves risk avoidance and risk retention not accounted for. These omissions are significant. Finance tends to approach risk management by emphasizing applications of the various risk-management products that are available in the financial marketplace. Limited attention is given to identifying methods of self-insuring or risk avoidance. Yet, these methods do receive attention in studies outside the financial risk-management arena. For example, a number of strategic management studies (e.g., Oxelheim and Wihlborg, 1997), propose techniques for strategic hedging that can lead to self-insurance as an outcome of active risk management. Similarly, strategic risk management preaches risk avoidance through natural hedging. These different potential approaches to risk management tend to take different views on the randomness that faces decision makers.

Assessing the relevance of these different views becomes more complicated when it is recognized that actuarial science, the mathematical science of insurance, is not concerned with the range of risks that are conventionally encountered in financial and commodity markets. Actuaries are concerned with the probability of loss versus no loss. Many of the risks encountered in financial and commercial markets are *speculative* risks, where there is a possibility of loss as well as a possibility of gain. Such risks can be distinguished from *pure* risks that involve situations with only the chance of loss or no loss (Vaughan, 1982, p. 8):

> The distinction between pure and speculative risks is an important one, because normally only pure risks are insurable. Insurance is not concerned with the protection of individuals against those losses arising out of speculative risks. Speculative risk is voluntarily accepted because of its two-dimensional nature, which includes the possibility of gain.

It is apparent that the study of risk management requires a careful and detailed discussion of the definition and classification of the types of risks that are going to be managed.

This observation extends to the comparison between financial risk management and strategic risk management. Financial risk management typically treats risks in isolation. The measurable component of randomness is modeled and estimates of possible gains and losses are assessed. In some cases, risks are considered in a portfolio context, by taking into account the relevant correlations between the measurable components. Extreme cases are approached by stress testing the modeling process using extreme observations. Strategic risk management focuses more on evaluating the uncertain component of randomness. The business operation is considered as a whole, and an attempt is made to provide a coordinated approach to the corpus of risk and uncertainty facing the firm. Compared to financial risk management, this process is considerably more difficult to implement in a quantitative fashion. In some situations, it may not be possible or desirable to engage in meaningful strategic risk management, outside of the realm of financial risk management. This argues for examining the techniques of financial risk management before considering strategic risk management.

C. WHAT IS VALUE AT RISK?

To say that the value at risk (VaR) methodology has revolutionized financial risk management is, arguably, an understatement. The importance of value at risk extends well beyond the implementation of the Bank for International Settlements (BIS) capital adequacy standards (BIS, 1996; Danielson *et al.*, 1998). For example, the introduction of FAS 133 has inspired firms, both financial and nonfinancial, to include VaR calculations in annual reports and other financial statements. The increased attention to risk management has led many firms to reform the process by which risk management is integrated into the hierarchy of managerial control. The VaR technique is, in and of itself, not much different than risk-management techniques that have been used for many years by more sophisticated firms. The VaR revolution is associated more with the systemwide adoption of these techniques, particularly by depository institutions and other financial intermediaries. Presumably, the systemwide introduction of VaR has resulted in a corresponding reduction in systemic risk in financial markets.

On balance, the VaR revolution has been more profound for financial firms (e.g., Jorion, 2001). Nonfinancial firms pose a somewhat different risk-management problem (Oxelheim and Wihlborg, 1997, p. 21):

> For a non-financial firm the primary risk would be its commercial risk—i.e., its uncertainty about the value of cash flows that can be generated by its physical assets producing output. Its liquidity risks are secondary in the sense that they merely enhance or modify the primary risk. The importance of a specific kind of risk can shift depending upon the situation.

As such, the VaR revolution is somewhat narrowly confined to financial firms, especially firms making markets in derivative securities and other leveraged instruments such as bond portfolios financed using repurchase agreements. VaR is also of importance for nonfinancial firms, particularly multinational firms, seeking to assess and control the financial risk associated with activities such as currency and interest rate risk management.

Wilmott (1998, p. 547) provides a useful definition for value at risk:

> Value at risk is an estimate, with a given degree of confidence, of how much one can lose from one's portfolio over a given time horizon.

The reliance on degree of confidence immediately suggests a connection to probability theory and the specific topic of hypothesis testing. The time horizon selected will vary according to the specifics of the situation. For example, a financial trading firm will do daily VaR calculations, while a portfolio manager will examine VaR when the portfolio is being rebalanced, a task that could be done monthly or quarterly. VaR has the irresistible attraction of providing a single number that summarizes the total risk of a position. The total risk can arise from a number of different situations, such as, the equity value of a financial firm, a derivatives trading portfolio, an internationally diversified portfolio of stocks, and so on.

A useful starting point for an introductory treatment of VaR is Hull (2000, p. 342):

> The VaR calculation is aimed at making a statement of the following form: "We are X percent certain that we will not lose more than V dollars in the next N days." The variable V is the VaR of the portfolio. It is a function of two parameters: N, the time horizon, and X, the confidence level. One attractive feature of VaR is that it is easy to understand. In essence, it asks the simple question: "How bad can things get?" In calculating a bank's capital, regulators use N = 10 and X = 99. They are, therefore, considering losses over a 10-day period that are expected to happen only

one percent of the time. The required capital for market risk is, at the time of writing, three times the 10-day 99% VaR.

Though the VaR methodology can conceptually be applied to a wide range of situations, applications have focused on situations involving market risk: the potential for changes in the value of a position resulting from changes in market prices.

An important impetus to the spread of VaR has been the widespread availability of software and technical material to support the implementation. For example, the RiskMetrics group at J.P. Morgan/Reuters has been an important promoter of the VaR methodology by providing detailed technical publications, such as the *RiskMetrics* manual (J.P. Morgan, 1996), and daily datasets for important financial variables free of charge at the J.P. Morgan website: www.jpmorgan.com / RiskMangement / RiskMetrics / RiskMetrics.html. The *RiskMetrics* manual describes a set of methodologies outlining how risk managers can compute VaR on a portfolio of financial instruments. *RiskMetrics* pays close attention to modeling the VaR for positions containing options. The nonlinear payoffs associated with options pose definite, if solvable, problems for the VaR methodology.

D. VaR for the One-Asset Case

Valve at risk can be calculated for a single component of the firm's operations (e.g., to assess the activities of a single trader) or for the full portfolio of a firm's activities. Because VaR can be affected by the presence of nonlinear payoffs arising from the presence of securities such as options, a number of different methods have been proposed to arrive at VaR estimates. The simplest of these methods is the *variance–covariance* method (e.g., Alexander and Leigh, 1997; Duffie and Pan, 1997). Though this method may produce inaccurate estimates if nonlinear payoffs are present, it is the easiest to understand and implement. As a consequence, the variance–covariance method is also the basis of the most widely used VaR applications. This method establishes an immediate connection between VaR and techniques of probability and statistics. As with all the VaR methodologies, risk is treated as a measurable quantity, ignoring the implications of uncertainty. Extreme deviations from previously observed financial price behavior are handled by stress testing (i.e., further assessing the impact that extreme observations can have on the VaR estimates).

Valve at risk calculations require a number of exogenous inputs. Before starting, the level of confidence and the time horizon for the VaR estimate are needed. In turn, these exogenous values depend on the degree of aversion to losses. Conceptually, as the aversion to loss increases, the level of confidence in the estimate will increase from, say, 95 to 99%. A similar comment applies to the selection of a time horizon, which can vary from daily to weekly to monthly. In theory, VaR for hourly intervals could be calculated. Large financial firms that face considerable market risk typically calculate a daily VaR. Nonfinancial firms that face a more limited range of market risk (e.g., the currency and interest rate risk for Coca-Cola) could calculate weekly or monthly VaR. It is sometimes maintained that the time horizon "is supposed to be the timescale associated with the orderly liquidation of the portfolio, meaning the sale of assets at a sufficiently low rate for the sale to have little effect on the market" (Wilmott, 1998, p. 548).

The other essential input to the VaR calculation is the data for the prices of the assets of interest. If the asset is traded, then market prices can be used. If the asset is not traded, then an estimate for the price has to be obtained from an appropriate pricing model (e.g., Hendricks and Hirtle, 1997). For financial institutions subject to BIS-style rules, the relevant pricing models have to conform to certain requirements. In-house models are acceptable, perhaps preferable, as long as the resulting prices are, on average, accurate. From such data, the relevant statistical parameters can be calculated using conventional formulas appropriate for the probability distribution selected. For the single-asset case, the mean (μ) and volatility (σ) of the asset return have to be calculated. For statistical reasons, the parameters are calculated for the rate of return distribution, as opposed to working directly with price levels or price changes. For the portfolio case, in addition to the individual asset return volatilities, the asset return covariances are also calculated and the VaR of the asset portfolio determined using the familiar formula for the portfolio variance that is covered in introductory investment analysis (see Chapter 6, Section III).

To illustrate the VaR methodology, consider the value of a portfolio containing a single, non-dividend-paying asset. Let $r_t = \ln(1 + R_t)$ where $R_t = (S_t - S_{t-1})/S_{t-1}$ and S is the asset price. Define the probability density associated with r as $\Phi[r]$. With this density, it is possible to obtain the probability that a future value of r will take a value less than r^*:

$$\text{Prob}[r_{t+1} < r^*] = \int_{-\infty}^{r^*} \Phi[r]dr = c$$

In this calculation, $c = (1 - \alpha)$ where α is the desired level of confidence (e.g., 5% or 1%), and r^* is defined by the level of confidence. Parameter estimation and calculation of confidence levels proceeds by assuming that $\Phi[r]$ is a normal (Gaussian) probability density.

Having assumed that r is normally distributed, parameter estimates for the volatility and mean of asset returns, σ and μ, respectively, are obtained from the available historical data, and the probability equation for, say, a 99% degree of confidence can now be determined by using the standard normal form:

$$\text{Prob}[r_{t+1} < r^*] = \text{Prob}\left[Z < \frac{r^* - \mu}{\sigma}\right] = c = .01$$

Using the appropriate value from the standard normal distribution tables (2.33 for a one-tailed test at the 99% level, 1.645 at the 95% level and so on), this equation can inverted to solve for r^* at the 99% level:

$$r^* = (\mu - 2.33\,\sigma)$$

Value at risk can now be determined by evaluating $QS_t r$ and $(QS_t r^*)$, where Q is the number of units of the asset held.

For short time horizons, such as daily VaR, it is usually assumed that $\mu = 0$ to produce the result:

$$\text{VaR} = -2.33\,\sigma(QS_t)$$

For longer time horizons, where $\mu \neq 0$, the solution is

$$\text{VaR} = (QS_t)(\mu - 2.33\,\sigma)$$

Some presentations of the calculation of the return form of VaR have an additional time scale factor to account for differences between the time scale used to estimate the volatility and the time horizon for the VaR; for example, if a weekly VaR is desired and the volatility estimate is for annual returns, scaling by $(1/52)^{1/2}$ is required. This adjustment is unnecessary if the sampling frequency of the data used to estimate the parameters is the same as the horizon for the VaR forecast.

E. Value at Risk, Normality, and Options

As evidenced by the numerous articles detailing potential problems associated with the variance–covariance VaR model, there are numerous pitfalls that can arise in VaR modeling and application (e.g., Duffie and Pan, 1997; Ju and Pearson, 1999). For example, Alan Greenspan (1996) observes that "disclosure of quantitative measures of market risk, such as value at risk, is enlightening only when accompanied by a thorough discussion of how the risk measures were calculated and how they relate to actual performance." It seems that even the regulators who proposed and promoted these quantitative risk measures have real reservations about the practical implications of naively using the techniques. To be sure, the VaR revolution has led to the institutionalization of quantitative risk management. Insofar as such techniques were not in place at various financial institutions, the revolution has produced a substantive reduction in systemwide exposure to market risks. Financial firms are required to identify and measure the set of risks that confront them. Yet, excessive reliance on quantitative risk measures can produce a chimera for individual firms and, possibly, for the financial system as a whole. Quantitative measures can provide false confidence that financial risk has been effectively identified and appropriate actions have been taken to deal with quantitative risk that has been identified.

As it turns out, there are a number of serious problems that can arise in determining the VaR for a given firm (e.g., Culp *et al.*, 1998; Marshall and Siegel, 1996). Some problems with VaR modeling are theoretically rectifiable. Other problems can be rectified only by significantly increasing the complexity of the VaR modeling process. Some problems may not be rectifiable at all and heuristic adjustment will be required. Because the set of problems facing a VaR modeler will vary from firm to firm, there is value added to considering the various limitations and extensions of the VaR model. Consider the assumption of normality, which is made for ease of implementation. It allows immediate application of techniques of hypothesis testing using the standard normal distribution inherited from elementary probability and statistics. Familiar estimators for μ and σ can be employed to determine the parametric inputs. The limitations of using normality to model financial prices are widely recognized. It is well known that the probability distribution for changes in financial prices are not normal, being typically fat tailed (leptokurtic) and often skewed. If the deviation from normality is significant, this will impact the critical (α) values; for example, testing at the 1% level may actually be testing at, say, the 12% level.

The problems associated with the normality assumption are in the realm of the theoretically rectifiable. A range of potential solutions has been proposed to deal with limitations of the normality assumption. The basic idea is to adjust the normal distribution to accurately reflect the true tail density. This can be done by empirically fitting a distribution to the past data, a task that is not without difficulties. Once the functional form for the distribution has been determined, tail densities can be accurately identified, with the VaR formulas given above being appropriately adjusted. As the whole distribution has to be modeled, this is a process that can be more difficult than required. A somewhat less complicated approach would be to use a series approximation, such as an Edgeworth expansion, to the true distribution. This would result in higher moments, such as skewness and kurtosis, being estimated and used to adjust the tail densities. Such approaches are less popular than approaches that make appropriate adjustments to the parameters that are needed for testing, such as the volatility and possibly the drift.

The most popular of these solutions revolve around providing improved volatility estimates. Important approaches include generalized autoregressive conditional heteroskedasticity (GARCH)-based estimators (Bollerslev *et al.*, 1992) recommended by the *RiskMetrics* group or, where available, implied volatility estimates backed out of option pricing models (see Chapter 8). In effect, the difficult problem of directly fitting the complete distribution is replaced by the more tractable problem of determining the parameter(s) of interest. However, which particular method will work best is not clear. The issues involved are similar to those in the debate surrounding whether advanced econometric estimators of volatility, such as GARCH, will provide more accurate forecasts of spot price volatility than estimates obtained using implied volatilities. Evidence on this issue is mixed, being complicated by various issues, such as determining precisely what the variable to be forecasted is and how the implied volatility estimate is determined (e.g., Takezawa, 1995). To assess whether the volatility estimate is reliable, it is recommended that techniques such as "back testing" the model be used (e.g., Kupiec, 1995; Jackson *et al.*, 1997; SBC Warburg, 1998; Lopez, 1999).

A more serious problem for the variance–covariance approach to VaR can arise with the types of cash flows being generated by the firm. In particular, many securities traded in financial markets, such as options, have nonlinear payoffs. Many real assets also contain various types of options that can have a nonlinear impact on firm valuation (see Chapter 7, Section IV). Nonlinear payoffs substantially complicate the problem of dealing with non-normality (e.g., Hull and White, 1998). To address these problems, the alternative delta and delta–gamma approaches to VaR have been proposed (e.g., *RiskMetrics*, 1996; Duffie and Pan, 1997). Much like the use of duration and convexity in fixed income analysis, these approaches use a Taylor series expansion (see Appendix I) to approximate the nonlinear payoff function. In fixed-income analysis, the payoff function is usually assumed to be convex, to reflect the inverse relationship between price and yield. This assumption may not be valid for situations involving options.

To see this, consider the VaR for a one-security portfolio containing a European call option, with price C, on a non-dividend-paying common stock with price S. The delta VaR approach uses the first-order Taylor series approximation:

$$C(S) - C(S_0) = (\partial C/\partial S)(S - S_0)$$

where the partial derivative, $(\partial C/\partial S)$, is evaluated at S_0. Chapter 9, Section I, derives a functional form for $(\partial C/\partial S)$ that could be used in this case, with the change in S being handled, say, in the same fashion as in the variance–covariance approach. For larger changes in the value of S, a second-order approximation will be needed. This can be done by using the second-order Taylor series expansion, which involves the second derivative or gamma term. However, to be consistent with option valuation theory, the most appropriate form for the expansion is second order in the state variable S and first order in time. Bookstaber (1997) discusses the difficulties of applying VaR to "globally managing" the range of risks facing a financial firm. Chapter 9 provides in-depth theoretical discussion of the behavior of delta and gamma for a number of trading stategies.

III. RISK MANAGEMENT AND SPECULATION

A. WHAT IS RISK MANAGEMENT?

Risk management is an immense subject, ranging from medicine to engineering to finance to political science.[10] Risk is a pervasive phenomenon. As such, methods for managing risk are a natural adjunct to everyday life. Risk-management decision problems range from the relatively straightforward, such as those involved in quality control on an assembly line, to the ethically and morally challenging, such as those involving treatment selection for a terminally ill patient. Though there are some general principles that apply to most risk-management situations, it is practical to narrow the focus to the specific types of risks that are of interest. Yet, this narrowing of focus is not without difficulty. Treating risks individually can oversimplify the problem, ignoring the complementarity that arises between different types of risk. Examining groups of risks together can also suggest different types of solutions. This problem of how best to structure risk-management decisions is relevant to financial and corporate situations.

  Consider the financial risk management situation of a depository institution. These firms are subject to at least three types of risk: market risk, credit risk, and operational risk. Market risk can be further subdivided into interest rate risk, currency risk, equity risk, and commodity risk. Liquidity risk could be added to this list or treated separately. Credit risk can be subdivided into liquidity risk, sovereign risk, corporate risk, and individual/personal risk. Operational risk can be subdivided into system and control risk, management failure risk, and the risk of human error. Though much discussion of financial risk management focuses on market risk, examination of the recent derivatives debacles reveals the importance of operational risk and credit risk (Kuprianov, 1995, p. 2). Within this environment, the risk-management process is decidedly complex. It is the goal of senior management to have in place "a risk management system that links capital, risk and

---

[10]A number of societies are dedicated to various aspects of risk management such as the Society of Actuaries, the Risk and Insurance Managers Association., Risk Management Association, and the Association of Financial Engineers.

profit in a way that enhances profitability whilst satisfying the . . . demands of regulators and the marketplace" (Arthur Anderson, 1998).

From a corporate perspective, the need for an integrated approach to risk management has been understood for many years. Dowd (1998, p. 9) captures the general approach required:

> The first point to appreciate is that all sensible approaches (to risk management) have the same first step, i.e., we formulate a corporate risk management philosophy to impose some guidelines on risk management decision-making. This tells us what kinds of risks we wish to bear, what risks we want to avoid, what sort of options we will consider to manage our risks, and so forth. Usually, we will readily bear those risks that we have some particular expertise in handling (e.g., risk unique to our particular line of business), but there will also be other risks that we will usually wish to avoid (e.g., the risk of our factory burning down). This philosophy should also give us some indication of what attitude we should take towards the many other types of risks that we might face—when we should bear them, when we should not bear them and the like.

Strategic risk management is the term often used to describe the process of formulating and implementing a corporate risk-management philosophy. This vital step in the risk-management process receives relatively little attention in conventional presentations of financial risk management that tend to focus on risk measurement and techniques of hedging, diversifying, and insuring.

The importance of the risk-management function has led to the creation of risk-management offices within larger corporations run by risk-management officers. Such offices engage in a whole range of activities that are of little or no relevance to financial risk management. Monitoring of Occupational, Health and Safety rules; internal security; and handling of various insurance plans for fire, theft, and the like are the types of activities that could be localized in the risk-management office. Depending upon the specific corporation, it is possible that the risk-management officer may have little or no financial expertise. By design, narrowing the focus to corporate financial risk management abstracts from the integrated risk-management process. This runs the risk of failing to make an adequate connection between the implementation of a financial risk-management program and the overall risk-management philosophy of the firm. Arguably, the failure to make such a connection has contributed to a number of recent and not so recent debacles (e.g., the Metallgesellschaft losses).

Developing a general framework for adequately identifying and managing the range of risks confronting the corporation is not feasible. There is so much variation across the types of risk encountered by the various firms that a general framework is unhelpful, at best, and could be misleading. Some method of simplifying the process is needed. Following Chance (1998, p. 672) and others, one possible method is to restrict the types of risks encountered: "Risk management is the practice of defining the risk level a firm desires, identifying the risk level a firm currently has, and using derivatives or other financial instruments to adjust the actual level of risk to the desired level of risk." In this approach, risk management is closely identified with the types of instruments that can be used to manage risk. Jorion (2001, p. 3) takes a similar tack: "Risk management is the process by which various risk exposures are identified, measured and controlled. Our understanding of risk has been much improved by the development of derivatives markets."

The modern approach to risk management typically proceeds by classifying risks into the categories encountered: business or commercial risks, market risks, credit risks, liquidity risks, operational risks, and legal risks, e.g., Culp (2001) and Crouhy et al. (2001). The importance of these classifications in practical risk management is reflected in the annual reports of major banks.[11] For both financial and nonfinancial firms, the risk-management process requires each of these risks to be assessed for the specific corporation involved. Decisions are then made on which of these risks will be assumed and which will be managed. Beyond this general intuition, things get more difficult as it is not possible to deal with all the various aspects in detail. Further focus is required. As a consequence, there is a myriad of different possible approaches to corporate risk management. Some treatments, e.g., Dowd, 1998; Jorion, 2001, and Crouhy et al. (2001) emphasize the measurement of market risks using VaR and other techniques; others, e.g., Oxelheim and Wihlborg, (1997) and Culp (2001) emphasize the integrated treatment of business risks. Still others, e.g., Smithson et al. (1995), examine the methods for handling financial risk in specific situations.

The modern, integrated approach to corporate risk management is a utopian ideal. It is conventional, if not essential, to treat risks in isolation in order to better conceptualize the methods of managing the risk. In certain situations, such as for financial firms making markets in securities, the risks being managed are primarily market risks, and utopian models, such as those derived from VaR, can be used effectively. These situations stand in stark contrast to cases where the risks are less amenable (e.g., Proctor and Gamble or Coca-Cola seeking to manage firm-wide business risks across different geographical markets). Even where the risks are perceived to be primarily market risks, the complexity of the risks being faced can defy adequate treatment (e.g., Long-Term Capital Management). In all of this, the traditional distinction between hedging and speculation seems misplaced. The is unfortunate, as there are useful lessons contained in the earlier discussions of risk

---

[11]Various examples of the risk-management sections of recent annual reports can be found at the website www.sfu.ca/~poitras. Follow the links to the book website.

management, which typically structure the discussion as a problem in hedging specific transactions.

The traditional approach to risk management predates the modern Renaissance of derivative securities. Products for managing risks were limited, both by legislation and market practices. Financial derivatives, so important in modern financial risk management, were largely traded over the counter (OTC) and were not widely used. Various types of financial risks, such as the volatility associated with flexible exchange rates, were still on the horizon. In this simpler world, risk management was typically associated with hedging using agricultural forward or futures contracts, where risks were treated in isolation and transactions involved in the hedge were emphasized. Considerable attention was dedicated to clarifying the distinction between hedging (risk management) and speculation. This distinction between risk management and speculation seems to have been lost in the modern approach to risk management. There is a modern belief that the engineering of risk is a precise enough science to make this distinction irrelevant.

B. HEDGERS VERSUS SPECULATORS: THE CARGILL CORN CASE

The traditional approach to risk management divides derivative market participants, particularly those operating in forward and futures markets, into the two general groups of *hedgers* and *speculators*. This distinction has both economic and legal implications. Cummins *et al.* (1998, p. 31) describe the economic distinction: "The terminology typically used is that if managers are attempting to reduce risk through their actions, they are said to be hedging; if managers are trying to increase the firm's risk exposure because they believe such a strategy will yield abnormal profits, they are said to be speculating." A number of the legal implications of the distinction between hedgers and speculators can be found in the Commodity Exchange Act, where a legal separation of traders in futures markets is identified and differential reporting requirements and position limits are specified. Commissions and margin requirements can and do vary between the two types of traders. The basic textbook distinction between hedgers and speculators has hedgers trading to reduce the risk associated with a cash market position while speculators are trading solely on the basis of expected price changes. While useful analytically, there is much more to this dichotomy that needs to be explained.

Historically, some legal distinction between the two types of traders was essential. The antispeculative sentiment surrounding the passage of the Commodity Exchange Act (1934) had to be tempered to accommodate commercial interests with a real need to trade derivative securities in order to manage risk.

Initial definitions of hedgers were quite restrictive. By the 1970s, the easing of antispeculative sentiment spurred on by the increasing needs of commercial enterprise was sufficient to produce a rethinking of the legal treatment of hedging and speculation. Of particular interest, as part of the process surrounding the revisions to the Commodity Exchange Act (1974), the Commodities Futures Trading Commission (CFTC) was required to provide a definition of hedging in order to determine which traders would be subject to position limits on speculative trade and which traders would be considered as hedgers, not subject to limits on trading positions. The CFTC definition for a hedger was released in 1977. Instead of attempting a precise legal definition, the CFTC opted for a long and involved definition, derived from the economic motivations for hedging. Though there is considerable scope in the CFTC definition for consideration on a case-by-case basis, the CFTC definition generally requires that (Leuthold *et al.* 1989, p. 71):

> (a) it must be economically appropriate to reduce risks; (b) risk must arise from operating the commercial enterprise; (c) the futures positions normally represent a substitute for transactions to be made later in the physical market; and (d) price fluctuations in futures markets must closely relate to fluctuations in the cash market value of assets, liabilities or services hedged. Thus, hedging is more than just enumeration of specific transactions and positions—it is a process of risk reduction. Prior to this definition, several legitimate hedging operations, especially cross and anticipatory hedges, were not recognized as hedges because futures positions did not meet the approximate equal and opposite requirement to the cash position.

While this explicit attempt to incorporate economic motivations into the definition of hedging is definitely an improvement over a strict legal approach, the underlying issues may be unresolvable. As discussed in Section I, there is a speculative element in the risk-management decision; optimal hedging involves an element of speculation.

The Cargill corn case (Falloon, 1998, ch. 8) provides a classic instance of the difficulties and associated implications of distinguishing hedging from speculation. The case originated from actions of Cargill, Inc., a grain marketing company that traded corn futures contracts on the CBOT during 1936 and 1937. Cargill was a major player in the grain industry, at that time handling approximately 12% of American grain being marketed (Broehl, 1992, p. 467), arguably the largest single private grain distributor. Also, at the time Cargill was the largest user of grain futures contracts on the CBOT. Despite being a major player in the markets, Cargill was something of an outsider in the CBOT hierarchy, having only grudgingly been admitted as a clearinghouse member in 1935. Cargill did not have a seat on any of the primary CBOT governing committees. As a result, Cargill reacted negatively to a series of adverse decisions from the CBOT that were implemented to prevent what was perceived as blatant market manipulation by Cargill. The resulting court cases that originated were the first major test of the market manipulation provisions of the Commodity Exchange Act.

As a major player in the corn market, Cargill was able to forecast tight conditions in U.S. corn supplies in 1936 and again in 1937. In response, during July 1936 Cargill bought corn offshore, in Argentina, for import and placed a large long position in September 1936 corn futures on the CBOT. Such activities are consistent with the role of Cargill as a grain distributor seeking to match orders with purchases. What was questioned by both the CBOT and the regulators was whether the size of the position was fully consistent with hedging activity. Did the position contain a significant speculative component? The size of Cargill's corn futures position constituted about 1/4 of the open interest and can be compared with the 22.5-million-bushels 4-year historical average for the "visible supply of corn in the U.S." at that time (Falloon, 1998, p. 190). As the end of the delivery month approached, the size of this position attracted the attention of the business conduct committee of the CBOT, which conducted meetings on the matter on September 25 with the president of Cargill. Despite assurances from Cargill that the position would be unwound in an orderly fashion and with no evidence to the contrary, the CBOT board of directors took action on September 29 allowing an extension of the deadline for notice of physical delivery. This action precipitated a substantial price drop in the cash corn price, adversely impacting Cargill.

Not surprisingly, Cargill management was incensed. The atmosphere was again poisoned on December 7, 1936, when the business conduct committee took action regarding Cargill's position in the December 1936 corn contract, which was deemed to be too large to be justified by legitimate hedging activity. The committee took the unprecedented action of ordering Cargill to reduce positions. Even though Cargill complied, at an estimated cost of 15¢ per bushel per contract, positions were only further hardened, setting the stage for the events of September 1937. Again confronted with supply shortages, during the summer of 1937 Cargill placed large long positions in CBOT corn futures, first in the July contract and then for the September contract. The September position was about double that of the previous year, being as large as 9.4 million bushels, about one half of the contract open interest. Based on past experience, Cargill surmised that the size of this position would come under intense scrutiny by the CBOT. To counteract such scrutiny Cargill entered into temporary futures-for-cash exchange contracts with the Continental Grain and Uhlmann Grain companies. The result was a reduction in Cargill's reported position to 2.2 million bushels.

The grain business being a closely knit community, it was not possible for Cargill to disguise the actual activities from the CBOT business conduct committee, which was only too aware of Cargill's controlling position in the September contract open interest. As the delivery month progressed, Cargill did little to reduce the size of its position, resulting in Cargill having an increasingly larger share of open interest in the contract. By September 22, the pressure on the price of deliverable stocks was evident. Despite apparent assurances to liquidate in an orderly fashion, Cargill did not move promptly to reduce its position. In response, on September 23 a cease-and-desist order was sent to Cargill, and on September 24 a trading halt was ordered and a settlement price for all outstanding contracts was set at $1.10\frac{1}{2}$ —2¢ below the close of September 22. The impact on the cash market was predictable; the cash price fell, resulting in significant losses for Cargill on the cash grain it held in company stocks, as well as on the cash corn it had acquired in the cash-for-futures swap it had done with Continental and Uhlmann. Cargill was incredulous, and a long series of CBOT committees as well as two court actions under the Commodity Exchange Act were initiated. Hearings of the CBOT board of directors in March 1938 resulted in the expulsion of Cargill from the CBOT. Resolution of the Commodity Exchange Act cases also went against Cargill, though only specific managers at Cargill were sanctioned. In the end, Cargill, Inc. was still able to use the futures markets to facilitate grain marketing.

Was Cargill engaged in legitimate hedging activities? Surely there was a significant hedging element behind some of Cargill's futures activities. Cargill maintained that insiders at the CBOT acted to undermine the legitimate activities of a grain distributor, with the members of the CBOT business conduct committee directly benefiting from the negative decisions made against Cargill. The accusation that the futures exchanges act as monopolies seeking to further the interests of the members has been replayed in other cases—for example, the Hunt silver manipulation. The apparent evidence of manipulative activities on the part of Cargill was confirmed in various forums, from CBOT hearings to court actions under the Commodity Exchange Act. Yet, somehow, the arguments are not clear cut. The boundary between legitimate hedging, speculation, and speculation supported by manipulative intent is not clear cut. The hedging decision involves a speculative component. Combined with sufficient impact in the cash market, it is possible to rig the game. Precisely when rigging the game is happening is not as easy to discern as might appear.

C. Speculation and Manipulation[12]

What is manipulation? The answer to this question is important, if only because manipulation is an activity that is considered illegal under a number

---

[12]Williams (1995) is an excellent source for more in-depth discussion of the issues surrounding the definition and legal application of manipulation. The following discussion draws liberally from that source.

of U.S. statutes. For example, the Commodity Exchange Act (1936) makes it a felony "to manipulate or attempt to manipulate the price of any commodity in interstate commerce". The CFTC licences futures exchanges with guidelines requiring rules to be in place to prevent manipulation. Various other statutes dealing with price fixing and monopoly also make manipulation a criminal activity. As illustrated in a number of civil cases (e.g., *Minpeco vs. Hunt*), there are also severe civil sanctions associated with attempts to manipulate markets. Yet, despite all this legal foundation: "The law governing manipulations has become an embarrassment—confusing, contradictory, complex, and un-sophisticated" (McDermott, 1979, p. 205).

The difficulties in the law surrounding manipulation speak to the difficulty in defining manipulation. Following Gray (1981), it is useful to make a distinction between *manipulation*, which is an economic concept, and *illegal manipulation*, which is a legal notion. There are two essential elements required for an illegal manipulation: intent and "the creation of an artificial price by planned action."[13] The issue of intent is primarily a legal concept that is difficult to capture in a legal sense. It often speaks to the specifics of the case at hand. Similarly, price artificiality is an economic concept that is also difficult to capture. Presumably, an artificial price is not a market-clearing price, the underlying forces of supply and demand have been circumvented for personal or corporate gain. But, this concept puts too much pressure on economic theory, a science that can usually provide only a vague estimate of what the "true" market price ought to be in a given situation. Various measures of artificiality have been proposed (e.g., Leuthold *et al.*, 1989, p. 383), with some of these measures being adopted in specific legal cases.

In approaching manipulation, the courts have chosen to proceed piece-meal. The Congress has stated quite clearly that manipulation is not a desirable economic activity. Yet, a precise definition of manipulation is not available in the relevant statutes. The number of legal cases dealing with manipulation in the United States is small; probably not more than 30 such cases have gone to trial since the 1950s (e.g., Johnson, 1981; Gray, 1981). Most of these cases have originated from trading on futures exchanges. From these cases, certain actions have been identified that are essential features of a manipulation: a controlling position in the appropriate deriva-tive contracts, a dominant position in the deliverable commodity, and the undertaking of specific actions that would produce an artificial price. The first activity is associated with a *squeeze*. The first two activities together constitute a *corner*, which encompasses what Williams (1995, p. 6) refers to as:

---

[13]*General Foods vs. Brannan*, 170 F.2d 220 (7th Circuit, 1948), p. 231; quoted in Williams (1995, p. 5).

A "rumor" manipulation, in which someone with a previously established position in the physical commodity or in futures convinces other traders through false reports that a shortage in that commodity will occur, for example, through a rumor of a freeze. The rumor must be believed by others only long enough for the manipulator to close out his position at top prices... (or)...An "investor-interest" manipulation, in which a series of trades and statements made by the manipulator convinces others of a broadly based desire to hold the commodity, thereby increasing its price. Until others realize that the underlying interest is merely temporary, the manipulator can sell her holdings at a high price.

The resulting confusion associated with applying all these standards in a specific legal situation is understandable.

The confusion surrounding manipulation extends to the jargon used to describe the possible strategies. Some sources (e.g., Williams, 1995, p. 6), use the terms *squeeze* and *corner* interchangeably. Others (e.g., Leuthold *et al.,* 1989), require a controlling position in both the derivative market and the cash market for there to be a corner. For a squeeze, the trader only takes advantage of cash market shortages (oversupply) by establishing long (short) positions in derivative contracts. Corners and squeezes can occur from both the short and long side of the market, though most attempts in practice are from the long side. For a long corner, the trader establishes long derivative positions, typically well in excess of available deliverable supplies. At the same time, the trader has attempted to obtain a controlling position in the available supply. The process of standing for delivery on the contracts forces the short side to pay high prices to bring available supplies onto the market. Yet, those available supplies are controlled by the holder of the long derivative positions. The shorts are forced to go "hat in hand" to the longs to cover their positions.

The textbook description of a long side corner is usually more involved in practice. The Hunt silver operations leading up to the silver price peak in 1980 had elements of a corner, but there are real questions about whether the Hunts and their confederates had controlling positions in both the spot and futures markets. The Sumitomo copper operation that ended in 1995 is a better example of a corner. This particular operation was spread over a long period of time, with the position in the deliverable spot commodity growing gradually, starting around 1986 when Yasuo Hamanaka assumed control of Sumitomo's team of copper futures traders. In the Sumitomo case, a plausible explanation was given for the buildup in stocks: Even before Hamanaka began his trading activities for Sumitomo, the firm was an important player in the international copper market.

The Hunt silver operation had many of the earmarks of a traditional corner: swashbuckling entrepreneurs making big bets on rigged games. The evolution of the Sumitomo copper corner has a decidedly more modern flavor. Hamanaka was a career man at Sumitomo, with a 20-year history in the company division. Whether more senior Sumitomo executives were aware of his activities is not clear. In any event, Hamanaka was legitimately able to assume huge positions in cash and futures on Sumitomo's behalf. He also had signing authority over various corporate bank accounts and access to corporate lines of credit and was able to geographically disperse his positions around the globe to exploit the laxness of regulators in specific jurisdictions. For example, Hamanaka did a considerable amount of trading on the London Metal Exchange (LME) which, together with the Commodity Exchange (COMEX) are the most important markets for forward and futures trading of copper. Despite being vigorously warned about possible wrongdoing by Hamanaka as early as November 1991, the LME did not get actively involved in serious investigations of Hamanaka until the CFTC became involved in October 1995.[14]

Due to filing requirements and other regulatory oversight, cornering activities in modern markets require considerable effort to avoid detection. The elaborate networks of traders involved in the Hunt silver operations was needed to avoid the appearance that large positions were being accumulated on one side of the market by one group of traders. Despite the laxness of the LME, Hamanaka had to enter into arrangements to hide the total size of Sumitomo's position in deliverable supplies of copper. A combination of LME regulatory laxness and careful planning permitted Hamanaka to successfully deny involvement in a market manipulation. This happened despite a number of instances of market turbulence, such as that in the extreme cash-futures price drop of September 1993, where evidence of a cornering operation was difficult to deny. The CFTC announced in April 1996, however, that it had uncovered sufficient irregularities in the Sumitomo accounts to proceed with regulatory actions.

Both the Hunt and Sumitomo operations were manipulations aimed at forcing up prices, to the detriment of the short side of the market. Operations aimed at driving down prices, to the detriment of the long side of the market, are much less common. Take the case of a corner aimed at squeezing the longs. The trader aims to acquire a controlling position in the cash commodity without significant impact on cash prices. Once this is done, the trader establishes a controlling short derivative position across a range of delivery dates and aims to deliver a large amount of the commodity against the nearby contracts. The trader may simultaneously engage in cash market sales in order to further depress the price. The combination of selling pressure from the

---

[14]In November of 1991, David Threlkeld, a U.S. copper broker operating on the LME, received a letter requesting him to backdate trade confirmation dates for a fake deal worth $425 million. This letter was apparently from Hamanaka. Recognizing the illegality of the request, Threlkeld passed the letter along to the head of the LME. The LME's view on the letter was, more or less, that Threlkeld was well advised to keep quiet over the matter to avoid getting sued. At this point, it is not clear whether the LME did anything to followup on the Threlkeld complaint.

short derivative positions and the weakness in the cash market permits the trader to profit from the excess short futures positions that are being held. The investment in the cash commodity that had been accumulated has now been recouped through deliveries on the futures contracts.

Manipulation is legally difficult to prove. When prosecuted, those involved in activities aimed at manipulating are often convicted of crimes associated with covering up the manipulation (e.g., forging documents or lying to regulators) and not for violation of statutes directly concerned with manipulation. The lines between manipulation and legitimate speculation are difficult to draw. Consider the case where an astute trader identifies a trading opportunity associated with the lack of deliverable supplies for a nearby contract delivery. The possibility of a squeeze causes the trader to take much larger nearby long positions than would be customary. Is this trader involved in manipulating markets? Say this trader was also a major player in the cash market and had what would be reasonably considered a potentially controlling position in the cash market. Would the unusually large long, nearby speculative position be manipulative in this case? Preventing the trader from taking positions aimed at profiting from the potential squeeze would be unreasonable, as other smaller traders without cash market influence would not be similarly restricted.

IV. STRATEGIC RISK MANAGEMENT

A. What is Strategic Risk Management?

Strategic risk management is becoming a popular buzz word in discussions of financial risk management (e.g., Dowd, 1998). Unfortunately, this terminology can cover a range of possible notions, creating some semantic confusions. Recognizing this lack of precision in the concept, various notions of strategic risk management have been adopted enthusiastically by numerous financial and nonfinancial corporations (e.g., Arthur Anderson, 1998). A rough description of strategic risk management applicable to all the various notions can be formulated as:

> *Strategic risk management is the process of identifying, implementing, and monitoring systems for managing the range of risks confronting the firm.*

The goal of strategic risk management is to deal with the risks facing the firm in a systematic and enterprise-wide fashion, instead of relying on the *ad hoc* and independent risk-management functions that often characterize traditional firm activities surrounding risk. As such, strategic risk management is squarely aligned with risk management for corporations.

The importance of the drive to strategically manage risks has not been lost on the management consulting industry. The perceived need for such a strategic management function has led the major players in that industry to develop programs for implementing the appropriate "business organization and management structures, geographic, regulatory and reporting matrices, and the mandates which underwrite these." Arthur Anderson (1998, p. 9) gives the following description of strategic risk management:

> An organization's risk management profile must reflect current business complexity as well as business dynamics, so that risk controls and risk management structures can be adjusted to changing business flows and regulatory requirements. The difficulty for many organizations is that risk management structures have evolved on an *ad hoc*, rather than organization-wide model. As a result, these structures are disjointed, with risk controls that are not aligned or comparable, and communications processes which do not yield the type or quality of management information required to meet both internal and regulatory requirements.

Upon closer inspection, it seems that the management consulting industry identifies strategic risk management with enterprise-wide risk management. This approach focuses on operational systems, such as reporting channels, methods of identifying risks, and solutions to information technology requirements.

The basic idea underlying the more general notion of strategic risk management is appealing. The process starts with the formulation of a risk-management philosophy for the firm. This requires an initial evaluation of the range of risks facing the firm. Decisions are then made about the exposures the firm wants to manage and what types of systems will be used to manage those risks. This step in the strategic risk-management process is referred to as *developing a philosophy*, because there is much that is subjective and intuitive, especially for nonfinancial firms. The correct method of identification and handling of risks is not obvious. Loosely put, philosophy has to do with ways of looking at the world. What risks are relevant and how these risks are to be handled depend on the managers' views of the world. This stage in the process is top–down, with senior management being an integral part of the decision-making process. It is likely that those senior managers responsible for risk management will be an essential cog in the process, due to the potentially limited knowledge about risk-management matters by those at the most senior levels of the firm.

A number of academic studies, many originating from the strategic management area (e.g., Ahn and Falloon, 1991; Oxelheim and Wihlborg, 1997), identify a specific type of risk-management philosophy as strategic risk management. This essence of this approach can be illustrated by examples. Consider Gallo Wines, a company that produces and sells the bulk of its outputs in the United States. Cash flows and assets are denominated primarily in U.S.

dollars. Does this firm need to manage foreign exchange (FX) risks arising from changes in the U.S. dollar? Seemingly no, but if it is recognized that the major competitors for Gallo are situated offshore with cost structures denominated in foreign currency, then Gallo's exposure to FX changes becomes apparent. What about the range of other macroeconomic risks? Oxelheim and Wihlborg (1997) examine the issues surrounding the management of macroeconomic risks and do a detailed analysis of Volvo. Shapiro (2000) gives numerous other examples, from U.S. ski resorts to Monsanto. These "soft" risks can be contrasted with the "hard" risks arising from pure financial decisions, such as funding of debt or investing in marketable securities. These types of issues can be considered as the *conceptual* aspect of the identification phase of strategic risk management.

The process of formulating a risk-management philosophy also involves an *empirical* aspect. The conceptual aspect requires detailed empirical data about the various risks facing the firm. These data have to be collected, processed, and evaluated. Decisions have to be made about which variables to include, the relevant sample periods to examine, and the types of techniques to use in evaluating the risks. There is feedback between the conceptual and empirical aspects. Whereas senior management is primarily involved in the conceptual aspect, the empirical aspect has to have wider involvement, with data inputs being collected and processed in the various risk management units within the firm. Once the basic empirical results have been obtained, decisions have to be made about the appropriate risk-management techniques to use for managing the risks. The data may require a fresh look at the firm's approach to risk management, a rethinking of the conceptual aspect, and a retooling of the empirical aspect.

Judging from the risk-management problems at various firms (e.g., Metall-gesellschaft, Barings, Proctor and Gamble, Orange County), the costs of ignoring the implementation phase of strategic risk management can be considerable. The first step of the implementation process is to determine the relevant chain of command, ensuring that each level in the chain understands the risk-management philosophy and subscribes to it. Implementation also requires putting decision-making systems in place to adequately manage risk. In this vein, Arthur Anderson (1998, p. 10) focuses on the importance of risk controls and management information systems: "Risk control is . . . the independent identification measurement, monitoring and reporting of risk, returns and capital utilization. . . . The quality of management information systems is central to management's ability to assess both business performance and risk management effectiveness."

In financial firms, monitoring of risk management is intimately connected with value at risk calculations. The practical experience of a number of financial firms indicates the importance of adequate monitoring. For example,

Jorion (1997) argues forcefully that the Orange County bankruptcy was due to inadequate monitoring. For nonfinancial firms, there have been some efforts to apply VaR techniques (e.g., Godfrey and Espinosa, 1998). Others, such as Culp, *et al.* (1998, p. 34), suggest that nonfinancial firms are more concerned with cash flow volatility than financial firms. In such situations, firms "are better off eschewing VaR altogether in favor of a measure of cash flow volatility." With all these competing *ad hoc* approaches to risk management on the landscape, conceptual guidance is needed. To this end, it is time to take a step back and undertake a careful discussion of the rationales for corporate risk management.

B. Arguments Against the Use of Derivatives in Corporate Risk Management

The problem of risk management for the corporation has been well studied using techniques adapted from traditional corporate finance. In traditional corporate financial management, because managers act as agents for the owners of the firm (the common stockholders), the appropriate primary objective is to *maximize the expected utility of the end-of-period wealth of stockholders.* Achieving this objective is complicated by the inability of managers to observe the expected utility functions of individual shareholders. Yet, under reasonable conditions, the primary corporate objective can be reformulated as *maximizing the long-run value of the firm's common stock.* Given Keynes's observations about the formation of prices in stock markets, this objective is not without difficulties (e.g., Poitras, 1994a). Proceeding on the assumption that long-run common stock prices will correctly reflect firm value, the market value of the firm can be determined as the sum of the net present values of the firm's ventures. Given this, net present value (NPV) increases due to corporate risk-management activities can arise from reductions in discount rates, increases in net cash flows, and increases in the real option value of projects.

Corporate financial managers facing exposure to, say, currency risks must address a natural question: Is hedging of currency risk consistent with the primary corporate objective? A number of persuasive arguments have been made *against* hedging corporate foreign exchange risk and other such market risks. The arguments against hedging are specific applications of more general arguments that claim that using derivative securities for corporate financial risk-management activities will not be value enhancing for common stockholders. Because such risk-management activities are costly to implement, monitor, and execute, firms are generally recommended to forego the use of derivative securities to manage risk. The general content of these arguments is that, in perfect markets, the role of derivative securities in the risk-management policy of the firm is irrelevant to the market valuation of the common stock (e.g., Siegel and Siegel, 1990, pp. 146–149).

There are a variety of arguments that have been advanced to attempt to demonstrate that the hedging policy or, more generally, the use of derivative securities to manage firm risks is irrelevant (e.g., Dufey and Srinivasulu, 1983; Levi and Sercu, 1991). Are the arguments that belie the importance of such financial risk management correct? To determine the answer to this question, it is helpful to classify the important arguments against corporate use of derivative securities into the following groups: Modigliani–Miller (MM) arguments, capital asset pricing model (CAPM) arguments, and, market efficiency (expected value) arguments.[15] There is a complementarity among the various irrelevance arguments. Irrelevance is demonstrated using perfect market assumptions (see Chapter 4, Section I). Because, in practice, the use of derivative securities involves an expenditure of firm resources that would not be required if derivatives were not used, it is argued that the use of derivatives is impractical. The firm is better off not using derivative securities at all.

In summarizing the irrelevance arguments, it is conventional to start with the MM arguments. The gist of the MM argument is captured by Levi and Sercu (1991): "It is a well-accepted principle of finance that managers of a firm will not increase the firm's value by doing anything the shareholders of the firm can do themselves at the same or lower cost." This argument is an extension of the MM arguments from traditional corporate finance that propose the financial policies of the firm are irrelevant in determining the market value of the firm. The original MM arguments focused on demonstrating that the capital structure and dividend policies of the firm have no implications (*are irrelevant*) for the market value of the firm.[16] Value is determined by the asset side of the balance sheet. The extension to the international arena is that, as a financial decision of the firm, the use of derivative securities to implement corporate FX risk-management decisions is irrelevant for the same reasons as those outlined by Levi and Sercu: The market will not increase the value of the firm for engaging in practices that can be done directly by investors.

The MM irrelevance argument relies on the perfect market assumptions. Within the MM framework, violations of key assumptions can dramatically change the results. For example, when corporate taxes are admitted and tax deductibility of interest payments on the debt is allowed, then, instead of debt irrelevance, the simple MM model indicates that all debt financing is the

---

[15]A standard reference on the basics of the CAPM is Alexander and Sharpe (1990). A more detailed discussion of the CAPM in an international context can be found in Adler and Dumas (1983), which is also a useful reference on PPP and other issues.

[16]The MM theorems and subsequent literature are discussed in numerous sources, including Brealey and Myers (1992).

optimal method to maximize the market value of the firm. Though introducing taxes can also provide a rationale for the use of derivative securities, this type of motivation does not appear to be widespread in practice and will not be examined here (see, for example, Siegel and Siegel, 1990, pp. 150–151, for an illustration of when taxes could provide a motive for hedging). More importantly, the MM argument is not exempt from the implications of relaxing perfect market assumptions such as no bankruptcy costs. If the market value of the firm is affected by bankruptcy risk, then reducing the total variability of cash flow allows hedging and other risk management activities to increase the market value of the firm by lowering the default premium and thereby lowering the discount rate in the long-run NPV calculation.

Though it is possible to demonstrate selected weaknesses in the MM argument by making appeals to the differences between perfect financial markets and actual financial markets, it is not as simple to completely dismiss the MM arguments as it would appear. For example, Levi and Sercu (1991) maintain that it is not possible to argue that there are economies of scale of various kinds that are available when the firm, not the individual shareholder, engages in risk-management activities such as hedging. Shareholders may not want the firm to engage in the types of risk-management policies being pursued. In spite of the scale economies, the hedge that the firm puts on may be considerably different than what the individual investor desires. While appealing, this view is subject to the same criticism, that it fails to directly account for the primary goal of management: maximization of the (long-run) market value of the firm.

Following Knight, firms earn economic rents from correctly handling uncertainty. Measurable risks, which can be handled by conventional risk-management techniques such as purchasing insurance, are part of the cost structure, not a source of economic value added. In many cases, firms that do not accurately handle measurable risks will, in the long run, suffer the consequences of the market place. This is all too apparent from the Metallgesellschaft Refining and Marketing debacle. Yet, if the use of derivative securities is aimed at increasing expected net cash flows, then it does not follow that the firm will also be able to reduce discount rates by reducing the variability of future cash flows. Using derivative securities to increase expected cash flow will likely increase the firm's cash flow variability. As demonstrated by Long-Term Capital Management, sophisticated use of derivatives can be a source of economic profit (i.e., increased net cash flow) only by moving out of the realm of measurable risks and into the grayer area of uncertainty. As demonstrated in Section I, the optimal hedge ratio is composed of a risk-minimizing component and a speculative component. Optimal use of derivative securities may increase bankruptcy risk to achieve a speculative gain.

Because they are derived using perfect market assumptions, CAPM arguments have many similarities with the MM arguments. A version of the CAPM argument can be found in Levi and Sercu's discussion of FX hedging (1991, p. 26):

> It is surprisingly common to hear it argued that hedging is a good idea because it reduces the variance of the value of an asset or liability when translated into a reference currency. . . . Of course this rationale for hedging can be quickly dismissed when it is recognized that investors do not care about the variance of the value of an individual asset or liability, *but rather the risk the asset or liability contributes to an efficiently diversified portfolio.* That is, it is only the undiversifiable or systematic part of risk that matters, and this can be defined only in the context of an investment portfolio. [emphasis added]

The CAPM argument is based on an analysis of variance argument. Total risk is decomposed into systematic (nondiversifiable) and unsystematic (diversifiable) risk. The argument is that in an efficiently diversified portfolio, the unsystematic component will be unimportant. Because FX risk is primarily unsystematic, there are no stock price implications to hedging unsystematic risk. FX risk is not likely to be priced and, if it is, any systematic risk would be incorporated in forward exchange rates, thus, all that hedging would do is to move the firm's stock along the security market line. Again, no benefit is obtained from risk-management activities such as hedging.

To better appreciate the CAPM argument, examine the discussion of the future basis from Chapter 3, Section I. Does the futures price provide an unbiased prediction of the future spot price? If not, then what factors determine the difference between $F(0,T)$ and $E[S(T)]$? The CAPM provides a solution to these questions by providing an elegant solution to the relationship between $S(0)$ and $E[S(T)]$. More precisely, the CAPM requires that all assets earn a return consistent with the level of systematic risk for that asset: $E[R_{i,T}] = R_f + \beta_i(E[R_{m,T}] - R_f)$, where $E[R_{i,T}]$ is the conditional expected return on asset i, R_f is the return on the riskless asset, β_i is the measure of systematic risk, and $E[R_{m,T}]$ is the expected return on the market portfolio at time T. If the CAPM holds, it follows that if S is the price of asset i then $E[S(T)] = S(0)(1 + E[R_{i,T}])$. Because $F(0,T) = S(0)(1 + ic(0,T))$, the CAPM can be used to solve the future basis: $E[S(T)] - F(0,T) = S(0)(E[R_{i,T}] - ic(0,T))$ or $F(0,T) = E[S(T)] - S(0)(E[R_{i,T}] - ic(0,T))$. (Where relevant, it is possible to reduce this result by netting out the pecuniary carry returns.) As a consequence, the CAPM implies that $E[S(T)]$ will typically be higher than $F(0,T)$.

To extend this result to firm valuation, make the conventional assumption that the value of the firm is determined by the discounted value of the expected net cash flows generated by the firm. Now, for simplicity, consider the case of the market value of an all-equity financed silver mining firm. The firm has not yet started production, but exploratory drilling results indicate an ore body of 10 million ounces (with no other economically recoverable by-product ores). If it takes one year to recover this ore and the firm does *not* *hedge*, then the market value of the firm's output will be the 10 million ounces times the expected price of the silver in one year's time. Assuming without loss of generality that there are also 10 million shares of stock outstanding, then the share price of the company will be given by: $S_U(0) = E[S(1)]/(1 + E[R_{s,1}])$, where the discount rate is determined by the CAPM.

To demonstrate that hedging is irrelevant to the market value of the firm, consider the value of a share if the firm decides to *fully hedge* and uncertainties in production are ignored: $S_H(0) = F(0,1)/(1 + R_f)$. Because the output price has been locked in by hedging, the discount rate will be lower than for the unhedged firm. The CAPM argument involves making sufficient assumptions to ensure $S_U(0) = S_H(0)$. This requires $E[S(1)]$ to be higher that than $F(0,1)$ by precisely the amount needed to offset the difference in the discount rates. Using the notation from Chapter 4, Section I, and observing that silver is typically near full carry, then it is possible to assume that $R_f = r(0,1)$. Similarly, because this company is a pure silver mining play, the discount rate for this company can be assumed to be the same as the CAPM discount rate for holding spot silver, $E[R_{s,1}] = E[R_{i,1}]$. Given this, $S_U(0) = S_H(0) = S(0)$, and the CAPM argument is validated. The market price of the firm's stock will be equal to the current spot price of silver. This is consistent with the company being a pure play on the deterministic stock of silver that will be marketed in one year's time.

Survey evidence on motivations for firm hedging presented in Chapter 1, Section IV, reveals that the most important determinant of firm derivatives usage was the desire to reduce the volatility of firm cash flows. By exhibiting less volatile cash flows firms can potentially lower the cost of capital. However, the CAPM argument maintains that this motivation is fictional. *Any decrease in the cost of capital from hedging is exactly offset by a decrease in the expected cash flows of the firm.* This follows from the equilibrium underlying the determination of forward prices. The forward price will differ from the expected spot price by just the amount needed to offset the gain associated with the reduction in the cost of capital. Yet, as the discussion in Chapter 3, Section III, illustrates, the CAPM argument imposes unrealistic empirical conditions on the futures basis. In addition, the full hedge assumption implies that the motivation for using derivative securities is to only to reduce the volatility; no attempt is made to identify the optimal hedge and to examine the associated valuation implications of employing such a hedge.

Much like the MM argument, the CAPM argument can be criticized by demonstrating that relaxation of the underlying assumptions substantively changes the results. Under the perfect markets assumptions required for the CAPM to hold, the CAPM argument could have considerable validity; however, the CAPM assumptions are relatively severe. Of particular interest are the assumptions that would make total instead of systematic variability a concern. *No bankruptcy costs* is, again, a key CAPM assumption. The basic hedging framework explicitly identifies risk affordability as an essential element in establishing a hedging program. While there are numerous possible examples, two that could be used are the B.C. Hydro (a Crown corporation producing electricity) case, where the combination of U.S. dollar borrowing and Canadian dollar revenues meant that a significant exchange rate change could more than eliminate firm capital, and, the (now defunct) Vancouver Grizzlies professional basketball team who earned the bulk of revenues in Canadian dollars but were obliged to incur expenses, including but not limited to salaries, in U.S. dollars. Among other things, the presence of bankruptcy costs can affect a firm's cost of and accessibility to capital.

Another difficulty with the CAPM argument is the significant restrictions on diversification associated with real assets. The CAPM framework was developed to explain optimal portfolio selection, where the assets involved are highly liquid and divisible. However, real assets may be "lumpy" and not easily divisible. The alternative assets needed to adequately diversify may not be available for purchase. Where such assets are available, capital constraints may prevent their acquisition. In short, it may not be possible to construct "an efficiently diversified portfolio." Again, factors such as the lumpiness of assets and the inability to adequately diversify, means there is an element of uncertainty in business decisions that cannot be reduced to the type of measurable risk argument that underlies the CAPM.

Another group of arguments against the use of derivatives in risk management can be classified as "expected return" arguments. These arguments make the empirical observation that risk-management activities involving derivatives will be, on average, a negative expected value operation, once the fixed costs of the risk-management program are considered. To see this, consider the case of a futures hedge. Assuming that futures prices are unbiased predictors of future spot rates, a policy of continuous hedging will just reflect back the price changes. Sometimes hedges will make money; sometimes hedges will lose money. On balance, the gains and the losses will net out and the hedged position will have the same expected value as the unhedged position. In effect, the expected values of the returns on the hedged and unhedged positions will be equal.

As it turns out, this argument may have validity in both practical and theoretical settings. For example, due to the costs associated with initiating, monitoring, and executing a derivatives program, practical concerns dictate that such activities are unnecessary for many firms. As Cummins *et al.* (1998, p. 34) conclude: "Whatever the underlying value-related motive for risk management, the existence of fixed costs associated with using derivative instruments may make it more likely that only larger firms, with the resources to pay these large up-front costs, will manage risk through derivatives trading." Theoretically, in perfect markets with risk neutral participants, traders are indifferent between risky prospects with the same expected values, independent of the variance of the prospect. However, the theoretical assumptions required to generate such results are associated with models that do not have a well-defined general equilibrium. In a world with risk-averse participants, the dependence solely on expected value omits one of the primary reasons for hedging: controlling the total variability of the firm's cash flows due to changes in financial prices such as exchange rates, interest rates, commodities, and equities. Following Perold and Schulman (1988), by not hedging the firm is foregoing a "free lunch" opportunity. A practical objective of hedging could be to cause fluctuations in the firm's market value to arise from changes in the firm's business activities, not (random) changes in financial prices. As in the MM and CAPM arguments, this could enhance long-run share prices by reducing bankruptcy cost, thereby reducing the cost of capital.

It could be further argued that the expected return arguments against using derivative securities for risk management do not fully develop the implications of observing that such activities have zero expected value. For example, consider the statement that, "It is just as likely to be surprised on a foreign exchange hedge as on the cash position." Given the additional costs associated with having a derivatives program, an expected return argument would conclude this is a reason for not hedging. However, situations when the hedge loses money (i.e., provides an unanticipated negative "surprise") will likely be situations where other offsetting positive surprises would have occurred as a result of favorable changes in other variables impacting firm cash flows. For example, a reduction in jet fuel prices would likely occur when the positive macroeconomic impact of lower oil prices was stimulating passenger growth. In order to reduce volatility, the hedge trades off both downside and upside changes in the cash prices being hedged. This allows the firm to concentrate on production problems without having to worry about complications related to unexpected changes in financial or commodity prices. The important question is whether, in this situation, firms that successfully pursue active financial risk management will have a substantive competitive advantage over firms that are continuously fully hedged (or do not hedge at all).

C. Arguments in Favor of Using Derivatives in Corporate Risk Management

Compared to the limited number of arguments against currency hedging, there is a daunting number of arguments in favor of using derivative securities for corporate risk management. Some of these arguments have already been mentioned in passing, (e.g., Chapter 1, Section IV). There are various ways these theories could be organized. For example, based on empirical evidence from risk-management practices in the gold mining industry, Tufano (1996, p. 1099) distinguishes between theories that focus on managerial characteristics, such as stock option ownership by management (e.g., Smith and Stulz, 1985), and "theories that explain risk management as a means to reduce the costs of financial distress, to break the firm's dependence on external financing, or to reduce expected taxes." This is a substantial break from the conventional corporate finance classifications which, based on the elements of the NPV calculation, identify theories supporting derivative use with reductions in the discount rate, increases in expected net cash flow, or increases in real option value of projects. If Tufano is correct, explanations for risk management that sustain share-value maximization may be a blind for managers engaging in activities that may be value reducing for shareholders. In opposition, Cummins et al. (1998) and Phillips et al. (1998) suggest that Tufano's empirical results may not apply in other industries.

In examining MM and CAPM theories regarding the use of derivatives in corporate risk management, it has been pointed out that the presence of bankruptcy costs would undermine both arguments. Yet, there is not strong empirical evidence to suggest that firms with a high probability of financial distress engage in higher levels of risk management compared to firms with lower levels. For example, while Wall and Pringle (1989) find the use of swaps is more likely for firms with lower credit ratings than for higher rated financial firms, more recently, Géczy et al. (1997), Mian (1996), and Nance et al. (1993) have been unable to find a link between derivatives usage and the capital structure of nonfinancial firms. Financial firms provide similar mixed results (Cummins et al., 1998, p. 38). The conclusion to be drawn from this is that, while financial distress may be a factor for some firms to use derivatives, this explanation does not seem to be generally reflected by the data.

It is difficult, if not unwise, to abandon the notion that managers act to maximize long-run share value in favor of a model of derivative usage that focuses on managerial incentives. Perhaps, as Copeland and Copeland (1999) argue, the financial distress hypothesis needs to be reformulated. Yet, it does seem that, if the MM and CAPM arguments against corporate use of derivatives are to be voided, another perfect markets assumption will have to be altered. Along this line, Froot et al. (1994, p. 98) maintain that by stabilizing cash flows firms can use derivative securities to align the internal supply and demand of funds. By stabilizing cash flows, corporate risk management permits the firm to participate in investment opportunities that may arise at inopportune times: "Managers who adopt our approach should ask themselves two questions: How sensitive are cash flows to risk variables such as exchange rates, commodity prices, and interest rates? and How sensitive are investment opportunities to those risk variables? The answers will help managers understand whether the supply of funds and the demand for funds are naturally aligned or whether they can be better aligned through risk management."

According to Froot *et al.*, by stabilizing cash flow, risk management permits firms to undertake some positive NPV projects that would be avoided in the absence of such activities. This hypothesis could be targeted at any of the elements in the NPV calculation. By stabilizing cash flows, the firm is better able to access sources of internal financing, which is less expensive to use than external financing. This will lower the discount rate. By using derivative securities to avoid under investment, risk management increases expected future cash flow by increasing the potential number of positive NPV projects. In the absence of other capital constraints, this will increase expected net cash Flows. Finally, stabilizing cash flows can permit the firm to exercise real options, such as the development option, thereby increasing the value of these options to shareholders. Gay and Nam (1998) provide evidence for the under-investment hypothesis. Using a sample of 325 firms using derivatives and 161 firms not using derivatives, it was estimated that "firms with enhanced investment opportunities, lower liquidity, and low correlation between investment expenditures and internally generated cash flows tend to be more likely users of derivatives" (Copeland and Copeland, 1999, p. 74).

Other promising explanations for corporate risk management have been advanced. Key factors in these explanations include: the ownership structure of the firm (Smith, 1995), resolving conflict between firms by enhancing the contracting relationship between firms (Pennings and Leuthold, 2000), risk shifting within the firm (Smith, 1995), and lowering expected tax costs (Smith and Stulz, 1985). Ownership structure can be related to both managerial incentives and shareholder wealth maximization. "Managers whose human capital and wealth are poorly diversified strongly prefer to reduce the risk to which they are exposed. If managers judge that it will be less costly (to them) for the firm to manage this risk than to manage it on their own account, they will direct their firms to engage in risk management" (Tufano, 1996, p. 1109). Similarly, concentrated ownership, whether in the hands of management or not, likely means that owners do not have well-diversified portfolios, again providing an incentive for the firm to engage in risk management. This supports the argument against the CAPM case against risk management: assets could be lumpy and, it is not easy to hold an efficiently diversified portfolio.

BOX 1

Tufano on Risk Management by Gold Mining Companies

Tufano (1996) is a useful source on risk management practices of gold mining companies:

Most of the 48 North American gold mines studied...are not well diversified. Risk management strategies can be implemented using explicit derivative transactions, such as the forward sale of gold, or they can be combined with financing activities. For example, in borrowing via a gold or bullion loan, a mining firm combines dollar-base financing with a forward sale of gold.

Hedging instruments include over-the-counter forward sales of gold, exchange-traded futures contracts, gold or bullion loans, gold swaps, and spot deferred contracts (which are economically similar to rolling forward contracts.) Firms wishing to establish *insurance* strategies can use either exchange-traded or over-the-counter gold put options, or can dynamically replicate puts by trading forwards and futures.

...The rich menu of risk management instruments gives firms an ability to customize their gold price exposure, and firms have embraced risk management. For example, over four years American Barrick Resources Corporation used put and call options, gold warrants, bullion loans, forward sales, spot deferred contracts, and customized gold-linked equity financing as part of its risk management program.

D. A SIMPLE GUIDE TO DESIGNING A RISK-MANAGEMENT PHILOSOPHY

The theoretical rationales for corporate risk management using derivatives provide a foundation for the discussion of practical issues involved in engaging in such risk-management decisions. Translating academic discussion into practice is facilitated by detailing some heuristic guidelines. The development of a risk-management philosophy for a specific firm is an essential step in developing an effective risk-management program. Yet, the search for an appropriate risk management philosophy may be difficult. It is possible that two firms, identical in all respects, could formulate dramatically different risk management philosophies, both of which are appropriate *ex ante*. For example, in the gold industry, Newmont Mining has a philosophy that hedging any gold price risk is contrary to the interests of shareholders who buy Newmont common stock in order to have exposure to changes in gold prices. Barrick Gold Corp. takes precisely the opposite view. Due to a combination of the contango in gold forward prices and the secular downtrend in gold prices over the last two decades, Barrick claims that active hedging of the bulk of gold production has generated substantial cash flow gains due to higher selling prices received. Both firms have dramatically different risk management philosophies leading to diametrically opposed approaches to managing gold price risk. Because the differences in risk management strategies arise from differences in philosophy, it is possible for both firms to argue that optimal decisions are being made.

It is difficult to formalize the procedure for developing a risk management philosophy. As Culp (2001) observes, risk management is a process. This process can be motivated by identifying a number of basic considerations to be addressed in order to determine the type of derivatives trading program to be undertaken (e.g., Powers and Vogel, 1983). It is in formulating answers to the various questions that the elements of a risk-management policy become apparent. To this end, consider the following sequential list of questions that are of particular relevance for a firm considering the implementation of a derivatives trading program:

1. What are the Firm's Aggregate and Specific Risk Exposures?

This step requires data and analysis. It is essential to make detailed calculations of the possible losses if no derivatives trades are made. Adjustment for expectations about future movement in prices may be incorporated, producing a range of scenarios. Unfortunately, in many cases, the calculations required are not obvious. For example, Gallo Wines was for many years a U.S. wine producer that produced and sold almost all of its output in the United States. However, even though almost all the cash flows for Gallo were denominated in U.S. dollars, the profitability of Gallo depended fundamentally on the price of competing wines from other countries. Hence, Gallo had a considerable risk exposure to changes in the value of the U.S. dollar. Another example is Metallgesellschraft Refining and Marketing (MGRM). In this case, the risk exposure was to changes in the value of the long-term forward oil by-product delivery contracts. Without a traded market price for these contracts, it is not possible to provide an objective estimate of a change in value when the spot price for the by-products change, say, $1.

The problem of determining risk exposures leads to the fundamental notions of *economic exposure* and *accounting exposure* (e.g., O'Brien, 1997), which underpin the optimal hedging strategy and the transactions hedging strategies discussed in Chapter 6. Accounting exposure measures on a transaction by transaction basis. This approach is reflected in conventional textbook presentations of risk management involving derivatives that assumes that there is only one transaction of interest. For example, a U.S. company books a sale in yen to be settled in 3 months. There is now an accounting exposure equal in size to the anticipated yen to dollar spot transaction that will take place in 3 months. The method of determining risk exposures can have severe consequences. For example, MGRM identified market risk using an accounting exposure. As a consequence, the size of the MGRM hedge position was set to be approximately equal to the number of barrels in the long-term delivery contracts with disastrous results.

In many situations, accounting exposure is a useful measure. For example, when basis risk is low, the number of derivative transactions is small and the objective is to minimize the variance of the firm's net cash flow, transaction hedges have desirable properties (see Chapter 6). Yet, in many cases there are numerous transactions that contribute to the risk exposure. These transactions can involve a large number of financial and commodity prices. Some process of aggregating the risk exposures is required. Economic exposure measures attempt to assess the impact of a specific financial or commodity price on the firm's net cash flow. An important example is the economic exposure of a financial institution to changes in the level and term structure of interest rates. Recognition of the difficulty in measuring risk exposure for financial institutions led to the development of measures such as the *duration gap* which is used in asset and liability management. Derivative securities such as interest rate swaps play a crucial role in allowing financial institutions to significantly reduce the duration gap. A substantial portion of interest rate swap market activity is derived from duration gap managing institutions, both financial and nonfinancial.

2. Are the Risks Affordable?

Answering this question involves comparing the calculated risk exposure with various measures of the capital invested in the business, also taking into account various possible remedies already in place, such as insurance policies and natural hedges. If the risk is affordable, the arguments in favor of implementing a derivatives trading program are substantively different than if the risk is sufficient to cause financial distress or bankruptcy. If the risk is not affordable, there can be real gains associated with implementing a derivatives trading program, such as a lower achievable cost of capital due to a lower probability of bankruptcy. It is also possible that competitive factors may impact whether a risk is affordable. For example, changes in jet fuel prices are an important component of cost variability in the airline industry. Firms that hedge jet fuel prices may be able to gain market share from those that do not hedge due, say, to being able to quote lower ticket or air freight prices when jet fuel prices are high and profits are being squeezed.

In some situations the decision to trade derivatives may be imposed by lenders. An example of this occurs with some Australian gold mines that have been required by their lender banks to implement a hedging program as a condition of being granted credit. Such hedging programs would dramatically alter the risk-management philosophy of a firm maintaining that shareholders want the share price to be fully exposed to changes in the gold price. Affordable for management is not necessarily consistent with affordable for shareholders which is not necessarily consistent with affordable for bondholders.

The risk affordability issue is also difficult to determine for government enterprises where, ultimately, affordability is determined by the ability to raise general tax revenue, borrow against future tax revenue, or levy increased user rates. For example, some government-owned Canadian electric utilities, such as B.C. Hydro, have had a large portion of debt denominated in U.S. dollars, while the bulk of cash flows are in Canadian dollars. Large, adverse changes in the exchange rate that would be sufficient to eliminate the net asset value of a private company would not have the same impact on the government-owned utility. It may be that the government, in some other enterprise, has a corresponding amount of U.S. dollar denominated assets. As such, the government's aggregate balance sheet would be fully hedged, without the need to manage the specific exposure at B.C. Hydro.

3. Can the Risks be Hedged?

This question addresses the problem of hedge design, a topic that is the central concern of Chapter 6. There may be a variety of possible hedging techniques that have to be considered. An important practical concern is whether there are derivative contracts available that qualify as feasible hedging instruments. In certain cases, forward contracts will be available that allow the cash position to be matched with the commodity underlying the forward contract. For example, money center banks can use forward exchange contracts and foreign exchange swap contracts to directly manage currency risk. In other cases, no forward contracting method is available and a *cross hedge* is required. In other cases, the pricing on the forward contract may be considered to be expensive relative to doing a cross hedge. For example, an airline may undertake a cross hedge using New York Mercantile Exchange (NYMEX) heating oil futures in lieu of doing a short-dated jet fuel swap in the OTC market because the cost of the swap is deemed to be too expensive relative to doing the NYMEX hedge and absorbing the basis risk.

Cross hedging involves managing a specific commodity risk using a derivative that is written for a commodity which differs from the cash commodity. For example, a copper scrap dealer can cross hedge using copper futures contracts that feature copper cathodes as the deliverable commodity, or a corporate bond issuer can hedge the issue cost using the T-note futures contract. Cross hedges can sometimes involve quite different commodities, such as hedging brass scrap with a combination of aluminum, copper, and lead futures/forward contracts. Cross hedging raises questions about the appropriate size for the derivative position relative to the cash position (an optimal hedging problem) and whether the hedge will be effective.

4. What are the Basis Relationships?

Examination of basis risk is a key part of the process in deciding whether a specific risk can be hedged. This is often a situation-specific problem. Some fundamentals regarding basis variation are discussed later in Chapter 3. Information on basis relationships is an essential element for determining the size and type of the hedge position to be initiated. Basis variation is an important impediment to implementing the transactions hedge described in Chapter 6.

5. What are the Costs of Hedging?

This could start with calculation of execution and transaction costs: bid/ask spreads, commissions, possible interest losses on margin, and administrative expenses to initiate and monitor trades. Except where the contracting process permits sufficiently precise specification, there will be an element of basis changes that needs to be calculated. Such changes appear to have come as a surprise to MGRM, for example. For substantial hedging programs, there can also be significant managerial costs in terms of the time required to monitor hedging operations. There will typically be considerable variation in the specific costs associated with various potential hedging instruments and programs. For example, firms aiming to use complicated risk-management products, such as exotic derivatives, need to provide internal checks for prices derived from proprietary dealer or internal pricing models.

6. What are the Tax and Accounting Implications of the Hedge?

The relevant issues involved here are discussed in other sources. These issues are not incidental and will have to be determined in order to precisely calculate the costs of hedging. In particular, the introduction of FAS 133 raises a host of questions and queries that lie outside the confines of the present inquiry.

By design, this general framework for designing a risk-management philosophy cannot deal with all important issues that may arise in specifying the appropriate risk-management/hedging program. It is only a guide to the appropriate mindset required to structure the risk-management process.

E. Measuring Corporate Economic Currency Exposure

The first question that has to be addressed in the development of a risk management philosophy is concerned with determining the firm's aggregate and specific risk exposures. To illustrate the potential differences which can arise at this step, consider the problem of measuring corporate currency exposure. The issue is of particular contemporary relevance because the increasing globalization of markets has put increasing pressure on corporate management to determine the appropriate method of handling exposure to currency fluctuations. As discussed previously, two general approaches to measuring corporate currency exposure can be identified: *accounting exposure* and *economic exposure*. The first of these is concerned with the implications of accounting rules, contained primarily in FAS 5 and FAS 52, that deal with the handling of accounting items which are denominated in foreign currency. When basis relationships permit, accounting exposure management typically leads to the use of transactions hedges (see Chapter 6, Section I). While useful within an accounting context, there are many forms of corporate currency exposure that are not captured using this measure.[17] For handling economic exposure, optimal hedging methods are needed.

Economic exposure is a broader concept that measures "the extent to which the value of the firm—as measured by the present value of its expected future cash flows—will change when exchange rates change" (Shapiro, 1992, p. 224). This occurs not only because components of a firm's cash flows are directly denominated in foreign currency, but also because the relative competitiveness of the firm can be affected. In order to identify how this happens, "the focus must be not on nominal exchange rate changes, but instead on changes in the purchasing power of one currency relative to another" (Shapiro, 1992, p. 225). This leads to the notion of "real" as opposed to nominal exchange rate change. It is changes in *real* exchange rates that produce the conventional economic result that exchange rate increases (decreases) will increase (decrease) imports and decrease (increase) exports. However, in the case of the multinational firm, a number of further complications have to be introduced.

---

[17]Accounting exposure identifies specific accounting items that are subject to risk of exchange rate changes. Hedging accounting items proceeds much as in the discussion in Chapter 6, Section I.

The real exchange rate is an implication of purchasing power parity (PPP): "If changes in the nominal exchange rate are fully offset by changes in the relative price levels between the two countries, then the real exchange rate remains unchanged. Alternatively, a change in the real exchange rate is equivalent to a deviation from PPP" (Shapiro, 1992, p. 155). Being based on PPP, the real exchange rate can be used to identify substantive changes in foreign currency values. In other words, if the economic implications of nominal exchange rate changes are offset by corresponding changes in price levels, then the real exchange rate is unchanged and, presumably, there is no incentive to change economic behavior.

This simplified model ignores various complications such as financial obligations that are fixed in nominal terms, including unhedged fixed rate debt, sales and labor contracts, and other types of receipts and disbursements denominated in foreign currency. In the absence of indexing, these factors cannot be readjusted when unanticipated changes in the *nominal* exchange rate occur. Hence, it is possible for the real exchange rate to be unchanged and still have substantive changes in economic behaviour. Similarly, it is possible for the nominal exchange rate to be unchanged and for changes in relative inflation rates to occur that will have substantive economic implications. Shapiro (1992, pp. 228–229) provides an illustration of this happening from 1979 to 1982 in Chile where a government attempt to fix the value of the Chilean peso led to a significant erosion in international competitiveness that had a disastrous impact on the Chilean economy.

A useful Canadian example of how economic currency exposure can affect firm profitability is the hotels and related businesses at the Whistler/Blackcomb ski resort in British Columbia.[18] Even though virtually all revenues and costs are in Canadian dollars, revenues are indirectly dependent on competition from overseas ski resorts. In effect, Whistler/Blackcomb is operating in a global market for skiing and other vacation services. Changes in the Canadian dollar will change the relative value of overseas ski vacations, for both domestic and foreign vacationers. More generally, even though a firm does not have any direct foreign currency exposure, the presence of foreign competition in either the input or output market means that there could be substantial economic currency exposure.

Another Canadian example of corporate currency exposure is provided by the Canadian mining industry. Because the price of metals is set in global markets in U.S. dollars, mining company U.S. dollar revenues will not be affected by changes in the Canadian dollar. While U.S. dollar revenues will not change, changes in the value of the Canadian dollar will alter the U.S. dollar cost of Canadian labor and supplies used in the production of metals. This

---

[18]An American example would be hotels and related businesses at Aspen, Colorado.

type of situation occurs in many other Canadian cases, where the product being produced is priced on international market in terms of U.S. dollars. This is the case with grains such as wheat and energy products such as oil, natural gas and hydroelectricity.

As a final example of corporate foreign exchange exposure, consider Toyota, an automobile manufacturer for which both revenues and costs are affected by exchange rate changes. On the revenue side, Toyota sells the bulk of its production overseas, concentrating on the United States. Changes in the value of the yen will force a pricing policy decision. For example, in the face of an appreciation of the yen, to maintain market share the U.S. dollar price has to be held constant, reducing yen revenues because the yen price per unit has fallen. If the yen price is held constant, market share will be reduced because of higher U.S. dollar prices. On the cost side, Toyota is a purchaser of commodities required in car production that are priced on international markets. Changes in costs will tend to offset changes in revenues, though not one for one. In the case of Toyota, because such a large component of revenues is in U.S. dollars while a relatively smaller portion of costs is not yen determined, the impact of appreciation in the yen is negative. Hence, there are numerous ways in which currency exposure can impact a given firm.

F. Natural Hedging of Corporate Currency Exposure

Another question of relevance to the development of a risk management philosophy was concerned with whether or how the risks could be hedged. Much as with the determination of risk exposures, there are a number of ways to approach this question. Consider again the problem of managing corporate currency exposure. While there are various strategies available for managing corporate currency exposure, it is possible to distinguish between two general types of strategies. One type is associated with traditional derivative security hedging techniques, suitable for nominal contracts stated in a foreign currency. Applications of these techniques include the important area of international asset/liability management, where relatively predictable cash flows originate from foreign financial assets. The techniques of swaps, futures, and options are well developed in this area. The other general type of strategy for managing corporate currency exposure involves natural hedges that are dependent on multinational firm management decisions. These techniques apply to corporate cash flows that are relatively indeterminate, consistent with cash flows that originate from many real assets.

The other group of strategies for managing corporate currency exposure involve assessment of the *competitive exposures* that originate from inherent differences in firm competitiveness due to costs and revenues being denominated in different currencies. Currency exposure management in these cases will typically involve adjustments to be made to operating procedures, encompassing marketing, production, and capital structure decisions. By design, this will require integrated, long-term decision making. Natural hedging techniques are inherent in these types of strategies. This is an essential, if not always well understood, point. Many risk-management situations, such as those faced by financial institutions in dealing with interest rate risk, can be most effectively managed using natural hedges.

Because competitive conditions can be altered by a real exchange rate change (Luehrman, 1990), the firm must attempt to anticipate such changes and decide whether a given change will be transitory or persistent (permanent). For example, a Japanese carmaker faced with an increase in the nominal US$/yen exchange rate, not matched by corresponding price level increases, must decide whether to increase dollar prices, attempting to sustain the yen price, or to hold dollar prices constant, thereby reducing the yen price. If the nominal exchange rate change was anticipated to be matched by price level adjustments in the near term, then the car manufacturer may be willing to hold the dollar price constant in order to maintain market share. This loss of income would have to be balanced against the cost of recovering market share when the real exchange rate is restored. On the other hand, if the real exchange rate change was anticipated to be persistent, then competitive conditions would require undertaking various adjustments such as lowering the yen cost of production. For example, this could be done by sourcing production of automobiles to the US and other countries where real production costs will be lower. There are various other possibilities.

Product strategy provides one potential method for adjusting to changes in currency exposure. Faced with long-term appreciations in their real domestic currencies relative to the dollar, both Volkswagen and the major Japanese car producers have had to adjust the nature of the product being sold in the United States. In effect, real exchange rate changes have made competition at the low end of the market unprofitable. As a result, these companies have made long-term product adjustments by offering higher priced automobiles targeted at middle to upper middle income consumers. In contrast to persistent real exchange rate changes, temporary exchange rate changes will usually not require substantial adjustments to product offerings. However, temporary depreciations may provide timing opportunities for firms seeking to penetrate foreign markets. This is an important point because the high fixed startup costs associated with overseas expansion are often incurred in the initial stages of establishing a market presence. Favorable, if temporary, exchange rate changes can partially offset these costs.

Perhaps the most widely recognized method for multinational firms to manage currency risks is to create natural hedges through appropriate *plant location* and input purchase decisions. Firms that have similar production facilities in areas with different currencies can, potentially, shift production to plants where production is least expensive. Where it is not possible to establish production facilities in the appropriate locales, a similar result can be achieved by spreading sources for inputs across countries in different currency areas. In practice, the benefits associated with multinational sourcing and production facilities have to be balanced against the costs associated with plant redundancy and loss of economies of scale. In a corporate context, this requires managerial decision makers to incorporate forecasts of exchange rate changes into company strategies. Hence, there is an element of active management in adjusting to currency exposure (in keeping with the results in Section I). In addition to the natural hedges provided by plant shifting and alternative sourcing, it is also possible to react to currency-related changes in competitive conditions in a more traditional fashion (i.e., by raising domestic productivity).

The final important method by which corporations can use natural hedges to manage currency exposure is by adjusting the *capital structure* of the firm. Conventionally, this involves taking advantage of the natural hedge provided by financing real assets with foreign debt. Where the cash flows of the real assets have an identifiable currency exposure, either because of foreign competition or dependence on foreign markets for inputs or sales, changes in operating cash flows arising from exchange-rate changes will be met by offsetting changes in debt service costs. As with any type of hedging situation, there will be situations when the hedge position is unprofitable (i.e., where the domestic currency value of the foreign borrowing increases). In these cases, it would be desirable to finance real assets with domestic debt. Because it may not be possible to adjust borrowing programs to keep pace with the numerous exchange rate changes, once again the natural hedge decision depends on active management of currency exposure to achieve the highest return. If management is not able to forecast or has a high degree of risk aversion, the optimal solution will be to establish a natural hedge that matches the foreign currency exposure.

In the face of the various complications, Table 2.5 provides a heuristic framework of key questions designed to identify exchange risk (Shapiro, 1992). The answers provided to these questions can be used to guide the implementation of natural hedging strategies. Luehrman (1990) and, more recently, Oxelheim and Wihlborg (1997) provide a theoretical development of these issues. Against this heuristic background, attempts have been made to provide a more formal approach to measuring currency exposure. Adler and

TABLE 2.5   Questions Relevant to Formulating Natural Hedging Strategies

1. What is the foreign/domestic breakdown of sales?
2. Are the company's key competitors foreign or domestic?
3. What are the short- and long-run price elasticities of demand for firm output?
4. What is the foreign/domestic breakdown of production activities?
5. What is the foreign/domestic breakdown of input sources?
6. What currency is used to determine the firm's inputs, outputs, assets, and liabilities?

Dumas (1984), Shapiro (1975), and others propose the use of regression analysis to identify the correlation between changes in the nominal exchange rate and the domestic currency value of the firm's cash flows. In effect, changes in a firm's cash flow (in domestic currency) are regressed on changes in nominal exchange rates.[19] The resulting estimated slope coefficient can be used as a proxy for currency exposure. While appealing, this approach suffers from a number of potential shortcomings. For example, the use of historical data for the regression requires that the nature of the firm has not changed substantively over the sample period (e.g., due to mergers or significant changes in unhedged foreign debt issues). Similarly, there should be no anticipated changes in the nature of the firm over the decision-making period for which the regression information will be used. In addition to these practical problems, the lead–lag relationship that is often associated with a currency change affecting firm cash flows may complicate identification of the appropriate regression equation. Various other problems also have to be addressed for this approach to be correctly implemented.

G. PURCHASING POWER PARITY ARGUMENTS

Purchasing power parity (PPP) plays a key role in decisions for naturally hedging currency risk. Though the roots of PPP can be found in Adam Smith and early 19th-century classical political economy, the PPP theory is usually credited to Gustav Cassels, writing in the 1920s. The earliest versions of PPP took the form of the Law of One Price: Assume a one-good world with no transactions or transportation costs; the price of that good denominated in different currencies will sell at the same price:

$$P_t^* S_t = P_t \quad \Rightarrow \quad S_t = \frac{P_t}{P_t^*}$$

[19]The specification given in Shapiro, 1975 (p. 243) is in terms of levels, not changes, as the relevant variables. This is not satisfactory on statistical grounds. Similarly, the discussion provided on the bottom of p. 243 about R^2 and significant beta coefficients also appears to be lacking.

where P^* and P are the foreign and domestic prices, respectively, of the good, with S being the spot exchange rate.

Extending the Law of One Price using price indices instead of individual prices is known as absolute purchasing power parity (APPP). Even in the unlikely event that the Law of One Price holds for each good individually, the APPP extension may be invalid if the index weights are not the same for both economies. The problem of traded and untraded goods also creates significant difficulties. Nevertheless, ignoring the various possible problems with APPP, substituting price index levels p^* and p into the Law of One Price and taking logs produces:

$$\ln S = \ln p - \ln p^* \Rightarrow \frac{1}{S}\frac{dS}{dt} = \frac{1}{p}\frac{dp}{dt} - \frac{1}{p^*}\frac{dp^*}{dt} \Rightarrow \dot{S} = \dot{p} - \dot{p}^*$$

Hence, APPP holds that foreign exchange rate changes are determined by the difference between foreign and domestic inflation rates. One implication of this appealing interpretation of exchange rate changes is that predicting domestic and foreign inflation rates will permit exchange rate changes to be forecasted accurately.

A more popular form for PPP to take is relative purchasing power parity (RPPP). This is the version used to define the real exchange rate as the nominal exchange rate adjusted for changes in the relative purchasing power of each currency since some base period. In a one-period framework, the relative form of the PPP condition can be expressed:

$$\frac{S_{t+1}}{S_t} = \frac{p_{t+1}/p^*_{t+1}}{p_t/p^*_t} = \frac{1 + \dot{p}_{t,\,t+1}}{1 + \dot{p}^*_{t,\,t+1}} \Rightarrow S_t = S_{t+1}\frac{1 + \dot{p}^*_{t,\,t+1}}{1 + \dot{p}_{t,\,t+1}}$$

where p is the appropriate price level index, $\dot{p}$ is the inflation rate, and $*$ denotes a foreign value. The real exchange rate (s_t) notion is an attempt to convert observed exchange rates back to some base period. Starting from some base year where $S_0 = s_0$, then:

$$s_1 = S_1\frac{1 + \dot{p}^*_{0,1}}{1 + \dot{p}_{0,1}} \Rightarrow s_n = S_n\frac{1 + \dot{p}^*_{0,n}}{1 + \dot{p}_{0,n}}$$

The multiperiod form of s_t involves compounding the inflation term over the time between the selected base year and the desired date. Some evidence on the historical behavior of nominal and real foreign exchange rates is given Shapiro (1999, p. 217). Casual examination of the empirical evidence reveals that real exchange rates for many currencies do deviate significantly from the PPP requirement that the real exchange rate must be relatively constant over time.

The basic approach of the PPP arguments is to attack the notion of exchange risk. This follows from the PPP implication that, in the long run, exchange rate changes will offset price level changes.[20] Take the example of a Canadian sugar refiner selling output in Canadian dollars (C$) but purchasing sugar in U.S. dollars (US$). The PPP argument indicates that a deterioration in the FX rate will be compensated for in price level increases. If, say, the US$/C$ increased by 50% (C$/US$ falls), causing the cost of raw sugar inputs to increase proportionately, then PPP dictates that the Canadian inflation rate will be such that the price of refined sugar in Canada will increase to completely offset the Canadian dollar increase in input costs. When appropriate assumptions are satisfied, PPP holds and the real foreign exchange rate is unchanged. In this case, there are no real implications to nominal foreign exchange rate changes.

The argument that PPP holds and, hence, corporate hedging is unnecessary has a number of obvious and not-so-obvious shortcomings. A list of these would include:

1. *Empirical applicability of PPP*: There is a sizable literature on the empirical validity of PPP (e.g., Corbae and Ouliaris, 1988). The long lead–lag time period for the relationship to hold makes PPP inconsistent with the typical types of business decision time frames; the greater applicability of PPP to tradeables than to nontradeables creates complications if the hedger is interested in nontradeables.
2. Slippage is created between the price index that underlies PPP and the specific prices that are of interest to the hedger. It is relative, not aggregate, prices that are of interest.
3. Financial and operating contracts are present that are fixed in nominal terms (i.e., cash flows that do not adjust when the aggregate price level changes).

In the context of an international firm, Shapiro (1984) has demonstrated that in the face of deviations from PPP (changes in real foreign exchange rates) a combination of forward exchange contracts, nominal debt, and fixed price sales are required in order to hedge against currency risk (composed of inflation and real exchange rate risk) and relative price risk.

---

[20]For a discussion of PPP, there are a number of useful sources. In addition to Shapiro (1999), see also Officer (1976), Roll (1979), and Shapiro (1983).

CHAPTER 3

Speculative Trading Strategies

... human decisions affecting the future, whether personal or political or economic, cannot depend on strict mathematical expectation, since the basis for making such expectations does not exist.

John Maynard Keynes (*The General Theory,*
chap. 12, 1936)

Throughout its long history, futures trading has been primarily associated with commodities having major seasonal patterns of production and inventory accumulation and liquidation. Prices of seasonally produced commodities are speculative.

Thomas Hieronymous (1977)

I. SPECULATIVE EFFICIENCY?

A. THE STUDY OF SPECULATION

The study of speculation is ancient. For example, Aristotle in the *Politics* (Book I, Chapter 11) examines speculation while discussing "the various forms of acquisition." Aristotle maintained that to consider "the various forms of acquisition . . . minutely and in detail might be useful for practical purposes; but to dwell upon them long would be in poor taste." At least two cases of speculation are considered. One case involved Thales, the philosopher, and the options he took on olive presses prior to a bumper crop. Another case involved a Sicilian who bought all the available supplies of iron. In both cases, Aristotle attributed the speculative profits to "the creation of a monopoly."

Aristotle's musings reveal two important historical themes in the study of speculation. One theme is the negative connotations attached to speculation, which has often suffered from a direct association with gambling (e.g., Emery,

1896). Yet, there are real differences between certain types of speculation, which can require both skill and expertise to be successful, and outright gambling, where outcomes depend purely on randomizers such as dice or playing cards. Yet, these differences are not always appreciated. At various times, speculative gains have been seen as ill gotten, achieved at the expense of some other group. Even Aristotle found more than a passing examination of speculation to be "in poor taste."

Another important theme is the role of market manipulation in obtaining speculative profits. Aristotle determined that the profits of both Thales and the Sicilian iron merchant originated from monopoly power. Writing about stock trading on the Amsterdam bourse, de la Vega was concerned with market manipulation. In the Fourth Dialogue of *Confusion de Confusiones* (1688), de la Vega lists twelve different "tricks" that compose "the most speculative part of the business . . . the climax of Exchange transactions, the acme of Exchange operations, the craftiest and most complicated machinations that exist in the maze of the Exchange and which require the greatest possible cunning." Writing about 18th century English security trading, Mortimer (1761) was also concerned about market manipulation involving speculating stockjobbers. Stories of speculation and manipulation in the 19th- and early 20th-century America have been addressed previously (see Chapter 1, Section II).

Modern opinion has been relatively kind to speculators. Vilifications are usually reserved for events such as large, anonymous speculators making an "attack" on a target currency. Various sophisticated types of speculation have become the grist of academic studies. For example, cash-and-carry arbitrages, even those as readily executed as covered interest arbitrage, are actually speculations, due to deviations from the perfect market assumptions that make these speculations riskless. Sophisticated speculation is inherent in the strategies underlying many hedge funds. Academic studies of speculative trading strategies abound that demonstrate there are numerous situations where market mis-pricing creates profitable trading opportunities (e.g., Poitras, 1997). In particular, many spread trading strategies are designed to mimic the payoffs on hedge positions. Profitability arises from correct modeling of the basis behavior.

B. THEORIES OF PURE SPECULATIVE EFFICIENCY

The speculative efficiency hypothesis is an extension of the more general notion that expected asset prices accurately reflect currently available information. As a consequence, it is not possible to systematically earn returns that are "abnormal." For a conventional equity investment, abnormal is defined to be more than adequate compensation as measured by the riskless rate plus an adjustment to compensate for the systematic risk of the asset. Because taking a purely speculative position in a derivative security such as a forward contract involves no investment of funds, adequate expected compensation is zero. From the discussion in Chapter 2, Section I, it can be readily shown that speculative efficiency implies that forward prices will be unbiased predictors of future spot prices. Yet, equilibrium considerations indicate that this requires speculators to be close to risk neutral in order for speculators to undertake market-clearing positions. By construction, speculative efficiency is concerned with random variables defined at different points in time. The resulting speculative trading strategies are risky. Unfortunately, the introduction of risk into the concept of efficiency significantly complicates the problem of determining whether a given market is "efficient." Unlike the arbitrage profit function, which is fully determined on the basis of contemporaneous information, the speculative profit function contains variables that are uncertain when the trading decision is initiated.

As a result of introducing risk, the concept of an efficient market equilibrium is more difficult to define. For example, the proper handling of risk requires some methodology for determining risk-adjusted profits. In addition, both the statistical properties of the random variables and the properties of the trader's objective function with respect to the relevant distributional parameters require specification. It follows that any test of "speculative efficiency" necessarily involves a joint hypothesis because a model of market equilibrium is required to formulate testable hypotheses about market efficiency. More significantly, when applied to a forward market it is difficult to test the hypothesis empirically without using variables observed at different points in time, most importantly $F(0,T) - S(T)$, the forecast error. Statistically, this can raise the problem of moving-average error terms if the forecast horizon has a greater length than the sampling frequency. Statistical fundamentals are an important component of one version of the speculative efficiency hypothesis: the unbiased prediction hypothesis.

In addition to being the focus of a large number of studies of forward foreign exchange market efficiency (e.g., Bilson, 1981; Boothe and Longworth, 1986; Gregory and McCurdy, 1984), the unbiased prediction hypothesis has also been applied to test efficiency in a wide range of markets, such as the when issued (*wi*) market in the United States (Ferri *et al.*, 1985) and the U.S. T-bill futures market (Howard, 1982; Hegde and McDonald, 1986; MacDonald and Hein, 1989). It is possible to theoretically derive the hypothesis using a number of not mutually exclusive theoretical justifications: imposing zero expected value on a specific class of speculative profit functions; in a mean-variance-expected utility framework, by assuming that either speculators are risk neutral or the second moments are unbounded; or working directly with the properties of the conditional expectation, by assuming that there is no systematic risk in futures price forecasts.

While there are a number of theoretical motivations for speculative efficiency, when the testable requirement for speculative efficiency is based on unbiased predictions, it is possible to take advantage of a range of econometric techniques. For example, applied to the *wi* market for T-bills, speculative efficiency requires:[1]

$$E[TB(N)] = WI(N - i)$$

where $E[\,\cdot\,]$ is the conditional expectations operator; $TB(N)$ is the issue price of the T-bill at the following auction; $WI(N - i)$ is the price of the to-be-issued T-bill observed in the *wi* market i days before the auction settlement date; and N is the auction settlement date. Under relatively weak conditions on the allowable functional form for the T-bill price process, the orthogonal decomposition can be formed:

$$TB(N) = E[TB(N)] + U(i, N)$$

where $U(i, N)$ is the forecast error of the conditional expectation formed at time $N - i$. Combining these two conditions provides for the specification of the *wi* forecast residual $(TB(N) - WI(N - i))$ that is equal to $U(i,N)$ under the null hypothesis. Hence, the speculative efficiency hypothesis is intimately connected with the statistical properties of the $U(i,N)$.

Although the unbiased prediction hypothesis can be tested statistically in a number of ways, implementation of the available methods is complicated by the unobservable expectation. One popular approach is to require $U(i,N)$ to be mean zero and serially uncorrelated. The empirical implications are illustrated in Poitras (1991), which plots a representative time series of the forecast errors $U(i,N)$ using 2-day *wi* contracts. The decidedly non-normal behavior of the forecast errors depicted in the data plot is confirmed for all contract maturities. Considerable research effort has been devoted to explaining the behavior of the forecast error in various financial markets. Recognizing the need to incorporate distributional properties, recent research has concentrated on time-varying finite volatility models (e.g., McCurdy and Morgan, 1988). In

---

[1]However, despite the considerable theoretical motivation, to date little attention has been given to the trading mechanics that support the unbiased prediction hypothesis. From a trading perspective, the underlying strategies are naive. Violation of the equality condition for unbiasedness induces a short *wi* trade when *wi* prices are greater (*wi* rates lower) than expected T-bill auction prices. A long *wi* trade is initiated when *wi* prices are lower (*wi* rates higher) than expected auction prices. Given the risks of these "naked position" strategies relative to other available strategies (e.g., Yano, 1989), there would have to be significant information-induced discrepancies to generate sizable trading activity. At best, such events would be discrete.

practice, this involves making unrealistic stationarity assumptions about the higher moments.

C. CONVENIENCE YIELD AND THE SUPPLY OF STORAGE

The notion of convenience yield and the closely related concept of the *supply of storage* were subjects of central interest in the early research on futures and forward markets.[2] Analytically, these notions have direct implications for explaining the behavior of the key variable in the speculator's profit function: $F(0,T) - E[S(T)]$, where $E[\,\cdot\,]$ is the conditional mathematical expectation of $S(T)$ given the information available at time $t = 0$. (For notational simplicity, the conditioning information is dropped because, in virtually every case encountered in the analysis of derivative securities, expectations are conditional.) Because convenience yield and the supply of storage are concerned with properties of the physical commodity, some approaches ignore the role of the futures market and examine $S(0) - E[S(T)]$. Brennan's (1958) two-period, two-agent equilibrium model of the supply of storage is a case in point. Supply and demand functions are derived for a consumer–merchant market. Brennan describes the market this way:

> During any period there will be firms carrying stocks of a commodity from that period into the next. Producers, wholesalers, etc. carry finished inventories from the periods of seasonally high production to the periods of low production. Processors carry stocks of raw materials. Speculators possess title to stocks held in warehouses. These firms may be considered as supplying inventory stocks or, briefly, supplying storage.... On the other hand, there will be groups who want to have stocks carried for them from one period...to another period....These consumers may be regarded as demanding storage.

In this case, the supply and demand functions for storage are behavioral and dependent on both the spread between the expected future spot price and the current spot price, as well as on the levels of stocks being held. The upshot is an identified supply of storage function that provides a (potentially nonlinear) montonically increasing relationship between physical inventory levels and $E[S(T)] - S(0)$.

The development of the partial equilibrium supply of storage model to include futures markets was provided initially by Weymar (1968) and extended by Turnovsky (1983). In Weymar's model, three agents are identified: merchants, manufacturers, and speculators. Futures markets provide cash market

---

[2]Relevant works include Working (1949), Brennan (1958), Muth (1961), Weymar (1968), Danthine (1978), and Turnovsky (1983).

participants with an additional method of carrying inventories. Equilibrium in the futures market is directly specified and a supply of storage function is derived. Much as in Brennan's case, there is a monotonically increasing relationship between physical inventory levels and $E[S(T)] - F(0,T)$. Using a more sophisticated, but similar, model, Turnovsky is able to show:

> ...with risk averse behaviour, the current futures price is a weighted average (with weights summing to less than unity) of the current spot price and the expected future spot price. Only if...producers and speculators are risk neutral...does $F(0,T) = E[S(T)]$ and the futures price become an unbiased predictor of the future spot price. Otherwise, the futures price is a biased predictor, with the direction of the bias depending on the magnitude of the (relevant) cost parameters.

A final implication of Turnovsky's model is that "under normal conditions," hedgers should be net short and speculators net long.

A graphical presentation of the supply of storage function is presented in Fig. 3.1. This figure illustrates the theoretical behavior of the convenience yield as the supply of inventory varies and the physical storage capacity is held fixed. Heuristically, Fig. 3.1 indicates that when inventory levels are "normal," fully hedged holding of stocks will earn storage operators a return to compensate for the costs of maintaining storage capacity. This return will be reflected in a forward price that is higher than the current price by the relevant cost of providing storage and, possibly, a small convenience yield to holding stocks. The differential between forward and spot prices is relatively constant across a wide range of inventory levels. However, when inventory levels approach the physical limit set by storage capacity, the costs of providing storage increase and, as a consequence, the convenience yield goes to zero or becomes negative. Conversely, at very low inventory levels stocks are in short supply relative to demand, and inventories have a high convenience yield.

The upshot of this discussion is that two potentially conflicting interpretations of futures price determination have been presented. In discussing the cash basis, it is demonstrated in Chapter 4, Section 1, how cash-and-carry arbitrages bind the futures prices to the current spot price. However, in discussing the supply of storage explanation for the expected *future* basis, $\{F(0,T) - E[S(T)]\}$, it was argued that forecasting accuracy of the futures price is the primary motivation for determining price. The confusion associated with these competing explanations has persisted into the contemporary literature, where the behavior of the future basis has attracted considerable attention, albeit in the form of the speculative efficiency hypothesis. In contrast to the requirement of arbitrage efficiency, speculative efficiency for a given market imposes a zero-expected-value condition on the speculative profit function. To see this, use the speculative profit function stated in Chapter 2, Section I, and

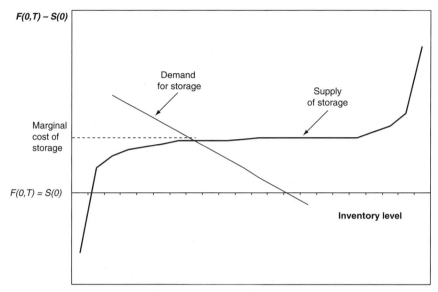

FIGURE 3.1   Supply of storage.

take expected values to get $E[\pi] = 0 = E[F(1,T)] - F(0,T) \rightarrow E[F(1,T)] = F(0,T)$.

D. THE THEORY OF NORMAL BACKWARDATION

To better understand the economic theory of forward price determination, it is useful to review the traditional explanation for future basis behavior (associated with Keynes and Hicks) which focused on the motivations of participants in forward (futures) markets. These participants are classified as *hedgers, speculators,* or *arbitragers.*[3] Observing that in the present context it is possible to ignore the role played by arbitragers because these traders are only concerned with the relationship between current prices, this leaves the future basis to be determined by hedgers and speculators.

---

[3]These participant categories are not mutually exclusive. For example, it is possible for the same trader to engage in arbitrage and hedging activities, just as it is possible for hedgers to also be speculators.

It is possible to provide precise definitions of hedgers and speculators as has been done in the Commodity Exchange Act (CEA) or in the trading regulations of the various exchanges. Information from traders subject to filing requirements is published by the Commodities Futures Trading Commission (CFTC) in "Commitments of Traders in Commodity Futures." Figure 3.2 provides a summary of such data for November 13, 2001. In this case, a "commercial hedger is a large trader who also deals in the commodity on a cash basis." As a consequence, contracts recorded in the hedger category will often, though not always, be associated with using the futures contract to cover a cash commodity position. A speculator, on the other hand, is a trader who takes positions to attempt to benefit from *expected* price changes, "a noncommercial trader who has no dealings in the underlying commodity."

By design, hedgers have a position, over time, in both the cash and futures market. From this, it is possible to classify hedgers according to the type of position taken in the futures market. *Short hedgers* have a long position in the cash commodity to protect from price fluctuation and, as a result, take a short futures position to offset this risk. While the classic example of a short hedger would be a grain farmer hedging the crop price to be received at harvest, other examples include a metals refinery hedging the price of future output or an insurance company hedging the price of its bond portfolio. *Long hedgers* have a short position in the physical commodity, or possibly a need for the commodity at some future point of time, and take a long position in futures as a hedge. Examples would include a flour mill hedging the cost of future wheat purchases, a fund manager hedging the interest rate on a future investment or an oil refinery hedging the price of future crude oil purchases.

Figure 3.2 reveals that short hedgers dominate the commercial hedger category for a number of commodities, most notably wheat, gold, and silver have a significantly greater short hedger position; however, there are closely related commodities, such as corn and copper, that have a significantly greater long hedger position. Hence, it does not appear that a particular, stylized type of hedger can be assumed. The type of hedging activity and the resulting net hedger position depends on the specifics of the commodity involved.

The traditional hedging situation features a short hedger; the use of this approach was based on the presumption that hedgers were net short in the bulk of forward and futures markets. Based on the evidence in Fig. 3.2 this does not seem well founded. However, many of these theories originated prior to the collection of the net hedger data by exchanges and regulatory bodies. Recalling the dictum that "for every short there is a long," it follows that if hedgers are net short then market clearing requires that speculators, *as a group*,

FIGURE 3.2 CFTC Commitments of Traders Report, allocation of open interest, November 13, 2001. (*Source*: CFTC *Commitments of Traders Report*, Nov. 13, 2001.)

Contract (Exchange) (Total Open Interest)	Large Speculator			Commercial Hedger		Small Trader	
	Long	Short	Spreads	Long	Short	Long	Short
Copper (COMEX) 87,982	9,344	22,245	6,831	58,306	48,419	13,501	10,487
Silver (COMEX) 82,969	30,820	25,152	6,500	26,279	43,677	19,370	7,639
Gold (COMEX) 150,368	29,495	19,449	26,184	62,759	93,977	31,930	10,758
Live Cattle (CME) 138,450	11,479	17,609	29,992	63,155	52,676	33,823	38,173
Canadian Dollar (IMM) 88,592	5,239	31,442	275	56,554	27,497	26,525	29,379
Japanese Yen (IMM) 119,631	17,177	23,557	4,163	85,981	65,183	12,310	26,728
S&P 500 Index (IMM) 600,563	29,622	38,882	23,752	400,893	438,655	146,296	99,274
Eurodollar (IMM) 8,472,519	18,406	56,937	2,636,041	4,732,839	5,272,191	585,233	507,351
Heating Oil (NYMEX) 201,815	2,204	13,496	27,357	139,228	129,676	33,026	31,285
Natural Gas (NYMEX) 737,519	3,436	15,663	93,950	597,906	608,581	42,227	19,326
Crude Oil (NYMEX) 745,005	6,551	38,671	133,385	542,884	518,670	52,185	54,279
Wheat (CBOT) 151,350	27,207	15,876	37,381	51,968	73,584	34,794	24,509
Corn (CBOT) 608,450	35,772	85,184	143,735	320,682	243,422	108,261	136,109
Soybeans (CBOT) 215,153	12,948	33,944	40,645	97,941	101,998	63,618	38,566
US T-bonds (CBOT) 777,055	77,319	90,217	96,291	471,132	497,970	132,314	92,578

Note: Results are for combined commitments including both futures and options trading. Large Speculator, Commercial Hedger and Small Trader categories are defined as per CFTC definitions. For further information, see the description of the Report on the CFTC website. Small Traders appear as non-reportable positions in the Report.

have to be net long. Assuming that hedgers have a tangible need for futures markets in order to shift the risk of price fluctuations to speculators, Keynes, Hicks, and other writers argued that speculators would have to be paid an "insurance premium" in order to be induced to hold the net long position. If they are correct, this insurance premium would be reflected in the future basis. If short (long) hedgers pay "insurance" to speculators, then the futures price would have to rise (fall) *on average* over the life of the contract. This result is known as the "normal backwardation hypothesis."[4]

The gist of the traditional position is well summarized by Hicks (1946):

> In normal conditions, when demand and supply are expected to remain unchanged, and therefore the spot price is expected to be about the same in a month's time as it is today, the futures price for one month's delivery is bound to be below the spot price now ruling. The difference between these two prices (the current spot and the currently fixed futures price) is called... "normal backwardation." It measures the amount which hedgers have to hand over to speculators in order to persuade the speculators to take over the risk of the price fluctuations in question.

The immediate implication is that, if hedgers are net short, the current futures price is a downwardly biased predictor of the spot price at delivery time. Houthakker (1968) argues that Hicks maintained this bias would only appear for normal conditions, while Keynes felt it would also hold if there were excessive inventories.[5] Historically, the views of Keynes and Hicks about normal backwardation are not supported by the 18th century Amsterdam stockjobber described by Wilson (1941), who indicates that contango was typical in prices from time bargains.

The normal backwardation hypothesis differs substantively from the speculative efficiency approach based on zero expected value for speculative trades. In effect, if markets are speculative efficient, the futures price will be an unbiased predictor of the future spot price. This approach is also known as the "unbiased expectations hypothesis."[6] Just as in the traditional approach, it is possible to specify a number of models that support this view. The presence of risk in the speculator's trading strategies significantly complicates the use of a hedger–speculator approach to explaining the future basis.

---

[4]In practice, the terms *normal backwardation* and *contango* are used to describe a number of different notions. In addition to the Keynes/Hicks usage that refers to futures prices being downward-biased predictors (normal backwardation) or upwardly biased predictors (contango), these terms are also used to refer to the relationship between current spot and futures prices. In cases where futures prices for succeedingly more distant deliveries are higher, the futures market is said to be in *contango*. When the futures prices fall as more distant deliveries are considered, the market is said to be in *backwardation*. Following a discussion provided by Hicks, the notion of normal backwardation is also applied to the term structure of interest rates where normal backwardation refers to higher yields for longer maturity bonds; that is, the term structure is upward sloping when the level of interest rates is expected to be unchanged. The "insurance premium" in this case is typically attributed to a liquidity premium embedded in shorter maturity securities.

[5]The early, empirically motivated debate on the normal backwardation hypothesis included Telser (1958), Cootner (1960), and Houthakker (1968).

[6]Included in this literature are Bilson (1981), Hansen and Hodrick (1980), Gregory and McCurdy (1984), and Boothe and Longworth (1986), and deRoon *et al.* (1998).

Unlike the cash-and-carry arbitrage strategies that only depend on current information, speculative profit functions contain variables that are not known when the trading decision is initiated. Accurate modeling requires the incorporation of risk into the speculator's objective function, as well as including considerations about the distributional properties of the relevant random variables. Given this, it is possible to derive the speculative efficiency hypothesis using a number of not mutually exclusive methods: directly imposing zero expected value on a relevant class of speculative profit functions; assuming mean-variance objective functions for hedgers and risk-neutral speculators; or working directly with the properties of the conditional expectation, assuming that there is no systematic risk in futures price forecasts.

A priori, it is not possible to demonstrate that either the normal backwardation or unbiased prediction hypothesis is correct. Houthakker (1968, p. 202) puts the point succinctly:

> ... The theory of normal backwardation does not merely follow from the imbalance of hedging and speculation; it also rests on an assumption concerning speculators, namely that in the long run they will only be net long if by doing so they will earn a profit, usually known as a "risk premium."

While it is possible that hedgers pay speculators an insurance premium, it is also possible that speculators may be willing to participate in futures markets without compensation from hedgers. In this case, hedgers would execute trades at prices determined by speculators pursuing zero-expected-value strategies. At present, while better understood, the issues involved still receive attention.

It is not possible to deal with all the theoretical issues surrounding normal backwardation in a concise fashion. Empirically, in certain markets, cash-and-carry arbitrage conditions provide a "tight" band around the futures price; this is the case for financial commodities. Relatively small deviations from the arbitrage conditions generate cash-and-carry trading activity. In addition, in commodities where the arbitrage is less restrictive, the accessibility of futures trading to small, speculative participants increases the potential for hedgers to trade at futures prices that reflect an expected value of zero for net (risk neutral) speculative participation. What is perhaps more instructive is to consider the less developed *forward* markets, dealing in the traditional agricultural and industrial commodities, that concerned Hicks and Keynes. Much as with the first futures trade, the lack of speculative liquidity in these markets may have dictated that the marginal hedger would have to pay the counter-party to the trade a premium in the form of a discount to the current spot price. Given the relatively low inflation of that era, "normal conditions" would dictate that the current spot price was an unbiased estimate of the future spot price. In effect, the need to pay a liquidity premium for forward contracting dissipates as the supply of speculative liquidity increases.

II. BASIC SPECULATIVE TRADING STRATEGIES

A. TRADING NAKED

Examine the profit functions for the short and long futures positions given in Chapter 2. Colloquially, these trades can be referred to as uncovered or *naked trades*, positions that are not covered or offset with any other position. Profitability depends on accurately predicting the change in the level of the futures price. This is also the case with naked trading in spot and forward markets. Considerable empirical evidence indicates that changes in prices for almost all commodities, physical and financial, are random. Appropriately adjusted price levels follow random walks, implying that such price changes are serially uncorrelated. This means that it is not possible to use past price behavior to profitably predict future price changes. Loosely put, if the commodity price goes up today, the price is equally likely to go up or down tomorrow. Given this, profitability in naked trading depends on having accurate fundamental information about price changes that is not reflected in current market prices. This type of information would typically be available only to traders intimately involved in cash market trading. Purely speculative traders must rely on a combination of intuition and luck in order to profitably use naked position strategies.

An exception to the empirical evidence about random price changes occurs with intra-day price movements. While the close-to-close price change is serially uncorrelated, numerous empirical studies confirm that within-the-day prices changes can have trends. As much of the volume in cash and futures trading is concentrated around the market opening, this trending behavior in futures markets is the source of profit opportunities for exchange-floor traders. A similar result holds for cash and forward markets where purely speculative traders are prevented by market rules from directly participating. Again, the profit opportunities are available only to those directly involved in the exchange process. Even when intra-day trending behavior is accessible to speculative naked position traders, unfavorable transaction costs put those not involved in the exchange process at a disadvantage. Even though betting on commodity price changes may provide a better chance at winning than, say, going to the racetrack or buying a lottery ticket, by using more sophisticated trading strategies it is possible to place bets that have a higher likelihood of profitability than for naked trades. This leads to the study of speculative spread-trading strategies using forward or futures contracts.

B. BASICS OF SPREAD TRADING

In the face of the uncertainties associated with naked position trading, the spread trade has decided advantages for the small speculative trader not able to access the less expensive execution costs available to floor traders. In addition, spreading techniques are also of considerable use to floor traders. The importance of spread trading is captured in the futures pits where there is, invariably, a specific pit location for spread traders. The significance of the spread trader in facilitating market liquidity is often misunderstood. Compared to naked positions, intracommodity spreads offer lower margin requirements and transaction costs. These advantages are combined with numerous potential trading strategies that can be pursued (see Exhibit 3.1). Spread trading techniques provide the ability to tailor speculative trades to make bets that are not accessible using naked position trades. Analytically, the similarity of the hedger and spread-trader profit functions permits numerous techniques from risk management to be applied to the design of spread trades.

EXHIBIT 3.1

A Taxomony of Spread Trades

Spread trades are sometimes referred to as *straddle* trades but this terminology is also used to describe a specific option trading strategy and can create semantic confusion. Schwager (1984, Part 5) provides a useful and practical introduction to spread trading.

Calendar spread, also referred to as an interdelivery spread, is a trade composed of a short and a long position in the same commodity involving different delivery dates. The number of contracts used for the short and long positions can be equal, a one-to-one spread, or unequal.

Tailed spread is a calendar spread where an unequal number of contracts is used for the short and long positions. The number of short and long contracts is chosen to achieve a specific type of trade payoff. It is possible to set the tail to have a spread trade payoff that depends on changes in the implied repo rate, an important feature for stereo and turtle trades.

(continues)

(*continued*)

Tandem spread is a trade combining calendar spreads in two different commodities (e.g., Kilcollin, 1982; Poitras, 1998a). The component spreads can be either one-to-one or tailed. The trade involves a hedge ratio to be calculated, usually to equalize the starting values of the positions in the two commodities. There is a wide range of possible rationales for doing tandem trades.

A *stereo* trade is a specific type of tandem trade designed to speculate on changes in the implied repo rates for different commodities (e.g., Yano, 1989); hence, a stereo is a specific type of tailed tandem where the tails are determined to have the calendar spread payoffs depend on changes in implied repo rates. The trade is usually triggered when the implied repo rates for different commodities are observed to deviate from typical historical relationships.

A *turtle* trade combines a tailed spread in one commodity with a short or long position in an interest rate future. The tail is determined to have the calendar spread payoff depend on changes in implied repo rates. The rationale for a turtle varies depending on the specific commodity. For T-bonds and T-notes, the turtle is triggered when the implied repo rate is observed to deviate significantly from the cash repo rate (e.g., Jones, 1981; Rentzler, 1986).

In turn, simplifications provided by futures trading permits spread design to go well beyond the narrow limits of risk management.[7]

The jargon associated with trading of derivative securities is often colorful but not always revealing. This is definitely the case with spread trading. One concept may be referred to by different terminology, while the same terminology may refer to different concepts. In order to avoid semantic confusion, some attention will be given to defining and explaining important basic notions. Spread trades can be classified into two general types. Intracommodity spreads, also referred to as *calendar spreads* or interdelivery spreads, involve taking a short position for one delivery date simultaneously with a long position for

---

[7]A Futures and Options Trading Game is available at www.sfu.ca/~poitras which is designed to familiarize students with some of the more well-known spreading strategies.

another delivery date.[8] While there are lesser margin requirements and transaction costs associated with taking an equal number of short and long contracts, there are often analytical and practical advantages to having an unbalanced spread position. The other general type of spread trade is the intercommodity spread, a category that includes a wide variety of possible trades including tandems, turtles, and stereos. In some cases, the profit function for an intercommodity spread can be developed from underlying production relationships. Examples include the soybean crush spread (Johnson *et al.*, 1991; Rechner and Poitras, 1993; Simon, 1999) and the crack spread (Schap, 1991, 1993).[9] The profit function for other types of intercommodity spreads can be derived using underlying cash-and-carry arbitrage conditions.

As discussed in Chapter 2, a basic building block for developing the analytics of spreading strategies is the profit function for the one-to-one intracommodity spread, a calendar spread involving equal position sizes on the two legs of the spread. Without loss of generality, assume that this trade is initiated at $t = 0$ and closed out at $t = 1$ and that the trader goes *short-the-nearby* (N) contract and *long-the-deferred* (T) contract. Taking $F(t,N)$ and $F(t,T)$ to be the futures prices observed at time t, the associated trading profile is given in Table 3.1. Spread profitability depends on the change in the *futures*

TABLE 3.1   Profit Function for a One-to-One Intracommodity Futures Spread Position

Date	Nearby position	Deferred position
$t = 0$	Short Q units at $F(0,N)$	Long Q units at $F(0,T)$
$t = 1$	Close-out position with long Q units at $F(1,N)$	Close-out position with short Q units at $F(1,T)$

Note: Taking Q to be always positive, the profit function (π) can be specified by observing that the profit for each leg of the spread is equal to the contract selling (short) price minus the purchase (long) price:

$$\pi/Q = \{F(0,N) - F(1,N)\} + \{F(1,T) - F(0,T)\}$$
$$= \{F(1,T) - F(1,N)\} - \{F(0,T) - F(0,N)\} \tag{3.1}$$

[8]Calendar spreads are also sometimes referred to as futures straddles (e.g., Peterson, 1977). However, both these terms also refer to option trading strategies. Schwager (1984, chap. 30–4) and Poitras (1997) provide a general overview of spread trading techniques.

[9]The soy crush spread involves trading the value of soybean contracts against the value of soybean meal and soybean oil contracts. The production relationship is defined by the number of pounds of meal and oil obtained when one bushel of soybeans is crushed. The crack spread connects the value of a crude oil contract with the gasoline and heating oil contracts. This spread refers to the process of "cracking" or distilling a barrel of oil into various components, the most important of which are heating oil and gasoline. Other types of possible production relationship spreads are discussed in Tzang and Leuthold (1990) and Schap (1992).

basis (not to be confused with the future basis of Section I). More precisely, the one-to-one intracommodity spread that is short-the-nearby and long-the-deferred will be profitable if the difference between the deferred and nearby prices widens (becomes more positive). The opposite would be true for the alternative spread, long-the-nearby and short-the-deferred.[10]

Analysis of Eq. (3.1) (Table 3.1) proceeds by introducing the general cash-and-carry arbitrage condition for futures contracts (e.g., Dubofsky, 1992; Poitras, 1991; Siegel and Siegel, 1990; Allen and Thurston, 1988; Hegde and Branch, 1985; Kawaller and Koch, 1984):

$$F(t,T) \equiv F(t,N)\{1 + ic(t,N,T)\} \tag{3.2}$$

In Eq. (3.2), the *implied carry*, $ic(t,N,T)$, is defined as the *net* cost of carrying the commodity from time N to time T observed at time t implied in the futures prices $F(t,N)$ and $F(t,T)$ (see Chapter 4, Section I). The cash-and-carry arbitrage interpretation of $ic(t,N,T)$ can be motivated by taking $F(t,N)$ to be $S(t)$, the price of the spot commodity, and examining the mechanics of the arbitrage connecting spot and futures prices. While somewhat more abstract, the futures-futures cash-and-carry arbitrage has the same logical mechanics as the spot-futures arbitrage. The functional determinants of the $ic(t,N,T)$ term will depend on the cash-and-carry arbitrage for a specific commodity. For example, gold will have an ic that depends primarily on interest charges of carrying gold through time while Treasury bonds will have an ic dependent on both the interest charges of carrying T-bonds as well as a carry return arising from interest earned on the underlying security.

Making appropriate substitutions of the arbitrage condition, Eq. (3.2), into the profit function, Eq. (3.1), and dropping the N, T notation for ic gives the result:

$$\pi/Q = F(1,N)\ ic(1) - F(0,N)\ ic(0)$$

Observing that $\Delta ic = ic(1) - ic(0)$ and $\Delta F = F(1,N) - F(0,N)$, basic algebra provides the fundamental result for the one-to-one spread profit function:

$$\pi/Q = ic(0)\ \Delta F(N) + F(1,N)\ \Delta ic \tag{3.3}$$

This demonstrates that π for the one-to-one spread depends on the change in two variables, ΔF and Δic. Except in special cases, the need to predict the behavior of two random variables in order to ascertain profitability can be problematic. Significantly, the technique of *tailing* the spread (e.g., Jones, 1981) involves altering the relative sizes of the nearby and deferred positions

[10]There are a number of pitfalls in the interpreting the spread trade profit function. For example, if the $t = 0$ difference between the deferred and the nearby prices were negative, then profitability for the short-nearby/long-deferred spread would require that the absolute value of the difference between the prices narrow.

in such a way that the ΔF term disappears. In this fashion, tailed intracommodity spreads can be used to speculate on changes in the implied *net* cost of carry without needing to adjust for changes in price levels. In addition, tailed spreads can be combined with other positions to create trading strategies such as the turtle.

As an example of how price level changes can affect spread profitability, consider the case of gold for the period November 9, 1979, to February 15, 1980. Over this period, interest rates were relatively unchanged; the benchmark 3-month T-bill rose only 11 basis points from 12.25 to 12.36. During this period, the Handy and Harman spot price rose from $389.75 to $667. Examining the June 80–June 81 Commodity Exchange (COMEX) gold futures spread for this period, the June 1980 contract rose from $420.80 to $703.50, while the June 1981 contract rose from $471.20 to $843. This resulted in a change in the futures spread from $50.40 to $139.50. Remembering that the futures spread *ic* for gold is primarily determined by interest rates, the impact of interest rate changes on the gold spread was reflected over the period March 3, 1980, to August 25, 1980. Over this period, the Handy and Harmon spot price was relatively unchanged, going from $633.75 to $634.75. During this period, interest rates, as reflected in the 3-month T-bill rate, fell from 13.38 to 9.41. Examining the October 1980–October 1981 COMEX gold futures spread over this period, the October 1980 contract fell from $709.50 to $629.70 while October 1981 fell from $849.50 to $719.40. This reflects a decline in the gold futures spread from $140 to $89.70.

C. Tailing the Spread

To motivate the profit function for a tailed spread, consider the trading profile for an intracommodity spread with potentially unequal position sizes. Letting the contract amounts be Q_N and Q_T, the short-the-nearby, long-the-deferred trade is depicted in Table 3.2. The tail for an intracommodity spread can be set

TABLE 3.2 Profit Function for a General Intracommodity Futures Spread Position

Date	Nearby position	Deferred position
$t = 0$	Short Q_N units at $F(0,N)$	Long Q_T units at $F(0,T)$
$t = 1$	Close-out position with long Q_N units at $F(1,N)$	Close-out position with short Q_T units at $F(1,T)$

Note: In this case, the profit function can be specified:

$$\pi(1,T) = \{F(0,N) - F(1,N)\}\, Q_N + \{F(1,T) - F(0,T)\}\, Q_T \tag{3.4}$$

by holding either spread leg constant and varying the other leg. To see this, set $Q_T = 1$. It can now be verified that $Q_N = F(0,T)/F(0,N)$ will give a trade profit function that depends only on Δic. Observing that $F(0,T)/F(0,N) = \{1 + ic(0)\}$ and substituting this result and $Q_T = 1$ into Eq. (3.4) (Table 3.2) gives:

$$\pi(1) = F(1,N) \Delta ic \qquad (3.5)$$

The case where $Q_N = 1$ and $Q_T = F(0,N)/F(0,T)$ gives virtually the same result:

$$\pi(1) = \{F(1,N)/(1 + ic(0))\} \Delta ic$$

Because the change in ic is the only random variable (Δ) in either profit function, the difference is not of practical importance.

To illustrate the use of a tail, consider the following gold futures prices that were available in February 1989:

June 1989	$379	August 1989	$382.90
June 1990	$404.80	August 1990	$409.20

For the June contracts, the 1-year spread gives $1 + ic(0) = 1.068$; for the August contracts, $1 + ic(0) = 1.069$. Using the tailing method that sets the number of deferred contracts equal to one involves taking 1.068 June 1989 nearby contracts for every one June 1990 deferred contract. By tailing, the dollar value of the gold underlying the nearby and deferred positions is equalized. In futures market terminology, this method of spread tailing is a *dollar equivalency* technique. Because futures contracts are only traded in whole numbers, it is necessary to gross the number of contracts up until an acceptable ratio is found. In this case, $14(1.068) = 14.952$. Hence, a ratio of 15 nearby for every 14 deferred contracts would appear to be acceptable; however, as the size of the spread trade positions grows, the more accurate the tail can be.

Because gold is typically at or near full carry, the size of the tail will depend on the prevailing level of interest rates. To see this, consider the following prices for gold futures prices for June 16, 1992:

June 1992	$343.10	August 1992	$344.90
June 1993	$355.80	August 1993	$358.40

Observing that for the June contracts $1 + ic(0) = 1.037$ and for the August contracts $1 + ic(0) = 1.039$, using the method that sets the deferred contract equal to one involves taking 1.039 August 1992 nearby contracts for every one August 1993 deferred contract. Again observing that futures contracts are only traded in whole numbers, it is necessary to gross the number of contracts up until an acceptable ratio is found. In this case, $24(1.039) = 24.936$. Hence, a ratio of 25 nearby for every 24 deferred contracts would appear to be an acceptable hedge ratio, subject to the caveat that as the size of the spread trade position grows, the more accurate the tail can be. The unusually large number of contracts required to tail the spread in June 1992 was driven by the historically low interest rates of this period.

The need to tail a spread depends on both the shape of the term structure of futures prices and the length of time between N and T. When prices across delivery months are relatively the same level or if there is no distant deferred deliveries available for trading, it is not necessary to tail. This is the case in a number of commodities. For example, in currencies there is often no trade in futures contracts over one year to delivery. Taking, say, a 6-month (September 1994/March 1995) spread in German DM, using the price quotes for August 8, 1994 (see Fig. 4.3) gives a tail of $.6311/.6327 = 1.0004$. For the Canadian dollar on that date, the same maturity for the contracts gives a tail of 1.0047. Neither of these numbers indicates that a tail is required unless the trade sizes go well beyond the allowable position limits. The story is different again for T-bond futures that admit both distant delivery dates and a typically sloped futures term structure. Using August 8, 1994 (see Fig. 3.3) quotes gives a September 1994/September 1995 tail of 1.0274. As will be seen when the specifics of intercommodity trades such as the turtle are considered, dollar equivalency is not the only possible tailing method. The process of setting the tail can also be done to attain profit functions that are dependent on components of ic and not just ic itself.

One interesting application of the concept of tailing occurs with the intra-commodity T-bond spread. In this case, the tailed spread can be used for speculating on changes in the shape of the yield curve (see Table 3.3). From Table 3.3, the connection between the payoff on a tailed T-bond spread and

TABLE 3.3 Profit Function for a Tailed T-Bond Spread

Date	Nearby (N) position	Deferred position (T)
$t = 0$	Short $[F(0,T)/F(0,N)]$ Q T-bonds at $F(0,N)$	Long Q T-bonds at $F(0,T)$
$t = 1$	Long $[F(0,T)/F(0,N)]Q$ at $F(1,N)$	Short Q at $F(1,T)$

Note: From Eq. (3.5), the profit function for the short-the-nearby, long-the-deferred tailed T-bond spread takes the form:

$$\pi(1) = F(1,N)\,\Delta ic = F(1,N)\{\Delta irr(N,T) - \Delta R(N,T)\}$$

where irr is the implied repo rate, the repurchase agreement financing rate implied in T-bond futures prices, and R is the return earned on the cash T-bond position during the period between the two delivery dates, N and T. With suitable modification, this type of profit function also applies to all other debt futures contracts.

shifts in the term structure of interest rates should be apparent. While more precise examination of the determination of the implied repo rate (*irr*) can be found in a number of sources (e.g., Siegel and Siegel, 1990, chap. 6; Rentzler, 1986), for purposes of analyzing the tailed T-bond spread *irr* can be taken to be a short-term interest rate, while the cash T-bond rate, being for > 15-year maturities, is a long-term rate.[11] From $F(0,T) = F(0,N)\{1 + irr(0,N,T) - R(0,N,T)\}$, where R $(0,N,T)$ is the carry return on the underlying T-bond (see Chapter 5, Section I) it follows that $F(0,T) < F(0,N)$ and the futures price term structure is downward sloping when the yield curve is upward sloping. By considering a variety of yield curve changes and allowing for changes in the spot T-bond rate, it can be verified that π on the tailed T-bond spread depends only on changes in yield curve shape; the level of the spot T-bond interest rate does not affect the profitability of the trade undertaken. This is not surprising, given that the spread is tailed; however, the positions involved in the tailed spread must be reversed when the yield curve is inverted. While a short-the-nearby, long-the-deferred spread is profitable when an upward sloping yield curve flattens, a long-the-nearby, short-the-deferred spread is profitable when an inverted yield curve flattens. Similarly, the positions will be reversed when a flat yield curve either inverts or becomes upward sloping.

Figure 3.3 and 3.4 provide various interest rate futures prices from August 8, 1994. Examining the T-bond futures prices in Fig. 3.3 reveals a downward-sloping futures price term structure. The more deferred the delivery date, the lower the price. This futures price structure is theoretically a result of the upward-sloping yield curve in the Treasury debt market, a result that is supported empirically by the Treasury yield curve observed on August 8, 1994 (see Fig. 4.4). A similar result applies for the Eurodollar futures prices (Fig. 3.4) and reflects the presence of an upward-sloping cash market yield curve. The theoretical motivation for the connection between the cash market yield curve and the term structure of Eurodollar futures prices is demonstrated in Chapter 6, Section III. That is the term structure of Eurodollar futures prices reflects the implied forward interest rates embedded in the Eurodollar cash market yield curve.

The analysis of the tailed T-bond spread can be illustrated diagrammatically. The discussion extends naturally to other types of interest rate futures contracts, such as Eurodollars. The two basic graphs required are provided in Graph 3.1, which captures the shape of the term structure of interest rates in the cash market, and Graph 3.2, which takes the information from the

[11]It is not possible to deal adequately with the various issues that are raised here. For example, direct comparison of the *irr* and the actual repo rate is distorted because of the various sellers' options to select the cheapest deliverable T-bond. In addition to illustrating how to derive the *irr* from T-bond futures, Siegel and Siegel (1990) also provide a more complete development of the *irr* − R relationship.

INTEREST RATE

TREASURY BONDS (CBT)—$100,000; pts. 32nds of 100%

	Open	High	Low	Settle	Change	Lifetime High	Lifetime Low	Open Interest
Sept	103-00	103-16	102-30	103-09	+ 6	118-26	90— 12	390,284
Dec	102-10	102-24	102-08	102-17	+ 5	118-08	91-19	73,842
Mr95	101-22	101-30	101-22	101-25	+ 5	116-20	98-20	4,218
June	101-05	101-08	101-04	101-04	+ 5	113-15	98-12	1,638
Sept	....	....	....	100-17	+ 5	112-15	97-28	673

Est vol 200,000; vol Fri 509,266; op int 470,763, +7,397.

TREASURY BONDS (MCE)—$50,000; pts. 32nds of 100%

	Open	High	Low	Settle	Change	Lifetime High	Lifetime Low	Open Interest
Sept	103-02	103-16	103-02	103-09	+ 8	115-20	100-02	14,067
Dec	102-14	102-24	102-14	102-17	+ 7	114-00	99-10	359

Est vol 3,500; vol Fri 5,328; open int 14,430, +51.

TREASURY NOTES (CBT)—$100,000; pts. 32nds of 100%

	Open	High	Low	Settle	Change	Lifetime High	Lifetime Low	Open Interest
Sept	104-01	104-09	103-31	104-05	+ 2	115-01	101-18	241,497
Dec	103-03	103-10	103-01	103-06	+ 1	114-21	100-25	24,587

Est vol 40,000; vol Fri 152,073; open int 266,143, +9,983.

5 YR TREAS NOTES (CBT)—$100,000; pts. 32nds of 100%

	Open	High	Low	Settle	Change	Lifetime High	Lifetime Low	Open Interest
Sept	03-295	04-025	03-295	104-00	....	10-195	102-12	180,491
Dec	03-075	103-10	03-055	03-075	....	104-18	101-26	10,898

Est vol 20,000; vol Fri 61,379; open int 191,389, +4,901.

2 YR TREAS NOTES (CBT)—$200,000, pts. 32nds of 100%

	Open	High	Low	Settle	Change	Lifetime High	Lifetime Low	Open Interest
Sept	02-232	102-25	02-232	02-235	− ¾	104-31	102-04	31,300
Dec	102-05	02-055	02-045	02-045	− ¾	02-187	02-045	610

Est vol 2,000; vol Fri 2,112; open int 31,910, +145.

30-DAY FEDERAL FUNDS (CBT)-$5 million; pts. of 100%

	Open	High	Low	Settle	Change	Lifetime High	Lifetime Low	Open Interest
Aug	95.56	95.57	95.56	95.57	+ .01	96.58	95.05	4,662
Sept	95.32	95.33	95.31	95.33	+ .02	96.44	94.81	3,083
Oct	95.08	95.10	95.08	95.09	+ .01	95.63	94.63	807
Nov	94.88	94.91	94.88	94.89	+ .01	95.52	94.50	311
Dec	94.62	94.62	94.62	94.62	....	96.00	94.46	102

Est vol 2,222; vol Fri 2,743; open int 9,053, +1,000.

TREASURY BILLS (CME)—$1 mil.; pts. of 100%

	Open	High	Low	Settle	Chg	Discount Settle	Chg	Open Interest
Sept	95.24	95.26	95.25	95.24	....	4.76	....	18,533
Dec	94.68	94.70	94.65	94.66	− .02	5.34	+ .02	9,198
Mr95	94.38	94.40	94.37	94.39	....	5.61	....	3,245

Est vol 1,559; vol Fri 3,962; open int 30,994, −905.

LIBOR-1 MO. (CME)—$3,000,000; points of 100%

	Open	High	Low	Settle	Chg	Discount Settle	Chg	Open Interest
Aug	95.27	95.30	95.27	95.29	+ .02	4.71	− .02	22,148
Sept	95.06	95.08	95.06	95.06	+ .01	4.94	− .01	9,640
Oct	94.86	94.87	94.86	94.86	+ .01	5.14	− .01	2,602
Nov	94.70	94.70	94.70	94.69	+ .01	5.31	− .01	2,376
Dec	93.97	93.97	93.97	93.97	....	6.03	....	1,594
Ja95	....	....	....	94.31	− .01	5.69	+ .01	384
Feb	....	....	....	94.19	− .01	5.81	+ .01	112
Mar	....	....	....	94.06	....	5.94	....	109
May	....	....	....	93.81	....	6.19	....	205

Est vol 5,304; vol Fri 12,937; open int 39,263, +2,351.

FIGURE 3.3 Interest rate futures prices. (*Source: The Wall Street Journal*, August 8, 1994. With permission.)

EURODOLLAR (CME) – \$1 million; pts of 100%

	Open	High	Low	Settle	Chg	Yield Settle	Chg	Open Interes
Sept	94.82	94.83	94.80	94.81	+ .01	5.19	– .01	427,28(
Dec	94.09	94.12	94.08	94.09	....	5.91	....	496,26!
Mr95	93.85	93.87	93.84	93.85	....	6.15	....	333,92;
June	93.55	93.55	93.52	93.53	....	6.47	....	249,69;
Sept	93.26	93.27	93.25	93.26	....	6.74	....	215,03;
Dec	93.00	93.00	92.97	92.99	....	7.01	....	150,22!
Mr96	92.93	92.93	92.90	92.92	....	7.08	....	130,65(
June	92.82	92.82	92.80	92.81	....	7.19	....	106,41&
Sept	92.72	92.73	92.71	92.72	+ .01	7.28	– .01	97,391
Dec	92.56	92.58	92.55	92.56	+ .01	7.44	– .01	76,780
Mr97	92.55	92.57	92.54	92.56	+ .02	7.44	– .02	68,643
June	92.47	92.49	92.46	92.48	+ .02	7.52	– .02	57,107
Sept	92.40	92.42	92.39	92.41	+ .02	7.59	– .02	52,734
Dec	92.26	92.28	92.25	92.27	+ .02	7.73	– .02	50,066
Mr98	92.27	92.29	92.26	92.28	+ .02	7.72	– .02	36,539
June	92.19	92.21	92.18	92.20	+ .02	7.80	– .02	31,795
Sept	92.11	92.14	92.11	92.13	+ .02	7.87	– .02	23,814
Dec	92.00	92.02	91.99	92.01	+ .02	7.99	– .02	19,722
Mr99	92.02	92.04	92.02	92.03	+ .02	7.96	– .02	15,964
June	91.95	91.98	91.95	91.96	+ .02	8.04	– .02	8,867
Sept	91.89	91.91	91.89	91.90	+ .02	8.10	– .02	8,182
Dec	91.78	91.79	91.78	91.78	+ .02	8.22	– .02	6,986
Mr00	....	....	....	91.81	+ .01	8.19	– .01	7,109
June	....	....	....	91.76	+ .01	8.24	– .01	5,273
Sept	....	....	....	91.71	+ .01	8.29	– .01	7,028
Dec	....	....	....	91.61	+ .01	8.39	– .01	5,862
Mr01	....	....	....	91.67	+ .01	8.33	– .01	6,923
June	....	....	....	91.64	+ .01	8.36	– .01	4,428
Sept	....	....	....	91.62	+ .01	8.38	– .01	2,373
Dec	....	....	....	91.54	+ .01	8.46	– .01	2,429
Mr02	91.59	91.59	91.59	91.60	+ .01	8.40	– .01	2,009
June	91.60	91.60	91.60	91.61	+ .01	8.39	– .01	2,141
Sept	....	....	....	91.60	+ .01	8.40	– .01	1,785
Dec	....	....	....	91.52	+ .01	8.48	– .01	1,354
Mr03	....	....	....	91.57	+ .01	8.43	– .01	1,516
June	....	....	....	91.55	+ .01	8.45	– .01	1,158
Sept	....	....	....	91.56	+ .01	8.44	– .01	1,071
Dec	....	....	....	91.50	+ .01	8.50	– .01	1,385
Mr04	....	....	....	91.56	+ .01	8.44	– .01	1,124

Est vol 193,687; vol Fri 775,986; open int 2,692,116, +42,309.

FIGURE 3.4   Eurodollar futures prices. (*Source: The Wall Street Journal*, August 8, 1994. With permission.)

assumed term structure shape and translates this into a term structure of T-bond futures prices using the fundamental arbitrage relationship for futures. The specific shapes that appear in the graphs apply to an upward-sloping (normal backwardation) yield curve. From $F(0,T) = F(0,N)$ $\{1 + irr(0,N,T) - R(0,N,T)\}$, it follows that $F(0,T) < F(0,N)$ and the futures

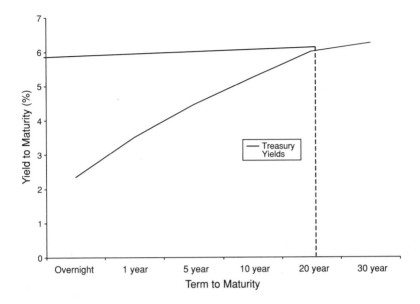

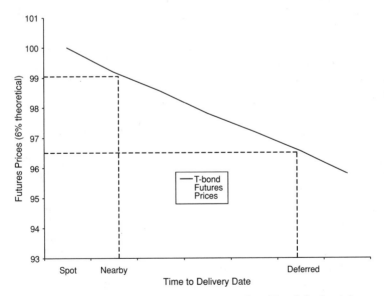

GRAPHS 3.1 AND 3.2   The relationship between the cash yield and the bond futures term structure. (Cheapest deliverable is 20 year maturity.)

price term structure is downward sloping when the yield curve is upward sloping. Analysis of the trading implications of specific changes in yield curve shape now follows by superimposing the "new" yield curve and futures price structure over the initial values.

The method required for determining the position type and trade profitability of the tailed T-bond spread is illustrated in Graphs 3.3 and 3.4, where the "new" yield curve is flat ($irr = R$). In these graphs the yield curve is assumed to pivot in such a way that the 15- to 20+-year yield remains unchanged. In this way, the cash price that anchors the futures price structure is unchanged. Taking points on the initial price schedule to be lower case, and the "new" schedule to be upper case, then the profitability of the short-nearby, long-deferred spread follows: $(a - A) + (B - b) > 0$. It follows from switching the time dates that a long-nearby, short-deferred spread will be profitable when the yield curve steepens and the cash T-bond yield is unchanged. By redrawing the "new" yield curve to allow for changes in the spot T-bond rate, it can be verified that the level of the spot rate does not affect the type of trade undertaken. This is not surprising, given that the spread is tailed. However, as illustrated in Graphs 3.5 and 3.6, the trades are reversed when the yield curve is inverted. In other words, the long-nearby, short-deferred spread is profitable when an inverted yield curve flattens. Similarly, the short-nearby, long-deferred spread is profitable when the yield curve inverts.

In addition to intracommodity spread trades such as tailed T-bond or T-note spreads, *intercommodity* spreads with naked positions in futures for different securities also provide an array of spreading opportunities. For purposes of speculating on changes in yield curve shape, examples would include T-notes with T-bonds (the NOB spread); T-notes with T-bills, and T-bonds with T-bills (the BOB spread).[12] The profit functions for these types of spreads are of the form:

$$\pi = \{Q_1[F(1,T)] - Q_2[G(1,T)]\} - \{Q_1[F(0,T)] - Q_2[G(0,T)]\}$$

These types of intercommodity spreads usually leave a hedge ratio to be calculated. To illustrate the method involved, recall that "equalization of basis points" is a convenient method for calculating dollar value hedge ratios. For a T-bill/T-bond spread, the T-bill has a basis point (bp) value of $25. The T-bond bp value depends on the level and direction of change in rates. Suppose, for example, that rates are expected to change from 8 to 7% ($100\,bp$). Using the old 8% coupon T-bond futures contract, observe that the T-bond at 8% has $F(0,N) = \$100,000$. The price of the T-bond at 7% is calculated as $110,590; a $10,590 change in value for a 100-bp change results in $105.90 per bp. This gives a hedge ratio of slightly more than 4/1. Similar calculations for going

---

[12]Yano (1989) provides an excellent discussion of these and various other strategies.

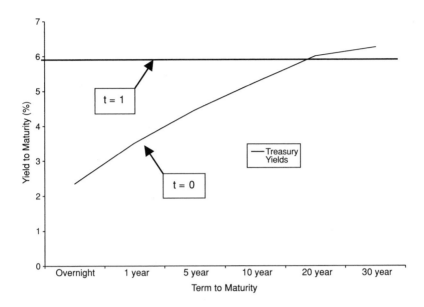

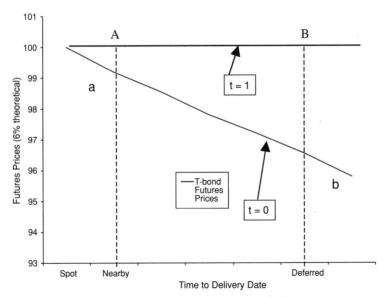

GRAPHS 3.3 AND 3.4   Example: upward-sloping to flat yield curve.

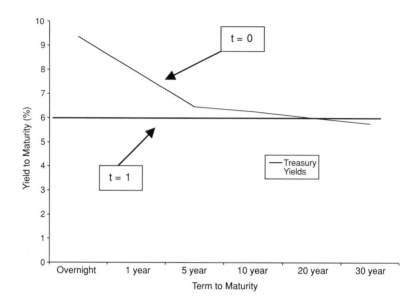

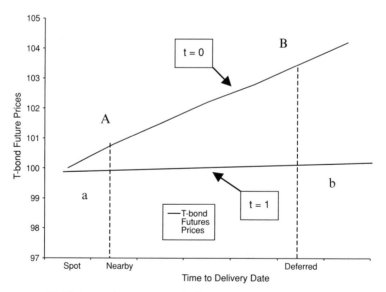

GRAPHS 3.5 AND 3.6   Example: from inverted to flat yield curve.

from 8 to 9% gives a \$9130 change or \$91.30 per *bp*. A hedge ratio of approximately 42 to 10 is indicated. This illustrates the heuristic result that the BOB hedge ratio is 4/1 when the T-bond is around par.

Another type of spreading strategy involves trading spread positions against spread positions. This can be done both intra- and intercommodity. When the spreads are all intracommodity, the resulting trades are known as butterflies and condors. When the spreads are in different commodities, the trades are generically referred to as tandems or stereos. Analytically, some of the most interesting trades, such as the stereo NOB (Yano, 1989) and the Treasury bill with Eurodollar (TED) tandem (Poitras 1989b, 1998a), are of this variety. A final type of spreading strategy arises from production relationships. Examples of these intercommodity trades are the soy crush (Rechner and Poitras, 1993) and the crack spread (Poitras, 2001b). The soy crush is based on the crushing of soybeans into soybean meal and soybean oil. The crack spread is based on the distillation of crude oil into heating oil and gasoline. The hedge ratios for the various positions are based on the underlying production relationships. While these relationships are relatively exact in the soy crush and crack spreads, other types of less deterministic production spreads are also possible, such as live cattle with feeder cattle and corn.

III. BASIS RELATIONSHIPS

A. TYPES OF BASIS

In market terminology, a *basis* refers to the difference between two prices. The study of basis relationships is fundamental to understanding cash markets as well as futures and forward markets.[13] Various types of basis relationships are of interest. One basis relationship that is of theoretical interest is the *maturity basis*, the difference between the delivery date price of a futures contract and the corresponding spot price. It is often theoretically convenient to assume that the maturity basis is zero, implying that $F(T,T) = S(T)$. The maturity basis is usually zero for forward contracts, which are typically written with delivery in mind. For futures the maturity basis will only be zero where the spot and futures prices both refer to the deliverable commodity. When the maturity basis for a deliverable spot commodity deviates from zero, a profit opportunity is provided for delivery arbitragers operating on the futures exchange. Evaluation of the maturity basis is often complicated by the grade

---

[13]Even though the following discussion is presented in terms of futures contracts, the relevant concepts also apply directly for forward contracts. However, the diversity of forward trading requires numerous secondary qualifications and asides to be introduced that obscure the presentation of the essential points. For this reason, futures contracts are used.

and location characteristics of the spot commodity. Even for futures contracts, the deliverable standard grade specified in the futures contract often permits multiple delivery grades or locations. For example, Chicago Board of Trade (CBOT) Treasury bond futures contracts permit delivery of any Treasury bond with maturity greater than 15 years, and nonferrous London Metals Exchange (LME) contracts can allow for delivery in ports such as Bristol or Hamburg.[14] In addition to the complications this presents to delivery arbitragers, the presence of *multiple delivery specifications* requires the *cheapest deliverable* commodity to be identified in order to determine the precise commodity grade and location being traded with a futures or forward contract.[15]

The *quality basis* is a development on the maturity basis. The quality basis relates to the difference between prices for different grades of a commodity. Consumers encounter various types of quality basis decisions everyday. For example, automobile drivers have to decide whether to buy regular or premium gas when filling up. The difference between these two prices is a quality basis. When the maturity basis is not zero, the difference between spot and futures prices on the delivery date will be a quality basis. Numerous examples of the quality basis are provided in Figs. 3.5–3.7. In Fig. 3.5, for New York delivery, Brazilian coffee is selling for $1.74/lb while Colombian coffee is selling for $1.84/lb. Engelhard-refined industrial- and fabrication-quality platinum are selling for $408 and $508 per troy ounce, respectively. Copper cathodes and copper scrap are selling for $1.11 and $.87 per pound, respectively. In Fig. 3.7, Arabian heavy and light oil in Rotterdam are selling for $15.05 and $16.25 per barrel, respectively.

Price differences due to variations in quality are determined by market considerations and are not typically constant. This variation will be of concern to hedgers for determining the hedge position for the spot commodity and identifying the appropriate deliverable commodity to use for calculating the cash-futures basis. Because of possible variation in the quality basis, futures contracts with multiple delivery specifications must provide an acceptable method to account for changes in the quality basis of deliverable commodities. The quality basis is also of relevance for some financial commodities. For example, because the contract permits a range of bonds to be deliverable, delivery arbitragers in T-bonds require quality basis information for determining the cheapest T-bond to deliver.

---

[14]The specifications for the T-bond deliverable often are stated as 20 years to call. However, due to the introduction of strip issues in the mid-1980s, the U.S. Treasury dropped the use of the 5-year call provision on long-term bonds. Presently, there are no callable T-bonds eligible for delivery. Hence, the 15-year maturity is the applicable minimum maturity.

[15]A number of useful studies, both theoretical and empirical, are available on multiple delivery specifications and the cheapest deliverable application (e.g., Hemler, 1990; Chance and Hemler, 1993; Cita and Lien, 1992; Kamara and Siegel, 1987; Lien, 1989a,b; Cornell, 1997).

CASH PRICES

Monday, August 8, 1994.
(Closing Market Quotations)

GRAINS AND FEEDS'

	Mon	Fri	Yr.Ago
Barley, top-quality Mpls., bu	2.30-.50	2.50	2.35
Bran, wheat middlings, KC ton	63.-65.0	63.-65.0	53.00
Corn, No. 2 yel. Cent. III. bu	bp2.11	2.09½	2.23½
Corn Gluten Feed, Midwest, ton ..	88.-95.0	88.-95.0	78.00
Cottonseed Meal,			
Clksdle, Miss. ton	140-142½	140.00	172.50
Hominy Feed,Cent. III. ton	60.00	60.00	58.00
Meat-Bonemeal, 50% pro. III. ton.	192.50	192.50	n.a.
Oats, No. 2 milling, Mpls., bu	1.39¼-44¼	1.38½-43½	1.61¾
Sorghum, (Milo) No. 2 Gulf cwt ...	4.30	4.26	4.36
Soybean Meal,			
Cent. III., 44% protein-ton	164-168	163½-67½	206.00
Soybean Meal,			
Cent. III., 48% protein-ton	177-181	176½-80½	218.00
Soybeans, No. 1 yel Cent.-III. bu ..	bp5.60	5.58	6.57½
Wheat,			
Spring 14%-pro Mpls. bu	3.77¼-82¾	3.77¾-82¾	4.91¼
Wheat, No. 2 sft red, St.Lou. bu ...	bp3.17½	3.17½	3.02½
Wheat, No. 2 hard KC, bu	3.54¼	3.54¼	3.24¼
Wheat, No. 1 sft wht, del Port Ore	3.51	3.52	3.41

FOODS

	Mon	Fri	Yr.Ago
Beef, Carcass, Equiv.Index Value,			
choice 1-3,550-700lbs.	103.60	103.75	111.60
Beef, Carcass, Equiv.Index Value,			
select 1-3,550-700lbs.	95.85	96.40	108.05
Broilers, Dressed "A" NY lb	x.5330	.5373	.5690
Broilers, 12-Cty Comp Wtd Av	.5385	.5379	.5985
Butter, AA, Chgo., lb.	.75½	.75½	.78
Cocoa, Ivory Coast, $metric ton ...	g1,627	1,667	1,176
Coffee, Brazilian, NY lb.	n1.74	1.97	.64½
Coffee, Colombian, NY lb.	n1.84	c2.05	.80½
Eggs, Lge white, Chgo doz.	.60-.65	.60-.65	.69½
Flour, hard winter KC cwt	9.40	9.40	9.95
Hams, 17-20 lbs, Mid-US lb fob	.53	.53	.63½
Hogs, Iowa-S.Minn. avg. cwt	43.25	43.25	48.00
Hogs, Omaha avg cwt	44.00	43.50	47.50
Pork Bellies, 12-14 lbs Mid-US lb ..	.42-.44	.39-.42	.47½
Pork Loins, 14-18 lbs. Mid-US lb ...	1.16-.17	1.16-.17	1.11
Steers, Tex.-Okla. ch avg cwt	70.50	z	76.75
Steers, Feeder, Okl Cty, av cwt ...	89.50	88.50	97.50
Sugar, cane, raw, world, lb. fob ...	.1187	.1196	.0949

FATS AND OILS

	Mon	Fri	Yr.Ago
Coconut Oil, crd, N. Orleans lb. ...	xxn.29¾	.29½	.22½
Corn Oil, crd wet mill, Chgo. lb. ..	n.25	.25	.21
Corn Oil, crd dry mill, Chgo. lb. ...	n.28¼	.28¼	.21½
Grease, choice white, Chgo lb.	n.16¾	.16¾	.14
Lard, Chgo lb.	n.18¼	.18¼	.15½
Palm Oil, ref. bl. deod. N.Orl. lb. .	n.30	.28	.20
Soybean Oil, crd, Decatur, lb.	.2454	.2468	.2354
Tallow, bleachable, Chgo lb.	n.18¼	.18¼	.15¼
Tallow, edible, Chgo lb.	n.19	.19	.16

FIGURE 3.5   Cash prices for selected commodities. (*Source: The Wall Street Journal*, August 8, 1994. With permission.)

FIBERS AND TEXTILES

Burlap, 10 oz 40-in N Y yd	n.2750	.2750	.2400
Cotton 1 1/16 str lw-md Mphs lb ...	.6985	.7087	.5423
Wool, 64s, Staple, Terr. del. lb.	2.30	2.30	1.37

METALS

Aluminum			
ingot lb. del. Midwest	q.69-.71	.69-.71	.56½
Copper			
cathodes lb.	p1.11	1.11	.90
Copper Scrap, No 2 wire N Y lb	h.87½	.87½	.65½
Lead, lb.	q.36988	.38150	.33½
Mercury 76 lb. flask N Y	q200.00	200.00	185.00
Steel Scrap 1 hvy mlt Chgo ton	135.-138.	135.-138.	112.50
Tin composite lb.	q3.4652	3.4752	3.3252
Zinc Special High grade lb	p.46500	.46500	.44750

MISCELLANEOUS

Rubber, smoked sheets, N Y lb. ...	n.66¾	.65	.43¼
Hides, hvy native steers lb., fob ...	.89	.89	.79

PRECIOUS METALS

Gold, troy oz			
Engelhard indust bullion	378.89	379.59	383.00
Engelhard fabric prods	397.83	398.57	402.15
Handy & Harman base price	377.60	378.30	381.70
Handy & Harman fabric price ..	379.10	379.80	z
London fixing AM 377.70 PM ...	377.60	378.30	381.70
Krugerrand, whol	a384.00	384.50	385.50
Maple Leaf, troy oz.	a390.00	390.50	397.00
American Eagle, troy oz.	a390.00	390.50	397.00
Platinum, (Free Mkt.)	406.00	410.50	394.50
Platinum, indust (Engelhard)	408.00	411.00	396.00
Platinum, fabric prd (Engelhard)	508.00	511.00	496.00
Palladium, indust (Engelhard) ...	152.00	152.00	141.00
Palladium, fabrc prd (Englhard)	167.00	167.00	156.00
Silver, troy ounce			
Engelhard indust bullion	5.140	5.175	4.730
Engelhard fabric prods	5.551	5.589	5.108
Handy & Harman base price	5.130	5.160	4.720
Handy & Harman fabric price ..	5.156	5.186	z
London Fixing (in pounds)			
Spot (U.S. equiv. $5.1130)	3.3165	3.3670	3.1260
3 months	3.3590	3.4100	3.1705
6 months	3.4085	3.4605	3.2140
1 year	3.5225	3.5835	3.2920
Coins, whol $1,000 face val	a3,643	3,673	3,397

a-Asked. b-Bid. bp-Country elevator bids to producers. c-Corrected. d-Dealer market. e-Estimated. f-Dow Jones International Petroleum Report. g-Main crop, ex-dock, warehouses, Eastern Seaboard, north of Hatteras. h.-Reuters. i.-f.o.b. warehouse. k-Dealer selling prices in lots of 40,000 pounds or more, f.o.b. buyer's works. n-Nominal. p-Producer price. q-Metals Week. r-Rail bids. s-Thread count 78x54. x-Less than truckloads. z-Not quoted. xx-f.o.b. tankcars.

FIGURE 3.5 *(continued)*

GRAIN

BY PARRISH and HEIMBECKER

(Prices quoted in tonnes)
Domestic 1 CW 13.5 wheat, Thunder Bay, 187.24, Export 1 CW 13.5 wheat, St. Lawrence, 235.86, Export 1 CW durum, St. Lawrence, 289.28.

Domestic milling wheat — CIF Bayports: 1 CW durum wheat 270.21, 1 CW 14.5 wheat 236.23, 1 CW 13.5 wheat 208.24, 2 CW 13.5 wheat 200.93, 1 CW 12.5 wheat 206.93; 2 CW 12.5 wheat 198.38.

FEEDING GRADES

Sample wheat DGC 119.20; 3 CW oats 140.50; 1 CW barley 112.00, 1 feed screening 108.00.

ONTARIO GRAIN

Approximate bid price track shipping point.
2 white oats 115.00; Ontario feed oats 90.00; Ontario barley 95.00; 2 winter wheat milling 169.58, 2 soybeans 273.10, 2 rye 100.00; 2 yellow corn 129.82; 3 yellow corn 128.63.

WINNIPEG CASH PRICES

Feed oats: 1 cw 106.40; 2 cw 106.40; 3 cw 104.40; mixed grain oats; 94.40.

Feed barley (Thunder Bay): 1 cw 94.90; 2 cw 92.90; mixed grain barley 84.90.

Rye: 1 cw 112.60; 2 cw; 110.60; 3 cw 82.60.

Flax: 1 cw 271.60; 2 cw 269.60; 3 cw 236.60.

Canola: In store Thunder Bay No. 1 Canada 473.60; In store Vancouver No. 1 Canada 481.30.

Feed Wheat: 3 red spring: 109.70; Can Feed: 103.70.

WHEAT BOARD

Export wheat, St. Lawrence: 1 cw 13.5 pct; 235.86; 1 cw 11.5 pct; 225.26; 2 cw 13.5 pct; 230.26; 2 cw 11.5 pct; 220.26; 3 cw 220.26; 1 durum 294.37; 2 durum 289.53; 3 durum 284.53.

Malting barley (domestic), Thunder Bay: Special Select 6-row; 169.00; Select 6-row 166.50; Special Select 2-row; 176.00; Select 2-row 173.50.

FIGURE 3.6   Cash prices for Canadian grain. (*Source: Globe and Mail*, August 8, 1994. With permission.)

Another related type of basis relationship is the *location basis*, which refers to the difference between the price of the same commodity at two different locations (e.g., live hogs in Des Moines and Chicago or winter wheat in Topeka and Kansas City). An example of a location basis is provided in Fig. 3.6 for No. 1 canola in Vancouver ($481.30/tonne) and in Thunder Bay ($473.60/tonne). For many of the nonfinancial commodities, including canola, transportation costs have an important impact on the location basis. In addition to transport costs, a number of other factors can impact the location basis, such as local supply-and-demand considerations. Information on the behavior of the location basis is important for hedgers to determine hedging strategies. For hedgers, the relevant location basis is the difference between the local price of the relevant spot commodity being hedged and the price of the commodity deliverable against the futures contract. Where multiple delivery locations are permitted, the location basis can also be important for determining which location is the cheapest for purposes of making delivery. For many commodities, price quotes combine the grade and location basis, such as W. Texas intermediate crude oil in Cushing, OK, at $19.75 per barrel and Brent Sea crude at $17.85 per barrel in Rotterdam (see Fig. 3.7).

When referring to *the basis*, without further adjectives, reference is usually being made to the difference between an appropriate forward or futures price and the cash price: $F(0,T) - S(0)$. This form of basis is also referred to as the cash basis or the cash-futures/cash-forward basis. Certain markets have

OIL PRICES

Monday August 8, 1994.

CRUDE GRADES	Mon	Fri	Yr. Ago
OFFSHORE-d			
European "spot" or free market prices			
Arab lt.	h16.25	16.55	13.95
Arab hvy.	h15.05	15.35	11.55
Iran, lt.	h17.30	17.60	14.90
Forties	h17.95	18.15	16.60
Brent	h17.85	18.15	16.50
Bonny lt.	h18.05	18.35	16.95
Urals-Medit.	h17.05	18.55	14.85

DOMESTIC-f
Spot market
W. Tex. Int Cush

	Mon	Fri	Yr. Ago
(1775-1875) (Sep)	h19.40	19.30	17.55
W.Tx.sour, Midl (1550-1740) .	h18.50	18.40	15.65
La. sw. St.Ja (1750-1870)	h19.50	19.35	17.80
No. Slope del USGULF	hn17.75	17.65	15.80

Open-market crude oil values in Northwest Europe around
17:50 GMT in dlrs per barrel, for main loading ports in country
of origin for prompt loading, except as indicated.

REFINED PRODUCTS

Fuel Oil, No. 2 NY gal.	g.4975	.4905	.4790
Diesel Fuel, 0.05 S.			
NY harbor low sulfur	g.5100	.5010	n.a.
Gasoline, unlded, premium			
NY gal.	g.7110	.7145	.6145
Gasoline, unlded, reg.			
NY gal.	g.5915	.5880	.5345
Propane, Mont Belvieu,			
Texas, gal.	g na	.3040	.3065
Butane, normal, Mont Belvieu,			
Texas, gal.	g na	.3540	.3615

RAW PRODUCTS

Natural Gas

Henry Hub, $ per mmbtu .	g1.57½	1.65	n.a.

a-Asked. b-Bid. c-Corrected. d-as of 11 a.m. EST in Northwest Europe. f-As of 4 p.m. EST. Refiners' posted buying
prices are in parentheses. g-Provided by Telerate Systems.
h-Dow Jones International Petroleum Report. n.a.-Not available. z-Not quoted. n-Nominal. r-Revised.

FIGURE 3.7   Cash prices for oil. (*Source: The Wall Street Journal*, August 8, 1994. With permission.)

specialized terminology for the basis; for example, in foreign exchange markets the basis is referred to as the *swap rate* or *swap points*. Comparing the cash prices in Figs. 3.5–3.7 with the futures prices for grain and oil in Figs. 3.8 and 3.9 reveals that, when the price of the deliverable spot commodity is correctly identified, the nearby futures contract price is almost identical with

Monday, August 8, 1994
Open Interest Reflects Previous Trading Day

	Open	High	Low	Settle	Change	Lifetime High	Low	Open Interest

GRAINS AND OILSEEDS

CORN (CBT) 5,000 bu.; cents per bu.

	Open	High	Low	Settle	Change	High	Low	Int
Sept	216¼	222½	215½	219¾	+ 2½	292¼	214¾	39,811
Dec	218½	225¼	217¾	222¾	+ 3	277	217	123,332
Mr95	226½	233¾	226½	231½	+ 3	282½	226	24,926
May	233¼	240¼	233	238¼	+ 3¼	285	232½	10,169
July	237½	244¾	237	242½	+ 3¼	285½	236½	9,160
Sept	245	245	244	244	+ 3	270½	239	610
Dec	241¾	247	241¾	245¼	+ 2½	263	235½	4,920
Dc96	....	....	....	243	+ 2	257	239	129

Est vol 50,000; vol Fri 22,558; open int 213,057, −906.

OATS (CBT) 5,000 bu.; cents per bu.

Sept	118¼	121	118¼	120¼	+ ¾	154½	111½	5,327
Dec	119¾	122	119¾	121	+ ¼	157¼	116	6,882
Mr95	126¾	127¼	126¼	126¼	+ ¼	152¾	121½	483
May	....	....	....	129¾	+ ¼	151	125	1,025

Est vol 2,000; vol Fri 1,606; open int 13,657, −81.

WHEAT (CBT) 5,000 bu.; cents per bu.

Sept	333½	336½	333	334½	....	357¼	302	14,594
Dec	347	350½	346½	348¼	− ½	365	309	35,556
Mr95	354	357	353½	354½	− ¾	364½	327	9,145
May	349	349¾	347	348¾	− 2	356½	325	557
July	331½	332½	331¼	332	− ¼	342¾	311½	1,135

Est vol 11,000; vol Fri 9,206; open int 60,989, −275.

WHEAT (KC) 5,000 bu.; cents per bu.

Sept	344½	347	343¾	344¾	− ¼	355	302½	15,052
Dec	352¾	354½	351	351¾	− 1	360	312½	16,992
Mr95	353	354½	352¾	352½	....	359½	326½	5,189
May	346	346	345	345	+ 2½	346½	321½	418
July	332½	332½	332	332	+ ¾	343	316½	389

Est vol 4,431; vol Fri 6,054; open int 38,042, −252.

WHEAT (MPLS) 5,000 bu.; cents per bu.

Sept	342	344	341	342¾	....	358	300	6,124
Dec	345	347½	344¾	346¼	+ ¾	360	304	5,359
Mr95	351	352	350	351½	+ 1½	363	325¼	683

Est vol 2,649; vol Fri 2,564; open int 12,264, −356.

RICE-ROUGH (MCE) 2000 cwt; $ per cwt

Sept	6.580	6.580	6.550	6.580	− .010	10.100	5.990	1,008
Nov	6.730	6.800	6.730	6.780	+ .055	9.650	5.950	930
Ja95	....	....		6.990	+ .040	9.700	6.230	122
Mar	....	....		7.180	+ .040	9.630	6.340	480

Est vol 100; vol Fri 187; open int 2,624, −89.

CANOLA (WPG) 20 metric tons; Can. $ per ton

Aug	394.00	404.00	394.00	404.00	+ 15.00	514.50	321.50	623
Sept	366.00	382.40	366.00	381.40	+ 13.20	412.00	315.00	7,047
Nov	361.50	377.50	361.50	375.70	+ 12.40	401.00	316.00	26,829
Ja95	364.00	379.00	364.00	376.00	+ 11.40	401.50	317.50	9,829
Mar	367.00	380.00	367.00	378.10	+ 11.10	403.90	331.00	11,444
June	380.50	383.70	376.00	381.00	+ 11.30	409.50	346.50	1,887

Est vol 5,625; vol Fri 3,700; open int 57,659, +714.

FIGURE 3.8 Futures prices for grains and oilseeds. (*Source: The Wall Street Journal*, August 8, 1994. With permission.)

SOYBEANS (CBT) 5,000 bu.; cents per bu.

Aug	574½	588½	574	584	+ 7½	735	571¼	7,519
Sept	562½	577	562½	570¾	+ 4¼	708½	560½	14,448
Nov	557	569	556	563¼	+ 3	699	551	71,774
Ja95	565½	576½	564	571¼	+ 2¾	704	560	11,040
Mar	573	585	573	580½	+ 3	705	569	4,068
May	580	591½	580	587¼	+ 3¼	705½	575½	3,094
July	585	596	585	590¾	+ 3	706½	578½	5,571
Aug	588	591	588	590½	+ 2½	594½	579	128
Nov	589½	595½	589	592	+ 2½	645	578½	2,610

Est vol 50,000; vol Fri 27,974; open int 120,274, + +171.

SOYBEAN MEAL (CBT) 100 tons; $ per ton.

Aug	174.00	175.90	173.30	174.90	+ .20	225.00	173.30	8,491
Sept	171.70	174.90	171.60	173.30	+ .60	210.00	171.60	19,098
Oct	171.00	173.90	170.80	172.00	+ .40	207.50	170.80	10,081
Dec	170.70	174.00	170.70	172.00	+ .80	209.00	170.60	31,963
Ja95	171.50	174.40	171.50	173.00	+ .60	207.50	171.50	4,527
Mar	173.50	176.00	173.30	174.90	+ .60	207.50	173.00	4,971
May	174.80	176.80	174.50	175.20	+ .20	207.00	174.00	3,178
July	175.90	179.00	175.90	177.20	+ 1.20	206.00	175.80	1,595
Aug	179.50	179.50	179.50	178.50	+ 1.70	181.30	178.00	108

Est vol 20,000; vol Fri 15,593; open int 84,036, +593.

SOYBEAN OIL (CBT) 60,000 lbs.; cents per lb.

Aug	24.60	24.84	24.49	24.54	− .12	30.65	21.65	4,739
Sept	24.55	24.82	24.45	24.49	− .11	30.34	22.40	22,168
Oct	24.30	24.60	24.21	24.30	− .10	29.54	22.10	15,528
Dec	23.95	24.39	23.90	24.07	+ .04	28.87	22.00	36,035
Ja95	23.95	24.25	23.90	24.05	+ .05	28.55	22.65	4,344
Mar	23.97	24.24	23.92	24.03	+ .01	28.30	22.95	4,808
May	23.90	24.04	23.90	23.99	− .01	28.05	22.93	3,510
July	23.85	24.05	23.85	23.96	+ .04	27.85	23.00	1,583
Aug	23.75	24.10	23.75	23.90	+ .10	27.20	22.95	154

Est vol 22,000; vol Fri 20,625; open int 92,922, −2,168.

FIGURE 3.8 (*continued*)

the spot price of the appropriate deliverable commodity. To make the relevant comparisons needed to evaluate the basis, it is necessary to identify the deliverable commodity associated with the futures contract of interest by referencing the contract specifications from the relevant exchange website. This exercise will reveal that, even though it is not always possible to precisely reconcile cash market quotes with futures market quotes, various commodities such as gold, silver, crude oil, and soybean meal can be seen to have a near zero maturity basis.

Having established the correspondence between the prices of the cash commodity and nearby futures contract, examine Figs. 3.8 and 3.9 to determine the behavior of prices for futures contracts as delivery dates get progressively more deferred. Significant deviations between spot and futures prices can be observed. For example, in Fig. 3.8 soybean futures prices exhibit a

CRUDE OIL, Light Sweet (NYM) 1,000 bbls.; $ per bbl.

Sept	19.35	19.70	19.35	19.42 +	.11	20.78	14.50	86,504
Oct	na	19.35	19.06	19.10 +	.13	20.73	14.65	62,136
Nov	na	19.05	18.84	18.87 +	.15	20.69	14.82	33,481
Dec	na	18.85	18.64	18.68 +	.16	21.25	14.93	47,835
Ja93	na	18.66	18.49	18.53 +	.17	20.12	15.15	22,220
Feb	na	18.53	18.38	18.44 +	.18	19.60	15.28	14,297
Mar	na	18.45	18.30	18.37 +	.19	20.66	15.42	14,039
Apr	na	18.37	18.25	18.31 +	.20	19.68	15.55	6,516
May	na	18.30	18.24	18.27 +	.20	19.23	15.69	9,622
June	18.30	18.32	18.27	18.26 +	.20	21.21	15.73	19,267
July	na	18.32	18.25	18.27 +	.20	18.85	16.28	6,554
Aug	....	....		18.28 +	.20	18.85	16.90	4,600
Sept	18.35	18.35	18.35	18.29 +	.20	19.84	16.28	7,002
Oct		....	....	18.30 +	.20	20.08	16.42	2,192
Nov		....	....	18.32 +	.20	18.87	17.15	3,507
Dec	18.40	18.45	18.40	18.34 +	.20	20.80	16.50	17,754
Ja96		....	....	18.37 +	.21	18.89	18.35	749
Feb		....	....	18.40 +	.22	18.84	18.54	376
Mar		....	....	18.43 +	.22	18.80	17.15	5,132
June		....	....	18.49 +	.22	20.40	17.22	12,218
Dec		....	....	18.73 +	.24	20.40	17.65	21,007
Ju97	na	19.00	19.00	19.00 +	.29	19.60	18.50	6,200

Est vol 90,686; vol Fri 152,056; open int 403,208, −3,516.

HEATING OIL NO. 2 (NYM) 42,000 gal.; $ per gal.

Sept	na	.5060	.4950	.4985 +	.0067	.5717	.4380	32,980
Oct	na	.5130	.5075	.5085 +	.0073	.5730	.4490	19,861
Nov	na	.5230	.5190	.5190 +	.0068	.5830	.4600	14,438
Dec	na	.5380	.5290	.5290 +	.0039	.5900	.4680	26,556
Ja95	na	.5390	.5345	.5345 +	.0039	.5850	.4745	15,521
Feb	na	.5410	.5375	.5355 +	.0039	.5875	.4795	5,500
Mar	na	.5335	.5270	.5260 +	.0034	.5750	.4700	6,049
Apr	.5225	.5235	.5200	.5165 +	.0029	.5500	.4525	1,775
May	.5200	.5200	.5110	.5095 +	.0029	.5350	.4700	2,094
June	na	.5120	.5090	.5060 +	.0029	.5300	.4679	4,458
July	.5115	.5130	.5110	.5080 +	.0029	.5290	.4785	4,635
Aug	.5200	.5200	.5165	.5150 +	.0029	.5390	.4740	809
Sept	.5295	.5295	.5265	.5240 +	.0029	.5060	.4845	669
Dec		....	....	.5495 +	.0029	.5265	.5370	1,096

Est vol 32,038; vol Fri 67,508; open int 136,525, +816.

GASOLINE-NY Unleaded (NYM) 42,000 gal.; $ per gal.

Sept	.5810	.5920	.5805	.5844 +	.0023	.6105	.4390	42,076
Oct	na	.5560	.5475	.5493 +	.0016	.5750	.4310	17,173
Nov	na	.5300	.5240	.5265 +	.0044	5480	.4275	11,869
Dec	na	.5790	.5720	.5770 +	.0049	.6000	.5080	6,817
Ja95	na	.5660	.5600	.5635 +	.0034	.5860	.5080	2,622
Feb	na	.5580	.5550	.5585 +	.0029	.5825	.5110	1,750

Est vol 20,713; vol Fri 39,678; open int 82,307, −598.

FIGURE 3.9   Oil complex futures prices. See Fig. 3.8 for column headers. (*Source*: *The Wall Street Journal*, August 8, 1994. With permission.)

pattern related to the soybean harvest cycle. In Fig. 3.9, heating oil exhibits futures prices that are seasonal. The precise pattern of the futures price deviations for different delivery dates varies considerably across commodities;

for example, the financial commodities, including the precious metals, exhibit futures prices that increase or decrease monotonically. The basis relationship between the prices of futures contracts for different delivery dates is the *futures basis*. An essential objective of Chapter 4 is to demonstrate how the basis and the futures basis are determined by arbitrage considerations. More precisely, differences in the basis and the futures basis will be determined by the specific arbitrage trades applicable to the commodity involved.

IV. SPECULATION AND HEDGE FUNDS

A. WHAT IS A HEDGE FUND?

The term "hedge fund" is generic, being used to describe a variety of different fund strategies that loosely share some similar characteristics. The President's Working Group on Financial Markets (PWGFM) (1999, p. 40) defines the term "to refer to a variety of pooled investment vehicles that are not registered under the federal securities laws as investment companies, broker–dealers, or public corporations." Both of these features—pooled investment vehicle and absence of registration—are important to identifying whether a given fund qualifies as a hedge fund. More precisely, in order to avoid the registration requirements specified under U.S. federal securities laws for securities companies, hedge funds have to be privately structured and closely held. As such, the primary investors in hedge funds are high-net-worth individuals and institutional investors.

BOX 1

An excerpt from the testimony given by George Soros to the U.S. House Committee on Banking, Finance and Urban Affairs, April 13, 1994:

I must state at the outset that I am in fundamental disagreement with the prevailing wisdom. The generally accepted theory is that financial markets tend toward equilibrium and, on the whole, discount the future correctly. I operate using a different theory, according to which financial markets cannot possibly discount the future correctly because they do not merely discount the future; they help to shape it. In certain

(continues)

(*continued*)

circumstances, financial markets can affect the so-called fundamentals which they are supposed to reflect. When that happens, markets enter into a state of dynamic disequilibrium and behave quite differently from what would be considered normal by the theory of efficient markets. Such boom/bust sequences do not arise very often, but when they do they can be very disruptive, exactly because they affect the fundamentals of the economy.

. . . Generally, *hedge funds* do not act as issuers or writers of derivative instruments. They are most likely to be customers. Therefore, they constitute less of a risk to the system than the dynamic hedgers at the derivatives desks of financial intermediaries. Please do not confuse dynamic hedging with hedge funds. They have nothing in common except the word "hedge."

I am not here to offer a blanket defense for hedge funds. Nowadays the term is applied so indiscriminately that it covers a wide range of activities. The only thing they have in common is that the managers are compensated on the basis of performance and not as a fixed percentage of assets under management.

Our type of hedge fund invests in a wide range of securities and diversifies its risks by hedging, leveraging and operating in many different markets. It acts more like a sophisticated private investor than an institution handling other people's money. Since it is rewarded on absolute performance, it provides a healthy antidote to the trend-following behavior of institutional investors.

. . . But the fee structure of hedge funds is not perfect. Usually there is an asymmetry between the upside and the downside. The managers take a share of the profits, but not of the losses; the losses are usually carried forward. As a manager slips into minus territory, he has a financial inducement to increase the risk to get back into the positive fee territory, rather than to retrench as he ought to. This feature was the undoing of the hedge fund industry in the late 1960s, just as I entered the business.

Hedge funds are not the only securities that seek such specific exemptions from U.S. securities laws. For example, venture capital pools, asset securitization vehicles, family estate planning vehicles, and investment clubs can receive such treatment. Another defining feature of hedge funds is the types of strategies that the funds pursue. Yet, in this area, hedge funds exhibit considerable variation: "There is no single market strategy or approach pursued by hedge

---

BOX 2

The President's Working Group (1999) on Hedge Funds

Hedge funds are not a recent invention, as the founding of the first hedge fund is conventionally dated to 1949. A 1968 survey by the Securities and Exchange Commission identified 140 hedge funds operating at that time. During the last two decades, however, the hedge fund industry has grown substantially. Although it is difficult to estimate precisely the size of the industry, a number of estimates indicate that as of mid-1998 there were between 2500 and 3500 hedge funds managing between $200 billion and $300 billion in capital with approximately $800 billion to $1 trillion in total assets. Collectively, hedge funds remain relatively small when compared to other sectors of the U.S. financial markets. At the end of 1998, for instance, commercial banks had $4.1 trillion in total assets; mutual funds had assets of approximately $5 trillion; private pension funds had $4.3 trillion; state and local retirement funds had $2.3 trillion; and insurance companies had assets of $3.7 trillion.

---

funds as a group. Rather, hedge funds exhibit a wide variety of investment types, some of which use highly quantitative techniques while others employ more subjective factors" (PWGFM, 1999).

The diversity of hedge fund strategies extends to the types of securities traded (PWGFM, 1999, p. 9):

> Many hedge funds trade equity or fixed income securities, taking either long or short positions, or sometimes both simultaneously. A large number of funds also use exchange-traded futures contracts or over-the-counter derivatives, to hedge their portfolios, to exploit market inefficiencies, or to take outright positions. Still others are active participants in foreign exchange markets. In general, hedge funds are more active users of derivatives and of short positions than are mutual funds and many other classes of asset managers.

However, behind all the confusion about hedge fund typology, the basic intuition is relatively clear: Hedge funds combine long positions is certain securities with short positions in other securities. Inherently, hedge fund strategies will, directly or indirectly, involve leveraging.

Hedge funds are not conventional investment vehicles. Investor liquidity is often compromised with "lock-up periods of one year for initial investors and subsequent restrictions on withdrawals to quarterly intervals" (Ackermann *et al.*, 1999, p. 834). The regulatory exemptions under which hedge funds work severely restrict the ability of hedge funds to advertise. Another untypical feature of hedge funds concerns the management of them (Ackermann *et al.*, 1999):

> Hedge funds are . . . characterized by strong performance incentives. On average, hedge fund managers receive a 1 percent annual management fee and 14 percent of the annual profits. For most funds this bonus incentive fee is paid only if the returns surpass some hurdle rate or "high-water mark"—meaning there is no incentive fee until the fund has recovered from past losses. Although incentive fees and high-water marks could lead to excess risk taking under some conditions, there are countervailing forces that may dampen risk. Hedge fund managers often invest a substantial amount of their own money in the fund. Furthermore, the managers of U.S. hedge funds are general partners, so they may incur substantial liability if the fund goes bankrupt.

BOX 3

The MARhedge Hedge Fund Categories

MARhedge is an important source of information and news about the hedge fund industry. Data available through MARhedge has been thoroughly examined in Ackermann *et al.* (1999). In order to provide some degree of organization to the mish-mash of hedge fund strategies, MARhedge (www. MARhedge.com), classifies hedge funds into eight broad categories:

Global macro funds: Take positions on changes in global economic conditions in equity, foreign-exchange, and debt markets. Use derivatives, including index derivatives, and leverage.

Global funds: Similar to macro funds but targeted at specific regions, often involving stock picking.

Long-only (U.S. *opportunistic*) *funds*: Like traditional equity funds but with the hedge fund characteristics of leveraging and incentive fees for managers. Strategies for these funds include value, growth, and short-term trading.

Market-neutral funds: The basic objective of these funds is to be long in one group of securities and short in another group, such that market

(continues)

(continued)

risk is controlled or neutralized. This can be done in a number of ways: by going long one group of stocks and short another group, seeking to benefit from superior stock-picking skills; conversion arbitrages, which are long in underpriced convertibles and short in the underlying stocks; stock index arbitrages; and fixed income arbitrages, which are long, say, off-the-run Treasuries and short on-the-run Treasuries.

Sectoral hedge funds: Have an industry focus; includes some short-sale funds, which short sell over-valued sectors, investing the balance in indexes or fixed-income securities.

Event-driven funds: Target special situations, specifically distressed securities of firms in reorganization or bankruptcy as well risk trading in takeovers (e.g., buying the target and selling the acquirer).

Short sales funds: Fund is positioned to benefit from market declines, these funds can be index driven or can be based on stock picking.

Funds of hedge funds: Funds of hedge funds, sometimes leveraged.

Within each of these general groups, a variety of different strategies could be pursued. Similarly, some funds may be involved in activities covering more than one fund category.

In contrast to mutual funds, which have been intensively studied, hedge funds have only started to receive attention, though work on managed futures funds and commodity pools, which started somewhat earlier, is also applicable (e.g., Irwin and Brorsen, 1985; Elton, *et al.*, 1987; Edwards and Ma, 1988; Cornew, 1988; Irwin *et al.*, 1993; Edwards and Liew, 1999; Edwards and Caglayan, 2001). Some useful recent studies directly on hedge funds include Klein and Lederman (1995), Fung and Hseih (1997, 2000), Brown *et al.* (1999), Schneeweis and Spurgin (1998), Ackermann *et al.* (1999), and Liang (2000). A useful overview of studies of hedge fund performance is given by Caldwell (1995, p. 13):

> Considerable caution must be used when reviewing performance statistics for the hedge fund industry and its various segments. Even the best statistics are skewed by asset weighting (or lack thereof), voluntary selection and a strong survivorship bias. It's highly unlikely that hedge fund performance statistics accurately reflect the true, weighted average return to investors for any segment of this industry.

Though more recent studies have come some of the way toward correcting these difficulties, there is still considerable uncertainly about how to measure and assess hedge fund performance.

B. History of Hedge Funds

In a sense, the essence of a hedge fund is inherent in the process of financial intermediation. Prior to the availability of derivatives for financial commodities, hedging of market risks for, say, a stock portfolio involved going short a similar bundle of stocks. Such practices date back to early trading in financial securities. Yet, the modern hedge fund has evolved considerably from these beginnings. Caldwell (1995) dates the beginning of the modern hedge fund to 1949, when Alfred Jones (1901–1989) set up a general partnership operating a fund with the requisite elements.[16] Prior to establishing this fund, Jones had led a full life. In addition to earning a Ph.D. in sociology from Columbia in 1941, Jones was an associate editor for *Fortune* and was a business writer for *Time* and other publications. Prior to this, Jones had traveled the world, including a stint as vice consul at the U.S. embassy in Berlin during the early days of Hitler's reign.

Apparently, it was the research that Jones did for an article published by *Fortune* in March 1949 that provided the foundation for establishment of his hedge fund. The research involved Jones interviewing many of the important players on Wall Street. The basic strategy guiding the fund was to combine short selling and leverage to create a relatively conservative investment portfolio aimed at capturing stock-picking opportunities. At the time, this was a novel approach, given that both leverage and short sales were generally used to increase return variability, not reduce variability. Jones went beyond this to develop a measure of market exposure for his fund. The result was the first of the *market-neutral* hedge funds.

Caldwell (1995, p. 7) describes the Jones approach to fund management:

> Jones regularly calculated the exposure of his capital to market risk. . . . His method of quantifying market exposure is highly valued by traditional hedge fund managers for its intuitive relevance, yet it is largely ignored or misunderstood by academics and the financial media.

> Market Exposure = (Long Exposure − Short Exposure)/Capital

> A typical asset allocation for Jones would look like this: Given $1000 in capital, he would employ leverage to purchase shares valued at $1100 and sell shares short valued at $400. His gross investment of $1500 (150 percent of capital) would have a net market exposure of only $700 ($1100 − $400), making this portfolio "70

---

[16]The fund was converted to a limited partnership in 1952.

percent net long." Although Jones valued stock picking over market timing, he increased or decreased the net market exposure of his portfolio based on his estimation of the strength of the market. Since the market generally rose, Jones was generally "net long."

As with other modern hedge funds, there was an uncommonly high management fee. Though there were no high-water marks or loss paybacks, the 20% of realized profits to the general partner is in the realm of more recent arrangements. Similar with recent hedge funds, Jones also kept his entire investment capital in the fund, providing a strong managerial incentive for positive performance.

Jones introduced another innovation in 1954, reducing fund risk by bringing in other fund managers to run part of the portfolio, effectively starting the fund-of-funds approach to hedge fund management. Though there was oversight to ensure that duplication and cancellation were not occurring, managers were given wide latitude to make investment decisions. Over the years, Jones would have as many as eight managers working the fund portfolio. With this move, the Jones fund became an incubator for new hedge fund creation. Two of his early manager selections, Dick Ratcliffe and Carl Jones, eventually moved on to start their own hedge funds, Ratcliffe establishing Fairfield Partners in 1965 and C. Jones establishing City Associates in 1964. Certain elements of hedge fund structure were adapted by other funds. For example, the notion of hedge fund management fees (i.e., incentive-based partnership agreements) was adopted by, among others, Warren Buffett with Buffett Partners and Walter Schloss with WJS Partners. However, though possessing some elements of hedge funds, these funds did not regularly use short sales to create market neutral positions.

Caldwell (1995, p. 9) identifies another turning point in hedge fund history as being an article by C. Loomis published in *Fortune* magazine in April 1966. This article detailed the performance of the Jones fund, demonstrating that this fund was easily the best performing fund over the previous 5 years, even when account was taken of the 20% management fees. Loomis also provided a reasonably accurate description of how the Jones fund was run. Fueled on the demand side by investors eager for such investment vehicles and on the supply side by fund managers attracted by the high management fees, the result was creation of a wave of new hedge funds (Caldwell, 1995, p. 10):

> Although we don't know how many hedge funds were established in the three-year flurry following Loomis's article, estimates range from 140 to several hundred. Michael Steinhardt and George Soros were among those setting up funds at this time. The SEC found 215 investment partnerships in a survey for the year ending 1968 and concluded that 140 of these were hedge funds, with the majority formed that year.

The market contraction that started at the end of 1968 and continued until the end of 1974 demonstrated that there was considerably more to running a hedge fund than desire and marketing. Considering just the 28 largest U.S. hedge funds at year end 1968, within 2 years 5 funds had shut down and fund asset values were down 70% due to losses and withdrawals.

Some hedge funds survived the tough years between 1968 and 1974 while others foundered. Why? There are no detailed empirical studies of hedge fund strategies during this period. Hedge funds are closely held and such information was and is difficult to obtain. Anecdotal evidence is strongly in favor of the hypothesis that most fund managers did not adequately establish sufficient short positions. Many so-called hedge funds were decidedly long, not market neutral. In effect, these "hedge funds" were more like traditional mutual funds, only with the high performance fees. Not surprisingly, the Renaissance in derivative securities has seen a remarkable resurgence of hedge funds. Armed with new risk-management technologies, (e.g., value at risk, or VaR), a number of new-style hedge funds today actively use derivatives to leverage underlying capital. Yet, there is a vast number of hedge fund strategies in place, some of which are similar to the Jones model. Others, such as Long-Term Capital Management (LTCM), are creatures of the Renaissance in derivative securities.

C. Regulation of Hedge Funds

The recent collapse of LTCM raised numerous quandries for regulators. For example, a formal legal definition of a hedge fund is lacking: "The term 'hedge fund' is not defined or used in the federal securities laws" (PWGFM, 1999, p. 40). One of the attractive features of hedge funds is the avoidance of certain legalities associated with registration, information filing, taxes, and so on. More precisely, a hedge fund can be characterized as a pooled investment vehicle that is privately organized, closely held among a small number of partners, and run by professional investment managers, typically on an incentive-fee basis. Such funds are often domiciled outside the United States, often being incorporated in havens such as the British Virgin Islands or Bermuda.

The various features of a hedge fund all interact to create a security that falls through many of the cracks in the U.S. securities laws. In addition to the Securities and Exchange (SEC) Act, hedge funds that are properly created also do not fall under the Investment Company Act (PWGFM, p. 41):

> To maximize flexibility, hedge funds operating in the U.S. are structured so as to be exempt from regulation under the Investment Company Act of 1940. Most hedge funds rely on the "private" investment company exclusions in Sections 3(c)(1) and 3(c)(7) of the Investment Company Act. These exclusion exempt certain pooled

investment vehicles from the definition of "investment company" and from substantive regulation under the Investment Company Act.

The 3(c)(1) exemption used by many hedge funds requires two qualifying factors: The number of investors may not exceed 100, and the fund cannot make a public offering of its securities. A 3(c)(7) exemption requires investors to have not less than $5 million in investments. Using this exemption would also serve to limit the number of investors to less than 500 which avoids an SEC filing rule.

Even though hedge funds do not fall within the scope of the SEC Act or the Investment Company Act, they still could be subject to a number of other U.S. statutes. Indirectly, hedge funds are regulated through the regulations that are imposed on the array of financial institutions with which hedge funds need to conduct business. For example, the SEC imposes capital, margin, and reporting requirements on broker–dealers, which are essential counterparties or clearing members for hedge funds. Included among these requirements are risk-assessment rules specified in the SEC Act to "establish recordkeeping and reporting requirements for subject broker–dealers and their affiliates whose business activities are reasonably likely to have a material impact on the financial and operational conditions of the broker–dealer" (PWGFM, 1999, p. 42).

One potential regulatory body for hedge funds is the CFTC, yet the scope of CFTC regulation is quite narrow: "The term *hedge fund* is not defined under the Commodity Exchange Act. Thus, no rule of the CFTC applies specifically to hedge funds as a separate category of regulated entity. However, to the extent that hedge funds trade commodity futures or options interests and have U.S. investors, their operators or advisors become subject to CFTC registration and reporting requirements" (PWGFM, 1999, p. 49). These reporting requirements apply only to large positions held on markets regulated by the CFTC and the associated speculative limits. There is no requirement that hedge funds report activities in other markets.

In addition to filing requirements, another aspect of CFTC regulation covers the operators of the hedge fund. Again, the scope of regulation is somewhat narrow: "If hedge funds have U.S. investors and trade commodity futures or commodity options, these funds would be commodity pools under the CEA. The CEA subjects the operators of commodity pools and their advisors—but not the pools themselves—to regulation" (PWGFM, 1999, p. 49). The objective of the regulating commodity pool advisors is to protect investors against fraud and overreaching by fund managers. These regulations require registration, disclosure, reporting, and recordkeeping requirements but do not include rules for capital adequacy or other financial standards.

D. Hedge Funds and Speculation

The collapse of LTCM, has attracted considerable attention to hedge funds from the popular press and policymakers. Yet, until the recent flood of articles on hedge fund performance, little attention had been given to hedge funds in academic studies. The comparison with mutual funds, for which there are literally thousands of studies, is striking. This asymmetric treatment reflects an underlying asymmetry in what passes for the received theory of finance. Modern finance theory, starting with Markowitz and continuing with Sharpe and Fama, up to the present, depends fundamentally on the assumption of efficient markets. In this framework, investment vehicles that depend on speculative outcomes, such as hedge funds, are treated as anomalies. However, unlike other anomalies such as the January effect and the small firm effect, there is no cohesive economic rationale for hedge funds.

Financial theory is often motivated by the assumption of perfect markets. Numerous results, from the Modigliani–Miller theorems to the Black–Scholes option-pricing model, use this assumption. It is a clean and efficient structure for seeking out theoretical results. Under perfect markets, there is no rationale for hedge funds. More precisely, a fund that is simultaneously long and short in a homogeneous commodity and its related derivatives can only earn the riskless rate of interest on the capital that is invested in the position. Such is the logic of the riskless hedge portfolio of Black–Scholes. Hedge funds arise in inefficient markets, driven by mis-pricing in different markets. There are numerous sources of the mis-pricing, from informational advantages to market liquidity to price noise to regulatory arbitrage. For example, the sheer size and volume of LTCM trades reflects the number of potential strategies.

All of this discussion is not meant to impugn the pure theory of finance; rather, the objective is to recognize that the theory of speculation, in general, and hedge funds, in particular, lies outside the scope of conventional finance theory in the Markowitz tradition. The efficient markets hypothesis requires that appropriately discounted prices follow a random walk, yet speculators aim to profit from superior price forecasts. Current prices are not accurate forecasts of future prices; mis-pricing occurs. Hedge funds are involved in shorting one portfolio and buying another portfolio, with the objective of achieving abnormal returns from the inherent leveraging. This process involves predicting the behavior of random variables: stock prices, exchange rates, interest rates, and so on. The gambles involved are often sophisticated, involving combinations of prices for different commodities. Because random variables are involved, optimal speculation will implicitly be improved by incorporating some type of risk management, a point that was, apparently, overlooked by the Hunt brothers, among others.

V. QUESTIONS

1. Discuss the distinctions among investment, speculation, and gambling. What are key elements that distinguish a speculative decision from the other two types of financial decisions?

2. Comment on the contemporary implications of the following statement from Ben Graham in *The Intelligent Investor*: "The distinction between investment and speculation in common stocks has always been a useful one and its disappearance is a cause for concern. We have often said that Wall Street as an institution would be well advised to reinstate this distinction and to emphasize it in all dealings with the public. Otherwise, the stock exchanges may some day be blamed for heavy speculative losses, which those who suffered them had not been properly warned against." To what extent does this comment also applying to trading in derivative securities?

3. As discussed in Chapter 5, Section I, a butterfly is a trade involving a spread of two calendar spreads, whereby the nearby spread is, say, short and the deferred spread is long. This would result in a trade that is long one nearby contract, short two intermediate contracts, and long one deferred contract. Using current market prices, explain how a butterfly trade can be used to speculate on the seasonal basis in oil complex contracts.

4. Derive the hedge ratio for the BOB Spread using the (new) 6% theoretical T-bond contract, i.e., rework the calculations in Section II which used the (old) 8% theoretical T-bond contract.

PART II

Futures and Forward Contracts

CHAPTER 4

Arbitrage and the Basis

I. THE CASH-AND-CARRY ARBITRAGE

A. CASH-AND-CARRY ARBITRAGE: THE CASE OF GOLD

For storable commodities, the behavior of the basis and the futures basis is determined by the execution of cash-and-carry arbitrage trades. The use of the term *arbitrage* in this context has a technical meaning. What is colloquially called an "arbitrage" by market practitioners may, under a more technical definition, be little more than a potentially profitable trading strategy with limited risk of losses. An arbitrage opportunity is defined here as: *a riskless trading strategy that generates a positive profit with no net investment of funds.*[1]

---

[1]The terminology "self-financing trading strategy" is also used, typically in mathematical finance. An arbitrage trade is similar to the notion of hedge portfolios, which are central to the Black-Scholes models of Chapters 8 and 9. By construction, hedge portfolios involve net investment of funds, which are then hedged using options trading strategies. If the initial purchase of stock was fully financed, the hedge portfolio would be an arbitrage portfolio. Hence, the hedge portfolio can be constructed as an arbitrage.

By construction, for any commodity there will be two associated arbitrage trades: the *long arbitrage*, where the arbitrage transactions involve holding a long position in the cash commodity, and the *short arbitrage*, where the arbitrage involves holding a short position in the cash commodity. In some presentations, the long arbitrage is referred to as the cash-and-carry arbitrage, with the short arbitrage being the reverse cash-and-carry.

A fundamental requirement of financial market equilibrium is that observed prices do not permit arbitrage opportunities. In other words, arbitrage profits cannot be positive. This requirement is considerably stronger than the conventional notion of "market efficiency" that requires security price changes to be serially uncorrelated. Arbitrages impose restrictions on spot and derivative prices that, under perfect market assumptions, have to be satisfied. Practical considerations dictate that the short and long arbitrages will provide upper and lower bounds on the derivative price. In turn, these boundary restrictions can be used to formulate speculative trading strategies, as in Chapters 3 and 5.

By design, arbitrages are defined only in terms of *current* prices and interest rates. If dependence on expected future values is admitted, the trading strategies are not riskless. For much the same reason, arbitrages cannot involve a net investment of funds. Where the purchase of a commodity is involved, a cash-and-carry arbitrage is executed by (risklessly) borrowing all necessary funds at the current interest rate and using those funds to purchase the spot commodity, simultaneously contracting to sell the commodity at some future date at the current futures price. Hence, the cash-and-carry arbitrage provides a relationship between the futures and spot prices that depends on the net price of carrying the commodity until delivery. Similarly, other derivative securities such as options on futures contracts also provide instances of arbitrage trades that may or may not involve purchase of the physical commodity. In this fashion, arbitrages determine relationships among current prices of derivative securities.

In practice, the execution of cash-and-carry arbitrages and the associated behavior of the basis depends on the type of commodity under consideration. Various questions must be addressed to identify the details involved in a specific arbitrage. Is the commodity storable, storable with loss, or not storable? What costs are associated with storage? Is the commodity harvestable? Is there an offsetting carry return? To illustrate how arbitrage trading determines the *basis* for a specific commodity, it is convenient to develop the trades assuming that markets are perfect. In other words, there are no transaction costs, either in the form of commissions or bid/offer spreads. Other components of perfect markets include no taxes or other regulatory restrictions and equal lending and borrowing rates at riskless rates of interest. Relaxing these assumptions converts the cash-and-carry equality conditions to be derived into upper and lower bounds on forward or futures prices associated with the long and short arbitrage conditions.

BOX 1

What are Perfect Capital Markets?

Various presentations of perfect capital markets are available, with different versions emphasizing elements that are of importance to the issues at hand. One particularly complete set is provided in Haley and Schall (1979):

Costless capital markets: No capital market transaction costs (including commissions and bid/offer spreads), no government restrictions which interfere with capital market transactions, and the costless ability to make financial assets infinitely divisible.

Neutral taxes: No personal or corporate taxes are in effect.

Competitive markets: There are many perfect substitutes for all securities of a firm at any point in time and there is no discrimination in the pricing of these securities such that any security can be acquired at the same market price by all investors. In addition, firms and investors are price takers in investing, borrowing, and lending activities.

Equal access: Investors and firms can borrow, lend, and issue claims on the same terms. This assumption requires that borrowing and lending rates be equal.

Homogeneous expectations: All capital market participants have the same expectations about relevant random variables.

No information costs: Firms and individuals have the same available information and this information is acquired at zero cost.

No costs of financial distress: Firms and individuals incur no costs of financial distress or bankruptcy such as legal costs and disruption of operations. This assumption does not rule out the possibility of bankruptcy.

Perhaps the simplest cash-and-carry to consider is the case of gold, a commodity that is storable at low cost, earns no carry return, and is not affected by harvests. Assuming for simplicity that there are no storage costs other than financing charges (i.e., ignoring insurance, vault charges, and administrative expenses), a long-the-spot cash-and-carry arbitrage for deliverable gold is described in Table 4.1.[2] Recalling that absence of arbitrage requires that the arbitrage profit be non-positive, $\pi \leq 0$, and observing that $Q > 0$ gives a *long* cash-and-carry arbitrage restriction on the gold futures price: $F(0,T) \leq S(0)\{1 + r(0,T)\}$. If this condition is violated, the long arbitrage can be profitably executed. When the equality is binding, the futures price is said to be at *full carry*, that is, it reflects the full carrying charges.

Consider the gold futures price data for August 8, 1994, given in Fig. 4.1. Examining the December 1994/December 1995 price relationship for the associated closing prices of \$382.30 and \$403.20, respectively, the interest rate implied in the gold futures prices is 5.467%, while June 1995/June 1996 contracts give an implied interest rate of 5.75% This is consistent with the London Interbank Offer Rate (LIBOR) offered on Euro-U.S. deposits for one year: On August 8, 1994, they were trading at 5 13/16%. Examination of the futures price structures for other commodities reveals a range of different relationships. Silver, for example, exhibits a carry rate of 6.45% for December 1994/December 1995. Soybeans exhibit 5.22% for the same November 1994/ November 1995 differential. The price structure of copper is inverted, with prices for deferred delivery being lower than the nearby contracts. Most of the agricultural commodities exhibit some form of kinking or reversal in the direction of futures prices as delivery dates get more distant (e.g., the Chicago Board of Trade [CBOT] wheat contract). The diversity of futures price spread behavior should be apparent. Full-carry relationships are the exception, usually applying to the precious metals futures complex.

TABLE 4.1   Profit Function for a Long Gold Cash-and-Carry Arbitrage

Date	Cash position[a]	Futures position
$t = 0$	Borrow $\$[Q_G S(0)]$ at interest rate $r(0,T)$ and buy Q_G ounces of gold at $S(0)$ for storage until $t = T$	Short Q_G units at $F(0,T)$
$t = T$	Deliver the Q_G units against the maturing futures contract and use the proceeds to repay the maturity value of the loan, $\$[Q_G S(0)]\{1 + r(0,T)\}$	

[a]The cash gold position provide no pecuniary return between $t = 0$ and $t = T$.

Note: In this case, the profit function can be specified as $\pi(0) \leq \{F(0,T) - S(0)(1 + r(0,T))\}Q_G$.

[2]The interest rate $r(i,j)$ is assumed to have been adjusted for the period over which interest is paid. This means that the interest rate has *not* been annualized.

METALS AND PETROLEUM

COPPER-HIGH (CMX)–25,000 lbs.; cents per lb.

Aug	108.60	108.60	108.25	108.30	+	1.65	116.00	75.30	159
Sept	107.25	109.10	107.25	108.60	+	1.75	116.90	74.90	25,595
Oct	....	....	108.75	+	1.65	115.05	75.20	623	
Nov	109.00	109.00	108.90	108.95	+	1.60	112.80	77.75	513
Dec	107.70	109.40	107.70	108.95	+	1.50	115.20	75.75	12,617
Ja96	108.80	108.80	108.80	108.70	+	1.45	111.30	76.90	341
Feb	....	....	108.45	+	1.40	111.30	87.85	245	
Mar	107.90	108.50	107.80	108.25	+	1.40	113.70	76.30	2,492
Apr	....	....	107.90	+	1.35	110.40	90.10	143	
May	106.70	107.90	106.70	107.55	+	1.35	111.40	76.85	1,062
June	....	....	107.15	÷	1.30	107.30	106.70	100	
July	107.05	107.05	107.05	106.75	+	1.30	112.50	78.00	814
Sept	....	....	105.95	+	1.30	110.05	79.10	621	
Dec	....	....	105.15	÷	1.30	109.00	88.00	853	
Mr96	....	....	104.15	+	1.30	105.00	99.20	134	

Est vol 12,000; vol Fri 10,861; open int 46,371, −1,025.

GOLD (CMX)–100 troy oz.; $ per troy oz.

Aug	377.00	377.80	376.40	376.70	−	.60	415.00	341.50	1,107
Oct	379.80	380.00	379.10	379.30	−	.60	417.00	344.00	10,661
Dec	382.60	383.10	381.90	382.30	−	.60	426.50	343.00	91,590
Fb95	386.00	386.30	385.70	385.70	−	.60	411.00	363.50	11,195
Apr	....	....	389.00	−	.60	425.00	385.50	6,497	
June	392.10	392.20	392.10	392.30	−	.60	430.00	351.00	10,014
Aug	....	....	395.90	−	.60	412.50	380.50	4,191	
Oct	....	....	399.50	−	.60	413.30	401.00	1,077	
Dec	403.30	403.30	403.30	403.20	−	.60	439.50	358.00	4,807
Fb95	....	....	407.00	−	.60	424.50	412.50	1,249	
Apr	....	....	410.90	−	.60	430.00	418.30	1,141	
June	....	....	414.90	−	.60	447.00	370.90	2,865	
Dec	....	....	427.40	−	.60	447.50	379.60	2,696	
Ju97	....	....	440.20	−	.60	456.00	436.00	1,168	
Dec	....	....	453.20	−	.60	477.00	402.00	1,392	
Ju98	....	....	466.80	−	.80	489.50	483.90	1,553	
Dec	....	....	480.30	−	1.00	505.00	468.00	1,388	

Est vol 14,000; vol Fri 25,886; open int 154,591, +394.

SILVER (CMX)–5,000 troy oz.; cents per troy oz.

Aug	....	....	510.3	−	4.0	558.0	525.0	0	
Sept	512.0	514.5	510.5	511.3	−	4.0	590.5	376.5	73,304
Dec	519.0	521.5	517.5	518.3	−	4.0	597.0	380.0	29,258
Mr95	529.0	529.0	526.0	526.0	−	4.0	604.0	416.5	6,751
May	....	....	531.3	−	4.0	606.5	418.0	3,834	
July	539.0	539.0	539.0	536.9	−	4.0	610.0	403.0	3,279
Sept	545.0	545.0	545.0	542.8	−	4.0	615.0	493.0	647
Dec	553.0	553.0	553.0	552.0	−	4.0	628.0	434.0	2,114
J196	....	....	574.4	−	4.0	630.0	524.0	943	
Dec	596.0	596.0	596.0	592.0	−	4.0	670.0	454.0	1,238
J197	....	....	618.5	−	4.0	655.0	588.0	483	
Dec	....	....	639.2	−	4.0	695.0	502.0	307	
Dc98	....	....	688.5	−	4.0	731.0	694.0	107	

Est vol 14,000; vol Fri 16,133; open int 122,386, −1,126.

FIGURE 4.1 Futures prices for selected metals. See Fig. 3.8 for column headers. (*Source: The Wall Street Journal*, August 8, 1994. With permission.)

Because each futures contract involves both a long and a short position, the arbitrage relationship between cash and futures prices involves two trading strategies. In addition to the long-the-cash strategy described above which involves combining a fully leveraged purchase of the spot commodity with a short futures position, it is also possible to combine a short position in the cash commodity with a long futures position, a *short cash-and-carry arbitrage* trade. Hence, cash-and-carry arbitrage strategies for futures contracts are said to be *two sided*, having both a long and a short arbitrage trade to be satisfied. While there are differences across commodities, in practice, due to restrictions on the ability to short the cash commodity, execution of the short or *reverse* cash-and-carry arbitrage can be substantially more difficult than the long arbitrage, which only involves purchase of the spot commodity.[3] In these cases, the cash-futures basis will be determined by what Siegel and Siegel (1990) call *quasi-arbitrages*, typically involving trades with natural hedges in the spot commodity. A classic example would be a jewelry manufacturer holding a silver inventory. If the futures price falls "too far" below full carry, then silver inventories would be sold (or purchases deferred), the funds invested, and the required silver inventory hedged using a long futures position. As will be illustrated in Chapter 6, Section I, banking activities provide a number of excellent examples of natural hedges in currency and other financial commodities.

In the case of gold, numerous mining companies engage in forward-selling activities, particularly in North America (where approximately 30% of mine output is sold forward), Australia, and, more recently, South Africa (15% of mine output).[4] Forward sales by mines are combined with deferred delivery of spot transactions which enables the forward-selling mining company to defer or roll forward the delivery date, thereby benefiting from upward price movements. In addition to quasi-arbitrage, in recent years short selling requirements have been facilitated by the use of central bank gold stocks as a source of gold for loan. In addition to other charges, shorting costs involve making a leasing payment to the central bank or other market participant supplying the physical gold for the short. In addition to arbitrage activities,

---

[3]In some cases neither the long nor the short cash-and-carry is executable, i.e., nonstorable commodities in short supply.

[4]These numbers are approximate and date from the early 1990s. During the 1990s, the general downward trend in the gold price level combined with a full contango futures price structure contributed to a significant increase in hedging activities by gold-mining companies. In 1990, the South African Reserve Bank introduced a forward selling facility called the Stabilised Contango Scheme that involves a mining company selling forward a specific amount of gold over either a 12- or 24-month period, at a fixed price, thereby fixing the producer price for gold output. The best single source for following developments in the gold market is the annual *Gold*, published by Gold Fields Mineral Services.

the gold leasing market is also affected by companies involved in gold loans seeking to cover a short-term deficiency in physical supplies. Compared to the long arbitrage, the gold lease payment is an offset to the nonfinancing costs of storage that are associated with carrying a long commodity position through time.

To execute the short cash-and-carry arbitrage for gold, the funds received from the sale of the borrowed gold will be invested at a different, probably lower, rate of interest than the long arbitrage. Taking $i(0,T)$ to be the all-in lending rate and again ignoring incidental costs, the short arbitrage is described in Table 4.2. Recalling that absence of arbitrage implies $\pi \leq 0$ and observing that $Q > 0$ gives the short cash-and-carry arbitrage restriction on the gold futures price: $F(0,T) \geq S(0)\{1 + i(0,T)\}$. If this inequality is violated, the short arbitrage can be profitably executed.

The combination of the long and short arbitrage conditions imposes upper and lower boundaries on the gold futures price:

$$S(0)\{1 + r(0,T)\} \geq F(0,T) \geq S(0)\{1 + i(0,T)\}$$

In an idealized world where $r(0,T) = i(0,T) = r$, the equality condition is binding and $F(0,T) = S(0)\{1 + r\}$: The futures price will be fully determined at $t = 0$ by the current spot price and the cost of financing. This idealized result requires that lending and borrowing rates are equal, there are no short-sale costs or restrictions, the commodity earns no carry return and is costless to store, and transaction costs such as those associated with the bid/offer spread are ignored. When the futures prices for gold obey this condition, the commodity is at full carry.

Given the idealized full-carry model for gold $(r(0,T) = i(0,T))$, it is useful to evaluate what happens to basis behavior as maturity of the contract approaches. Defining $\Delta X \equiv X(1) - X(0)$ and substituting $X(1) = X(0) + \Delta X$ permits the profit function for a one-to-one long spot/short futures gold position to be expressed as:

TABLE 4.2 Profit Function for a Short Gold Cash-and-Carry Arbitrage

Date	Cash position	Futures position
$t = 0$	Borrow Q_G ounces and sell at $S(0)$. Invest the funds received at interest rate $i(0,T)$	Long Q_G ounces at $F(0,T)$
$t = T$	Take delivery of the Q_G units against the maturing futures contract, pay with the proceeds of the investment, $\$[Q_G S(0)]\{1 + i(0,T)\}$, returning the Q_G units to settle the short position	

Note: In this case, the profit function can be specified as $\pi(0) = \{S(0)(1 + i(0,T)) - F(0,T)\}Q_G$.

$$\pi/Q = \{F(0,T) - S(0)\} - \{F(1,T) - S(1)\}$$
$$= \{r(0,T)S(0)\} - \{r(1,T)S(1)\} = -\{r(0,T)\Delta S + S(1)\Delta r\}$$

This result is useful for interpreting the profitability of inventory hedges. Recalling that $r(i,j)$ is not annualized but, rather, reflects the actual return over the i to j holding period, $r(0,T)$ will typically be larger than $r(1,T)$. This is due to the one-period reduction in the number of days until maturity for both the loan and the futures contract. Hence, even if $\Delta S = 0$ and the level of annualized interest rates is unchanged, there is a time decay in the basis associated with $\Delta r < 0$ that is fundamental to understanding hedge profit determination. There is a "time clock" at work in a hedge, acting to reduce the difference between the spot and futures price. The time clock continues to wind down to the point where $r = r(T,T) = 0$ and $F(T,T) = S(T)$. Significantly, this time decay is *not* present in the futures basis.

B. FACTORS IMPACTING THE BASIS: GENERALIZED CASH-AND-CARRY ARBITRAGE CONDITIONS

As it turns out, the idealized, perfect market conditions required for the long and short arbitrages to be combined and produce an equality condition do not occur in practice. Allowing for the conditions associated with actual markets converts the equality conditions to upper and lower boundaries on the futures (or forward) price provided by the long and short arbitrage conditions. Due to restrictions on the ability to execute the short arbitrage trade, the lower bound on the futures price will often provide a weaker boundary than the upper bound that is determined by the long arbitrage. In some cases, the short arbitrage cannot be executed and the cash-and-carry is said to be *one sided*. An example of this situation is described in Section II. In other cases, most notably for some nonstorable commodities, neither the short nor long cash-and-carry arbitrage can be executed. Commodities in this group have included potatoes, eggs, and onions. The price performance of futures or forward contracts for these commodities is decidedly more erratic when compared to storable commodities.[5] Without the ability to do cash-and-carry arbitrages, price determination relies on expectations about future spot prices. At times, this can create market-clearing problems, due to lack of liquidity on one side of the market. Empirically, while a number of different types of contracts have been offered over the years, there are currently only a few futures contracts for truly nonstorable commodities.

---

[5] A number of the relevant studies on this point can be found in A. Peck, *Selected Writings on Futures Markets*, Chicago Board of Trade, Chicago, IL, 1977.

In addition to the truly nonstorables, certain other commodities do not satisfy strict requirements of storability, such as Treasury bills and feeder cattle, insofar as a delivery in one contract month cannot be carried for delivery against the next contract as would be the case for, say, gold or silver. However, in these cases, nonstorability does not significantly affect cash-futures price determination because there are other similar commodities that can be used to do the cash-and-carry arbitrage. For example, in the case of T-bills, even though a 3-month T-bill taken for delivery cannot be carried 3 months to the next delivery date (when the T-bill will be maturing), the current 6-month T-bill is available to do the arbitrage. Similarly, for feeder cattle, there are numerous opportunities to purchase feed stock which is at a point in the growth cycle that the stock will qualify for future delivery. On balance, it is safe to say there is considerable diversity across commodities in the execution of the short and long cash-and-carry arbitrages.

For analytical purposes, the diversity of arbitrage execution across commodities can be captured by generalizing the profit function for the cash-and-carry arbitrage to include both fixed costs and variable carry costs and carry returns. More precisely, for a transaction starting at $t = 0$ and ending at $t = T$:

$$F(0,T) = S(0)\{1 + cc(0,T) + CC(0,T) - cr(0,T) - CR(0,T)\}$$
$$= S(0)\{1 + r(0,T) + oc(0,T) + CC(0,T) - d(0,T) - cy(0,T) - CR(0,T)\}$$

where $cc(0,T)$ is the variable carry costs, expressed as a rate; $cr(0,T)$ is the variable pecuniary and nonpecuniary returns to holding the commodity, also expressed as a rate; $r(0,T)$ is the interest rate portion of carry costs; $CC(0,T)$ is the fixed cost component of carry costs; $cc(0,T) - r(0,T) = oc(0,T)$ is that portion of variable carry costs not attributable to interest carrying costs; $d(0,T)$ is the pecuniary interest or dividend return associated with carrying the commodity; $cy(0,T) = cr(0,T) - d(0,T)$ is that portion of cr not associated with pecuniary interest or dividend return; and $CR(0,T)$ is any fixed return earned while holding the commodity. This approach allows for all elements of cost to be introduced, including allowance for spoilage of the commodity during storage. Many commodities, even other metals such as copper and aluminum, have a significant storage component in carry costs.

Historically, the agricultural and industrial commodities were associated with futures and forward trading. For these commodities, it is possible to consider carry costs to be either relative (variable) or absolute (fixed). Relative carry costs are dependent on the value of the commodity and will change as the value of the commodity changes. The most significant relative cost is usually interest expenses. Absolute carry costs are associated with the quantity of the commodity to be stored and do not vary as the price of the commodity changes. These costs include storage, wastage, and insurance. It is important to recognize that the basis will behave quite differently depending on whether carry costs are predominately relative, as in the case of gold and other financial commodities, or absolute, as with the grains and industrial commodities.

It is possible to define $ic(0,T) = cc(0,T) - cr(0,T)$ combining the carry cost and carry return elements. For notational convenience, this was done in Chapter 3. Yet, for present purposes, it is expedient to ignore fixed costs and fixed returns and to work with the additional variable, $cr(0,T)$, to explicitly allow for potential returns the commodity may provide during the arbitrage period. The return captured by cr can be either pecuniary or nonpecuniary:

$$F(0,T) = S(0)\{1 + cc(0,T) - cr(0,T)\}$$

Financial futures such as T-bond and stock index futures contracts provide examples where this formulation is useful because of the pecuniary return in the cash-and-carry arbitrage associated with holding the commodity. Following the discussion of the long spot/short futures inventory hedge for gold, this formulation can be directly applied to the profit function for an inventory hedge for a general commodity. In this case, the profit function can be written:

$$\pi/Q = \{F(0,T) - S(0)\} - \{F(1,T) - S(1)\}$$
$$= [S(0)\{cc(0,T) - cr(0,T)\}] - [S(1)\{cc(1,T) - cr(1,T)\}]$$

Again, letting $\Delta X \equiv X(1) - X(0)$ and using $X(1) = X(0) + \Delta X$ permit this form of the profit function to be expressed as:

$$\pi/Q = S(0)\{\Delta cr - \Delta cc\} + \{cr(1,T) - cc(1,T)\}\Delta S$$
$$= -\{S(0)\Delta ic + ic(1)\Delta S\}$$

This provides a general framework for examining the profitability of an inventory hedge as well as numerous other hedge trades. Application to specific cases requires correct interpretation of cr. For example, while there are no direct financial returns involved in carrying commodities such as wheat and other grains, there are other benefits. In these cases, cr can be interpreted as the *convenience yield* from holding stocks. (Convenience yield is discussed in more detail in Chapter 3, Section I). This is based on the notion that stocks of a commodity provide some net benefit to the owner. When stocks are low, the convenience yield is high; when stocks are plentiful, the convenience yield is low. The cr may, at times, be an important element of basis behavior, especially for commodities with high absolute carry costs such as grains and industrial metals.

In practice, the role of cr depends intimately on the importance of absolute carry costs. Commodities with a cash-futures basis determined by relative carrying costs, such as financial futures and gold, usually adhere closely to the cash-and-carry arbitrage condition. When the cash-futures basis depends predominately on absolute carry costs, the arbitrage conditions provide only wide boundaries on the cash-futures basis, and convenience yield can act to offset the costs of carrying the physical commodity. Numerous instances of this are provided in the futures price quotes. For example, this explains how harvestability affects the basis. Stocks of grain are most plentiful after the harvest. The value of stocks carried from one crop year to another will fall by the amount of the associated loss in convenience yield. This will be reflected in futures prices, typically resulting in a discontinuity in the futures price structure occurring with the harvest delivery contract, when stocks of grain will be high and the convenience yield low. This type of discontinuity can be seen in the futures prices for corn, soybeans, and wheat. Convenience yield is also important in commodities such as the oil complex and copper contracts.

C. THE TERM STRUCTURE OF FUTURES PRICES

At any time t, there are a range of futures prices for a given commodity. This is apparent from a casual inspection of the futures prices in Chapter 3 and Table 4.2. One unresolved question concerns the relationship between $F(t,T)$ and $F(t,N), N \leq T$. Returning to the perfect markets assumption, the cash-and-carry arbitrage conditions for any two futures prices can be specified:

$$F(0,N) = S(0)(1 + ic(0,N))$$
$$F(0,T) = S(0)(1 + ic(0,T))$$

Taking the ratio of $F(0,T)$ to $F(0,N)$ provides:

$$F(0,T)/F(0,N) = (1 + ic(0,T))/(1 + ic(0,N))$$
$$= \{(1 + ic(0,N))(1 + ic(0,T - N))\}/(1 + ic(0,N))$$

It follows that:

$$F(0,T) = F(0,N)(1 + ic(0,T - N))$$

This relationship holds between any two delivery dates.

The equation $F(0,T) = F(0,N)(1 + ic(0,T - N))$ can be conceptualized as a deferred cash-and-carry transaction. Consider a trade that is established at $t = 0$ and is long $F(0,N)$ and short $F(0,T)$. Ignoring fixed costs and revenues, at time $t = N$ the long position is settled by borrowing $QF(0,N)$ at $r(N,T)$ and incurring other possible carry costs $oc(N,T)$ where $cc(N,T) = r(N,T) + oc(N,T)$. The borrowed funds are used to settle the long position by buying the spot commodity at the agreed price $F(0,N)$. This spot position is carried for $T - N$ periods, where applicable, earning a carry return of $cr(N,T)$. At time

$t = T$, the spot commodity is then used to settle the short position at $F(0,T)$. This sequence of transactions can be used to specify $ic(0,T - N)$ as the implied carry cost, reflected in $F(0,T)$ and $F(0,N)$ at time $t = 0$, for a cash-and-carry arbitrage that will begin at $t = N$ and end at $t = T$. Observe that the actual implied carry earned on the cash-and-carry transaction between N and T, $cc(N,T) - cr(N,T)$, will not usually be the same as that reflected in futures prices at time $t = 0$.

II. COVERED INTEREST ARBITRAGE

A. Early Forward Exchange Markets

Unlike some other commodities where trading in time bargains had been conducted at least since the 17th century, large-scale forward trading in currencies did not develop until probably the late 1840s in Vienna (Einzig, 1937).[6] The emergence of this trade can be attributed to wide fluctuations in the Austrian gulden during the 19th century. For a number of reasons, traditional methods of handling foreign exchange risk, such as trading in foreign bills of exchange, were inadequate for dealing with this exchange-rate volatility. While forward trade in sterling developed much later, initial Vienna trading was in German mark notes with delivery dates up to 6 months in the future. Following the customs of the continental stock exchanges, forward contracts were settled at month end, with speculators covering their positions by settling the differences and renewing their forward contracts for the next end-of-month settlement. The impact of speculative activity on the foreign exchanges was evident in the movement of end-of-month exchange rates, which were impacted by speculative covering activities.

The presence of forward trading in Vienna gave impetus to the development of forward trading in Russian rubles, another unstable currency, and Austrian gulden in Berlin. Higher interest rates in Vienna led to active and fully covered interest arbitrage between the two centers. Forward trading also emerged in other centers, such as St. Petersburg. Active forward trading of British sterling, the international unit of account for the 19th and early 20th centuries, did not develop in London until just before World War I. The

---

[6]This statement refers only to forward foreign exchange contracts that are the same form as contracts traded in the modern era, a pure agreement to exchange currency at a specified later date at an exchange rate that is determined on the date that the contract is created. It would be possible to effectively achieve a forward exchange transaction using bills of exchange. Such trades could have been done at a much earlier time, possibly even in ancient times. However, bills of exchange did have certain features that would pose real complications, such as a geographical separation in the contract initiation and settlement locations.

absence of a forward market in London can be attributed to the relative stability of sterling up to the period following World War I. In the United States, there probably was forward trading in U.S. dollars associated with the currency turbulence created by the Civil War. In the late 1880s, a forward market in French francs emerged in New York, New Orleans, and Chicago. This trading was unusual in that there was no forward market for francs in France. In the period before World War I, active forward currency trading also occurred in Latin America, Shanghai, and Japan, where there had been trading in forward exchange since before introduction of the gold standard.

An important element leading to the emergence of forward currency markets was instability in the foreign exchanges. Stabilization of the Austro-Hungarian currency (now the krone) in 1892 led to a reduction in commercial forward exchange transactions, even though there still was considerable forward trading associated with stock arbitrage. Forward dealing in currency gradually declined towards the end of the 19th century, being replaced by forward trading using bills of exchange. Vienna, Berlin, and St. Petersburg all developed active markets in sterling bills. For many traders, foreign bills of exchange could provide the requisite currency hedging function. In addition, foreign bills were desirable instruments for conducting covered and uncovered interest arbitrage: "Interest arbitrage between Vienna and Berlin on the one hand and the Western European centers on the other attained a high state of development in the 1890s, but it was usually the central European markets that took the initiative. Very little was known about the forward exchange business in London or Paris in those days. To secure a high yield on swap transactions in those days was still the privilege of the select few, who jealously safeguarded the secret of their knowledge.... During the years that preceded [World War I], interest arbitrage combined with swap operations between Vienna and other markets assumed such dimensions that the Austro-Hungarian Bank at times considered it necessary to adopt special tactics to counteract its effect" (Einzig, 1937, p. 42).

A significant difference between a forward currency market and a forward market in bills was the deliverable instrument involved; one contract involved future delivery of foreign exchange and the other a short-term debt instrument denominated in sterling, almost invariably involving an offshore issuer. The forward bill arose in a number of ways, typically with the objective of protecting against changes in the bank rate. Because stability in the exchanges under the gold standard was usually achieved by significant fluctuations in the bank rate, this source of risk was often greater than currency changes. For example, a bill secured by a crop to be harvested in the autumn could be sold forward in the spring. Delivery of the crop would give rise to a bill of exchange that would then be used for settlement of the forward position. There was a forward market in foreign sterling bills in London for decades before World

BOX 2

Keynes on Forward Exchange Rates

John Maynard Keynes, in his *Tract on Monetary Reform*, was one of the early popularizers in Britain of forward exchange trading. Writing in 1923, Keynes finds: "The nature of forward dealings in exchange is not generally understood. The rates are seldom quoted in the newspapers. There are few financial topics of equal importance which have received so little discussion or publicity. The present situation did not exist before the war (although even at that time forward rates for the dollar were regularly quoted), and did not begin until after the 'unpegging' of the leading exchanges in 1919, so that the business of the world has only begun to adapt itself. Moreover, for the ordinary man, dealing in forward exchange has, it seems, a smack of speculation about it. Unlike the Manchester cotton spinners, who have learnt by long experience that it is not the hedging of open cotton commitments on the Liverpool futures market, but the failure to do so, which is speculative, merchants, who buy or sell goods of which the price is expressed in a foreign currency, do not yet regard it as part of the normal routine of prudent business to hedge these indirect exchange commitments by a transaction in forward exchange." (p. 121)

War I, with delivery dates as far as 6 months in the future. The presence of the London forward discount market together with an active market in short-term funds gave considerable impetus to the development of a forward foreign exchange market in sterling. Despite playing a significant role in the functioning of the forward markets, the speculative element in the markets was not officially encouraged.

B. Covered Interest Arbitrage

While there are a number of possible arbitrages involving foreign exchange rates, covered interest arbitrage is sufficient to determine the forward foreign exchange rate. Section I gave a brief overview of the notion of a cash-and-carry arbitrage. While such arbitrages are associated with virtually all futures and forward contracts, covered interest arbitrage is perhaps the most well known example of a cash-and-carry arbitrage. Covered interest arbitrage is based on the notion that, in markets where arbitrage is active and unrestricted, securities that differ only by currency of denomination should exhibit fully hedged returns that are approximately equal. The resulting *covered interest parity* (CIP) condition establishes an arbitrage relationship between domestic and foreign interest rates and the current forward and spot exchange rates. CIP arbitrages have been executed almost from the beginning of forward exchange trading, though as late as the 1920s Keynes observed that: "It must be remembered that the floating capital normally available, and ready to move from center to center for the purpose of taking advantage of moderate arbitrage between spot and forward exchange, is by no means unlimited in amount, and is not always adequate to meet the market's requirements" (Keynes, 1923, p. 129).

BOX 3
—————————

A Stylized Example of Covered Interest Arbitrage

Patrick Lim, a trader in the foreign exchange department of Citicorp, Singapore office, specializes in arbitraging U.S. dollars against Deutschemarks (DM). He observes the following rates at 9:10 a.m. Singapore time:

Spot rate:	DM1.8200 = $1.0000
3-month forward rate:	DM1.8000 = $1.0000

Lim can borrow or invest U.S. dollars for 3 months at 9% per annum or Deutschemarks for 3 months at 5% per annum. He has a borrowing limit of $5,000,000 or the equivalent in DM.

(a) Ignoring transaction costs, how can Lim make a riskless arbitrage profit? Assume that Lim desires to take any profits in dollars.

(b) If the dollar 3-month interest rate on U.S. dollars were 10% instead of 9%, all other factors remaining the same, would Lim still make a profit using the strategy outlined in item (a)? If not, is there another set of transactions that would provide an arbitrage profit?

(c) If the transactions costs in a) or b) were above $7000 and were to be paid out of final proceeds, would this change the strategies described in (a) or (b)?

BOX 4

Solution to Lim's Stylized Arbitrages

(a) LiM can make an arbitrage profit by doing a short covered interest arbitrage trade. The arbitrage is short because it involves borrowing in US$ and investing in DM. This arbitrage involves the following sequence of transactions which will all be executed at 9:10 a.m. Singapore time:

- Borrow $5,000,000 for 3 months. In 3 months' time, the amount owing on this borrowing will be $(5 \text{ mil})(1 + (.09/4)) = \$5,112,500$
- Exchange the $5 million at the spot exchange rate to get ($5 mil)(1.82) = 9.1 mil DM.
- Invest the 9.1 million DM for 3 months. In 3 months' time, the investment will mature to a value of $(9.1 \text{ mil})(1 + (.05/4)) = 9,213,750$ DM.
- Sell the maturing value of the DM investment for US$ using a 3-month forward exchange contract. At the quoted forward exchange rate of 1.8, the DM investment will produce (9,213,750/1.8) = $5,118,750.
- In 3 months' time, the DM investment will mature and the proceeds will be delivered on the forward exchange contract. The proceeds of the forward contract will be used to settle the maturing 3-month loan, producing an arbitrage profit of $5,118,750 − $5,112,500 = $6250.

(b) If the U.S. interest rate is 10% instead of 9%, then the cost of the US$ borrowing would be $(5 \text{ mil})(1 + (.1/4)) = \$5,125,000$. Because this exceeds the covered return which could be received on the DM investment, the short arbitrage would not be profitable. However, in the absence of transaction costs, it would now be possible to do the *long* arbitrage, which would involve borrowing in DM and investing in US$. In this case, the profit would be $5,125,000 − $5,118,750 = $6250.

(c) The presence of a $7000 transaction cost would prevent either the long or the short arbitrage from being executed. This illustrates the point that covered interest arbitrage only provides upper and lower boundaries on the available combinations of interest rates and exchange rates that are consistent with absence of arbitrage at a specific point in time.

(continues)

(continued)

Note: In actual practice, the presence of transaction costs dictates that the spot and forward transactions will be combined into one transaction, a foreign exchange swap.

For expository purposes, development of the CIP condition requires a number of assumptions and definitions to be introduced. For example, the method of determining the exchange rate must be given as either units of domestic to foreign currency or the converse. To see the difference, consider that on April 12, 1983, the $/£ exchange rate was 1.5285 while the £/$ exchange rate was .6542.[7] Similarly, for the August 27, 1992, cash exchange rates, the C$/US$ rate was 1.196 and the US$/C$ rate was .8361. Figure 4.2 provides the foreign exchange rate data from the *Globe and Mail* for August 8, 1994. Following the convention on U.S. currency futures markets, so-called *U.S. direct terms* will be used which involve units of US$ to units of foreign currency (or domestic currency for non-U.S. traders).[8] This will also apply to the spot exchange rate, meaning $S(0)$ will be measured in U.S. direct terms. Using the opposite convention of quoting the exchange rate, so-called *foreign direct terms*, changes the identification of the foreign and domestic interest rate; however, the substance of the CIP condition is unchanged.

The basics of the arbitrage trading strategy can be illustrated by considering a stylized cash-and-carry arbitrage trade between U.S. dollars and a foreign currency for 1-year securities. If the covered foreign interest rate *exceeds* the rate on a comparable U.S. security, the trade described in Table 4.3 can be executed at $t = 0$. Assuming perfect capital markets, this trade will generate an arbitrage profit by assumption because the amount received on the covered foreign investment will be more than the cost of the U.S. dollar borrowing.

To see how the series of transactions in Table 4.3 translates into an arbitrage profit function, consider that the fully covered value of the foreign asset at

---

[7]The notational convention selected here (e.g., to use $/£ to mean number of US$ per £) is not general. There are various sources, including certain textbooks and journals, that use the *opposite* convention where $/£ would mean the number of £ per $. For example, using the reverse quotation US$/MR 1.7220 would mean 1.7220 Malaysian ringit per US$. Another less confusing convention involves using five significant digits when the FX rate is less than one and four significant digits when the FX rate is greater than one.

[8]More generally, "domestic direct terms" is defined as units of domestic currency to units of foreign currency; for example, for Canadian investors this would be $C/$US (Stigum, 1983). However, the Canadian dollar futures contract is traded in US$/C$. Hence, to avoid complications, the U.S. dollar is considered the "domestic" country for present purposes.

CROSS RATES

	Canadian dollar	U.S. dollar	British pound	German mark	Japanese yen	Swiss franc	French franc	Dutch guilder	Italian lira
Canada dollar	—	1.3797	2.1289	0.8735	0.013610	1.0362	0.2550	0.7777	0.000875
U.S. dollar	0.7248	—	1.5430	0.6331	0.009864	0.7510	0.1848	0.5637	0.000634
British pound	0.4697	0.6481	—	0.4103	0.006393	0.4867	0.1198	0.3653	0.000411
German mark	1.1448	1.5795	2.4372	—	0.015581	1.1863	0.2919	0.8903	0.001002
Japanese yen	73.48	101.37	156.42	64.18	—	76.14	18.74	57.14	0.064291
Swiss franc	0.9651	1.3315	2.0545	0.8430	0.013135	—	0.2461	0.7505	0.000844
French franc	3.9216	5.4106	8.3486	3.4255	0.053373	4.0635	—	3.0498	0.003431
Dutch guilder	1.2858	1.7741	2.7374	1.1232	0.017500	1.3324	0.3279	—	0.001125
Italian lira	1142.86	1576.80	2433.03	998.29	15.554286	1184.23	291.43	888.80	—

Mid-market rates in Toronto at noon, Aug. 8, 1994. Prepared by the Bank of Montreal Treasury Group.

		$1 U.S. in Cdn.$ =	$1 Cdn. in U.S.$ =
U.S./Canada spot		1.3797	0.7248
1 month forward		1.3808	0.7242
2 months forward		1.3818	0.7237
3 months forward		1.3827	0.7232
6 months forward		1.3862	0.7214
12 months forward		1.3973	0.7157
3 years forward		1.4457	0.6917
5 years forward		1.4917	0.6704
7 years forward		1.5622	0.6401
10 years forward		1.6547	0.6043
Canadian dollar	High	1.3083	0.7644
in 1994:	Low	1.3990	0.7148
	Average	1.3712	0.7293

Country	Currency	Cdn. $ per unit	U.S. $ per unit
Britain	Pound	2.1289	1.5430
1 month forward		2.1294	1.5421
2 months forward		2.1297	1.5412
3 months forward		2.1297	1.5402
6 months forward		2.1320	1.5380
12 months forward		2.1385	1.5304
Germany	Mark	0.8735	0.6331
1 month forward		0.8739	0.6329
3 months forward		0.8751	0.6329
6 months forward		0.8787	0.6339
12 months forward		0.8891	0.6363
Japan	Yen	0.013610	0.009864
1 month forward		0.013650	0.009886
3 months forward		0.013728	0.009928
6 months forward		0.013873	0.010008
12 months forward		0.014211	0.010170
Algeria	Dinar	0.0436	0.0316
Antigua, Grenada and St. Lucia	E.C.Dollar	0.5119	0.3711
Argentina	Peso	1.38205	1.00170
Australia	Dollar	1.0213	0.7402
Austria	Schilling	0.12403	0.08990
Bahamas	Dollar	1.3797	1.0000
Barbados	Dollar	0.6933	0.5025
Belgium	Franc	0.04245	0.03077
Bermuda	Dollar	1.3797	1.0000
Brazil	Real	1.509519	1.094092
Bulgaria	Lev	0.0258	0.0187
Chile	Peso	0.003281	0.002378
China	Renminbi	0.1604	0.1162
Cyprus	Pound	2.8744	2.0833
Czech Rep	Koruna	0.0490	0.0355
Denmark	Krone	0.2220	0.1609
Egypt	Pound	0.4076	0.2954

Country	Currency	Cdn. $ per unit	U.S. $ per unit
Fiji	Dollar	0.9548	0.6920
Finland	Markka	0.2662	0.1929
France	Franc	0.2550	0.1848
Greece	Drachma	0.00578	0.00419
Hong Kong	Dollar	0.1786	0.1294
Hungary	Forint	0.01258	0.00912
Iceland	Krona	0.01972	0.01429
India	Rupee	0.04397	0.03187
Indonesia	Rupiah	0.000636	0.000461
Ireland	Punt	2.1068	1.5270
Israel	N Shekel	0.4531	0.3284
Italy	Lira	0.000875	0.000634
Jamaica	Dollar	0.04415	0.03200
Jordan	Dinar	1.9852	1.4388
Lebanon	Pound	0.000824	0.000597
Luxembourg	Franc	0.04245	0.03077
Malaysia	Ringgit	0.5346	0.3874
Mexico	N Peso	0.4074	0.2953
Netherlands	Guilder	0.7777	0.5637
New Zealand	Dollar	0.8340	0.6045
Norway	Krone	0.1999	0.1449
Pakistan	Rupee	0.04519	0.03275
Philippines	Peso	0.05276	0.03824
Poland	Zloty	0.0000603	0.0000437
Portugal	Escudo	0.00859	0.00623
Romania	Leu	0.0008	0.0006
Russia	Ruble	0.000661	0.000479
Saudi Arabia	Riyal	0.3679	0.2667
Singapore	Dollar	0.9164	0.6642
Slovakia	Koruna	0.0437	0.0317
South Africa	Rand	0.3821	0.2770
South Korea	Won	0.001719	0.001246
Spain	Peseta	0.01062	0.00770
Sudan	Dinar	0.0445	0.0322
Sweden	Krona	0.1787	0.1295
Switzerland	Franc	1.0362	0.7510
Taiwan	Dollar	0.0524	0.0380
Thailand	Baht	0.0553	0.0401
Trinidad, Tobago	Dollar	0.2475	0.1794
Turkey	Lira	0.0000441	0.0000320
Venezuela	Bolivar	0.00812	0.00589
Zambia	Kwacha	0.002090	0.001515
European Currency Unit		1.6701	1.2105
Special Drawing Right		1.9950	1.4460

The U.S. dollar closed at $1.3772 in terms of Canadian funds, down $0.0095 from Friday. The pound sterling closed at $2.1201, down $0.0182.

In New York, the Canadian dollar closed up $0.0050 at $0.7261 in terms of U.S. funds. The pound sterling was down $0.0026 to $1.5394.

FIGURE 4.2   Selected foreign exchange rates. (*Source: Globe and Mail*, August 8, 1994. With permission.)

TABLE 4.3   Short Covered Interest Arbitrage Trade

Date	U.S. asset	Exchange market	Foreign (Canadian) asset
$t = 0$	Borrow $\$Q$ for 1 year at $r(0,1)$	Buy $\$Q/S(0)$ Canadian dollars, spot	Invest $\$Q/S(0)$ for 1 year at $r^*(0,1)$
		Sell $(\$Q/S(0))(1 + r^*(0,1))$ Canadian dollars forward at $F(0,1)$	
$t = 1$	Use the funds from the maturing foreign asset to settle the forward exchange position by paying the foreign currency and receiving US dollars. Use these dollars to settle the US dollar loan.		

Note: $F(0,1)$ is the 1-year forward exchange rate in U.S. direct terms; $S(0)$ is the spot exchange rate in U.S. direct terms; $r(0,1)$ is the domestic (U.S.) interest rate on a 1-year zero-coupon security (quoted on a 365-day basis); $r^*(0,1)$ is the foreign (Canadian) 1-year interest rate (quoted on a 365-day basis).

maturity is $F(0,1)\{Q/S(0)\}(1 + r^*)$ while the amount to be repaid at maturity of the loan is $Q(1 + r)$. This produces the arbitrage profit function associated with the *short arbitrage*:

$$\pi_s(0) = F(0,1)\{Q/S(0)\}(1 + r^*) - Q(1 + r) \leq 0$$

The ≤ 0 condition is required for absence of arbitrage.

To this point, much of the discussion of arbitrage transactions has assumed perfect markets. This assumption permits the profit functions for both the short and long arbitrages to be combined to produce an equality relationship involving forward and spot prices. When markets are not assumed to be perfect, as is the case in actual markets, then the short and long arbitrage conditions provide upper and lower boundaries on the futures or forward price. To see how this occurs, relax the assumption that lending and borrowing rates are equal by letting y and y^* denote the interest rates applicable to the long covered interest arbitrage trade done using covered Canadian borrowing to finance a U.S. asset position. A sequence of transactions similar to those in Table 4.3 produces the arbitrage profit function:

$$\pi_L(0) = Q(1 + y) - F(0,1)\{Q/S(0)\}(1 + y^*) \leq 0$$

In this case, $y = y(0,1)$ is a lending rate, and $y^* = y^*(0,1)$ is a borrowing rate; for the short arbitrage, r is a borrowing rate and r^* is a lending rate.

Manipulating the long arbitrage condition gives:

$$F(0,1) \geq \{(1 + y)/(1 + y^*)\}S(0)$$

while manipulation of the short arbitrage condition gives:

$$F(0,1) \leq \{(1+r)/(1+r^*)\}S(0)$$

The upper and lower arbitrage boundaries can now be expressed as:

$$\frac{1+y}{1+y^*} \leq \frac{F(0,1)}{S(0)} \leq \frac{1+r}{1+r^*}$$

These boundaries can be equivalently expressed as:

$$\frac{y-y^*}{1+y^*} \leq \frac{F(0,1)-S(0)}{S(0)} \leq \frac{r-r^*}{1+r^*}$$

The validity of these boundary conditions can be verified by observing that $y^* > r^*$ and $r > y$, because rationality requires that borrowing rates are always at least as high as lending rates. A number of studies further develop the upper and lower arbitrage boundaries by further relaxing the perfect market assumptions, particularly the assumption of no transaction costs (e.g., Deardorff, 1979; Clinton, 1988).

BOX 5

Bids and Offers in Foreign Exchange

Quoting of bid/offer rates in the FX market is complicated because two units of account are being exchanged. This requires a convention as to how the quotation method relates to which currency is being sold and which is being purchased. A further complication is the presence of conflicting market conventions for stating exchange rate quotes.

For example, say the bid/offer rates on the C$/US$ are 1.4955 and 1.4975, respectively, which means that FX dealers are willing to *buy* one US$ at the bid in exchange for 1.4955 C$. The dealer will give the customer 1.4955 C$ in exchange for a US$. Similarly, the dealer offers to *sell* one US$ to customers in exchange for 1.4975. This is consistent with the intuitive result that the bid rate will be less than the offer rate in order for the dealer to earn the spread, .0020 in this example.

The potential confusion arises because buying US$ involves selling C$. Buying one currency involves selling another. To see how to avoid possible confusion, consider the corresponding US$/C$ bid/offer quotes of .66778/.66867. Using these quotes, FX dealers are willing to *buy* one C$ in exchange for .66778 US$ and to *sell* one C$ in exchange for .66867 US$. Again, the dealer will make the spread, which is .00089 when rates are expressed as US$/C$.

(continues)

(continued)

To avoid potential confusions that can arise, make reference to conventional bid/offer rates for other commodities, for example, the bid/offer on gold being $260/$261. These quotes are $/oz and involve buying or selling gold in exchange for dollars. The ounce of gold that is being bought and sold appears in the denominator of the quote. Similarly, the bid/offer quotes for the currency that is being bought and sold is associated with the currency appearing in the denominator of the quote. If the exchange rate is quoted as US$/C$, then the bid/offer quotes will refer to C$ transactions.

In order to arrive at the conventional equality conditions, assume that both the long and short arbitrages impose the binding restriction that $\pi = 0$. This result is achieved by going back to the perfect markets assumption where $y = r$ and $y^* = r^*$ or, in other words, lending rates and borrowing rates in each country are equal. Imposing this condition on the long and short arbitrage profit functions and manipulating give an equality relationship. Recognizing the wide range of possible maturity dates for forward contracts, the conventional CIP condition can be stated:[9]

$$F(0,T) = \frac{1 + r(0,T)}{1 + r^*(0,T)} S(0)$$

In terms of the cost-of-carry model in Section I, $F(0,T) = \{1 + cc(0,T) - cy(0,T)\}S(0)$, the CIP condition can be expressed as:

$$F(0,T) = \left\{ 1 + \frac{r(0,T) - r^*(0,T)}{1 + r^*(0,T)} \right\} S(0) \text{ or}$$

$$cc(0,T) - cy(0,T) = \frac{r(0,T) - r^*(0,T)}{1 + r^*(0,T)}$$

where r is the approximate carry cost and r^* is the approximate carry return.

---

[9]In the stylized form $F = S(1 + ic)$, the CIP formula implies $(1 + ic) = (1 + \{(r - r^*)/(1 + r)\})$. The term $(1 + r)/(1 + r^*)$ is sometimes referred to as the *interest agio*. Depending on the relative sizes of r and r^*, the interest agio can be either greater or less than one. When the interest agio is less than $1 (r < r^*)$, then $F(0,T) < S(0)$ and the spot currency is said to be at a *premium*. When the interest agio is greater than one $(r > r^*)$, then $F(0,T) > S(0)$ and the spot currency is said to be at a *discount*. The difference between the spot and forward rate, $S(0) - F(0,T)$ is known as the *swap rate* and is the "price" of doing a swap transaction. Finally, $\{F(0,T) - S(0)\}/S(0) = \{r - r^*\}/(1 + r^*)$ is known as the *forward exchange agio*.

Extending this result to currency futures, the nearby contract can be taken as a replacement for the spot position:[10]

$$F(0,T) = \frac{1 + i(0,T-N)}{1 + i^*(0,T-N)} F(0,N)$$

$$= \left\{ 1 + \frac{i(0,T-N) - i^*(0,T-N)}{1 + i^*(0,T-N)} \right\} F(0,N)$$

where $i(0,T-N)$ and $i^*(0,T-N)$ = the time 0 domestic (U.S.) and foreign (Canadian) interest rates adjusted by $(T-N)/365$ to account for the trading horizon. (This notation takes no account of the term structure of interest rates implied by currency futures.) Figure 4.3 provides data for currency and Eurocurrency deposit futures prices on August 8, 1994 (see Questions at the end of this chapter for a useful exercise concerning this table and the CIP condition). These CIP relationships apply to money market instruments. A number of issues require attention before applying CIP to long-term, $T > 1$ year, forward contracts.

In the discussion of cash-and-carry arbitrages in Section I, it was demonstrated that, for a number of reasons, the short and long arbitrages would only provide upper and lower boundaries on the futures price. Only in idealized conditions would equality conditions be binding. In the case of CIP, transaction costs and other factors provide the basis for precisely specifying the boundaries. Clinton (1988) demonstrates the importance of considering how the arbitrage trade is executed in the foreign exchange market, correcting one of the numerous errors in the 1970's literature on calculating transaction costs for CIP trades (e.g., Deardorff, 1979).

Consider the short covered interest arbitrage trade described previously that involved both a spot and a forward foreign exchange transaction, in addition to the two security market transactions. Assuming no broker fees were incurred on these transactions and that trading limits on forward exchange positions are not binding, the primary source of transactions costs for a CIP trade done in the forward market will be the bid/offer spread. (In practice, while there are futures contracts for a wide range of currencies, the bulk of covered interest arbitrage activity takes place in the interbank forward and spot markets.) In order to reduce the transaction costs associated with foreign

---

[10]By the nature of trade in futures on the IMM, these relationships will also hold for forwards. There are specific institutional arrangements within the IMM to ensure that a direct link is maintained between the currency futures and outright forward market. An arbitrage role is performed by traders whose function is to purchase and sell futures contracts at the IMM, simultaneously covering the positions in the forward market with a commercial bank. Because the IMM does not release information figures on this type of arbitrage trading, market participants such as central banks rely on the commercial banks to provide information on the activities of these IMM traders.

CURRENCY

	Open	High	Low	Settle	Change	Lifetime High	Low	Open Interest

JAPAN YEN (CME) – 12.5 million yen; $ per yen, (.00)

	Open	High	Low	Settle	Change	High	Low	Int
Sept	1.0012	1.0016	.9850	.9878	– .0129	1.0408	.8942	65,543
Dec	.9985	.9985	.9920	.9948	– .0131	1.0490	.9525	6,056
Mr95	1.0130	1.0130	1.0000	1.0025	– .0133	1.0560	.9680	1,052
Jun	....	....	....	1.0114	– .0135	1.0670	.9915	268

Est vol 24,931; vol Fri 24,956; open int 72,941, +687.

DEUTSCHEMARK (CME) – 125,000 marks; $ per mark

Sept	.6336	.6338	.6301	.6311	– .0018	.6595	.5364	89,149
Dec	.6310	.6332	.6308	.6315	– .0018	.6606	.5351	4,567
Mr95	....	....	....	.6327	– .0018	.6595	.5798	1,532

Est vol 23,876; vol Fri 43,379; open int 95,294, +2,455.

CANADIAN DOLLAR (CME) – 100,000 dlrs.; $ per Can $

Sept	.7214	.7258	.7214	.7255	+ .0052	.7740	.7068	32,802
Dec	.7195	.7242	.7195	.7239	+ .0055	.7670	.7038	2,534
Mr95	.7170	.7221	.7170	.7221	+ .0058	.7618	.7020	700
June	.7150	.7180	.7150	.7188	+ .0061	.7600	.6990	377

Est vol 15,365; vol Fri 3,365; open int 36,494, +1,096.

BRITISH POUND (CME) – 62,500 pds.; $ per pound

Sept	1.5420	1.5456	1.5366	1.5382	– .0028	1.5764	1.4440	31,389
Dec	1.5362	1.5400	1.5350	1.5360	– .0028	1.5760	1.4400	766
Mr95		....	....	1.5340	– .0020	1.5750	1.4530	152

Est vol 6,930; vol Fri 11,704; open int 32,307, -343.

SWISS FRANC (CME) – 125,000 francs; $ per franc

Sept	.7518	.7522	.7478	.7490	– .0015	.7817	.6590	39,514
Dec	.7495	.7532	.7495	.7506	– .0015	.7840	.6885	1,561

Est vol 12,166; vol Fri 17,207; open int 41,106, +531.

AUSTRALIAN DOLLAR (CME) – 100,000 dlrs.; $ per A.$

Sept	.7415	.7430	.7385	.7388	– .0039	.7467	.6645	8,418

Est vol 806; vol Fri 3,067; open int 8,472, +842.

U.S. DOLLAR INDEX (FINEX) – 1,000 times USDX

Sept	89.65	90.23	89.61	90.11	+ .29	98.55	86.85	6.557
Dec	89.95	90.50	90.28	90.37	+ .29	99.00	87.08	3,108

Est vol 2,300; vol Fri 2,711; open int 9,675, +784.
The index: High 90.02; Low 89.50; Close 89.91 +.28

FIGURE 4.3 Currency futures and Eurodeposit futures. (*Source: The Wall Street Journal*, August 8, 1994. With permission.)

STERLING (LIFFE) – £500,000; pts of 100%

	Open	High	Low	Settle	Change	Lifetime High	Low	Open Interest
Sept	94.10	94.15	94.09	94.13	+ .02	95.25	90.10	97,877
Dec	93.33	93.42	93.33	93.40	+ .06	95.23	90.10	171,388
Mr95	92.78	92.84	92.74	92.82	+ .06	95.10	90.70	64,708
June	92.31	92.37	92.28	92.37	+ .08	94.23	91.73	51,323
Sept	91.92	92.01	91.90	92.00	+ .09	94.81	91.46	42,165
Dec	91.63	91.72	91.61	91.70	+ .09	94.66	91.14	35,157
Mr96	91.39	91.49	91.37	91.49	+ .11	94.61	90.82	23,179
June	91.20	91.30	91.20	91.29	+ .08	94.25	90.60	21,963
Sept	91.05	91.10	91.05	91.10	+ .06	93.64	90.40	11,912
Dec	90.88	90.92	90.88	90.92	+ .07	93.50	90.20	11,484
Mr97	90.77	90.79	90.77	90.78	+ .04	93.33	90.05	9,549
June	90.65	90.69	90.65	90.66	+ .04	90.90	89.92	2,686

Est vol 33,164; vol Fri 55,930; open int 543,391, +5,775.

EUROMARK (LIFFE) – DM 1,000,000; pts of 100%

	Open	High	Low	Settle	Change	Lifetime High	Low	Open Interest
Sept	95.06	95.07	95.05	95.06	– .01	95.54	91.81	169,353
Dec	94.96	94.97	94.94	94.94	– .03	95.73	91.83	168,509
Mr95	94.68	94.69	94.66	94.68	– .02	95.83	92.45	155,996
June	94.35	94.37	94.33	94.35	– .01	95.91	93.15	97,541
Sept	94.09	94.09	94.06	94.07	– .03	95.83	93.62	63,420
Dec	93.81	93.82	93.78	93.81	– .01	95.74	93.43	54,859
Mr96	93.61	93.63	93.60	93.61	– .02	95.62	93.25	38,230
June	93.46	93.47	93.43	93.46	– .01	95.45	93.05	19,193
Sept	93.31	93.32	93.31	93.30	– .03	94.26	92.82	8,911
Dec	93.12	93.12	93.12	93.10	....	94.10	92.22	11,788
Mr97	....	....	....	92.98	....	93.99	92.45	6,556
June	92.86	92.86	92.81	92.82	– .01	93.10	92.29	4,327

Est vol 46,083; vol Fri 154,991; open int 798,683, –1,972.

EUROSWISS (LIFFE) – SFr 1,000,000; pts of 100%

	Open	High	Low	Settle	Change	Lifetime High	Low	Open Interest
Sept	95.62	95.64	95.61	95.61	– .02	96.75	95.37	25,024
Dec	95.51	95.52	95.48	95.48	– .04	96.80	95.14	12,280
Mr95	95.31	95.31	95.27	95.27	– .04	96.15	94.80	10,933
June	95.02	95.02	94.97	94.97	– .05	95.22	94.42	3,237

Est vol 3,650; vol Fri 6,892; open int 51,474, ÷1,548.

3-MONTH EURO LIRA (LIFFE) – Itl 1,000,000; pts of 100%

	Open	High	Low	Settle	Change	Lifetime High	Low	Open Interest
Sept	91.30	91.30	91.26	91.27	– .03	91.35	91.02	27,631
Dec	90.93	90.93	90.89	90.90	– .05	91.00	90.74	48,506
Mr95	90.52	90.54	90.51	90.53	– .05	90.58	90.40	13,359
June	90.07	90.08	90.07	90.06	– .06	90.15	89.97	12,035
Sept	89.85	89.85	89.85	89.80	....	89.85	89.68	8,117
Dec	89.55	89.55	89.55	89.48	– .03	89.55	89.41	3,336

Est vol 1,915; vol Fri 5,479; open int 112,984, –656.

GERMAN GOVT. BOND (LIFFE)

250,000 marks; pts of 100%

	Open	High	Low	Settle	Change	Lifetime High	Low	Open Interest
Sept	93.36	93.39	93.04	93.08	– .33	97.25	89.91	153,857
Dec	92.66	92.66	92.31	92.35	– .36	93.75	89.52	23,761

Est vol 59,860; vol Fri 113,802; open int 177,618, –2,389.

ITALIAN GOVT. BOND (LIFFE)

ITL 200,000,000; pts of 100%

	Open	High	Low	Settle	Change	Lifetime High	Low	Open Interest
Sept	102.71	103.02	102.70	102.73	– .27	114.30	99.60	81,037
Dec	101.71	101.71	101.50	101.46	– .34	103.90	100.00	317

Est vol 8,618; vol Fri 25,730; open int 81,354, –2,799.

FIGURE 4.3 (continued)

BOX 6
_____

Triangular Arbitrage and Bid/Offer Rates

Triangular arbitrage ensures consistency between exchange rate quotes for different currencies. More precisely, given the FX quote for currency A/currency B and the FX quote for currency B/currency C, triangular arbitrage ensures consistency of the FX quote for currency A/currency C. In practice, triangular arbitrage provides outer boundaries for the bid/offer rates that prevail for a given currency, relative to other traded currencies. The actual observed bid/offer rates will depend on competitive factors prevailing in the market for a given currency.

To see how triangular arbitrage constrains the bid/offer rate, consider the following quotes for S$/US$ and DM/US$: S$/US$ bid = 1.3410, S$/US$ offer = 1.3490, DM/US$ bid = 1.4035, and DM/US$ offer = 1.4100. Constructing the offer rate for S$/DM consistent with triangular arbitrage involves starting with S$ and then exchanging these into US$ at the offer rate, 1.3490, and using these US$ to buy DM at the bid rate, 1.4035. The resulting calculation, 1.3490/1.4035 = .9612, is the FX rate at which triangular arbitrage _offers to sell_ S$ for DM. Similarly, the bid rate to buy S$ in exchange for DM involves selling DM for US$ at the offer rate of 1.4100 and using these US$ to buy S$ at the bid rate, 1.3410. The resulting calculation of 1.3410/1.4100 = .9511 is the FX rate that triangular arbitrage _bids to buy_ S$ for DM. Hence, the triangular arbitrage bound on the bid/offer rate for S$/DM is .9511/.9612.

---

exchange transactions, banks do matched spot/forward transactions by combining the trades in the form of a _foreign exchange swap_.[11] This involves only one swap trade bid/offer transaction cost instead of the two bid/offers arising from the spot and forward trades. Hence, to be consistent with the actual arbitrage execution, the stylized example above should have one swap transaction instead of a spot/forward combination.

---

[11]Numerous excellent references on this subject are available including Grabbe (1996). In practice, the volume of swap transactions is far greater than for forwards. A minor complication arising from the use of swaps involves the need to adjust the increment of the forward position to account for the difference in principal values due to the interest paid. Stigum (1983, p.167) recognizes this point: "On swap transactions, interest payments generate a residual foreign exchange exposure. For example, if a bank takes in a 3-month DM deposit and swaps it into dollars, the bank assumes a foreign exchange risk because it is committed to pay interest in DM on

A fundamental observation that can be made about the CIP condition concerns the number of variables involved in the CIP condition: given the spot exchange rate, two interest rates determine the forward rate. Given that there is only one forward-spot pairing for a given delivery date, there can only be one interest rate pair, domestic and foreign, that can determine the forward rate. At least since Einzig (1970), it has been recognized that the smallest empirical deviations from CIP occur when Euromarket interest rates are used (e.g., Marston, 1976; Poitras, 1988b). Conditions in this market are close to providing the idealized conditions required for CIP to hold precisely. In addition, the primary participants in the Eurocurrency deposit markets are also the most important participants in the swap, forward, and spot markets for foreign exchange.

Because interest rates for different money market securities tend to follow different paths, deviations from CIP for any given interest rate pairing can be considerable. This basic point was misunderstood by Frenkel and Levitch (1975, 1977, 1981), Otani and Tiwari (1981), Bahmani-Oskooee and Das (1985), Sharpe (1985), Overturf (1986), and Prachowny (1970), who used interest rates other than Eurocurrency deposit rates and incorrectly drew conclusions about excess deviations from covered interest arbitrage. In particular, when treasury bills are used to evaluate the CIP condition, neither the short nor long arbitrage is executable. (This follows because it is not possible for arbitragers to borrow in the T-bill market). For this reason, it is not possible to draw any conclusions about deviations from arbitrage conditions when T-bills are selected as the operative lending and borrowing rates.

In addition to pairing T-bill rates together, a number of other pairings can be considered. Interest rate pairings for securities that could be used by arbitragers for borrowing programs, such as U.S./Canadian commercial paper or bankers' acceptances tend to exhibit small (but still larger than Euro) deviations from CIP, consistent with institutional limitations on accessing these types of funds. To see this, consider the Canadian dollar exchange rates and money market interest rates on August 8, 1994, given in Figs. 4.3 and 4.4. The U.S. direct terms spot is .7248 and the 3-month forward is .7232. This translates into a 3-month interest agio of 0.9977924. Using the appropriately adjusted U.S. (4.77%, 360-day basis) and Canadian (5.61%, 365-day basis) 3-month Banker's Acceptance (BA) rates, the interest agio is calculated

---

the DM deposit at maturity, while it will earn interest at maturity in dollars on the dollars it has loaned. If the bank chooses to avoid this risk, it can lock in a fixed spread on the overall swap by buying DM (selling dollars) *forward* in an amount equal to the interest to be paid in DM." In terms of Table 4.3 the swap would involve a spot exchange of US$Q for $Q/S(0)$ Canadian dollars combined with a return of the $$Q/S(0)$ in 1 year at $F(0,1)$. To make the transaction riskless, the trader would have to enter an outright forward contract for an additional $[Q/S(0)]r^*(0,1)$ at $F(0,1)$.

MONEY RATES

ADMINISTERED RATES		UNITED STATES	Certificates of Deposit by
Bank of Canada	5.70%	NEW YORK (AP) — Money	dealer: 30 days, 4.47; 60 days,
Canadian prime	7.25%	rates for Monday as reported by	4.67; 90 days, 4.80; 120 days,
MONEY MARKET RATES		Telerate Systems Inc:	4.91; 150 days, 5.12; 180 days,
(for transactions		Telerate interest rate index:	5.21
of $1-million or more)		4.820	Eurodollar rates: Overnight,
3-mo. T-bill(when-issued)	5.58%	Prime Rate: 7.25	4.25-4.375; 1 month, 4.50-4.5625;
1-month treasury bills	5.21%	Discount Rate: 3.50	3 months, 4.8125-4.875; 6
2-month treasury bills	5.40%	Broker call loan rate: 6.00	months, 5.25-5.3125; 1 year,
3-month treasury bills	5.50%	Federal funds market rate:	5.75-5.8125
6-month treasury bills	6.10%	High 4.375, low 4.3125, last	London Interbank Offered
1-year treasury bills	7.20%	4.3125	Rate: 3 months, 4.75; 6 months,
10-year Canada bonds	9.03%	Dealers commercial paper:	5.1875; 1 year, 5.5625
30-year Canada bonds	9.18%	30-180 days: 4.48-5.15	Treasury Bill auction results:
1-month banker's accept.	5.46%	Commercial paper by fi-	average discount rate: 3-month
2-month banker's accept.	5.56%	nance company: 30-270 days:	as of Aug. 8: 4.43; 6-month as of
3-month banker's accept.	5.61%	4.43-4.71	Aug. 8: 4.93
Commercial Paper (R-1 Low)		Bankers acceptances dealer	Treasury Bill, annualized rate
1-month	5.60%	indications: 30 days, 4.45; 60	on weekly average basis, yield
2-month	5.68%	days, 4.64; 90 days, 4.77; 120	adjusted for constant maturity,
3-month	5.73%	days, 4.86; 150 days, 5.05; 180	1-year, as of Aug. 1: 5.51
Call money	5.25%	days, 5.12	Treasury Bill market rate, 1-
Supplied by Dow Jones		Certificates of Deposit Pri-	year: 5.29-5.27
Telerate Canada		mary: 30 days, 3.40; 90 days,	Treasury Bond market rate,
		3.85; 180 days, 4.23	30-year: 7.53

FIGURE 4.4   Money market interest rates. (*Source: Toronto Globe and Mail*, August 8, 1994. With permission.)

by first converting the U.S. discount rate to the coupon yield equivalent and then calculating the agio using annualized rates that have been divided by four (90/365 to be exact), to account for the 90-day maturity. The resulting value of 0.99826 differs from the arbitrage value by about 4 basis points (not annualized). Similar calculations for U.S. (4.80%) and Canadian (5.73%) commercial paper gives 0.9980177, a smaller differential.

Other pairings to consider include when one of the rates can be used to borrow while the other cannot. These situations lead to *one-sided* arbitrage conditions. To see this, observe that the ready availability of arbitrage funds at the Euro–U.S. rate defines an arbitrage relationship between the Euro–U.S. rate and other non-Eurocurrency assets.[12] For example, when the other rate is for treasury bills, whenever the covered domestic treasury bill rate rises above

[12]Following Kreicher (1982), institutional factors such as reserve requirements and deposit insurance costs may affect the rate determination processes in the Eurocurrency and domestic deposit markets. As a result, appropriate adjustments have to be made to domestic rates before examining the arbitrage relationship. These institutional factors are not as important in the Canadian case because of the limited institutional restriction on Canadian banks operating in the Euro–U.S. market (though foreign banks arbitraging the Euro–U.S./Canadian t-bill differential will be subject to the requirements imposed by their country of origin).

the Euro–U.S. rate, arbitragers will borrow funds at the Euro–U.S. rate, convert the funds into domestic dollars, and purchase domestic treasury bills. At the same time, the amount of funds to be received upon maturity of the treasury bill will be covered forward. If the maturity of the treasury bill and the Eurodollar-deposit are the same, the trade will generate a theoretically riskless profit. This arbitrage establishes an *upper* bound on the domestic treasury bill rate—the covered Euro–U.S. deposit rate.

The arbitrage trade when the covered domestic treasury bill rate exceeds the Euro–U.S. rate is apparent. Yet, there is no practical arbitrage trade when the Euro–U.S. rate exceeds the covered domestic treasury bill rate. In this case, when the treasury bill rate falls below the covered Euro–U.S. rate, the implied covered interest arbitrage trade would involve borrowing at the domestic treasury bill rate, converting to U.S. dollars, and investing in an appropriately dated Euro–US deposit—simultaneously selling forward the funds to be received upon maturity of the Euro–U.S. deposit. This trade cannot be executed because only the domestic government has the ability to issue liabilities in the domestic treasury bill market. As a consequence, the connection between these two rates is limited; the Euro–US rate can move to a substantial premium over the covered domestic treasury bill rate. The size of this potential premium depends on what can be descriptively defined as quasi-arbitrage support where cash market investor activity assumes importance.

The need for quasi-arbitrage support extends to the case where U.S. and domestic T-bill rates are considered. For example, investors may not want the additional risk associated with a Euro–US investment, opting instead to buy U.S. T-bills that are perceived by the market to be less risky than say, Government of Canada treasury bills (t-bills). Hence, substitution between U.S. T-bills and Canadian t-bills by asset holders would be based on covered parity plus an adjustment for the differential risk characteristics of the two instruments. This type of quasi-arbitrage support will provide a weak lower bound on the Canadian t-bill rates. For this lower bound, T-bill investors and other important players are required to react to the size of the covered differential with U.S. T-bills or Euro–U.S. deposits primarily by making portfolio adjustments. The adjustment process is conditioned by the level of overnight foreign and Canadian interest rates, tax rates, foreign exchange market conditions, Canadian monetary policy, and so on.

C. FORWARD–FORWARD ARBITRAGE AND SWAP ARBITRAGE

Forward–forward covered interest arbitrage determines the relationship between the price of forward contracts for different delivery dates. The arbitrage is interesting both in the method used to construct the underlying trades and in the associated covered interest arbitrage conditions. The arbitrage extends naturally to arbitrage between swap contracts. As illustrated in the description of the short forward–forward arbitrage in Table 4.4, the trades involve careful selection of the principal amounts of the borrowings and the forward contracts. Extending the arbitrage to swap contracts imposes additional restrictions on the principal amounts. These additional restrictions can be satisfied by "tailing" the initial swap trades. This is accomplished using additional outright forward positions to supplement the forward contracts embedded in the initial swap transactions.

At $t = 0$, the forward–forward arbitrage involves borrowing and investing offsetting market values in both the foreign and domestic markets. In the U.S. or domestic market, the amount borrowed and invested is equal to $\$Q(1 + r^*(0,N))$ while in the foreign market the amount borrowed and invested is $(\$Q/F(0,N))(1 + r(0,N))$. Because the maturity dates of the investments and borrowings are different, these cash market transactions result in a forward starting loan. For example, when the U.S. investment matures at $t = N$, the investment will still have $T - N$ days to go. In the absence of the foreign transactions, the trader would raise the funds required by borrowing at $t = N$ at $r(N, T - N)$, an interest rate that is *uncertain* at $t = 0$. The forward–forward arbitrage avoids this uncertainty by paying the balance due on the domestic loan using the fully covered proceeds of the foreign loan. This offset is achieved by careful selection of the market values of the initial foreign and domestic transactions.

TABLE 4.4   Short Forward–Forward Arbitrage

Date	U.S. (domestic) market	Exchange market	Foreign market
$t = 0$	Borrow $\$Q(1 + r^*(0,N))$ at $r(0,T)$	Sell US$ forward $\$Q(1 + r^*(0,N))$ $(1 + r(0,N))$ at $F(0,N)$	Borrow $(\$Q/F(0,N))$ $(1 + r(0,N))$ at $r^*(0,N)$
	Invest $Q(1 + r^*(0,N))$ at $r(0,N)$	Buy US$ forward $(\$Q/F(0,N))$ $(1 + r(0,N))(1 + r^*(0,T))$ at $F((0,T)$	Invest $(\$Q/F(0,N))$ $(1 + r(0,N))$ at $r^*(0,T)$
$t = N$	The U.S. investment will mature to give $\$Q(1 + r^*(0,N))(1 + r(0,N))$ that is used to deliver on the forward position that matures at $t = N$. The amount of foreign currency received will be $\$(Q/F(0,N)(1 + r^*(0,N))(1 + r(0,N))$ which is the amount owing on the foreign borrowing maturing at $t = N$. The cash flows at $t = N$ all cancel.		
$t = T$	The T-period foreign investment will mature to $(\$Q/F(0,N))(1 + r(0,N))(1 + r^*(0,T))$. This amount is delivered against the forward contract to obtain US$ which can be used to settle the loan. The resulting US$ cash flow will have to be less than or equal to the maturing value of the US$ T-period loan in order to ensure absence of arbitrage opportunities.		

The result of these transactions is a forward-starting covered interest arbitrage trade that commences at $t = N$. At $t = T$, the short arbitrage profit function provides the restriction:

$$\pi_s = \frac{\$Q}{F(0,N)}(1 + r(0,N))(1 + r^*(0,T))\ F(0,T)-$$

$$\$Q(1 + r^*(0,N))(1 + r(0,T)) \leq 0$$

Much as with the spot-forward covered interest arbitrage, this condition can be manipulated and combined with the long arbitrage condition to produce the perfect markets result:

$$F(0,T) = \frac{\dfrac{1 + r(0,T)}{1 + r(0,N)}}{\dfrac{1 + r^*(0,T)}{1 + r^*(0,N)}}\ F(0,N) = \frac{1 + i(0,T - N)}{1 + i^*(0,T - N)}\ F(0,N)$$

Closer examination of this condition reveals a direct connection between i and i^*, the interest rates determining the relationship between forward exchange rates for different delivery dates and implied forward rates determined from the cash market, $[r(0,T), r(0,N)]$ and $[r^*(0,T), r^*(0,N)]$.

More precisely, the *implied forward rate* for money market securities can be defined:

$$1 + i(0,T - N) = \frac{1 + r(0,T)}{1 + r(0,N)}$$

$$\rightarrow (1 + i(0,T - N))(1 + r(0,N)) = 1 + r(0,T)$$

In effect, the $t = 0$ implied forward rate $(i(0,T - N))$ is the *breakeven interest rate* that will equate the buy and hold return on a T-period security with the return earned on a rollover investment. The rollover investment involves buying an N-period security, holding to maturity, and investing the proceeds at $t = N$ in a $T - N$ period security that matures at time T. Remembering that the arbitrage is done in the Eurocurrency deposit markets is significant because the major currencies also have actively traded interest rate futures/forward contracts. Because these contracts provide the market with a traded implied forward rate, this means that the relevant Eurocurrency interest rate futures for the appropriate maturity can be used as the operative interest rates in evaluating the forward–forward arbitrage condition.[13]

[13]To see that the Eurocurrency deposit futures rate is a substitute for the implied forward rate, observe that the rollover strategy can be constructed as investing in a one-period Eurodeposit and simultaneously entering into a long Eurodeposit forward contract with a delivery date that matches the maturity date on the one-period Eurodeposit. For example, at $t = 0$ the investor buys a 6-month Eurodeposit at $\$Q$ and simultaneously goes long a 6-month forward contract for a

Where implied forward rates are calculated using money market securities, there is a subtle difference when compared to implied forward rates from bonds. For example, if T is 6 months and the annualized T period interest rate is 10%, then $r(0,T) = 5\%$. If N is 3 months and the associated N-period rate is also 10% annualized, then $r(0,N) = 2.5\%$. In this case, $i(0,T - N)$, which is the 3-month interest rate starting in 3 months, is determined as $(1.05) = (1.025)(1 + i(0,T - N))$ or $i(0,T - N) = 2.439\%$. Using a straightforward application of intuition associated with implied forward rate calculations from bond markets, it may seem that $i(0,T - N)$ would have to be 2.5%, but this does not happen because of the linear relationship among money market interest rates.

The forward–forward arbitrage extends naturally to the case where the forward contracts are embedded in swap transactions. However, in the swap arbitrage it is not possible to offset both the spot/forward foreign exchange (FX) transactions as well as the cash market transactions in both the foreign and domestic markets at $t = 0$. Much as with the spot-forward covered interest arbitrage that is executed using a swap, this complication is handled by adjusting one of the forward positions using an outright forward contract.

For example, consider the case where the trader is short the swap for forward delivery at $t = N$ and long the swap for delivery at $t = T$. Using Table 4.4 as a reference point, having the $t = 0$ value of the spot FX transactions equal can be accomplished by having the spot FX values being exchanged at $t = 0$ set equal to $\$Q(1 + r(0,N))(1 + r^*(0,N))$. In this case, the trader has no position in spot currency. However, unlike the forward–forward arbitrage, the trader now has *uncertainty* associated with the principal value applicable to the forward transactions for $t = T$. The cash market transactions require that $\$(Q/F(0,N))$ $(1 + r(0,N))(1 + r^*(0,T))$ units of FX be delivered for exchange into US$ at $F(0,T)$. But, the corresponding spot FX transaction only provided for $\$(Q/S(0))(1 + r(0,N))(1 + r^*(0,N))$. This leaves a residual forward position to be covered that is equal to $\$(Q/S(0))(1 + r^*(0,N))(r^*(0,T) - r(0,N))$.

D. Designing Speculative Trading Strategies

The CIP condition can be used to specify various types of speculative currency spread trading strategies, including speculative trades used by banks in the

Eurodeposit with an initial 6-month maturity. The principal value (M) for the forward contract is set to equate the maturity value of the 6-month Eurodeposit $\$(Q(1 + r(0,6 \text{ months})))$. In other words, $M = (\$Q(1 + r(0,6 \text{ months}))) (1 + e(0,6 \text{ months})))$, where $e(0,T)$ is the $t = 0$ interest rate quoted on the Eurodeposit forward contract that requires delivery of a 6-month Eurodeposit in 6-months. For the return on this rollover strategy to equal the buy-and-hold return, $e(0,T)$ has to be the implied forward rate.

swap market. For illustrative purposes, the general results can be done using the CIP condition expressed in terms of forward contracts. Assuming that the CIP condition holds with equality, manipulation of the CIP equation gives:

$$i(0,T-N) = i = i^*(0,T-N) + (1 + i^*(0,T-N))\frac{F(0,T) - F(0,N)}{F(0,N)}$$

$$= i^* + (1 + i^*)\frac{F(T) - F(N)}{F(N)}$$

Now consider a first difference equation for this CIP condition:[14]

$$\Delta i - \left\{\Delta i^* + (1 + i^*)\Delta\left[\frac{F(T) - F(N)}{F(0,N)}\right] + \frac{F(T) - F(N)}{F(N)}\Delta[(1 + i*)]\right\} = 0$$

Assuming that the last term can be safely ignored for present purposes, as it is of second order, expanding and manipulating gives an approximation to the condition desired, where $FPS(t) = \{F(t,T) - F(t,N)\}$:

$$\Delta i = \Delta i^* + (1 + i^*)\left[\frac{\Delta(FPS)}{F(N)} - \frac{FPS}{F(N)}\frac{\Delta F(N)}{F(N)}\right]$$

$$= \Delta i^* + (1 + i^*)\frac{\Delta(FPS)}{F(N)} - (i - i^*)\frac{\Delta F(N)}{F(N)}$$

This result can be rearranged to get the profit function for a one-to-one currency spread:

$$\Delta FPS = \Delta\{F(T) - F(N)\} = \frac{F(1,N)}{(1 + i^*)}\{\Delta i - \Delta i^*\} + \frac{(i - i^*)}{(1 + i^*)}\Delta F(N)$$

Examining this result, it can be seen that the profit function for a one-to-one currency spread depends on the difference in changes of U.S. and Canadian interest rates and on the change in the level of the exchange rate. Insofar as $(i - i^*)$ is small, there is no need to tail the spread; in other words, the ΔF term is effectively zero. In this case, the profit function will be dominated by the first term, the difference in the changes of domestic and foreign interest rates. Poitras (1997) provides a substantial development of these concepts.

Application of this profit function to swap speculation follows from inspection of Table 4.5, where the profit function can be written as:

[14]For ease of exposition, it is assumed that the relevant variables satisfy the conventional calculus regularity conditions. In practice, this assumption requires that the futures positions be continuously adjusted.

TABLE 4.5   Bankers' Foreign Exchange Swap Speculation

Date	Nearby (N) swap contract	Deferred (T) swap contract
$t = 0$	Short the swap that sells $\$Q$ of domestic currency in exchange for a forward purchase of $\$[Q/S(0)]$ of FX at $F(0,N)$. *Note*: The $\$Q$ spot FX transactions at $t = 0$ cancel.	Long the swap that buys Q of domestic currency in exchange for selling forward $[Q/S(0)]$ of FX at $F(0,T)$.
$t = N$	Receive delivery of domestic currency from the maturing nearby swap $= [\$Q/S(0)]$ at $F(0,N)$ that is immediately swapped by entering into a $T - N$ period swap that delivers $[Q/S(0)]F(0,N)$ of domestic currency in exchange for receiving $[(Q/S(0))F(0,N)]/S(N)$ at $F(N,T)$ at time T.	The swap from $t = 0$ is required to deliver domestic currency of $[Q/S(0)]$ at $F(0,T)$ while the swap from $t = N$ receives domestic currency of $[(Q/S(0))(F(0,N)/S(N)]$ at $F(N,T)$.

$$\pi(T) = [Q/S(0)]\{[F(N,T)/S(N)] - [F(0,T)/F(0,N)]\}$$
$$= [Q/S(0)]\{(1 + ic(N,T)) - (1 + ic(0,T-N))\} = [Q/S(0)]\{ic(N,T) - ic(0,T-N)\}$$

Note: Observing that $ic = (r - r^*)/(1 + r^*)$ and substituting where appropriate reveals the connection between the profit function of the bankers' swap speculation and the profit function for a 1–1 spread.

$$\pi(T) = \frac{Q}{S(0)}\left[\frac{F(N,T)}{S(N)} - \frac{F(0,T)}{F(0,N)}\right]$$
$$= \frac{Q}{S(0)}\{ic(N,T) - ic(0,T-N)\}$$
$$= \frac{Q}{S(0)}\left[\frac{r(N,T) - r^*(N,T)}{1 + r^*(N,T)} - \frac{i(0,T-N) - i^*(0,T-N)}{1 + i^*(0,T-N)}\right]$$
$$\cong \frac{Q}{S(0)}\{(r(N,T) - r^*(N,T)) - (i(0,T-N) - i^*(0,T-N))\}$$

The logic associated with the profit function for the one-to-one currency spread can be applied directly to the swap speculation. Hence, the analysis of speculative profits on interbank swap speculation can be approached using the techniques developed for the general analysis of speculative trading strategies.

E. LONG-TERM FORWARD EXCHANGE RATES

Extending the Table 4.3 conventional covered interest arbitrage formula for pricing short-term forward exchange contracts to long term, N-year forward contracts gives:

$$FF_N = \frac{(1 + z_N)^N}{(1 + z_N^*)^N} S$$

where FF_N is the N-year, theoretical, arbitrage-consistent, forward exchange rate in domestic direct terms; S is the spot exchange rate in domestic direct terms; z_N is the N-year, domestic, *zero-coupon* interest rate; and z_N^* is the N-year zero-coupon foreign interest rate.[15] Consistent with an arbitrage relationship, all variables in the long-term CIP equation are available at the same date, say $t = 0$. Manipulation of the CIP condition leads immediately to an expression for the covered interest rate deviations:

$$z_N - z_N^* - \left[\left(\left\{ \frac{F_N}{S} \right\}^{1/N} - 1 \right)(1 + z_N^*) \right] = \text{deviation}_N$$

where F_N is the forward exchange rate quoted in the foreign exchange market. Figure 4.5 provides long-term FX rates for August 8, 1994 (see also Fig. 4.2).

As it turns out, empirical analysis of deviations from long-term covered interest arbitrage is complicated by the market preference for using coupon bonds to raise long-term funds. Hence, while the CIP condition is applicable to short-term money market instruments, such as Eurodeposits, BAs, T-bills, and commercial paper that feature zero coupons, it is not immediately applicable to markets that feature coupon-bearing securities. Even though zero-coupon instruments are traded in the long-term market, such as U.S. Treasury strips (Gregory and Livingston, 1992), the bulk of market liquidity is focused on trading coupon-bearing securities.[16] Hence, coupon bonds are most representative of actual, long-term market interest rates. Given this, appropriate calculation of the covered interest deviations requires that observed coupon bond rates be converted to zero-coupon rates before being used to determine the deviations. This involves the use of a bootstrap technique to "back-out" the zero-coupon rates implied in the coupon bond term structure. A worked example of the bootstrapping methodology is given in Box 7 and, for semi-annual bonds, in Table 4.6.[17]

---

[15]Domestic direct terms is defined as units of domestic currency to units of foreign currency.

[16]In addition, due to pricing anomalies, there are difficulties associated with using the observed zero-coupon yields quoted for U.S. Treasury strips (Daves and Ehrhardt, 1993).

[17]There are two methods for determining the spot interest rate. Box 7 describes the par bond approach using semiannual coupon bonds. This method uses the result that when a bond sells at par then the coupon percentage is equal to the stated yield to maturity. In this case, par value can be used for the price of the bond being used to determine the spot interest rates and the yield to maturity used as the coupon. The alternative approach is to work directly with the observed prices and coupons. Instead of using par value, the price used is the observed price and the stated coupon is used for the coupon. There are some computational advantages to using the par bond approach.

Currency Cross Rates

Supplied by Royal Bank of Canada - indicative wholesale late afternoon rates

	C$	US$	DM	Yen	£	Fr. fr.	Sw. fr.	A$
Canadian $	...	1.37775	0.87026	0.01357	2.12070	0.25399	1.03164	1.01905
U.S.$	0.72582	...	0.63165	0.00985	1.53925	0.18435	0.74878	0.73965
Deutschmark	1.14908	1.58315	...	0.01559	2.43686	0.29185	1.18544	1.17098
Japanese yen	73.69	101.53	64.13	...	156.27	18.72	76.02	75.09
British pnd.	0.47154	0.64967	0.41036	0.00640	...	0.11977	0.48646	0.48053
French franc	3.93722	5.42450	3.42640	0.05343	8.34966	...	4.06177	4.01223
Swiss franc	0.96933	1.33550	0.84357	0.01315	2.05567	0.24620	...	0.98780
Australian $	0.98130	1.35199	0.85399	0.01332	2.08105	0.24924	1.01235	...

Forward Exchange Rates

Supplied by Royal Bank of Canada - indicative wholesale late afternoon rates

Per US$	Spot	1-mo	3-mo	6-mo	1-yr	2-yr	3-yr	4-yr	5-yr
Canadian $	1.3778	1.3789	1.3808	1.3844	1.3960	1.4198	1.4428	1.4633	1.4883
Japanese yen	101.53	101.33	100.89	100.10	98.58	94.53	91.83	89.62	87.33
Deutschmark	1.5832	1.5839	1.5839	1.5816	1.5754	1.7032	1.7531	1.8032	1.8532
British pound*	1.5393	1.5386	1.5367	1.5347	1.5275	1.5768	1.6118	1.6517	1.6868

Per C$									
U.S.$	0.7258	0.7252	0.7242	0.7224	0.7164	0.7043	0.6931	0.6834	0.6719
Japanese yen	73.69	73.49	73.06	72.30	70.61	66.58	63.65	61.25	58.68
Deutschmark	1.1491	1.1487	1.1471	1.1424	1.1285	1.1996	1.2151	1.2323	1.2452
British pound*	2.1207	2.1214	2.1219	2.1246	2.1324	2.2386	2.3254	2.4169	2.5103

* inverted

Mid-market rates in Toronto at noon, Aug. 8, 1994.

		$1 U.S. in Cdn.$ =	$1 Cdn. in U.S.$ =
U.S./Canada spot		1.3797	0.7248
1 month forward		1.3808	0.7242
2 months forward		1.3818	0.7237
3 months forward		1.3827	0.7232
6 months forward		1.3862	0.7214
12 months forward		1.3973	0.7157
3 years forward		1.4457	0.6917
5 years forward		1.4917	0.6704
7 years forward		1.5622	0.6401
10 years forward		1.6547	0.6043
Canadian dollar	High	1.3083	0.7644
in 1994:	Low	1.3990	0.7148
	Average	1.3712	0.7293

FIGURE 4.5 Long-term forward exchange rates. (*Source: Globe and Mail* and *Financial Post*, August 8, 1994. With permission.)

TABLE 4.6 Bootstrapping Spot Interest Rates for Semiannual Bonds

The bootstrapping technique (e.g., Smith, 1991; Iben, 1992), is an iterative process for calculating implied zero-coupon interest rates, so-called spot interest rates, from observed coupon bond rates. The process requires the observed yields for coupon bonds of each relevant term to maturity along the yield curve. In practice, spot rates would typically be extracted from a fitted yield curve for federal government bonds, Treasury bonds in the United States or Government of Canada bonds in Canada. Because these types of bonds pay semiannual coupons, precision requires that the bootstrap be executed at semiannual intervals.

For purposes of illustration, assume that the relevant bonds are sold at par and pay coupons semiannually. Further assume that the observed 6-month yield is 8.87%. Taking this yield to be quoted ex-dividend means that the quoted yield is for a 6-month zero-coupon bond. If the observed yield on a 1-year semiannual coupon bond is assumed to be 9.04, for a $100 par value bond this implies a semiannual coupon payment of 4.52. Given this, the iteration for solving a sequence of implied zero coupon rates begins by discounting the first semiannual coupon payment at the 6-month, zero-coupon rate and solving for the implied 1-year zero coupon rate. For a bond sold at par this requires that:

$$100 = \frac{4.52}{1 + \frac{.0887}{2}} + \frac{104.52}{\left(1 + \frac{z_1}{2}\right)^2}$$

where z_1 is the implied 1-year zero coupon rate, that can be calculated as 0.090438.

Having solved for z_1, the next step in the iteration involves using z_1 to solve the implied zero coupon rate, $z_{1.5}$, using a 1.5-year par coupon bond. If the observed rate on 1.5-year coupon bonds is 9.155, then this implies a semiannual coupon payment on a $100 par bond of 4.5775. This leads to:

$$100 = \frac{4.5775}{1 + \frac{0.0887}{2}} + \frac{4.5775}{\left(1 + \frac{z_1}{2}\right)^2} + \frac{104.5775}{\left(1 + \frac{z_{1.5}}{2}\right)^3}$$

Substituting the value for the z_1 determined previously and solving gives $z_{1.5} = 0.091629$. The next step in the iteration involves solving for z_2. Taking the observed 2-year yield to be 9.2% produces:

$$100 = \frac{4.6}{1 + \frac{z_5}{2}} + \frac{4.6}{\left(1 + \frac{z_1}{2}\right)^2} + \frac{4.6}{\left(\frac{1+z_{1.5}}{2}\right)^3} + \frac{104.6}{\left(1 + \frac{z_2}{2}\right)^4}$$

This formula can be used to solve for z_2 using the previously computed values for z_1 and $z_{1.5}$. This iterative process continues until the zero-coupon rate for the desired term to maturity is calculated. The relevant zero-coupon rate can then be used to do calculations involving long-term covered interest arbitrage.

Box 7 provides the spot interest rates needed to find a solution for the following problem: On August 8, 1994, the spot and 5-year forward rates for the C$/US$ exchange rate were $1.3797 and $1.4917, respectively. Using interest rate and exchange rate information provided in Figs. 4.4, 4.5, and 4.6, what "arbitrage-free" interest rate on 5-year, zero-coupon, US$ instruments would be consistent with CIP? To answer this question it is necessary to pick

CANADIAN BONDS

Selected quotations, with changes since the previous day, on actively traded bond issues, provided by RBC Dominion Securities. Yields are calculated to full maturity, unless marked C to indicate callable date. Price is the midpoint between final bid and ask quotations Aug. 8, 1994.

Issuer	Coupon	Maturity	Price	Yield $ Chg	Issuer	Coupon	Maturity	Price	Yield $ Chg
GOVERNMENT OF CANADA					NEWFOUNDLAND	10 13	22 NOV 14	101.025	10.002 + 0.950
CANADA	4.75	15 MAR 96	95.625	7.708 + 0.300	NOVA SCOTIA	9.60	30 JAN 22	97.325	9.884 + 0.950
CANADA	6.50	1 AUG 96	97.505	7.887 + 0.360	ONTARIO HYD	10.88	8 JAN 96	103.930	7.837 − 0.240
CANADA	7.75	15 SEP 96	99.795	7.852 + 0.420	ONTARIO HYD	7.25	31 MAR 98	95.725	8.644 + 0.450
CANADA	7.50	1 JUL 97	98.225	8.197 − 0.425	ONTARIO HYD	9.63	3 AUG 99	103.400	8.765 + 0.700
CANADA	6.25	1 FEB 98	93.600	8.418 + 0.450	ONTARIO HYD	8.63	6 FEB 02	96.575	9.269 + 0.700
CANADA	6.50	1 SEP 98	93.350	8.474 + 0.500	ONTARIO HYD	9.00	24 JUN 02	98.325	9.301 − 0.700
CANADA	5.75	1 MAR 99	89.850	8.486 + 0.600	ONTARIO	8.75	16 APR 97	100.775	8.411 + 0.800
CANADA	7.75	1 SEP 99	96.800	8.542 + 0.600	ONTARIO	9.00	15 SEP 04	97.200	9.434 + 0.800
CANADA	9.25	1 DEC 95	102.550	8.634 + 0.600	ONTARIO	7.50	7 FEB 24	78.600	9.713 + 0.900
CANADA	9.75	1 JUN 01	104.625	8.821 + 0.700	P E I	9.75	30 APR 02	101.125	9.555 − 0.550
CANADA	9.50	1 OCT 01	103.425	8.836 + 0.700	P E I	11.00	19 SEP 11	108.300	9.976 + 0.900
CANADA	9.75	1 DEC 01	104.750	8.848 + 0.700	QUEBEC	8.00	30 MAR 98	97.625	8.774 − 0.450
CANADA	8.50	1 APR 02	97.950	8.672 − 0.700	QUEBEC	10.25	7 APR 98	104.375	8.813 − 0.450
CANADA	7.25	1 JUN 03	89.650	8.973 + 0.700	QUEBEC	10.25	15 OCT 01	103.550	9.549 − 0.750
CANADA	7.50	1 DEC 03	90.800	8.977 + 0.750	QUEBEC	9.38	16 JAN 23	93.425	10.079 − 1.200
CANADA	10.25	1 FEB 04	107.750	9.014 + 0.650	SASKATCHEWAN	9.88	6 JUL 99	103.975	8.852 + 0.700
CANADA	6.50	1 JUN 04	84.000	8.938 − 0.750	SASKATCHEWAN	9.50	16 AUG 04	99.625	9.559 − 0.750
CANADA	9.00	1 DEC 04	99.863	9.017 + 0.953	SASKATCHEWAN	9.60	4 FEB 22	98.300	9.779 − 1.100
CANADA	10.00	1 JUN 08	106.650	9.139 + 0.900	TORONTO-MET	10.38	4 SEP 01	106.250	9.151 + 0.650
CANADA	9.50	1 JUN 10	102.850	9.152 − 0.950	**CORPORATE**				
CANADA	9.00	1 MAR 11	98.650	9.159 + 0.950	ALTA ENERGY	8.15	31 JUL 03	91.250	9.628 − 0.625
CANADA	10.25	15 MAR 14	109.400	9.204 + 1.000	BELL CANADA	9.20	1 JUN 99	101.375	8.836 − 0.500
CANADA	9.75	1 JUN 21	105.650	9.177 − 1.150	BELL CANADA	9.50	15 JUN 02	100.750	9.358 − 0.625
CANADA	8.00	1 JUN 23	88.150	9.174 + 1.000	BELL CANADA	9.70	15 DEC 32	99.375	9.760 − 1.000
CMHC	8.25	3 AUG 99	98.200	8.703 + 0.600	BC TELEPHONE	9.65	8 APR 22	99.875	9.661 − 1.000
REAL RETURNS	4.25	1 DEC 21	94.500	4.606 + 0.125	CDN IMP BANK	7.10	10 MAR 04	85.375	9.454 − 0.625
PROVINCIAL					CAN TRUST M	10.05	4 AUG 14	101.375	9.890 − 0.675
ALBERTA	7.00	20 AUG 97	95.650	8.278 + 0.500	CDN UTIL	8.73	1 JUN 04	95.875	9.379 − 0.625
ALBERTA	6.50	1 SEP 99	99.190	8.700 + 0.620	CDN UTIL	9.40	1 MAY 23	97.375	9.669 − 0.875
ALBERTA	5.38	1 JUN 04	82.238	9.158 − 0.700	FINNING LTD	8.35	22 MAR 04	90.375	9.925 − 0.625
B C	7.00	9 JUN 99	93.700	8.621 + 0.650	IMASCO LTD	8.38	23 JUN 03	92.625	9.628 − 0.625
B C	9.00	9 JAN 02	99.425	9.105 + 0.650	INTERPRV PIP	8.20	15 FEB 24	85.000	9.757 − 0.875
B C	9.00	21 JUN 04	98.400	9.248 + 0.750	MOLSON BREW	8.20	11 MAR 03	92.125	9.565 − 0.500
B C	8.50	23 AUG 13	91.550	9.466 − 1.000	MOLSON BREW	8.40	7 DEC 18	87.000	9.811 − 0.750
B C	8.00	8 SEP 23	85.225	9.505 + 1.000	MAR TEL + TEL	10.13	31 JUL 97	104.000	8.563 − 0.500
HYDRO QUEBEC	9.25	2 DEC 95	102.025	8.254 + 0.350	NVA SCOT PWR	6.50	15 DEC 99	91.750	8.828 − 0.500
HYDRO QUEBEC	10.88	26 JUL 01	106.775	9.517 − 0.800	NVA SCOT PWR	7.70	15 OCT 03	88.500	9.612 − 0.625
HYDRO QUEBEC	11.00	15 AUG 20	108.725	10.049 + 1.350	NVA SCOT PWR	9.75	2 AUG 19	99.375	9.817 + 1.000
HYDRO QUEBEC	9.63	15 JUL 22	95.825	10.073 + 1.250	NRTH TELECOM	7.45	10 MAR 98	96.000	8.776 − 0.375
MANITOBA	6.75	24 AUG 95	99.425	7.340 − 0.150	NOVA CORP	8.30	15 JUL 03	92.250	9.611 + 0.625
MANITOBA	7.00	19 APR 99	93.500	8.717 + 0.650	ROYAL BANK	10.50	1 MAR 02	106.000	9.371 − 0.500
MANITOBA	7.88	7 APR 03	92.125	9.213 + 0.650	SUNCOR INC	7.40	23 FEB 04	86.375	9.616 − 0.625
MANITOBA	10.50	5 MAR 31	109.400	9.569 + 1.350	THOMSON CORP	9.15	6 JUL 04	97.250	9.584 − 0.625
NEW BRUNSWIC	7.00	17 MAR 98	95.225	8.570 + 0.400	TRANSCDA PIP	9.45	20 MAR 18	96.625	9.818 + 0.875
NEW BRUNSWIC	8.38	26 AUG 02	95.250	9.224 + 0.550	UNION GAS	8.75	3 AUG 18	89.875	9.858 − 0.875
NEW BRUNSWIC	8.50	28 JUN 13	90.375	9.613 + 0.850	WSTCOAST TRN	8.50	4 SEP 18	87.750	9.837 + 0.750

BOND INDEX
ScotiaMcLeod Bond Indexes

Index	Close	% chg	Yield	Chg	52 wk High	52 wk Low
Short	222.03	0.38	8.249	−0.14	231.91	215.83
Mid	232.90	0.59	9.071	−0.10	258.78	223.77
Long	243.42	0.79	9.439	−0.09	282.93	232.20
Universe	234.84	0.56	8.857	−0.11	258.29	226.21

BENCHMARK
INTERNATIONAL BONDS

Issuer	Coupon	Maturity	Price	Yield $ chg
U.S. Treasury	6¼	Aug/23	84 29/32	7.54 + 3/32
British gilt	9	Oct/08	104 24/32	8.41 + 12/32
German	6¼	Sep/04	98.76	6.93 −0.36
Japan # 164	4.5	2003	96.54	4.630 + 0.03

FIGURE 4.6 Canadian bond interest rates. (*Source: Globe and Mail*, August 8, 1994. With permission.)

out the appropriate Canadian interest rates to use for determining the spot interest rates. For our purpose, it is sufficient to assume that all bonds pay annual coupons. (The gain in precision using semiannual calculations, as in Table 4.6, is lost in the slippage required to identify bonds with appropriate maturities.) For the first spot interest rate, use the 1-year t-bill rate. For the

---

BOX 7

Example: Roughly Solving the Canadian Spot Interest Rates

Assume annual coupon payments. From Figs. 4.4 and 4.6 pick the following bills/bonds:

1 year t-bill $z_1 = .0720$
6.5% 1 Aug. 1996; $P_2 = 97.505$ $(y_2 = 0.07887)$
7.5% 1 Jul. 1997; $P_3 = 98.225$ $(y_3 = 0.08197)$
6.5% 1 Sept. 1998; $P_4 = 93.350$ $(y_4 = 0.08474)$
7.75 1 Sept. 1999; $P_5 = 96.800$ $(y_5 = 0.08542)$

The two possible bootstrap solution techniques are the direct approach and the par bond approach. The direct approach involves using the observed price and coupon to solve for the spot interest rate. Solving for z_2:

$$97.505 = 6.5/(1 + z_1) + 106.5/(1 + z_2)^2$$

Using this method, $z_2 = .0792$.

For the par bond approach, use the result that when the stated yield to maturity equals the coupon divided by the par value, then the bond sells at par:

$$100 = 7.887/(1 + z_1) + 107.887/(1 + z_2)^2$$

Using this method, $z_2 = 0.0791428$.

Why the difference, when the method would appear to be exactly the same? Yields used are semiannual, not annual, compounded while the prices/coupons are exact (except that annual coupon payments have been assumed in making the calculations). The differences involved are generally small:

Par bond: $z_3 = 0.082423$; $z_4 = 0.0854697$; $z_5 = 0.0861374$

Price/coupon: $z_3 = 0.08232$; $z_4 = 0.08595$; $z_5 = 0.08630$

appropriate bonds, select the Government of Canada bond with a maturity closest to August 4. The relevant bonds would be 6.5% of August 1, 1996; 7.5% of July 1, 1997; 6.5% of September 1, 1998; and 7.75% of September 1, 1999.

In addition to limitations on issuing appropriate long-term zero-coupon instruments, there are a number of other institutional factors that impose significant restrictions on arbitrage trading of long-term forward exchange contracts (e.g., Popper, 1993). For example, because the bulk of trading activity involving currency hedged bond issues is done in the currency swap market, the relevant trading strategy to consider is between a fully hedged borrowing and the related currency swap.[18] In the special case of a zero-coupon currency swap these two trades are equivalent; however, this is not the case when coupon bonds are involved. The resulting trading strategies involve comparing cash flows that are unequal at future payment dates, creating a significant problem for specifying the arbitrage portfolio. Other factors such as taxes and transaction costs (e.g., wider bid/offer spreads and longer execution times) also complicate the analysis.

III. WHEN-ISSUED ARBITRAGE

A. THE WHEN-ISSUED MARKET FOR GOVERNMENT OF CANADA TREASURY BILLS

Each week, the Government of Canada issues 3 and 6 month treasury bills (t-bills) at auction.[19] Barring holidays, this price discrimination auction now takes place on Tuesday with delivery (and maturity) of the t-bills occurring on Wednesday. Announcement of the size of the following week's offerings is made at the same time (2:00 p.m. Tuesday) as the results for that week's auction are announced. Unlike the United States, where limited public participation and noncompetitive tenders at the weekly T-bill auction are permitted, only banks and investment dealers eligible to act as primary distributors of new Government of Canada issues are eligible to submit "sealed" competitive tenders at the Canadian t-bill auction. No commissions are paid on

---

[18]The relevant trading strategies and arbitrage conditions are discussed in Popper (1993) and Poitras (1992, 1999).

[19]The Government of Canada also can issues 12-month t-bills at the weekly auction that are also traded on a wi basis. However, in Poitras (1991) for part of the sample, 12-month t-bills were only issued biweekly, creating sampling problems. In addition, the 12-month cash and wi markets are the thinnest of the three available maturities.

allotted tenders. Investors with "jobber" status are expected to actively participate at the auction.

T-bills to be auctioned at the next tender are traded on a *when-issued* (*wi*)
basis from the time of the announcement of the size of the tender until the
auction takes place. In other words, the *wi* t-bill market is a forward market
for t-bills with maximum contract maturities of one week.[20] More precisely, a
when-issued t-bill is a contract either to purchase or sell t-bills that are to be
auctioned at the next tender. Settlement of *wi* transactions is made in t-bills on
the next business day following the auction. Typically, active *wi* trading begins
on the Wednesday preceding the tender and continues up to the actual
auction.[21] Active participants in the *wi* market are the investment dealers,
the banks, and major institutional investors. While there was some *wi* trade
prior to 1978, the formal beginning of the *wi* market in Canada can be traced
to the introduction of screen-oriented, brokered *wi* trading in the fall of 1978.
By the early 1990s, more than half of trading in *wi*s was done through screen-
oriented broker services.[22] The widespread use of screen-oriented trading
means that *wi* activity is highly visible to other participants in the t-bill
market.

The *wi* market provides large t-bill cash market participants with a relatively inexpensive method for forward trading Canadian t-bills. Like other
forward markets, there is an essential connection between forward trading and

[20]The structure of the Canadian t-bill auction process differs somewhat from that in the United
States. For example, as well as having different auction days and somewhat different auction
procedures, there is a 3-day settlement lag in the United States and only a 1-day lag in Canada. As a
result, in the United States *wi* T-bill trading often refers to trade in new T-bills in the period
between auction and settlement (Stigum, 1983). In Canada, *wi* t-bill trade refers only to the trade
in to-be-issued t-bills occurring between the announcement of tranche sizes and the auction.
When-issued trading also occurs in instruments other than t-bills—such as Government of
Canada marketable bonds. Finally, there is no formal restriction on *wi* trade limiting the maximum
maturity to 1 week. Rather, it is the requirements of t-bill traders that determine the available
contract maturities.

[21]While there is some *wi* trade on the auction date, in the period between auction and
settlement the market is primarily concerned with sorting out of cash positions arising from the
auction. Hence, the market does not usually start focusing on *wi* trading for the next auction until
the day following the auction.

[22]In screen-oriented trading, bids and offers are listed on computer terminal screens in the
offices of subscribers to the service. Bids, offers, and amounts for *wi* trades are entered directly
onto the screen by the trader. Trades are executed by accepting one the positions listed on the
screen, again by making the appropriate terminal data input. Once a trade is executed, the broker
is responsible for recording the relevant transaction information. Off-screen brokered trading of
*wi*s is conducted like conventional over-the-counter (OTC) trading. Usage of *wi* brokers is
significantly affected by the ability of investment dealers to do *wi* trades directly with their
accounts. Typical broker commissions for *wi*s are one half a basis point each way.

cash market participation. For example, only eligible auction participants, a significant subset of all *wi* traders, have the ability to effectively short sell *wi* positions. While there is some purely speculative participation by forward market participants (e.g., from small banks seeking to make a rate play without the costs of acquiring t-bills), the bulk of contracts are initiated to reflect t-bill purchases at the ensuing auction. This lack of small speculative participation makes the *wi* market unlike a t-bill futures market. In the Canadian context, this is significant because the only futures contract for Canadian t-bills has been delisted by the Toronto Futures Exchange.[23] The *wi* market differs in a number of other ways from a typical futures market: While the deliverable commodity is homogeneous, *wi* contracts are not standardized in size. Also, a smaller performance deposit (margin) is required,[24] there is no marking to market, and trading is not on a centralized exchange. Most importantly, the 1-week trading horizon for *wi*s differs markedly from the maturity dates typically associated with futures.

Regarding the liquidity of the market, there is at best only limited quantitative information. Typically, there is a considerable narrowing of the bid/offer for a *wi* contract as the auction date approaches. In terms of the net position of traders and the absolute size of outstanding contracts, the data are limited. However, Fig. 4.7 demonstrates that the major dealers are generally net short. Theoretically, net short positions by dealers could arise from a number of factors, most importantly speculating on increasing yields, hedging inventory against increasing yields, and hedging anticipated auction winnings. In practice, it appears as though the use of *wi*s to hedge anticipated auction winnings is an important part of the dealer's use of *wi*s. Based on this, it is useful to examine the actual arbitrage mechanics for *wi*s and verify what types of restrictions affect these trades in practice. In particular, transactions costs are a necessary, but not usually sufficient, adjustment. The introduction of transaction costs effectively transforms the arbitrage equality restriction into upper and lower arbitrage boundary restrictions providing an arbitrage band within which some variation from the frictionless arbitrage condition is permitted.

---

[23]In 1989, the Montreal Exchange launched a new Government of Canada bond contract. More recently, a Bankers' Acceptance contract has been offered. For more on other available hedging instruments see the Montreal Exchange website. By draining off liquidity, the growth of the *wi* market has undoubtedly contributed to the lack of success of the t-bill futures contract.

[24]The margin requirements for *wi*s arise out of the Investment Dealers Association (IDA) regulations. For IDA purposes, *wi*s are treated as contingent liabilities, much as with futures contracts. Margin requirements are capital sufficient to cover 1% of the outstanding contingent liability.

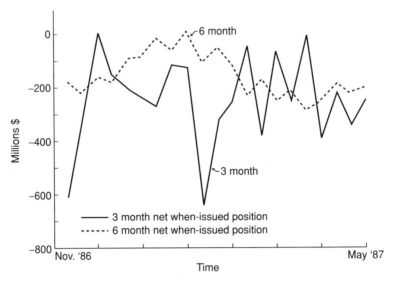

FIGURE 4.7   When-issued positions of major dealers. (*Source:* Poitras, G., *Canadian Journal of Economics*, 24, 604–623, 1991. With permission.)

B. THE WHEN-ISSUED CASH-AND-CARRY ARBITRAGE

To derive the long cash-and-carry arbitrage condition for a 3-month wi, the profit function at $t = 0$ involves the *purchase* of a 3-month + N-day T-bill financed at the term call loan rate. Term financing is required for the borrowing rate to be riskless. The call loan rate is used because this market typically provides the best combination of availability of funds and competitive rates. This purchase is simultaneously covered with the sale of a 3-month wi maturing in N days. In other words, the t-bill being purchased is the "old" 6-month t-bill that is to be reopened at the next 3-month auction, $N < 7$. This cash t-bill purchase is simultaneously covered with a wi short. Schematically, the long arbitrage trade is described in Table 4.7. While this profit function is consistent with the idealized full carry model, it is somewhat misleading in the case of t-bills in that $P(0)$ will increase over time due to the effect of maturity reduction. This is reflected in the $r(0,N)$ term that incorporates the return on the underlying t-bill. In terms of yields, it can be shown (Poitras, 1997) that the profit function can be approximated as:

$$\pi(0,N) = i^* - [i + (N/91)(i - R)] \leq 0$$

TABLE 4.7   Derivation of the Yield Version of the Cash-and-Carry

---

Assume that the t-bill purchase can be financed at the term call (or term repo) rate, that the par values of the t-bill and *wi* have been normalized to 1, and that the deliverable t-bill has 91 days (i.e., only the 3-month *wi* case is being considered). Given this, $P(0) = 1/(1 + (i(91 + N)/365))$ and $wi(0) = 1/(1 + (i^*(91/365)))$ where i is the T-bill rate and i^* is the *wi* rate at time 0. The cost of carrying the t-bill from time 0 to N at the term repo rate is $P(0)((R)(N/365)) = P(0) R(0,N)$ where R is the annualized term call rate.

With these assumptions and ignoring transaction costs, the no arbitrage profit condition is

$$\pi(0) = wi(0) - [P(0)(1 + r(0,N))] = 0$$

where $r(0,N) = R(0,N) - i(0,N) = (R(0) - i(0))(N/365)$

Evaluating individual terms:

$$\frac{(wi(0) - P(0)) = ((i^* - i)(91/365)) + (i(N/365))}{(1 + (i(91 + N)/365))(1 + (i^*(91/365)))}$$

Similarly, the interest expense can be derived:

$$P(0)R(0,N) = (R(N/365))(1/(1 + (i(91 + N)/365)))$$

After manipulating the two expressions, evaluation of the resulting numerator gives:

$$i^* - i \le i(N/91) - (R(N/91))(1 + (i^*(91/365)))$$

The result in the text follows from ignoring the second order term $Ri^*(N/365)$.

---

where i^* is the promised yield at $t = 0$ on the 91-day *wi* t-bill, i is the secondary market yield on the (to-be-reopened) $91 + N$-day t-bill, and R is the term call loan rate with all interest rates expressed in annualized form. In other words, the *wi* rate is bounded from above by the t-bill rate and the cost of carrying the t-bill between time 0 and N.

The profit function for the short cash-and-carry arbitrage requires the 3-month $+$ N-day) t-bill to be "shorted". The implied acquisition of the appropriate t-bill can be done by doing a term *reverse* repo at annualized rate RR using the correctly dated t-bill as underlying collateral. This t-bill is then sold and the funds acquired are used to cover the cost of doing the reverse. Simultaneously, the short t-bill position is covered by taking an equal par value amount of long *wi* contracts. At delivery, the t-bills acquired from the long *wi* position are used to cover the short position created by the reverse and the profit function is

$$\pi(0,N) = i^* - [i + (N/91)(i - RR)] \ge 0$$

In words, the short cash arbitrage provides a lower bound on the *wi* rate. Hence, in addition to transaction costs, the upper and lower boundaries use different borrowing/lending rates.

While these profit functions provide theoretical upper and lower bounds on
wi rates, the adherence of wi rates to the boundary restrictions depends on the
ability of market participants to execute the arbitrages. From a trading perspective, there are considerably more impediments to executing the wi arbitrages than there are on similar arbitrages for, say, U.S. t-bill futures. In
particular, unlike the term repo market in the United States, the term call
(or repo) market in Canada is quite thin. This is especially so for reverses. In
practice, the long wi arbitrage would likely have to be financed in the overnight call market. This would require the cash position to be refinanced on a
daily basis.[25] Given the short trading horizon, this will not severely restrict
execution, only the level of riskiness. On the other hand, the reverse would
likely require the participation of an institutional t-bill account that would
require some form of short sale fee. By implication, as is in a number of other
financial markets, the short arbitrage provides a significantly weaker restriction than the long arbitrage. This means that large deviations from zero
arbitrage would tend to be positive.

In order to assess the performance of the wi cash-and-carry trade, Poitras
(1991) uses cash and wi transactions in which the bid/offer spread[26] as well as
broker commissions on the wi are taken into account. Assuming wi bid/offer
spreads of 2 basis points, cash T-bill spreads of 1 basis point, 1 basis point in
wi broker commissions, and 1 basis point for the bid/offer on the financing
rate, transaction costs provide a 5-basis-point buffer on either side of the
theoretical arbitrage value. Given this, Poitras (1991) provides evidence that,
when account is taken of transaction costs, wi rates have on a number of
occasions deviated substantially outside of the arbitrage boundaries of 5 basis
points in the direction of the long arbitrage and 10 basis points in the short
arbitrage direction. Positive arbitrage profits were observed. Given a number
of qualifications, detailed examination of the empirical evidence reveals that
the instances of unexploited arbitrage opportunities arose mostly during
unsettled market conditions. Especially when markets are unsettled, speculative traders have incentive to use the wi market as an inexpensive vehicle to
make an interest rate play. Because of the limited amount of arbitraging
activity, speculative trade is able to move the wi rate significantly outside the
arbitrage bounds. Based the prevalence, timing, and size of the differentials, it
appears that the wi market was under-arbitraged, during the period studied by
Poitras (1991).

---

[25]The introduction of auctions of Receiver General Balances in 1986 increased the supply of
term call money, especially from the near banks.

[26]In market parlance, "the edge." While the trader does not have to give up the edge on each
trade, the required passive trading tactics (e.g., putting out bids instead of hitting offers) would
increase the execution time (risk). Active execution of the arbitrage would necessitate that the
transactions costs be paid.

IV. STOCK INDEX ARBITRAGE

Due to the role that stock index futures played in the market crash of October 1987, stock index arbitrage has, arguably, received the most public attention of all the futures arbitrages. Careful analysis of the specific mechanics of the arbitrage transactions was required to determine the connections between trading in the cash and futures markets for equities. The general public ignorance of stock index futures reflected in the public discussion surrounding the crash of 1987 is understandable. Trading in stock index futures is a product of the modern Renaissance in derivative security trading. Not only is exchange trading of stock index futures contracts relatively new, but the underlying commodity is not the garden variety agricultural or industrial commodity, featuring multiple delivery specifications of a particular commodity. Stock index futures are written on an index, an appropriately weighted bundle of underlying securities. One arbitrage transaction in this commodity can generate anywhere from dozens to hundreds of trades in the underlying equities.

The first stock index futures contract, based on the Value Line Index, was introduced in February 1982 on the Kansas City Board of Trade (KCBT). The most important stock index futures contract, the Standard & Poor (S&P) 500, traded on the Chicago Mercantile Exchange/International Money Market, was introduced shortly thereafter in April 1982. A raft of stock index futures contracts have appeared since that time, starting with the introduction of the New York Stock Exchange (NYSE) Composite on the NYFE in May 1982 and the Major Market Index on the Chicago Board of Trade (CBOT) in 1984. More recently, there have been the introduction of foreign indexes traded on U.S. exchanges, such as the Nikkei 225 on the CME. This has been accompanied by the trading of domestic equity indexes on futures markets around the world, including markets in Japan, Hong Kong, Holland, Australia, England, France, Germany, Switzerland, and Canada. Another development has been the start of trading in the Dow Jones Industrial Average (DJIA) index futures in October 1997. The slow pace associated with the introduction of the DJIA was not due to a lack of interest in such a contract. On the contrary, perceiving considerable demand, the CBOT had attempted to introduce a DJIA contract as early as July 1984; however, these plans were thwarted by Dow Jones and Company, which initiated legal action to prevent trading of the contract. What ensued was a process lasting over a dozen years and ending with the CBOT eventually introducing DJIA futures and options contracts.

Stock index futures were a success almost from the beginning. In conjunction with the Eurodollar contract and the oil complex contracts, the introduction of trading in stock index futures redefined the landscape of derivative security trading. By 1986, in terms of total number of contracts traded, the

S&P 500 futures contract was the second most successful futures contract in the world. Stock index futures contracts are cash settled, eliminating complications associated with multiple delivery specifications. This simplification is offset by the differing methods by which stock indexes are calculated. A range of possible indexing schemes are available. The DJIA is price weighted and the S&P 500 is value weighted. Though indexes do not typically adjust for dividends, there are exceptions such as the German Stock Index (DAX), which is a *performance index*. By reinvesting coupons back into the index, a performance index is cumulative dividend adjusted. The price behavior of such an index is similar to that of a non-dividend-paying stock. The specifics of index construction are essential to actual execution of the arbitrage.

Given the practical importance of stock index arbitrage, numerous studies have been conducted on this arbitrage and the implications for derivative pricing (e.g., Eytan and Harpaz, 1986; Neal, 1996), in addition to a range of studies on program trading (e.g., Grossman, 1988; Harris *et al.*, 1994; Hill and Jones, 1988; Kamara *et al.*, 1992). As discussed in Chapter 9, Section III, program trading is a collection of strategies in which computerized trading techniques are an integral part. Program trading includes dynamic portfolio insurance, stock index futures arbitrage, and dynamic hedging of equity option books. Analysis of stock index arbitrage activities surrounding the crash of 1987 generally supported the notion that such activities were stabilizing (e.g., Tosini, 1988), though such conclusions were based primarily on the narrow implications of the arbitrage transactions.

To better appreciate how the cash-and-carry arbitrage condition for stock indexes, consider the arbitrage trades involved for a stylized stock index future described in Table 4.8. For stock index arbitrage, $cc(0,T)$ is given by

TABLE 4.8   Profit Function for a Long S&P 500 Cash-and-Carry Arbitrage

Date	Cash position[a]	Futures position
$t = 0$	Invest $\$Q_S$ in the Stock Index at $S(0)$ financed with a loan at the broker call loan interest rate, $i(0,T)$.	Short Q_S of the Stock Index at $F(0,T)$
$t = T$	Sell the $\$Q_S$ of the stock index at $S(T)$ to receive the value of the stock index futures $F(T,T) = S(T)$. Cash settle the futures position, repaying the broker call loan with the net proceeds of the investment and dividend income, $\$[Q_S S(0)]$ $\{1 + i(0,T) - d(0,T)\}$.	

[a]Position will earn the dividend yield $d(0,T)$ on the S&P between $t = 0$ and $t = T$.
Note: Because the value of the cash and futures positions at T are equal, in this case the cash-and-carry arbitrage profit function can be specified as $\pi(0) = \{F(0,T) - S(0)(1 + i(0,T) - d(0,T)\}$ $Q_S \leq 0$.

INDEX

S&P 500 INDEX (CME) $500 times index

	Open	High	Low	Settle	Chg	High	Low	Open Interest
Sept	457.35	458.45	457.00	457.95 +	.55	485.20	436.75	195,724
Dec	460.00	460.75	459.60	460.40 +	.60	487.10	438.85	16,365
Mr95	....	....		463.70 +	.60	479.00	441.45	2,859
June	....	....		467.20 +	.70	472.70	449.50	1,357

Est vol 33,151; vol Fri 55,440; open int 216,305, −1,921.
Indx prelim High 458.30; Low 457.10; Close 457.89 +.80

S&P MIDCAP 400 (CME) $500 times index

Sept	170.20	171.80	170.10	171.70 +	1.50	186.70	161.50	12,140

Est vol 365; vol Fri 682; open int 12,239, +96.
The index: High 171.12; Low 169.84; Close 171.12 +1.15

NIKKEI 225 STOCK AVERAGE (CME)—$5 times index

Sept	20750.	208.50	207.50	208.20 +	2.45	21775.	16240.	22,596
Dec	208.60	209.10	208.60	209.10 +	2.45	21800.	17030.	477

Est vol 2,039; vol Fri 848; open int 23,074, +155.
The index: High 20638.93; Low 20502.20; Close 20635.83 +114.13

GSCI (CME)—$250 times GSCI nearby prem.

Oct	179.40	179.40	178.30	178.50	....	184.40	171.90	4,731
Dec	....	....		182.30 +	.20	187.20	178.70	736

Est vol 476; vol Fri 1,618; open int 5,467, −738.
The index: High 178.82; Low 176.93; Close 177.30 −.38

MAJOR MARKET INDEX (CME)—$500 times index

Aug	385.50	386.45	385.30	386.20 +	1.05	388.55	369.90	3,206
Sept	386.20	386.60	386.20	386.50 +	1.05	399.35	360.55	709
Dec	....	....		388.10 +	1.05	400.45	361.75	187

Est vol 107; vol Fri 1,361; open int 4,102, +800.
The index: High 386.98; Low 385.05; Close 386.69 +1.64

NYSE COMPOSITE INDEX (NYFE)—500 times index

Sept	252.65	253.30	252.50	253.10 +	.55	267.90	241.00	3,587
Dec	253.70	254.20	253.70	254.10 +	.60	264.50	244.15	261

Est vol 1,374; vol Fri 2,609; open int 3,962, +214.
The index: high 253.05; Low 252.50; Close 252.99 +.49

KR-CRB INDEX (NYFE)—500 times index

Sept	232.70	233.15	231.80	232.05 −	.95	241.50	221.10	2,101
Dec	234.15	235.00	233.80	233.90 −	.95	241.00	225.00	1,757
Mr95	....	....		235.75 −	.95	242.75	228.70	968
May	....	....		237.25 −	.95	240.75	238.75	655

Est vol 184; vol Fri 240; open int 5,481, +9.
The index: High 232.31; Low 231.03; Close 231.05 −.93

FIGURE 4.8   Stock index futures prices. (*Source: The Wall Street Journal*, August 8, 1994. With permission.)

the broker call loan rate, and $cr(0,T)$ is given by the dividend yield. Consistent with all the financial commodities, the cash-and-carry arbitrage condition only takes account of borrowing charges paid and pecuniary returns earned while holding the commodity during the period of the arbitrage. Complications arise with stock index arbitrage because the dividend yield, $d(0,T)$ is not known at $t = 0$ and, for distant delivery dates, there may be some difficulty in obtaining broker call loan financing without a substantial *haircut*. The uncertainty of the dividend yield introduces some risk into the arbitrage while the haircut requires the trader to finance a fraction of the position, again undercutting the pure arbitrage notion because a net investment of funds is required. In order to reduce transaction and other execution costs, additional uncertainty may be intentionally introduced by trading only a subcomponent of the index that is deemed to track the index sufficiently well.

As noted, stock index futures are a commodity without the complications of multiple delivery specifications and cheapest deliverable grades. Stock index futures contracts are cash settled. As indicated in Fig. 4.8 the bulk of market interest centers on the nearby contracts, reducing the difficulties of obtaining longer term financing for arbitragers but complicating the use of strategies that aim to replicate the long-term payoff on the underlying equity index by forming portfolios of cash T-bills and stock index futures. Such portfolios have to be rolled over at regular intervals, creating a slippage between the underlying equity index return and the replicating portfolio.

V. QUESTIONS

1a. Explain the *arbitrage* underlying the covered interest parity theorem discussed in Section II. What assumptions are being made about both the execution of the arbitrage and the underlying securities?

1b. Will CIP hold for all types of money market instruments? Which money market security will produce the smallest deviations from the covered interest parity conditions? Why? What institutional characteristics of Bankers' Acceptances, commercial paper, and Treasury bills would make it difficult for CIP transactions to be instantaneously executed in those markets? Be as complete as possible in explaining your answer.

1c. On March 1, 1990, the spot and 3-month forward rates for the Canadian dollar (per U.S. dollar) were $1.1922 and $1.2072, respectively. What "risk-free" discount rate on U.S. dollar instruments would be consistent with the interest-rate-parity theorem if the 3-month (annualized) risk-free rate on Canadian dollar instruments was 13.10%?

1d. On August 8, 1994, the spot and 5-year forward rates for the C$/US$ exchange rate were $1.3797 and $1.4917, respectively. Using interest rate and exchange rate information provided in Figs. 4.4, 4.5, and 4.6 what "arbitrage-free" interest rate on 5-year, zero-coupon U.S. dollar instruments would be consistent with CIP?

2. On August 8, 1994, the price of the September Treasury bill futures is 95.24. The spot market for 91-day T-bills is quoted at a discount rate of 4.45, while the 182-day rate is 5.08. Estimate the forward rate on 91-day T-bills and compare it with the rate implied by the futures market. Repeat your calculations using similar quotes for Eurodollar cash and futures prices.

3. Define the following: (a) basis, (b) location basis, (c) maturity basis, (d) contango, (e) backwardation (f) arbitrage, (g) cash-and-carry arbitrage. Explain how the cost of carry affects the relationship between spot and futures prices. How do changes in the cost of carry affect the basis over the life of a futures contract? What factors are significant for determining the quality basis for Treasury bond futures?

4a. Are forward prices unbiased predictors of future spot prices?

4b. It is often stated that futures price levels follow random walks. What is the relationship of this hypothesis with the hypothesis that forward prices are unbiased predictors of future spot prices?

4c. If futures prices are at full carry, is this inconsistent with the hypothesis that futures prices are unbiased predictors and that there are zero expected profits to speculation? If so, what type of trading strategy could be used to profit from this discrepancy?

5. From Section I, rework the condition $S(0)\Delta ic + ic(1)\Delta S$ to include fixed as well as variable cost components. Explain the impact of the additional terms on the pricing of forward and futures prices.

6. Using data from the current *Wall Street Journal*, calculate the size of the deviation from CIP using T-bills and Eurodollars together with foreign t-bills and Eurocurrency deposits. To do this requires the CIP condition to be manipulated to obtain:

$$i(0,T) - i^*(0,T) - \left\{ \frac{F(0,T)}{S(0)} - 1 \right\}(1 + i^*(0,T)) = \text{Deviation}$$

To do the calculations it is sufficient to use the nearby interest rate futures for the interest rate.

7. Extend the results of Section II to the calculation of bankers' profits from doing foreign exchange swap transactions over three delivery periods. Is there a substantive difference in the solution? *Hint:* Are implied forward interest rates unbiased predictors of future interest

rates? Consider the case of a locking in a 3-year return vs. locking in a 2-year and then rolling into an uncertain 1-year security vs. locking in for 1 year and then taking on either another 1-year or locking in for 2 years.

CHAPTER 5

The Mechanics of Spread Trading

Spreading as a futures technique is as old as the markets themselves and is probably the single largest source of market liquidity, particularly in the forward months. Indeed, spread participants are the backbone of market liquidity, without which no viable futures market can exist.

Leo Melamed, former chairman of CME and IMM

I. BUTTERFLIES, TANDEMS, TURTLES, AND STEREOS

A. BUTTERFLIES

A natural extension of the intracommodity futures spread trades described in Chapter 3 is the *butterfly* (e.g., Schwager, 1984). Because the butterfly can be interpreted as an intracommodity tandem trade, it also provides a useful introduction to intercommodity trades. Recognizing that there are a number of possible variations on butterfly trades, consider the following generic version: short (long) one nearby contract; long (short) two contracts of an intermediate delivery date contract; and, short (long) one distant delivery contract. The interpretation of the trade can be captured as a "spread of spreads," a combination of a short (long) nearby spread and a long (short) deferred spread. The trades supporting the profit function are described in Table 5.1.

For this trade to be profitable, the nearby futures basis is expected to widen more (become more positive) than the deferred futures basis.

Analysis of the butterfly proceeds expediently by assuming that the trade has been "tailed"—unlikely in practice, but an assumption typically only

TABLE 5.1   Profit Function for a Butterfly Spread

Date	Nearby (N) position	Intermediate (T)	Distant position (T*)
$t = 0$	Short 1 at $F(0,N)$	Long 1 at $F(0,T)$	
		Long 1 at $F(0,T)$	Short 1 at $F(0,T^*)$
$t = 1$	Long 1 at $F(1,N)$	Short 1 at $F(1,T)$	
		Short 1 at $F(1,T)$	Long 1 at $F(1,T^*)$

Note: The profit function for the short–long–short butterfly is

$$\pi_b/Q = \{[F(1,T) - F(1,N)] - [F(0,T) - F(0,N)]\} + \{[F(1,T) - F(0,T^*)]$$
$$- [F(0,T) - F(0,T^*)]\}$$
$$= [F(0,N) - F(1,N)] + 2[F(1,T) - F(0,T)] + [F(0,T^*) - F(1,T^*)] \qquad (5.1)$$

resulting in second-order differences from Eq. (5.1). In this case, the profit function can be approximated as:[1]

$$\pi_b/Q = F(1,N)\Delta ic(N,T) - F(1,T)\Delta ic(T,T^*)$$

In other words, profitability of the butterfly depends on the behavior of the term structure of futures prices. For non-exchange members subject to higher transaction costs, this type of trade would usually not provide interesting opportunities because the associated price movements are small relative to the costs of trading as a non-exchange member.[2] On the other hand, floor traders can use this trade, for example, to flatten out the term structure of the futures prices. This could occur if the price of an intermediate contract became mispriced due, say, to a large position being placed in a particular delivery month because of cash market considerations. As it turns out, the most interesting applications of trading spreads against spreads arise when the spreads are in different commodities. In this case, the trade is referred to as a *tandem*.

A variation of the butterfly trade, known as the *condor*, is constructed by separating the spreads contained in the butterfly. Instead of short (long) one nearby contract, long (short) two contracts of an intermediate delivery date contract and short (long) one distant delivery contract involving three

---

[1] The profit function is approximate because the exact profit function requires two tails to be specified for the trade. The precise method of specifying the two tails is similar to setting a hedge ratio in the stereo trades.

[2] Commodities where the butterfly may be a feasible trading strategy for traders with higher transactions costs are those with a significant seasonal factor in the term structure of futures prices, such as heating oil. For example, by forming the spread using fall–winter–summer contracts, changes in the butterfly could be used to speculate on, say, the appearance of an unexpectedly cold winter, without being concerned with changes in the level of heating oil prices.

different delivery dates, the condor requires four delivery dates. The two contracts in the intermediate delivery date required for the butterfly are established in two distinct, but still intermediate contract delivery dates. In this case, the tailed profit function would look like:

$$\pi_c/Q = F(1,N)\Delta ic(N,T) - F(1,T^*)\Delta ic(T^*,T^{**})$$

While, typically, $T^{**} > T^* > T > N$, it is also possible that $N < T^* < T < T^{**}$. Because the condor requires at least four distinct and actively traded delivery dates, this trade is not applicable to all commodities. As with the butterfly, because the potential profits from this trade will often be small, it is usually of more interest to exchange floor speculators than to off-exchange traders subject to higher transactions costs.

B. Tandems and Stereos

A *tandem* involves combining spreads in two different commodities. Interpreting the tandem as an intercommodity butterfly, the profit function for a tandem follows immediately from the butterfly, allowing for differing position sizes in the two commodities. The profit function for the *untailed short-the-nearby, long-the-deferred* spread in the first commodity would be

$$\pi_1 = Q_1\{[F(1,T) - F(1,N)] - [F(0,T) - F(0,N)]\}$$

And, for the second commodity, where the untailed spread is *long-the-nearby, short-the-deferred*:

$$\pi_2 = Q_2\{[G(0,T) - G(0,N)] - [G(1,T) - G(1,N)]\}$$

Combining these two component spreads gives the general profit function for the tandem trade:

$$\pi_{tan} = \{Q_1[F(1,T) - F(1,N)] - Q_2[G(1,T) - G(1,N)]\} \\ - \{Q_1[F(0,T) - F(0,N)] - Q_2[G(0,T) - G(0,N)]\} \tag{5.2}$$

Determining the hedge ratio, the number of spreads in the second commodity for each spread in the first commodity involves dividing Eq. (5.2) through by Q_1 Substituting in the cash-and-carry equilibrium conditions gives the cash-and-carry arbitrage form of the profit function:

$$\frac{\pi_{tan}}{Q_1} = [F(1,N)\Delta ic_F + ic_F(0)\Delta F(N)] \\ - \frac{Q_2}{Q_1}[G(1,N)\Delta ic_G + ic_G(0)\Delta G(N)] \tag{5.3}$$

Later sections provide specific examples of calculating hedge ratios for inter-commodity trades.

Unfortunately, the presence of two commodities in the tandem trade means that interpretation of the profit function can be somewhat complicated, such as, the TED tandem (see Section III) (Landau and Wolkowitz, 1987; Kawaller and Koch, 1992; Poitras, 1989b, 1998a). Following the approach used for the butterfly, in order to simplify the cash-and-carry profit function for the tandem analysis can proceed expeditiously by taking both sides of the trade to be tailed spreads. In this case, Eq. (5.3) becomes:

$$\frac{\pi_{tt}}{Q_1} = [F(1,N)\Delta ic_F] - \frac{Q_2}{Q_1}[G(1,N)\Delta ic_G]$$

$$\pi_{tt}^* \equiv \frac{\pi_{tt}}{Q_1 F(1,N)} = \Delta ic_F - \frac{Q_2 G(1,N)}{Q_1 F(1,N)}\Delta ic_G$$

Choosing a dollar equivalent hedge ratio involves setting $[Q_2 G(1,N)] = [Q_1 F(1,N)]$, permitting the profit function to depend solely on the difference in the ic changes for the two commodities involved. In order to determine the hedge ratio in practice, $G(0,N)$ and $F(0,N)$ are used to approximate the unobserved prices, $G(1,N)$ and $F(1,N)$. This approach to interpreting the profit function provides an immediate connection between tailed tandems and stereo trades.

A *stereo* trade has a profit function that depends on the difference in changes for the cost-of-carry interest rates implied in arbitrages for the selected futures contracts. A simple example of a stereo trade occurs with a tailed tandem involving gold and silver. For these commodities, there is no significant return to holding the cash commodity, and non-interest carrying charges involved in the cash-and carry arbitrage are small relative to interest charges. As a result, the profit function depends on the difference in the changes for the interest rates implied in gold and silver futures prices. More complicated forms of stereo trades occur for debt futures contracts, where the commodity has an interest carrying cost, the implied repo rate, and an interest carry return. Recognizing that the tailing procedure can be adjusted such that the profit function for the spread in each commodity depends only on the implied repo rate changes, the tailed tandem again becomes a stereo:

$$\pi_s^* \equiv \frac{\pi_s}{F(1,N)Q_1} = \Delta irr_1 - \frac{G(1,N)Q_2}{F(1,N)Q_1}\Delta irr_2$$

where irr_j is the interest carrying cost implied by the cash-and-carry arbitrage for commodity j (i.e., the implied repo rate for financial futures). For a number of reasons, not all tailed tandem trades are stereos. In order for a stereo trade to occur, the tailing method must convert the profit function to depend only on the change in interest carrying charges. Except in special cases, untailed tandems will not be stereos.

The tailed tandem stereo trades are specific instances of "differential repo arbitrage" trades, a class of trades that also includes the turtle trades (Yano, 1989). The profit functions for these intercommodity trades depend either on the difference in the implied repo rates for two sets of financial futures contracts or on the difference in an implied repo rate and a surrogate for the cash market repo rate. Trading opportunities are identified when the irr for a given futures contract deviates significantly, either from the irr for other futures contracts, generating a stereo trade, or from the cash market, generating a turtle trade. Specific examples of these trades include the stereo NOB, which trades the irr from T-note and T-bonds futures, and the stereo NUN, which involves irr from futures contracts for T-notes with different term to maturity for the underlying T-notes. To illustrate these trades, consider the stereo NOB. This trade is constructed using tailed spreads in bonds and notes, where the tail is $(1 + irr)$ with resulting profit functions of the form $F(1,N)\Delta irr$. The appropriate hedge ratios are calculated in the same fashion as for the naked NOB. Yano (1989) provides an elegant and slightly more precise method of arriving at the relevant position sizes.

C. TURTLES AND STEREOS

Variations on tailed tandem trades occur where one of the positions is not an appropriately tailed spread but, rather, an open position. These types of trades are known generically as turtle trades. The basic idea of the turtle is to trade the difference between the ic or irr embedded in the futures price structure against some other variable, usually an interest rate. The simplest version of this trade is a metal turtle, which is discussed in more detail later in this chapter. This trade involves, for example, combining a tailed gold spread with a Eurodollar futures position (Poitras, 1987). The objective is to speculate on changes in the difference between the implied interest rate in gold futures and the Eurodollar rate. Among other reasons, this trade is of interest because there is a one-sided arbitrage relationship between gold futures prices and Eurodollar interest rates that can be used to fine-tune the spread trading decision. Because absence of arbitrage prevents the gold ic from being greater than the relevant Euro rate, the difference between the two rates can be used to identify trading opportunities. To calculate the "dollar value" hedge ratio for this trade, the technique of equalizing the value of a basis point movement for the naked Euro and the tailed gold spread is used.

In turtle trades involving debt futures, such as the turtle (Rentzler, 1986; Easterwood and Senchack, 1986) between T-bond spreads and T-bills, it is the *irr* and not the *ic* that is of interest. Much as in the stereo trades, which speculate on changes in $(\Delta irr_1 - \Delta irr_2)$, the turtle is concerned with speculating on $\Delta irr - \Delta i$, where i is the interest rate on the appropriate open (naked) interest rate futures contract. This requires specification of the tail for the intracommodity spread to be readjusted such that the resulting profit function is of the form: $\pi_{irr} = F(1,N)\Delta irr$. To identify the appropriate tail for this situation, observe that for debt futures $ic = irr - R$ or $irr = ic + R$. More precisely, taking the current yield to be a sufficient approximation to R:

$$irr(0,N,T) = \frac{F(0,T) - F(0,N)}{F(0,N)} + \frac{C}{F(0,N)}\frac{T-N}{365}$$

$$= ic(0,T,N) + R(0)$$

(5.4)

where C is the annual stated coupon on the underlying theoretical bond or note. Taking $\pi_{ts} = F(1,N)\Delta ic = F(1,N)(\Delta irr - \Delta R)$, to derive the appropriate tail, observe that:

$$F(1,N)\Delta R = F(1,N)\left\{\frac{C^*}{F(1,N)} - \frac{C^*}{F(0,N)}\right\} = -\frac{C^*}{F(0,N)}\Delta F$$

where $C^* = C((T - N)/365)$. Combining this with the result:

$$\pi_{ts} = [1 + ic(0)][F(0,N) - F(1,N)] + [F(1,T) - F(0,T)]$$

$$= [1 + ic(0)][-\Delta F(N)] + [F(1,T) - F(0,T)]$$

Substituting from the definition for π_{irr} gives:

$$\pi_{irr} = \pi_{ts} + F(1,N)\Delta R = \pi_{ts} - R(0)\Delta F(N)$$

$$= [1 + ic(0) + R(0)][F(0,N) - F(1,N)] + [F(1,T) - F(0,T)]$$

Hence, for spreads involving profit functions using the implied repo rate, the appropriate tail is $\{1 + irr(0)\}$ and not $\{1 + ic(0)\}$ where *irr* is calculated using Eq. (5.4).

Compared to precious metal turtles, factors determining profitability of turtle trades involving debt futures are somewhat more complicated. As with the $(1 + ic)$ tailed T-bond spread and the (naked) NOB, the turtle can be used to speculate on changes in yield curve shape, albeit only at the short end. More frequently, turtle trades involving debt futures are used to capture deviations of the implied repo rate from the actual or cash repo rate. These deviations emerge because the repurchase agreement used to finance cash transactions is primarily an overnight rate, with some term repo available in short maturities but, effectively, no terms to maturity that correspond to the deliveries of the relevant debt futures contract. Because the cash market does not provide a direct financing vehicle for doing arbitrages involving, say, T-bonds, it is possible for the *irr* associated with T-bonds to deviate substantially from the *irr* observed in the cash market (Allen and Thurston, 1988). Turtles takes the form of a cash-and-carry quasi-arbitrage trade designed to exploit the observed deviation. This intuition for the turtle trade relies on the type of interest rate futures position being used as a surrogate for the cash repo rate.

Motivations for doing turtle trades with U.S. Treasury debt futures can be illustrated by considering a profit function that has been simplified by assuming the hedge ratio has been set appropriately:

$$\pi_{turt} \propto [\Delta irr(N,T)] - [\Delta tbr(N,T)]$$

where *tbr* is the interest rate reflected in the relevant T-bill futures, and *irr* is the implied repo rate for the relevant T-note or T-bond futures contract. When the hedge ratio is set appropriately, the payoff on the turtle is dependent on the difference in the implied repo and T-bill rate changes.[3] From this, turtle trades can be generalized to trades involving $(1 + irr)$ tailed spreads and any other relevant money market futures contracts. Other possible configurations include $(1 + irr)$ tailed T-note spreads with Euros. Because the profit functions for the various possible turtle trades involve differencing two interest rates that are, invariably, determined by differing market forces, it is necessary to construct a behavioral foundation for explaining the profitability of each specific trade. Yano (1989) recognizes this point: "The turtle trade is not riskless arbitrage. There seems to be a widespread fallacy that the [difference in the implied repo rates is] zero on average, but there is no necessary reason for this to be true." Referring to turtles derived from financial futures: "Different configurations will have their idiosyncrasies due to, but not limited to, heterogeneous expectations along the yield curve" (p. 446).

II. METAL TURTLES

In contrast to the currency tandem, for which the profit function was somewhat complicated to derive, the profit function for a metal turtle trade is straightforward. Ignoring the hedge ratio, $\pi = \Delta ic - \Delta r$, where *r* is the

---

[3]Significantly, the *irr* depends fundamentally on the cheapest deliverable commodity. For T-bond spreads, it is possible to have numerous changes in the cheapest deliverable bond over longer trading horizons. This can give rise to variations in trade profitability.

interest rate on the interest rate futures contract selected for the specific turtle trade. One conceptual difficulty with a turtle occurs with specifying the time at which the trade is initiated. In the case of the precious metals gold and silver, turtle profitability depends on the relationship between the *ic*, which is largely determined by interest charges, and the upper arbitrage boundary provided by the Eurodollar rate. For gold, this relationship is illustrated in Fig. 5.1. Inspection of Fig. 5.1 reveals that when the gold *ic* gets either "too close to" or "too far from" the Eurodollar boundary rate, a golden turtle trade can be established and held until the gold *ic* comes back to a more normal relationship with the boundary. At this time, the position is closed out and profit on the trade calculated. This approach to defining a trading strategy differs from other studies (e.g., Monroe, 1992; Monroe and Cohn, 1986; Rentzler, 1986) that use techniques such as moving averages and standard deviations to generate trading decisions.

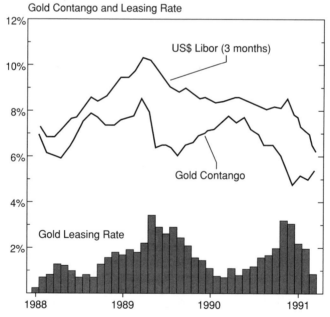

FIGURE 5.1   Gold contango and leasing rate. (*Source*: Poitras, G. (1997). *Journal of Derivatives* 5: 71–87. With permission.)

A. TRADE TRIGGERS

In order to identify the appropriate number of basis points to use in determining when to initiate and close out the golden turtle trade, Poitras (1987) introduces an additional interest rate, the U.S. T-bill rate, to serve as a lower boundary. The golden turtle trading strategy then involves evaluating the relationship between the three relevant rates: the gold ic, the Eurodollar rate, and the T-bill rate. Poitras (1987) considered the following method of identifying golden turtle trading opportunities: For a period starting approximately 15 months prior to the delivery date of the front gold contract and lasting until 2 months prior to the last delivery date on the front gold contract, an appropriate trade was initiated if at any time during this period the annualized gold ic traded within a predetermined number of basis points of a boundary rate. The trade was then examined daily to assess whether it should either be reversed or closed out. The reverse/close-out decision was again made according to whether the gold ic traded within a predetermined number of basis points of the other boundary rate. At this time, if there was more than 6 months left in the trading period the trade was reversed and the daily evaluation process was restarted; otherwise, trading for that trading horizon was complete. If the trade had not been closed out by the end of the last month of the trading period, the trade was closed out at market.[4]

An unanswered question in this trading strategy is determining the number of basis points from a boundary rate the gold ic must be in order for a trade to be initiated or closed out. The problem of specifying a strict rule is further complicated by occasional convergence of the boundaries (i.e., where the Eurodollar rate approaches the T-bill rate). With this in mind, Poitras (1987) selected a censored-percentage trigger rule. This rule works by determining the number of basis points from the boundary the gold ic must be to trigger a trade as a percentage of the size of the T-bill/Eurodollar differential. For example, if the Eurodollar/T-bill differential is 80 basis points, a 10% rule would initiate or close a trade if the annualized gold ic came with 8 basis points of a boundary.[5] Using this trading technique, it was demonstrated that the golden turtle provided significant trading profits. The number of trades decreased with the number of basis points in the trigger rule, while profits increased monotonically. The holding periods were typically several months,

---

[4]The reason for avoiding the delivery month is that the gold ic drops well below the T-bill rate as the delivery period progresses. As there is no arbitrage relationship between gold futures and T-bills, this is not a violation of absence of arbitrage.

[5]In devising this trigger strategy, two types of rules can be considered: censored percentage rules and censored fixed rate rules. Fixed rate rules establish the trade if the gold ic approaches the boundaries by an *ad hoc* number of basis points, say 20 for both the upper and lower boundary, but

indicating that the golden turtle depends more on underlying fundamentals than pure noise trading.

B. Calculating the Tail and Hedge Ratio: Golden Turtle

In order to determine the number of gold and Euro contracts to be used in the trade it is necessary to specify the tailing procedure and the method of determining the hedge ratio between gold spreads and Euro contracts. Recognizing that there are different methods of determining the tail, in the golden turtle the objective is to isolate ic. As discussed in Chapter 3, Section II, the tailed spread in this case can be specified such that for every long (short) deferred contract there will be $F(0,T)/F(0,N)$ short (long) nearby contracts. For every unit of the deferred contract, there will be $(1 + ic(0))$ units of the nearby contract. The profit function for a short-the-nearby, long-the-deferred tailed gold spread is: $\pi_{TGS}/(100oz) = G(1,N)\Delta ic(N,T)$. Assuming the trade is being initiated on August 8, 1994 (see Fig. 4.1) and taking the gold price $G(1,N)$ to be equal to $379, the $G(0,N)$ for the October 1994 delivery on August 8/94, then the hedge ratio follows by observing that one basis point equals .0001, that the Commodity Exchange (COMEX) gold contract is written for 100 oz, and that the value of one basis point for a Eurodollar contract is $25. Hence, the hedge ratio for the number of gold spreads per Euro contract is $\{\$25/[(\$379)(100)(.0001)]\} = 6.596$. The value is combined with the value for the spread tail to determine the appropriate number of the three contracts to use for the trade.

To see this more precisely, the basic problem is to derive the number of tailed gold spreads that, for a given basis point change, will (locally) have the same dollar value change as the corresponding dollar value change in the Euro contract. The profit function for a golden bear turtle, long one Euro contract and short Q^* tailed gold spreads is

$$\pi_{gt}(1) = \$2500[r_{EU}(0,T) - r_{EU}(1,T)] + 100Q^*G(1,N)[ic(1) - ic(0)]$$

$$= \$2500[EU(1,T) - EU(0,T)] + 100Q^*G(1,N)[ic(1) - ic(0)]$$

where: $r_{EU}(i,T)$ is a whole-number, *annualized* interest rate calculated as 100 minus $EU(i,T)$, the quoted Euro contract price at time i. When Q^* is selected to be consistent with the dollar equivalent hedge ratio, the golden bear turtle

---

restricts (censors) trades if the Eurodollar/T-bill differential is less than an *ad hoc* number of basis points, say 80. The main difficulty with this approach is that it does not account for variations in the differentials due to changes in the level of rates and other related factors.

will be profitable when the differential between the annualized gold ic and the Eurodollar rate narrows. The converse would hold for the golden bull turtle; the trade will be profitable when the differential between the annualized gold ic and the Euro rate widens. Correct calculation of Q^* follows appropriately.

Given that the π for a Euro is \$25 per basis point, the dollar equivalency hedge ratio problem is to calculate the value of 1 basis point (per $Q_T = 1$ spread) for a tailed gold spread. Recalling that one basis point is .0001, what remains is to set $\Delta ic = .0001$ and solve the tailed gold spread profit function. On a per-contract basis this produces:

$$\pi_{TGS} = (100)G(1,N)(.0001) = (.01)G(1,N)$$

Because $G(1,N)$ is not known at $t = 0$ when the trade is initiated, a proxy is required. In the absence of a better value, $G(0,N)$ is appropriate. Recalling that this value for the October 1994 delivery on August 8, 1994, is \$379.30, then \$3.793 is the value of one basis point (per contract) in a tailed gold spread. Relating this basis point value to a Euro again provides the appropriate hedge ratio for the golden turtle:

$$Q^* = HR = \$25/\$3.793 = 6.591 = \text{number of tailed gold spreads per Euro}$$

This number can now be used to construct the trade.

Because of the need to match the (whole) number of contracts in the tailed spread with the hedge ratio, the golden turtle is somewhat more complicated to implement than the tailed gold spread. Recall that in order to get a correct trade size for the tail, it was necessary to gross up $\{1 + ic(N,T)\}$ until a "comfortable" integer relationship was established for the two legs of the spread. Using the one-year, October/October spread values from August 8, 1994, produced: $1 + ic(N,T) = (399.5/379.3) = 1.0533$. Observing that $(3)(6.591) = 19.77$ and $(19)(1.0533) = 20.013$, it follows that the trade can be roughly done using 19 deferred gold, 20 nearby gold, and 3 naked Euro contracts. Slippage between trading profits and the theoretical profit function due to rounding involved in the calculations is reduced if a proportionately larger number of contracts are used.

What remains is to analyze various scenarios where the difference between the Euro rate and the annualized gold ic is expected to change. Consider the case where the difference between the Euro rate and the gold ic is expected to widen. This can happen a number of ways; for example, the ic could stay constant and the Euro rate could increase. In this case, $r(1) - r(0) > 0$. Because the profit function for a long position is $\pi = \$2500\Delta EU = \$2500$ $(-\Delta r)$, when r is expected to rise a short position in Euros is profitable. Similarly, if the widening occurs because the Euro rate is unchanged $r(1) - r(0) = 0$, with the gold ic falling, $ic(1) - ic(0) < 0$, then it follows that a spread that is long-the-nearby and short-the-deferred is indicated. Further examples confirm that when the Euro/gold ic interest rate spread is expected to widen the appropriate trade involves a short Euro combined with a tailed spread that is long-the-nearby and short-the-deferred. Similarly, when the interest rate differential is expected to narrow then the appropriate trade is long the Euro combined with a tailed gold spread that is short-the-nearby and long-the-deferred. The appropriate combination of these positions involves calculation of the size of the tailed spread, adjusted for the appropriate hedge ratio.

C. SILVER TURTLE

Analysis for the silver turtle and other precious metal turtles follows in the same fashion as for the golden turtle trade. The hedge ratio for the silver turtle is developed from the profit function for the $(1 + ic)$ tailed intracommodity spread:

$$\frac{\pi_{TSS}}{5000 \text{ oz}} = S(1,N)\Delta ic$$

Again, solve for one basis point in tailed silver spread profit per $(Q_T = 1)$ contract. For the December 1994, COMEX silver price observed on August 8, 1994, $S(0,N) = \$5.183$, for the 5000-oz COMEX futures contract:

$$\pi_{st} = (5000)(5.183)(.0001) = \$2.5915$$

Using the \$25 per basis point value for the Euro produces a hedge ratio of \$25/ \$2.5915 = 9.647. The August 8, 1994, December 1995/December 1994 tailed silver spread produces $(1 + ic) = (552/518.3) = 1.065$. From the basic calculations $(9.647)(3) = 28.941$ and $(28)(1.065) = 29.82$, it follows that on August 8, 1994, a trade with some slippage can be constructed as 3 December 1994 Euros combined with 28 deferred December 1995 and 30 nearby December 1994 COMEX silver futures contracts.

D. COPPER TURTLE

The copper turtle differs from the precious metal turtles because ic is often dominated by factors other than interest charges. Following the approach used for the gold and silver turtles, the relevant per pound profit function for the $(1 + ic)$ tailed spread using COMEX copper futures is

$$\frac{\pi_{TCS}}{25,000} = C(1,N)\Delta ic_c$$

Using the August 8, 1994, prices (see Fig. 4.1) and, again, taking the Euro basis point value to be \$25 with $C(0,N) = \$1.0895$ as a proxy for the copper price $C(1,N)$, then calculating the value of $\Delta ic = .0001$, the per-contract $(Q_T = 1)$ profit of one basis point for the tailed copper spread is

$$\pi = \$1.0895(25,000)(.0001) = \$2.724$$

This yields a hedge ratio of $9.178 = \$25/\$2.724$. For the December 1995/ December 1994 tailed copper spread, $(1 + ic) = (\$1.0515/\$1.0895) = .965$. Observing that $(6)(9.178) = 55.07$ and $(56)(.965) = 54.04$, it follows that on August 8, 1994, a copper turtle could be constructed using 6 December 1994 Eurodollar contracts combined with 56 deferred December 1995 and 54 nearby December 1994 contracts.

Spread behavior in copper futures can be considerably more volatile than for precious metals. For example, the August 8, 1994, prices reflected a backwardation in futures prices, $F(0,T) < F(0,N)$ with $[F(0,T) - F(0,N)] = -\$.038$ for the December 1995/December 1994 prices. This level of backwardation was not unusual during the decade of Hamanaka's activities in the copper market (see Chapter 2, Section III), though copper had largely been a contango market during the 1980s and, following the collapse of the scheme, the contango relationship in copper has re-emerged; for example, as of September 9, 2001, for the December 2001 and December 2002 COMEX copper contracts, $F(0,T) = \$.7065$ and $F(0,N) = \$.6775$. During the period of the scheme, there was variation in the degree of backwardation. For example, on June 16, 1992, copper prices for a 1-year December 1992/December 1993 spread were $F(0,T) = \$1.1515$ and $F(0,N) = \$1.0755$, which is a wider backwardation than on August 8, 1994, with $(1 + ic) = .934$ and $[F(0,T) - F(0,N)] = -.076$. Backwardation in COMEX copper futures prices reached a peak during September 1993 and continued until some time after the collapse of the Sumitomo scheme. To the astute spread trader, the collapse of the scheme presented a predictable reduction in the degree of backwardation that, in turn, presented a profitable trading opportunity for a copper turtle— a tailed copper spread would also have been profitable.

To see the profit potential in the copper turtle, consider the August 8, 1995, prices, which reflect a severe backwardation in futures prices. Using the December 1996/December 1995 COMEX copper futures prices: $[F(0,T) - F(0,N)] = (\$1.1145 - \$1.3155) = -\$.201$ with $(1 + ic) = .847$. This yields a hedge ratio of $\$25/\$3.29 = 7.60$, and a copper turtle could be roughly established with 26 deferred, 22 nearby, and 3 Euros. If the speculation at that time was that backwardation would disappear into contango within the following year, then a trade of long the December 1995 Euro combined with short the December 1995 nearby and long the December 1996 deferred is appropriate. Because the nearby contracts will reach maturity before the end of the trade horizon is reached, to calculate the trade profit it is necessary to assume the contracts in the trade could be "rolled forward" with no cost. Given this, evaluating the approximate profit for the trade held to August 8, 1996, produces: $(3)(2500)(94.2 - 94.3) + 25,000[26(.889 - 1.1145) + 22 (1.3155 - .9085)] = -750 - 146,575 + 223,850 = \$76,525$.

Treating a copper turtle to be similar to a precious metal turtle presents complications similar to using a $(1 + ic)$ T-bond spread in the turtle trade. Unlike the precious metals that are typically at or near full carry or full contango, copper has a term structure of futures prices that depends on convenience yield. In some periods, copper is at full carry while at other times there is backwardation where $F(0,N) > F(0,T)$. During the period of the Sumitomo copper corner, backwardation was often the case. Unlike the T-bond case where there is an observable price and coupon allowing the ic to be decomposed into two parts and a $(1 + irr)$ tail to be specified, convenience yield for copper is not so readily observable. To deal with this problem, assume the copper ic can be decomposed as $ic_c \cong irr_c - cy$, where irr_c is the implied interest charges associated with carrying copper and cy is the convenience yield that copper stocks provide. Taking $cy = irr_c - ic_c$ and using, say, the implied interest rate for gold, ic_G, as a surrogate for irr_c, it is possible to define a $(1 + cy)$ tailed copper spread that can be used to construct a $(1 + cy)$ tailed copper spread for the copper turtle (see Question 4 at the end of the chapter).

III. TED TANDEMS AND CURRENCY TANDEMS

A. THE TED SPREAD

To futures traders, a TED spread is an intercommodity spread trade that combines a short (long) Eurodollar future with a long (short) U.S. Treasury bill future (the acronym TED comes from combining Treasury bill with Eurodollar). The trade is put on for a number of reasons. For example, the trade can be used to speculate on cash market credit spreads.[6] Combining TED spreads with different delivery dates produces the TED tandem. Due to the gradual disappearance of liquidity in T-bill futures contracts with more than 6 months to delivery, the TED tandem is at present more a pedagogical

---

[6]Further discussion of the naked TED spread can be found in Siegel and Siegel (1990, pp. 262–266). It is also possible to develop complex tandem trading strategies that combine TEDs with spreads in other futures.

device than a practical trading strategy. Yet, for instructional purposes, the TED tandem is still useful for illustrating how trading strategies can be developed by exploiting differences in the arbitrages which determine prices for different money market futures contracts. Both the TED spread and TED tandem have the desirable analytical feature that the position sizes $Q_1 = Q_2 = Q$ due to the equal maturity (3 month), par value ($1 million), and $25 basis point value of the contracts. Applying the general tandem profit function of Section II using a hedge ratio of one to correspond to the TED tandem produces:

$$\pi/Q = \{[F(1,T) - F(1,N)] - [G(1,T) - G(1,N)]\}$$
$$- \{[F(0,T) - F(0,N)] - [G(0,T) - G(0,N)]\}$$

where the Euro quote is $G(\cdot)$ and the T-bill quote is $F(\cdot)$. This profit function will be developed in more detail shortly.

To consider the intuition behind the TED tandem trade, assume the current date is September 11, 1990, when the following set of futures prices was available:

	Euro	Basis	T-bill
Cash (%)	8.06	0.65	7.41
Nearby (September 1990)	91.95	0.69	92.64
Nearby (December 1990)	92.02	0.84	92.86
Deferred (September 1991)	91.65	1.10	92.75
Deferred (December 1991)	91.38	1.05	92.43

This pattern, where the deferred basis is wider than the cash basis, combined with the requirement that the nearby basis must converge to the cash basis is the motivation for tandem trading opportunities.

Figure 5.2 provides a representative plot of the behavior of cash and futures TED spreads. It suffices to say that the TED tandem is designed to benefit from futures to cash convergence. At delivery, the futures TED must equal the cash TED. For a number of reasons, the distant contracts are less affected by the cash-and-carry arbitrage than the nearby contracts. As a result, futures to cash convergence will impact the nearby more than the deferred, generating a potential profit opportunity.

The history of TED spread trading on futures markets begins with the introduction of Eurodollar futures contracts on the Chicago Mercantile Exchange's International Monetary Market (IMM) in December of 1981. Following an initially disappointing debut, the Eurodollar futures contract has grown to be arguably the most successful futures contract ever introduced. In addition, Eurodollar futures have been successfully introduced on other futures exchanges, most notably the London International Financial Futures

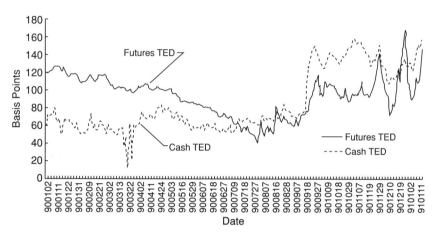

FIGURE 5.2   Cash and futures TED, January 1990 to January 1991. Cash TED is the difference between 3 month Eurodollar and T-bill (add-on) interest rates; futures TED is for March 1991 delivery contracts.

Exchange (LIFFE) in September 1982. The other half of the TED spread, the U.S. T-bill contract, has not performed as well. In the period following the introduction of IMM T-bill futures contracts in January 1976 to the start of trading in Eurodollar futures, the T-bill contract was a marked success. However, in the period since December 1981, volume and open interest in T-bills have declined to the point where TED spreaders are now a crucial component of distant contract liquidity in the T-bill pit. In other words, over time Eurodollar futures have added more distant contracts at the IMM, while T-bill futures are losing liquidity in the distant contracts.

Given this background, the history of TED trading can be roughly divided into two parts: an early period (1982 to 1983), when there was substantial divergence between the cash and futures TED spreads creating significant arbitrage opportunities, and a later period (1983 to present), when deviations in the cash–futures TED from arbitrage equilibrium have substantially narrowed. The differences between the two periods can be attributed to market learning and the ensuing creation of trading operations to arbitrage significant divergence between cash and futures prices. Short-term TED trades based on cash–futures divergence that were profitable in the earlier period are, typically, no longer available. TED spreaders have had to adapt to changing conditions by either increasing position sizes on smaller anticipated moves or by basing trades on longer term fundamentals such as "flight to quality." In both cases, the nature of trading the TED spread has changed.

B. THE CASH-AND-CARRY ARBITRAGES FOR MONEY MARKET FUTURES

One aspect of the TED spread that has not changed is the arbitrage-based fundamentals for the relationship between the cash and futures TED spreads. Briefly, because of the mechanics of cash–futures arbitrage, there is an inherent bias causing the cash TED to differ from the nearby futures TED. In addition, the distant TED is generally undetermined because of the lack of a financing vehicle to execute the cash–futures T-bill arbitrage. Hence, there is sound basis for identifying profitable TED tandem trades. To see this, consider the cash–futures arbitrage trades for nearby T-bill futures contracts (e.g., Dym, 1988; Hegde and Branch, 1985). This trade is similar to the cash-and-carry arbitrage for wi in Chapter 4, Section III. At time $t = 0$ ($<N$), the long cash arbitrage involves purchasing a T-bill deliverable on a futures contract maturing at $t = N$ at price $P(t,91 + N)$, financing the purchase at the term repurchase agreement (repo) rate $(R(t,N)(N/360))$, and covering the cash purchase by shorting a dollar equivalent amount of futures contacts at (invoice) price $TB(t,N)$. Observing that the cash T-bill will also earn a carry return $r(t,N)N/360$, the no-arbitrage condition is[7]

$$P(t, 91 + N)\{1 + (N/360)[R(t,N) - r(t,N)]\} \geq TB(t,N)$$

In other words, the net cost of purchasing the deliverable T-bill today and carrying it to delivery must be greater than the price received from simultaneously selling the same T-bill in the futures market. Violation of this condition will generate arbitrage opportunities.

The short cash arbitrage is similar. A T-bill deliverable at $t = N$ is acquired by doing a term *reverse* repo at the reverse repo rate $[RR(t,N)]$ with the appropriately dated T-bill as the underlying collateral. This T-bill is then sold at $P(t,91 + N)$, creating a short position. Simultaneously, the short is covered by taking a dollar equivalent number of long T-bill futures contracts. In this case, no arbitrage dictates that:[8]

$$P(t, 91 + N)\{1 + (N/360)[RR(t,N) - r(t,N)]\} \leq TB(t,N)$$

It follows from combining these two conditions that $TB[t,N]$ is bounded:

$$P(t, 91 + N)\{1 + (N/360)[RR(t,N) - r(t,N)]\} \leq$$
$$TB(t,N) \leq P(t, 91 + N)\{1 + (N/360)[R(t,N) - r(t,N)]\}$$

---

[7]This arbitrage condition ignores variation margin costs as well as the related transactions costs including bid/offer differences. Relevant interest rates are annualized.

[8]In doing this arbitrage, it assumed that the funds received from doing the short are used to repay the funds used to originate the term reverse.

From this it can be shown that (see Poitras, 1998):

$$RR(t, N)(N/360) \leq RTB(t, 91 + N)(N/360) + [RTB(t, 91 + N) - r^t(N)](91/360) \leq R(t,N)(N/360)$$

where $RTB(t, 91 + N)$ and $r^t(N)$ are the appropriate interest rates for the $91 + N$ day cash T-bill and the T-bill futures positions.

For expository purposes, assume that the equality holds in the above weak inequality relationships; that is, that the repo (borrowing) and reverse (lending) rates are equal. In other words, $R = RR$. In this case, the conditions simplify to:

$$r^t(N) = RTB(t, 91 + N) + \{(N/91)[RTB(t, 91 + N) - R(t,N)]\}$$

This result provides a direct relationship between the interest rate implied in a specific T-bill futures contract, with the cash rate for a T-bill that is deliverable on that contract and the financing rate applicable for the underlying arbitrage. However, because there is no deliverable cash T-bill for contracts more than 9 months to delivery, the cash-and-carry arbitrage can only hold for nearby T-bill futures contracts. In addition, there is only a thin market for term repo in that maturity range.[9] Hence, the arbitrage fundamentals that drive the nearby T-bill futures rates differ from the deferred futures.

The arbitrage for Eurodollar futures differs fundamentally from that for nearby T-bill futures. This follows because arbitrage financing is done in the repo market for T-bills while, for Eurodollars, financing is done in the cash market. As a consequence, the financing rate for Eurodollars is determined by the implied forward rate in the cash market. To see this, consider a long arbitrage for Eurodollar futures. At time t, funds for the arbitrage are borrowed by issuing a Eurodollar deposit (at the bid rate, $RS(t,N)$) that matures on the delivery date for the Euro contract N days away. These funds are then invested for $91 + N$ days (at the offer rate, $RL(t, 91 + N)$, and the resulting tail is covered by shorting the Euro contract at $EU(t,N)$ with implied interest rate $r^e(N)$. Unlike the T-bill case, the long Euro position is not deliverable on the futures contract, both because the Euro contract involves cash settlement and because the Euro deposit is nonnegotiable. The position must be refinanced (at the bid rate) with the gain (or loss) on the futures position providing a mechanism to "lock in" the borrowing rate.

---

[9]More precisely, as the financing term increases the difference between the repo and reverse rates widens significantly to the point where the reverse rate is almost zero. In other words, while it may be possible to do term repos (and reverses) for distant months, the quoted financing rates are sufficient to deter the arbitrage.

Ignoring the bid/offer difference for ease of notation, the long arbitrage implies:[10]

$$\{1 + RL(t, 91 + N)[(91 + N)/360]\} =$$
$$[1 + RS(t,N)(N/360)][1 + r^e(N)(91/360)]$$

Taking logs and ignoring second order terms gives:

$$r^e(N) = RL(t, 91 + N) + \{(N/91)[RL(t, 91 + N)] - RS(t,N)]\}$$

As shown in Poitras (1989b, 1998a), this indicates that the "arbitrage" equilibrium condition for Euros has the relevant implied forward rate in the cash market equivalent to the interest rate implied in the relevant Euro futures price (see Sundaresan (1991) for some complications).

These equations can now be used to determine the equilibrium value for the TED:

$$r^e(N) - r^t(N) = [TED(t, 91 + N)] + \{(N/91)[(TED(t, 91 + N))]$$
$$- [RS(t,N - R(t,N))]\}$$
$$= \{[1 + (N/91)][TED(t, 91 + N)]\}$$
$$- \{(N/91)[RS(t,N) - R(t,N)]\}$$

where $TED(t, 91 + N) = RL(t, 91 + N) - RTB(t, 91 + N)$. In other words, the futures TED spread is determined by the cash TED with an adjustment for the difference between the (short) Euro rate and the term repo rate. When $N = 0$, this equation reduces to the arbitrage condition that cash and futures rates must be equal at maturity.

Given this, the formula for the term structure of the TED spread, essential to determining the profitability of the TED tandem, can now be calculated. More precisely, suppressing time dating for ease of notation:

$$[r^e(T) - r^t(T)] - [r^e(N) - r^t(N)]$$
$$= [1 + (N/91)]$$
$$[TED(91 + T) - TED(91 + N)] \qquad (5.5)$$
$$- \{(N/91)[EUROYC(T,N)] - [R(T) - R(N)]\}$$
$$+ [(T - N)/91]\{[TED(91 + T)] - [RS(T) - R(T)]\}$$

$EUROYC(T,N) = RS(T) - RS(N)$. Hence, the difference between the nearby and deferred TEDs depends theoretically on the relative slopes of the Eurodollar and T-bill yield curves. However, at some point, the actual TED term

---

[10]For Euros, dropping the bid/offer difference is much the same as assuming R and RR are equal for T-bills; the inequality conditions reduce to equality conditions. Hence, it is not necessary to consider the short arbitrage condition.

structure will deviate from this condition due to restrictions on the underlying arbitrage. This divergence can provide a basis for designing profitable trading rules.

C. TED SPREAD AND TED TANDEM TRADING STRATEGIES

As a spread trade, the TED has the desirable property of having equivalent basis point value for changes in the two contracts involved, $25 per basis point on both Euro and T-bill contracts. Hence, the dollar equivalence ratio of the number of Euro contracts to T-bill contracts in the TED is one to one. Given this, consider the payoff on a long TED trade (short the Euro and long the T-bill) that was established at t and closed out at $t + 1$:

$$\pi_{TED} = [EU(t) - EU(t+1)] + [TB(t+1) - TB(t)]$$
$$= [EU(t) - TB(t)] - [EU(t+1) - TB(t+1)]$$

In terms of futures price quotes:

$$\pi_{TED} = \{[100 - r^e(t,N)] - [100 - r^b(t,N)]\} - \{[100 - r^e(t+1,N)]$$
$$- [100 - r^b(t+1,N)]\}$$
$$= [r^e(t+1,N) - r^b(t+1,N)] - [r^e(t,N) - r^b(t,N)]$$

Briefly, the *long* TED will be profitable when the price difference between *EU* and *TB* narrows or, put differently, $(r^e - r^t)$ widens. It follows that the *short* TED will be profitable when $(r^e - r^t)$ narrows. While futures to cash convergence may have some marginal impact, the payoff on this trade depends primarily on changes in the cash TED. Factors driving the cash TED include flight to quality and instrument supply considerations. Hence, the TED spread involves forcasting cash market fundamentals and putting on the appropriate TED trade to speculate on the forcast.

In contrast to the TED spread, the TED tandem is a different type of speculation. Based on analysis of the profit function for the TED tandem, there are arbitrage factors that cause the cash, nearby, and deferred TED spreads to differ. However, on the delivery date for the futures contract, the cash and futures TEDs must be approximately equal. To exploit these discrepancies requires trading strategies that have payoffs based on spread convergence. For intermarket spreading, tandem trades have the practical advantage of combining spreads in different commodities. Each side of the trade being a spread allows for substantially lower transaction costs and margin requirements.[11] Defining the long tandem as *short-the-deferred* Euro and *nearby* T-bill and *long-the-nearby* Euro and *deferred* T-bill, the associated payoff is

$$\pi_{\text{tan}} = \{[r^e(t+1,T) - r^b(t+1,T)] - [r^e(t+1,N) - r^b(t+1,N)]\}$$
$$- \{[r^e(t,T) - r^b(t,T)] - [r^e(t,N) - r^b(t,N)]\}$$

Hence, the long tandem profits when the difference between $[r^e(T) - r^b(T)]$ and $[r^e(N) - r^b(N)]$ widens over time. Similarly, the short tandem is profitable when the difference between $[r^e(T) - r^t(T)]$ and $[r^e(N) - r^t(N)]$ narrows over time. For example, assume at $t = 0$ that the nearby spread is 115 basis points and the deferred is 123. Further assume that at $t = 1$ the nearby spread falls to 95 basis points while the deferred spread stays relatively constant at 120 (due, say, to futures–cash convergence factors affecting the nearby spread). In this case, a long tandem would have generated a profit of 17 basis points.

Based on this analysis, it is possible to heuristically specify a trading rule based on the implied convergence behavior. To see this, assume that for large N the TED spread basis is constant. As N declines (the nearby contracts approach maturity) the front contracts become increasingly more affected by cash–futures arbitrage considerations. This drives $[r^e(N) - r^t(N)]$ down relative to $[r^e(T) - r^t(T)]$ creating a spread-trading profit opportunity. An example of this type of behavior is exhibited in Fig. 5.2, which tracks the cash–futures TED spreads as the contract moves from creation to maturity. By trading spreads against spreads, both legs of the trade are protected against changes in the level of interest rates. A primary source of risk in the trade is the possibility that perverse yield curve shifts that distort the cash–futures convergence behavior could occur at the end of the trade horizon. In addition, the maturity dates for futures contracts selected should be far enough apart that the nearby contract can be affected by cash–futures arbitrage factors while the deferred contracts are not.

Because the payoff on the tandem depends on relative changes in interest rates, profits on this trade are dependent on small basis point moves. Given the underlying variability in the spread relationships, trade performance will be dependent on the selection of the trade's trigger and kill rules. Unfortunately, there is a sizable number of such possible rules with the practical selection criteria being empirical performance. The type of trigger rule considered in Poitras (1989b, 1998a) is naive: The trade is mechanically established a prespecified number of months prior to the delivery month for the

---

[11]Until the introduction of SPAN for setting margins (see Chapter 1), the TED spread proper was not treated as a spread in assessing transactions costs and margin requirements; that is, both the Euro and T-bill positions were considered "open" positions. Even before SPAN, the tandem TED trader did qualify for spread treatment.

nearby contracts. The kill rule can also be naive with trades can be closed out a prespecified number of days before the beginning of the delivery period for the nearby contracts. Naive rules are useful to provide a benchmark against which rules incorporating judgmental factors can be measured. Trades based on triggers that incorporate qualitative factors may outperform naive rules. For example, a more sophisticated rule could be based on fundamentally motivated factors such as the "cheapness" of the cash yield curve relative to a Euro or T-bill futures strip.

D. Currency Tandem

Analytically, currency tandems are one of the most interesting of all spread trades. The background for this trade has already been considered in some detail in Chapter 4, Section II. From Eq. (3.3), it follows that:

$$\Delta[F(T) - F(N)] = \theta(0)\Delta F + F(1,N)\Delta\theta$$

By working directly with the covered interest parity (CIP) condition from Eq. (4.1), this exact result can be used to derive a precise expression for the profit function.

Using the discrete time version of the differential in Chapter 4, Section II, evaluating the $\Delta\theta$ term gives:

$$\begin{aligned}
\Delta\theta &= \frac{\Delta(i - i*)}{(1 + i*)} + (i - i*)\Delta\frac{1}{(1 + i*)} \\
&= \frac{(\Delta i - \Delta i*)}{(1 + i*)} - (i - i*)\frac{\Delta i*}{(1 + i*)^2}
\end{aligned}$$

Substituting this result into Eq. (3.3) and collecting terms gives:

$$\pi_{ct} = \Delta[F(T) - F(N)] = F(1,N)\left[\frac{\Delta i - \Delta i*}{(1 + i*)}\right] + \frac{i - i*}{1 + i*}\Delta F(N)$$

Observing that $(i - i^*)\Delta i^*$ is a product of differences in interest rates, it follows that this term on the righthand side is, to a first approximation, second order and can be set equal to zero. If the spread is tailed, or tailing is unnecessary, the ΔF term is removed and this leaves only the first term on the righthand side to determine the spread:

$$\pi_{ct} \cong \frac{F(1,N)}{1 + i*}(\Delta i - \Delta i*)$$

Recalling that currency futures are quoted as the amount of U.S. dollars per unit of foreign currency, the upshot is that the profitability of an intracommodity currency futures spread depends on the relative change in the appropriate interest rates for the United States and the foreign country. This result for a one-to-one currency spread extends naturally for a tandem, which can be used to speculate on changes in interest rates that are not U.S. The tandem permits speculation on relative foreign interest rate changes even when there is no liquid foreign currency futures contracts directly quoted in terms of the two foreign currencies.

Before proceeding to consider the currency tandem, one practical problem about the intracommodity currency spread needs to be considered: Under what conditions is it possible to simplify the profit function by ignoring the tail on the spread (e.g., Poitras, 1997)? This question can be resolved by observing that the ΔF term in Eq. (3.3) is associated with the tail, with $\theta(0)$ representing the appropriate size of the tail. It follows that if foreign and domestic interest rates are approximately equal ($\theta(0) \cong 0$), then it is not necessary to tail the spread. However, in cases where there is a significant difference a tail may be required. To see this, assume that $F(0,N) = 1, i = .1$, and $i^* = .04$. If the exchange rate falls by 20%, then $\Delta F = .2$ and $[\theta(0)\Delta F]$ is around .012. If $(\Delta i - \Delta i^*)$ changes by .02, then $F(1,N)\Delta\theta$ is around .016. However, while there are definitely situations in which a tailing a currency spread is advisable, it is also possible to construct numbers for which a tail is not required for the currency spread. In general, because it is a product of two differences, the difference in foreign and domestic interest rate levels and the change in exchange rates, the $\theta(0)\Delta F$ term is likely to be of second order though this result does not apply when the difference between foreign and domestic interest rates is large.

Assuming, for simplicity, that it is not necessary to tail the two currency spreads comprising the tandem, calculation of a hedge ratio is required for the tandem. Reexpressing the currency tandem profit function gives:

$$\pi_{ct}* = (\Delta i - \Delta i_F) - \frac{Q_G G(1,N)(1 + i_F)}{Q_F F(1,N)(1 + i_G)}(\Delta i - \Delta i_G)$$

where * indicates that profit has been appropriately scaled. If the hedge ratio is chosen to be dollar equivalent $[Q_G G(1,N)(1 + i_F) = Q_F F(1,N)(1 + i_G)]$, then the U.S. interest rate terms Δi will cancel, and this profit function will depend on the difference in the two foreign interest rates:

$$\pi_{ct}^* \cong \Delta i c_G - \Delta i c_F$$

Hence, when the hedge ratio is set appropriately and tailing is done when necessary, the profitability of a currency tandem depends on the difference in the two foreign interest rate changes, with the U.S. interest rate impact canceling out.

In practice, calculation of the hedge ratio involves solving the approximation $[Q_2G(0,N)] = [Q_1F(0,N)]$. This requires equalizing dollar value on both
legs of the tandem at $t = 0$. To see how this is accomplished for the currency
tandem, consider a trade where the objective is to speculate on relative
changes in Canadian and British interest rates using currency futures denominated in terms of US$. In this case the US$ value of the Canadian dollar
contract is (US$/C$) $\$100,000 = F(0,N)Q_1$. And the U.S. dollar value of the £
contract is (US$/£) (£62,500) $= G(0,N)Q_2$. Hence, $[G(0,N)Q_2/F(0,N)Q_1] =$
[(US$/£) (£62,500)]/(US$/C$) $\$100,000 = $ (C$/£) (62,500/100,000). The
hedge ratio is the product of the current Canadian to British exchange rate
times .625.[12]

IV. SYNTHESIZING FOREIGN INTEREST RATES

The absence of a viable futures market for foreign money market securities
could pose a legitimate problem for money market participants seeking to
hedge foreign cash positions. In some circumstances hedging objectives can be
achieved through some other means (e.g., in the Government of Canada t-bill
market through the use of when-issued t-bill positions). However, for some
hedging situations, a potentially more practical alternative is to make use of
instruments traded on U.S. exchanges, specifically foreign currency and Eurodollar futures contracts. Use of U.S. money market futures by foreign hedgers
will be complicated by basis risk considerations and by the hedge profit
function being denominated in two different currencies. This section provides
examples for hedging cash Canadian t-bill positions, though the result generalizes in a straightforward fashion to the hedging of any admissible foreign
money market security. Application to the design of speculative trading strategies is also possible. The strategies examined exhibit differing position sizes
for the U.S. money market futures used in forming the hedge. Theoretically, it
is demonstrated that the minimum variance hedge ratios can be interpreted
and estimated as coefficients in an appropriately specified multivariate regression.

To accurately hedge a cash Canadian t-bill position with U.S. money market
futures, hedge design should account for the interest and exchange rate
relationships implied by CIP. In Chapter 4, Section II, it was demonstrated

---

[12]To be exact, the hedge ratios involve variables defined at $t = 1$. These obviously are not
known at $t = 0$ and, as a result, must be approximated. In the absence of information that may
improve the estimate, the ratio of current values can be used. In certain cases, hedge ratio
adjustment during the life of the trade may be required and this will have to be incorporated
into trade design. This practical substitution of current for future values occurs in virtually all the
hedge ratio evaluation situations.

that for arbitrage involving securities identical in all respects except currency denomination, the annualized CIP relationship is often restated as:

$$r = r^* + \frac{F - S}{S}(1 + r^*)$$

The CIP condition provides the framework for hedging Canadian t-bill positions with U.S. money market futures. The basics of the hedge strategy follow from the textbook short covered interest arbitrage trade (long Canadian t-bills). Converting the CIP trade to a synthetic interest rate futures trade involves substituting a short U.S. money market futures position for the borrowed U.S. funds and, to reflect the currency transactions, a tailed currency spread that is short the deferred and long the nearby. Given this, the hedge design problem is concerned with specifying appropriate hedge ratios for the futures positions.

Basis risk in the hedge arises from two factors: deviations from CIP for the relevant Canadian and U.S. instruments and discrepancies arising from the use of futures positions as replacements for cash transactions. Of these sources, the replacement of cash transactions with futures positions introduces only limited difficulties. Basis risk arising from CIP deviations is another matter. CIP holds as an equality for instruments that are identical in all respects except for currency of denomination. This is not the case when Canadian t-bills are compared with either Eurodollars or U.S. T-bills. Each of these instruments possesses differential risk characteristics. Due to a combination of risk and arbitrage considerations, either the Eurodollar (Euro) or U.S. T-bill futures (or both) could be used in constructing the hedge. Both these rates can be considered to provide effective inequality bounds on the covered Canadian rate, that is, the covered Canadian rate is bounded above by the Euro rate and below by the U.S. T-bill rate. This implies that deviations from CIP are also bounded and, hence, variation of the hedge position is constrained. This provides some scope for designing hedging strategies that exploit the systematic portion of the basis risk to improve hedge performance. To understand how this is done it is necessary to examine the specific mechanics of how covered interest arbitrage applies to the relevant instruments under consideration.

As discussed in Chapter 4, for equality to hold in CIP the arbitrage must be two sided. In the Euro/Canadian t-bill case, the arbitrage is one sided. One of the arbitrage trades cannot be executed because only the Canadian government has the ability to issue liabilities in the Canadian t-bill market. The Euro rate only provides an upper boundary on covered Canadian t-bill rates (omitting time dating for convenience): $r^e \geq \{r^* + [(F(0,T) - F(0,N))/F(0,N)] (1 + r^*)\}$, where, for present purposes, r^* is the Canadian t-bill rate and r^e is the Euro-U.S. dollar rate. Considering the other direction for the arbitrage, a lower bound on the covered Canadian t-bill rate is provided by a risk arbitrage with the U.S. T-bill rate, when r^u is the U.S. T-bill rate and the inequality extends naturally: $r^u \leq \{r^* + [(F(0,T) - F(0,N))/F(0,N)](1 + r^*)\}$. The lower bound is not driven by the pure arbitrage activity that drives the upper boundary. Given that the Euro rate will always lie above the U.S. T-bill rate because of the differing risk characteristics of those two instruments, this implies that the covered Canadian t-bill rate will fluctuate within boundaries provided by the Euro and U.S. T-bill rates.

Given this, the key practical questions in implementing the hedge are which U.S. money market futures contracts to use and how to determine the appropriate hedge ratios for the interest rate futures and currency futures spread positions. Selection of the appropriate interest rate futures contract is primarily an empirical question. Two hedge ratio specification procedures are examined: dollar value and minimum variance. The dollar value approach computes the hedge ratio directly from the value of the cash market transactions used in the textbook covered interest arbitrage trade. This approach produces accurate hedging outcomes when the price behavior of the futures contracts used closely matches that of the cash instruments. The greater the basis risk, the more likely it is that hedges based on the dollar value approach will be less effective. The dollar value approach can be used as a benchmark against which outcomes of the minimum variance hedge ratios can be compared.

To evaluate the dollar value hedge ratios, analysis of the CIP conditions developed in Chapter 4, Section II, is required. For ease of exposition, assume that the relevant variables satisfy the conventional calculus regularity conditions. (In practice, this assumption requires that the hedge positions be continuously adjusted.) Specifically, in Chapter 4, Section II, it was derived that:

$$dr = dr^* + (1 + r^*)\frac{d(FPS)}{F(0,N)} - (r - r^*)\frac{dF(0,N)}{F(0,N)}$$

Examining this result, it can be seen that a dollar value hedge involves combining a U.S. interest rate futures position and an appropriately tailed currency futures spread with the appropriate hedge ratios given as the coefficients for the $dFPS$ and $dF(0,N)$ terms.

Following the discussion in Chapter 6, Section I, the accepted method for deriving minimum variance hedge ratios is to exploit the first-order conditions for hedge variance minimization.[13] For the case at hand, this requires specifi-

---

[13]The hedge ratio calculation and estimation problem is examined in a number of sources (e.g., Toevs and Jacob, 1986; Bell and Krasker, 1986; Hill and Schneeweis, 1981; Cecchetti et al. 1988). Benninga et.al. (1984) show that if futures prices are unbiased then the minimum variance hedge ratio is also an optimal hedge ratio for hedgers with quadratic utility functions.

cation of the expected profit and variance of profit for the hedge position. For a hedge done with Euros:

$$E(\pi) = Q[r^*(0)' - E(r^*(1)'')] + A\{E[FPS(1)] - FPS(0)\} + B[eu(0) - E(eu(1)]$$
$$var(\pi) = Q^2\sigma_*^2 + A^2\sigma_f^2 + B^2\sigma_e^2 + 2[QA\sigma_{*f} - (QB\sigma_{*e} + AB\sigma_{fe})]$$

where Q is the value of the cash position, A is the value of the legs of the currency futures spread (FPS), B is the value of the interest rate futures position, and σ is either a variance or a covariance defined by the subscripts f for futures spread, e for Euro, and $*$ for Canadian t-bill. The $'$ and $''$ superscripts allow for possibly differing times between settlement and maturity for the cash instrument. Given the variance function $var(\pi)$, generalized hedge ratios for both A and B unconstrained can be derived. This can be done by solving the two first order conditions for the minimum variance problem.

Specifically, differentiating $var(\pi)$ with respect to A and B gives two first-order conditions that can be solved to get:

$$A^* = \frac{B\sigma_{fe} - Q\sigma_{*f}}{\sigma_f^2} \qquad B^* = \frac{Q\sigma_{*e} + A\sigma_{fe}}{\sigma_e^2}$$

Solving for A:

$$A^* = \frac{Q}{1 - R^2}\left\{\sigma_{*e}\frac{\sigma_{fe}}{\sigma_e^2\sigma_f^2} - \frac{\sigma_{*f}}{\sigma_f^2}\right\} \qquad \text{where:} \qquad R^2 = \frac{\sigma_{fe}^2}{\sigma_e^2\sigma_f^2}$$

In other words, R^2 is the squared correlation between e and f. Rearranging A^* gives:

$$A^* = Q[(\sigma_{*e}\sigma_{fe} - \sigma_{*f}\sigma_e^2)/(\sigma_e^2\sigma_f^2 - \sigma_{ef}^2)]$$

This is a special case of the multivariate hedge ratio discussed in Chapter 6, Section I; the minimum variance hedge ratio for the currency spread position is equivalent to the currency spread regression coefficient in a regression of Canadian t-bill rates on Euro rates and currency spreads. Solving for B gives a similar result.

In order to transform the hedge ratio problem into its more familiar bivariate regression interpretation, one of the two hedge positions can be constrained, thereby reducing the solution to a single first-order condition. This can be done by setting the exchange rate adjusted value of the Eurodollar position to be equal to the value of the Canadian t-bill position or by setting the value of the currency futures positions equal to the implied CIP values; that is, set $B = Q/F(0,T)$ or set $A = Q/F(0,T)$. If $B = Q/F(0,T)$, then differentiating $var(\pi)$ with respect to the single choice variable A gives:

$$A^{**} = Q \left(\frac{1}{F(0,T)} \frac{\sigma_{fe}}{\sigma_f^2} - \frac{\sigma_{*f}}{\sigma_f^2} \right)$$

A similar result holds for B^* if A is constrained. In this form, the hedge ratio expression involves bivariate regression coefficients. However, the variances and covariances are based on the *conditional* distribution and, as a result, imply a different regression specification than in the unconditional case.

Econometrically, use of regression to estimate minimum variance hedge ratios raises a number of interesting points (e.g., Kroner and Sultan, 1993). One basic question involves specification of the variables in the regression: Should levels or first differences be used? Toevs and Jacob (1986) attempt to cast some doubt on the conventional wisdom (e.g., Hill and Schneeweis, 1982) that first-difference regressions are superior to regressions done in levels. However, regressions based on levels typically have undesirable statistical properties (e.g., nonstationarity as reflected in Durbin–Watson values significantly different from two). As a result, the minimum variance hedge ratio regressions should be based on *changes* in rates (or prices) and futures spreads. Because the ultimate objective is to minimize the variation in *prices*, regression results based on rates require some manipulation before being used as hedge ratios. Specifically, the following coefficient trans-formation is required: $\Delta P = -\Delta r / [1 + r(0) + r(1) + r(0)r(1)]$. In practice, rates must be adjusted to be comparable in maturity to the maturity of the currency spread. In addition, the coefficient on the interest rate futures position must be adjusted by the (US\$/C\$) exchange rate to get dollar equivalency. Poitras (1988b) provides more detailed discussion and various estimation results.

QUESTIONS

1. Derive the profit profile for a spread trade with equal position sizes. What factors determine the profitability of this trade? Derive the profit profile for a tailed spread and explain how this trade is different from one with one-to-one position sizes. Does your answer depend on the commodity under consideration?
2. What factors determine the profitability of a copper turtle trade, an oil butterfly, a tandem combining T-notes and T-bonds? What trading strategy is most applicable to trading the TED spread?
3a. Assume you are convinced that the spread between long- and short-term interest rates is going to *widen* within the next few months but you do not know whether rates in general will be higher or lower than they are at present. As reflected in market prices, other investors appear

to disagree with your prediction: They expect the spread to remain constant. How could you profit from your superior predictive ability by using tailed T-bond futures spreads or a turtle trade combining U.S. T-bond spreads and T-bill futures? Does your answer depend on whether the yield curve is inverted?

3b. Assume that you are convinced that the spread between the implied carry return in gold futures will narrow relative to the implied carry return in silver futures. How would you design a trade to profit on your predictive ability in this case?

4. From Section II construct a $(1 + cy)$ spread for the August 8, 1994, copper futures prices. Do the same calculations for crude oil futures. Explain the factors that would drive profitability for the two trades.

CHAPTER 6

Risk Management: Hedging and Diversification

I. TRANSACTIONS HEDGING AND OPTIMAL HEDGING

A. RISK MANAGEMENT OBJECTIVES

As discussed in Chapter 2, Merton (1993), Tufano (1996), and others state that corporate risk management can be achieved through diversification, hedging, and insurance. In some situations, such as Tufano's gold mining sample, the firms involved have little opportunity to exploit diversification opportunities to manage business risk. In other cases, such as globally diversified investment funds, diversification is an integral part of risk management. Situations vary, and the identification of an optimal risk-management strategy depends on the objective function specified. Though it is difficult to formulate general rules, the results in Chapter 2 do provide useful guidance. Difficult does not mean impossible, and this chapter focuses on implementing corporate risk management through diversification and hedging with derivatives. The viability of a given technique will depend on the risk-management philosophy adopted by the firm and the empirical characteristics of the firm's risk profile.

Drawing from the analysis in Chapter 2, Section I, it is possible to decompose the optimal solution for the risk management decision problem into a speculative component and a risk-minimizing component. Factors determining the speculative part can be significantly different than the elements of the risk-minimization problem. Faced with an inability to forecast key variables, the firm is reduced to seeking risk-management solutions aimed at minimizing the variability of a target variable, such as direct transactions cash flow, cash flow from firm operations, firm earnings before interest and taxes (EBIT) and so on (e.g., Culp et al., 1998). This theoretical observation is consistent with the rationales expressed by numerous nonfinancial and financial firms for using derivatives. Yet, even when the speculative component does not affect the optimal solution (i.e., the firm is seeking only to minimize the variance of firm profit by eliminating risks that can be managed with derivative securities), there is still a considerable range of risk-management solutions that could be selected, depending on the empirical characteristics of the firm's operations.

To see this, consider the problem of a financial institution managing interest-rate risk. The risk-management objective often specified in this situation is to have the firm choose the composition of assets and liabilities such that the duration of surplus is equal to zero (e.g., Reitano, 1991, 1992, 1996). In theory, the best method to achieve this objective is to use "cash flow matching" to match each liability cash flow with an asset having the same cash flow. Except in special cases, cash flow matching is not possible—for example, due to a lack of assets with cash flows that match liabilities and the large number of transactions and planning periods involved. The resulting risk-management rules that have been developed seek to aggregate the various transactions and planning periods, for example, for a zero surplus fund, set the duration of assets equal to the duration of liabilities (e.g., Bierwag, 1987). This situation can be contrasted with that of, say, a hog producer seeking to lock in the price to be received for animals nearing the end of the feed cycle. In this case, there is only one transaction and one planning period. For these situations, using cash flow matching to implement the risk-management strategy would be feasible and, possibly, desirable.

In what follows, hedging techniques will be illustrated using two approaches. The *transaction hedging* approach emphasizes the trading mechanics involved in fully hedging a specific transaction. A cash position is identified, and the appropriate forward position is described and determined. It is conventional to have spot and derivative positions that have little or no basis risk, although, as will be seen, this does not have to be the case. Various examples of transaction hedges are provided in the following discussion. The transaction hedging approach does not address what the optimal size of the hedge position needs to be for a specific cash position. This is addressed in the optimal hedging approach. Transaction hedging involves cash flow matching, so it is desirable to have only a small number of transactions to manage. The transaction hedging approach would be optimal in situations where the risk-management objective is to minimize the variance of firm cash flow (i.e., where the firm has no view on expected prices and has no ability or desire to speculate). In addition, the optimality of transaction hedging requires that there is little or no basis risk associated with the derivative securities being used.

While transaction hedging takes the optimal hedge ratio to be one, optimal hedging requires estimating the hedge ratio from empirical data. The transactions hedging approach is the basis for arguments involving the relative benefits of hedging versus no hedging, such as those that appear in the free-lunch argument (Perold and Schulman, 1988). The optimal hedging approach avoids these questions, starting from the premise that full hedging and no hedging are only two of a theoretically infinite number of possible hedge ratios. In a sense, a transaction hedge is a special case of an optimal hedge, applicable under certain specific situations. However, in general, transaction hedges will not be optimal. For example, there may be considerable basis risk associated with the hedging instruments. In addition, transaction hedging does not admit the possible use of derivatives as an essential component of a business plan (e.g., as evidenced in numerous hedge funds). The downside risks of using a transaction hedge approach when an optimal hedge is needed are evident in the Metallgesellschaft Refinery and Marketing (MGRM) case. Business risks are speculative. Integrating derivative securities into a program to optimally manage business and market risks is the ultimate goal.

The relevance of these two different approaches to hedging extends well beyond academic pedagogy, as illustrated by the MGRM saga. This firm was in the business of intermediating the long-term forward market for oil. Faced with liquidity constraints on available contract maturities, MGRM employed a rolling-stack hedge that featured a concentration of nearby contracts being used to hedge a deferred spot commitment. The hedging decision was modeled using the transaction hedging approach. Mello and Parsons (1995b, p. 19) concluded that MGRM had to:

> ...incorporate the fact of cash flow variability across months into a decision about whether and how much to hedge. When the time pattern of cash flows matters—as it typically does for corporations looking to hedge—a smaller size hedge may be preferable to a one-for-one rolling stack or other strategy that actually increases initial cash flow variability.

In effect, MGRM used a transaction hedging approach when the situation was theoretically better suited to using an optimal hedge due to the substantial amount of basis risk facing MGRM. However, given the difficulty of determining a market value for the forward delivery contracts, how an optimal hedge would have been estimated in the MGRM case is not obvious.

The airline industry provides another illustration of the contrast between an optimal hedge and a transaction hedge. Based on information contained in annual reports, this industry is characterized by a range of risk-management activities using derivative securities. Some firms (e.g., Thai Airways) engage in only limited use of derivatives, such as for hedging specific foreign exchange (FX) or jet fuel transactions. Other firms (e.g., Singapore Airlines) have a sophisticated program to cover the range of market risks. Although it is only about 10% of the cost of goods sold, the most volatile cost component for airlines is jet fuel prices. A transaction hedge of this commodity price risk would fully hedge the quantity of jet fuel to be purchased over the planning horizon. An optimal hedge would attempt to estimate the impact of changes in jet fuel prices on changes in net cash flows. Industry practice among firms using sophisticated derivative strategies indicates a hedge ratio of approximately one half; about half of near-term jet fuel purchases are hedged.

B. PRICE RISK VERSUS BASIS RISK

In Chapter 2, hedgers were taken to be traders who are using the derivatives market to cover a cash position. While there are some legal and regulatory interpretation problems with this broad definition of hedgers, analytically there is little problem using this approach. The analytical difficulties arise in handling interaction of the two basic components of hedge design: risk minimization which is inherent in hedging, and speculation, which is required in order to design optimal trades. To see how speculation affects the problem, consider the unhedged grain elevator case (see Table 6.1). As a random variable, π will have a conditional mean and variance that can be used to assess the risk (volatility) of the unhedged position (see Appendix I).

Application of the definition for conditional variance (where the conditioning notation has been dropped for convenience), $\mathrm{var}[\pi] = E(\pi - [\pi])^2$ provides the result that the conditional variance is

TABLE 6.1   Profit Function for an Unhedged Grain Elevator

Date	Cash position	Futures position
$t = 0$	Buy Q_A units of grain at $S(0)$ for storage in grain elevator	None
$t = 1$	Q_A units are sold at $S(1)$ and loaded for shipment	None

Note: Ignoring carrying costs, the profit function can be specified:

$$\pi(1) = [S(1) - S(0)]Q_A$$

$$\text{var}[\pi] = Q_A{}^2 \, \text{var}[S(1)]$$

In the case of unhedged cash positions, risk depends on the size of the position and the volatility of the cash price. Despite some stylized textbook treatments to the contrary, futures hedging does not typically eliminate all the risk of cash price fluctuations. To see this, recall the profit function for the *one-to-one* grain elevator hedge from Chapter 2, Section I:

$$\pi = Q\{[F(0,T) - S(0)] - [F(1,T) - S(1)]\}$$

It was remarked that the profitability of the hedged position depends on the change in the basis. This discussion can now be extended to observe that the conditional variance for the hedged position is

$$\text{var}[\pi] = Q^2 \, \text{var}[F(1,T) - S(1)]$$

In other words, *a transaction hedge substitutes basis risk for price risk*. Basis risk is only zero when the deliverable and spot commodities are the same and the spot commodity is delivered to settle the futures contract.

The importance of understanding basis behavior for designing effective hedges is apparent from the variance of the one-to-one hedge profit function. Basis information can be used to make various adjustments to improve

---

BOX 1

Types of Hedges

Borrowing liberally from Working (1962), Leuthold *et al.* (1989, pp. 145–146) provide a partial taxonomy of hedges in which two of the most important types, optimal hedges and natural hedges, are not identified.

Carrying-charge hedge: A carrying-charge hedge is associated with the storage of a commodity. A merchant purchases and stores the commodity and hedges it to profit from storage. The merchant seeks to profit from changes in the price relationship (basis), rather than price level changes.

Operational hedge: An operational hedge facilitates merchandising or processing operations. A merchant hedges to establish the price of an input or output, usually holding it for only a short time, often ignoring

(continues)

(continued)
change in price while a product is being processed or transported. Typical examples of an operational hedge include a flour miller buying wheat futures to offset a forward sales contract of flour to a baker or a shipper, exporter, or importer selling futures against a cash purchase. These hedges act as temporary substitutes and are liquidated as soon as the trader takes a corresponding cash position.

Selective hedge: The trader decides whether to hedge or not according to price expectations. The holder of the commodity hedges if prices are expected to fall and does not hedge if prices are expected to rise. Selective hedging introduces an additional speculative element to hedging as traders hedge only under certain price expectations. This common hedging procedure is often done to prevent large losses, and it can relate to optimal hedging.

Anticipatory hedge: An anticipatory hedge is usually not matched or offset by an equivalent stock of goods or merchandising commitment. The anticipatory hedge serves as a temporary substitute for merchandising to be done later, that is, an expected future cash purchase or sale. The anticipatory hedge involves either the purchase of futures contracts against raw material requirements or the sale of contracts by producers in advance of the completion of production. For example, flour millers and soybean processors may buy futures contracts in anticipation of subsequent purchases of wheat and soybeans, respectively. Livestock feeders may sell live cattle and live hog futures long before the animals are ready for market. Similarly, grain farmers forward sell their crops before harvest.

Cross hedge: To cross hedge is to assume a futures position opposite an existing cash position, but in a different commodity. Typically, there is no active futures contract in the commodity corresponding to the cash position, so the trader must select a related commodity for hedging. To be effective, the prices and commodity values of the cash commodity and futures contract must have a fairly high positive correlation. Examples include hedging corporate bonds in the Treasury-bond market, grain sorghum in corn, and boneless beef in live cattle.

hedging performance. For example, a refiner seeking to hedge the price of purchasing copper scrap using the high-grade copper contract will want to know the basis relationship between the grade of refined copper being produced from the scrap as well as the approximate amount of refined copper that can be produced per unit of scrap. With this information, appropriate adjustments can be made to Q. When will the hedge completely eliminate price risk? This will occur when $F(1,T) = S(1)$. Accomplishing this result requires a delivery hedge where the commodity being hedged is the same as the commodity specified in the forward or futures contract and $T = 1$. In this case, $F(1,1) = S(1)$, and the contract is satisfied by delivery of the commodity. This result is typically easier to achieve with the use of *forward* contracts that can be tailored to match the size, grade, location, and other factors that can impact the basis relationship.

C. Transaction Hedging Example: Issuing Commercial Paper

Basis variation in a transaction hedge can originate from three sources: *cross-hedging*, when the cash instrument being hedged is an imperfect match to the deliverable commodity; deviation from *dollar equivalency*, when the implied market value of the futures position differs from that of the cash commodity; and *cost-of-carry considerations*, which include the "time decay" (to $F(T,T) = S(T)$) built into the cost-of-carry relationship that determines the futures price. To see the role of these factors in basis variation consider the trading profile for a perfect transactions hedge involving a corporation (circa 1981) seeking to lock in the cost of funds on a future issue of $20 million of 3-month commercial paper (see Table 6.2). This hedge was perfect because the cash and futures positions moved up and down in unison. The commercial paper issuer was able to fully lock in the borrowing rate that prevailed when

TABLE 6.2   Perfect Transaction Hedge for a Commercial Paper Issuer (*circa* 1981)

Date	Cash position	Basis	Futures position
$t = 4/13$	Decide to issue $20 million in 3-month commercial paper on June 3 and want to lock in current rate of 15.25%	1.93%	Short $20 million June (3-month) T-bill contracts at 13.32%
$t = 6/3$	Issue is offered and sold at 17.50%	1.93%	Close out position with long contract at 15.57%
Change	+2.25%	0	−2.25%

the original hedging decision was made. Given that this trade involved a cross hedge (i.e., a commercial paper position is being hedged with T-bills), this is an unlikely outcome.

A more likely result for the cross hedging situation would be the following example of an actual hedge (see Table 6.3). For this hedge, the issue cost was 15.44%, not 15.25% as in the perfect hedge. Hence, while the hedge was not perfect, the bulk of the considerable increase in interest rates that took place was offset. The effectiveness of the hedge will depend on basis behavior of the cash and futures commodities. For some hedges (e.g., corporate bonds hedged with T-bonds or Iowa corn hedged with Chicago corn), the basis variation will be small relative to potential changes in cash prices. In other cases (e.g., tungsten hedged with platinum or kerosene hedged with crude oil), basis variation could be greater than the change in cash prices. This chapter examines some techniques for determining the hedge position in the face of cross hedging considerations.

Compared to the vagaries of cross hedging, basis variation arising from dollar equivalency is straightforward: "Dollar equivalency refers to the process of structuring the hedge in such a way that one gets equivalent dollar movement in the two (cash and futures) positions even if the per-unit dollar changes in the two are not equal" (Powers and Vogel, 1983, p. 183) For some commodities, such as grains and metals, dollar equivalency can be handled by *tailing* the hedge (tailing is discussed in Chapter 3). For financial futures the problem is slightly more complicated. In this case, dollar equivalency requires adjusting the number of futures contracts such that a basis point change in the futures yield will produce the same dollar value change as a basis point change in the cash position. For example, Appendix II derives the values for an 01 (basis point) for $1 million par value of 3- and 6-month T-bills as $25 and $50, respectively. Hence, to hedge a 6-month T-bill position with the 3-month International Money Market (IMM) T-bill contract, two $1 million par value futures contracts would be required to hedge, on a dollar

TABLE 6.3   Actual Transaction Hedge Profit for a Commercial Paper Issuer

Date	Cash position	Basis	Futures position
$t = 4/13$	Decide to issue $20 million in 3-month commercial paper on June 3 and want to lock in current rate of 15.25%	1.93%	Short $20 million June T-bill contracts at 13.32%
$t = 6/3$	Issue is offered and sold at 17.50%	2.12%	Close out position with long contract at 15.38%
Change	+2.25%	−0.19%	−2.06%

equivalent basis, the equivalent par value in 6-month T-bills. Given this, it does not follow that dollar equivalent hedge ratios will be optimal hedge ratios. This point will be addressed later in this chapter.

The final component of basis variation to consider is issues related to the cost of carry. More precisely, this aspect is concerned with deviations of futures from (and deviations due to) cash-and-carry arbitrage conditions during the life of the hedge. In its simplest form, this systematically occurs with the implied "time decay" in the hedge. Depending on the commodity, associated factors would include a combination of fluctuations in carry costs, changes in the cheapest deliverable commodity, term-structure effects, distortions arising from delivery, and the time to maturity of the futures contract. These factors can impose some limitations on hedge design. For example, because of the impact that delivery considerations have on futures prices during the delivery month of the contract, the nearby contract selected should not enter the delivery month during the anticipated life of the hedge (unless "rolling the hedge forward" is incorporated as part of the hedging strategy or futures delivery is the objective).

Given the various issues associated with basis variation, an essential feature of hedge design involves the incorporation of cash and futures price expectations into the hedge decision; that is, at some point hedge design has to deal with the speculative aspect of hedging. Armed with accurate price forecasts, it is clear that transaction hedges will not always produce the most profitable outcomes. This is because the futures position in an effective hedge will only be profitable when the cash price moves adversely. In cases where the cash price moves favorably, the futures position in the hedge portfolio will lose money and the hedger would have been better off (made a higher profit) *not* hedging. To see this, consider the commercial paper issuer given in Table 6.4. In this case, if the hedger had chosen not to hedge, then the issue rate would have been 17.50% instead of the 18.20% associated with the hedged offering. Hence, to be optimal, in the sense of maximizing profit on the hedge the

TABLE 6.4 Transaction Hedge Profit for a Commercial Paper Issuer (*circa* 1981)

Date	Cash position	Basis	Futures position
$t = 4/13$	Decide to issue \$20 million in 3-month commercial paper on June 3 and want to lock in current rate of 18.75%	2.67%	Short \$20 million June T-bill contracts at 16.08%
$t = 6/3$	Issue is offered and sold at 17.50%	2.12%	Close out position with long contract at 15.38%
Change	−1.25%	+0.55%	−0.70%

hedger must build in expectations of future price changes and, as a result, engage in speculation.

D. Transaction Hedging: Using a Eurodollar Futures Strip Hedge

The considerable discussion and debate surrounding the MGRM rolling-stack hedging strategy illustrates the potential complexity that a transaction hedge can assume, examples illustrating the MGRM stack hedge abound (e.g., Edwards and Canter, 1995; Culp and Miller, 1994; Mello and Parsons, 1995a,b). Faced with massive position sizes to hedge, MGRM could not pursue a maturity and quantity matching hedging strategy, the strip hedge. Due to the substantial liquidity in nearby deliveries, MGRM was able to implement a rolling-stack hedge. Because the MGRM cash position was not marked to market, such a hedging strategy can incur substantial variation margin costs, in addition to the usual basis risk. In a rolling-stack hedge, the rollover can also add mark-to-market basis charges to the variation margin costs arising from spot price changes. The MGRM case illustrates that such charges can be enormous and can constitute a serious complication when designing certain hedging programs. Conversely, it is also possible for the rolling-stack hedge to generate enormous positive cash flows from variation margin. Such is the element of speculation inherent in the underlying business plan.

The application of the rolling-stack hedging strategy is not confined to oil complex contracts. Dubofsky and Miller (2002) provide an excellent example comparing a stack hedge with a strip hedge for hedging a multiperiod interest rate cash flow. The example proceeds as follows: Suppose that on July 28, 1999, a bank plans to make a 1-year fixed-rate loan for $50 million beginning on September 13,1999, with loan payments to be made in quarterly install-ments. The fixed interest rate is 7.50%. The bank plans to fund the loan by using quarterly borrowing in the Eurodollar cash market. This funding takes place in 47 days. To execute a strip hedge for this borrowing, the bank sells 200 Eurodollar futures contracts, 50 in each of the four available different delivery months. To execute a stack hedge, the bank initially sells 200 futures contracts in the nearby delivery month, rolling the position forward into the next available nearby as expiration arrives.

Because the bank will borrow $50 million in September and, again, ap-proximately every 90 days three more times thereafter, the bank starts the strip hedge by selling 50 Eurodollar futures contracts in each of four delivery months: September, December, March, and June. The short positions in these 200 futures contracts are all entered on July 28. This implies that a strip hedge is constructed as a portfolio of single-period hedges. In the strip hedge, the hedger has hedged borrowing costs over four successive quarters. Table 6.5 contains a schematic of the strip hedge example. Interest rates and prices that are known on July 28, 1999, appear in italics. In this example, the firm has transformed the uncertain borrowing stream into a fixed loan rate over the four successive quarters.[1] In order to read the table, "S 50 @ 94.555" means go short 50 contracts at a futures price of 94.555, and "L 50 @ 94.35" means go long 50 contracts at a futures price of 94.35 (Dubofsky and Miller, 2002).

In this example, the locked-in borrowing rate for each quarter is the implied futures rate at the time the hedge is placed, just as it is in the one

TABLE 6.5   Strip Hedge Using Eurodollar Futures

Date	Spot LIBOR (%)	Sept. 1999	Dec. 1999	March 2000	June 2000
7/28/1999	5.3125	S 50 @ 94.555	S 50 @ 94.19	S 50 @ 94.185	S 50 @ 93.95
9/13/1999	5.65	L 50 @ 94.35			
12/13/1999	5.85		L 50 @ 94.15		
3/13/2000	6.00			L 50 @ 94.00	
6/19/2000	5.90				L 50 @ 94.10
Futures LIBOR rate (on 7/28/99)		5.445%	5.81%	5.815%	6.05%
Gain (loss) in Eurodollar futures		$25,625	$5000	$23,125	($18,750)[a]

Quarter	Firm's borrowing rate (%)	Quarterly interest expense ($)	Gain (loss) on futures positions ($)	Net interest expense ($)	Effective borrowing rate (%)
9/99–12/99	5.650	706,250[b]	25,625	680,625	5.445
12/99–3/00	5.850	731,250	5000	726,250	5.810
3/00–6/00	6.000	750,000	23,125	726,875	5.815
6/00–9/00	5.900	737,500	(18,750)	756,250	6.050
				Average:	5.78

[a]The $18,750 loss occurs because the futures price rose from 93.95 to 94.10. This is a loss of 15 ticks. With each tick worth $25 and the bank short 50 futures contracts: (−15 ticks) ($25/tick)(50 contracts) = −$18,750.
[b]($50 million)(0.0565)(90/360) = $706,250.

[1]In this example, as well as those presented in Tables 6.6 and 6.7, interest expenses are calculated assuming a 90-day period where the actual days between dates are 9/13/1999 to 12/13/1999 = 91 days; 12/13/1999 to 3/13/2000 = 91 days; 3/13/2000 to 6/19/2000 = 98 days; 6/19/2000 to 9/12/2000 = 85 days.

cash flow case. It follows that the strip hedge can be viewed as a portfolio of one-period hedges. However, as Mello and Parsons (1995b, p. 18) point out, "...even when constructing a hedge using a strip of futures, it is important to think about the cash flow effects of the maturity structure. If the hedge is constructed using OTC instruments, then there is greater flexibility in designing the terms: It may be possible to negotiate a deviation from the mark-to-market rules necessary for exchange-traded instruments so that payments on the hedge instruments better match payments under the delivery contracts." This speaks to both basis variation and variation margin cost. The futures example in Table 6.5 disguises certain elements involved in practical execution.

In terms of the strip hedge example in Table 6.5, the basis variation is avoided by assuming that the spot London interbank offer rate (LIBOR) = futures LIBOR on each date; the firm goes to the capital market and actually borrows $50 million for another 3 months at the spot rate prevailing at the same time as the futures contract expires. In this example, this is evident from the four diagonal futures prices (L 50 @ 94.XX) equaling (100 - spot LIBOR) on these four dates. This can be assured only if the firm borrows using each of the futures contracts. In addition, the example does not take any account of variation margin. Gains or losses on futures are calculated at delivery. Observing that interest rates swaps can be priced using Eurodollar strips, this discussion can be extended to provide insight into motivations for using interest rate swaps.

E. Transactions Hedging: Using a Eurodollar Futures Stack Hedge

A stack hedge is sometimes referred to as a rolling hedge or a rolling-stack hedge. In this transaction, for example, the hedger sells 200 September 99 futures contacts on July 28, 1999. Instead of having 50 contracts spread over the four contract delivery dates, the 200 nearby contracts are substituted for the protection provided by 50 futures contracts for four quarters. If the firm only sold 50 September futures contracts, then the firm would only be hedging the first quarter's borrowings. Thus, the firm "stacks" the hedges for subsequent quarters in one nearby delivery date. In this example, this is the September futures contract. Because the Eurodollar futures contract is cash settled, the firm will hold the 200 September futures contracts until just prior to the expiration on September 13, 1999, at which time the firm will close out the September contracts and sell 150 December futures contracts, holding these contracts until just prior to expiration on December 13, 1999, at which time the firm sells 100 March delivery contracts. This process continues for March, when 50 June contracts are rolled forward. Finally, the June futures contracts are closed out just prior to expiration. Due to possible basis risk, the end result is a less certain locking in of the quarterly borrowing rate over 1 year than in the strip hedge.

Table 6.6 contains data for a stack hedge example comparable to the example in Table 6.5. The only difference between the tables is that the futures prices at the time of the hedge placement differ, with the futures prices at the time the hedge is lifted being the same. This implies that the spot LIBOR at the expiration of the futures contracts is the same in both examples.

To calculate the uncertain borrowing rate in the stack hedge as described in the lower part of Table 6.6 involves allocating gains and losses from previous quarters' futures trading to the current quarter. For example, one fourth of the $102,500 gain from the Eurodollar futures hedge in place during the September 1999/December 1999 quarter must be allocated to the December 1999/March 2000 quarter. The net interest expense during this quarter will reflect a $25,625 Eurodollar futures gain from the previous quarter as well as a $20,625 Eurodollar futures loss in the current quarter (one third of $61,875). Casual inspection of Tables 6.5 and 6.6 reveals an average effective borrowing rate of 5.78% for both transactions. This is comparable to the perfect hedge of a single cash flow from Table 6.2. In Table 6.5, the September futures rate is 0.132% above the spot LIBOR on July 28; on July 28, the December futures rate is 0.365% higher than the September futures rate; the March futures rate is 0.005% higher than the December futures rate; and the June futures rate is 0.235% higher than the March futures rate. This can be compared with the basis in Table 6.6; on July 28, the September futures rate is also 0.132% higher than the spot LIBOR rate; on September 13, 1999, the December futures rate is 0.365% higher than the spot LIBOR rate; on December 13, 1999, the March futures rate is 0.005% higher than the spot LIBOR rate; and, on March 13, 2000, the June futures rate is 0.235% higher than the spot LIBOR rate.

F. CHOOSING BETWEEN A STRIP HEDGE AND A STACK HEDGE

Movements in the futures yield curve determine the relative effectiveness of a stack hedge versus a strip hedge. When the futures term structure shifts in this parallel fashion, a strip hedge or a stack hedge will result in the same effective borrowing rate. Other changes in the futures term structure will favor one hedge over the other. For most futures contracts, the advantage of the stack hedge is that the hedger is always trading the most liquid futures contract. Casual inspection of the volume and open interest for Eurodollar futures (readily available on the exchange website or in the financial press) reveals considerable liquidity out to 5 years. Volumes can exceed 1000 contracts in

TABLE 6.6   Stack Hedge Using Eurodollar Futures

Date	Spot LIBOR (%)	Sept. 1999	Dec. 1999	March 2000	June 2000
7/28/1999	5.3125	S 200 @ 94.555			
9/13/1999	5.65	L 200 @ 94.350	S 150 @ 93.985	S 100 @ 94.145	S 50 @ 93.765
12/13/1999	5.85		L 150 @ 94.150	L 100 @ 94.000	L 50 @ 94.100
3/13/2000	6.00				
6/19/2000	5.90				
Futurs LIBOR rate		5.445% (on 7/28/99)	6.015% (on 9/13/99)	5.855% (on 12/13/99)[a]	6.235% (on 3/13/00)
Gain (loss) in ED futures		$102,500	($61,875)	$36,250[a]	($41,875)

Quarter	Firm's borrowing rate (%)	Quarterly interest expense ($)	Gain (loss) on futures positions ($)	Net interest expense ($)	Effective borrowing rate (%)
9/99–12/99[b]	5.650	706,250	25,625	680,625	5.445
12/99–3/00	5.850	731,250	(20,625)	726,250	5.810
From Sept./Dec.			25,625		
3/00–6/00	6.000	750,000	18,125	726,875	5.815
From Sept./Dec.			25,625		
From Dec./March			(20,625)		
6/00–9/00	5.900	737,500	(41,875)	756,250	6.050
From Sept./Dec.			25,625		
From Dec./March			(20,625)		
From March/June			18,125		
Average					5.78

[a] The $36,250 gain occurs because the futures price fell from 94.145 to 94. This is a profit of 14.5 ticks, worth $25/tick. The bank was short 100 futures contracts. 14.5 ticks × $25/tick × 100 contracts = $36,250.

[b] The futures price on 9/13/99 is 94.35. It follows that $100 − 94.35 = 5.65$; $(0.0565/4) × \$50$ million $= \$706,250$; $(680.625/50.000.000)(4) = 5.445\%$.

contracts over 20 expirations in the future. In contrast, the futures contract volume and open interest for various commodities (e.g., T-bills, stock indexes, currencies) is concentrated in the nearby delivery date. Hence, in some commodities hedgers have a choice to use a strip or stack hedge, while in others only a stack hedge is available.

What is the rationale for using a stack hedge when contract liquidity permits the use of strip hedges? For the risk manager willing to speculate on future price movements, the risks inherent in stack hedging can be a blessing. In particular, stack hedges in liquid markets can offer the hedger the opportunity to take advantage of relative mispricings when switching to later delivery months. More precisely, if the hedger sees mispricing between two deferred futures contracts, the hedger can roll the hedge into (sell) the relatively higher priced futures contract. An important disadvantage of stack hedges is the higher transaction costs compared to a strip hedge. The importance of transaction costs in strip hedging has inspired the Chicago Mercantile Exchange (CME) to introduce, starting in 1994, trading in packs and bundles of Eurodollar futures. A Eurodollar bundle is the simultaneous sale or purchase of one contract each of a series of consecutive Eurodollar futures contracts. Bundles are a convenient way to construct a Eurodollar strip position because all contracts are entered concurrently. That is, the trader does not have to construct the strip contract by contract, eliminating execution risk and reducing transactions costs.

In practice, the relative performance of stack hedges versus strip hedges depends on the uncertain future yield curve shape. Table 6.7 provides an example for which the futures term structure slopes subsequently upward. As discussed in Chapter 4, the change in the futures term structure is due to changes in the difference between the implied carry cost and the carry return, in effect a change in the short-term Eurodollar yield curve. In Table 6.6, on July 28, the September futures rate is still 0.132% higher than the spot LIBOR rate. However, on September 13, 1999, the December futures rate is now 0.23% higher than the spot LIBOR rate. On December 13, 1999, the March futures rate is now 0.33% higher than the spot LIBOR rate, and on March 13, 2000, the June futures rate is now 0.43% higher than the spot LIBOR rate. As a result, the average effective borrowing rate for the stack hedge is 5.89% in this case. Under these conditions, the firm would have been better off, in terms of interest costs, with a strip hedge instead of a stack hedge. However, if the futures term structure slope subsequently decreases, a stack hedge would have outperformed a strip hedge (Dubofsky and Miller, 2002).

The decision to choose a stack hedge or a strip hedge is an excellent illustration of the rich texture of decisions involved in implementing risk-management decisions. Even when transaction hedging is employed, there are decisions involving business risks that have to be identified. Recognizing the

TABLE 6.7 Stack Hedge with a Futures Term Structure Slope that Subsequently Increases

Date	Spot LIBOR (%)	Sept. 1999	Dec. 1999	March 2000	June 2000
7/28/1999	5.3125	S 200 @ 94.555			
9/13/1999	5.65	L 200 @ 94.350			
12/13/1999	5.85		S 150 @ 94.12	S 100 @ 93.82	S 50 @ 93.57
3/13/2000	6.00		L 150 @ 94.15	L 100 @ 94.00	L 50 @ 94.10
6/19/2000	5.90				
Futures LIBOR rate		5.445%	5.88%	6.18%	6.43%
Premium (discount) to spot LIBOR at hedge		0.1325% (5.445–5.3125)	0.230% (5.88–5.65)	0.330% (6.18–5.85)	0.430% (6.43–6)
Gain (loss) in ED futures		$102,500	($11,250)	($45,000)	($66,250)

Quarter	Firm's borrowing rate (%)	Quarterly interest expense ($)	Gain (loss) on futures positions ($)	Net interest expense ($)	Effective borrowing rate (%)
9/99–12/99	5.650	706,250	25,625	680,625	5.445
12/99–3/00	5.850	731,250	(3750)	709,375	5.675
From Sept./Dec.			25,625		
3/00–6/00	6.000	750,000	(22,500)	750,625	6.005
From Sept./Dec.			25,625		
From Dec./March			(3750)		
6/00–9/00	5.900	737,500	(66,250)	804,375	6.435
From Sept./Dec.			25,625		
From Dec./March			(3750)		
From March/June			(22,500)		
Average					5.89

speculative component in the risk-management decision is an essential element in the development of an effective business plan. An essential limitation of the transaction approach is the failure to allow for the size of the hedge position to vary significantly from the size of the cash position. For some hedging situations, this approach is more than adequate. However, in other situations, the transactions approach does not capture observed behavior. For example, airlines seeking a hedge against oil prices do not necessarily take a hedge position that is equal in size to expected fuel usage; rather, hedge ratios around say one half may be more appropriate. Ultimately, there are many possible uses for derivative securities. Whether a transactions approach or an optimal hedging approach is used to structure derivative usage decisions depends on the specifics of the situation.

G. Multivariate Optimal Hedge Ratio Estimation

Chapter 2, Section I, dealt with the mean-variance optimal univariate hedge ratio—that is, solutions for the optimal univariate hedge ratio associated with the expected utility function: $EU = E[\pi] - b \, var[\pi]$. The problem is univariate because a single cash position is being hedged using a single derivative security. The mean-variance solution was composed of two parts: the minimum-variance hedge ratio and the optimal speculative position. While the minimum-variance component depends on the ratio of statistical parameters, the speculative component depends on the hedger's risk attitudes as reflected in b. Hedgers who are less risk averse will have lower b (*ceteris paribus*) and, as a result, will be more willing to take speculative positions in the form of over or under hedges. In addition, because the futures price variance enters in the numerator of the "speculative" term, as the *perceived* volatility increases the hedger will be less willing to take positions over or under the minimum variance hedge. Because variances as well as expectations are conditional on the information available on the hedge date and the subjective probability assessments of the hedger, the less capable or willing the hedger is to make forecasts the less important is the speculative component of the hedge.

In some hedging situations, it is possible to reformulate the hedging problem to have not one but many different futures contracts involved in the hedge. One example would be hedging a portfolio of foreign assets denominated in a number of different currencies. In this case, currency futures for all the relevant currencies could be used to construct a hedge. Another example is a commodity, such as tungsten or titanium, where there is no traded futures contract available. A hedge could be constructed by using an appropriately weighted combination of a number of different futures contracts. Yet another example would be a portfolio of mortgages, for which there is not a precise traded futures contract. Instead a hedge could be constructed using a number of different futures contracts. Chapter 5, Section IV, discusses a sophisticated example where a currency spread and an interest rate future are used to hedge a foreign interest rate.

The objective of increasing the number of different future contracts used in the hedge is, ultimately, to improve hedge performance. At some point, this will be a fruitless exercise because there would be so many futures contracts to monitor, and transaction costs would increase accordingly. The obvious question is how to optimally construct multivariate futures hedges. Theoretically, it would be most appropriate to develop an equilibrium model explaining the relationship between the commodity being hedged and the commodities underlying the futures contracts being used to construct the hedge. The approach used here is to assume that such a model has been specified and to work with the general profit function for a multivariate hedge position.

Two problems will be considered: the minimum variance hedge and the mean-variance optimal speculative solution. These two solutions will then be combined to produce the mean-variance optimal multivariate hedge solution. As with the univariate hedge solution, it is assumed that there is one random variable to be hedged, the price risk of the cash position. The size of the cash position is fixed, and the relevant components of perfect markets are adopted. Given this, consider the general profit function for a hedge involving k futures contracts and a fixed cash position:

$$\pi(1) = \overline{Q}_s(S_1 - S_0)$$
$$- Q_1[F_1(1,T) - F_1(0,T)] - Q_2[F_2(1,T) - F_2(0,T)]$$
$$- \ldots - Q_k[F_k(1,T) - F_k(0,T)]$$

where the bar on Q_s indicates that the size of the cash position is not a choice variable. Like the previous univariate hedge where it was assumed that the cash position was long and that the futures position was short when $Q > 0$, this formulation also permits futures to be short or long with the $Q_i > 0$ solution denoting a short futures position matched with a long cash position and $Q_i < 0$ denoting a long futures position matched with a long cash position.

The key step in transforming the general profit function into a form suitable for estimating a minimum variance solution is to reformulate the problem in the form:

$$y = X\beta + u$$

where $y = Q_s\Delta S$, $X = (1, \Delta F_1, \Delta F_2 \ldots, \Delta F_k)$, $\beta = (\alpha, Q_1, Q_2, \ldots, Q_k)$, and u is an equation error that captures the unexplained variation in y not accounted for by $X\beta$ and α is the equation constant term. It is possible to normalize this formulation by dividing through by Q_s, in which case β would refer to the hedge ratios Q_i/Q_s. The general formulation with Q_s on the lefthand side allows the use of income as the random variable to be hedged. It is also useful for deriving the mean-variance optimal solution.

Using $y = X\beta + u$ to specify the problem permits the ordinary least squares (OLS) solution ($\hat{\beta}$) to be immediately specified as:

$$\hat{\beta} = \left(X^T X\right)^{-1} X^T y$$

In a time-series estimation framework, this is an OLS regression estimator where y is a $T \times 1$ vector containing ΔS_t and X is a $T \times (k+1)$ matrix containing k columns of $T \times 1$ vectors of ΔF_{it} together with a $T \times 1$ column of ones to represent the constant term. (This specification for y assumes that Q_s has been used to normalize and that β represents hedge ratios.) For a long cash position, $\beta_i > 0$ indicates the fraction of the cash position that will be hedged with a short position in commodity future i. $\beta_i < 0$ indicates the fraction of the cash position that will be hedged with a long position in commodity future i. Extensions of this solution to generalized least squares (GLS) follow naturally.

Transforming the solution for the multivariate minimum variance hedge ratio estimator to an equilibrium framework involves ignoring the constant and taking expectations at the appropriate point to produce the result that:

$$\left(X^T X\right)^{-1} = \Sigma^{-1}$$

$$X^T y = \{\sigma_{1,s}, \sigma_{2,s}, \ldots, \sigma_{k,s}\}^T \overline{Q}_s = \text{cov}[F,S]\overline{Q}_s$$

where Σ is the variance-covariance matrix of the ΔF_i:

$$\Sigma = \begin{bmatrix} \sigma_1^2 & \sigma_{1,2} & \cdots & \sigma_{1,k} \\ \sigma_{2,1} & \sigma_2^2 & \cdots & \cdots \\ \cdots & \cdots & \cdots & \sigma_{k-1,k} \\ \sigma_{k,1} & \cdots & \sigma_{k,k-1} & \sigma_k^2 \end{bmatrix}$$

and the individual σ_{ij} refer to variances and covariances for changes in the relevant futures prices. It follows that:

$$Q_{mv} = \frac{Q^*}{Q_s} = \Sigma^{-1} \text{cov}[F,S]$$

This result is identical to the estimation solution, with the proviso that the equilibrium solution involves conditional population parameters while the estimated solution involves estimates of the population parameters determined using T observations of data on the ΔF_i and ΔS.

As an example of the multivariate solution, consider the case of a minimum variance hedge using two futures contracts. In this case:

$$\Sigma^{-1} = \frac{1}{\det}\begin{bmatrix} \sigma_2^2 & -\sigma_{1,2} \\ -\sigma_{1,2} & \sigma_1^2 \end{bmatrix} \quad X^Ty = \begin{bmatrix} \sigma_{s,1} \\ \sigma_{s,2} \end{bmatrix}\overline{Q}_s$$

$$\det = \sigma_1^2\sigma_2^2 - \sigma_{1,2}^2$$

The conventional result follows:

$$\frac{\hat{Q}_1}{\overline{Q}_s} = \frac{\sigma_2^2\sigma_{s,1} - \sigma_{1,2}\sigma_{s,2}}{\sigma_1^2\sigma_2^2 - \sigma_{1,2}^2} \quad \frac{\hat{Q}_2}{\overline{Q}_s} = \frac{\sigma_1^2\sigma_{s,2} - \sigma_{1,2}\sigma_{s,1}}{\sigma_1^2\sigma_2^2 - \sigma_{1,2}^2}$$

These results are intuitively the same as those given previously, with the proviso that the sign of β has positive coefficients reflecting short hedge positions combined with long cash positions and negative coefficients representing long futures combined with a long cash position.

As in the univariate hedge case, the optimal mean-variance solution is a combination of the minimum-variance solution and the mean-variance optimal speculative solution. To derive the *optimal speculative solution*, observe that the objective is to maximize expected utility which, in this case, is specified using the mean and variance of speculative profit:

$$L = E[\pi] - b\,\mathrm{var}[\pi] = Q_1E[\Delta F_1] + Q_2E[\Delta F_2] + \ldots + Q_kE[\Delta F_k] - b[Q^T\Sigma Q]$$

$$= Q^T\begin{bmatrix} E[\Delta F_1] \\ E[\Delta F_2] \\ \cdot \\ \cdot \\ \cdot \end{bmatrix} - b\{Q^T\Sigma Q\}$$

Differentiating the objective with respect to the choice variables Q^T produces the solution:

$$Q^* = \begin{bmatrix} Q_1^* \\ Q_2^* \\ \cdot \\ \cdot \\ \cdot \end{bmatrix} = \frac{1}{2b}\Sigma^{-1}\begin{bmatrix} E[\Delta F_1] \\ E[\Delta F_2] \\ \cdot \\ \cdot \\ \cdot \end{bmatrix}$$

where * denotes an optimum value.

Solving the general mean-variance optimal speculative solution for the case of two futures positions gives:

$$\begin{bmatrix} Q_1^* \\ Q_2^* \end{bmatrix} = \frac{1}{2b\,\det}\begin{bmatrix} \sigma_2^2 & -\sigma_{1,2} \\ -\sigma_{1,2} & \sigma_1^2 \end{bmatrix}\begin{bmatrix} E[\Delta F_1] \\ E[\Delta F_2] \end{bmatrix}$$

where det is the same as that given in the minimum variance hedge example given above. Solving for the specific case of Q_1^*:

$$Q_1^* = \frac{[\sigma_2^2 E[\Delta F_1] - \sigma_{1,2} E[\Delta F_2]]}{2b\left(\sigma_1^2 \sigma_2^2 - \sigma_{1,2}^2\right)}$$

The result for Q_2^* follows appropriately.

This result has much the same implications as in the univariate case. As $b \to \infty$, the speculator's risk aversion becomes so high that the optimal speculative solution goes to zero, and as $b \to 0$ the speculator's risk aversion approaches risk neutrality, and the size of the speculative position is very sensitive to even small expected changes in futures prices. Similarly, the speculator's ability to forecast price changes, as reflected in the size of the elements in Σ, also affects the solution. In the univariate case, the result was that if the speculator has limited ability to forecast the next price change then the variance of the forecast (σ_f^2) will be large and the difference between current and expected prices will have to be large in order to induce a significant speculative position. The multivariate case has similar intuition but adjusts this result to account for the covariances between the various contracts involved in the position as well as the variances of the forecasts for the prices of other contracts involved in the position.

Having derived the minimum variance and optimal speculative solutions, it is now possible to derive the mean-variance optimal solution for a multivariate hedge. The objective function for this problem is

$$EU[\pi_{mh}] = \overline{Q}_s E[\Delta S] - Q_1 E[\Delta F_1] - Q_2 E[\Delta F_2] - \ldots - Q_k E[\Delta F_k] - b\{\text{var}[\pi_{mh}]\}$$

where, using the definitions from the previous derivation of the equilibrium minimum variance solution:

$$\text{var}[\pi_{mh}] = \overline{Q}_s^2 \sigma_s^2 + Q^T \Sigma Q - 2\{\overline{Q}_s Q_1 \sigma_{s,1} + \overline{Q}_s Q_2 \sigma_{s,2} + \ldots + \overline{Q}_s Q_k \sigma_{s,k}\}$$

The first-order condition for futures position 1 gives:

$$\frac{\partial EU}{\partial Q_1} = -\{E[\Delta F_1]\} - 2b\{Q_1^* \sigma_1^2 + Q_2 \sigma_{1,2} + \ldots + Q_k \sigma_{1,k} - \overline{Q}_s \sigma_{s,1}\} = 0$$

where, as before, the * indicates an optimum value. Solving Q_1^* involves determining the solution of the other $k - 1$ positions.

Proceeding with determining all k derivatives and expressing the solution in matrix form:

$$\Sigma \frac{Q^*}{Q_s} = -\frac{E[\Delta F]}{2b\overline{Q}_s} + \text{cov}[F,S]$$

Inverting Σ gives the solution:

$$\frac{Q^*}{\overline{Q}_s} = -\Sigma^{-1}\frac{E[\Delta F]}{2b\overline{Q}_s} + \Sigma^{-1}\text{cov}[F,S] = Q_{mv} - \frac{Q_{os}}{\overline{Q}_s}$$

where Q_{mv} is the minimum-variance solution and Q_{os} is the mean-variance optimal speculative solution. This verifies the generalization of the univariate result: the mean-variance optimal hedge ratio is determined by combining the minimum-variance hedge ratio and the mean-variance optimal speculative solution.

Again considering the example where two futures contracts are being used to hedge a fixed cash position, the optimal mean-variance solution can now be specified as:

$$\frac{Q_1^*}{\overline{Q}_s} = \frac{\sigma_2^2\sigma_{s,1} - \sigma_{1,2}\sigma_{s,2}}{\sigma_2^2\sigma_1^2 - \sigma_{1,2}^2} - \frac{\sigma_2^2 E[\Delta F_1] - \sigma_{1,2}E[\Delta F_2]}{2b\overline{Q}_s\left(\sigma_1^2\sigma_2^2 - \sigma_{1,2}^2\right)}$$

From this it follows that if the different futures contracts involved in the hedge have price changes that are uncorrelated ($\sigma_{1,2} = 0$), then the individual hedge ratios will be equal to the univariate solutions. The dependence of the optimal solution on the utility parameter b casts doubt on the *general* validity of the numerous empirical studies that have taken the minimum-variance solution to be the optimal solution.

The two-period structure of the profit function leads to a number of other qualifications about the generality of the optimal mean-variance solution. Extending to a multiperiod framework raises the possibility of readjusting the hedge position over time, producing a different hedge ratio at each hedge readjustment date. In addition, the solution to an intertemporal, multiperiod optimization problem will not necessarily produce the decomposition of the hedge ratio into the minimum variance and optimal speculative solution (Heaney and Poitras, 1991). Among other reasons, this is because as prices evolve over the life of the hedge, risk propensities will affect the desire to adjust to observed data.

H. Optimal Hedge Ratios for Different Utility Functions

Regarding the minimum variance component of the optimal hedge, it has long been recognized that ordinary least squares (OLS) is optimal for only a restricted set of expected utility functions. Work on hedge ratio estimation has demonstrated that the "optimal" futures hedge ratio does depend on the objective function selected. For example, significantly different empirical estimates of the hedge ratio for T-bonds have been obtained from log and minimum-variance expected utility functions (Cecchetti *et al.*, 1988). However, available evidence to date has been restricted to comparisons of a small number of specific objective functions. With this in mind, it is possible to formulate further solutions to the general expected utility problem underlying the hedge ratio optimization. Two types of solutions are considered here. First, under the assumption of bivariate normality of the spot and futures returns, a general relationship between the OLS estimate and the hedge ratio implied by a general expected utility function will be specified and a number of specific expected utility functions examined as illustrations. Second, admitting riskless lending and borrowing in the wealth dynamics, the hedge ratio can be shown to be independent of preferences (i.e., depending solely on parameters of the joint distribution of the return-generating processes). These results are derived for the traditional, single-period, "myopic" objective function.

While there are a number of roughly equivalent specifications of the hedger's optimization problem, following Heaney and Poitras (1991) and Cecchetti *et al.* (1988) another approach to the relevant hedger's problem can be expressed as maximizing the expected utility of terminal wealth for a hedged portfolio with wealth (W) determined by:[2]

$$W_{t+1} = W_t[1 + R_s(t+1) - h_t R_f(t+1)] \tag{6.1}$$

where h_t is defined to be the ratio of the values (price times quantity) of the spot and futures positions at time t, $R_s(t+1)$ and $R_f(t+1)$ are the t to $t+1$ returns to holding spot and futures, and $t \ \varepsilon \ [0, \ldots, T]$, that is, $R_A(t+1) = (A_{t+1} - A_t)/A_t$ where A is either the spot or futures price at t and $t+1$. By construction, the selection of Eq. (6.1) to specify the wealth dynamics restricts the problem in order to derive implementable solutions. In particular, Eq. (6.1) assumes a single-period decision framework with no potential for variation in the quantity of the spot commodity being held.

Another significant feature of Eq. (6.1) is the absence of portfolio theoretic considerations. In particular, by not incorporating lending and borrowing into the specification of the profit function, the size of the cash position has been fixed. In effect, the resulting hedging optimization assumes away the portfolio decision by having the hedger fully invested in the spot commodity. If lending and borrowing are admitted, considerations of leveraging to buy the spot commodity and short selling the spot to invest in the riskless asset enter the hedger's decision process. Theoretically, this is translated into a change in the underlying wealth dynamics to:

$$W_{t+1} = W_t\big(1 + x_t R_s(t+1) + (1 - x_t)r(t+1) - H_t R_f(t+1)\big) \tag{6.2}$$

---

[2]Because h_t enters with a minus sign, this defines a short futures position to be a positive quantity.

where x is the fraction of total wealth invested in the spot commodity, H is the value (price times quantity) of the hedge position divided by initial wealth (not the value of the spot position), and r is the riskless interest rate. In turn, Eq. (6.2) can be used as the argument in the hedger's optimization problem. In practice, the primary advantage of using Eq. (6.1) over (6.2) is analytical simplification: The optimal hedge ratio requires specification of only a joint probability distribution and a utility function. The addition of lending and borrowing results in the introduction of an additional choice variable.

Given this, the conventional hedge ratio optimization problem can be generalized to admit any type of well-behaved utility function. Using Eq. (6.1):

$$\max_{h_t} E\{U[\pi(t+1)]\}$$

$$\Rightarrow \quad \max_{h_t} \int_{R_f} \int_{R_s} U\{W_t[1 + R_s(t+1) - h_t R_f(t+1)]\}dP_{sf}(t) \tag{6.3}$$

where the conditional expectation $E[\,\cdot\,]$ has been formally defined using an appropriately specified conditioning information set. In this form, the joint conditional probability distribution (measure) associated with the expectation is P_{sf}, the profit function is either $\pi(t+1) = W_t[R_s(t+1) - h_t R_f(t+1)]$ or $\pi(t+1) = W_t[x_t R_s(t+1) + (1 - x_t)r(t+1) - H_t R_f(t+1)]$.[3] In practice, there are restrictions on the types of commodities for which the EU optimization using Eq. (6.1) is the appropriate hedging problem. For example, because no allowance has been taken of unexpected variation in quantity of the spot commodity, the hedged portfolio would not fully capture the wealth dynamics associated with many harvestable crops. However, Eq. (6.3) would be appropriate in the case of financial futures, such as T-bonds, money market securities, and currencies.

In terms of solutions, under some strong distributional assumptions, the minimum variance solution leads to an optimal hedge ratio that equals the slope coefficient in an OLS regression of spot on futures prices. By construction, OLS depends fundamentally on the selection of joint probability distributions that are constant over time. This assumption results in equality of conditional and unconditional parameters. When time variation in the joint probability distributions is permitted (e.g., due to ARCH errors), the decision problem can be more complicated. In this case, specification of the optimal hedging problem typically takes on a more complicated form and has to be

---

[3]The transformation from terminal wealth, W_{t+1}, to terminal profit, π_{t+1}, follows because the expectation of $U[W_t]$ reduces to a constant that does not affect the optimization. In addition, it will always be assumed that the only state (conditioning) variables of interest are R_s and R_f. However, in general, this need not be true.

solved using some dynamic optimization procedure (e.g., dynamic programming), that takes account of the state variable time paths. The resulting solutions are potentially intractable and difficult to interpret. However, in the special case of *log utility* (Cecchetti *et al.*, 1988), the dynamic solution will reduce to a sequence of one-period solutions (Samuelson, 1969). This important simplification permits the introduction of certain types of temporal variation in the conditional variances and covariances without significantly complicating the solution.

In addition to complications arising from non-constant distributional parameters, when the structure of the optimal hedging problem is altered by the introduction of riskless lending and borrowing, variation in the size of the spot position means that the hedge ratio cannot be determined by choosing the relative size of the futures position. There are now two choice variables, the fraction of initial wealth invested in the riskless asset and the size of the hedged position. Again, while there has been explicit recognition of riskless lending and borrowing, analysis has been restricted to special cases, particularly mean-variance (Bond and Thompson, 1986; Turvey and Baker, 1989). In certain special cases (e.g., Poitras, 1989a), the resulting optimal hedge ratio has been shown to be independent of hedger risk preferences, depending solely on the parameters of the (un)conditional joint distribution of returns.

This section provides two propositions corresponding to the two different formulations of the "myopic" optimal hedge ratio problem, where myopia is a direct consequence of single-period specification of the optimization problem. The first formulation is based on the conventional approach that omits lending and borrowing from the portfolio decision, where Eq. (6.1) is the basis of the objective function. The second approach uses Eq. (6.2), thereby admitting portfolios that allow riskless lending and borrowing. In this analysis, myopia dictates that future time paths of the conditioning variables be ignored; the trade is initiated at time t and profits are taken at $t + 1$. This permits use of the unconditional distributions. Given this, Proposition 6.1 extends the conventional constant distributional parameter solution to include a general expected utility function. It is shown that the optimal hedge ratio can be decomposed into the OLS-based hedge ratio (h_{OLS}) and a utility function dependent term. Proposition 6.2 incorporates riskless lending and borrowing to determine a market equilibrium hedge ratio that is shown to be independent of the utility function selected.

Conventionally, h_{OLS} has been the foundation of empirical estimation of hedge ratios; hence, it is important to know the relationship between specific solutions to Eq. (6.3) and the OLS estimate. More precisely, the linkage between Eq. (6.3) and the minimum variance hedge ratio is given by the following propositions (proofs for Proposition 6.1 and 6.2 are provided in Heaney and Poitras, 1991). In other words, Proposition 6.1 demonstrates that,

---

PROPOSITION 6.1

Optimal Myopic Hedge Ratio

Under the assumption of constant parameter bivariate normality of $R_s(t)$, and $R_f(t)$, the generalized optimal hedge ratio can be specified as:

$$h^* = h_{OLS} + \frac{E[R_f]}{var[R_f]} \frac{E[U'[\cdot]]}{W_t E[U''[\cdot]]}$$

where $E[\cdot]$ is the (un)conditional expectation taken with respect to the joint density; U' and U'' are the first and second derivatives of the selected utility function with respect to π; $var[R_f]$ is the (un)conditional variance of R_f; h_{OLS} is from a regression of spot on futures prices.

PROPOSITION 6.2

Quasi-Separation of the Hedge Ratio

In the presence of riskless lending and borrowing, the myopic optimal hedge depends solely on expectations and other statistical parameters and is not affected by risk attitudes or initial wealth. Specifically, the optimal hedge ratio is given by:

$$H^* = \frac{var[R_s]}{var[R_f]} \frac{(\beta[F,S](E[R_s - r]) - E[R_f])}{((E[R_s - r]) - \beta[S,F]E[R_f])}$$

where $\beta[S,F] = (cov[R_s,R_f]/var[R_f])$; $\beta[F,S] = (cov[R_s,R_f]/var[R_s])$.

---

for myopic agents, the optimal hedge ratio can always be decomposed into a sum of the OLS-based hedge ratio and an additional term that is fully determined by statistical parameters and the risk aversion propensity of the selected utility function.

The primary upshot of Proposition 6.1 is that in addition to h_{OLS} consideration must be given to the risk-aversion-adjusted, variance-deflated, expected return on the futures position. When the expected return is nonzero, the properties of the particular expected utility function assumed (i.e., the inverse of the coefficient of relative risk aversion) takes on importance. Examining the effect of the statistical parameters, an important *general* corollary follows: When the current futures price is an unbiased predictor of the distant futures price ($E[R_f] = 0$), h_{OLS} is optimal. Thus, results that apply for specific utility functions (e.g., Benninga *et al.*, 1984; Poitras, 1989) can be generalized to any type of admissible utility function, albeit under the restriction of bivariate normality. However, for many commodities, $E[R_f] = 0$ is not observed, in which case the issue of selecting an appropriate utility function is raised.

To better illustrate, consider some specific examples. Because of the normality assumption, if utility is taken to be negative exponential, $U = -\exp\{-\alpha W\}$, this is equivalent to assuming mean-variance expected utility, a case for which a solution has already been provided using a slightly different approach (see question 5 at the end of this chapter). The resulting optimal solution reflects the different approaches:

$$h^*{}_{MV} = h_{OLS} - \frac{E[R_f]}{\alpha W_t \, \text{var}[R_f]}$$

This form of solution also emerges for other methods of generating mean-variance expected utility, such as quadratic utility where $U = \pi - \frac{1}{2} b (\pi - E[\pi])^2$. In order to contrast constant absolute and relatives aversion utility functions, consider the power utility function, $U = (\pi^p / p)$, where $p < 1$. In this case:

$$h^*{}_{pow} = h_{OLS} - \frac{E[R_f]}{\text{var}[R_f]} \frac{E[\pi^{p-1}]}{W_t(1-p)E[\pi^{p-2}]}$$

For the important specific power utility case of log utility, $U = \ln(\pi)$, the solution reduces to:

$$h^*{}_{\ln} = h_{OLS} - \frac{E[R_f]}{\text{var}[R_f]} \frac{E[\pi^{-1}]}{W_t E[\pi^{-2}]}$$

From these results it follows that a given optimal hedge ratio depends on parameters of both the conditional distribution and the expected utility function.

Significantly, Proposition 6.1 demonstrates that, *when $E[R_f] \neq 0$, it is not "optimal" to use OLS hedge ratios without making further assumptions about the return- and profit-generating processes and the form of expected utility*. In practice, given specific distributions for the relevant processes, the h^* of interest can be approximated with numerical methods (e.g., Cecchetti *et al.*, 1988). It is also possible to empirically model and estimate the conditional hedge ratio (e.g., Kroner and Sultan, 1993). However, such applications typically result in a substantive increase in the complexity of the estimation problem. Unfortunately, it is not possible to establish, theoretically, whether there will be corresponding increases in the value of the resulting hedge ratio estimates. While there is related work on portfolio specification that would indicate there may be potential benefits (e.g., Grauer and Hakansson, 1987), the value added of more direct specification of the both the expected utility function and return-generating processes is largely an unresolved empirical issue.

Turning to specification of the underlying optimization problem, within the myopic model the introduction of riskless lending and borrowing alters the objective function such that the wealth dynamics are now given by Eq. (6.2). Solution of the resulting optimization problem leads to Proposition 6.2. Because this result depends only on parameters of the joint (un)conditional distribution, the optimal hedge ratio with riskless borrowing and lending is independent of both the specification of the expected utility function and initial wealth.

While not immediately apparent, the relationship between Propositions 6.1 and 6.2 can be seen by evaluating h^* in Proposition 6.2 where $E[R_f] = 0$. In this case, $h^* = \beta[S,F] = h_{OLS}$. Significantly, as is the case without lending and borrowing, h_{OLS} is optimal when the current futures price is an unbiased predictor of the distant futures (spot) price. Hence, while it is not possible to provide a revealing closed-form expression, the introduction of lending and borrowing into the hedger's optimization problem does not alter the general result that the optimal hedge ratio is decomposable into h_{OLS} and another term that depends on statistical parameters. However, admitting the ability to short sell and leverage eliminates the need to consider the risk aversion properties of the selected utility function. The upshot is that, in practice, optimization problems based on Eq. (6.2) may produce more implementable solutions than those based on Eq. (6.1).

On a more critical level, as demonstrated by Cecchetti *et al.* (1988), Poitras (1988a), Sephton (1992), Kroner and Sultan (1993), and many others, hedge ratio estimation is complicated because both the means and the variance–covariance matrix of the relevant variables are not typically constant through time as required for OLS regression.[4] In addition, because the minimum-variance hedge ratio does not take the mean return on the hedge portfolio into account, regression-based hedge ratios will not necessarily be optimal for all types of hedger expected utility functions.

---

[4]More precisely, the variables exhibit autoregressive condition heteroskedastic (ARCH) behavior. Estimating and testing in ARCH models is currently an active area of research in econometrics (e.g., Engle, 1982). In addition to the ARCH problem, conventional estimates of hedge ratios typically confuse *ex ante* and *ex post* distributions.

Theoretically correct estimation of hedge ratios suggests the use of sophisticated (e.g., ARCH) estimation procedures.[5] However, straightforward implementation of ARCH assumes that only minimum variance solutions are relevant to the hedger. In an intertemporal model that permits changing means and variances, Heaney and Poitras (1991) demonstrate that minimum variance techniques will only be valid for log utility. To date, there is little empirical evidence indicating that introducing more advanced estimation methods, such as ARCH techniques, substantially improves OLS-based hedge ratio estimates. On the contrary, Cecchetti *et al.* (1988, p. 21) present results for U.S. Treasury bonds indicating that the *profitability* of hedging strategies based on OLS estimates are not substantially different from those based on hedge ratios derived from ARCH procedures. Similarly, while it is possible to incorporate information on the mean returns of the hedge portfolio into the estimation procedure, this also leads to considerably more complicated estimation procedures.

Figure 6.1 provides an example from Kroner and Sultan (1993) comparing OLS and ARCH hedge ratios for a number of currency hedges. The conventional hedge is the OLS estimate, which is constant over the sample. The conditional hedge is an ARCH estimate of the hedge ratio. The relevance of ARCH has been examined in various sources (e.g., Hsieh, 1988). ARCH takes account of the conditional movement of volatility over the sample. A bivariate regression hedge ratio is determined as the ratio of a covariance between the dependent and independent variables divided by the variance of the independent variable; thus, if these parameters change conditionally as time evolves, the associated hedge ratio will also change. This is the basis for the conditional hedge that is reported in Fig. 6.1. Unfortunately, evaluation of the relative performance of the ARCH and OLS hedge ratios is difficult. Following Leitch and Tanner (1991) to compare different hedge ratios using statistical criteria (e.g., by examining the minimum mean square forecast error) fails to account for the profitability of the hedge. To date, while a wealth of studies have examined the estimation problem, there is still little direction on the most appropriate method of evaluating hedge performance.

I. DETERMINING THE DYNAMIC HEDGE RATIO

Poitras and Heaney (1991) and others have extended the static framework to the dynamic case. This involves reformulation of the underlying optimization problem, Eq. (6.3). While of considerable practical interest, Propositions

---

[5]A number of sources have shown that ARCH models are a specific form of random coefficient model.

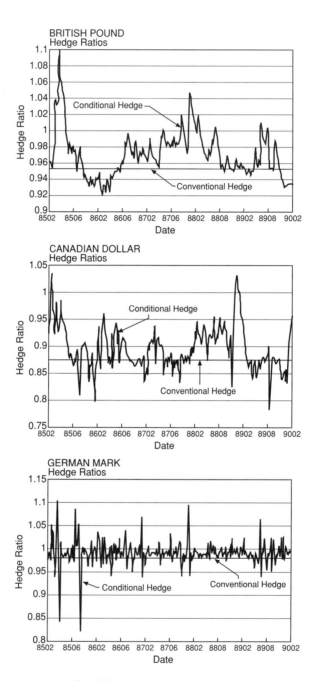

FIGURE 6.1   Comparison of ARCH and OLS currency hedge ratios. (*Source*: Kroner, K. and Sultan, J., *J. Financial Quantitative Anal.*, vol. 28, p. 546, 1993. With permission.)

6.1 and 6.2 are theoretically imprecise due to the assumption of myopia that allows expected utility of terminal wealth to be optimized without considering the entirety of lifetime consumption. This is an important theoretical development because it permits the future time paths of the conditioning variables to affect the optimization problem. As in the previous section, the results in this section feature a general expected utility function. In addition, conditional probability measures with state-dependent parameters are admitted. All the results depend on the assumption of conditional joint normality of the underlying returns. While it is possible to further generalize to include other types of joint distributions, this typically reduces the sharpness of the results.

The problem of maximizing the expected utility of lifetime consumption (not terminal wealth) can be solved expediently by assuming additive separability of the utility function. Given this, at any time t the hedger's more general "intertemporal" optimization problem is

$$J[W_t, X_t] = \max_{C_i, i=\{t, \ldots, T\}} E\left[\sum_{i=t}^{T} U[C_i] + D_T|X_t\right] \tag{6.4}$$

where $X(t)$ are the conditioning variables, C_i is consumption in period i, and D_T is the bequest function for the terminal date T (e.g., Ingersoll, 1987). The introduction of consumption into the intertemporal problem is dependent on using a different specification for the wealth dynamics. More precisely, W for the intertemporal case is

$$W_{t+1} = (W_t - C_t)[1 + R_s(t+1) - hR_f(t+1)] \tag{6.5}$$

In addition to incorporating consumption, the intertemporal problem involves conditional distributions that require the relevant state variables to be identified. While it is possible to be more general, for present purposes the rate processes (R_s and R_f) are the only state variables considered. Given this, the general solution to the optimization problem must now incorporate compensation for the hedger's "nervousness" about future changes in the state variables.

Applying Bellman's dynamic programming principle (e.g., Malliaris and Brock, 1982), the dynamic generalization of Proposition 6.1 into Proposition 6.3 reveals the corresponding complications. In addition to h_{OLS} now being a conditional estimate, the role of preferences in the intertemporal optimal hedge ratio is more complicated than in the myopic case. More significantly, h_{OLS} is no longer generally optimal when $E[R_f] = 0$.

Specifically, the additional preference-dependent terms arise from expected changes in the state variables affecting the marginal utility of wealth. In this situation, utility function selection takes on added importance. For example, log utility possesses the important simplifying property that $J_{ws} = J_{wf} = 0$, which allows the intertemporal solution to correspond directly to the myopic

---

PROPOSITION 6.3

Optimal Intertemporal Hedge Ratio

Under the assumption of conditional bivariate normality of $R_s(t)$ and $R_f(t)$, the generalized optimal hedge ratio using Eqs. (6.4) and (6.5) can be specified as:

$$H_t^* = (1 + \gamma)\, h_{OLS}|_{x(t)=c} + \frac{E[R_f]}{\text{var}[R_f]} \frac{E[J_W]}{E[J_{WW}]'} + \frac{E[J_{Wf}]}{E[J_{WW}]'}$$

where:

$$\gamma = \frac{E[J_{Ws}]}{E[J_{WW}]'} \qquad E[J_{WW}]' = (W_t - C_t)E[J_{WW}]$$

and where c is the observed values on the state variables (X) up to and including t, and all expectations are taken conditionally on $X(t)$ with:

$$E\left[\frac{\partial J}{\partial W_{t+1}}\bigg| X(t)\right] \equiv J_W \qquad E\left[\frac{\partial^2 J}{\partial W_{t+1}^2}\bigg| X(t)\right] \equiv J_{WW}$$

$$E\left[\frac{\partial^2 J}{\partial W_{t+1}\,\partial R_{s,t+1}}\bigg| X(t)\right] \equiv J_{Ws} \qquad E\left[\frac{\partial^2 J}{\partial W_{t+1}\,\partial R_{f,t+1}}\bigg| X(t)\right] \equiv J_{Wf}$$

---

case, with the caveat of potential inequality of conditional and unconditional statistical parameters. Empirical estimation proceeds by assuming a specific form of conditional distribution (e.g., ARCH) (Cecchetti *et al.*, 1988). Significantly, other important types of utility functions such as quadratic and power are not so well behaved. Estimation of intertemporal optimal hedge ratios for these types of functions can be problematic.[6]

Similar complications arise when riskless lending and borrowing are admitted. In this case, the wealth specification is

$$W_{t+1} = (W_t - C_t)[1 + (1 - x_t)r(t+1) + x_t R_s(t+1) - H_t R_f(t+1)]$$

In an intertemporal context this leads to the introduction of an additional conditioning (state) variable, r, which has to be taken into account. As in Proposition 6.3, the risk associated with the potential changes in the state

---

[6]Numerous studies have approached this problem using advanced estimation techniques (e.g., Scott, 1989).

variables must be compensated. This leads to an equilibrium condition for the generalized hedge ratio that has terms that involve J_{ws}, J_{wf}, and J_{wr} (i.e., indirect utility function $[J]$ terms appear). However, J_{ww} terms do not appear and, as a result, the hedge ratio does not depend on risk attitudes of the hedger. The exact expression for the optimal hedge ratio is quite complicated and not revealing; therefore, it is not given here, although, as before, the log utility provides an important simplification: Because the J_{ws}, J_{wf}, and J_{wr} terms are zero, the myopic results of Proposition 6.2 apply.

J. THE FARMER'S HEDGING PROBLEM

One of the limitations of the conventional optimal hedging model is that there is only one source of uncertainty that has to be hedged. This is reflected, for example, in the assumption of a nonstochastic cash position. Another example occurs when hedging the domestic currency value of the return on a foreign stock, where both the exchange rate and the foreign stock price interact to determine the variable to be hedged. Hence, in a number of hedging situations, it is not practical to assume there is only one source of uncertainty. This section considers the case where both price and quantity to be hedged are random. This means that *income*, not price, is the variable to be hedged. This problem is motivated by a stylized farming situation: At planting time, the farmer must estimate the size of the future crop in order to determine the size of the futures hedge (see Table 6.8). More generally, this problem also applies to hedging situations where future inputs to the (uncertain) production process have to be estimated. For the farmer's problem, because Q_S is not fixed at $t = 0$, it must be estimated. At $t = 0$, the farmer plants with the objective of reaping $\hat{q}$ where $\hat{q}$ is generated by some production function, $f(K, L, Land)$, and offered for sale at some expected price, $E[S(1)]$. Even at this basic level, the complexities of the farmer's problem are apparent. To

TABLE 6.8   Profit Function for a Non-Cross-Hedging Farmer

Date	Cash position	Futures position
$t = 0$	Plant with expectation of reaping $\hat{q}$ at $t = 1$ (based on price $S(0)$ and $f[K, L, Land]$	Short $\hat{q}$ at $F(0,T)$
$t = 1$	Reap $\bar{q}(1)$ and sell at $S(1)$	Close out position with long $\hat{q}$ at $F(1,T)$

Note: The associated profit function can now be derived as:

$$\pi = [\bar{q}(1) - \hat{q}]S(1) + \hat{q}[S(1) - S(0) + F(0,T) - F(1,T)]$$

make the problem more manageable, a number of simplifying assumptions are required.

In the analysis of the minimum variance hedge ratio (see Chapter 2, Section I) it was shown that the relevant objective function was $EU = -\text{var}[\pi]$. This functional form can be compared to the mean-variance EU. Given the similarities in the mean-variance and minimum-variance optimal hedge ratios, it is possible to rationalize the minimum-variance approach by assuming that hedgers (in this case, farmers) do not forecast spot prices. In effect, the price in the future is expected to be the same as it is today. This form of myopia permits use of the minimum-variance hedge ratio by eliminating the need to consider expected price change. Another simplifying assumption is the requirement that the hedge position put on at $t = 0$ is held and not changed until harvest at $t = 1$. More formally, no dynamic hedge adjustment is permitted. Given these two assumptions, two situations can be considered: where $\hat{q} = Q_H = Q$ (no cross hedging) and where $\hat{q}$ and Q_H are allowed to differ (cross hedging). If farm output realized at $t = 1$ is taken to be $\tilde{q}$, then it is possible to define the profit function for the farmer doing a delivery hedge (where no cross hedge is involved).

Creating a new random variable $\tilde{q}(1)S(1) = Y(1)$, which effectively represents future farm income, it is possible to define an associated variance of profit function that can be used to solve for the minimum-variance hedge ratio:

$$\text{var}[\pi] = \sigma_Y^2 + Q^2\sigma_F^2 - 2Q\sigma_{YF}$$

$$\frac{\partial \text{var}[\pi]}{\partial Q} = 2[Q\sigma_F^2 - \sigma_{YF}] = 0$$

$$Q^* = \frac{\sigma_{YF}}{\sigma_F^2}$$

While interesting, this form of the optimal hedge ratio has little practical value. Expanding the solution to allow for Q_H to differ from the expected size of the crop position does not substantially change the practicality of the solution. The primary analytical difficulty is the presence of a random variable, farm income, which is the product of two random variables. Only one of these variables, spot prices, can be hedged using futures contracts written on the spot commodity price. With this in mind, it is possible to reconstruct the optimal problem into the form used in Propositions 6.1 and 6.2.

The basic model is discrete. Farmers have access to a variety of possible risk-management instruments to hedge production decisions. The representative farmer plants a crop at time t and harvests it at time $t + 1$. Both the price at harvest and the quantity harvested are unknown at time t, the date the relevant risk-management and planting decisions are initiated. As conceived here, in addition to choosing the usage of hedging instrument(s), the farmer's optimization problem also involves choosing the amount of initial wealth to invest in crop production. Hence, the production decision is treated in a portfolio context. As a result, the costs associated with planting the given acreage are also determined. Starting from a given initial level of wealth, the farmer's objective is to maximize the value of terminal wealth, assuming that the balance (possibly negative) of initial wealth that is not allocated to planting costs will earn (pay) the risk-free rate of interest.

Given this basic structure, it will initially be assumed that the only hedging instrument available is futures contracts. In this case, the underlying wealth dynamics can be specified:

$$W_{t+1} = AY_{t+1}P_{t+1} + [W_t - C(A)](1 + r) + Q_f(f_{t+1} - f_t)$$

where W_{t+1} is wealth at time $t + 1$ and W_t is the known level of initial wealth; A is the number of acres planted; Y_{t+1} is the random yield per acre observed when the crop is harvested at $t + 1$; P_{t+1} is the random spot price at $t + 1$; $C(A)$ is the known cost function associated with planting the A acres; r is the risk-free interest rate; Q_f is the quantity of futures contracts sold $(-)$ or bought $(+)$; and f_{t+1} and f_t are the futures prices observed at $t + 1$ and t, respectively. Manipulation gives:

$$\begin{aligned} W_{t+1} &= W_t[x(1 + R) + (1 - x)(1 + r) + HR_f] \\ &= W_t[(1 + r) + x(R - r) + HR_f] \\ &= W_t + \pi_{t+1} \end{aligned} \tag{6.6}$$

where π_{t+1} is the profit realized at time $t + 1$; x is $[C(A)/W_t]$, the fraction of initial wealth invested in the crop production; H is the value $(f_t \times Q_f)$ of the hedge position divided by initial wealth (not the value of the spot position); R_f is $(f_{t+1} - f_t)/f_t$; and $(1 + R)$ is $[(AY_{t+1}P_{t+1})/C(A)]$, one plus the rate of return on planting.

Given this, the farmer's optimal risk management decision problem is to choose x and H such that the expected utility of terminal wealth is maximized. The decision problem is modeled with a general expected utility function. However, in order to achieve analytically concise results, joint normality of R and R_f is invoked. This leads to Proposition 6.4. Significantly, while the derivation of Proposition 6.4 reveals that the individual optimal solutions (denoted by *) to the farmer's risk-management problem (x^*, H^*) depend on preferences, the ratio (H^*/x^*) only involves statistical parameters.

The portfolio-theoretic intuition behind the proposition is as follows: The farmer faces two problems, one involving hedging and the other involving the scale of production. To determine the fraction of the crop to hedge, the farmer must solve a portfolio problem involving two risky "assets" with returns

---

PROPOSITION 6.4

Crop Investment and Hedging Decision

Assuming that the returns R and R_f are jointly normal random variables and that the farmer chooses x and H so as to maximize the expected utility of terminal wealth given by Eq. (6.6) then:

$$\left\{\frac{H}{x}\right\}^* = \frac{\dfrac{E[R_f]}{\sigma_f^2} - \rho\dfrac{E[R] - r}{\sigma_R\sigma_f}}{\dfrac{E[R] - r}{\sigma_R^2} - \rho\dfrac{E[R_f]}{\sigma_R\sigma_f}}$$

where:

$$\rho = \frac{\sigma_{Rf}}{\sigma_R\sigma_f} \qquad \sigma_{Rf} = Cov[R,R_f] \qquad \sigma_f^2 = Var[R_f] \qquad \sigma_R^2 = Var[R]$$

and U is the farmer's utility function for wealth $(U' > 0, U'' < 0)$.

$(R - r)$ and R_f. From mean-variance portfolio theory, it is well known that if asset returns are jointly normal and riskless borrowing and lending are permitted, then all investors, regardless of preferences, hold the same portfolio of risky assets. In addition, the ratio of any two assets in an optimal portfolio will be independent of risk preferences. Because the farmer's choice of the fraction of initial wealth to invest in crop production (x) is unconstrained, as long as returns are independent of the scale of production—and the other assumptions relevant to Proposition 6.4 are satisfied—(H^*/x^*) will not involve preferences.

When used to analyze (H^*/x^*), the practical implication of Proposition 6.4 is that the fraction of the investment in crop production to be hedged, $[Q_f f_t/C(A)]$, is independent of the size of the crop. Further, when the futures price is unbiased $(E[R_f] = 0)$, only joint normality of R and R_f is required to motivate OLS as the optimal hedge ratio estimation technique. Though similar types of conditions have been derived for related problems (e.g., Benninga *et al.*, 1984; Heaney and Poitras, 1991), this result has not been recognized as applying to the farmer's hedging problem with both price and production uncertainty. On balance, Proposition 6.4 is significant because it establishes the connection between the results of portfolio theory and the farmer's hedging problem, providing a motivation for the use of regression analysis to estimate the farmer's optimal hedge ratio.

II. CURRENCY HEDGING FOR INTERNATIONAL ACTIVITIES

A. TRANSACTION HEDGING EXAMPLE: MANAGING CURRENCY EXPOSURE

The final transaction hedging example being considered involves hedging currency exposure. As discussed previously, a fundamental difficulty of textbook discussions of hedging involves the assumption that a single transaction is involved. While this may work for the grain elevator or the hog farmer, assessing interest rate exposure for a financial institution or currency risk for a multinational firm is much more complicated. For example, financial institutions such as pension funds have a systemic exposure to changes in the level and shape of the term structure of interest rates due to a structural imbalance between the duration of liabilities and assets. Even if derivatives with sufficiently distant expiration dates were available, it is often not feasible to hedge each individual transaction due to the large number of implied trades. A similar problem faces financial institutions such as chartered banks, which also have a large number of interest- and exchange-rate-sensitive transactions. Despite this, there are numerous practical situations where interest rate and exchange rate hedges are treated as individual transactions. These simplified cases require the specifics of the hedge to be known at the time the hedge is initiated. Illustration of these cases is the objective of this section.

Predictable foreign currency cash flows permit the use of a range of conventional hedging instruments associated with foreign asset/liability management to be applied. The procedures for implementing some of these techniques, such as currency swaps and options, will be discussed in later sections. The textbook use of a long currency futures hedge to cover a foreign currency cash flow is illustrated in Table 6.9 where a U.S. firm is making a purchase in pounds for sale in dollars. The hedge requires that the amount of the cash flow and the payment date be known with certainty. The anticipated transaction is approximately fully hedged. The position is long because futures contracts are measured in U.S. direct terms (US$/£) and profit will be positive if the (US$/£) increases over time. The hedger expects the pound to strengthen. In the example, the hedger was correct and the pound increased from $1.5430 to $1.5842. The hedge was profitable and was able to more than offset the loss on the purchase of British radar systems. This was a best-case scenario. It was also possible for the pound to weaken and for the hedge to lose money.

Table 6.10 illustrates the use of a short currency hedge using forward contracts. In this example, a transfer of funds from Japanese yen into dollars

TABLE 6.9   Long Transaction Hedge using Foreign Currency Futures Contracts

Scenario: On Aug. 8, 1994, an American defense contractor enters into a contract to purchase 10 British radar systems with cash payment to be made in British pounds on Nov. 8, 1994. Each radar system will cost £70,000. The American firm is concerned that the pound will strengthen over the next few months causing the radar systems to cost more in dollars.

Date	Spot market	Futures market
August 8	The current exchange rate is $1.5430 per pound. The forward rate for the pound is $1.5402.	December pound contract is at $1.5360. US$ value per contract = 62,500 ($1.5360) = $96,000.
	US$ forward cost of 10 radars: 10(70,000)($1.5402) = $1,078,140	Number of futures contracts for the hedge: $\frac{\$1,078,140}{\$96,000} = 11.23$
		Buy 11 contracts (closest whole number)
November 8	The spot rate is $1.5842. Pay £700,000 pounds to purchase 10 radars. Cost in dollars: 700,000($1.5842) = $1,108,940.	December pound contract is at $1.5820.US$ value per contract: 62,500($1.5820) = $98,875
		Sell 11 contracts (close out position)

Ex post analysis:

The cost of not forward hedging the radar system is: $1,108,140 − $1,078,140 = $30,800 more.

The profit on the futures transaction hedge is:

11 ($98,875) =	$1,087,625	(US$ value of futures position on Nov. 8)
−11 ($96,000) =	−$1,056,000	(US$ value of position on Aug. 8)
	$ 31,625	(gain on futures transactions)

The profit on the futures is sufficient to fully offset the higher US$ cost of the radar systems, leaving a small net gain of $825 compared to using a forward hedge. The defence contractor effectively paid $1,108,940 − $31,625 = $1,077,315 for the 10 radar systems.

at a future date is involved. Again, the details of the transaction are known with certainty when the hedge is initiated. The risk in this transaction is that the yen (¥) will weaken, the (US$/¥) will fall, and the number of dollars that can be purchased will be less in the future than at the time the hedge is being considered. Once again, a full hedge is established, and the hedger is correct about the direction of the exchange rate change. The forward hedge was able to exactly offset the loss on the spot position. Why did the futures gain and spot loss not fully cancel out in the full hedge in Table 6.9? This has to do with the basis. On August 8, the date the hedge was initiated, the basis was $F(0,T) − S(0) = \$1.5360 − \$1.5430 = −0.0070$. On November 8, the date of the payment and the end of the hedge, the basis was $1.5820 −1.5842 = −0.0022$. The difference of 0.0048 times the size of the cash

TABLE 6.10   Short Transaction Hedge using Foreign Currency Forward Contracts

Scenario: On April 9, 1994 a U.S. investment firm with a Japanese subsidiary decides it will need to transfer 900 million Japanese yen from an account in Tokyo to U.S. dollar account with a New York bank. Transfer will be made on Aug. 8, 1994. The firm is concerned that over the next two months the Japanese yen will weaken.

Date	Spot market	Forward market
April 9	The current exchange rate is $0.9982 per 100 yen. The forward rate for 100 yen is $0.9998. Forward value of funds: 9,000,000($0.9998) = $8,998,200.	Sell 900 million yen forward for delivery on August 8 at $0.9998.
August 8	The spot rate is $0.9864.	Deliver yen and receive 9,000,000($0.9998) = $8,998,200.

Ex post analysis:

The value on the yen on August 8 is $8,877,600. The gain to the forward transaction can be calculated as: $8,998,200 − $8,877,600 = $120,600. Due to the absence of basis risk associated with the forward contract the investment firm was able to lock in an exchange rate which was higher than the April 9 value. Had the forward transaction not been done, the firm would have converted the yen at the Aug. 8 spot rate of $0.9864 and received only $8,877,600.

position, adjusted for the rounding error incorporated in the number futures contracts (11.23 versus 11) used in the hedge, produces the appropriate excess value earned by the hedge. The bulk of the basis change is due to the impact of covered interest parity on the reducing maturity of the futures contract being used in the hedge.

In the short and long currency hedges, expected profit on the hedge was achieved because the hedger was correctly able to predict the expected change in the spot exchange rate. For many types of international transactions, such as bidding on contracts denominated in foreign currency, other sources of risk also enter the hedging problem. For example, bidding on a construction contract where the contract payments and, possibly, the construction expenses are denominated in foreign currency involves the additional risk that the bid will be unsuccessful. If futures are used to hedge expected change in the currency between the time the bid is submitted and the time of the payments and expenses, and the bid is *unsuccessful*, then the firm will face significant potential losses. For some firms, this would present a significant barrier to bidding on foreign contracts. Because the outcome of the bidding process is a contingency, it is decidedly more efficient to use options than futures to hedge the currency risk. Some of the comparative advantages of options over futures in theses types of hedging situations are listed in Table 6.11.

TABLE 6.11 Comparison of a Different Methods of Hedging a Contingent Foreign Currency Position

Scenario: A U.S. telecommunications firm is planning a hostile takeover of a British firm. If the takeover is successful, payment of a fixed number of British pounds is required. If the takeover is unsuccessful, no pound payments are required. The U.S. firm is concerned that the pound will strengthen during the uncertain time period during which the takeover bid is in effect. The table below indicates various possible combinations of forward, futures or option contracts which could be used to hedge the pound exposure.

Outcome of takeover	No hedge	Long futures hedge	Long forward hedge	Option hedge (buy call)	Option hedge (buy call, write put)
Successful					
Pound increases	Cost of takeover in US$ increases	Increased US$ payment offset by hedge gain;	Increased US$ payment offset by hedge gain;	Call exercised; increased US$ payment offset by gain on option	Call exercised; put expires; increased US$ payment offset.
Pound decreases	Cost of takeover in US$ decreases	Lower US$ payment offset by hedge loss;	Lower US$ payment offset by hedge loss;	Call expires; lower US$ payment but loss of option premium	Call expires, put is exercised; lower US$ payment offset by put payout
Unsuccessful					
Pound increases	No effect	Cash inflow from gain on hedge	Cash inflow from gain on hedge	Call exercised	Call exercised; put expires; cash inflow from call.
Pound decreases	No effect	Cash outflow from loss on hedge	Cash outflow from loss on hedge	Call expires; premium lost	Call expires, put exercised; cash outflow from put exercise
Advantages	No hedging cost	Easy to unwind	No basis risk	Contingent payoff	Ability to set different put and call exercise prices

B. When is Hedging Foreign Assets Effective?

Textbook presentations of currency hedging indicate that a hedged foreign asset position will have a less variable return (cash flow) than an unhedged foreign asset. This intuition is, unfortunately, not always correct. To see this, consider the calculation for the return on a domestic asset, R:

$$R = (P_1 - P_0 + div)/P_0 = [(P_1 - P_0)/P_0] + [div/P_0]$$
$$= [P_1/P_0] + [div/P_0] - 1 = \text{capital gain (loss)} + \text{dividend (or coupon) yield}$$

The return calculation can be contrasted with the domestic currency return on a foreign asset. Showing the distinction requires some notation for the domestic currency return on a foreign asset position, $R_\$$. The return on a foreign asset denominated in foreign currency terms is $R_\pounds$; $e = S_1/S_0$ is the growth rate of the currency; div is the single dividend that is known to be paid at $t = 1$; P is the asset price in foreign currency terms; and S is the spot exchange rate:

$$1 + R_\$ = 1 + \frac{[P_1 + div_1]S_1 - P_0 S_0}{P_0 S_0} = \frac{P_1 + div_1}{P_0}\frac{S_1}{S_0} = [1 + R_\pounds][1 + e]$$

In effect, the asset return can be decomposed into the returns associated with local factors, $R_\pounds$, and currency changes, e.

In order to evaluate the behavior of hedged portfolios, an appropriate specification of the hedging rule is required. A naive specification is to assume all currency risk is fully hedged. In practical applications, this requires determining at $t = 0$ a hedge amount. To see how this is done, consider the following:

$$1 + R_H = 1 + \frac{[P_1 + div_1]F(0,1) - P_0 S_0}{P_0 S_0}$$
$$= \frac{P_1 + div_1}{P_0}\frac{F(0,1)}{S_0} = [1 + R_\pounds][1 + fp]$$

where R_H is the return on the fully hedged foreign asset position. The fully hedged U.S. dollar return can then be calculated from the observed domestic currency return and the forward premium (fp). Hence, the hedged U.S. dollar return on, say, a Japanese government bond will be higher than the Japanese yen denominated return by the amount of the forward premium, where:

$$fp = \frac{F(0,1)}{S_0} = \left[\frac{1 + r(0,1)}{1 + r^*(0,1)}\right]$$

This condition follows from covered interest arbitrage.

It is now possible to demonstrate that hedging foreign assets will not necessarily reduce the variability of the asset's cash flow (e.g., Benari, 1991).

This requires a direct comparision of $[R_\$]$ and $\text{var}[R_H]$. For expedience, it is useful to use the approximation $\ln\{1 + r\} = r$. Given this, then $\text{var}[R_\$] = \text{var}[R_\pounds] + \text{var}[e] + 2\,\text{cov}[R_\pounds, e]$. Assuming that the hedge size can be completely determined at $t = 0$, then application of the log approximation gives $\text{var}[R_H] = \text{var}[R_\pounds]$. This follows because the forward premium is known at $t = 0$. Given this, what is now required is the conditions for which $\text{var}[R_\$] < \text{var}[R_H]$ or, in other words, the variance of the hedged return is larger than the unhedged return. Using $\rho\sigma_\pounds\sigma_e = \text{cov}[R_\pounds, e]$ gives a result that can be referred to as Benari's condition:

$$\rho < -\frac{\sigma_e}{2\sigma_f}$$

As stated, if Benari's condition is satisfied, then the hedged return will be more volatile; that is, if the observed conditional correlation between the return on the foreign asset and the foreign exchange rate is sufficiently negative, then hedging can increase risk.

While it might seem intuitively unlikely for a hedged asset position to have a more volatile cash flow than an unhedged position, Tables 6.12 and 6.13, from Madura and Tucker (1992), confirm that Benari's condition may hold in practice. Table 6.12 provides the relevant hedged and unhedged returns for three monthly sample periods: a weak dollar from January 1985 to July 1987; a strong dollar period from 1981–1984; and an August 1987 to November 1988 sample impacted by the October 1987 market crash. The benchmark portfolio is an equally weighted collection of the market indices for the seven countries listed. Significantly, Madura and Tucker find that the results for the crash period indicate that "during the period surrounding the 1987 world stock market

TABLE 6.12   Hedging and Crash of 1987: Intertemporal Comparison of Fully Hedged and Unhedged Portfolios[a]

	Unhedged Portfolios			Hedged Portfolios		
Subperiod	Mean return (%)	Standard deviation (%)	Coefficient of variation	Mean return (%)	Standard deviation (%)	Coefficient of Variation
1. 1981–1984 (strong $)	0.174	3.924	22.55	1.049	3.052	2.91
2. Jan. '85–July '87 (weak $)	3.330	4.011	1.20	2.178	3.302	1.52
3. Aug. '87–Nov. '88	0.133	6.313	47.46	−0.004	6.881	NA

[a]Monthly returns with equal weight.

Source: Reprinted from Madura and Tucker (1992). With permission.

TABLE 6.13   Hedging and Crash of 1987: Market Risk Characteristics

Stock market	Sub-period	Variance of stock market movements	Variance of exchange rate movements	Covariance between stock market and exchange rate movements	Correlation between market and exchange rate movements	Variance of exchange rate-adjusted stock market movements
Canada	1	31.69	1.53	3.10	0.45	39.43
	2	13.39	2.01	1.90	0.34	19.21
	3	47.05	1.96	1.90	0.19	52.81
France	1	38.81	11.28	1.20	0.05	52.50
	2	40.57	13.76	−2.50	−0.09	49.34
	3	101.60	11.69	−11.00	−0.32	91.30
Germany	1	17.64	10.95	0.76	0.05	30.11
	2	50.41	15.81	−3.20	−0.08	59.85
	3	86.67	13.91	−19.00	−0.54	62.58
Japan	1	20.79	14.13	4.70	0.25	44.33
	2	30.14	14.06	2.90	0.14	50.00
	3	38.31	20.61	−11.00	−0.36	36.92
Switzerland	1	10.30	12.60	1.80	0.15	26.50
	2	21.99	20.07	−7.30	−0.35	27.46
	3	68.39	17.72	−24.00	−0.70	38.11
United Kingdom	1	19.09	8.41	−0.30	−0.02	26.90
	2	21.71	16.16	5.10	0.27	48.07
	3	72.76	16.48	−12.00	−0.37	65.24
United States	1	14.13	—	—	—	14.13
	2	15.52	—	—	—	15.52
	3	49.98	—	—	—	49.98
Average across markets	1	21.77	9.82	1.88	0.16	33.41
	2	27.67	13.64	−0.52	0.04	38.49
	3	66.39	13.73	−12.52	−0.35	56.71

Source: Reprinted from Madura and Tucker (1992). With permission.

crash, international portfolios that were hedged with forward contracts exhibited more total risk than those that were not hedged" (Madura and Tucker, 1992).

Table 6.13 contains information required for evaluation of Benari's condition. Examining, say, Japan in period 3 gives $-0.36 < -\{\sqrt{20.61}\}/2\{\sqrt{38.31}\}$, which indicates the condition is not satisfied, but only just. Hence, hedging the currency risk of Japanese stocks would provide virtually no risk-reduction benefit. Germany, Switzerland, France, and the United Kingdom all satisfy the condition for the crash period, meaning that hedging these international stock groups during the crash would have increased volatility. In effect, in an international context, the risk-reduction benefits of hedging depend on the correlation between stock market and exchange rate movements. The October 1987 crash was a stock market contagion triggered by an information event that had strong negative implications for the U.S. dollar. This contagion spread from the United States to international stock markets, which experienced severe stock market declines at the same time there was marginal strengthening of their currencies.

Tables 6.12 and 6.13 illustrate that Benari's condition is not satisfied in most periods. Currency hedging does typically reduce return volatility. This much is apparent from a casual inspection of the condition. When the correlation is positive, Benari's condition is automatically satisfied. Even if the correlation is negative, hedging is still risk reducing if the variability of the exchange rate is sufficiently greater than that of the foreign stock market. Because it is not possible for $\rho < -1$, it follows that if $\sigma_e > 2\sigma_{\pounds}$ then the condition cannot be satisfied. On balance, Benari's condition serves to emphasize the importance of selective hedging. Following the analysis of Chapter 2, Section I, selective hedging should be used unless the investor is unable to forecast effectively, the exchange rate forecast indicates that $F_{(0,1)} = E[S]$, or there is a high degree of investor risk aversion (b large).

Some of the issues raised by Benari's condition are quite subtle and require further elaboration. Benari's basic result is a special case of a more general result: When using one derivative to hedge the product of two random variables, even if the derivative has no basis risk with one of the variables, an unhedged position could have less cash flow volatility than a hedged position. This can happen when the correlation between the two random variables is negative and the derivative contract is written on the variable that has the least volatility. It is possible to generalize this result further to where n derivatives are hedging k random variables ($n > k$). Madura and Tucker use an *ex post* conditional empirical analysis to demonstrate that Benari's condition did apply during the year surrounding the October 1987 stock market crash. All this raises the question: How can this result be used to facilitate *ex ante* hedging decisions?

The distinction between *ex ante* and *ex post* analysis is fundamental to the analysis of risk-management tactics and strategies. It is one thing to show that, *ex post*, a particular strategy was optimal; it is quite another for that strategy to translate *ex post* into *ex ante* performance. This is a fundamental criticism of the Markowitz mean-variance portfolio optimization model when the investment universe includes both domestic and foreign assets. The *ex post* optimality does not seem to translate into *ex ante* performance (e.g., Jorion, 1985; Eun and Resnick, 1994; Wilcox, 2000). In the absence of some method of accurately predicting changes in the relevant parameters, Benari's condition would have to rely on unconditional parameter estimates obtained from a specific sample. Tables 6.14 and 6.15 report some relevant estimates from Eun and Resnick (1994) for seven countries using monthly data from January 1978 to December 1989. Of particular interest, Eun and Resnick report the results using two different reference currencies: U.S. dollars and Japanese yen. Both intermediate-term bond returns and stock market index returns are examined.

The first column in Tables 6.14 and 6.15 give the total variance of the monthly asset return, where the return is denominated in the reference currency. The next four columns fully decompose this variance into its components. Recalling that $(1 + R_\$) = (1 + R_£)(1 + e) = 1 + R_£ + e + R_£ e$, the last column is associated with the cross product term that was ignored above by assuming that $R_\$ = R_£ + e$. The fourth column of Tables 6.14 and 6.15. measures the contribution of the cross-product term. The insignificant numbers in this column confirms the validity of the approximation, at least for monthly returns. Whether this conclusion would change for quarterly or annual returns is another matter. This term is small because the cross product is small relative to the levels. Larger differencing intervals could produce some pairs of large returns that could alter this result for specific countries.

TABLE 6.14 Decomposition of the Variance of the US$ Currency Return for Six Foreign Equity and Bond Indices, 1978–1989[a]

		Components of var($R_{i\$}$)			
	var[$R_{i\$}$]	var[R_i]	var[e_i]	2 cov[R_i,e_i]	Δvar
Bonds					
Canada	15.29	10.82	1.72	2.67	0.08
France	16.48	2.82	12.74	0.60	0.32
Germany	21.53	2.59	13.84	4.91	0.19
Japan	24.70	3.03	15.13	6.09	0.45
Switzerland	21.16	1.14	17.64	2.34	0.04
United Kingdom	27.67	8.88	12.39	6.08	0.32
United States	10.24	10.24	0.00	0.00	0.00
Stocks					
Canada	37.70	30.58	1.72	5.37	0.03
France	59.75	43.03	12.74	3.75	0.23
Germany	43.82	29.27	13.84	0.00	0.71
Japan	41.47	19.45	15.13	5.83	1.06
Switzerland	34.81	20.07	17.64	−3.76	0.86
United Kingdom	40.96	29.27	12.39	−1.52	0.82
United States	21.16	21.16	0.00	0.00	0.00

[a]The variances are computed using monthly percentage returns.
Reprinted from Eun and Resnick (1994). With permission.

TABLE 6.15   Decomposition of Variance of Yen Currency Return for Six Foreign Equity and Bond Indices, 1978–1989[a]

	var[$R_{i\$}$]	Components of var[$R_{i\$}$]			
		var[R_i]	var[e_i]	2 cov[R_i,e_i]	Δvar
Bonds					
Canada	24.90	10.82	14.75	−1.01	0.34
France	10.43	2.82	8.58	−1.08	0.11
Germany	14.52	2.59	9.86	2.02	0.05
Japan	3.03	3.03	0.00	0.00	0.00
Switzerland	12.25	1.14	10.43	0.69	−0.01
United Kingdom	22.85	8.88	11.42	2.93	−0.38
United States	21.16	10.24	14.59	−3.91	0.24
Stocks					
Canada	51.27	30.58	14.75	5.96	−0.02
France	50.84	43.03	8.58	−0.38	−0.39
Germany	40.45	29.27	9.86	0.68	0.64
Japan	19.45	19.45	0.00	0.00	0.00
Switzerland	32.04	20.07	10.43	1.16	0.38
United Kingdom	42.90	29.27	11.42	2.45	0.24
United States	37.58	21.16	14.59	2.11	−0.28

[a]The variances are computed using monthly percentage returns.

In column three, Tables 6.14 and 6.15 directly address the possibility of negative correlations, which is necessary for Benari's condition to apply. Few negative values are observed. There were two cases where the negative values were large enough to be of interest: US$ bond returns with yen as the reference currency and Swiss stock returns with US$ as the reference currency. In both these cases, the volatility of exchange rates was larger than the volatility of local returns, another violation of a necessary condition. In total, in only one of the 24 variances were two of the necessary conditions satisfied: negative covariance and exchange-rate volatility less than one half the local return volatility. That case was French stocks with yen as the reference currency. Yet, this case had the lowest covariance of the six negative covariances that were observed. Benari's condition is far from being satisfied in this case.

C. THE OPTIMAL HEDGE RATIO FOR A SINGLE FOREIGN ASSET

In deriving Benari's condition, the following assumption was used: The currency risk of the foreign asset could be fully hedged at $t = 0$. In practice, it is not always possible to determine the terminal payoff on the foreign asset at $t = 0$. In other words, the exact size of the foreign currency hedge will be indeterminate because the precise payoff on the foreign asset at $t = 1$ will be unknown when the hedge is initially established. Though it may be possible to start the hedge at the $t = 0$ market value and sequentially increment the hedge at discrete intervals, such a strategy would be path dependent and would give an uncertain outcome. Another possible approach would be to set the size of the hedge position equal to the expected value of the position at the end of the hedge horizon. The success of this approach would depend on the accuracy of the estimate of future values.

Eun and Resnick (1994, p. 147) examine this point in more detail. Consider the return on a hedged foreign asset position, where the size of the hedge position is determined by estimating the value of the position at the end of the investment horizon. Unexpected gains or losses are left uncovered to be converted back at S_1. Letting R_{eh} be the return to a hedged foreign asset where the size of the hedge position is established by estimating the value of the position, it follows that:

$$1 + R_{eh} = (1 + E[R_£])(1 + fp) + (R_£ - E[R_£])S_1$$

This result is derived from the payoff on the hedged position:

$$1 + R_{eh} = \frac{E[P_1 + div_1]}{P_0 S_0} F(0,1) + \frac{P_1 + div_1 - E[P_1 + div_1]}{P_0 S_0} S_1$$

Manipulation produces:

$$R_{eh} = R_£ + fp + eR_£ + (fp - e)E[R_£] \cong R_£ + e + (fp - e)E[R_£]$$
$$= R_\$ + (fp - e)E[R_£]$$

$R_{eh} - R_\$$ depends on $(fp - e)$. Hence, if forward exchange rates are unbiased predictors of future spot interest rates, then establishing the size of the hedge position by estimating the value of the asset at the end of the investment horizon will on average produce much the same result as for the stylized full hedging problem.

The full hedging concept is useful in developing certain basic properties of currency hedges, such as the free-lunch argument of Perold and Schulman (1988). However, the full (or transaction) hedge ignores the possibility that assuming a fully hedged position is consistent with the best method of determining the hedge position. Armed with this observation, it is possible to proceed to the more difficult question of determining the optimal currency hedge ratio for a portfolio containing a single foreign asset. To accomplish this, let h be the fraction of the value of the foreign asset position (P_0) that is being hedged. With the value of the hedge being determined as $h[P_0 F(0,T)]$. Table 6.16 gives the profit profile for the optimal hedge. Some presentations of the

TABLE 6.16   Profit Profile for an Optimal Currency Futures Hedge

Assume: One unit of the foreign asset is being purchased; hedge position is constructed using a contract that matures at the end of the investment horizon

Date	Cash	Futures
$t = 0$	Convert at S_0 and buy the foreign asset at P_0	Short $h P_0$ of the foreign currency at $F(0,T)$
$t = 1$	Sell the asset at P_1, receive dividend of div_1 and convert back to domestic currency at S_1	Go long $h P_0$ at $F(1,T)$

Note: The profit function for this trade can be now stated as:

$$\pi(1) = (P_1 + div_1)S_1 - P_0 S_0 + h P_0 (F(0,T) - F(1,T))$$

profit function (e.g., Glen and Jorion, 1993) use forward contracts where delivery takes place at $t = 1$, using the proceeds from the foreign asset to settle the forward position.

Using R_{oh} for the return on the optimal hedged position, it follows that:

$$\frac{\pi(1)}{P_0 S_0} = R_{oh} = \frac{(P_1 + div_1)S_1}{P_0 S_0} - 1 - h \frac{P_0 \Delta F}{P_0 S_0}$$

$$= (1 + R_£)(1 + e) - 1 - h \frac{\Delta F}{S_0} \cong R_£ + e - h \frac{\Delta F}{S_0}$$

From this the variance can be determined and df is defined:

$$var[R_{oh}] = var[R_\$] + h^2 \, var[\Delta F/S] - 2 \, h \, cov[R_\$, \Delta F/S]$$

$$\equiv var[R_\$] + h^2 \, var[df] - 2 \, h \, cov[R_\$, df]$$

With this it is now possible to determine the optimal hedge ratio using the minimum variance solution (e.g., Eaker *et al.*, 1993). The size of the hedge position (h^*) is the choice variable:

$$\frac{d \, var[R_{oh}]}{dh} = 2h \, var[df] - 2cov[R_\$, df] = 0 \quad \rightarrow \quad h^* = \frac{cov[R_\$, df]}{var[df]}$$

By observing that the covariance term can be further expanded as:

$$R_\$ \cong R_£ + e \quad \rightarrow \quad cov[R_\$, df] \cong cov[R_\$, df] \cong cov[e, df] + cov[R_£, df]$$

With this result the minimum variance hedge ratio can be expressed:

$$h^* \cong \frac{cov[e, df]}{var[df]} + \frac{cov[R_£, df]}{var[df]}$$

Eaker *et al.* (1993) provide selected empirical estimates for this form of the optimal currency hedge ratio.

Closer inspection of the minimum variance hedge ratio provides some useful information. Consider the term $cov[e,df]/var[df]$:

$$\frac{cov[e,df]}{var[df]} = \frac{cov[(S_1 - S_0)/S_0, (F(1,T) - F(0,T))/S_0]}{var[F(1,T) - F(0,T)/S_0]}$$

Substituting the value of F from covered interest arbitrage reveals that this term will be close to one. If changes in the local asset return, $R_£$, are uncorrelated with changes in the forward exchange rate, an empirically plausible assumption, then the optimal currency hedge ratio for a single foreign asset will be close to one. Hence, the conditions under which full hedging is optimal may be empirically valid. Unfortunately, this relatively sharp result only applies to the restricted case of hedging a single foreign asset. Given this, it is natural to consider extending the analysis to allow for two assets: one domestic and one foreign (see Table 6.17).

TABLE 6.17   An Example of the Diversification Benefits of a Domestic/Foreign Portfolio

Question: You are considering purchasing two portfolios. One portfolio is composed 50/50 of two domestic assets each with $E[R] = 0.1$ and $\sigma = 0.15$ and with a 0.5 correlation between the asset returns. The other portfolio is also 50/50 and contains one of these domestic assets and a foreign asset. The foreign asset has $E[R_\$] = 0.1$ with $\sigma_£ = 0.15$ and $\sigma_e = 0.03$. The correlations between the foreign and domestic asset returns and between all the asset returns and the exchange rate are zero. Which portfolio is less risky?

Solution: The portfolio variance for the domestic assets is just the conventional result. To get the portfolio variance when there is a foreign asset observe that the return on a foreign asset when the return in denominated in domestic currency ($R_\$$) is given as: $R_\$ = (1 + R_£)(1 + e) - 1$. Taking logs and observing $\ln(1 + x)$ is approximately equal to x when x is sufficiently small produces the result:

$$var[R_\$] = \sigma_\$^2 = \sigma^2 + \sigma_e^2 + 2\sigma_{£,e}$$

Using the variance formula for two securities and doing appropriate substitutions, it follows that for a portfolio containing a foreign asset:

$$\sigma_p^2 = W_d^2\sigma_d^2 + W_\$^2\sigma_\$^2 + 2\ W_dW_\$\sigma_{d,\$}$$
$$= W_d^2\sigma_d^2 + W_\$^2\{\sigma_£^2 + \sigma_e^2 + 2\ \sigma_{£,e}\} + 2\ \{W_\$W_d(\sigma_{£,d} + \sigma_{e,d})\}$$

Evaluating the relevant formulas gives for the domestic portfolio $var[R_{dp}] = 0.016875$ ($\sigma_{dp} = 0.13$) and for the foreign/domestic portfolio $var[R_p] = 0.011475$ ($\sigma_p = 0.107121$)

Due to the much lower correlation between domestic asset returns and foreign asset returns and the exchange rate (than with other domestic asset returns) including foreign assets enhances the diversification process considerably.

D. Optimal Hedge Ratio for the Domestic/ Foreign Portfolio[7]

The single foreign asset case is pedagogically interesting because it allows illustration of the general principles of optimal hedging for single transactions. Yet, in practice, the problem of optimal hedging for foreign assets is often considerably more complicated, if only because foreign assets are typically part of a larger portfolio that also contains domestic assets. Extending the portfolio to include a domestic asset and a foreign asset follows naturally. As in the single-asset case, the problem is to determine the optimal size of the currency hedge, where optimal is defined using a minimum-variance objective function. The reformulation requires the use of value weights, W_d and $W_£$, the fractions of the total market value of the portfolio invested in the domestic and foreign assets, respectively. The budget constraint requires: $W_d + W_£ = 1$.

Using the Eaker *et al.* (1993) approach, substitution of the budget constraint produces:

$$R_{p2} = (1 - W_£)R_d + W_£(R_£ + e - h \, df)$$

The variance follows appropriately:

$$\text{var}[R_{p2}] = (1 - W_£)^2\sigma_d^2 + W_£^2(\sigma_£^2 + \sigma_e^2 + h^2 \, \sigma_F^2)$$
$$+ 2[(1 - W_£)W_£(\sigma_{£d} + \sigma_{ed} - h \, \sigma_{Fd}) + W_£^2(\sigma_{£e} - h \, \sigma_{F£} - h \, \sigma_{Fe})]$$

where for ease of notation, $F = df$ has been used in the subscripts. The minimization problem produces the solution (e.g., Filatov and Rappoport, 1992):

$$h^* = \frac{W_£}{1 - W_£}\frac{\sigma_{Fd}}{\sigma_F^2} + \frac{\sigma_{F£} + \sigma_{Fe}}{\sigma_F^2} \cong 1 + \frac{W_£}{1 - W_£}\frac{\sigma_{Fd}}{\sigma_F^2} + \frac{\sigma_{F£}}{\sigma_F^2}$$

This implies the following approach to determining the optimal currency hedge ratio. Determine (σ_{Fd}/σ_F^2) and $(\sigma_{F£}/\sigma_F^2)$ by regressing the foreign and domestic returns on $df = (\Delta F/S)$. Starting from a fully hedged position $(h = 1)$, increment the hedge by taking the values of the regression coeffi-

---

[7]A number of possible approaches could be taken after the single-asset case is considered. Recent work that has addressed this issue includes Filatov and Rappoport (1992), Adler and Jorion (1992), and Black (1989). For example, Black and others claim that there is a "universal currency hedge" that applies to all investors, regardless of nationality. The theoretical underpinnings for this result are derived from the international CAPM, which prescribes that all investors should hold a combination of the riskless asset and the world market portfolio, with currency exposure fully hedged. In practice, the optimal hedge ratios are estimated using regression analysis. Unfortunately, a number of theoretical and empirical criticisms of this approach have been offered (e.g., Solnik, 1991, pp. 29–30).

cients into account and, adjusting the coefficient from the domestic return regression by the relative size of the domestic asset in the portfolio.

The domestic/foreign asset case immediately suggests the next step in the analysis of risk-management decision problems involving foreign currency risk: solving for the optimal weight $W_£^*$. More precisely, it is immediately possible to solve for the minimum-variance solution. Following Filatov and Rappaport (1992), the following reformation of R_{p2} is possible:

$$R_{p2} \cong (1 - W_£)R_d + W_£(R_£ + (1 - h)e + h\,fp)$$

It follows that:

$$(1 - W_£)^* = \frac{\sigma_£^2 - \sigma_{£d} + (1 - h)[(1 - h)\sigma_e^2 + 2\sigma_{£e} - \sigma_{ed}]}{\sigma_d^2 + \sigma_£^2 + (1 - h)^2 - 2[\sigma_{£d} + (1 - h)\sigma_{ed} - (1 - h)\sigma_{£e}]}$$

When the $h = 1$, the solution reduces to the minimum variance solution familiar from basic financial economics:

$$(1 - W_£)^{**} = \frac{\sigma_£^2 - \sigma_{£d}}{\sigma_£^2 + \sigma_£^2 - 2\sigma_{£d}}$$

Comparing this solution with the $h = 0$ case is useful for revealing the intuition behind the impact of hedging on diversified portfolios.

III. MEAN VARIANCE ANALYSIS AND OPTIMAL INTERNATIONAL DIVERSIFICATION

A. BENEFITS OF INTERNATIONAL DIVERSIFICATION

Going back to Grubel (1968) and Levy and Sarnat (1970), numerous writers have demonstrated the potential benefits to international diversification of investment portfolios (e.g., Solnik, 1974; Lessard, 1976; Grauer and Hakansson, 1987; Burik and Ennis, 1990; Fosburg and Madura, 1991; Eaker *et al.*, 1991; Jorion and Goetzmann, 1999). Early writers on this subject demonstrated that the introduction of international securities into portfolios composed solely of domestic securities results in a significant outward movement in the *ex post* efficient frontier, as depicted in Graph 6.1. In effect, when international diversification is permitted it is possible to form portfolios with higher expected returns for the same level of risk. Another method of presenting this information is provided in Graph 6.2. It is possible to achieve a lower level of systematic risk than is achievable with domestic securities alone.

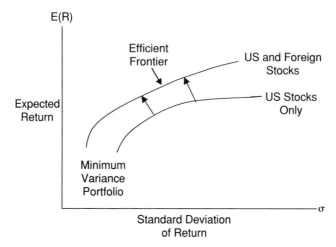

GRAPH 6.1   International diversification pushes out the effective frontier.

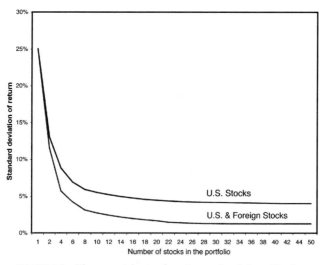

GRAPH 6.2   The potential gains from international diversification.

The diversification advantages of forming international portfolios arise due to low correlation of the returns for securities denominated in different currencies. By construction, it would seem that the greatest diversification benefits would require that the investor accept foreign exchange rate exposure. Upon closer inspection, many questions are raised by the results on the benefits of international diversification. For example, what are the implications of including hedged, as opposed to unhedged, foreign securities? Can currency risk be eliminated by fully hedging? How much diversification is necessary to achieve the bulk of the risk reduction benefits? What type of asset mix between the various countries and assets (i.e., stocks and bonds) is indicated? What are the implications of allowing short sales? Is a riskless asset permitted and, if so, is leveraging using the riskless asset permitted? Does the selection of the reference currency, which is used to denominate the return, matter? At present, there is only a limited amount of empirical information available to answer such questions.

To begin addressing these types of questions, further information about the decomposition of the risk of foreign securities into the currency and local components is needed. Ignoring for the moment that the efficient frontier may contain other securities in addition to unhedged common stocks, consider the evidence provided by Fosberg and Madura (1991) for a sample of 67 non-U.S. stocks from France (7), Japan (24), Switzerland (7), U.K. (14), and West Germany (15). Using quarterly US$ returns over 1976–1989, the variances of equally weighted, unhedged, randomly selected portfolios are calculated for portfolios containing 1–16 stocks. The variance is calculated using the familiar Taylor series approximation that $\ln\{1 + R\} = R$, which reduces the portfolio return to $R_\$ = R_\pounds + e$. The resulting variance relationship is $\text{var}[R_\$] = \text{var}[R_\pounds] + \text{var}[e] + 2\,\text{cov}[R_\pounds, e]$.

Fosburg and Madura calculate the average variance of the portfolio with 16 stocks is less than 1/10 the average variance of a portfolio with only one stock. Close to this amount of variance reduction can be achieved with only half that number of stocks. This rapid decrease in portfolio variance is consistent with the results of previous studies (e.g., Solnik, 1974).

These diversification benefits arise from stock returns being not as highly correlated across countries when compared to correlations between domestic stocks. Evidence of this for stocks has been provided in various sources, at least since Ibbotson et al. (1982). An important practical implication is that only a relatively small number of stocks is required to achieve significant diversification. For example, the evidence presented by Fosburg and Madura indicates that, for well-diversified portfolios, at least 40% of the returns of unhedged portfolios can be attributed to currency-related movements (see also Tables 6.14 and 6.15). Such results are based on unhedged common stock returns which raises practical questions about whether this result also applies to other asset specifications, such as foreign bond holdings. Answering such questions is facilitated by introducing the Markowitz model framework.

B. The Markowitz Model

The Markowitz model is a central paradigm of modern finance. The essence of the model is captured in the following optimization problem (e.g., Elton and Gruber, 1995; Luenberger, 1998):[8]

$$\min_{\{W_i\}} \ \text{var}[R_p] = \sum_{i=1}^{k} \sum_{j=1}^{k} W_i W_j \sigma_{ij}$$

subject to: $\sum_{i=1}^{k} W_i = 1$

$$E[R_p] = \sum_{i=1}^{k} W_i \, E[R_i] = \bar{c}_n \quad \text{for} \quad \bar{c}_n \in \{c_0 > c_1 > c_2 > \dots \dots\}$$

where $c_0 = c_{mv}$, the expected return on the minimum variance portfolio; k is the number of risky assets available for investment; $E[R_i]$ is the (conditional) expected return on asset i; $E[R_p]$ is the expected return on the portfolio; and $\text{var}[R_p]$ is the variance of portfolio return. In this model, the $\{W_i\}$ are the value weights, the fraction of the total value of the portfolio invested in each asset. For example, if there are four assets in the portfolio and the market value of each asset is equal, then the W_i for each asset is .25. It follows that the restriction requiring the sum of the weights to be equal to one is a budget constraint requiring that the sum of market values of all the assets held in the portfolio equals the total amount of money invested. The optimization problem is to determine the value weights for each asset that minimize the variance of the return on the portfolio, subject to a target level of expected return. Because there is range of possible expected returns that can be chosen, the solution to the optimization problem will be a set of portfolios, each with its own set of optimal weights.

The number of variations that have emerged from this basic model is staggering.[9] Initially, implementation of the model was impeded by the large number of parameters required to make the model operational. In addition

---

[8]The σ_{ij} term is interpreted as being a covariance when $i \neq j$ and as a variance when $i = j$. Because the basic optimization problem is quadratic, it follows that the optimal solutions will take the form of an ellipse or a parabola. In the case where the $\{W_i\}$ are restricted to be non-negative, the solution will be an ellipse. At any given target level of expected return, there will be two values of σ that solve the optimization problem. In evaluating the solutions, it is conventional to ignore the optimal solution that has the higher level of σ and to consider only the portfolios that have the lowest σ.

[9]Markowitz (1999) reviews the historical development of the model.

to the k individual asset returns, $E[R_i]$, there are k variances, σ_i^2, and $[k(k - 1)]/2$ covariances that have to be estimated from past data. Even if these parameters are available, the model is only capable of generating a set of mean-variance optimal portfolios, the *efficient frontier*. Additional structure is needed to select a specific portfolio from the set of optimal portfolios. Sharpe and others handled this problem by introducing a riskless asset. This permits the investor to form portfolios that combine the riskless asset with an efficient frontier portfolio. In this fashion, the investor is able to achieve the same level of expected return as that generated by an efficient frontier portfolio, again with a lower level of risk. Effectively, the addition of a riskless asset transforms the investment opportunity set from a convex function, the efficient frontier, to a set of linear functions, the capital allocation lines.

By exploiting the properties of mean-variance expected utility, Sharpe was able to show that the efficient frontier portfolio that would be selected is that portfolio associated with the capital allocation line just tangent to the efficient frontier. This particular capital allocation line is identified as the *capital market line*. This tangency portfolio can be determined by solving the following optimization problem (e.g., Eun and Resnick, 1994):

$$\max_{\{W_i\}} \frac{E[R_p] - r}{\sigma_p}$$

subject to:

$$\sum_{i=1}^{k} W_i = 1$$

where r is the risk-free interest rate and σ_p is the standard deviation of the return on the portfolio. On theoretical grounds, the tangency portfolio is the *ex ante* mean-variance expected-utility-optimizing, risky portfolio.[10] Even though the precise combination of riskless asset and risky tangency portfolio for any given investor requires specification of the relevant parameters for the investor's mean-variance expected-utility function, the optimal risky portfolio has been determined.

Yet, despite the theoretical importance of the tangency portfolio, practical identification of the value weights for this portfolio requires *ex post* estimates of the relevant means, variances, and covariances. Once the set of parameter estimates has been obtained and the optimality problem is solved, the resulting tangency portfolio will represent the optimal, *in-sample* portfolio. Whether this in-sample optimality translates into superior out-of-sample (*ex ante*) performance is an open question. The answer to this question becomes even more complex when foreign assets are admitted into the asset universe.

---

[10]It is possible to derive the optimal solutions in a number of different ways.

In particular, the domestic currency return on a foreign asset depends on a combination of two random variables: the return denominated in foreign currency terms and the change in the exchange rate. The correlation between foreign and domestic asset returns will tend to be lower than the correlations between domestic assets, making foreign assets excellent candidates for diversification. In addition, foreign assets can also provide the possibility of significantly higher returns than domestic assets.

The basic *ex post* returns and volatilities associated with hedged and unhedged international portfolios can be found in numerous sources (e.g., Burik and Ennis, 1990). Unhedged common stocks are found to have a higher mean return, at the expense of higher total volatility. For U.S. investors, when the dollar strengthens, hedging currency risk of foreign stocks will be profitable, resulting in higher returns; however, in periods when the dollar is weakening, hedging loses money, lowering the return relative to an unhedged position. Consistent with the theoretical results of Chapter 2, Section I, this evidence confirms that the appropriate hedging decision should incorporate speculative factors, if possible, in order to improve hedge performance. Burik and Ennis also provide information on the composition (optimal value weights) of the portfolios that lie on the efficient frontier (i.e., the set of optimal portfolios that achieve the highest level of return for a given level of risk). For a wide range of expected return/standard deviation combinations, the bulk of the portfolio is composed of a short-term money market fund and hedged foreign stocks. Only at high risk/return levels does portfolio composition shift to unhedged stocks. Unhedged foreign bonds are almost never held, with hedged foreign bonds playing a role over the intermediate risk/return combinations.

C. CRITICISM OF MEAN-VARIANCE PORTFOLIO ANALYSIS

While the mean-variance rationalization for international diversification has considerable appeal, attempting to capture the gains, *out-of-sample*, has proved to be illusive. In practice, the use of *ex post* data to estimate the relevant *ex ante* parameters creates numerous problems, not the least of which is instability in both the mean and variance–covariance parameter estimates. This is especially the case where expected returns are of interest. As pointed out by Eaker *et al.* (1991): "The problem with including returns in the portfolio selection decision is that such portfolios generally perform poorly in out-of-sample tests." The first wave in the assault on the mean-variance approach can be credited to Jorion (1985, p. 265), who describes the problems emphatically:

> Mean-variance analysis has serious shortcomings which are too often ignored.... Perhaps the most serious defect in the classical (portfolio) approach is the poor out-of-sample performance of the optimal portfolios. Performance measures always deteriorate substantially outside the sample period, and the supposedly optimal choice is sometimes dominated by a naive method.... Another problem is the instability in the optimal portfolio: the proportions allocated to each asset are extremely sensitive to variations in expected returns, and adding a few observations may change the portfolio distribution completely. Also, optimal portfolios are not necessarily well diversified. Often a corner solution appears, where most of the investments are zero and large proportions are assigned to countries with relatively small capital markets and high average returns.

As it turns out, this attack is decidedly overstated. However, the basic point remains: *ex post* estimates of expected returns, based on arithmetic or weighted average estimators, are not reliable estimates of future returns. Relative to estimates of variances and covariances, Jorion (1985), Eun and Resnick (1988), and others have demonstrated that estimates of expected returns are considerably more unstable over time.[11]

Empirically, the parameter instability problem has a number of implications. For example, *ex ante* results concerning the return on a given portfolio may vary significantly from sample to sample. Jorion (1985) examines the out-of-sample performance of the two *ex post* optimal portfolios identified by Grubel (1968) and Levy and Sarnat (1970), together with two "naive" portfolios: the equally weighted and global market-value-weighted portfolios. As measured by the Sharpe ratio, Jorion found that over the next investment horizon, the *ex ante* performance of the two mean-variance efficient portfolios was inferior to the performance of the naive equally weighted portfolio. Jorion (1985) also provides evidence that, in estimating *ex post* returns, longer sampling windows (e.g., 5 years for monthly data) provides superior *ex ante* forecasting when compared with shorter sampling windows (e.g., 1 year of monthly data). The practical difficulty with longer sampling windows is that it takes a longer time interval for the estimates to reacte to changing market conditions.[12]

In addition to the length of the sampling window, the type of estimator also can have a significant impact on the *ex ante* results. In applications, means and variances are estimated from the most recent data available at the time the portfolio is rebalanced. Grauer and Hakansson (1992) provide data on the behavior of the mean-variance efficient portfolio over time, using quarterly

---

[11]Various other writers (e.g., Maldonado and Saunders, 1981) have demonstrated the instability of intercountry correlations for periods longer than two quarters.

[12]Such is the reason for using moving sampling windows instead of using all the data available. For example, 100 years of monthly data produces estimates of the arithmetic average that would not be affected by an additional observation, hence, the optimal weights would not change over time.

rebalancing of the portfolio based on the most recent 40 quarters of data. The investment universe includes U.S. equities and bonds, seven non-U.S. equities (Canada, Japan, United Kingdom, Switzerland, Netherlands, Germany, and France). The simulations try four different methods of estimating the mean and provide results over a wide range of possible investor preferences. Their results indicate the importance of mean return estimation to portfolio composition. When simple historical averages are used, the average portfolio contains three risky assets or less for the "typical" range of investor preferences. When the capital asset pricing model (CAPM) is used, eight to the maximum possible ten risky assets are common in the average portfolio.

In addition to the estimation method used to determine the relevant parameter inputs, the presence or absence of short selling has been found to be fundamental in assessing the performance of mean-variance efficient portfolios. Even though the early studies implicitly assumed short selling was not permitted, at least since Jorion (1985) it has been recognized that odd results can be obtained when short selling is permitted. For example, Jorion reports results for the time-series properties of the optimal weight on domestic assets in the *ex post* tangency portfolio. A considerable amount of short selling is indicated at various times, as much as -2.4 times the total principal value of the portfolio at one point in 1978. For many types of investment situations (e.g., pension funds or life insurance companies), this amount of short selling would be unacceptable and unobtainable. Evidence on portfolio composition with short-selling restrictions (e.g., Glen and Jorion, 1993) indicates that a dramatic narrowing of the number of assets held in the portfolio is likely, amplifying the concentration of a given portfolio in a small number of assets.

D. EUN AND RESNICK (1994)[13]

Almost a decade after Jorion (1985), issues surrounding the difficulties of diversifying internationally were examined in Eun and Resnick (1994), who provide a detailed examination of the *ex ante* performance of three mean-variance efficient portfolios derived from the Markowitz framework: the tangency portfolio, the minimum-variance portfolio, and the Bayes–Stein portfolio. Allowing short sales, Eun and Resnick (1994) consider an impressive number of variations on the basic optimization model. Three different types of asset groups are used to form portfolios: stocks only, bonds only, and combinations of stocks and bonds. Both hedged and unhedged returns are examined. In

[13]The work of Eun and Resnick (1994) is not without shortcomings. For example, risk-free interest rates are set to zero (p. 148) and there seems to have been problems in identifying some of the *ex ante* optimal tangency portfolios for 7 of the 36 months in the U.S. sample (p. 149).

addition, two different reference currencies are used to denominate returns: U.S. and Japanese. Over the *ex post* sample period, Japan was a high-return country and the U.S. was a low-return country. The returns from seven countries are included: Canada, France, Germany, Japan, Switzerland, United Kingdom and the United States. Results on the decomposition of var[$R_\$$] for each of these countries, over the sample, have been given in Tables 6.14 and 6.15.

After providing summary statistics for the securities involved, Eun and Resnick report the *ex post* optimal weights derived for the *tangency portfolio* derived from a sample of monthly returns covering 1978–1989 (see Table 6.18). Results are reported for both U.S. and yen denominated returns. Observing that in the table ME = mean, SD = standard deviation, and SHP = Sharpe ratio, a number of interesting results emerge. For U.S. investors, both the bond and stock portfolios reflect the full benefits of international diversification. There is a reduction in portfolio return volatilty *and* an increase in expected returns. The combined stock/bond portfolio does exhibit an increased volatility but this is offset by the higher expected return. Examining the specific weights, a definite home-country bias is observed, with the positive weight on the domestic asset being significantly larger than weights for other countries. There is also evidence of significant short selling, with

TABLE 6.18   *Ex Post* Optimal International Portfolios 1978–1989

	U.S. perspective			Japanese perspective		
Market	Bond portfolio	Stock portfolio	Bond/stock portfolio	Bond portfolio	Stock portfolio	Bond/stock portfolio
Canada	0.0218	−0.0579	−0.0764/0.0009	−0.0255	−0.0956	−0.0499/−0.0079
France	0.4488	0.0509	0.2379/0.0245	0.2392	0.1165	0.1531/0.0145
Germany	0.0204	0.0550	0.1747/−0.0177	−0.1294	−0.0170	−0.0905/0.0139
Japan	0.2838	0.3945	−0.1278/0.3650	0.8064	0.6700	0.6049/0.1896
Switzerland	−0.4896	0.0006	−0.3988/0.0500	−0.0483	0.1252	−0.0301/0.0428
United Kingdom	0.0895	0.0770	−0.0055/0.0836	0.0319	0.1011	−0.0032/0.0349
United States	0.6254	0.4792	0.5145/0.1752	0.1257	0.0998	0.0930/0.0348
ME	1.06%	1.72%	1.59%	0.61%	1.55%	0.89%
SD	3.15%	4.19%	3.49%	1.51%	3.65%	1.68%
SHP	0.34	0.41	0.46	0.41	0.42	0.53
Domestic strategy[a]						
ME	0.86%	1.34%	1.10%	0.61%	1.66%	1.14%
SD	3.20%	4.60%	3.20%	1.74%	4.41%	2.57%
SHP	0.27	0.29	0.34	0.35	0.38	0.44

[a]For the domestic strategy, the bond/stock portfolio consists of domestic bond and stock indices, with 50% weight each.
ME is the mean; SD is the standard deviation; SHP is the Sharpe ratio. ME and SD are expressed as monthly returns.
Source: Eun and Resnick (1994), with permission.

the negative weight on the Swiss being particularly noticeable (e.g., a short position equal to about half the initial principal value being indicated for the bond-only portfolio).

The results for the *ex post* optimal portfolios using returns denominated in Japanese yen are also revealing. Again, there is a decided home-country bias, only in this case Japanese investors desire Japanese assets. This can be explained by observing that investing in domestic assets allows domestic investors to avoid the exchange risk.[14] This evidence calls into question the hypothesis that an optimal diversified international portfolio will be the same, regardless of the currency of denomination. However, unlike the U.S. case, where including international assets resulted in an increase in portfolio expected returns, international diversification only produced a reduction in portfolio return volatility. For both the stock and stock/bond portfolios, Japanese investors had a reduction in portfolio return. The increase in the Sharpe ratio was due to the substantial reduction in return volatility.

While interesting, the *ex post* results only confirm what is available in a number of sources. Eun and Resnick (1994) also examined the *ex ante* performance of the mean-variance optimal portfolios for the 3 years, 1990–1992. The optimization exercise is conventional. Each month the relevant means, variance, and covariances are estimated using the 60 most recent observations. The portfolio weights are determined and the portfolio is held for one month, at which point the parameters are re-estimated and the optimal portfolios determined. This continues for 3 years, at which point the *ex ante* returns are calculated. The naive benchmarks selected to compare the performance are an equally weighted portfolio and the domestic-only portfolio. Two types of results are reported: the average portfolio weights and the *ex ante* performance results (see Tables 6.19 and 6.20). Both the results are revealing and require close inspection.

Examining the average weights for an unhedged U.S. portfolio reported by Eun and Resnick (but not reported here) indicates disturbing behavior for the weights in the tangency portfolio. Several of the weights, particularly on the Swiss, French, and German bonds in the stock/bond portfolio, indicate average weights well in excess of invested principal. The −4.75 *average* weight on Swiss bonds is almost frightening. The contrast with the minimum variance and Bayes–Stein portfolios is evident. For these portfolios, only the Swiss securities in the stock/bond Bayes–Stein portfolio have weights in excess of one. As expected, the minimum-variance portfolio typically has the smallest weights. Evidence of a home-country bias is apparent for all the mean-variance optimal portfolios. Examining the weights associated with the hedged portfolios reveals some dramatic changes. The largest weight for any

---

[14]Coval and Moskovitz (1999) propose an alternative explanation for the home-country bias.

TABLE 6.19   Average Out-of-Sample Performance Results of the *Ex Ante* Investment Strategies: United States[a]

		Bonds	Stocks	Bonds and stocks
Unhedged				
CET	ME (%)	1.50	1.65	6.74
	SD (%)	6.48	4.98	21.10
	SHP	0.32	0.37	0.31
MVP	ME (%)	1.20	1.86	2.23
	SD (%)	2.61	4.38	4.71
	SHP	0.40	0.51	0.41
EOW	ME (%)	1.29	2.07	1.68
	SD (%)	3.07	4.40	3.08
	SHP	0.41	0.55	0.54
BST	ME (%)	1.33	1.80	3.77
	SD (%)	3.92	4.46	14.68
	SHP	0.37	0.48	0.35
US	ME (%)	0.91	1.32	1.11
	SD (%)	2.67	4.84	3.14
	SHP	0.31	0.33	0.36
Hedged				
CET	ME (%)	0.78	1.77	0.88
	SD (%)	1.09	4.78	1.27
	SHP	0.74	0.49	0.72
MVP	ME (%)	0.73	1.72	0.86
	SD (%)	0.90	4.39	1.12
	SHP	0.87	0.51	0.81
EOW	ME (%)	0.83	1.60	1.21
	SD (%)	1.37	4.24	2.37
	SHP	0.63	0.53	0.60
BST	ME (%)	0.75	1.79	0.90
	SD (%)	1.05	4.58	1.21
	SHP	0.75	0.51	0.79

[a]In each cell, the three numbers represent the average of 29 out-of-sample values.

CET is the tangency portfolio; MVP is the minimum variance portfolio; BST is the Bayes-Stein portfolio, ME and SD expressed as monthly returns. US is the domestic return. See notes to Table 6.18.
Source: Eun and Resnick (1994), with permission.

asset is a .77 weighting on Swiss bonds in the stock/bond minimum-variance case. The tangency portfolio weights now appear to be similar to the weights in the other two portfolios. The home-country bias disappears, to be replaced by a Swiss bias. This is strong evidence of the impact that hedging has on the results of international diversification. The average weights for the Japanese

TABLE 6.20   Average Out-of-Sample Performance Results of the *Ex Ante* Investment Strategies: Japan[a]

		Bonds	Stocks	Bonds and stocks
Unhedged				
CET	ME (%)	0.92	1.34	1.15
	SD (%)	1.95	4.57	2.66
	SHP	0.53	0.35	0.46
MVP	ME (%)	0.65	1.53	0.93
	SD (%)	1.47	4.21	2.00
	SHP	0.53	0.47	0.51
EOW	ME (%)	0.37	1.18	0.78
	SD (%)	2.14	4.38	2.87
	SHP	0.17	0.37	0.32
BST	ME (%)	0.78	1.48	1.07
	SD (%)	1.59	4.21	2.13
	SHP	0.59	0.45	0.54
JA	ME (%)	0.75	2.18	1.46
	SD (%)	1.64	5.24	2.97
	SHP	0.59	0.44	0.52
Hedged				
CET	ME (%)	0.59	1.28	0.64
	SD (%)	1.28	5.83	3.81
	SHP	0.49	0.26	0.21
MVP	ME (%)	0.52	1.81	0.14
	SD (%)	0.89	5.30	4.76
	SHP	0.64	0.40	0.04
EOW	ME (%)	0.67	1.89	1.04
	SD (%)	1.33	5.40	3.24
	SHP	0.52	0.43	0.38
BST	ME (%)	0.04	1.45	0.44
	SD (%)	4.85	5.52	4.47
	SHP	0.06	0.30	0.14

[a]In each cell, the three numbers represent the average of 36 out-of-sample values.
JA is the Japanese domestic return. See notes to Table 6.19.
Source: Eun and Resnick (1994), with permission.

returns are somewhat confounding. The large weights on certain assets in the unhedged tangency case have disappeared, being replaced by a strong home-country bias. No weights in excess of one are reported, and there is not much difference between the weights for the different portfolios. Examining the hedged results again reveals the domestic bias being replaced by a Swiss bias, albeit not as dramatic a reduction in the home-country weights as in the U.S. case.

The final and most important results reported by Eun and Resnick are associated with the *ex ante* performance results. The monthly unhedged U.S. returns in Table 6.19 indicate, for bonds, that the naive equally weighted portfolio had the best Sharpe ratio, followed closely by the minimum variance portfolio. The tangency portfolio, which financial theory suggests will have the best performance, outperforms only the domestic-only portfolio, though the tangency portfolio did report the highest return. There is a similar story for stocks, albeit with the tangency portfolio now reporting a mean return that is higher than only the domestic-only strategy. The results for the combined portfolio are dramatic. Despite having a mean value that is huge, the Sharpe ratio ranks the tangency portfolio dead last in performance. The hedged results repeat this general story. For bonds and stock/bonds, the minimum variance portfolio has the highest Sharpe ratio, with the naive equally weighted portfolio having the best performance for stocks. The tangency portfolio is either last or second to last in all cases. The weakness of the mean returns for the tangency portfolio indirectly indicates the difficulty of using *ex post* estimates of returns to achieve *ex ante* results.

The *ex ante* Japanese results in Table 6.20 repeat this general story, with some provisos. For the unhedged results, the equally weighted naive portfolio, which had such good performance in the U.S. case, now does poorly. The performance of the Bayes–Stein portfolio improves considerably, with minimum variance continuing a strong relative showing. In the stock case, for example, minimum variance has both a higher mean and lower volatility than the tangency portfolio. Compared to the U.S. case, there is a strong performance by the domestic Japanese portfolios. The unhedged case is somewhat confounding. Despite having the highest Sharpe ratio for bonds and second highest for stock, the reported result for the minimum variance bond/stock portfolio gives the appearance of a typographical error. The upshot of all these results is that the Markowitz model, which holds so much promise from a theoretical standpoint, may have serious difficulties in delivering an *ex ante* performance consistent with the *ex post* predictions.

Recognizing the connection to the results of Chapter 2, Section I, the apparently poor *ex ante* performance of the tangency portfolio, relative to the minimum-variance portfolio, can be attributed to the poor forecasting performance of the arithmetic averages in predicting actual returns. This poor *ex ante* performance is happening despite the use of foreign markets that have relatively high correlation with each other. Introducing emerging markets almost certainly would confound the Markowitz optimization procedure. An inspection of world stock market performance for 1996 (Table 6.21) reveals the extreme return distributions that occur when emerging markets are considered. A number of the countries in the top 10 could be found in the bottom 10 in the previous year. As Chapter 2, Section I,

TABLE 6.21   World Stock Market Performance, 1996[a]

Rank	Market	% change in price index	Rank	Market	% change in price index
1	Bangladesh*	196.0	45	Trinidad & Tobago*	10.9
2	Russia*	155.9	46	Italy	10.8
3	Venezuela*	131.8	47	Swaziland	9.9
4	Hangary*	94.6	48	Belgium	8.8
5	China*	89.4	49	Colo d'Ivoire*	5.3
6	Lithuania*	82.0	50	Colombia*	4.5
7	Poland*	71.1	51	Austria	3.2
8	Paraguay	59.9	52	Slovenia*	2.6
9	Zimbabwe*	59.6	53	Malta	1.2
10	Nigeria*	55.6	54	Swltzerland	1.2
11	Iran	52.7	55	Peru*	0.7
12	Turkey*	42.4	56	Kyrgyz Republic	0.3
13	Jamaica*	39.8	57	Greece*	−1.0
14	Egypt*	38.8	58	Barbados	−3.1
15	Morocco*	38.4	59	India*	−3.5
16	Spain	36.5	60	Jordan*	−3.6
17	Costa Rica	36.3	61	Israel	−5.4
18	Taiwan, China*	36.1	62	Tunisia*	−6.5
19	Namibia	36.0	63	Mauritius*	−6.9
20	Sweden	35.4	64	Singapore	−8.0
21	Finland	31.7	65	Kenya*	−9.9
22	Brazil*	30.4	66	Sri Lanka*	−14.0
23	Hong Kong	28.9	67	Ecuador*	−15.2
24	Ireland	28.8	68	Japan	−16.0
25	Norway	26.8	69	Chile*	−17.2
26	Canada	26.4	70	South Africa*	−19.2
27	Oman	26.1	71	Bolswana*	−20.3
28	Panama	24.9	72	Ghana*	−21.4
29	Portugal*	24.9	73	Pakistan*	−21.8
30	Netherlands	24.5	74	Thailand*	−38.1
31	U.K.	23.3	75	Korea*	−39.2
32	Malaysia*	22.9	76	Bulgaria*	−83.0
33	USA	21.4			
34	Denmark	20.0	*Regional indexes*		
35	Czech Republic*	20.0	1	IPCG Latin America	16.0
36	France	19.4	2	IFCI Latin America	14.0
37	Philippines*	19.1	3	MSCI World	11.7
38	Argentina*	18.8	4	IFCI Asia	8.9
39	Indonesia*	18.0	5	IFCI Composite	7.0
40	Mexico*	16.2	6	IFCG Composite	5.8
41	Slovakia*	15.7	7	MSCI EAFE	4.4
42	New Zealand	13.5	8	IFCG Asia	4.2
43	Australia	13.4	9	FT/S&P, Europac	3.6
44	Germany	12.1	10	IFCI EMEA	−5.2

[a]Ranked by 1996 percent change in price indexes in US$.

Notes: Markets marked by an asterisk indicate IFC Global Index as source; developed market returns are from Morgan Stanley Capital Markets International.

Source: International Financing Corporation, *Emerging Markets Factbook*, 1997.

demonstrated, if the firm is unable to accurately forecast the future expected return, then the rational procedure is to use the minimum-variance weights gaining risk reduction benefits without "speculating" on forecasts of expected returns. Based on the results provided by Eun and Resnick, this intuition seems to work well empirically.

E. THE CAPM AND INTERNATIONAL DIVERSIFICATION

The CAPM is a central paradigm of modern finance. This *ex ante* model can be stated as:

$$E[R_j] = r + \beta_j[E[R_M] - r]$$

where $E[R_j]$ is the expected return on asset j; $E[R_M]$ is the expected return on the closed economy market portfolio; $\beta_j = (\text{cov}[R_j, R_M]/\text{var}[R_M])$; and R_F is the risk-free rate of interest. Among other uses, the CAPM provides a methodology for estimating discount rates to be used in capital budgeting problems and the like. The CAPM also implies an investment strategy for rational investors. More precisely, if the CAPM is true, it follows that the tangency portfolio associated with the capital market line is the market portfolio. Operationally, this two-fund separation theorem requires that the rational investor hold portfolios composed of the riskless asset and the market portfolio. Risk-averse investors will be net long the riskless asset and the market portfolio while high levels of risk tolerance would permit leveraging (i.e., borrowing by shorting the riskless asset in order to leverage the position in the market portfolio). This powerful and persuasive *ex ante* investment philosophy is confounded by the observation that diversification using international and domestic assets will shift the efficient frontier upward when compared with diversification using only domestic assets, as in Graph 6.1. Various problems arise immediately concerning specification of the global market portfolio, the riskless asset, and how currency risk will be handled.

The difficulties that have been identified with operationalizing the Markowitz mean-variance model lend considerable support to efforts to generalize the CAPM, which is typically derived under closed-economy assumptions. Various approaches can be taken to generalizing to the international context. The particular approach selected depends on a key assumption about the handling of exchange-rate risk. Solnik (1974) and Sercu (1980) assume that exchange risk is unhedged. It is observed that the international CAPM is unlike the closed-economy CAPM, where systematic risk is related to the relationship between the individual asset returns and the market return, with appropriate adjustment for the riskless rate of return. In the international case, there is an additional risk dimension associated with the exchange rate. The additional risk is captured by modeling the return on the exchange rate using a "pure exchange risk asset." For a non-U.S. investor, the pure exchange risk asset is the U.S. T-bill.[15] In addition, the return on the domestic market portfolio is replaced by the global market portfolio.

Using * to denote the foreign (U.S.) rate, it follows that the domestic risk-free rate r can be expressed as $r = r^* + e$. As before, the cross-product term has been ignored for simplicity. Using a replicating portfolio argument, Uppal and Sercu (1995) are able to derive the international CAPM as:

$$E[R_j] = r + \beta_j(E[R_W] - r) + \gamma_j(r^* + e - r)$$

where $E[R_W]$ is the expected return on the world market portfolio, and $\gamma_j = \text{cov}[R_j, e]/\text{var}[e]$. If $\gamma_j = 0$, then the international CAPM reduces to a variation of the closed-economy CAPM, albeit with the global market portfolio replacing the domestic market portfolio. Yet, this presentation is constructed with a two-country format (e.g., the domestic asset/foreign asset portfolio encountered previously). Where there are $n + 1$ countries, then there would be n exchange rate γs to estimate, all of which would have to equal zero in order to reduce the international CAPM to the closed-economy CAPM. In practice, this model extends the bivariate regression of the closed-economy CAPM to a multivariate regression involving exchange rates and the market portfolio.

The international CAPM represents a substantive theoretical extension of the closed-economy model. Whether this theoretical contribution translates into improved empirical performance is, at present, an open question. The difficulties inherent in estimating *ex ante* asset pricing models are well known, and it will be difficult to resolve the validity of the closed- or open-economy version.[16] Nevertheless, the questions involved are fundamental and require attention. In particular, are assets priced in domestic markets or in international markets? By estimating βs using the domestic market index, the convention is to assume a closed economy model. This approach avoids the problem of specifying the world market portfolio, a seeming quandary for the international CAPM. This and other difficulties associated with implementing the international model have meant that the international CAPM has

---

[15]The use of the T-bill to model the riskless asset is a common convention in presentations of the closed-economy CAPM. This selection embeds an underlying assumption about the investment process driving the rational investor. In particular, the riskless asset is required to have no default risk or price risk. If the investor does rebalancing at regular 3-month intervals, then the purchase of a 3-month T-bill will represent a riskless return over that interval. If the rebalancing period is annual, then a 1-year T-bill is needed, and so on.

[16]Many of the difficulties associated with estimating the closed-economy CAPM have been gathered under the heading of Roll's critique (Roll, 1978).

received surprisingly little attention in empirical studies (e.g., Uppal and Sercu, 1995, pp. 607–608).

Why is the specification of the global market portfolio a quandary for the international CAPM? Consider the case of a Dutch investor. Extending the approach of specifying the closed-economy market portfolio, presumably the world market portfolio would be a value-weighted portfolio of the world's capital assets, which is proxied by a value-weighted world equity portfolio. Though the precise value weights would depend on valuations at a specific point in time, at present such a portfolio would be more than 60% in U.S. equities, with a further 15–20% in Japanese equities. The Dutch component in such a global index would be negligible. Hence, the international CAPM dictates that the expected return on a Dutch capital asset (e.g., an equity security), will be determined by the expected return on a world market portfolio that is not capable of capturing the Dutch country-specific risk. In effect, country-specific risk, outside of pure exchange-rate risk, will not be priced. This puts considerable pressure on international capital flows to equalize returns across countries. The upshot is that the international CAPM lacks the intuitive appeal needed for practical applications.

Another approach to specifying an international CAPM is suggested by extending the Arrow–Debreu theorem, a fundamental result from microeconomics about the Pareto optimality of a perfect market economy under uncertainty. This theorem requires complete markets: a traded security for each source of uncertainty. The resolution of uncertainty is provided by market participants hedging the uncertainty using the traded contingent claims. Given this, there is also considerable empirical evidence in favor of fully hedged versus unhedged portfolios in specifying the international CAPM. Early research on this issue by Madura and Reiff (1985) demonstrates that, *ex post*, efficient frontiers of fully hedged portfolios dominate unhedged portfolios.

Tables 6.19 and 6.20, from Eun and Resnick (1994), provide empirical results on the *ex ante* performance of hedged and unhedged portfolios. For US\$ returns, hedged portfolios dominate unhedged portfolios for bonds. This confirms similar results found in Glen and Jorion (1993). Yet, for yen returns, the *ex ante* results are ambiguous. It is not possible to determine whether hedged or unhedged portfolios are superior. This incongruity in results seems to be due primarily to the differing performance of hedge profitability. For both reference currencies, *ex ante* unhedged returns are found to be generally higher than hedged returns, as reflected in the spreads between the mean returns for the hedged and unhedged portfolios for the two reference currencies. Yet, the Sharpe ratio gains seem to originate primarily from the reduction in return volatility.

The results for bonds do not carry forward to stock portfolios or stock/bond portfolios. If anything, for yen returns unhedged portfolios of stocks generally outperformed hedged portfolios. Results for stock portfolios using US$ returns are ambiguous. There is little difference either in the mean returns or the Sharpe ratios. Eun and Resnick (1994, p. 149) also make an insightful if unexplored observation about the *ex ante* results:

> The portfolio weight vectors under hedging for U.S. and Japanese investors look remarkably similar for all asset classes. The reason for this is that regardless of which numeraire currency is used, a particular hedging strategy will identify a similar *ex ante* optimal investment weight vector to the extent that the forward premiums or discounts are small relative to the local currency mean returns.

Glen and Jorion (1993) use a variation on this result to design conditional hedging strategies based on the forward premium that can capture a significant increase in *ex ante* portfolio performance.

As initially conceived, the benefits of diversification were related to unhedged portfolios of securities, the rationale being that hedging would be redundant. If enough currencies were included, all sources of country-specific currency risk would be diversified away, leaving only the systematic currency component. However, a number of authors have argued that hedged portfolios may be a more appropriate method of capturing the full benefits of diversification (e.g., Perold and Schulman, 1988; Fosburg and Madura, 1991; Eaker *et al.*, 1991; Filatov and Rappoport, 1992; Adler and Jorion, 1992). Others have argued against holding specific securities such as hedged foreign bonds (e.g., Burik and Ennis, 1990).[17] On balance, though considerable insight has been achieved, at this point the issues surrounding the appropriate method of implementing mean-variance efficient international portfolio diversification are still largely unresolved.

IV. CURRENCY SWAPS AND FULLY HEDGED BORROWING

A. HISTORY OF CURRENCY SWAP TRADING

The history of currency swap trading is difficult to trace, if only because it is difficult to identify precisely when swap trading began. In a sense, swap trading is inherent in the activities of all financial intermediaries. For example, when a Singapore customer enters a local bank and purchases a Canadian dollar (C$) term deposit, a current cash flow (S$) is being exchanged for a

---

[17]Others such as Levy and Lerman (1988) take the opposite view, arguing in favor of stock/ bond portfolios composed largely of foreign bonds (West German for their 1960–80 data). The Levy and Lerman results also indicate mean-variance efficient portfolios that are heavily concentrated in a small number of risky assets, with many asset groups not held.

future cash flow, the return of principal and interest at maturity that depends on the future value of the C$. This type of transaction has ancient roots. One example is the 16th-century bill of exchange. This security involved the payment (receipt) of cash in one geographical location for return (payment) of principal plus interest to be paid in another geographical location in the currency of that location. In modern parlance, this transaction is a zero-coupon currency swap or a short-dated foreign exchange swap. Such contracts reach back to antiquity; for example, there are laws regarding bills of exchange to be found in the Code of Hammurabi. Such contracts were actively traded on the 16th-century Antwerp bourse (e.g., de Roover, 1948).

Numerous modern writers date the beginning of swap trading to the mid-1970s for interest rate swaps and the early 1980s for currency swaps. This historical interpretation is based on a subtle change in the definition of a swap transaction, narrowing the focus to derivative contracts that are bundles of spot and forward exchange contracts. Swaps, such as those traded in the short-dated foreign exchange market, would not be included under this modern swap definition. Such zero-coupon, currency swap contracts will be referred to as foreign exchange swaps, as opposed to currency swaps, to avoid semantic confusion. Under this historical interpretation, currency swap financing evolved from the shortcomings associated with parallel and back-to-back loans (e.g., Price and Henderson, 1988; Antl, 1986). While a number of proprietary currency swap deals were done prior to 1981, the first widely publicized deal was a currency swap between IBM and the World Bank. Among other factors, currency swaps were an important legal advance over parallel and back-to-back loans that are governed by securities law, in which default provisions are unclear. Swaps fall within the realm of contract law, in which default provisions are more straightforward.

While initially motivated by security and accounting difficulties arising from borrowing in different currencies, by the early 1980s it was widely recognized that currency swaps could be used for numerous purposes. With the growth of swap financing, intermediaries have been willing to take initially unmatched (i.e., dealer), swap positions. The result has been a liquid market where various types of currency swap quotes are available on a regular basis. In turn, this has permitted increasingly sophisticated swap trades to be executed, while at the same time requiring techniques for hedging the temporary dealer swap risk to be "engineered." To facilitate the standardization of swap terms, the International Swap and Derivatives Association (ISDA, formerly the International Swap Dealers Association) has been formed by the major players.

To facilitate the increased liquidity in the currency swap market, the ISDA provided a uniform set of definitions and contracts to standardize swap trading. From these early beginnings, the growth of swap trading, particularly for interest rate swaps, has been phenomenal. Examining Table 6.22, one can see that there were over US\$22 trillion in notional principal of outstanding interest swaps and US\$1.8 trillion in currency swaps. The use of notional principal is somewhat misleading, as the actual cash flows are dramatically less, especially for interest rate swaps, where there is usually no exchange of principal at initiation and maturity. Table 6.23 indicates that the interest rate swap activity was not concentrated solely in US\$. The relative importance of interest rate swaps compared to currency swaps and the "building block" character of many actual swap transactions dictate that the mechanics of interest rate swaps get some attention, in addition to examining currency swaps.

B. The Mechanics of Swap Trading

While numerous variations on swap contracts are possible (e.g., Beidleman, 1992; Das, 1994), the basic principle of a swap is an exchange of cash flows that are deemed to be equal in value at the time the swap is initiated. Given this prerequisite, two basic types of "plain vanilla" swaps are available (Abken, 1991): currency swaps and interest rate swaps.[18] In an interest rate swap, the net cash flows being exchanged are based on fixed and floating interest rate borrowings. One borrower issues fixed-rate debt and exchanges the resulting periodic net debt payments with another borrower issuing floating-rate debt. A currency swap involves exchanging net cash flows arising from debt issues denominated in different currencies. Principal values are exchanged at initiation and maturity, with both these cash flows, together with the periodic payments, being valued at the spot exchange rate prevailing at the time the swap was initiated. In "building block" fashion, these basic types of swaps are often combined in practical applications, resulting in an exchange of borrowings in different currencies that can involve either fixed or floating interest rates.

Exhibits 6.1–6.4, provide an illustration of the mechanics of a "plain vanilla" interest rate swap. The situation being described is stylized and is not meant to capture all the various rationales for doing an interest rate swap. Exhibit 6.1 describes the initial situation: There are two financial institutions with a duration gap mismatch. Counterparty A has an asset portfolio

---

[18]Various developments and combinations on these general types of swaps, not considered here, are possible, e.g., cross-currency floating-to-floating interest rate. Antl (1986), Price and Henderson (1988), Beidleman (1992), and Das (1994) provide more in-depth discussion of the various types. Swap trading techniques can be used in asset. as well as liability, management, e.g., by combining a domestic fixed-rate bond purchase with a swap. In addition, various combinations of swaps can be combined to "complete" a given, intermediated transaction.

TABLE 6.22 Currency and Interest Rate Swaps: Annual Activity and Outstanding (US$ billions of notional principal)

Year ending	Interest rate swaps		Currency swaps		Interest rate options		Totals	
	Activity	Outstandings	Activity	Outstandings	Activity	Outstandings	Activity	Outstandings
1987	$387.8	$682.80	$85.8	$182.80			$473.6	$865.6
1988	568.1	1,010.20	122.6	316.80		$327.30	690.7	1,654.3
1989	833.6	1,502.60	169.6	434.80	$335.5	537.30	1,338.7	2,477.7
1990	1,264.3	2,311.50	212.7	577.50	292.3	561.30	1,769.3	3,450.3
1991	1,621.8	3,065.10	328.4	807.20	382.7	577.20	2,332.9	4,449.5
1992	2,822.6	3,850.80	301.9	860.40	592.4	634.50	3,716.9	5,345.7
1993	4,104.6	6,177.30	295.2	899.60	1,117.0	1,397.60	5,516.8	8,474.5
1994	6,240.9	8,815.60	379.3	914.80	1,513.2	1,572.80	8,133.4	11,303.2
1995	8,698.8	12,810.70	454.1	1,197.40	2,015.4	3,704.50	11,169.3	17,712.6
1996	13,678.2	19,170.90	759.1	1,559.60	3,337.2	4,722.60	17,774.5	25,453.1
1997	17,067.1	22,291.30	1,135.4	1,823.60	3,978.4	4,920.10	22,180.9	29,035.0
1998								50,997.0
1999								58,265.0
2000								63,009.0

Sources: Compiled from International Swap and Derivatives Association website (www.isda.org) and Bank for International Settlements website (www.bis.org).

TABLE 6.23　Notional Principal of Interest Rate Swaps by Currency and Category[a]

Currency	June 1999	June 2000	June 2001
Euro	17,483	22,948	22,405
Japanese Yen	10,207	12,763	11,278
Pound Sterling	4,398	4,741	5,178
US dollar	16,073	17,606	23,083
Other	5,911	6,067	5,521
Total Contracts	54,072	64,125	67,465
Category			
Counterparty			
With reporting dealers	27,065	32,208	32,319
With other financial institutions	21,149	25,771	28,653
With nonfinancial costumers	5,863	6,146	6,494
Forward rate agreements	7,137	6,771	6,537
With reporting dealers	3,769	3,556	3,310
With other financial institutions	2,630	2,849	2,484
With nonfinancial costumers	739	356	743
Swaps	38,372	47,993	51,407
With reporting dealers	20,080	24,803	24,907
With other financial institutions	14,463	18,875	22,037
With nonfinancial costumers	3,828	4,315	4,463
Options	8,562	9,476	9,521
With reporting dealers	3,210	4,012	4,102
With other financial institutions	4,056	4,066	4,132
With nonfinancial costumers	1,296	1,399	1,288

[a]Billions of U.S. dollars.

Source: Bank for International Settlements Quarterly Review, December 2001, pg. 91.

composed of fixed-rate mortgages with a duration of 8 years and paying a fixed-rate cash flow of 6.25%. Counterparty B has an asset portfolio composed of floating-rate commercial loans, paying prime rate which resets every 3 months (on average). Against these assets, A has floating-rate liabilities arising from a program of rolling 3 month CDs while B has a 10-year fixed-rate liability of 7% from a fixed coupon Eurobond issue. Par values of all the assets and liabilities are equal. The duration gap for both counterparties is apparent. A has mismatch between the longer duration cash flow of assets and the shorter duration of the liability cash flow. B is facing the opposite situation.

As indicated in Exhibits 6.2–6.3, Swap Dealer is able to step into this situation and resolve the duration gap mismatch by providing an interest rate swap to both parties. This step captures two essential features of a

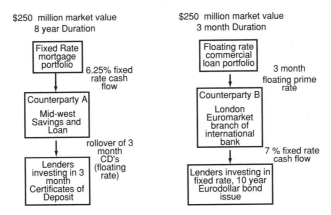

EXHIBIT 6.1   Initial situation confronting the counterparties to the interest rate swap.

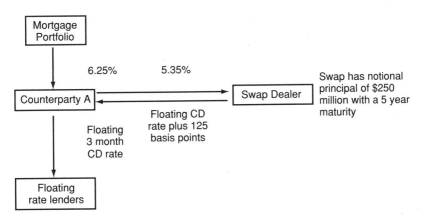

EXHIBIT 6.2   Counterparty A's interest rate swap agreement with Swap Dealer.

"plain vanilla" interest swap: The transactions are intermediated by a swap broker or dealer and there is no initial exchange of cash flows; the "plain vanilla" interest rate swap only involves (net) payments of the periodic coupons. Subject to certain arbitrage restrictions, the fixed-to-floating/floating-to-fixed rates at which the swap is initiated, together with the

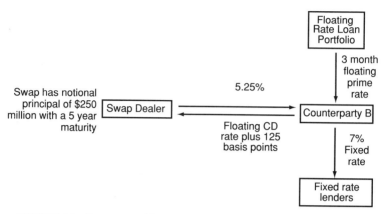

EXHIBIT 6.3   Counterparty B's interest rate swap agreement with Swap Dealer.

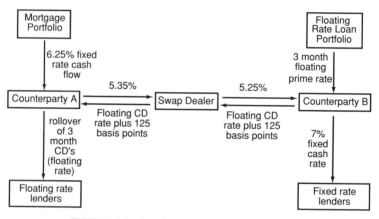

EXHIBIT 6.4   Complete interest rate Swap Structure.

intermediary's margin, will be determined by market conditions. In the example, the intermediary is quoting a 5 year fixed-to-floating swap of 5.35% in exchange for a 3 month floating CD rate plus 125 basic points (bp) with a floating-to-fixed swap quoted as the same floating rate in exchange for 5.25%.

The benefits of the swap to *A* are apparent. *A* will receive 6.25% on the asset portfolio and pay 5.35% to the intermediary and receive the floating rate payment with which A is able to satisfy the liability cash-flow requirement. A has gone from a situation where end-of-period cash flows were uncertain, with a downside risk that CD rates would move up, to a situation where there is a locked-in spread of 215 basis points: $(6.25 - 5.35) - CD + (CD + 125\,bp) = 215$ basis points. In contrast to A, counterparty B has to absorb basis risk, making the final outcome of the swap uncertain. B has assets with a floating interest rate tied to the commercial prime rate. The swap only provides a floating rate payment based on the CD rate. Hence, B has to absorb the credit risk associated with changes in the difference between CD and prime rates. At the time the swap was initiated, the prime rate was 7.25% and the CD rate 3.40%, a basis of 385 basis points. Assuming this basis does not change over the life of the swap, B will "lock-in" a spread of 85 basis points $= (7.25 - 3.40\%) - 1.25\% - (7.00 - 5.25\%)$. This compares to the somewhat precarious situation confronting B before the swap where a floating rate payment, currently at 7.25%, is being used to fund a liability which requires a payment of 7% fixed. B is seriously exposed to the risk that interest rates on the asset portfolio will fall. A complete picture of the swap structure is depicted in Exhibit 6.4, where it can be observed that Swap Dealer is able to clear 10 basis points at each payment date.

Despite being grouped in the category of swaps, currency swaps are substantively different than interest rate swaps. Figure 6.2 illustrates the transactions involved on one side of a currency swap. The two key features distinguishing currency swaps and interest rate swaps are evident. Unlike interest rate swaps, currency swaps do involve an exchange of principal at initiation and maturity. The textbook objective of a currency swap is to acquire a borrowing in some target currency. As such, the receipt of that currency at the initiation of the swap is required. The other key feature is that the spot exchange rate on the trade-initiation date governs all the cash flows. In effect, the currency swap involves counterparty A borrowing in currency X and counterparty B borrowing in currency Y. Given that the market values of the two borrowings are deemed to be equal on the trade-initiation date, A and B then exchange borrowings. In practice, values are equalized through the market determined currency swap rates, the quoted borrowing rates on the underlying debt issues.

In Fig. 6.2, the fixed-to-fixed currency swap rates involve a 5% yen borrowing being exchanged for a 10% U.S. dollar borrowing. These are the quoted swap rates. As discussed later, unless foreign and domestic interest rate levels are equal (from CIP, this implies $S = F$), these rates will differ from rates observed for (unswapped) borrowings done directly in the domestic and foreign debt markets. At $t = 0$, the transaction is initiated with an exchange of principal, ¥5 billion for US$40 million. This translates to a spot exchange rate of ¥/US$ = 125. At each coupon payment date there is an exchange of

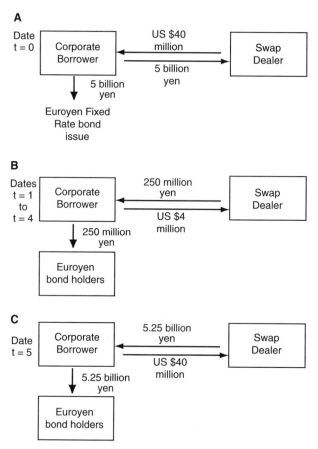

FIGURE 6.2   Illustration of a plain vanilla fixed-to-fixed currency swap. *Scenario:* The borrower seeks to acquire a US$ borrowing and has a funding advantage when borrowing in Japanese yen. The borrower makes a par value, 5 year fixed rate borrowing of 5 billion yen in the Euroyen market bearing an annual coupon of $r_Y = 5\%$. The corporation is then able to exchange the principal of 5 billion with a swap dealer for US$40 million, together with the agreement to make an annual US$ coupon payment of $r_{US} = 10\%$. The implied spot exchange rate used to value the transaction is: (5 billion yen)/ (US$40 million) = 125 yen/US$. (A) Fixed-to-fixed cash flows at the commencement of the currency swap. (B) Fixed-to-fixed cash flows on each of the first four annual coupon payment dates. (C) Fixed-to-fixed cash flows when the swap is completed (principal plus last coupon).

coupons. The trade being described, borrows yen and swaps for US$. Over the life of the swap, this involves receiving yen payments of 5% to offset the yen borrowing. This yen payment inflow is exchanged for a dollar outflow of 10%.

This fixed-to-fixed exchange of cash flows is equal at each payment date, a consequence of $S(0)$ being applied to each cash flow. In practice, coupon payments are usually netted, using the spot exchange rate applicable at the time the coupon payments are being made. At $t = T$, the swap concludes with payment of the final coupon and return of principal.

C. Fully Hedged Borrowings and Currency Swaps

In a fixed-to-fixed currency swap, an agreed-upon (usually spot) foreign exchange rate applicable to the closing date governs the exchange of principal at initiation and maturity, as well as the periodic net interest payments. In turn, the fixed periodic net payments are determined by negotiations, usually based on the interest differential in the different currencies prevailing at the time of closing; i.e., the issuer subject to the highest interest rate will usually receive the net payment. On the other hand, in a fully hedged foreign borrowing, the borrowing is made directly in the target currency and the principal is exchanged into the desired currency at the current spot rate. The resulting (fixed) coupon payments and return of principal are then fully hedged using the currency forward market. In addition to generating a different sequence of cash flows from a currency swap, this type of borrowing also depends on the availability of the appropriate forward exchange quotes.

Ignoring the issue of long-term forward market liquidity, there are often practical benefits to doing currency swaps instead of fully hedged borrowings. For example, in many countries investor preferences favor domestic credits; e.g., in Switzerland or Japan, a well-known domestic corporation is likely to get a significantly lower borrowing rate than, say, a U.S. or Canadian corporation that does not have a substantial international reputation. A similar situation could prevail in reverse in the United States or Canada. In this case, borrowers requiring funding in foreign currency can exploit the borrowing advantage in their domestic market and swap into the desired currency, thereby significantly reducing foreign borrowing costs for both issuers.

A variation of differential credit assessment is differential credit-spread compression. In this case, there are inter-country differences in the short- and long-term borrowing rate spread between strong and weak credits. Such differentials would generate cross-currency swap opportunities. In a fully hedged borrowing, which can be used to acquire either domestic or foreign funds, the "counterparty" is the forward foreign exchange market. Hence, the potential to exploit funding advantages arising from differential credit assessments is only indirectly available (i.e., insofar as these benefits are reflected in long-term forward exchange rates). In the case of a fully hedged (foreign) borrowing to acquire domestic funds, credit assessment may have a negative effect.

In addition to funding advantages arising from differential credit assessments across countries, there are a number of other factors that could favour a currency swap over a fully hedged borrowing. For example, the ability to structure a currency swap as a series of foreign exchange transactions instead of as a foreign borrowing can lead to accounting and taxation advantages, both for the borrower and, particularly in the case of banks, for lenders (e.g., Hull, 1989). Other possible factors favoring a currency swap could include the borrowing corporation wanting to conserve forward exchange lines of credit for other purposes; favorable pricing (i.e., given the borrower's view of future exchange rates and interest rates, in the case of cross-currency interest rate swaps, the swap may be cheaper); and, finally, avoiding regulatory restrictions imposed on overseas borrowings.

To illustrate the fully hedged transaction, consider the following sequence of C\$/US\$ FX rates quoted by the Royal Bank of Canada for August 8, 1994 (see Fig. 4.5):

$$S_0 = 1.3778$$
$$F(0,1) = 1.3960$$
$$F(0,2) = 1.4198$$
$$F(0,3) = 1.4428$$
$$F(0,4) = 1.4633$$
$$F(0,5) = 1.4833$$

where $F(0,T)$ is the long-term forward exchange observed at $t = 0$ for delivery at $t = T$. Assume, for example, that the Canadian borrower raised C\$137,780 using a 5-year fixed-coupon borrowing. When translated at the spot FX rate, the principal value of the borrowing would provide US\$100,000. If the fixed C\$ borrowing had a coupon of, say, 10%, paid annually, then the resulting fully hedged US\$ cash flows would be

$t = 1$: C\$13, 778/1.3960 = US\$9869.63

$t = 2$: C\$13, 778/1.4198 = US\$9704.18

$t = 3$: C\$13, 778/1.4428 = US\$9549.49

$t = 4$: C\$13, 778/1.4633 = US\$9415.70

$t = 5$: (C\$13, 778 + C\$137, 780)/1.4833 = US\$102,176

This sequence of uneven US\$ cash flows can be compared with the US\$ cash flows from the fixed-to-fixed currency swap that would be five *equal* annual coupon payments of (US100, 000) (rs_T^*) each period plus the return of principal of US\$100,000 at maturity where rs_T^* is the fixed interest rate for U.S. payments in the currency swap.

Compared to a fully hedged C\$ borrowing, the currency swap would require lower US\$ cash flows at the beginning, with the difference progressively narrowing to the point where the currency swap cash flows are higher than the fully hedged borrowing, with the highest differential occurring at maturity. The opposite situation would apply for the fully hedged US\$ borrower. Comparing a fully hedged borrowing in US\$ to acquire C\$ with a fixed-to-fixed currency swap out of US\$ and into C\$, the fully hedged borrower would issue fixed-coupon US\$ debt, exchange at the spot exchange rate to acquire C\$, and fully hedge each of the C\$ cash flows required to make payments on the US\$ issue. If the US\$100,000 issue were made at, say, 9.25%, then using the August 8, 1994, long-term foreign exchange (LTFX) rates the cash flows would be[19]

$$t = 1: (US\$9250)(1.3960) = C\$12,913$$
$$t = 2: (US\$9250)(1.4198) = C\$13,133.20$$
$$t = 3: (US\$9250)(1.4428) = C\$13,345.90$$
$$t = 4: (US\$9250)(1.4633) = C\$13,535.50$$
$$t = 5: US\$(100,000 + 9250)(1.4833) = C\$162,051$$

The associated (rs_T C\$ fixed)-to-(rs_T^* US\$ fixed) currency swap would have higher C\$ cash flows at the beginning, narrowing to the point where the currency swap cash flows become lower at maturity.

As before, the perfect markets assumption is retained.[20] It is further assumed that there is no funding advantage for either currency swaps or fully hedged borrowing arising from implicit differences between quoted interest rates on C\$/US\$ swaps, interest rates quoted for direct borrowings in the cash market, or the implied zero-coupon rates associated with LTFX. This *assumption*, that there is *no* funding advantage for either currency swaps or fully hedged borrowings, permits differences in borrowing rates to be analyzed as deviations from

[19]The rate of 9.25% is not necessarily consistent with absence-of-arbitrage for the 10% C\$ offering used in the previous example. Given the sequence of forward exchange rates for different maturities, the precise fixed-coupon US\$ interest rate that is consistent with absence-of-arbitrage will depend on the sequence of spot interest rates in the U.S. and Canadian debt markets, so at this point the arbitrary rate of 9.25% can be chosen without significant loss of intuition.

[20]The perfect markets assumption does suppress some important issues involved in comparing currency swaps and fully hedged borrowings. For example, assuming that transaction costs are zero favors fully hedged borrowing. This is because the currency swap involves only one transaction, while the fully hedged borrowing involves a sequence of forward exchange transactions together with the initial and terminal debt market and foreign exchange transactions. This is an extension of a similar result observed for short-term covered interest parity (e.g., Clinton, 1988).

the equilibrium conditions. For the fully hedged borrowing to acquire US$, the cash flows are denominated in US$ even though the actual debt payments are made in C$. Hence, the fully hedged borrower is providing a sequence of US$ cash flows in exchange for the U.S. dollar value of the borrowing (PUX_0). All cash flows are in US$ and can be discounted using U.S. spot interest rates, appropriately adjusted for credit risk. Because the perfect markets assumption involves no default risk in LTFX and, as before, the relevant default risk associated with the inherent risk of the borrower generating sufficient US$ cash flows (which, due to institutional rigidities, may be different than that of the borrower's ability to generate C$ cash flows) is also ignored.

In a fully hedged borrowing, the bond is issued directly in the Canadian debt market, such that:

$$PC_0 = \sum_{t=1}^{T} \frac{CV}{(1 + r_T)^t} + \frac{MV}{(1 + r_T)^T} = \sum_{t=1}^{T} \frac{CV}{(1 + z_t)^t} + \frac{MV}{(1 + z_T)^T}$$

where $z_t(t = 1,2...T)$ are is the spot interest rate associated with a direct borrowing in the debt market at yield to maturity r_T. For a par bond, $CV = (r_T)(PC_0)$ and $MV = PC_0$. The associated fully hedged US$ cash flows that are used to pay the C$ borrowing are discounted using the US$ spot interest rates (z_t^k) of the fully hedged borrower:

$$\frac{PC_0}{S_0} = PUX_0 = \sum_{t=1}^{T} \frac{[CV/F(0,t)]}{(1 + z_t^*)^t} + \frac{[MV/F(0,T)]}{(1 + z_T^*)^T}$$

The discounting is done with z_t^* because a sequence of US$ cash flows is generating a US$ denominated borrowing unconstrained by the requirement of a specific yield to maturity. By equating the C$ cash flows (CV, MV) for two distinct sets of US$ cash flows and fully covering any unmatched future cash flows, it is possible to derive an absence-of-arbitrage condition under which the fully hedged borrowing and the currency swap will be equivalent. This condition is complicated by forward cover associated with the potential mismatching of the US$ cash flows and the need to adjust principal values at maturity (Poitras, 1999). More expediently, it is also possible to derive a less-complicated *equilibrium* condition connecting fully hedged borrowings and currency swaps that does not fully cover the mismatched cash flows.

Derivation of the main equilibrium condition for LTFX proceeds by dividing the equation for PC_0 by S_0 and equating with the formula for PC_0 which uses spot interest rates. For each $t = 1$ to T it follows:

$$\frac{CV/S_0}{(1 + z_t)^t} = \frac{CV/F(0,t)}{(1 + z_t^*)^t} \quad \Rightarrow \quad F(0,t) = \frac{(1 + z_t)^t}{(1 + z_t^*)^t} S_0$$

This condition must hold in equilibrium because the cash flows in the two borrowings PC_0 and PUX_0 have been constructed to be equal in C$ terms at each point in time. The equilibrium condition connecting LTFX and the foreign and domestic spot interest rates involves exploiting the covered interest arbitrage condition for LTFX (see Chapter 4, Section II):

$$F(0,t) = \frac{(1 + zz_t)^t}{(1 + zz_t^*)^t} S_0$$

where, as before, zz_t^* and zz_t are the implied zero-coupon interest rates associated with covered interest arbitrage trades between time 0 and time t. Using this condition, the equilibrium condition for LTFX derived from the fully hedged borrowing becomes, for each $t \in [1,T]$:

$$\frac{1 + z_t}{1 + z_t^*} = \frac{1 + zz_t}{1 + zz_t^*}$$

In other words, for each t, the spot interest rate agio derived from the foreign and domestic debt markets must equal the implied zero-coupon interest agio from the LTFX market.

QUESTIONS

1. Outline appropriate questions to be addressed by a commercial or chartered bank undertaking a financial futures hedging decision. Explain in detail the appropriate hedging strategies for the following:
   a. In April, a bank wants to lock-in today's interest rate on a $1 million issue of 6-month negotiable CDs due to take place in 3 months.
   b. A money market trader wants to hedge against possible capital losses on a 1-year Government of Canada t-bill that is about to be purchased. The bill may be sold at any time between purchase and maturity.
   c. In June, a bank wants to lock-in today's interest rates on a $10 million purchase of 3-month T-bills in September.
   d. A bond dealer expects interest rates to rise and wants to protect itself against capital losses on its T-bond inventory.
   e. In June, a metals refinery wants to lock-in today's price on a purchase of 50,000 pounds of copper cathodes due to take place in September.
   Why will basis variation affect the performance of the hedge? Which of your answers involves a cross hedge?

2a. Derive a closed-form expression for the risk-minimizing hedge ratio. In what sense is this ratio an optimal hedge ratio? How is your answer affected if the commodity being hedged is undetermined at the time the hedge is "put on" (e.g., a wheat farmer hedging the output for a crop that has just been planted).

2b. Assuming mean-variance agents, derive an expression for the optimal speculative position size. What happens to this position as the sensitivity of the agent to risk diminishes? Based on this, what can you conclude about the equilibrium in a market dominated by risk-neutral speculators?

3. Derive the profit function for a hedger facing a stochastic output. What are the related expected profit and variance of profit? How would the profit function be affected by the addition of output (e.g., crop) insurance?

4. What is portfolio insurance and what role do stock index futures play in insuring portfolios? What role did stock index futures play in the October 1987 market break? Identify and explain some factors that restrict the execution of stock index futures arbitrages.

5. From Section II, discuss the relationship between the mean-variance optimal hedge ratios, h_{MV}^*, which is given in terms of R_f, and (Q_H^*/Q_S), which is given in terms of $F(1,T)$.

6. In calculating the *ex post* rate of return, what is the difference between the arithmetic average and the geometric average? Describe situations where these two methods of calculating rates of return will differ.

7. Suppose a U.K. zero-coupon bond was purchased by a U.S. investor and held for 1 year. The bond was purchased for £500 when the £/US$ exchange rate was $2. (The bond cost $1000.) Due to increases in U.K. interest rates, the bond was sold for £475 when the exchange rate was $2.20.

   a. What was the rate of return on the bond in £?

   b. What was the rate of return on the bond in US$?

   c. What portion of the US$ return was due to exchange rate changes?

8. Derive Eq. (6.4) from p. 146 of Eun and Resnick (1994):

$$\mathrm{var}(R_{p,\$}) \cong \sum_{i=1}^{N}\sum_{j=1}^{N} X_i X_j \ \mathrm{cov}(R_i,R_j)$$

$$+ \sum_{i=1}^{N}\sum_{j=1}^{N} X_i X_j \ \mathrm{cov}(e_i,e_j)$$

$$+ 2\sum_{i=1}^{N}\sum_{j=1}^{N} X_i X_j \ \mathrm{cov}(R_i,e_j)$$

PART III

Options Contracts

CHAPTER 7

Option Concepts

I. BASIC OPTION PROPERTIES

A. Some Distribution-Free Properties of Options[1]

The celebrated Black–Scholes option pricing formula depends fundamentally on the assumption that stock prices are log-normally distributed. While it is not possible to develop an option pricing formula without making a distributional assumption, a number of distribution-free properties can still be identified. Several of these basic properties of options have already been developed in previous chapters. For example, the max [·] function associated with the expiration date value of an option describes one distribution-free property of options. Put–call parity is another property. For completeness, even those properties already derived will be listed here.

---

[1]The seminal source of this material is Merton (1973). Gibson (1991) and other general sources give a comprehensive treatment.

Given the notation provided in Chapter 1, Section I, unless otherwise stated, the following properties are stated for the case of a *non-dividend-paying stock* (or deliverable commodity that does not earn a carry return). This case is examined for traditional reasons, as early statements of the distribution-free properties of options (e.g., Merton, 1973) used this case. Extensions to other cases, such as options on dividend-paying stocks, spot commodities, and futures contracts, are provided when appropriate, either in this section or elsewhere (e.g., in the discussion of early exercise of American currency options in Chapter 8, Section IV). The distribution-free properties rely on conventional perfect markets assumptions: no transaction costs, no taxes, and riskless lending and borrowing at the constant riskless interest rate.

Property 1: Non-Negative Prices

$$C[S,\tau,X] \geq 0; \; C_A[S,\tau,X] \geq 0$$
$$P[S,\tau,X] \geq 0; \; P_A[S,\tau,X] \geq 0$$

This property holds for every $t \leq T$.

Property 2: Expiration Date Value

$$C_A[S(T),0,X] = C[S(T),0,X] = \max[0,S(T) - X]$$
$$P_A[S(T),0,X] = P[S(T),0,X] = \max[0,X - S(T)]$$

As with other properties stated in this section, this property ignores transaction costs and other related expenses such as taxes.

Property 3: Non-Negative Value to Exercising Early

$$C_A[S,\tau,X] \geq C[S,\tau,X]; \quad P_A[S,\tau,X] \geq P[S,\tau,X]$$

This property can also be expressed as:

$$C_A[S,\tau,X] = C[S,\tau,X] + EEP_C[S,\tau,X] \text{ and}$$
$$P_A[S,\tau,X] = P[S,\tau,X] + EEP_P[S,\tau,X]$$

where $EEP[S,\tau,X]$ is the early exercise premium with the subscripts C and P referring to calls and puts, respectively. Property 3 then implies that $EEP \geq 0$ with almost sure equality for deep out-of-the-money options. This is because early exercise is only rational if the option is in-the-money and the probability of a deep out-of-the-money option being exercised is negligible. Hence, the prices of European and American calls will be approximately equal for deep out-of-the-money options. For calls and puts with the same exercise value and time to maturity, increasing (decreasing) EEP_C implies decreasing (increasing) EEP_P.

Property 4: No Early Exercise Arbitrage Profits

$$C_A[S,\tau,X] \geq S(t) - X; \quad P_A[S,\tau,X] \geq X - S(t)$$

The value of the American option is bounded below by the exercise value. This is *not* a property that applies to European options; it is possible for European options on dividend paying securities to trade below the intrinsic exercise value $S(t) - X$ for calls and $X - S(t)$ for puts (see Chapter 8, Section IV).

Property 5: Non-Negative Value to Earlier Exercise

$$C_A[S,\tau_1,X] \geq C_A[S,\tau_2,X], \quad \text{for } \tau_1 > \tau_2$$
$$P_A[S,\tau_1,X] \geq P_A[S,\tau_2,X], \quad \text{for } \tau_1 > \tau_2$$

The right to earlier exercise has a non-negative value.

Property 6: Exercise Prices and Options Premiums for $X_1 > X_2$

$$C[S,\tau,X_1] \leq C[S,\tau,X_2]; C_A[S,\tau,X_1] \leq C_A[S,\tau,X_2]$$
$$P[S,\tau,X_1] \geq P[S,\tau,X_2]; P_A[S,\tau,X_1] \geq P_A[S,\tau,X_2]$$

The lower the exercise price the more (less) valuable is the call (put) option.

Property 7: Calls with Zero Stock Prices

$$C_A[0,\tau,X] = C[0,\tau,X] = 0$$

The right to purchase a stock or commodity with no value has no value.

Property 8: Perpetual American Call with Zero Exercise Price

$$C_A[S,\infty,0] = S$$

The perpetual property requires the American early exercise feature. Given this, the spot commodity (e.g., common stock) can be described as a perpetual option with a zero exercise price. This is one sense in which the common stock can be described as an option.[2] This property is a special case of the price for perpetual American call options, the only general case where a pricing formula for American call options is generally available (see Chapter 9, Section IV).

Property 9: Put Premium Upper Bound

$$X \geq P_A[S,\tau,X] \geq P[S,\tau,X]$$

While call option values are unbounded above, put options prices are bounded above by X because the stock price can only fall to zero, due to limited liability. This property of put options is important in distinguishing American put and call options. Unlike American calls, there is an additional incentive to exercise American put options early: When the stock price is sufficiently close to zero, the value of the potential interest on the exercise premium exceeds the expected gain from holding the put option until expiration.

Property 10: Call Plus Debt Versus Stock

Let $PV[r,\tau]$ be the present value of $1 to be paid in τ days discounted at the discrete annualized interest rate r. In discrete form, $PV[\tau]$ can be expressed as:

$$PV[r,\tau] = \frac{1}{1 + r\dfrac{\tau}{365}} = \frac{1}{1 + rt^*}$$

In continuous form, with continuous (annualized) interest rate r:

$$PV[r,\tau] = \exp\left\{-r\frac{\tau}{365}\right\} = \exp\{-rt^*\} \equiv e^{-rt^*}$$

where t^* is the fraction of the year remaining on the security (see Appendix I). With appropriate specification of the continuous or discrete r:

$$C[S,\tau,X] \geq \max[0, S(t) - X\,PV[r,\tau]]$$

This condition has considerable practical value. Demonstrating this result requires a specific portfolio: The portfolio shorts the spot commodity generating $S(t)$. For the short position, in all states of the world at time T, $-S(T)$ is the payoff. The portfolio involves taking the money from the short and purchasing a call option with exercise price X and τ days to maturity as well as buying a

---

[2]In the following, the spot commodity will be assumed to be common stock. In general, dividend payments relate to carry returns on the spot commodity. When the option is written on a futures contract, there is no carry return by construction.

pure discount bond that has τ days to maturity and a par value of X. Whenever $S(T) < X$, then the call will expire worthless and the portfolio will earn only the maturing value of bonds, X, and $-S(T)$, the cost of the short. In this case, the terminal value of the portfolio is positive, by construction. When $S(T) > X$, the call will have the value $S(T) - X$, which, when combined with the maturing value of the bond and the short, gives a value of zero. Hence, because the call option and lending portfolio has a greater value than the short stock position in one state of the world and the same value in the other state, the portfolio must involve a net investment of funds at t such that $C + X \, PV[r,\tau] - S \geq 0$. Manipulating and combining this condition with Property 1 give the desired result.

In practice, this property can provide a mechanism for "replicating" the return on the stock position: The value of the call plus lending will be close to the value of the stock, providing a viable trading opportunity.[3] In other words, instead of buying the stock and holding for some horizon τ it is also possible to invest in bonds and buy calls. From put–call parity arbitrage, the cost of this position will exceed the cost of buying the stock by the cost of buying a put with exercise price X and time to expiration τ. It follows that a call plus bond portfolio will have the same payoff as an "insured" stock portfolio. The advantages and disadvantages of this strategy will be discussed in Chapter 9, Section III. Recognizing that transaction costs for puts and calls will be approximately the same, insofar as execution costs for bonds are lower than for stocks, the call plus bond strategy will be preferred.

A Property 10 condition is available for puts. In this case, the relevant portfolio involves a long stock position combined with buying a put with exercise price X and time to maturity τ with the funds obtained from a borrowing with maturity value of X using a pure discount bond from t until T. In all the future states of the world where $S(T) > X$, the stock will be worth $S(T)$, the put will expire worthless, and the borrowing will be worth $-X$. This is positive by construction. In the future state of the world where $S(T) \leq X$, the put will be worth $X - S(T)$; the stock, $S(T)$; and the borrowing, $-X$, for a portfolio value of zero. The implication is that at time t, the value of the put plus the stock minus borrowing must be positive: $P + S - X \, PV[r,\tau] \geq 0$. Manipulating and combining with Property 1 produces:

$$P[S,\tau,X] \geq \max[0,X \, PV[r,\tau] - S(t)]$$

As with the call plus bond portfolio, the implication is that a portfolio of a stock with a put must sell for more than a bond with par value equal to X. From put–call parity, the difference will equal the amount paid for an appropriate call.

Another practical implication of Property 10 follows from combining this result with Property 3 to get:

$$C_A[S,\tau,X] \geq C[S,\tau,X] \geq \max\,[0,S(t) - X\,PV[r,\tau]] \geq S(t) - X$$

This result fills in the inequality given in Property 4. Upon some consideration, it is apparent that, except in extreme cases such as described in Property 7, the value of the American call option at any time t will almost surely be greater than the exercise value, $S(t) - X$. Colloquially, the American call on a non-dividend-paying stock is always worth more alive than dead; it will always be worth more to the call option holder to sell an American call rather than to exercise it prior to maturity.

Property 11: American and European Call and Put Options On Non-Dividend-Paying Stocks

Property 10 raises a quandary: If the American call on a non-dividend-paying stock will never rationally be exercised early, what value does the right of early exercise have in this case? This leads to the following property for calls on non-dividend paying stocks:

$$C_A[S,\tau,X] = C[S,\tau,X]$$

This result follows directly from Property 10 because, for $\tau > 0$, $\max\,[0,S(t) -X\,PV[r,\tau]] \geq S(t) - X\,PV[r,\tau] > S(t) - X$. Recognizing that $S(t) - X$ is the immediate exercise value of the American call, the value of the American call on a non-dividend-paying stock is always strictly greater than the exercise value. Hence, the value of the early exercise premium is zero because the call will never be exercised early. Property 11 is specific to calls and does not extend to either American put options on non-dividend-paying stocks or to American call options on dividend-paying stocks. The latter cases are examined in Section III.

Early exercise for American puts can be motivated by examining the European put condition from the discussion in Property 10:

$$P[S,\tau,X] \geq \max\,[0,X\,PV[r,\tau] - S(t)]$$

For puts that are in the money, it is *not* the case that $\max\,[0,X\,PV[r,\tau] -S(t)] \geq X - S(t)$. Because the value of the American put is not supported by portfolio trading involving long the stock, long the put combined with borrowing $X\,PV[r,\tau]$, as the put goes deeper in the money the put price will fall to the early exercise boundary of $X - S(t)$.[4] In this case, if the put is exercised,

---

[4]Precisely when this will happen depends on a combination of factors such as the time to expiration, the size of $X - S(t)$, the volatility on the stock, liquidity in the option, and so on.

the holder will receive $X - S(t)$ that can be invested at r to provide $[X - S(t)] \exp\{rt^*\}$ on the expiration date. If the put is held to maturity, the holder will receive max $[0, X - S(T)]$.

Comparing $[X - S(t)] \exp\{rt^*\}$ with max $[0, X - S(T)]$ reveals that the early exercise decision for the deep in-the-money put depends on the tradeoff between the interest income associated with exercising immediately and the potential gain associated with expected falls in the stock price. In the extreme case, $S(t) = S(T) = 0$ and the decision is obvious (for $X > 0$). There is no possibility for further gain from spot price changes and rationality requires immediate exercise of the put option. Once the put price has reached the arbitrage boundary of $X - S(t)$, the general condition for early exercise of the American put on a non-dividend-paying stock is $X(\exp\{rt^*\} - 1) > S(t) \exp\{rt^*\} - E[S(T)]$. It follows that if $S(t)$ is expected to stay the same, then the put will be exercised.

Property 12: Exercise and Call Prices

$$C[S,\tau,X_1] - C[S,\tau,X_2] \leq PV[r,\tau]\{X_2 - X_1\}, \text{ where } X_2 > X_1$$

This implies that a \$1 increase in the exercise price reduces the value of the option by less than \$1. The proof of this condition is given as an assignment in the Questions at the end of chapter.

A combination of Properties 2, 7, 8, 10, and 12 can be used to construct a graphical presentation of call option price behavior. A plausible relationship between the call option price and the stock price without Property 10 is given in Graph 7.1.[5] While the precise shape of the $C[S; \cdot]$ function will be examined in Section II, it is sufficient to know that:

$$1 \geq \frac{\partial C}{\partial S} \geq 0 \qquad \left.\frac{\partial C}{\partial S}\right|_{S \to \infty} = 1$$

The inclusion of Property 10, combined with the above restriction on $C[\cdot]$, produces Graph 7.2, which illustrates the type of intertemporal behavior associated with the call option. One of the applications arising from the Black–Scholes formula is the analytical expression that can be derived to capture the precise nature of the call price, as various parameters are allowed to change (see Chapter 9, Section I).

---

[5]It is important to recognize that Graph 7.1 is not an expiration-date profit diagram (i.e., the horizontal axis measures the current stock price, $S(t)$, while the vertical axis measures the call price).

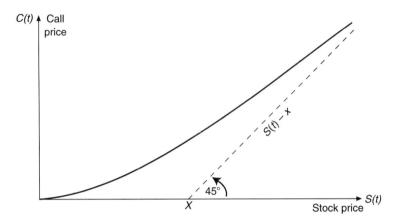

GRAPH 7.1   Value of a call as a function of stock price ($t > 0$).

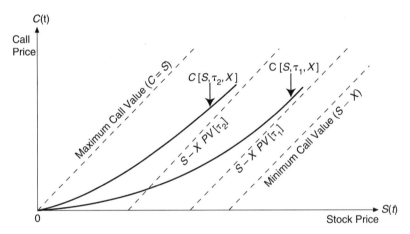

GRAPH 7.2   Value of a call for different time to maturity ($t_2 > t_1$).

B. Expiration Date Profit Diagrams

Exchange-traded stock options differ substantively from warrants insofar as exercise of an exchange-traded option does not have any implications for the amount of common stock outstanding; i.e., there is no dilution of the common stock associated with exchange-traded stock options. For analytical purposes, it is most expedient to assume exchange-traded options for illustrating the relevant option payoff functions using the *expiration-date profit diagram* technique. While the presentation may differ from source to source, the relevant profit function is usually derived by subtracting the option premium paid from the max [·] function that gives the value of the option at expiration. For a call option, the value of the call option, $C[\,\cdot\,]$, depends on the expiration date T and exercise price X. At expiration, the value of the call option $C[T,X]$ is

$$C[T,X] = \max[0, S(T) - X]$$

For the put option price, $P[T,X]$:

$$P[T,X] = \max[0, X - S(T)]$$

It follows that the profit function for the call purchaser is $\pi(T) = C[T,X]$ $-\{\text{call premium paid}\}$, and, for the put purchaser, $\pi(T) = P[T,X] - \{\text{put premium paid}\}$. While it is theoretically correct to include an allowance for foregone interest on the premium over the life of the option, this issue is ignored at this point for simplicity.

The combination of puts and calls with writers and purchasers leads to four versions of the expiration-date profit diagram for naked option positions. Graph 7.3 is a collection of the various elementary expiration-date profit diagrams. Be careful to observe that the expiration-date profit is being plotted against the expiration-date stock price. The diagrams of the profit functions for the written positions are a mirror image of the diagrams for the purchased positions, because the gains (losses) on written positions are the losses (gains) of the associated purchased positions. (Following the definitions given in Chapter 1, Section I, written positions are "short" positions and purchased positions are "long".) Given this, these diagrams are best interpreted as describing the payoff for a $t = 0$ option trader planning to hold the position until $t = T$. This suppresses certain essential elements of the option valuation problem (e.g., how the premium is determined or admitting the possibility of early exercise). While perhaps most descriptive of the earlier over-the-counter (OTC)-style options, the diagrams do illustrate the essential features of naked options: The purchased call (put) has value when the stock price at expiration is *above* (*below*) the exercise price; the maximum possible loss on the purchased option is loss of premium; possible losses (gains) on a written (purchased) call are unbounded; and possible loss (gain) on a written (purchased) put is bounded by the exercise price minus the premium.

C. EVALUATION OF DIFFERENT POSITIONS

While of limited analytical value when applied to naked positions, expiration-date profit diagrams are of greater value when applied to more complicated options positions. For example, consider the case of a *covered*, as opposed to

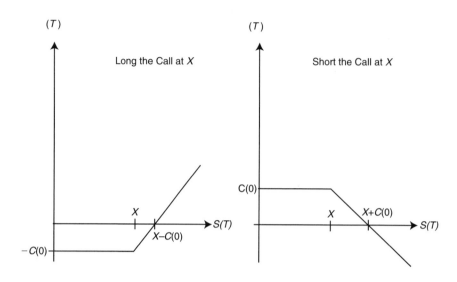

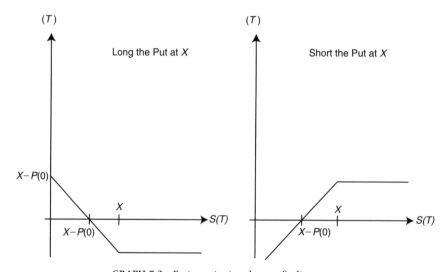

GRAPH 7.3   Basic expiration-date profit diagrams.

naked or uncovered, option position. In this case, the option is purchased in conjunction with some spot position (e.g., long [short] IBM stock combined with an IBM options position). To see this, consider the associated expiration-date profit diagram for a long position in a non-dividend-paying stock: $\pi = Q\{S(T) - S(0)\}$. Both the long and short spot positions expiration date profit diagrams are used to construct Graphs 7.4 to 7.7. If dividend payments are permitted, the profit function for the long (short) will shift up (down) by the amount of the dividends received (paid). As with the payment of interest, this complication will be ignored for present purposes. It is now possible to derive the diagrams for covered positions by geometrically combining the profit functions for the two components of the relevant covered position. Because each of the four uncovered positions can theoretically be combined with either a long or a short cash position, this gives rise to eight different possible scenarios. Graphs 7.4–7.7 provide the four most commonly encountered cases.

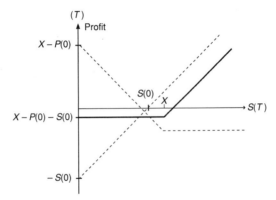

GRAPH 7.4   Long the stock at $S(0)$, buy a put at X.

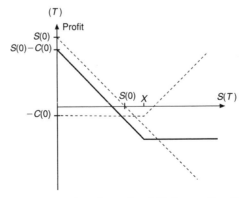

GRAPH 7.5   Short the stock at $S(0)$, buy a call at X.

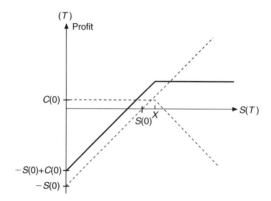

GRAPH 7.6   Long the stock at S(0) write a call at X.

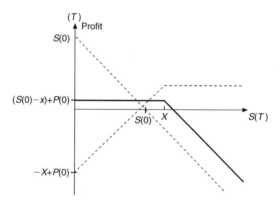

GRAPH 7.7   Short the stock at S(0), write a put at X.

Analysis of the expiration-date profit diagrams for covered positions reveals some of the fundamental replication properties of options. Consider the standard strategy of using purchased puts to insure the value of a cash position against downside moves (Graph 7.4). Subject to the caveats associated with transaction costs, size of premium, dividends and interest on the cash position, and so on, the payoff on this covered position is identical to the payoff on a purchased uncovered call position with exercise price X. Similarly, the covered position that combines short-the-cash with a purchased call is shown to be equivalent to an uncovered purchased put with exercise price X (Graph 7.5). The replication strategies for naked written positions follow appropriately: Long-the-cash combined with a written call replicates a written put

(Graph 7.6), and short-the-cash combined with a written put replicates a written call (Graph 7.7). The remaining four types of covered positions do not produce replication.[6] Rather, these positions will tend to increase exposure to volatility of the underlying cash position.

The final group of (uncovered) replication strategies to consider use options to replicate either a long or a short position in the underlying commodity or stock (Graph 7.8). In order to replicate a long stock position, a purchased call is combined with a written put with the same X and time to expiration. Taking the premiums paid $(-)$ or received $(+)$ on the call and put at $t = 0$ to be $C(0)$ and $P(0)$, the expiration-date profit diagram (again ignoring foregone interest on premiums) is

$$\pi[T] = P(0) - C(0) + \max [0, S(T) - X] - \max [0, X - S(T)]$$

Similarly, for the replicated short stock position that combines a put purchase with cash outflow of $P(0)$ with a written call cash inflow of $C(0)$:

$$\pi[T] = C(0) - P(0) + \max [0, X - S(T)] - \max [0, S(T) - X]$$

Replication of the short stock position is left as an exercise (see Questions at the end of the chapter). The combination of the max [·] functions provide a 45° line through X. In interpreting these diagrams, the net premium terms shift the 45° line along the horizontal axis. Due to differences in the time premium for puts and calls, this operation typically will not produce a payoff that is exactly centered at $X = S(0)$.[7] This point is also important for interpreting these replication strategies when the options involved are not at-the-money.

To understand this, consider the nature of the payoffs on a replicated long stock position when $X = 50$ and $S(0) = 60$. In this case, the combination of max [·] functions produce a 45° line through $X = 50$. The call premium will generate a cash outflow that is a combination of intrinsic expiration value ($\$60 - \$50 = \$10$) and a time premium. The cash inflow from the put will depend solely on the time premium, as an out-of-the-money put has *zero* intrinsic expiration value. In this case, as discussed in Section II, the time premiums for the put and call will not be equal. Given this, the net cash outflow at $t = 0$ will be $\$10$ plus the difference in the call and put time premiums. This will shift the 45° line to the right by this amount, producing a replicated long stock (spot commodity) position that has a breakeven close to, but not precisely, $S(0)$. Similarly, for the short stock position, with $X = 50$ and $S(0) = 60$, the written call will generate a cash inflow of $\$10$ plus the difference in the call and put time premiums. This will result in a shift of the 45° line to the right by the

---

[6]These combinations are short the stock and write a call, short the stock and buy a put, long the stock and buy a call, and long the stock and write a put.

[7]However, this difference between X and the breakeven $S(T)$ for the replication strategies will not usually be large.

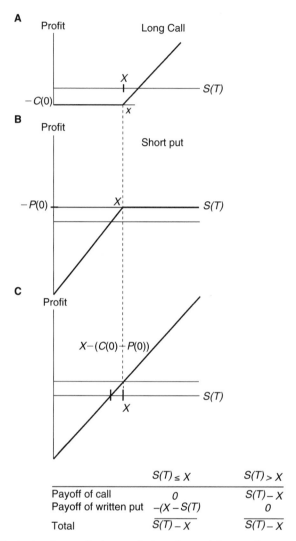

	$S(T) \leq X$	$S(T) > X$
Payoff of call	0	$S(T) - X$
Payoff of written put	$-(X - S(T))$	0
Total	$S(T) - X$	$S(T) - X$

GRAPH 7.8 Expiration-date profit diagram for long-the-stock buy a call at X, write a put at X (where $P(0) > C(0)$).

amount of the net cash inflow.[8] A similar analysis holds when the put is in-the-money and the call is out-of-the money. In this case, the $45°$ lines will shift to

---

[8]Shifting both $45°$ lines in the same direction, even though one strategy involves a cash inflow and the other a cash outflow, is due to the different slopes (i.e., the short position has slope -1 while the long position has slope $+1$).

the left by the amount of the expiration value of the put plus the net time premiums. In all cases, a payoff is created that is approximately centered at $S(0)$, as illustrated in Chapter 9 Section I, but there will be substantive differences between the sensitivity to changes in stock prices of the various possible in- and out-of-the-money positions.

D. HEDGING WITH OPTIONS AND HEDGING FOR OPTIONS

The expiration-date profit diagrams illustrate the wide range of possible payoffs constructed by combining options with options or options with spot positions. In the specific context of using options in stock portfolios, Bookstaber and Clarke (1983, p. 5) observe: "Potentially, the use of options in combination with a portfolio of stocks can provide the investor with a portfolio containing a wide range of return characteristics. The use of options allows the investor to 'mold' the return distribution of the portfolio to fit a given set of investment objectives. Indeed, the range of returns that can be created through the use of the option market makes the two-dimensional tradeoffs of conventional mean-variance portfolio theory obsolete." This observation can be readily extended to commodities other than stocks. In general, the presence of options substantively complicates analysis of the hedging decision, compared to the case where only futures contracts are available.

A significant difference between using options and futures for hedging purposes is that options involve the payment of a premium at $t = 0$, while futures do not involve any initial cash flow (ignoring margin and transactions costs). In addition, the sensitivity of options and futures prices to spot price changes also differs. While it is possible to use options to "replicate" a futures position, this will involve incrementally adjusting (dynamically trading) the size of the options position to account for changes in the spot price. To see this, consider a *hedge portfolio* in stocks involving one unit of stock and β units of written call options. The net value of this portfolio, V, will depend on the cash outflow associated with the price of the stock, S, and the cash inflow associated with selling β units of call options at price C. In order to replicate the payoff for a hedge portfolio using options to hedge the stock position, it is necessary to determine β such that $\partial V/\partial S = 0$.

For the option hedge portfolio: $V = S - \beta_c C$. In this equation, V is the net investment in the portfolio and S is the value of the stock position which, for pedagogical purposes, can be taken to be one unit of stock. Observing that C is the price of a call option on the one unit of stock, β_c is the number of *written* call options per unit of stock. The value of $\beta_c C$ enters with a minus sign because the written options position generates a cash inflow that can be used to partially offset the cost of buying the stock. Because ΔS is the only source of randomness in the portfolio, the hedge portfolio condition can be used to determine the value of β_c:

$$\frac{\partial V}{\partial S} = 0 = 1 - \beta_c \frac{\partial C}{\partial S} \quad \Rightarrow \quad \beta_c = \frac{1}{\dfrac{\partial C}{\partial S}}$$

Because the value of a call option will change as the stock price changes, it is necessary to *dynamically* determine β_c, the appropriate number of options to write to maintain the hedge portfolio. One of the useful analytical features of the Black–Scholes option pricing formula is that β can be solved in closed form.

The above discussion involved hedging with options. The inverse problem is encountered by option market makers: How many units of stock to hold in order to hedge a book of traded options positions. As option books usually involve (net) written option positions, the problem of hedging for options involves the value equation: $V = \delta_c S - C$. The choice variable in the hedge is the δ_c, the number of units of stock to purchase (short) to hedge a written (purchased) call option written on one unit of stock. The associated solution for the hedge ratio is

$$\frac{\partial V}{\partial S} = 0 = \delta_c - \frac{\partial C}{\partial S} \quad \Rightarrow \quad \delta_c = \frac{\partial C}{\partial S} = N[d_1]$$

The last equality is solved in Chapter 9 and is included here to illustrate the pedagogical basis for using the hedging-for-options formulation of the riskless hedge portfolio.

Similar conditions can be derived for puts, which can also be used to *dynamically* hedge the stock position. In this case, purchased puts are used and the hedge portfolio has the form: $V = S + \beta_p P$, where P is the price of a put option, and β_p is the number of puts needed to be purchased in order to hedge one unit of stock. The hedge portfolio condition can now be applied to solve for the number of puts:

$$\frac{\partial V}{\partial S} = 0 = 1 + \beta_p \frac{\partial P}{\partial S} \quad \Rightarrow \quad \beta_p = -\frac{1}{\dfrac{\partial P}{\partial S}}$$

Anticipating the discussion in Chapter 9, the Black–Scholes formula can be used to show that the number of purchased put options is directly related to the number of written call options required to construct the two hedge portfolios.

The dynamic hedging of the options hedge portfolio can be contrasted with the case of the futures hedge portfolio, where the spot position is approximately hedged without further need for dynamic adjustment once a futures position has been established. However, like the hedge portfolio with puts or calls, it could be necessary to dynamically adjust a hedge portfolio created with futures. Using the hedging for futures formulation, the futures hedge has the value function: $V^* = \beta^* S - F$. Assuming that the spot commodity is the same as the commodity underlying the futures hedge, it is possible to construct a delivery hedge. Using the cash-and-carry arbitrage condition, $F = (1 + ic)S$, it follows that:

$$\frac{\partial V^*}{\partial S} = \beta^* - \frac{\partial F}{\partial S} \quad \Rightarrow \quad \beta^* = \frac{\partial F}{\partial S} = (1 + ic) + S\frac{\partial ic}{\partial S}$$

The sensitivity of the futures position is not one-to-one with the spot position, though the futures sensitivity is considerably different than the sensitivity of the call option to changes in the stock price, where the *delta* of the call determines the size of the hedge. As demonstrated in Chapter 9, the delta of a call option will be bounded between 0 and 1, making β_c, the inverse of the delta, a positive number greater than 1.

E. Do Replicated Positions Differ?

The basic replication properties for covered and uncovered option positions can be illustrated using expiration-date profit diagrams. Because this technique suppresses accurate accounting for the foregone interest associated with the option premium, it is possible to provide more precise statements of the replication strategies. Heuristically, the basic insights can be illustrated by considering two possible approaches to capturing the payoff of a long (short) spot position. One approach is to directly take a long (short) spot position. The alternative approach to capturing the long spot payoff given by the expiration-date profit diagram approach is to buy a call and write a put with the same T and $X = S(0)$. However, the investment required to purchase a stock position is significantly larger than the long call plus short put alternative. Hence, combining a purchased call plus a written put does not provide accurate replication of a long stock position. (From put–call parity, for $P = C$ it is equivalent to buying stock using 100% margin borrowing.)

Invoking an absence-of-arbitrage approach, it is possible to identify the accurate replication trading strategy. More precisely, if the call and put options are correctly priced, investing the remaining balance between the stock price and the net premium on the put and call options in a fixed-income security maturing on the expiration date of the options will equate the initial cost of the two approaches. In order for the expiration date payoff on the purchased call plus written put plus fixed income position to be exactly equal to the payoff on the long stock position, the maturity value of the fixed-income security must be X. This is the basis of put–call parity arbitrage. There are alternative ways of specifying the transactions involved in the arbitrage, such as using the cost of buying the spot position and an appropriate put option for comparison. For absence-of-arbitrage, the cost of purchasing this position is just equal to the price of an appropriate call option combined with an investment of the balance in an appropriately dated fixed-income position, with maturity value equal to the exercise price.

Perhaps the most useful application of put–call parity is to specify the relationship between the price of a call and a put. Once the value of the call is determined, the put–call parity arbitrage condition provides the price of the put having the same X and T. As discussed in Chapter 9, Section III, it is possible to use the put–call parity condition to develop similar but more complicated strategies applicable to replicating the payoff on naked options positions that use *dynamic hedging strategies* involving active trading of fixed-income and spot positions. One important instance of the dynamic strategies involves replicating the payoff on a long stock position combined with a purchased put—in other words, portfolio insurance. This payoff can be replicated by actively trading a portfolio that contains only stocks and bonds, with no derivatives. Because many institutional investors already possess stock/bond portfolios and are often involved in making active trading decisions, the dynamic trading approach is appealing. The advantages of using one particular approach over another will be examined in later sections.

The possibility of using a number of different methods to achieve a given type of payoff raises some practical considerations. Speaking in the context of stock options, many of the relevant issues are captured by Gibson (1991, p. 179):

> We cannot ignore the institutional characteristics of the stock, option markets, and trading restrictions that investors in those markets are actually facing. They are often in sharp contrast with the "perfect markets" paradigm of most option pricing models.... These models often ignore the transactions costs and bid/offer spreads investors actually incur. In addition, margin requirements,... short-selling restrictions,... differences between the lending and borrowing rates as well as tax considerations will also refrain investors from trading as frequently as predicted.

In effect, practical considerations associated with actual execution costs may determine whether a specific replication strategy is feasible. The practical importance of the institutional characteristics should not be underestimated. For example, certain hedge funds, such as Long-Term Capital Management (LTCM), can be characterized as: funds designed to exploit inefficiencies that arise in the market valuation of either side in a specific replication strategy. Firms making markets in exotic and mark-to-model OTC derivatives are also attempting to profit by spanning market inefficiencies.

II. PUT–CALL PARITY

A. EUROPEAN PUT–CALL PARITY
WITHOUT DIVIDENDS[9]

The most important of all the option replication strategies is the put–call parity arbitrage. There are two possible pedagogical approaches to demonstrating the supporting arbitrage transactions. One approach, which has a history predating the development of the Black–Scholes formula, involves demonstrating that the payoffs on two different portfolios are the same in all future states of the world. If the prices of the two portfolios differ, sell the overpriced portfolio and buy the underpriced portfolio. Hence, in equilibrium the two portfolios must sell for the same price. The alternative approach is more modern and involves specifying an arbitrage portfolio in which there is no net investment of funds. Much as in the discussion of arbitrages for forward and futures contracts, the equilibrium requirement that there be no arbitrage opportunities provides the restriction needed to specify the put–call parity condition. Tables 7.1 and 7.2 illustrate that both approaches provide identical results.

The two-portfolio approach demonstrates that the payoff functions for two different portfolios are equal for all possible future outcomes. The arbitrage-portfolio approach combines the two portfolios into a single portfolio and observes that the value of the portfolio is zero in all future states of the world. Assuming perfect markets, it follows that the cost of purchasing the two positions should be equal to avoid arbitrage profit opportunities. For a European option on a non-dividend-paying stock, at $t = 0$, the two portfolios are given in Table 7.1. As discussed in Appendix I, $PV[\tau]$ is a discounting

TABLE 7.1   Two-Portfolio Approach

Strategy A
    Buy a call for one unit of stock, with exercise price X and days to expiration T.

Strategy B
    Borrow $X\ PV\ [\tau]$.
    Buy one unit of stock.
    Buy a put for one unit of stock, with same X and T as for the call.

---

[9]There is a literature on put–call parity that predates the introduction of the Black–Scholes formula, e.g., Stoll (1969). Many studies of put–call parity have related the issue to market efficiency, e.g., Klemkosky and Resnick (1979, 1980, 1992), Finucane (1991), Nisbet (1992). Other studies have been concerned with developing the put–call parity conditions for specific instruments, e.g., Chance (1988); Wagner *et al.* (1996). A recent development has been the use of put–call parity conditions to identify the early exercise premium, e.g., Zivney (1991), de Roon and Veld (1996).

TABLE 7.2   Arbitrage-Portfolio Approach

Short-arbitrage portfolio

Strategy

Buy a call for one unit of stock, with exercise price X and days to expiration T.
Invest $X PV (\tau)$.
Short one unit of stock.
Write a put for one unit of stock, with same X and T as for the call.

Long-arbitrage portfolio

Strategy

Write a call for one unit of stock, exercise price X and days to expiration T.
Borrow $X PV (\tau)$.
Buy one unit of stock.
Buy a put for one unit of stock, with same X and T as for the call.

TABLE 7.3   Two-Portfolio Approach: *All Possible Values of the Strategies at Expiration*

	$X \geq S(T)$	$X < S(T)$
Strategy A	0	$S(T) - X$
Strategy B		
Stock	$S(T)$	$S(T)$
Put	$X - S(T)$	0
Loan	$-X$	$-X$
Total	0	$S(T) - X$

function, which can be expressed in continuous ($\exp\{-rt^*\}$) or discrete ($1/\{1 + rt^*\}$) form, where r is annualized and $t^* = \tau/365 = [(T - t)/365]$, the fraction of the year remaining to expiration. Portfolio A is the call option position and Portfolio B is the *replicating* portfolio. In the arbitrage portfolio approach, described in Table 7.2, there is only one portfolio which satisfies the condition that there is no net investment of funds in the position.

Observing that the only admitted source of randomness is the stock price, what is significant about portfolios A and B is the associated payoffs at time T, which are given in Table 7.3. Because there is only one random variable in this world, the stock price, all possible futures states of the world have been taken into account. Table 7.3 demonstrates that the two strategies have equal expiration-date values. Because market equilibrium requires that portfolios with identical payoffs sell at the same price, the relationship between the market price of puts and calls is established. This condition is specific to the particulars of the security involved in the arbitrage, which is assumed to pay no dividends. It is also specific to the type of option that is being traded, which

TABLE 7.4   Arbitrage-Portfolio Approach

	$X \geq S(T)$	$X < S(T)$
All possible values of the long strategy at expiration		
Call	0	$S(T) - X$
Stock	$-S(T)$	$-S(T)$
Put	$-[X - S(T)]$	0
Zero bond	X	X
Total	0	0
All possible values of the short strategy at expiration		
Call	0	$-[S(T) - X]$
Stock	$S(T)$	$S(T)$
Put	$(X - S(T))$	0
Zero bond	$-X$	$>-X$
Total	0	0

is a European option. Hence, the condition which is derived is referred to European put–call parity for non-dividend-paying securities. The same outcome is achieved with the arbitrage portfolio (see Table 7.4).

The put–call parity condition can now be expressed as shown in Box 1. This relatively simple formula has a number of significant practical implications. Taking the case where the options are at the money ($S = X$), then the call will sell for more than the put because $S = X > Xe^{-rt^*}$. The righthand side of the put–call parity condition is sometimes referred to as a *synthetic call*. It is possible to rearrange the put–call parity condition such that any one of P, S, Xe^{-rt^*}, or C appears on the lefthand side. In each of these cases, the righthand side is referred as the synthetic position. For example, a *synthetic put* would be short the stock, buy a call, and invest in bonds. Similarly, a synthetic borrowing would be short the stock, write a put, and long a call.

Examining the actual execution of the arbitrage condition, when the call is expensive relative to the synthetic portfolio or, put differently, the actual call is overpriced relative to the synthetic call:

$$C[S,\tau,X] + [X \, PV[\tau]] > P[S,\tau,X] + S(t)$$

BOX 1

European Put–Call Parity for Non-Dividend-Paying Securities

$$C[S,\tau,X] = P[S,\tau,X] + S(t) - [X \, PV[\tau]]$$

In this case, the arbitrager would sell the call and borrow money, using these funds to purchase the put and the stock. This particular trade, which is aimed at exploiting call option mispricing, is referred to as a *conversion*.[10] Assuming the "perfect markets" paradigm, the conversion would create an arbitrage profit on the expiration date if the call is overpriced.[11] When the inequality is reversed, the arbitrager would sell the put and short the stock, using the funds to buy the call and invest the balance in zero-coupon (pure discount) fixed-income securities with maturity date T days ahead. This strategy is known as a *reverse conversion* or reversal. The importance of the practical qualifications involved in trading alluded to previously, such as transaction costs, is an important element in determining the profitability of conversions and reversals.

Consideration of the actual trading mechanics involved in the arbitrage reveals the importance of the issues alluded to by Gibson (1991). For example, allowing for significant differences between lending (L) and borrowing (B) rates reduces the equality in put–call parity to a pair of inequality restrictions:

$$S(t) + P[S,\tau,X] - X\ PV[\tau]_B \geq C[S,\tau,X] \geq S(t) + P[S,\tau,X] - X\ PV[\tau]_L$$

The upper boundary refers to the long arbitrage case considered in the last paragraph. The lower bound is associated with the short arbitrage. Another important source of discrepancy that can arise between the short and the long arbitrages is short-selling costs. This tends to weaken the applicability of the lower boundary. For many types of options, liquidity may be a consideration, affecting the bid/offer spread for the various transactions involved in trading debt, stocks, and both the put and call options. Together with other factors such as margin requirements, marking-to-market, and tax, there is considerable scope for the distance between the put–call parity boundaries to be substantial.[12]

B. EUROPEAN PUT–CALL PARITY WITH DIVIDENDS

The discussion to this point has focused on European options on non-dividend-paying stocks. When discussing the extension of European put–call

[10]The use of conversions in options trading has a long history (e.g., Poitras, 2000, Chap. 9).

[11]To see this, observe that if $S(T) = X$ then the stock is sold to pay off the maturing value of the loan, both options expiring worthless. If $S(T) > X$, the put expires worthless and $C[S(T),0,X]$ which equals max$[0,S(T) - X]$ plus X, the maturity value of the loan, equals $S(T)$, the value of the stock that is to be sold to settle the position. If $S(T) < X$, the call expires worthless and $P[S(T),0,X]$ which equals max$[0,X - S(T)]$ plus $S(T)$ equals X, the maturing value of the loan. In all cases, the additional balance that was raised initially due to $C + X\ PV > P + S$ is the residual arbitrage profit.

[12]A number of articles have explored the validity of the put–call parity condition (e.g., Klemkosky and Resnick, 1979).

parity to options on stocks, assets, or commodities that pay dividends, it is conventional to assume that the option contract does not allow for dividend payout protection. Such protection could be accomplished in a number ways, including delivering the stock *plus* all dividends paid during the life of the option if the option is exercised. Another method would be to adjust the exercise price for any dividends paid. The absence of dividend payout protection benefits the option writer, who is entitled to receive any dividend payouts during the life of the option. Prior to the twentieth century, it was common for option contracts to include dividend payout protection. As option market makers typically write options, it is not surprising that the CBOE chose to use option contracts without dividend payout protection.

Extending the specification of put–call parity to allow a known future dividend on the underlying stock, or more generally a discrete carry return on the underlying commodity, is not a significant complication, as it only involves adjusting the cash flows to account for the known dividends. More formally, if D is taken to be the present value of all known dividends to be paid between the current date and the options expiration date, T:

$$S(t) + P[S,\tau,X] = X\ PV[\tau] + D + C[S,\tau,X]$$

In this case, the return on a position that is long (short) the stock combined with a purchased (written) put option can be exactly financed by writing (purchasing) a call and borrowing (investing) $X\ PV[\tau] + D$. At maturity, the value of the stock plus accumulated dividends plus the expiration value of the put will just equal the maturity value of the fixed income position, $X + DFV[\tau]$, plus the expiration value of the call position, where $FV[\tau]$ is the future value function that corresponds to $PV[\tau]$.

In contrast to known dividend payments, introducing either the early exercise provision of American options or unknown dividend payments undermines the ability to precisely determine the arbitrage transactions. Formally, these features violate requirements needed for *path independence* of the option price. For example, at any time $t = 0$, if prices are measured continuously, there are a theoretically infinite number of possible paths that the spot price can take. Path independence requires that the payoff on the trading strategy does *not* depend on the specific future time path that the spot price actually takes.[13] Otherwise, the strategy is *path dependent* and will give a payoff that is uncertain at the decision date, $t = 0$. For example, path dependence occurs with the American put because some spot price paths will be sufficiently close to zero that it is profitable to exercise early. Early

---

[13]Goldman *et al.* (1979), Kemna and Vorst (1990), and Wilmott (1998) are useful sources on path-dependent options.

exercise can also occur in other situations (e.g., just before the last ex-dividend date for an American call) on a dividend paying stock. Because the occurrence of these events is not known at $t = 0$, the associated strategies are path dependent. Similarly for stock options, unknown dividends on the underlying stock means that the payoff on the strategy cannot be determined at $t = 0$ and again path dependence emerges.

C. European Put–Call Parity for Options on Forward and Futures Contracts

Put–call parity for options on forward and futures contracts retains all the features associated with options on spot commodities, with the exception that the net investment in the position is different because, in perfect markets, the forward or futures contract is theoretically costless to create. This means that the net pure discount bond position in the replicating portfolio is equal to the difference between the put and call premiums. There is no longer funds required for investment in the spot position. For replicating portfolios involving the spot commodity, the portfolio always involved a pure discount loan if the spot position was long and a pure discount bond purchase if the spot position was short.

For options on forwards and futures contracts, the net investment is determined by the difference between $F(t,T)$ and X, which determines the relative size of the call and put premiums. If $F(t,T) > X$, then the call is in-the-money and the put is out-of-the-money. Using the two-portfolio approach, the small put premium has to be incremented by a discount bond purchase to offset the size of the call premium. Similarly, if $F(t,T) < X$, then the call is out-of-the-money and the put is in-the-money. The call premium in this case is small, requiring the cost of the large put premium to be financed by a discount bond borrowing (see Table 7.5). Using the arbitrage portfolio approach, the argument is messier to explain. The long arbitrage portfolio will require a discount bond purchase when $X > F(t,T)$ and a discount bond borrowing when $F(t,T) > X$ (see Table 7.6).

A minor complication in specification of the replicating portfolios using forward and futures contracts occurs with specification of the expiration date. For example, many futures options involve delivery of a futures contract with delivery at $T + 1$ on the expiration date T preventing the same T to be used for the delivery date of the futures and the expiration date of the option. Option expiration date settlement involves delivery of the relevant futures contract together with a cash payment reflecting the difference between the option expiration date futures price and the option exercise price ($\max[0, F(T, T + 1) - X]$) (see Table 7.7). For other futures options, the

TABLE 7.5   Two-Portfolio Approach to Put–Call Parity for Options on Forward Contracts[a]

Strategy A
  Purchase a call option on a forward contract with option exercise price X and expiration date T and forward contract delivery date T involving delivery of one unit of spot commodity.

Strategy B
  Lend $[F(t,T) - X]PV[\tau]$
  Establish a long forward position at price $F(t,T)$, requiring delivery of one unit of the spot commodity.
  Buy a put on the same forward contract with the same X and T as for the call.

[a]$F(t,T) > X$, call in-the-money, put out-of-the-money.

TABLE 7.6   Two-Portfolio Approach for Options on Forward Contracts: *All Possible Values of the Strategies at Expiration*[a]

	$X \geq S(T)$	$X < S(T)$
Strategy A	0	$S(T) - X$
Strategy B		
Forward	$S(T) - F(t,T)$	$S(T) - F(t,T)$
Put	$X - S(T)$	0
Lending	$F(t,T) - X$	$F(t,T) - X$
Total	0	$S(T) - X$

[a]$F(t,T) > X$; $F(T,T) = S(T)$.

TABLE 7.7   Two-Portfolio Approach to Put–Call Parity for $F(t,T+1)$[a]

Strategy A
  Purchase a call option on a forward contract with exercise price X and expiration date T, requiring delivery of one unit of a forward contract with delivery date $T + 1$.

Strategy B
  Borrow $[X - F(t,T+1)]PV[\tau]$.
  Establish a long forward position, requiring delivery of one unit of the spot commodity, at $F(t,T+1)$.
  Buy a put on the same forward contract with the same X and T as for the call.

[a]$F(t,T+1) < X$, call out-of-the-money, put in-the-money.

expiration dates of the futures and options are the same. In this case, the option payoff is a cash payment that reflects the difference between the futures expiration-date price and the option exercise price (max $[0,F(T,T) - X]$). For ease of illustration, forward contracts with the same T as for the option will be assumed for the $F(t,T) > X$ case and forward contract with different T from the option for the $F(t,T+1) < X$ case. With appropriate modification, the replicating portfolio argument also applies to the other cases as well as for futures contracts.

For the $F(t,T) > X$ case, the call is in-the-money and the put is out-of-the-money. The relevant theoretical portfolios are described in Table 7.7. As before, Portfolio A is the call option position and Portfolio B is the replicating portfolio. After allowing for the cost of paying the put premium, equating the values of the portfolios means that there will be money left over to lend in Portfolio B. Using the result that $F(T,T) = S(T)$, the resulting payoffs at expiration are determined.

For the $F(t,T) < X$ case, the put is in-the-money and the call is out-of-the-money. To equalize the value of the two portfolios it will be necessary to borrow money in Portfolio B. The relevant theoretical portfolios are described in Table 7.8. As before, Portfolio A is the call option position and Portfolio B is the replicating portfolio. Because expiration date (T) delivery of this option involves a forward contract with delivery at $T + 1$, the resulting payoffs at expiration are determined.

The relationship between the price of puts and calls for forward and futures contracts is given in Box 2. The two strategies have equal value on the expiration date. This is the put–call parity condition for options on forward and futures contracts with the same expiration date (see also the Questions at the end of this chapter).

TABLE 7.8   Two-Portfolio Approach for Options on Forward Contracts: All Possible Values of the Strategies At Expiration

	$X \geq F(T,T+1)$	$X < F(T,T+1)$
Portfolio A	0	$F(T,T+1) - X$
Portfolio B		
Forward	$F(T,T+1) - F(t,T+1)$	$F(T,T+1) - F(t,T+1)$
Put	$X - F(T,T+1)$	0
Invest	$F(t,T+1) - X$	$F(t,T+1) - X$
Total B:	0	$F(T,T+1) - X$

BOX 2

European Put–Call Parity Condition for Options on Forwards with the Same Expiration Date

$$C[F,\tau,X] = P[F,\tau,X] + [F(t,T) - X]PV[\tau]$$

D. American Put–Call Parity

Derivation of the condition for put–call parity on American options requires the use of a number of the distribution-free properties, especially Properties 10 and 11. One implication of Property 11 is that American call options on non-dividend-paying stocks will not be exercised early. It will always be better to sell the American option than to exercise it. Hence, because there is no rational reason to exercise the call early, the value of the European and American call options will be the same. This is not the case for American call options on dividend-paying stocks or for any type of American put option, whether the underlying commodity pays a dividend or not. So, for the case of American options on non-dividend-paying stocks, it is not possible to specify an equality relationship between the price of put and call options. Rather, all that can be derived are upper and lower boundary conditions on the put price provided by arbitrage transactions involving calls.

The lower boundary on the put follows from Property 3, which states that, if there is a possibility of early exercise, then the value of the American option will be greater than the value of the European option. Because the values of the European and American calls are equal for a non-dividend-paying security:

$$P_A[S,\tau,X] \geq C_A[S,\tau,X] + X\,PV[\tau] - S(t)$$

To derive the upper bound on the put option, let Portfolio A be long the put with price $P_A[S,\tau,X]$, let Portfolio B be long the call at $C[S,\tau,X]$ and short the stock at $S(t)$, and invest X in a bond earning $r(t,T)$ with maturity date T.

To evaluate the put–call parity conditions for American options requires examining the expiration date payoff, together with the value of the payoff if exercise is initiated prior to the expiration-date. The expiration-date payoff for the two portfolios is given in Table 7.9. Observing the $1/PV[\tau] = \exp\{rt^*\} > 1$, in all future states of the world Portfolio B will have a higher payoff than Portfolio A. Similarly, for all times prior to maturity, the same schematic

TABLE 7.9 American Option Put–Call Parity Values: *All Possible Values of the Strategies at Expiration*

	$X \leq S(T)$	$X > S(T)$
Strategy A	0	$X - S(T)$
Strategy B		
Stock	$-S(T)$	$-S(T)$
Call	$S(T) - X$	0
Invest	$X/PV[\tau]$	$X/PV[\tau]$
Total	$X(1/PV[\tau] - 1)$	$X/PV[\tau] - S(T)$

applies, with the proviso that T is changed to the exercise date. This produces the upper bound condition for the American put (see Table 7.8):

$$C_A[S,\tau,X] + X - S(t) \geq P_A[S,\tau,X]$$

Combining these two conditions produces the upper and lower put–call parity boundaries for the American put.

Extending the put–call parity condition to American options on dividend-paying stocks follows much the same procedure as for Europeans. It is assumed that the dividend payment streams are known with certainty, which permits the present value of future dividend payments (D) to be determined. It is left as an exercise to demonstrate that the arbitrage boundaries will be

$$C_A[S,\tau,X] + X + D - S(t) \geq P_A[S,\tau,X] \geq C_A[S,\tau,X] + X\ PV[\tau] - S(t)$$

In practice, because most traded options are American, it is unfortunate that the put–call parity conditions do not provide the same type of sharp restrictions on American put and call prices as are provided for European options.

E. Using Put–Call Parity To Estimate the Early Exercise Premium

In practice, almost all exchange-traded options have the American feature. Yet, closed form pricing formulas for options are usually only available for options with the European feature. As a consequence, information about the empirical behavior of the early exercise premium (EEP) is of considerable interest. For example, Zivney (1991) suggests that empirical estimates of the EEP can be used as inputs to the Hull and White (1988b) control variate technique to numerically obtain American option prices. There are various possible methods of estimating the EEP. For example, by examining foreign currency options Jorion and Stoughton (1989) derived comparative statics for the EEP under the assumption that the spot exchange rate follows a diffusion. Critical exercise values associated with specific values of the spot exchange rate are identified for both puts and calls. The comparative static conditions are then estimated empirically using regressions with the difference between the American and European prices for the same underlying spot exchange rate. Unfortunately, the reported empirical results were not impressive, indicating that the methodology is not the best technique to use in evaluating empirical EEP behavior.

Direct estimates of the *EEP* are not essential to obtaining American option prices. There are various methods available for numerically estimating American prices (e.g., Hull, 2000, chap. 16). Once the American option price is obtained, a value for the EEP can be estimated by taking the difference between the estimated American price and the European price obtained from Black–Scholes. Estimated over a range of times to expiration and exercise prices, it is possible to obtain an estimate for the early exercise boundary. Bodurtha and Courtadon (1995) provide an excellent example of how the early exercise boundary can be directly estimated using numerical methods. While useful, such methods are not readily accessible, and results depend on the accuracy of the pricing models selected. For example, Bodurtha and Courtadon (1995) report that if not all the options are exercised then the estimated early exercise boundary predicted would be imprecise.

The direct approach to evaluating EEP involves examining the difference in the prices of European and American options written on the same commodity. A major difficulty with the direct approach is the relative absence of European option prices. Zivney (1991) and de Roon and Veld (1996) have used a creative approach based on the European put–call parity condition. Recall that, for spot commodities paying dividends:

$$S(t) + P[S,\tau,X] = X\ PV[\tau] + D + C[S,\tau,X]$$

It follows that: $C - P = S - X\ PV - D$. Using the result that $C_A = C + EEP_C$ and $P_A = P + EEP_P$ it follows that:

$$
\begin{aligned}
C_A - P_A &= C + EEP_C - P - EEP_P = S - X\ PV - D + (EEP_C - EEP_P) \\
&\rightarrow EEP_C - EEP_P = C_A - P_A - (S - X\ PV - D)
\end{aligned}
\tag{7.1}
$$

The difference between the EEP for calls and puts is now represented by values that are obtainable from American option prices and observable cash market values.

An interesting development on this approach is provided by de Roon and Veld (1996) where the German stock market (DAX) index traded on the American Stock Exchange was used in place of the Standard and Poors (S&P) 100 index options used by Zivney (1991). The DAX index is a performance index where dividends paid on the underlying securities in the index are reinvested, unlike the S&P 100 index options, where dividends are not paid. In this case, the index call option will not be exercised early and any deviation in the righthand side of Eq. (7.1) can only be due to EEP_P. Zivney (1991) found that the EEP for puts was greater than for calls, *ceteris paribus*, and EEP increases with time to expiration, moneyness, and the riskless rate of interest. Similar results were found by de Roon and Veld (1996), though the time to expiration results did differ. Both studies suggest that commonly used American option pricing models may fail to capture all the nuances of the early exercise decision.

III. SPREAD TRADES AND STRATEGIES[14]

A. STRADDLES, STRAPS, AND STRANGLES

Two general types of speculative trading strategies for options can be identified.[15] The first type relies on option mispricing—effectively, deviations of observed options prices from theoretical values as determined by an applicable option pricing formula or a theoretical arbitrage boundary condition. Examples of these types of trades are conversions, reversals, ratio spreads, and box spreads. Due to transaction costs and difficulties in obtaining real-time option quotes, these strategies are difficult to execute profitably for non-exchange traders. The amount of mispricing is typically of a small enough order that access to low transaction and execution costs, associated with exchange-member trading, is required. The other types of strategies are natural extensions of the speculative trades examined in Chapter 3. The profitability of these trades requires a prediction about the direction or volatility of spot prices or some other variable such as interest rates. The associated trades, and their profit functions, will be the central concern of this section. For want of a better description, these trades will be referred to as *directional* trades.

Two general types of directional trades can be identified: *spreads* and *combinations*. Combinations involve taking positions in both puts and calls on the same security, as in a straddle, while a spread trade involves taking positions in two or more options of the same type: two (or more) calls, two (or more) puts, as in a butterfly or vertical spread. At a basic level, spreads involve the simultaneous purchase of one option and the sale of another, usually on the same spot commodity, with the two options differing in exercise price and/or time to expiration. If the options differ in exercise price, but have the same expiration date, the trade is a *vertical* spread. If the options differ in expiration date, with the same exercise price, the trade is a *horizontal* spread or time spread. If the options combine differences in both time and exercise price, the trade is a *diagonal* spread. As with futures, an intracommodity spread involves the same spot commodity for both options, while the intercommodity spread will use different commodities. Unlike spreads, combinations involve having

---

[14]Much of the literature on the various types of options trading strategies is somewhat dated, with much of the material available in trade publications and textbooks. Examples of early studies include Gombola *et al.* (1978) and Ritchken and Salkin (1981). There is also a substantial literature on the performance of covered call option writing strategies, e.g., Yates and Kapprasch (1980); Mueller (1981); Brown (1986).

[15]It is also possible to devise strategies that involve using options to generate premium income. This income can be used to finance various types of speculative positions in other assets. These types of strategies will not be explored here except where the positions are directly related to arbitrage trades.

the same type of position, either long or short, in the relevant options. A *straddle* involves combining a put and a call, on the same commodity, with the same exercise price and time to maturity. When the exercise price of the put is less than the exercise price of the call, the position is called a *strangle*. Variations on the straddle include the *strap*, two calls and one put, and the *strip*, two puts and one call. The expiration-date profit diagrams for these trades are not difficult and are given in an end-of-chapter question.

Using the assumption that interest on premiums is ignored, the expiration-date profit diagram can be used to illustrate the terminal payoffs associated with spreads and combinations. Prior to expiration, more advanced valuation techniques are required. These complications will be explored in Chapters 8 and 9. Consider the case of a purchased straddle, with both options having exercise price X—not necessarily at-the-money—and expiring on the same date. Selling the straddle, again with the same X and expiration date for both options, will be the negative of the purchased straddle.[16] The importance of stock price volatility to the profitability of these trades should be apparent. A purchased straddle requires that spot commodity prices move a greater amount, either up or down, than is implied in the option premium (plus the foregone interest that is being ignored by assumption). Selling the straddle is the reverse; the volatility of the spot commodity will be less than implied by the option premium (less the interest). The key feature of these trades is the reliance on volatility to determine trade profitability.

In certain cases, the speculative trader may have notions both about the direction of prices and about volatility. For example, there may be a potential takeover bid emerging for a company. If the bid is announced, the stock price will increase substantially; however, if the bid collapses, then prices may fall substantially. The weight of evidence may be in favor of either alternative. In either case, volatility will increase substantially. In these types of cases, if it is more likely that the bid will successfully materialize, it is possible to purchase a strap. Similarly, if the bid is viewed unfavorably and prices are felt to be more likely to fall than rise, then a strip could be purchased. It is also possible to exploit this type information by selling straps and strips. For example, instead of purchasing a strap (strip), it is also possible to write a strip (strap). However, as was the case with the straddle, the written positions have a bounded above expiration-date profit function versus the purchased positions where the profit functions are unbounded above. Hence, for the written position, straps and strips allow the seller to generate additional premium income based

---

[16]A variation on the straddle is the *strangle* where the exercise prices for the put are below the exercise price for the call positions. In this case, the expiration-date profit diagram is flat over the region between the exercise prices. The advantage of a strangle over a straddle is that it is cheaper to purchase. For the writer, while premium income is lower, there is a wider range of expiration-date stock prices that generate a profit.

on a prediction about the direction of spot prices. Variations on straps, strips, and straddles can be developed based on where the exercise price of the options is determined relative to the value of the spot commodity (i.e., whether the option is in-the-money, out-of-the-money, or at-the-money).

B. Vertical and Horizontal Spreads

While there are a number of similarities between speculative trading strategies in futures and options, there are notable differences in the nature of the payoffs. This is the case with option spread trades where, despite combining purchased (long) and written (short) positions, the futures/options payoffs differ significantly. As noted previously, three basic types of intracommodity spread trades can be identified: *vertical* spreads, where the options being combined have different exercise prices; *horizontal* spreads, where the expiration dates differ; and *diagonal* spreads, which involve combining options with different exercise prices and time to expiration.[17] Much as in the futures discussion in Chapters 3 and 5, it is possible to extend these notions to intercommodity trading, but this development will not be explored here. In addition, it is possible to use various types of replication strategies to approximate one or both of the options used in the spread position as well as to replicate the spread payoff function directly. This point will be developed more fully in Chapter 9, Section I, where the concepts of synthetic security design will be developed more precisely. Other extensions of spreads include the butterfly trade, which has a substantively different payoff function than for the futures case. In turn, the butterfly trade can be used to provide restrictions on the premiums for options with different exercise prices (see Questions at the end of the chapter).

Consider a vertical spread trade that combines a purchased call at X_1 with a written call at X_2, where $X_2 > X_1$ (Graph 7.9). This is sometimes referred to as a "bullish" vertical spread. The effect of the written call position is to trade off a portion of the upside potential of the purchased call for a reduction in the (net) premium paid. Similarly, a "bearish" vertical spread would involve writing a call at X_1 and purchasing a call at X_2 (Graph 7.10). In this case, the trader is seeking to eliminate the unbounded nature of the written call, in exchange for some reduction in (net) premium income received. Vertical spreads can also be established for puts (Graphs 7.11 and 7.12). In one case, the purchased put is at X_2 with a written put at X_1, where $X_2 > X_1$. This

---

[17]These descriptions correspond to the method in which option price quotes are typically observed in the financial press. Differences in prices across exercise prices are recorded vertically, while price differences across expiration dates occur horizontally.

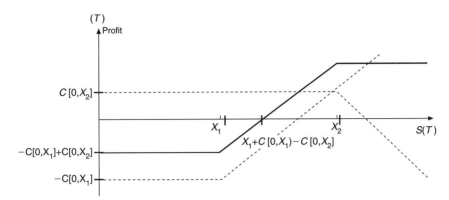

GRAPH 7.9 Bullish vertical call spread: buy a call at X_1, write a call at X_2.

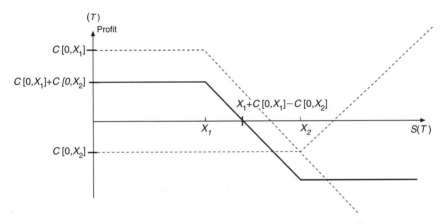

GRAPH 7.10 Bearish vertical call spread: write a call at X_1, buy a call at X_2.

reduces the (net) premium paid to purchase the put. Where the written put is at X_2 and the purchased put at X_1, (net) premium income is reduced in order to bound the payoff function. By recalling the replication strategies described previously, various extensions are possible—for example, the "bullish" vertical spread. The purchased call position can be replicated with long the cash plus buy at put at X_1. Hence, long the stock, combined with a purchased put at X_1 and a written call at X_2 will "replicate" the payoff on a vertical spread. At this point, the basic connection to caps, collars, and floors should be apparent.

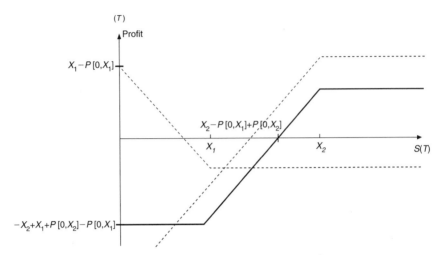

GRAPH 7.11 Bullish vertical put spread: write a put at X_2, buy a put at X_1.

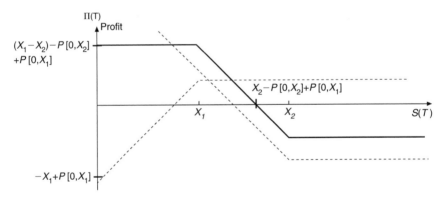

GRAPH 7.12 Bearish vertical put spread: buy a put at X_2, write a put at X_1.

While not difficult conceptually, horizontal, or time, spreads are problematic to depict using expiration-date profit diagrams. This is because the expiration date can only apply to one of the options; the value of the other option on the expiration date of the first option must be estimated. To see this, consider a horizontal spread in GM options observed on October 20 with a then-current GM stock price of $54 7/8 and an exercise price of $55:

December	2 7/8
March	4 3/4
June	5 1/4

If the horizontal spread involves purchasing the March (June) option and selling the December, then the "basis" on the trade is $-1\frac{7}{8}(-2\frac{3}{8})$. This is the net premium income that has to be paid to establish the spread on October 20. Consider the payoff on this trade on the expiration date of the December option given in Graph 7.13. In deriving this payoff profile, it was necessary to *estimate* the value of the March 55 (June 55) option that would prevail on the expiration date of the December 55 option.

C. BUTTERFLIES, SANDWICHES, AND OTHER TRADES

The expiration-date profit diagram for the time spread associated with the GM example is given in Graph 7.13. Because of the need to estimate the price of one of the options, the motivation for doing a horizontal spread is closely connected to the problem of how options are priced or, more precisely, how time decay affects options with different expiration dates. This problem will be addressed analytically in Chapter 9. Given this, the final spread trade to be considered is the intracommodity *butterfly*, which involves taking positions in options with three different exercise prices. Specifically, for $X_1 < X_2 < X_3$, a

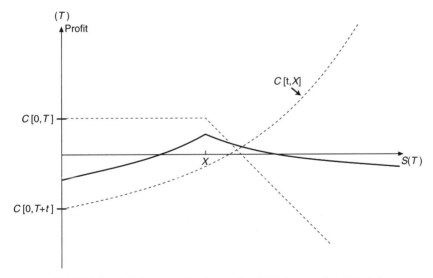

GRAPH 7.13   Call time spread: write a call at (X,T), buy a call at $(X,T+t)$.

butterfly involves selling one option at both X_1 and X_3 and buying two options at X_2. While similar in construction to its futures counterpart, the expiration-date profit diagram for the options butterfly trade has a shape that is responsible for the name attached to this trade (see Questions at the end of the chapter). Conceptually, a butterfly can be viewed as a bounded straddle. Because of the different shape of the expiration-date profit diagram, the opposite trade that involves purchasing options at both X_1 and X_3 and writing at X_2 is sometimes referred to as a *sandwich* (see Graph 7.14). Much as in the futures case, the small potential profits associated with the butterfly and sandwich trades restricts the usefulness of this trade primarily to exchange members.

The list of trades considered to this point has covered trades that depend on predicting the direction or volatility of some random variable, usually the spot price. Option strategies also include trades based on mispricing that are primarily of interest to traders on the option exchanges. The mechanics of the trades are more complicated, as evidenced in an examination of two important trades aimed at exploiting mispricing: the *ratio* spread and the *box* spread. A ratio spread is a trading strategy aimed at simultaneously selling an overpriced (correctly priced) option and buying a comparable correctly priced (under-priced) option on the same stock. The comparable option could differ either in time to expiration or exercise price. Execution of the ratio spread requires some method for determining the appropriate number of contracts to initiate in the two options in order to be properly hedged. As will be discussed in Chapter 9, the ratio of the derivatives of the Black–Scholes formula with respect to the spot price for the two options, the *option deltas*, provides the relevant hedge ratio.

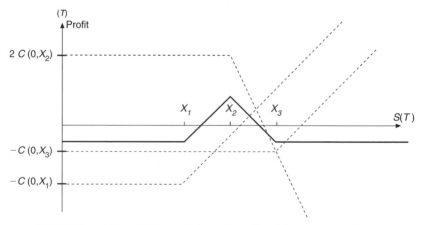

GRAPH 7.14   Call sandwich spread: buy calls at X_1 and X_3, write two calls at X_2.

A box spread combines bullish (bearish) vertical spreads using calls with bearish (bullish) vertical spreads using puts, using the same X_1, X_2, and T (e.g., Billingsley and Chance, 1985; Hemler, 1997). The trade is designed to exploit mispricing across exercise prices. To see this, consider the expiration-date payoff on a box spread. The bullish vertical spread using calls involves buying at X_1 and writing at $X_2(X_1 < X_2)$ to give max $[0,S(T) - X_1]$ − max $[0,S(T) -X_2]$. Similarly, the bearish vertical spread using puts gives max $[0,X_2 - S(T)]$ − max $[0,X_1 - S(T)]$. If $S(T) > X_2$, then the call positions pay off $X_2 - X_1$ and both puts expire worthless. If $X_1 < S(T) < X_2$, then the calls pay off $S(T) - X_1$ and the puts provide $X_2 - S(T)$ or, combining the two positions, $X_2 - X_1$. Finally, if $S(T) < X_1 < X_2$, then the calls expire worthless and the puts provide $X_2 - X_1$. Hence, in all future states of the world, the box spread will pay off $X_2 - X_1$. Mispricing occurs when the discounted value of $X_2 - X_1$ does not equal the net premium generated from the box spread for $t < T$. If the discounted value of $X_2 - X_1$ is greater than the net premium, the bullish call spread and bearish put spread are purchased. If the value is less than the net premium, a bearish call spread combined with a bullish put spread is purchased. This case involves generating *positive* net premiums at t that can be invested for t^* to earn a greater amount than the payout of $X_2 - X_1$ at T.

D. Caps, Floors, and Collars

Even though caps, collars, and floors are available for a number of different commodities, these instruments are most widely used in adjusting cash flows originating from floating-rate debt securities. There is an active OTC market in medium to long-term caps, collars, and floors, collectively known as the *cap market*. An interest rate cap is an agreement between two parties: the provider of the cap, typically a large financial institution, and a cap purchaser, often (though not always) a borrower in the floating-rate debt market. The cap agreement specifies a par value, a reference rate (typically the London Interbank offer rate, LIBOR), a term (e.g., 5 years), and a cap level or ceiling rate, often specified as some number of basis points above current LIBOR. If the reference rate goes above the cap level, the provider agrees to make payments, based on the par value, sufficient to keep the cap purchaser's interest payments at the cap level. If the reference rate stays below the ceiling rate, no payments are made. In exchange for entering into the cap agreement, the cap purchaser agrees to pay a premium to the provider. When incorporated into a debt issue, a cap provision adds some basis points to the cost of the borrowing.

A floor is the reverse of a cap. The floor is an agreement where the floor provider, often a borrower in the floating-rate debt market, agrees to make payments to the purchaser when the reference rate falls below the stated floor.

Again, the size of the payments depend on the par value and the number of basis points the reference rate is below the floor. Adding a floor to a floating-rate borrowing reduces the cost of the borrowing by some basis points. A collar is a combination of a cap and a floor. This agreement effectively limits the interest rate payments on a floating-rate borrowing to a band, determined by the cap and floor rates. An advantage of a collar over a cap is that the premium received for the floor will offset the cost of the cap, making the interest rate hedge less expensive. The resulting cash flows from the debt instrument are a hybrid possessing features of both floating-rate and fixed-rate debt. In the limit, adjusting a floating-rate debt issue by selling a floor and buying a cap, with a reference rate equal to the current interest rate, will transform the floating-rate debt into fixed-rate debt. Similarly, adjusting fixed-rate debt by buying a floor and selling a cap has the opposite affect.

The ability to combine debt issues with caps and floors to transform floating-rate debt into fixed-rate debt, and vice versa, implies that there is a direct connection between the pricing of interest rate swaps and the pricing of caps and floors. For the case of single cash flows, there is a direct connection between caps, floors, and options. In practice, a cap can be priced as a sequence of put options on individual cash flows, known as *caplets*. Consider what a caplet offers. If the reference interest rate rises above the ceiling rate, then a payment is made based on the size of the difference and the par value. The connection to options now follows from taking t^* to be the floating-rate reset interval; X to be the present value of the exercise price, discounted at the ceiling rate c; $X = \exp\{-ct^*\}$; and B to be the present value of a zero-coupon bond discounted at the observed reference rate r, $B = \exp\{-rt^*\}$. The payoff on the caplet can now be viewed as a put option: $P = \max[0, X - B]$. In discrete time, which is the way the swap payout is determined in practice, $P = \max[0, [(r - c)t^*]/(1 + rt^*)]$. Briys *et al.* (1991) demonstrate the approximate equivalence of these two formulations. The floor can be similarly interpreted as a sequence of call options on individual cash flows, with the exercise price determined by the floor rate and payments on the individual options made on the reset dates. The purchased collar can be interpreted as a long position in the cap, at exercise price X_1 and a short position in the floor at exercise price $X_2 (X_2 > X_1)$.

IV. REAL OPTIONS, INSURANCE, AND THE DEMAND FOR PUT OPTIONS

A. REAL OPTIONS

Options occur in many other forms than the OTC and exchange-traded variations. In some cases, the embedded option is apparent, as with a callable or convertible bond. A floating-rate loan with an interest rate cap, collar, or floor is another example. Less obvious examples are insurance and common stock. In response to shortcomings in the traditional net present value decision rule, corporate finance and real estate economics have developed valuation models that incorporate the numerous types of real options that arise in those areas (e.g., Dixit and Pindyck, 1994; Trigeorgis, 1996; Brennan and Trigeorgis, 2000). Real option notions have also had a significant impact in modeling the economics of capital investment. A list of the most important of these options includes the option to defer, the option to redevelop or reschedule, the time-to-build option, the option to alter operating scale, the option to abandon or mothball, the option to switch, and growth options. Like conventional options, real options have some exercise "price" and may be exercised if the option is in-the-money, but exercise is not required if the option is out-of-the-money. The exercise decision is typically irreversible. Unlike most conventional options, real options are usually long-dated and are often valued as perpetuals (e.g, Capozza and Li, 1994).

Real options also play a role in firm capital budgeting and real asset investment decisions. The traditional net present value (NPV) rule can be stated: In the absence of capital rationing, invest in projects that have NPV greater than zero (e.g., Brealey and Myers, 1992). Despite being central to capital budgeting and the macroeconomic theory of investment, this rule fails in many important situations due to the presence of real options that can induce a firm to forego investments with positive NPV. Important features of investment decision problems where the rule fails contain some combination of irreversibility, timing, and uncertainty. Irreversibility means that an investment has an element of sunk costs; for example, in real estate a decision to tear down an existing structure and build a more expensive structure designed to generate more rents is irreversible. The decision to redevelop the property involves foregoing the option to defer development to a later time, when expected rentals may be higher. In mining, a decision to abandon a mine is partially irreversible, because the costs associated with startup are similar to the costs of starting a new mining operation. Mine closure is an exercise of the real option to abandon, which depends on the quality of the ore being produced and the expected price of the metal.

Closely related to the real options, such as the development option, are executive stock options. Unlike real options, which are largely of theoretical interest and deal with the return on real assets, executive stock options (ESOs) are non-traded securities that have to be valued in order to satisfy generally accepted accounting principles (GAAP). ESOs are an important component of modern corporate finance, with roughly three quarters of larger corporations having such plans, with unexercised ESOs accounting for roughly 13% of the number of shares outstanding (Soffer, 2000). To address the important accounting implications of ESOs, FAS 123 (FASB, 1995) deals with "Accounting for Stock-Based Compensation" and provides a modified Black–Scholes model (see Chapters 8 and 9) to determine the fair value of ESOs for use in financial disclosure statements. Unlike exchange-traded options, ESOs are typically subject to numerous restrictions including forfeiture when an employee leaves the company and the inability to sell or hedge the ESO position. These restrictions make it difficult to obtain a precise value for an ESO. The Financial Accounting Standards Board (FASB) model uses empirical values for expected forfeiture and exercise behavior to determine an estimated option value. The adjustments result in a lower value for an ESO relative to an exchange-traded option.

Considerable debate still surrounds the question of whether FAS 123 is the appropriate method for valuing ESOs (e.g., Huddart and Lang, 1996; Carpenter, 1998; Soffer, 2000). There does not seem to be a consensus on whether FAS 123 results in option values which are too high or too low. For example, Cuny and Jorion (1995) argue that stock price performance and employee turnover are highly correlated. In assuming these two variables are uncorrelated, the FAS 123 methodology will undervalue ESOs. Hemmer et al. (1994) argue that by using the expected time to exercise instead of actual time to exercise, FAS 123 overstates the value of ESOs. Some options will be exercised earlier and some options will be exercised later than the expected exercise date. Yet, the option value is a concave function of the time to expiration, resulting in an overvaluation of the option by using the expected time to expiration. The FAS 123 methodology also has supporters. For example, working within a more sophisticated model that incorporates numerous elements not included in FAS 123 (e.g., employee risk aversion), Carpenter (1998) demonstrates that, despite the imperfections, FAS 123 does provide a reasonable estimate for the value of ESOs.

B. Insurance and Option Pricing

At least since Merton (1977) and Smith (1979), it has been recognized that insurance valuation is a potential application of the options pricing methodology discussed in Chapters 8 and 9. Though other methods of obtaining premium payments are available, it is possible to successfully price insurance premiums using options pricing methods (e.g., Doherty and Garven, 1986; Cummins, 1988; Shimko, 1992; Phillips et al., 1998). The extension of options pricing to insurance is not as easy as it might appear. It is possible, for example, to conceive of insurance as a form of put option. For example, car insurance involves the payment of a premium in exchange for the right to sell the car back to the insurance company (or at least the damaged part) under conditions laid out in the insurance policy. Similarly, a life-insurance premium is made in exchange for the right to receive a cash payment in the event that the death of a specific person occurs in the period up to when the next premium payment is due. Precisely how options pricing methodology could be used in these instances is not always apparent.

Shimko (1992, p. 229) identifies three reasons why insurance policies complicate option pricing:

> 1. For many lines of insurance, a policy holder may submit multiple claims. 2. Policies are typically written with prescribed deductibles and maximum coverage limits. The non-linear nature of these loss-sharing rules creates aggregation problems similar to those encountered in the valuation of portfolios of options. 3. The size and frequency of losses may vary systematically, which requires the calculation of a risk premium that is also affected by the option-like characteristics of the insurance policies.

Further complications for option pricing arise when it is recognized that most insurance companies write policies in a number of lines of business (e.g., automobile, property, general liability) and are subject to default risk (Phillips *et al.*, 1998). Multiple-line insurance companies hold equity in a common pool, where the different lines are subject to different risks. Option pricing methods can be used to determine how to allocate equity capital to the different lines of business.

C. SKEWNESS PREFERENCE AND THE DEMAND FOR PUT OPTIONS

Chapter 2, Section I, identified the maximization of expected utility for end-of-period wealth as an appropriate objective for risk-management decision making. At various points, optimal hedge ratios have been derived, using the mean-variance moment-preference function and other forms of expected-utility functions. These techniques can be applied to determine the optimal demand for options, as well as futures and forward contracts. Yet, the payoffs on futures and forward contracts are linear, while option payoffs are nonlinear. Linear payoffs work directly on the variance. For example, a full hedge with no basis risk effectively reduces the variance of hedge profit to zero. Options work by altering the shape of the return distribution. If desired, options can be used to reduce the dispersion of the return distribution (e.g., using a purchased put to truncate negative returns associated with a stock price falling below the exercise price). However, the nonlinear payoff on options will, of necessity, impact the higher moments of the return distribution, particularly the skewness. Bookstaber and Clarke (1983) have numerous useful graphs of the various distributional shapes associated with option usage in portfolios.

As risk-management products, options are much like insurance. As discussed in Chapter 2, Section II, insurance theory is concerned with pricing the risks associated with situations involving loss or no loss. As such, the main objective of insurance is to reduce the possibility of (extreme) negative returns. This is equivalent to saying that insurance is used to reduce negative skewness in the return distribution. If the firm is long the spot commodity being hedged, then purchased put options would be used. As such, the use of put options is equivalent to buying insurance on the spot commodity return. (The connection between purchased calls and insurance is less obvious.) Because options act on the skewness in the return distribution, it is natural to ask whether an improved estimate for the optimal hedge ratio can be obtained by adding a skewness term to the moment preference function as discussed in Chapter 2, Section I, where $U''' > 0$; i.e., positive skewness preference is assumed. Presumably, because put options act to reduce negative skewness, explicitly identifying skewness preference in the objective function will result in an increase in the optimal demand for put options, compared to the mean-variance case where only the put option impact on variance is taken into account. As it turns out, this is not the case.

In perfect markets, options will be priced on an actuarially fair basis implying that the expected return on purchasing an option will be zero. Hence, the mean part of the mean-variance and mean-variance-skewness objective functions will not enter the optimal solutions. Derivation of the optimal solutions now requires the variance and skewness for the terminal wealth function to be identified. While it is possible to do this in general, it is more instructive to consider a practical example. In particular, the choice of a stylized farmer regarding the optimal amount of privately issued crop insurance to purchase has attractive features. The stylized farmer plants one crop, which is subject to both price and yield uncertainty. To hedge this uncertainty, the farmer only has access to crop insurance. Three kinds of crop insurance schemes are possible:

1. *Quantity insurance*: The physical yield is restricted from falling below some minimum amount, usually set as some percentage of historical yields. This case is consistent with many traditional crop insurance plans.
2. *Price insurance*: The crop delivery price is restricted from falling below a minimum amount. This type of insurance can be accomplished using put options.
3. *Mixed or revenue insurance*: The total revenue is restricted from falling below a minimum amount. This case is consistent with farm income stabilization and, to a lesser extent, disaster relief programs.[18]

---

[18]Total revenue is the realized income from planting a given crop. Given that various types of farm income stabilization programs are possible (e.g., where payments are made prior to planting on the condition that farmers do not plant certain crops), the revenue insurance schemes being examined here are not fully descriptive of all possible plans.

The farmer is able to select only one of these types at a time from a given vendor.

In practice, there is no stylized farmer and it is useful to provide some context about how crop insurance schemes actually work. In the United States, crop insurance has undergone substantial changes. The crop insurance program that is federally administered is now managed by the Risk Management Agency of the U. S. Department of Agriculture (USDA) (www.act.fcic. usda.gov). Where the farmer traditionally only had access to a federal crop insurance scheme that was effectively a quantity-based insurance scheme with premiums priced at a subsidy, there are now an array of crop insurance plans offered by private insurance companies (e.g., www.cropinsurance.org), as well as a wider range of plans available from the federal governments. Virtually all the plans have restrictions on the fraction of the crop that can be insured. In addition to pure crop insurance programs, disaster relief programs are also available. The totality of income support, crop insurance, and other programs targeted at farmers is complicated to model. In Canada, all three types of crop insurance have been offered as alternatives under the Guaranteed Revenue Insurance Program (GRIP). Various schemes are offered in other countries (e.g., Hazell *et al.*, 1986).

The farmer's terminal wealth functions with crop insurance based on price and for futures hedging are given in Chapter 2, Section I. While the terminal wealth functions for the other forms of crop insurance (price and yield) follow appropriately, some motivation is required. In particular, in the absence of crop insurance and hedging, there is a natural minimum on R. Either a complete crop loss where $Y_{t+1} = 0$ or a spot price of zero at time $t + 1$ corresponds to the case $(1 + R) = 0$. Significantly, unlike revenue insurance, neither yield insurance nor price insurance by itself can guarantee a higher minimum return when $(1 + R)$ equals zero. For example, price insurance guaranteeing \$K a bushel $(P_{t+1} > K)$ cannot prevent a 100% crop loss due to drought, nor can quantity insurance providing for, say, Y bushels an acre $(Y_{t+1} > Y)$ prevent the future spot price from falling to zero. However, both price and quantity insurance do reduce the probability of the total return attaining low values and, as a result, alter the distribution for terminal wealth. As it turns out, there are substantive differences in how price and yield insurance accomplish this result.

D. The Farmer's Terminal Wealth Function

To see the formal implications of admitting insurance, it is useful to derive the terminal wealth functions for the price, yield, and revenue forms of crop insurance (see Chapter 2, Section I). Assuming the farmer buys revenue insurance against the full value of the crop $(AP_{t+1}Y_{t+1})$, the terminal wealth function can be specified:

$$\begin{aligned} W^i_{t+1} &= W_t\{(1+r) + x(\max[R,\underline{R}] - s - r)\} \\ &= W_t\{(1+r) + x[(R-r) + \max[0,\underline{R}-R] - s]\} \\ &= W_t + \pi_{t+1} + W_t\{x(\max[0,\underline{R}-R] - s)\} \end{aligned}$$

where s equals $(SA)/C(A)$, with S being the price (insurance premium) per acre for the revenue insurance, and $\underline{R}$ is the income floor specified in the insurance plan. It can be seen from the terminal wealth function that the effect of adding revenue insurance to the risk-management problem depends on assumptions made about both the pricing of the insurance premium (S) and the requirement that the full value of the crop be insured.

It can also be seen from the terminal wealth function that the effect of adding revenue insurance to the risk-management problem is to increase terminal wealth by x times the purchase price adjusted payout on a "put option" written on the return R, with exercise "price" $\underline{R}$. If the insurance (put option) is priced as an acutarially sound expected indemnity, then insurance will not change the farmer's expected wealth for the selected production level. All insurance does is limit downside risk. Whether this will affect the production level is discussed in Poitras (1993). The conclusion about the effect on expected wealth does not change if the farmer is permitted to choose the fraction of acreage insured; that is, where the terminal wealth function is given by:

$$W^i_{t+1} = W_t\{(1+r) + x(R-r) + x\theta \max[0,\underline{R}-R] - s\}$$

where θ is the fraction of the total planted acreage insured under the revenue insurance scheme.

In many respects, the yield and revenue insurance cases are identical. As in the revenue insurance case, it is the number of acres to insure that is the decision variable:

$$W^y_{t+1} = AY_{t+1}P_{t+1} + [W_t - C(A)](1+r) + Q_y(P_{t+1}\max[0,\underline{Y}-Y_{t+1}] - L)$$

where L is the price (insurance premium) per acre for the crop insurance, Q_y is the number of planted acres covered by the physical yield insurance, and $\underline{Y}$ is the yield floor provided by the insurance plan. In practice, $\underline{Y}$ is set based on a percentage ($< 100\%$) of relevant historical physical yield averages. While the price used would actually depend on a specific method of price election selected by the farmer, taking the price elected to be the harvest period cash price (P_{t+1}) is not unrealistic.

Assuming that $Q_y = A$ (i.e., all planted acres are insured) leads to the following:

$$W^y_{t+1} = W_t\{(1 + r) + x[(R - r)$$
$$+ \max [0, \frac{(P_{t+1}\underline{Y}A) - (P_{t+1}Y_{t+1}A)}{C(A)}] - l]\}$$

where l equals $(LA)/[C(A)]$. Observing that the expression inside the max function involves the difference between two random variables illustrates the primary analytical difference between the different forms of the terminal wealth function. This distinction depends crucially on assuming that both price and quantity are uncertain. Observing that it may be unrealistic to assume that all acreage is insured, allowing the farmer to choose the acreage insured leads to:

$$W^y_{t+1} = W_t\{(1 + r) + x(R - r) + x\lambda(\max [0, \underline{RR} - R] - l)\}$$

where λ is the fraction of the total planted acreage insured under the physical yield crop insurance scheme and $\underline{RR} = \{P_{t+1}\underline{Y}A\}/[C(A)]$. As with revenue insurance, fair pricing requires insurance to impact the decision problem through its effect on downside risk.

As in Chapter 2, Section I, examining the price insurance case involves introducing put options (written on the futures price). This leads to:[19]

$$W^z_{t+1} = AY_{t+1}P_{t+1} + [W_t - C(A)](1 + r) + Q_z(\max [0, K - f_{t+1}] - z)$$
$$= W_t\left\{x(1 + R) + (1 - x)(1 + r) + \frac{Q_z f_t}{W_t}\left(\max [0, \frac{K - f_{t+1}}{f_t}] - \frac{z}{f_t}\right)\right\}$$
$$= W_t\left\{x(1 + R) + (1 - x)(1 + r) + \gamma\left(\max [0, -R_f] - \frac{z}{f_t}\right)\right\}$$

where K is exercise price on the put option that is assumed to be at-the-money (i.e., $K = f_t$), z is the price per unit of output of the put, Q_z is the number (in output units) of puts purchased, and the ratio γ is the value of the option position divided by initial wealth.[20] As in the yield and revenue insurance cases, if the put option is "fairly priced," then the expected value of the last term in the terminal wealth function is zero and insurance only has relevance for maximizing the expected utility of wealth insofar as it limits downside risk. However, price insurance has a direct impact on the distribution for R_f and not R, as in the other two cases.

[19]Given the ability to replicate call positions by combining puts and futures, little is gained by introducing a term for a call option. Similarly, while a straddle position would have an interesting random variable distribution, this would add little when futures are present.

[20]It is also possible to specify the put option using cash prices. However, this significantly complicates the analysis. In addition, exchange-traded options are typically written using futures prices, so the present construction is potentially more realistic.

E. Mean-Variance Skewness and the Optimal Demand for Put Options

Following the discussion in Chapter 2, Section I, the terminal wealth function provides essential information required to derive conditions from the maximization of an appropriate expected utility (EU) function. Using the moment-preference approach, the presence of options argues for optimizing a mean-variance-skewness EU function because the nonlinear payoffs on options are designed to impact the higher moments of the return distribution. Poitras and Heaney (1999) use a mean-variance-skewness, moment-preference function to derive relatively robust results about the problem at hand, the optimal amount of put option (e.g., crop insurance) to purchase, and the more general issue of modeling optimal decisions involving options using moment preference object-ive functions.

The results in this section make use of results derived in Chapter 2, Section I, for the mean-variance-skewness, expected-utility function and the wealth process for a long spot position combined with a put option. This combination is of interest because options alter the skewness of the return distribution, so modeling the decision problem with an objective function that values skew-ness in addition to mean and variance seems intuitively desirable. Yet, pursu-ing this approach soon leads to counterintuitive results. Proposition 7.1 deals with the case of put options that are being used to reduce the negative skewness in the distribution of asset return. The simplest application would be to crop insurance, where a farmer wants to protect against flood, drought, disease, or some other outcome that reduces crop yield. Presumably, introdu-cing skewness preference into the expected-utility problem would increase the optimal hedge ratio for the put option. Proposition 7.1 demonstrates that this is not the case (Poitras and Heaney, 1999).

The results require assuming that the risk manager optimizes a moment-preference approximation to a general expected-utility function of the form, $EU_{MVS} = U\{E[W_{t+1}]\} - b \ \text{var}[W_{t+1}] + c \ \text{skew}[W_{t+1}]$, where b and c are meas-ures of the sensitivity of EU to changes in $\text{var}[\ \cdot\ ]$ and $\text{skew}[\ \cdot\ ]$, with $b, c > 0$; all options/insurance premiums are "fairly priced." It is also assumed that R has a negatively skewed probability density function, where $\text{skew}[R] < 0$.[21] Proposition 7.1 now applies.[22]

---

[21]This assumption involves somewhat more than is stated. More precisely, this assumption requires that the put option payouts will occur in states where the returns are low. Cases where put option payouts occur and revenue is high are excluded to avoid having to consider pathological cases.

[22]If the option is not fairly priced, in practice it will probably be underpriced due to government subsidies. In the crop insurance context, underpricing will produce an increase in

---

PROPOSITION 7.1

Optimal Demand for Put Options

Assuming that the risk manager optimizes a moment-preference object-ive function, defined over the mean, variance, and skewness of the farmer's terminal wealth function that includes put options, then the optimal demand for a put option with payoff depending on *yield* is

$$\lambda^* = -\frac{\sigma_{Rq}}{\sigma_q^2} + x\frac{3cW_t}{2b\sigma_q^2}\{cosk[\lambda; \underline{RR}]\}$$

where the subscript q corresponds to the random variable $\max[0,\underline{RR}-R]$ and the subscript R refers to the rate of return on the asset. The coskewness term, cosk $[\lambda; \underline{RR}]$, has the interpretation:

$$
\begin{aligned}
cosk[\lambda;\underline{RR}] \equiv cosk[\lambda] = & E\{\lambda^2(\max[0,\underline{RR}-R]-E[\max[0,\underline{RR}-R]])^3 \\
& + (\max[0,\underline{RR}-R]-E[\max[0,\underline{RR}-R]])(R-E[R])^2 \\
& + 2\lambda(\max[0,\underline{RR}-R]-E[\max[0,\underline{RR}-R]])^2(R-E[R])\} \\
\equiv & \lambda^2 skew[q] + \sigma_{qR^2} + 2\{\lambda\sigma_{q^2R}\}
\end{aligned}
$$

The mean-variance solution (λ_{MV}) is given by ignoring the second term on the righthand side of λ^*. The associated closed-form solution is

$$\lambda^* = \frac{(\sigma_q^2 - 2A\,\sigma_{q^2R}) - \sqrt{(\sigma_q^2 - 2A\,\sigma_{q^2R})^2 - 4A\,skew[q](A\,\sigma_{R^2q} - \sigma_{qR})}}{2A\,skew[q]}$$

where $A = x(3cW_t)/2b$.

The stated closed-form solution is one of two roots of the quadratic equation in λ. It is possible to verify by differentiating the first-order condition that the stated closed-form solution corresponds to a maximum, while the other root corresponds to a minimum (Poitras and Heaney, 1999).[23]

---

the usage of insurance. As a consequence, many subsidized government crop insurance programs restrict the allowable percentage of insurable acres.

[23]While seemingly identical, the optimal demand for a yield put option does differ from the price put option in that $\gamma^*/x = [Q_z P_t]/C(A)$ and $\lambda^* = Q_x/A$. These decision variables have a somewhat different interpretation. For the put option based on prices, it is the fraction of the initial dollar value of investment in the risky asset that is of interest, while for the yield put option

Closer analysis of the proposition can be used to identify conditions for which the optimal put option demand derived from the mean-variance-skewness objective, λ^*, is less than the mean-variance optimal demand, λ_{MV}. A result such as $\lambda_{MV} \geq \lambda^*$ is interesting because it is seemingly counterintuitive, as the mean-variance-skewness function explicitly values positive skewness and the put option is a security that reduces the negative skewness in asset returns. However, the λ that maximizes skewness of W is less than the λ that minimizes the variance of W, making the solutions considerably more complicated than simple intuition would suggest.[24] For example, from the proposition it is apparent that negative $\mathrm{cosk}[\cdot]$ at the λ^* optimum is required for $\lambda_{MV} \geq \lambda^*$ to apply. Observing that $\mathrm{cosk}[\cdot]$ is a quadratic function of λ leads to consideration of three points associated with the $\mathrm{cosk}[\cdot]$ function: the two roots of the quadratic that are associated with $\mathrm{cosk}[\cdot] = 0$ and the minimum point of the $\mathrm{cosk}[\cdot]$ function. Various methods can be used to show that $\mathrm{cosk}[\cdot] < 0$ at the minimum. It follows that the addition of the skewness term to the moment preference function results in a reduction of the optimal demand for put options compared to the mean-variance solution.

QUESTIONS

1. What is a speculative bubble? Can the use of derivative securities lead to speculative bubbles? What role did derivative securities trading play in the Dutch tulipmania?

2. From Section II, algebraically derive the profit functions for a bearish vertical put spread, a bullish vertical put spread, a time spread, and a butterfly spread.

3. On Friday June 16, 1989, three call options for IBM trading on the CBOT, all expiring in October 1989, sold for the following prices:

Exercise price	Option price
105	9
115	3.75
125	1.06

Consider a butterfly spread with the following positions: Buy one call at 105, sell (write) two calls at 115, buy one call at 125. What would be

---

it is the fraction of the physical size of the asset. The optimal demand for put options on revenue is the same as that for yield insurance, with the proviso that the actual value of the various parameters (i.e., variances, covariances and the like) will have different values.

[24]The underlying moment preference objective function requires that $dEU/d\ \mathrm{skew}[W] > 0$. Using the optimal solution it is now possible to do comparative static analysis on specific parameters to determine, for example, that $\{d\lambda^*/d\ \mathrm{skew}[q]\} < 0$.

the values at expiration of such a spread for various prices of IBM at the time? What investment would be required to establish the spread? Given information about the prices of the $105 and $125 options, what could you predict about the price of the $115 option?

4. A short stock position can be "protected" by either selling a put or buying a call. Determine the profit functions for these alternative strategies and determine the breakeven stock price at expiration together with the maximum and minimum profits.

5. Derive the expiration-date profit diagrams for the following trades: straddle, strap, vertical spread, and horizontal time spread. Verify the replication strategies for a written put, a written call, a purchased put, a purchased call, and a long cash position.

6. The discussion of replication trades in Section I uses the two-portfolio approach to derive the relevant conditions. Reconstruct these arguments using the arbitrage portfolio approach.

7. "A call option benefits from increases in the stock price and these increases can be very large. A put option benefits from stock price declines, but the stock price can only fall to zero. Therefore, if we have a put and a call on the same stock with the same terms, the put must sell for less than the call." Do you agree or disagree? Explain, making sure that you identify relevant restrictions on the underlying arbitrage.

8. Establish the relationships among caps, collars, and floors with a bearish vertical spread that is long the put and short the call.

9. In Section I, the derivation of the put–call parity boundary conditions for American options was left as an exercise. Using the two-portfolio approach, verify the boundary conditions given in that section. In addition, use the most recent put and call option prices for IBM together with the current stock price, interest rate, and estimated dividends to estimate the size of the difference between the upper and lower boundaries for options on that stock.

10. Draw the expiration-date profit diagram for the put–call combination that replicates a short stock position. Be sure to consider the three scenarios: $X > S(0)$, $X < S(0)$, and $X = S(0)$.

11. From Section III, draw the expiration-date profit diagrams for the straddle, the strangle, the strap, and the strip. Be sure to identify long and short positions (e.g., long the straddle and short the straddle).

12. Derive the put-call parity condition for options, with expiration date T, written on forward contracts with expiration date $T + 1$.

CHAPTER **8**

Option Valuation

I. MATHEMATICAL BACKGROUND

A. STOCHASTIC PROCESSES: BASIC DEFINITIONS[1]

The development of options pricing theory is intimately related to notions associated with *stochastic processes*. The first important work on options pricing, Louis Bachelier's (1900) doctoral dissertation, also represents a significant early contribution to the theory of Brownian motion. Bachelier's work predates and anticipates Einstein's work on Brownian motion 5 years later. Unfortunately, Bachelier's thesis passed largely unnoticed and was only "rediscovered" by Paul Samuelson around 1954, following the "rediscovery" by Leonard Savage of a 1914 Bachelier publication on speculation and

---

[1]The scope of the material covered in this chapter is large. In addition to numerous books, journals, and other academic efforts, courses in stochastic processes are part of the typical requirements for advanced degrees in mathematical statistics. Given this, it is not possible to be either fully comprehensive or adequately technical in treating this material. The development given here is aimed at introducing concepts and notions required to develop options pricing theory, no more.

investment (Bernstein, 1992). Bachelier entered the mainstream of financial economics in the mid-1960s when his thesis was included in Cootner's (1964) seminal book of readings on the random behavior of stock prices.[2]

The theory of stochastic processes, proper, has a much longer history. One possible starting point would be the work of Abraham de Moivre in the 1730s when he derived the normal distribution as the limit of the skew binomial. A more traditional starting point dates back to 1827 when the English botanist R. Brown observed that small particles, suspended in a liquid, exhibited "ceaseless irregular motions." This observation was subsequently applied to the behavior of various other physical objects, such as smoke particles suspended in the air.[3] The important modern contributions in stochastic processes can be traced to N. Wiener in 1918.[4] His role is recognized in the use of the term *Wiener process* to signify the fundamental building block of the theory of stochastic differential equations (SDEs). In recognition of the early work of Brown, the term *Brownian motion* is often used synonymously. Important later contributions were made by Kolmogorov and Feller. Excellent representations of the modern state of the theory can be found in Cox and Miller (1965), Gihman and Skorohod (1975, 1979), Arnold (1974), Karatzas and Shreve (1988), Karlin and Taylor (1981), and Rogers and Williams (1987).

Formally, a stochastic process can be defined:

> *Definition*: Let $\{X(t)\}$ be a family of random variables indexed by the linear (index) set $\Im$, where $t \in \Im$. Then $\{X(t)\}$ is said to be a *stochastic process*.

The terms *stochastic* (random) *process* and *time series* are often used interchangeably. Following Karlin and Taylor (1975, p. 32), "a stochastic process may be considered as well defined once its state space, index parameter and family of joint distributions are prescribed." Similar approaches can be found in Goldberger (1964, p. 142), "...a stochastic process is defined by a family of random variables $\{X(t)\}$...such that for all finite sets of choices of t... a joint probability distribution is defined for the random variables $X(t)_1$, $X(t)_2, \ldots, X(t)_n$," and Dhrymes (1974, p. 383): "The probability characteris-

---

[2]Written for the centenary of the *Theorie de la Speculation*, Courtault *et al.* (2000) provide an excellent overview of Bachelier's life.

[3]One of Einstein's important contributions in this area was the observation that this random behavior could be explained by the perpetual collision of the molecules between the suspending medium and the physical objects.

[4]This point is debatable. The beginnings could arguably be traced to the development of the Markov chain in 1907 by A. Markov. However, this result was aimed at the solution of a specific problem. The work of Wiener involves a complete development of the mathematical foundation for the theory of Brownian motion. There is also some disagreement about when Wiener's development of a rigorous theory of Brownian motion was developed, with Cox and Miller (1965, p. 203) using 1923 as the appropriate date.

tics of a stochastic process $\{X(t)\}$ are completely specified if we determine the joint density function of a finite number of members of the family of random variables comprising the process."

Heuristically, the theory of stochastic processes describes the behavior of random variables, the Xs, over time, $t \in \Im$. A random variable is a function that maps from a prespecified domain, or sample space, to some portion of the real line, R^1. In certain financial applications (e.g., where X refers to an asset price), X takes values only on the positive, half line. In this case, as well as when the X values are allowed to assume any value along the real line, it is conventional to assume that there is a zero probability of X being equal to plus or minus infinity. When t is fixed at a given point, $X(t)$ has the conventional interpretation of a random variable, with associated (one-dimensional) probability density function. Specification of the stochastic process for X requires further specification of the joint density functions that relate Xs at different points in time: The joint densities provide a probabilistic specification of how X evolves over time. This potentially complicated mapping can involve various combinations of discrete or continuous observation on X and t. While in financial applications X is usually continuous, time can be either. The terms *discrete stochastic process* and *continuous stochastic process* are used to refer to the time intervals at which $X(t)$ is observed. Applications of stochastic processes have contributed significantly in numerous fields (e.g., engineering, physics, biology, and statistics).

A number of important notions from stochastic processes have received considerable attention in financial economics. While martingales and random walks are possibly the most familiar,[5] most of the literature on options pricing is developed using diffusion processes. These concepts are all closely related. *Diffusions* are (strong) Markov processes, continuous in both X and t. In turn, diffusions are constructed from Wiener processes that are the continuous time representation of a discrete-time random walk. Both types of processes obey the martingale property. The essential concept of a *Markov* process is most readily illustrated in discrete time. Using the conditional probability distribution $P[\,\cdot\,]$, then the Markov property can be stated:

$$P[X(t+1) = j | X(0) = a,\, X(1) = b,\, X(2) = c,\, \ldots,\, X(t) = s]$$
$$= P[X(t+1) = j | X(t) = s]$$

In effect, the Markov process is "memoryless," as the past and future are statistically independent when the present is known.

While a number of subtle technical issues are associated with the precise definition of the Markov process, Markov families, and diffusions (e.g., Wentzel, 1981), for current purposes it is sufficient to define a diffusion process as a

---

[5]Malliaris and Brock (1982) survey the range of applications in economics and finance.

Markov process in which both time and the state variable X are continuous. When expressed in the form of a *stochastic differential equation*, diffusions can be used to concisely specify the joint density functions for the stochastic process. To adequately motivate stochastic differential equations, it is necessary to develop the basic concept of a Wiener process as the limit of a discrete "normal" random walk, defined by a stochastic difference equation. The discrete *random walk*, without drift, has the form:

$$X(t+1) = X(t) + Z(t+1), \text{ where } X(0) = 0, \text{ and } t \in \{1, 2, 3, \dots\}$$

where $Z(1)$, $Z(2)$, $Z(3)$, ... form a stochastic process of independent random variables with the standard normal probability distribution: $Z(t) \sim N[0,1]$. In other words, over the unit time interval ($\Delta t = 1$) $Z(t)$ is a normal random variable with mean 0 and variance of one.

B. TYPES OF DIFFUSIONS

Consider what happens to a normal random walk as the time interval Δt shrinks. In this case, $Z(t + \Delta t)$ is no longer $N[0,1]$, but rather $N[0,\Delta t]$, where the random walk now has the form:

$$X(t + \Delta t) = X(t) + Z(t + \Delta t) = X(t) + Z(t)\sqrt{\Delta t}$$

Reexpressing in difference form and using:

$$\lim_{\Delta t \to 0} \Delta t = dt$$

gives the stochastic differential equation (SDE) for the standard Wiener process:

$$dX(t) = Z(t)\sqrt{dt} \quad \Rightarrow \quad dX(t) = dW(t)$$

$W(t)$ is usually referred to as a standard Wiener process. The *ensemble* of sample paths for $X(t)$ conform to the evolution of a random variable that is standard normal on the unit time interval.

Geometrically, the behavior of the Wiener process can be illustrated in two dimensions by taking $X(t)$ on the vertical axis and time on the horizontal axis. Starting from $X(0)$, which is a predetermined point, the Wiener process specifies an infinite number of possible paths originating from $X(0)$. The pattern of these paths conform to $N[0,\Delta t]$. To see this, select any time $t_1 > 0$, take a "slice" across the X paths, and plot the distribution of the paths. The distribution of the paths will be a normal distribution, centered at $X(0)$ with variance t_1. Similarly, doing the same "slicing" operation for another time $t_2 > t_1$ and evaluating the density associated with the ensemble of X time paths will again produce normal distribution, centered at $X(0)$ but with a larger dispersion. In this fashion, it is possible to make a connection with the distribution theory familiar from traditional statistics, which is concerned with variables at a given point in time. The SDE technique is a method of describing the evolution over time of random variables that are a function of the class of normal random variables.

The Wiener process can be immediately generalized to allow for nonzero drift and variance that differs from Δt. When a trend or "drift" term μ and standard deviation $\sigma (\neq 1)$ are admitted then the *arithmetic Gaussian* stochastic process (with constant coefficients μ and σ) is defined:

$$dX(t) = \mu \, dt + \sigma \, dW(t)$$

This constant coefficient process is also referred to as an arithmetic or absolute Brownian motion. The ensemble of time paths for this process are also normal but differ from the standard Wiener process by allowing for a different amount of variation around a constant trend. The basic Wiener process can be used to construct a wide range of stochastic differential equations, each of which is associated with a different specification for the joint density of the stochastic process. The construction of the Wiener process requires these densities to be functionally connected to the normal.

In general, the drift and standard deviation can be functions of both the state variable and time, such that $\alpha[x,t]$ is the drift and $\beta[x,t]$ is the volatility. Consider a simple form of state dependence, where $\alpha[x,t] = \mu X$ and $\beta[x,t] = \sigma X$, with μ and σ being constants:

$$dX(t) = \mu \, X \, dt + \sigma X \, dW(t) \Rightarrow dX(t)/X = \mu \, dt + \sigma \, dW(t)$$

In this case, the instantaneous rate of change (dX/X) follows a Gaussian process. For this reason, the terms *geometric Gaussian process* or *geometric Brownian motion* are used to identify this process. It can be shown that for the geometric Gaussian process the paths of $X(t)$ correspond to a process that is log-normally distributed at each point in time. This is important for cases where $X(t)$ refers to prices that, like log-normal variables, cannot be negative (for $X(0) > 0$).[6]

The geometric Brownian motion has an important position in option pricing theory. Black and Scholes (1973) use the geometric Gaussian process to describe the behavior of the stock price in deriving their option pricing formula. The process is often encountered in a variety of option pricing situations

---

[6]To see this is not difficult. By construction, if y is lognormally distributed then for $\ln [y] = x$, x is normally distributed. A normally distributed variable is a real variable that can take values ranging over the real line from positive to negative infinity. Observing $\exp \{\ln[y]\} = y = \exp \{x\}$, if x takes the value of minus infinity, the lowest possible value for x on the real line, then y will take a value of zero. Hence, a log-normal variable is defined on the positive half line, ranging from 0 to positive infinity.

because geometric Brownian motion usually leads to a relatively simple closed-form solution. While the empirical validity of this assumption can be questioned, the process is sufficiently close to real-world processes so that in many cases a reasonable approximation is provided.[7] In addition, Nelson (1990) has shown that allowing for $\mu = \mu[X]$ and $\sigma = \sigma[X]$ produces the result that the geometric Gaussian process is the continuous limit of the popular generalized autoregressive heteroskedasticity (GARCH) discrete stochastic process.

For various reasons, it is useful to know the mean and variance of an assumed diffusion process. For example, a key step in the risk-neutral valuation of the European option requires this result. For geometric Brownian motion:

$$E[X(t)] = X(0)e^{\alpha t} = X(0)e^{\left(\mu + \frac{\sigma^2}{2}\right)t}$$

$$\text{var}[X(t)] = X(0)^2 e^{2\alpha t}[e^{\sigma^2 t} - 1]$$

Derivation of these results can be found in Dixit and Pindyck (1994).

Other important processes that are exploited in the pricing of options include variations of the regular *Ornstein–Uhlenbeck* (OU) process.[8]

$$dX(t) = \alpha X \, dt + \sigma \, dW(t)$$

In financial applications, the OU process is often presented as a *mean reverting* process:

$$dX(t) = \alpha[\mu - X]dt + \sigma \, dW(t)$$

where α can be interpreted as the speed of adjustment of $X(t)$ to the steady-state mean μ. Different variations of the OU process have appeared. For example, Brennan and Schwartz (1979) and many others use the process:

$$dX(t) = \alpha[\mu - X]dt + \sigma X \, dW(t)$$

In this case, dX/X reduces to a mean-reverting OU.

Unlike the geometric and arithmetic Brownian motions, the $X(t)$ distribution associated with the OU process changes over time. At any time t, $X(t)$ is governed by a non-steady-state distribution that is normal but with condi-

---

[7]The empirical literature on the distribution of security and derivative prices is voluminous. A useful introduction is included in Duffie (1989).

[8]In the form given, the OU process is a form of arithmetic Gaussian process. Unlike the geometric case, this type of process admits the possibility of negative values for X. In certain cases, this difficulty can be rationalized away by arguing that only short-term options are of interest. In other words, the probability of observing negative values increases with the length of the permissible time paths. If these paths are constrained to be short, then there will only be a negligible probability of observing negative values.

tional means and variances that are time dependent (e.g., Cox and Miller, 1965, pp. 225–227). For the regular OU:

$$E[X(t)] = X(0)e^{-\alpha t}$$
$$\text{var}[X(t)] = \frac{\sigma^2(1 - e^{-\alpha t})}{2\alpha}$$

Asymptotically, as $t \to \infty$, the OU converges to a normal steady-state distribution with mean zero and variance $\sigma^2/2\alpha$. This damping behavior of the OU is different from the geometric Brownian motion that increases indefinitely as $t \to \infty$. Similarly, the mean-reverting OU has conditional parameters:

$$E[X(t)] = \mu + (X(0) - \mu)e^{-\alpha t}$$
$$\text{var}[X(t)] = \frac{\sigma^2}{2\alpha}\left\{1 - e^{-2\alpha t}\right\}$$

As $t \to \infty$, the mean-reverting OU converges to a steady-state normal distribution with mean μ and variance $\sigma^2/2\alpha$. Cox, *et al.* (1985) and others use a diffusion process, the *square root* process, in which volatility depends on the square root of X. In mean-reverting form, the SDE for this process is represented:

$$dX(t) = \alpha[\mu - X]\, dt + \sigma\sqrt{X}\, dW(t)$$

This process can be shown to be the continuous limit of a non-central chi-squared distribution. In turn, the square root process is a special case of the more general constant elasticity of variance (CEV) process:

$$dX(t) = \alpha X\, dt + \sigma X^{\beta/2}\, dW(t)$$

where $\beta \in [0,2]$. Unlike the other diffusions examined to this point, the CEV model describes a class of processes defined over the range of β. For $\beta = 1$, the CEV process is equivalent to a square root process. For $\beta = 2$, the process is lognormal.

The *Brownian bridge* process is a development on the Brownian motion process that incorporates a drift term that forces the process to a fixed endpoint. For a Brownian bridge process that starts at zero and ends at zero, the unit variance process takes the form:

$$dX(t) = -[X(t)/(T - t)]\, dt + dW(t)$$

The Brownian bridge process has been used in a number of papers (e.g., Ball and Torous, 1983; Chaing and Okunev, 1993), to model the bond price process. For this purpose, the Brownian bridge is attractive because the bond price converges to par value at the term to maturity endpoint. Cheng (1991) explores problems that assuming a Brownian bridge has for arbitrage-free pricing.

Unfortunately, the number of diffusion processes for which readily inter-
pretable conditional probability densities can be derived is limited. While the
density function for the general CEV process has been derived, the formula is
complicated. In addition to the processes already described and immediate
extensions, such as the Brownian bridge, the only other class of processes that
have manageable density functions are *Bessel* processes, which, in squared
form, have the representation: $dX(t) = \alpha \, dt + 2\sqrt{X} \, dW(t)$. This form of the
Bessel process is typically used (e.g., Geman and Yor, 1993) because the
associated densities are stable under convolutions, a useful property not
shared by geometric Brownian motion. While not always the best empirical
fit to the distribution for financial random variables, the analytical advantages
of diffusion processes have played important roles in the application of
stochastic processes to problems in finance and economics.[9]

With relatively little analytical complication, the general SDE model can be
extended to include jump processes. One of the properties of the diffusion is
the continuity of its sample paths. This property can be generalized to permit
certain types of jumps in the state variable to take place, usually modeled as a
Poisson event process. In other words, the sample paths of the diffusion are
continuous except at a countable number of discontinuity points, where the
jumps are generated by a Poisson process. In this case, the SDE can be written:

$$dX(t) = \alpha[x,t]dt + \sigma[x,t] \, dW(t) + v[x,t]dQ(t)$$

where $v[x,t]$ obeys the same technical conditions imposed on α and σ, and
$dQ(t)$ is a Poisson process assumed to be distributed independently of $W(t)$.[10]
For this type of SDE, there is a generalized form of Ito's lemma (e.g., Malliaris
and Brock, 1982, p. 122). The usefulness of this result in applications is that,
theoretically, it permits the valuation of jumps in the underlying process (e.g.,
Merton, 1976; Cox and Ross, 1976).

Another complication that can be introduced to the SDE is to impose
absorbing or *reflecting barriers* on the process. An absorbing barrier occurs
when the process vanishes at a specific point. A natural example of this occurs
for price processes that vanish when the price process reaches zero. The
absorbing barrier is imposed by requiring the transition probability density
to equal zero when the state variable equals the absorbing value. The resulting
solution for the absorbed transition density typically has a solution that is the
difference of the unrestricted density and the density associated with the paths
that are absorbed (e.g., Karlin and Taylor, 1975, v. 1, p. 355). Situations where

---

[9]Analytically, the admissibility of a given diffusion for arbitrage-free financial pricing depends
on satisfaction of conditions required for Girsanov's theorem to hold. A discussion and application of
this point to using the Brownian bridge process to model bond prices are provided in Cheng (1991).

[10]Extending analysis to this type of process can be motivated by observing that a diffusion
process can be created from the countable combination of Poisson processes.

a reflecting barrier is imposed on the SDE have less immediate natural application in finance. The imposition of a reflecting barrier involves restrictions on the partial derivative of the transition density with respect to the state variable. The restricted transition density will be the difference between the unrestricted density and the density associated with the transients induced by the reflecting barrier (e.g., Cox and Miller, 1965, p. 224).

C. THE CHAPMAN–KOLMOGOROV EQUATIONS

Associated with a general SDE of the form $dX(t) = \alpha[X,t]dt + \sigma[X,t]\,dW(t)$, together with an initial condition $X(0) = c$, is an integral solution for $X(t)$:

$$X(t) = X(0) + \int_0^t \alpha[s]ds + \int_0^t \sigma[s]\,dW(s)$$

Considerable analysis has been done on identifying the conditions under which $X(t)$ can be derived from the SDE (e.g., Malliaris and Brock, 1982, chap. 2). The existence and uniqueness of such a solution depends on a number of technical conditions being satisfied, primarily associated with the behavior of α and σ.[11] Heuristically, the most commonly used form of these conditions, the Lipschutz and growth conditions, can be interpreted as restrictions that the coefficients cannot grow faster than the random variables.

Given a specific solution, $X(t)$, for the SDE, a number of important analytical results apply. One essential feature of a diffusion process is that the transition probability density, the probability law that determines how $X(t)$ evolves through time, will be Markov. If $X(t)$ is a solution to the SDE then, subject to the satisfaction of a number of technical conditions, the transition probability density $P[X_0, t_0; X, t]$ can be obtained from α and σ using the Kolmogorov forward and backward equations that are partial differential equations (PDEs) which the transition probability density obeys. For the arithmetic Gaussian process, which features constant coefficients, the forward or Fokker–Planck equation is

---

[11]Included in these conditions are the Lipschutz condition:

$$|\alpha[t,x] - \alpha[t,y]| + |\sigma[t,x] - \sigma[t,y]| \le K|x - y|, \quad \text{for some } K > 0$$

(for admissible x and y) and the restriction on growth condition:

$$|\alpha[t,x]|^2 + |\sigma[t,x]|^2 \le K^2\{1 + |x|^2\}$$

$$\frac{1}{2}\sigma^2 \frac{\partial^2}{\partial x^2} P[X_0,t_0; X,t] - \alpha \frac{\partial}{\partial x} P[X_0,t_0; X,t] = \frac{\partial}{\partial t} P[X_0,t_0; X,t]$$

In financial applications, this PDE equation is usually subject to the delta function initial condition $P[X_0,t_0; X,t] = \delta[X - X_0]$.

The forward equation is so named because the solution process starts from the initial values X_0 and t_0 and solves for the density function of the future values of $X(t)$. This is the usual method of solving valuation problems in finance. The forward equation for transition densities that have nonconstant coefficients is

$$\frac{1}{2}\frac{\partial^2}{\partial x^2}\{\sigma^2[X,t]P[X_0,t_0; X,t]\} - \frac{\partial}{\partial x}\{\alpha[X,t]P[X_0,t_0; X,t]\}$$

$$= \frac{\partial}{\partial t}P[X_0,t_0; X,t]$$

Related to the forward equation is the backward equation, which is similar in appearance to the forward equation and is used to derive the density function of X_0 starting from the density associated with $X(t)$. A demonstration of how to apply the forward equation to solve for specific functional form of a transition probability density for the OU and other processes in given in Cox and Miller (1965) and other sources.

D. UNIVARIATE ITO'S LEMMA

Calculus is an important mathematical technique with numerous useful applications. As conventionally presented, calculus is applied to functions that are deterministic. In effect, the familiar rules associated with dy/dx, such as $y = x^2 \rightarrow dy/dx = 2x$, only apply when x is known. When x is a random variable the usual rules of calculus no longer apply. The importance of Ito's lemma is that it specifies the procedures for applying calculus to functions that contain random variables. More precisely, Ito's lemma provides a method for evaluating the total derivative of a function of a stochastic variable that follows a Markov diffusion process. As discussed previously, the diffusion class includes a wide range of stochastic processes. Given this, the *univariate* form of Ito's lemma can be stated:[12]

> *Ito's lemma*: Let $u[x,t]$ be a continuous random function mapping from $R^1 x[0,T]$
> $\rightarrow R_1$ with continuous partial derivatives u_t, u_x, and u_{xx}. If $x(t)$ is a random process
> with a stochastic differential equation obeying a diffusion of the form:

[12]Various technical conditions associated with the lemma are suppressed (e.g., restrictions on $f[\cdot]$ and $\sigma[\cdot]$. These details can be found in various sources (e.g., Arnold, 1974). It should also be recognized that other approaches to differentiation and integration of stochastic functions is possible (e.g., Meyer 1976).

$$dx(t) = a(t)\, dt + v(t)\, dW(t)$$

where $W(t)$ is a standard Wiener process and $a(t)$ and $v(t)$ are the drift and volatility of the diffusion, then the function $y(t) = u[x(t),t]$ also has a differential on $[0,T]$ given by:

$$dy(t) = \{u_t + u_x a(t) + 1/2\, u_{xx} v(t)^2\} dt + u_x v(t)\, dW(t)$$

This form of Ito's lemma generalizes in a natural fashion to the case where x is multidimensional (e.g., Malliaris and Brock, 1982, pp. 85–86)[13].

While Ito's lemma has had numerous applications in financial economics, perhaps the most well known is the Black–Scholes application to call option valuation. In this case, the non-dividend-paying stock price is assumed to follow a log-normal diffusion:

$$dS = \alpha S\, dt + \sigma S\, dW$$

In this case, $a(t) = \alpha S$ and $v(t) = \sigma S$, where α and σ are constants. The functional relationship between the call option price (C) and the stock takes the form: $C = C[S,t; X]$. Application of Ito's lemma gives:

$$dC = \left\{C_t + C_S \alpha S + \tfrac{1}{2} C_{SS}\, \sigma^2 S^2\right\} dt + \{C_S\, \sigma S\}\, dW$$

This solution plays a central role in the derivation of the Black–Scholes price of a European call. In particular, Black–Scholes are able to use the *riskless hedge portfolio* construction to provide an additional condition that permits elimination of the dW term. In this fashion, the call option pricing problem is transformed from an SDE problem that is not solvable in closed form with standard techniques into a deterministic PDE problem that can be solved. However, complications associated with solving PDEs are such that closed-form solutions are not always possible which has at least two implications. First, there is an emphasis on problem specifications that can be solved in closed form (e.g., Black–Scholes), even though such solutions may not be fully realistic. And, second, there is the need to apply numerical simulation to "solve" problems in which a precise specification of the problem is required and no closed form is available.

Ito's lemma can also be used to transform one type of SDE into another. One useful example involves the function $G[S] = \ln[S]$ when the SDE for S is geometric Brownian motion. Application of Ito's lemma provides the SDE for $G[S]$, specified using the drift and volatility parameters for S. More precisely, $G_t = 0$, $G_S = 1/S$, and $G_{SS} = -(1/S)^2$. Using Ito's lemma it follows that:

$$dG = \left\{0 + \alpha - \tfrac{1}{2}\sigma^2\right\} dt + \sigma\, dW = \left\{\alpha - \tfrac{1}{2}\sigma^2\right\} dt + \sigma\, dW$$

---

[13]Cox (1987, pp. 348–349) motivates Ito's lemma using a Taylor series expansion and ignoring terms that are higher.

The result that the log of a log-normally distributed random variable follows an arithmetic Brownian process is not surprising, but the specification of the drift is not obvious.

A straightforward extension to the case of functions of two variables (and time) is provided by Fischer (1975), who examines the stochastic behavior of the real bond price $q = B/P$, where B is the nominal price of a riskless bond and P is the price level. In this case, the rate of change in the price level (dP/P) and the return on a zero-coupon, continuously compounded nominal bond (dB/B) can be specified:

$$dP/P = \pi\, dt + \sigma\, dW$$

$$dB/B = R\, dt$$

Observing that when $q = u(B,P) = B/P$:

$$u_t = 0,\; u_{BP} = -\{1/P\}^2,\; u_{BB} = 0,\; u_B = 1/P,\; u_P = -\{B/P^2\},\; u_{PP} = 2\{B/P^3\}$$

It is now possible to apply the multivariate form of Ito's lemma to get:[14]

$$dq = \left\{\frac{1}{P}RB + \frac{-B}{P^2}\pi P + \frac{B}{P^3}P^2\sigma^2\right\}dt + \frac{-B}{P^2}\sigma P\, dW$$

Factoring out B/P gives the desired result:

$$dq/q = \{R - \pi + \sigma^2\}\,dt - \sigma\, dW$$

More developed applications of the multivariate form of Ito's lemma can be found in various sources (e.g., Gibson and Schwartz, 1990; Schwartz, 1982).

E. Multivariate Ito's Lemma

It is useful to proceed by example to illustrate the multidimensional form of Ito's lemma. Briys and Solnik (1992) provide an interesting application to the case where x is multidimensional, involving two random variables. This requires a more involved form of Ito's lemma. The Briys and Solnik example involves the domestic currency value of a foreign asset, $V^* = VS$, where V is the random foreign currency value of the foreign asset and S is the random spot exchange rate, producing V^*, which is the random domestic currency value of the foreign asset. In this case, processes are given for dV and dS, with dV^* to be calculated using Ito's lemma.

---

[14]Because the nominal bond price does not have a Brownian component, no cross product terms of the form $\{dB\, dP\}$ appear. This simplification is what makes Fischer's derivation uncomplicated.

To evaluate Ito's lemma for this case requires application of the associated multivariate total derivative. The resulting solution for the two random variable case, $y(t) = u[t, \{x(t)\}] = u[t, \{x_1(t), x_2(t)\}]$, takes the form:

$$dy = u_t\, dt + u_x dx + \frac{1}{2} tr\left[\sum u_{xx}\right] dt$$

where Σ is the variance–covariance matrix of the state variables and $tr[\,\cdot\,]$ is the trace operator. Because there are n state variables in the general form, u_x is an $n \times 1$ column vector containing the first partial derivatives, dx is a row vector containing the diffusion processes, and u_{xx} is a symmetric $n \times n$ matrix of the second partial derivatives.

In the Briys and Solnik example, $dy = dV^*$ and V and S are assumed to follow the log-normal diffusions:

$$\frac{dV}{V} = \mu_V\, dt + \sigma_V\, dW_V$$

$$\frac{dS}{S} = \mu_S\, dt + \sigma_s\, dW_S$$

The covariance between dW_S and dW_V per unit time is $cov(dW_S, dW_V) = \rho_{vs}\, dt$. It follows that $\sigma_{VS} = \rho_{VS}\sigma_V\sigma_S$. Recognizing that $y = u[x,t]$ in this case is $V^* = VS$, it follows that:

$$u_1 = \frac{\partial V^*}{\partial V} = S, \quad u_2 = \frac{\partial V^*}{\partial S} = V, \quad u_t = \frac{\partial V^*}{\partial t} = 0$$

$$u_{11} = \frac{\partial^2 V^*}{\partial V^2} = 0 = \frac{\partial^2 V^*}{\partial S^2} = u_{22}, \quad \frac{\partial^2 V^*}{\partial V \partial S} = 1 = \frac{\partial^2 V^*}{\partial S \partial V} = u_{1,2}$$

Because there are now two state variables, V and S, the variance–covariance matrix Σ is 2×2 with variances on the diagonal and covariances on the off-diagonal. Remembering from the univariate log-normal example that $v(t)^2 = \sigma^2 S^2$, evaluating $\frac{1}{2} tr[\,\cdot\,]$ for this case gives:

$$\frac{1}{2} tr\left\{\begin{bmatrix} \sigma_{11} & \sigma_{1,2} \\ \sigma_{2,1} & \sigma_{22} \end{bmatrix}\begin{bmatrix} u_{11} & u_{1,2} \\ u_{2,1} & u_{22} \end{bmatrix}\right\}$$

$$= \frac{1}{2}\left\{\sigma_{11}u_{11} + \sigma_{1,2}u_{2,1} + \sigma_{2,1}u_{1,2} + \sigma_{22}u_{22}\right\} = \sigma_{1,2} = \sigma_{VS}VS$$

Using the result that $\frac{1}{2} tr[\,\cdot\,] = \sigma_{VS}VS$, the solution to the total derivative is found to be

$$dV^* = 0 + S(\mu_V V\, dt + \sigma_V V\, dW_V) + V(\mu_S S\, dt + \sigma_S S\, dW_S) + \sigma_{VS}VS\, dt$$

$$\frac{dV^*}{V^*} = (\mu_V + \mu_S + \sigma_{VS})dt + \sigma_V\, dW_V + \sigma_S\, dW_S$$

Given dV and dS, this is dV^*, the SDE for the domestic currency value of the foreign asset.

II. DERIVING THE BLACK–SCHOLES OPTION PRICING FORMULA[15]

A. DERIVING THE FORMULA

The seminal paper by Black and Scholes (1973) directly addresses the problem of providing a practical, closed-form expression for the price of a call option on a common stock prior to the maturity date. Extensions to options on futures and spot commodities follow with appropriate adjustments. Recognizing that a considerable amount of research effort preceded the development of Black–Scholes (e.g., Cootner, 1964), what is most significant about this contribution is that the formula depends only on observable inputs: stock price, exercise price, time to expiration, interest rate, and variance of the stock price. With a suitable choice of estimator for the variance, the accuracy of the formula has proved to be robust across a wide range of option pricing situations. Extensions of this option pricing approach can be used to value the debt and common stock of the firm; bond features such as callability, convertibility, and retractability; and tax and investment policy. As initially derived, the formula applies to a "perfect markets" world for a European call on a non-dividend-paying stock. The techniques used to derive the formula are consistent with the material on stochastic processes covered previously. With appropriate transform of variables, Black and Scholes were able to show that the call option pricing problem reduces to solving a special case of the heat equation from mathematical physics.

The Black–Scholes argument proceeds by implementing the essential concept of a *hedge portfolio*. Recognizing that there are both long and short hedge portfolios, the long portfolio involves combining a long stock position with β written call options on the stock. The hedge is created by selling just enough calls to offset changes in the value of the stock position. This portfolio will involve a net investment of funds because the premium income received from writing the calls will not be sufficient to purchase the stock position. Similarly, the short hedge portfolio involves shorting the stock, buying call options to hedge the position against upward changes in the stock price, and investing the balance of the funds in a riskless asset. Observe that, for both the long and short hedge portfolio, as the stock price changes the option hedge has to be continuously adjusted to maintain the hedge position.

---

[15]Black (1989a) discusses the process of developing and publishing the Black–Scholes formula.

BOX 1
_____

The Black–Scholes Assumptions

The Black–Scholes assumptions are

(a) Nondividend-paying stock
(b) European option
(c) The instantaneously riskless continuous interest rate r is constant over time (with a flat term structure)
(d) The model has only *one* source of randomness, the single-state variable, the price of the stock that follows a log-normal diffusion process; this log normal process is defined only over $S \in [0, \infty]$
(e) No transactions costs or taxes
(f) No penalties on short selling
(g) Riskless lending and borrowing at r
(h) Continuous trading

Assumptions (e) to (g) are the conventional perfect-markets assumptions.

For ease of exposition, consider the long hedge portfolio. In order to determine the number of call options to sell, let $V = S - \beta C$ be the value of the hedge portfolio. From the hedge portfolio construction:

$$\frac{\partial V}{\partial S} = 1 - \beta \frac{\partial C}{\partial S} = 0 \quad \Rightarrow \beta = \frac{1}{\frac{\partial C}{\partial S}} \quad \Rightarrow \frac{\partial C}{\partial S} = \frac{1}{\beta}$$

Given this specification for β, the change in the value of riskless hedge portfolio will earn the riskless rate of interest (this follows from the assumption that interest rates are riskless). In terms of arbitrage portfolios, this condition is necessary in order to prevent the execution of arbitrage trades by either borrowing at the riskless rate and buying the hedge portfolio or selling the hedge and investing the funds at the riskless rate. It follows that there are two dV conditions that have to be satisfied:

$$\left\{ S - \frac{C}{C_S} \right\} r \, dt = dV \quad \Rightarrow \quad dV = dS - \frac{dC}{C_S}$$

At this point, Ito's lemma can be applied to solve for dC:

$$dC = \left\{ C_t + C_S \alpha S + \tfrac{1}{2} C_{SS} \sigma^2 S^2 \right\} dt + C_S \sigma S \, dW$$

The solution for dV can be derived as:

$$dV = dS - \frac{dC}{C_S}$$

$$= \alpha S \, dt + \sigma S \, dW - \frac{1}{C_S} \left\{ [C_t + C_S \alpha S + \tfrac{1}{2} C_{SS} \sigma^2 S^2] dt + C_S \sigma S \, dW \right\}$$

$$= - \frac{1}{C_S} \left\{ C_t + \tfrac{1}{2} C_{SS} \sigma^2 S^2 \right\} dt = (S - \tfrac{C}{C_S}) r \, dt$$

Dividing through by $-\{ dt/C_S \}$ gives the *fundamental PDE* for a European call on a nondividend paying stock:

$$C_t = rC - rSC_S - \tfrac{1}{2} \sigma^2 S^2 C_{SS}$$

With appropriate transformation of variables, this equation reduces to the heat equation from mathematical physics.

The Black–Scholes option pricing formula is derived by solving the fundamental PDE, subject to appropriate boundary and terminal conditions: $C[S,0,X] = \max [0, S(T) - X]$; $C[0,\tau,X] = 0$. If Laplace transforms are used in the solution procedure, the condition $C_S[\infty,\tau,X] = 1$ is also used. As it turns out, solving the PDE problem involves considerable analytical manipulation. The ultimate solution is the Black–Scholes formula:[16]

$$C[S,t,X] = C[S,t^*; X,r,\sigma] = C = SN[d_1] - Xe^{-rt^*} N[d_2]$$

where $N[\cdot]$ is the *cumulative* standard normal distribution evaluated at the appropriate arguments:[17]

---

[16]An interesting implication of the Black–Scholes formula is the solution for pricing the perpetual option. When t approaches infinity, $N[d_1]$ and $N[d_2]$ both go to one, with the result that the discounted value of the exercise price goes to zero. The final result is that the value of the call option equals the current stock price. This seemingly incorrect result can be explained using the discussion of the perpetual option from Chapter 9, Section IV. When there is no dividend paid on the underlying stock, then the perpetual option will never be exercised because the optimal exercise boundary occurs at infinity. Hence, the stock price will eventually grow well beyond the exercise price and the option will be deep in-the-money. In this case, the delta will be one and the perpetual call option price will move one-for-one with the stock price. Effectively, the perpetual call option price will behave the same as the stock price. This explanation goes some, but not all, of the way to explaining the seemingly incorrect result for the price of a perpetual option on a non-dividend-paying stock.

$$d_1 = \frac{\ln\left[\dfrac{S}{X}\right] + \left(r + \dfrac{1}{2}\sigma^2\right)t^*}{\sigma\sqrt{t^*}}$$

$$d_2 = d_1 - \sigma\sqrt{t^*} = \frac{\ln\left[\dfrac{S}{X}\right] + \left(r - \dfrac{1}{2}\sigma^2\right)t^*}{\sigma\sqrt{t^*}}$$

The formula for pricing puts follows from put–call parity:

$$P = C + Xe^{-rt^*} - S = SN[d_1] - Xe^{-rt^*}N[d_2] + Xe^{-rt^*} - S$$
$$= S\{N[d_1] - 1\} - Xe^{-rt^*}\{N[d_2] - 1\} = Xe^{-rt^*}N[-d_2] - SN[-d_1]$$

This follows from observing that $1 - N[d] = N[-d]$ (see Appendix III).

Manual evaluation of the Black–Scholes formula requires familiarity with the calculation of specific values for $N(d)$, the cumulative normal distribution

---

BOX 2

Application of the Black–Scholes Formula

Assume the following: $S(t) = \$36$, $X = \$40$, $\tau = 3$ months $\Rightarrow t^* = .25$, $r = .05$, $\sigma = .5$. Both the interest rate and standard deviation are expressed in annualized form. For sigma, this requires estimating the standard deviation over the relevant sampling frequency and then annualizing as appropriate. Given this:

$$d_1 = \left\{\ln[36/40] + \left(0.05 + 0.5(0.5)^2\right)0.25\right\}/\left\{0.5\left(\sqrt{0.25}\right)\right\} \cong -0.25$$

$$d_2 = \left\{\ln[36/40] + \left(0.05 - 0.5(0.5)^2\right)0.25\right\}/\left\{0.5\left(\sqrt{0.25}\right)\right\} \cong -0.50$$

Evaluating the $N[\cdot]$ values—$N[-0.25] = 0.4013$, $N[-0.50] = 0.3085$, and $\exp\{(0.05)(0.25)\} = 0.9877$—it is possible to solve for the Black–Scholes call option price:

$$C = S[0.4013] - X[0.9877][0.3085] = 14.4468 - 12.1882 = \$2.26$$

---

[17]With some manipulation, it is possible to show:

$$\frac{\ln\left\{\dfrac{S}{X}\right\} + (r + \frac{1}{2}\sigma^2)t^*}{\sigma\sqrt{t^*}} = \frac{\ln\left\{\dfrac{S}{X\exp\{-rt^*\}}\right\}}{\sigma\sqrt{t^*}} + \frac{1}{2}\sigma\sqrt{t^*}$$

This form is used in Gibson (1991) and other sources.

function evaluated at d (see Table 8.1). Though it is easiest to work directly with $N[d]$, it is also possible to work with $n[d]$, the normal probability density

TABLE 8.1   Values of the Cumulative Normal
Distribution Function, $N[d]$

d	$N[d]$	d	$N[d]$	d	$N[d]$
		−1.00	0.1587	1.00	0.8413
−2.95	0.0016	−0.95	0.1711	1.05	0.8531
−2.90	0.0019	−0.90	0.1841	1.10	0.8643
−2.85	0.0022	−0.85	0.1977	1.15	0.8749
−2.80	0.0026	−0.80	0.2119	1.20	0.8849
−2.75	0.0030	−0.75	0.2266	1.25	0.8944
−2.70	0.0035	−0.70	0.2420	1.30	0.9032
−2.65	0.0040	−0.65	0.2578	1.35	0.9115
−2.60	0.0047	−0.60	0.2743	1.40	0.9192
−2.55	0.0054	−0.55	0.2912	1.45	0.9265
−2.50	0.0062	−0.50	0.3085	1.50	0.9332
−2.45	0.0071	−0.45	0.3264	1.55	0.9394
−2.40	0.0082	−0.40	0.3446	1.60	0.9452
−2.35	0.0094	−0.35	0.3632	1.65	0.9505
−2.30	0.0107	−0.30	0.3821	1.70	0.9554
−2.25	0.0122	−0.25	0.4013	1.75	0.9599
−2.20	0.0139	−0.20	0.4207	1.80	0.9641
−2.15	0.0158	−0.15	0.4404	1.85	0.9678
−2.10	0.0179	−0.10	0.4602	1.90	0.9713
−2.05	0.0202	−0.05	0.4801	1.95	0.9744
−2.00	0.0228	0.00	0.5000	2.00	0.9773
−1.95	0.0256	0.05	0.5199	2.05	0.9798
−1.90	0.0287	0.10	0.5398	2.10	0.9821
−1.85	0.0322	0.15	0.5596	2.15	0.9842
−1.80	0.0359	0.20	0.5793	2.20	0.9861
−1.75	0.0401	0.25	0.5987	2.25	0.9878
−1.70	0.0446	0.30	0.6179	2.30	0.9893
−1.65	0.0495	0.35	0.6368	2.35	0.9906
−1.60	0.0548	0.40	0.6554	2.40	0.9918
−1.55	0.0606	0.45	0.6736	2.45	0.9929
−1.50	0.0668	0.50	0.6915	2.50	0.9938
−1.45	0.0735	0.55	0.7088	2.55	0.9946
−1.40	0.0808	0.60	0.7257	2.60	0.9953
−1.35	0.0885	0.65	0.7422	2.65	0.9960
−1.30	0.0968	0.70	0.7580	2.70	0.9965
−1.25	0.1057	0.75	0.7734	2.75	0.9970
−1.20	0.1151	0.80	0.7881	2.80	0.9974
−1.15	0.1251	0.85	0.8023	2.85	0.9978
−1.10	0.1357	0.90	0.8159	2.90	0.9981
−1.05	0.1469	0.95	0.8289	2.95	0.9984

function, and to construct $N[d]$ values from $n[d]$ tables. This is possible because the value of the cumulative normal distribution function evaluated at x, $N[x]$, is the area under the normal density function between $-\infty$ and x.

To evaluate the Black–Scholes formula using the standard normal probability density table, refer to Tables 8.1 and 8.2, which have both $N[d]$ and $n[d]$. The potentially simple exercise of producing the required cumulative $N[d]$ values is complicated by the form in which the $n[d]$ table is presented. To illustrate the use of the table, observe that when the calculated value of d in $N[d]$ is greater than zero, the value in the $n[d]$ table is added to $0.5 = N[0]$.

TABLE 8.2 Value of the Normal Density Function, $n[d]$

d	0.00	0.01	0.02	0.03	0.04	0.05	0.06	0.07	0.08	0.09
0.0	0.0000	0.0040	0.0080	0.0120	0.0160	0.0199	0.0239	0.0279	0.0319	0.0359
0.1	0.0398	0.0438	0.0478	0.0517	0.0557	0.0596	0.0636	0.0675	0.0714	0.0753
0.2	0.0793	0.0832	0.0871	0.0910	0.0948	0.0987	0.1026	0.1064	0.1103	0.1141
0.3	0.1179	0.1217	0.1255	0.1293	0.1331	0.1368	0.1406	0.1443	0.1480	0.1517
0.4	0.1554	0.1591	0.1628	0.1604	0.1700	0.1736	0.1772	0.1808	0.1844	0.1879
0.5	0.1915	0.1950	0.1985	0.2019	0.2054	0.2088	0.2123	0.2157	0.2190	0.2224
0.6	0.2257	0.2291	0.2324	0.2357	0.2380	0.2423	0.2454	0.2486	0.2517	0.2540
0.7	0.2580	0.2611	0.2642	0.2673	0.2704	0.2734	0.2764	0.2794	0.2823	0.2852
0.8	0.2881	0.2910	0.2939	0.2967	0.2995	0.3023	0.3051	0.3078	0.3106	0.3133
0.9	0.3150	0.3186	0.3212	0.3238	0.3264	0.3289	0.3315	0.3340	0.3365	0.3389
1.0	0.3413	0.3438	0.3461	0.3485	0.3508	0.3531	0.3554	0.3577	0.3599	0.3621
1.1	0.3643	0.3665	0.3686	0.3708	0.3729	0.3740	0.3770	0.3790	0.3810	0.3830
1.2	0.3849	0.3869	0.3888	0.3907	0.3925	0.3944	0.3962	0.3980	0.3997	0.4015
1.3	0.4032	0.4049	0.4066	0.4082	0.4099	0.4115	0.4131	0.4147	0.4162	0.4177
1.4	0.4192	0.4207	0.4222	0.4236	0.4251	0.4265	0.4279	0.4292	0.4306	0.4319
1.5	0.4332	0.4345	0.4357	0.4370	0.4382	0.4394	0.4406	0.4418	0.4429	0.4441
1.6	0.4452	0.4463	0.4474	0.4484	0.4495	0.4505	0.4515	0.4525	0.4535	0.4545
1.7	0.4554	0.4564	0.4573	0.4582	0.4591	0.4599	0.4608	0.4616	0.4625	0.4633
1.8	0.4641	0.4649	0.4656	0.4664	0.4671	0.4678	0.4686	0.4693	0.4699	0.4706
1.9	0.4713	0.4719	0.4726	0.4732	0.4738	0.4744	0.4750	0.4756	0.4761	0.4767
2.0	0.4772	0.4778	0.4783	0.4788	0.4793	0.4798	0.4803	0.4808	0.4812	0.4817
2.1	0.4821	0.4826	0.4830	0.4834	0.4838	0.4842	0.4846	0.4850	0.4854	0.4857
2.2	0.4861	0.4864	0.4868	0.4871	0.4875	0.4878	0.4881	0.4884	0.4887	0.4890
2.3	0.4893	0.4896	0.4898	0.4901	0.4904	0.4906	0.4909	0.4911	0.4913	0.4916
2.4	0.4918	0.4920	0.4922	0.4925	0.4927	0.4929	0.4931	0.4932	0.4934	0.4936
2.5	0.4938	0.4940	0.4941	0.4943	0.4945	0.4946	0.4948	0.4949	0.4951	0.4952
2.6	0.4953	0.4955	0.4956	0.4957	0.4959	0.4960	0.4961	0.4962	0.4963	0.4964
2.7	0.4965	0.4966	0.4967	0.4968	0.4969	0.4970	0.4971	0.4972	0.4973	0.4974
2.8	0.4974	0.4975	0.4976	0.4977	0.4977	0.4078	0.4979	0.4979	0.4980	0.4981
2.9	0.4981	0.4982	0.4982	0.4983	0.4984	0.4984	0.4985	0.4985	0.4986	0.4986
3.0	0.4987	0.4987	0.4987	0.4988	0.4988	0.4989	0.4989	0.4989	0.4990	0.4990

Note: For $d > 0$, add 0.5 to the value in the table. For $d < 0$, subtract the value in the table from 0.5.

Similarly, when $d < 0$, then the value in the $n[d]$ table is subtracted from 0.5. In the example provided, d_1 was approximately -0.25. To identify the appropriate $N[\cdot]$ value, look down the vertical axis in the $n[d]$ table to find the first digit (in this case, 0.2) and then read across to get the second digit (in this case, 0.05). Examining the table, the value in that cell is 0.0987. Subtracting this value from 0.5 (because $d_1 < 0$) gives 0.4013, the value used in the example. Evaluating d_2 at -0.50 gives a table value of 0.1915 and $N[d_2] = 0.3085$. These are the same values as those obtained by working directly from $N[d]$. This method of calculating d using the relevant standard normal densities can be used because the distribution is symmetric, making the values for one half of the distribution redundant. Presenting the table using only half of the distribution information as in the table allows a larger number of "useful" cells to be presented.

B. INTERPRETING THE FORMULA

The first step in interpreting the Black–Scholes formula involves interpreting $N[d]$, particularly as S and X change. Consider an at-the-money option, $S = X$, where t^* is small. In this case, $\ln[S/X] = \ln[1] = 0$ and, due to small t^*, the remaining values will be small, and $N[d] \to N[0] = 0.5$. Similarly, when the option is deep in-the-money, $S >> X$ and $N[d] \to N[+\infty] = 1$, which implies that, for an European call option on a non-dividend-paying security, $C \to S - X\exp\{-rt^*\} > S - X$. Observing that $S - X$ is the early exercise value, it follows that European call options on non-dividend-paying securities will, if the Black–Scholes formula is correct, not be exercised early. For puts, deep in the money requires $X >> S$ where $N[-d] \to N[+\infty]$, which implies for a put option that $P \to X\exp\{-rt^*\} - S < X - S$. It follows that European puts on non-dividend-paying securities can be rationally exercised early. This asymmetry is an artifact of the upper bound on the value of the put position resulting from the restriction that $S \geq 0$. If the spot price falls far enough, the expected gain of interest due to early exercise will exceed the expected possible gains due to further price declines.

It has been demonstrated that as an option goes deeper into the money, the $\ln[S/X]$ term in d_1 and d_2 tends to dominate the value of d. The same is true as the options goes deeper out-of-the-money. For the call option, deep out-of-the-money requires $X >> S$, which produces $N[d] \to N[-\infty]$ because $\ln[0] = -\infty$. Hence, as the spot price goes to zero, $C \to 0$. A similar result holds for puts, with the proviso that deep out of the money requires $S >> X$ for puts. In this case, $N[-d] = N[-(+\infty)] = 0$. Similar intuition can be used to evaluate the formula as $t^* \to 0$. In this case, only the term involving $\ln[S/X]$ matters, due to the t^* cancellation of $\sqrt{t^*}$ leaving a $\sqrt{t^*}$ term to multiply $(r + 0.5\sigma^2)$. If the option is in the money on the expiration date, then $C = S - X$, whereas if the option is out-of-the-money then $C = 0$. This is verification that the formula satisfies the boundary condition that $C[X, t = T] = \max [S - X, 0]$.

Other basic interpretations of the formula are associated with the relevant partial derivatives. Analytically, the partial derivatives:

$$\frac{\partial C}{\partial t}, \quad \frac{\partial C}{\partial S}, \quad \frac{\partial^2 C}{\partial S^2}$$

of the fundamental PDE, together with other partial derivatives of the Black–Scholes formula, are demonstrated in Chapter 9, Section II to play a central role in applications to the management of portfolios. As it turns out, for portfolios containing derivative securities, one or more of the partial derivatives become choice variables. To illustrate possible applications, consider the riskless hedge portfolio. In this case, the delta of the portfolio is constructed to have $\partial V / \partial S = 0$.

Another simple example is a portfolio containing only a call option. By setting, say, $\partial^2 C / \partial S^2 = 0$ by choosing to write only options that are deep in-the-money, the fundamental PDE provides restrictions on the remaining two partial derivatives of the form:

$$\frac{\partial C}{\partial t} + rS \frac{\partial C}{\partial S} = rC$$

Recognizing that $\partial C / \partial S = 1$ when the option is deep in-the-money provides a solution for $\partial C / \partial t$ in terms of the interest expense of the funds invested in the position. Chapter 9 provides numerous more developed extensions of this approach to the construction of portfolios containing options.

C. Implied Volatility

Practical application of the Black–Scholes formula requires some method of estimating the variance, σ^2, of the continuously compounded rate of return on the stock (dS/S).[18] Unlike the other values required to calculate the Black–Scholes option price (S, X, r, τ), the value for volatility is not directly observed. Some method of estimating σ is required. Starting with the first empirical studies on Black–Scholes, it has been recognized that using the past history of returns to estimate volatility can produce undesirable results,

---

[18]In addition, a number of other more mundane issues associated with practical application remain. For example, in some presentations of the Black–Scholes formula (e.g., Turnbull, 1987), monthly or quarterly frequencies are used for r and σ. This requires minor adjustments in the form but not the substance of the formula.

such as inconsistency between Black–Scholes and observed option prices (e.g., Latane and Rendleman, 1976; Macbeth and Merville, 1979).[19] Lauter-bach and Schultz (1990) report: "Our findings indicate that the constant equity variance assumption is the most serious deficiency in the Black–Scholes model." Over time it has been recognized that, given an observed call option price, Black–Scholes can be "inverted" and used to solve for an estimate of volatility. In other words, given S, X, r, τ and C it is possible to use Black–Scholes to solve for σ. For this purpose, computer programs that solve for Black–Scholes prices also provide a routine for solving the implied standard deviation or implied volatility (IV).[20]

Not surprisingly, the behavior of implied volatility has been intensely studied from a number of different angles. From the beginning, study of implied volatility has revealed that Black–Scholes is not a formula for pricing

---

BOX 3

Malz (2000) on OTC Foreign Currency Option Trading

In foreign exchange markets, options are traded among dealers using the delta as a metric for exercise price and the Black-Scholes volatility as a metric for price. The volatility smile can then be represented as a schedule of implied volatilities of options on the same underlying (currency) and with the same maturity but different deltas. This convention is unambiguous, since a unique exercise price corresponds to each call or put delta and a unique option premium in currency units corresponds to each implied volatility. The most liquid option markets are for at-the-money forward and for 25-delta calls and puts. There are also somewhat less actively traded markets in 10-delta calls and puts.

---

[19]A useful study on the use of the implied standard deviations to predict future stock price variability is Beckers (1981). In the case of currency options, Shastri and Tandon (1986a) demonstrate that implied standard deviations result in significantly more accurate Black–Scholes prices than those based on historical estimates. In particular, the historical standard deviation "yields model prices which are, on an average, lower than market prices" (p. 150) Similarly, Chesney and Scott (1989) also confirm that the Black–Scholes model using a constant variance "performs poorly."

[20]Various studies have investigated the empirical validity of Black–Scholes and its immediate variants discussed in Section IV (e.g., Macbeth and Merville, 1979; Bhattacharya, 1980; Geske and Roll, 1984; Sterk, 1983; Wiggins, 1987; Lauterbach and Schultz, 1990). Most studies find some small sources of bias in the prices, usually associated with deep in or deep out-of-the-money options.

options; instead, because the traded call price is observed and the only unobserved variable in the Black–Scholes model is the volatility, Black–Scholes is more appropriately viewed as a formula for determining an estimate of the underlying spot price (S) volatility.[21] Various properties of the implied volatility have been examined in numerous studies. One property of interest is the ability of the implied volatility to predict future volatility, typically using the most advanced econometric volatility predictor (e.g., GARCH) as a benchmark. This type of comparison can be found in Stein (1989), Canina and Figlewski (1993), Lamoureux and Lastrepes (1993), Heynen et al. (1994), Takezawa (1995), Xu and Taylor (1994, 1995), Sabatini and Linton (1998), and Dumitru (1999).

Volatility forecasts have a number of potential uses, including being used as input for market markers determining appropriate bid/offer quotes for option trading or as inputs to value at risk (VaR) calculations. For a number of reasons, it is difficult to formulate definitive tests of implied volatility performance in forecasting future spot volatility. Given this, there is conflicting evidence as to whether IVs from option pricing models provide superior forecasts to those obtained from spot data using appropriate econometric techniques (such as GARCH estimators). Some studies, such as Takezawa (1995), Canina and Figlewski (1993), and Stein (1989), find that the IVs tend to be poor forecasts of future realized volatility compared to econometric estimators. Among other reasons, this is attributed to implied volatilities "overreacting" to volatility surprises. Other studies (e.g., Xu and Taylor, 1994) find that implied volatilities are the best predictors of future volatility.

One difficulty in identifying the forecasting properties of implied volatilities concerns the sampling windows being used. On the IV side, there is the problem of how best to combine IV information. Implied volatilities change over time and numerous studies have demonstrated that averages, including weighted averages, of past IVs have better performance than using just the previous IV (e.g., Latane and Randleman, 1976; Beckers, 1981). IVs from at-the-money options are also found to be better predictors than deep out-of-the-money and, where applicable, deep in-the-money options. Short-dated options and options written on extremely high or low volatility spot markets also have poor performance. There is also the question of how to combine the estimates from options on the same security, with the same time to expiration but different exercise prices. Another complication concerns the variable being forecasted. Is accuracy in pricing subsequent options the criterion or is it the tracking of actual spot market volatility, or is it profitability of a trading

---

[21]Reference to spot price is intended to include all underlying commodities, securities, and assets upon which the option could be written. This also, implicitly, includes futures and forward prices.

strategy based on option mispricing (e.g., Galai, 1977)? All these questions are complicated by option and spot quotes not being simultaneous, as well as the problem of accounting for the bid/offer spread (e.g., Rubinstein, 1985).

From these early results, the study of implied volatilities progressed to the detailed comparison of volatilities extracted from different options for the same commodity or security, concentrating on currencies and stocks. More precisely, at any point in time a number of options with varying term-to-maturity and exercise prices are available for the same spot commodity. The implied volatilities for the different option prices reveal a significant degree of heterogeneity. In particular, comparing implied volatilities for different exercise prices reveals a *volatility smile* or *volatility smirk* when currency option prices are used to calculate the IVs.[22] The IV is lowest for at-the-money options, with the IV having progressively higher values as the option price moves in-the-money or out-of-the-money (e.g., Heynen, 1994; Dumitru, 1999; Xu and Taylor, 1994; Malz, 2000).[23] This empirical result for currency options is stylized, and the precise shape of the smile varies across time and currencies. For example, a smirk is sometimes observed where the IVs for at-the-money and in-the-money options are approximately equal, while the out-of-the-money options have higher IVs.

The IV smile of currency options does not carry over to stock options and stock index options where a volatility skew is observed (e.g., Dumas *et al.*, 1998). In a volatility skew, IV decreases as the strike price increases. Low strike price options, where the call is deep in-the-money and the put is deep out-of-the-money have the highest IVs. IV declines progressively, reaching the lowest levels for high strike price options, where the put is deep in-the-money and the call is deep out-of-the-money. For both currency and stock options, differences in calculated IVs are also observed when different terms to expiration are used, with the shorter maturity options typically exhibiting higher IVs. All this variation in empirical IV has led to considerable theoretical analysis in an attempt to explain the IV variation.

If the Black–Scholes model were perfect, then volatilities derived from option prices would be the same irrespective of the expiration date and exercise price of the option used to derive the IV. However, in practice, volatilities derived from in-, at-, and out-of-the-money options differ; sometimes the IV plot reveals a smile when implied volatility is plotted against moneyness of the option (e.g., Heynen, 1994) and sometimes the plot reveals a smirk or a skew. A first possible step in dealing with observed IV behavior is to

---

[22]In some cases, a volatility frown is observed (e.g., Wilmott, 1998, p. 290).

[23]Another stylized fact associated with implied volatility is "that the differences in implied volatilities becomes less pronounced as options with greater time-to-maturity are considered" (Das and Sundaram, 1997, p. 2).

evaluate the *vega risk* of the position. For a position containing only one option, the vega risk can be approximated by taking the derivative, with respect to σ, of the appropriate Black–Scholes formula (e.g., Hull and White, 1987; Malz, 2000). This approach is discussed in Chapter 9. It is possible to incorporate vega risk into VaR calculations.

Another possible approach to accounting for observed IV behavior is to model the stochastic behavior of volatility directly. This involves introducing an additional stochastic process into the model. Unfortunately, the presence of two random variables, volatility and commodity price, significantly complicates the modeling process (e.g., Scott, 1987, 1997; Hull and White, 1987, 1988a; Heston, 1993; Ball and Roma, 1994; Duan, 1995; Ritchken and Trevor 1999). The basic problem of introducing volatility is captured by Ball and Roma: "Since volatility is not spanned by assets in the economy, the volatility risk may not be eliminated by arbitrage methods. Therefore, its market price of risk explicitly enters into the PDE." Hull and White (1987) were able to partially circumvent this problem by taking volatility to be uncorrelated with the commodity price, allowing the Black–Scholes price to be determined by integrating over the probability distribution of the average variance during the life of the option.

The Hull and White approach can be motivated using a power series expansion of the option price. Ball and Roma (1994) demonstrated that the Hull and White approach can be extended "to any security price process that is conditionally log-normal and for which the MGF of the average variance possesses a known analytical form". This follows because, if a tractable stochastic process for volatility has been specified, it is possible to solve for the expected variance by direct integration. This approach can be extended to demonstrate how stochastic volatility leads to a smile effect (Ball and Roma, 1994, p. 662). To see this, expand the option price in a univariate Taylor series, expanded in volatility around the expected value of the true variance of the underlying process. Ignoring terms higher than second order gives:

$$C^* = C[E[\hat{\sigma}^2]] + \frac{1}{2} \frac{\partial^2 C[E[\hat{\sigma}^2]]}{\partial(\hat{\sigma}^2)^2} \text{var}[\hat{\sigma}^2] = C[\Omega] + \frac{1}{2} C'' \text{var}[\hat{\sigma}^2]$$

where C^* is the true option price that takes account of stochastic volatility, C is the Black–Scholes price, $E[\hat{\sigma}^2] = \Omega$ is the expected value of the average variance, and var $[\hat{\sigma}^2]$ is the variance of the average variance.

From this point, it is possible to adapt an argument similar to that in used in Chapter 2, Section I, to capture the cost of risk. Recall that IV is the implied volatility calculated from the Black–Scholes formula using the observed option price. While it is conventional to solve for IV using observed option prices, it is also possible to solve for the IV associated with the option price calculated from the pricing model that accounts for stochastic volatility. With this in mind, let $IV^* = \Omega + \omega$; the implied volatility calculated from the Black–Scholes model using the option prices determined from the "true" stochastic volatility model is equal to the expected variance of the true process generating the commodity price *plus* any deviation of IV^* from the expected variance of the process that accounts for stochastic volatility. It follows that the first-order Taylor series approximation gives:

$$C^* = C[IV^*] = C[\Omega + \omega] = C[\Omega] + \omega \frac{\partial C[\Omega]}{\partial(\hat{\sigma}^2)} \rightarrow \omega = \frac{1}{2}\,\mathrm{var}[\hat{\sigma}^2]\,\frac{C''}{C'}$$

The relationship between the deviations of the true stochastic volatilities from the implied volatilities calculated from Black–Scholes prices, can now be determined by directly evaluating the derivatives C'' and C'.

Ball and Roma (1994) give an approximation to the solution for ω as:

$$4\omega = \frac{\mathrm{var}[\hat{\sigma}^2]}{\Omega}\left[-\left\{\frac{\Omega\,t^*}{4}\right\} + \frac{\ln\,[S/\{X\,e^{-rt}\}]^2}{\Omega\,t^*} - 1\right]$$

Solving this for at-the-money reveals $\omega < 0$. As Ball and Roma (1994) observed: "This is not surprising since the Black–Scholes option price is only everywhere concave in variance for at-the-money options and, hence, a straightforward application of Jensen's inequality implies that the stochastic volatility option is priced below the Black–Scholes counterpart evaluated at the mean of average variance." With this result the presence of a smile effect in the calculated IV using actual option prices can now be determined by observing that there are different ωs for the various exercise prices. Some caution is needed in applying these results due to the initial assumption that the randomness in volatility is uncorrelated with randomness in commodity prices. Failure of this assumption contributes to the volatility skew in equity option IVs.

Ultimately, only so much can be accomplished by dealing with σ, which is just one parameter from the underlying commodity or security price distribution. It is natural that attention has also focused on modeling or extracting the complete distribution for the underlying commodity price process. Improving pricing accuracy by better modeling the distribution of commodity prices has been of interest almost since Black–Scholes (1973). One potential approach along these lines is to empirically evaluate the commodity price distributions to assess which empirical assumption is most appropriate. For example, Bates (1996) and others examine the empirical fit of jump diffusion, stochastic volatility, and mixed jump–stochastic volatility models. One inherent difficulty with this approach is that the distributional model that has the best goodness of fit (e.g., the skew-stable) may not be manageable theoretically, especially if the objective is a closed-form solution.

Once it is recognized that there are only a few cases where closed forms can be derived, approximation methods gain appeal. Various approximation techniques, including Edgeworth expansions, Hermite–Fourier expansions (Chiarella et al., 1999), Laguerre expansions (Dufresne, 2000), and Gram–Charlier expansions, have been examined (e.g., Jarrow and Ruud, 1982; Shimko, 1994; Corrado and Su, 1996). However, these methods are decidedly in the direction of numerical evaluation of option prices (e.g., using finite difference methods). While these methods can be used to accurately solve for option prices, the intuition and appeal of the closed-form solution is lost. Another related approach is to estimate the volatility surface directly (e.g., Derman and Kani, 1994; Jackwerth and Rubinstein, 1996; Avellaneda et al., 1997). To date, this approach has been found to be "no better than an *ad hoc* procedure that merely smooths Black–Scholes implied volatilities across exercise prices and times to expiration" (Dumas et al., 1998, p. 2059).

III. SOLVING THE BLACK–SCHOLES PDE

A. POSSIBLE METHODS OF SOLVING BLACK–SCHOLES

At least six methods are available for deriving the Black–Scholes option pricing formula from the fundamental PDE. These methods are, in no particular order of importance, the original approach proposed by Black–Scholes, which involves making relevant substitutions into available solutions to the heat equation derived using Fourier series methods; the risk-neutral valuation approach of Cox and Ross, which involves solving the discounted expected value of the option's expiration date payoff function; evaluating the PDE as the limit of the binomial process; taking Laplace transforms; the Feynman and Kac approach which is closely related to the risk-neutral valuation approach and involves expressing the solution of the fundamental PDE as the expected value of a functional of Brownian motion; and, finally, direct verification that the derivation of the Black–Scholes formula satisfies the PDE and boundary condition. While the last suggested method is consistent with "proof by knowledge of the solution," it is also consistent with the *ad hoc* method, sometimes used in mathematical physics and engineering, of guessing a solution and then verifying that the proposed solution satisfies the PDE.

The method that has been found to have useful applications to a range of pricing situations, particularly where the solution to the pricing problem is not apparent, is the risk-neutral valuation method proposed by Cox and Ross. For the European call option on a non-dividend-paying stock, this method involves directly evaluating the expectation:

$$
\begin{aligned}
C_t &= e^{-rt^*} \, E\{ \max [0, S_T - X] \} \\
&= e^{-rt^*} \{ E[S_T - X | S_T \geq X] + E[0 | S_T < X] \} \\
&= e^{-rt^*} \{ E[S_T - X | S_T \geq X] \} \\
&= e^{-rt^*} \{ E[S_T | S_T \geq X] - X \, \text{Prob}[S_T \geq X] \}
\end{aligned}
\tag{8.1}
$$

where $E[\,\cdot\,]$ is the time t expectation taken with respect to the risk-neutral density Prob$[\,\cdot\,]$. Stoll and Whalley (1993) provide a worked solution for this problem.

As for the "proof by knowledge of the solution" method of solving the Black–Scholes call option pricing formula, while this method is not conceptually satisfying, it is immensely practical in many situations. The method proceeds by examining the solutions for PDE problems with similar structure. As discussed in texts on PDEs (e.g., Berg and McGregor, 1966), there is an elaborate classification scheme for PDE problems that facilitate this exercise. Having determined the solution to a closely related problem, a solution to the pricing problem is then guessed and derivatives of the pricing problem are taken to verify whether the PDE and boundary conditions are satisfied. This starts an iterative process that combines intuition and brute force to arrive at a solution. This method relies on the guidance of the existence and uniqueness theorems for PDEs from advanced mathematical analysis to determine when a solution will be available and if that solution is unique. Of course, a trivial variation of this method is to know the solution at the start and verify that it satisfies the PDE and boundary condition.

Yet another method to solve the Black–Scholes PDE involves applying the technique of Laplace transforms. Applied to the function $f[t]$, this transform is defined as:

$$
L[f[t]] = \int_0^\infty e^{-qt} f[t] \, dt
$$

Solutions to the Laplace transform for a wide range of functions are available. After making an appropriate transformation of variables, the Laplace transform technique permits the fundamental PDE to be converted to an ordinary differential equation (ODE) that is easier to solve. In the Black–Scholes case, the Laplace transform solution involves the erf$[\,\cdot\,]$ function, which often appears in Laplace transformations involving probability distributions. The Laplace transform method is quite tedious and, without prior knowledge of the solution provided by Black–Scholes, it is not obvious how to proceed to the desired solution. Though widely used in engineering, the Laplace transform approach is not common is finance applications (e.g., Buser, 1986).

B. THE ORIGINAL BLACK–SCHOLES SOLUTION

The original notation in Black and Scholes (1973) differs somewhat from what is currently in common use. To retain the flavor of the Black–Scholes discussion, some of the original notation will be adopted. In Black–Scholes (1973), the notation used for the call price was w (to refer to warrants) and the PDE has the form:

$$\frac{\partial w}{\partial t} = rw - rS\frac{\partial w}{\partial S} - \frac{1}{2}v^2 S^2 \frac{\partial^2 w}{\partial S^2}$$

where v^2 is the variance of the stock price. This PDE is also subject to the boundary condition applicable to the exercise value of the option on the maturity date T:

$$w(S,T) = S(T) - X \text{ for } S(T) \geq X; \text{ and } w = 0 \text{ otherwise } (S(T) < X)$$

(Note that round brackets are being used instead of square brackets to denote functions in the following discussion.) At this point, it is possible for analysis to proceed with "proof by knowledge of the solution." In other words, the Black–Scholes solution is "proved" by verifying that the Black–Scholes call option pricing function satisfies the PDE. This exercise will be carried out in Chapter 9, Section I. Restrictions imposed on the state space then make it possible to infer that the Black–Scholes solution is the unique solution to the PDE problem.

However, not knowing the solution to the PDE, Black and Scholes found it necessary to proceed by solving the boundary value problem directly. The method used is cumbersome and has since been superceded by other solution methodologies, such as direct evaluation of the discounted expectation problem used in risk-neutral valuation. To better appreciate the more difficult and direct method of solving the PDE used by Black and Scholes, consider the following guide provided by Black and Scholes as to the method of finding a solution (1973, pp. 643–644):

To solve this differential equation, we make the following substitution:

$$w(S,t) = e^{-r(t-T)} y\left[\left(\frac{2}{v^2}\right)\left(r - \frac{1}{2}v^2\right)\left[\ln\frac{S}{X} - \left(r - \frac{1}{2}v^2\right)(t-T)\right],\right. \tag{9}$$

$$\left. -\left(\frac{2}{v^2}\right)\left(r - \frac{1}{2}v^2\right)^2 (t-T)\right]$$

With this substitution, the differential equation and boundary condition become:

$$\frac{\partial y}{\partial s} = \frac{\partial^2 y}{\partial u^2}$$

$$y(u,0) = 0, \quad u < 0$$

$$y(u,0) = X\left[\exp\left\{\frac{u\left(\frac{v^2}{2}\right)}{r - \frac{v^2}{2}}\right\} - 1\right], \quad u \geq 0$$

This differential equation is the heat-transfer equation of physics, and its solution is given by Churchill (1963, p. 155). In our notation, the solution is

$$y(u,s) = \frac{1}{\sqrt{2\pi}} \int_{\frac{-u}{\sqrt{2s}}}^{\infty} X\left[\exp\left\{\frac{(u + q\sqrt{2s})\left(\frac{v^2}{2}\right)}{\left(r - \frac{v^2}{2}\right)}\right\} - 1\right] \exp\left\{\frac{-q^2}{2}\right\} dq$$

Substituting (this result) back into Eq. (9) from the Black–Scholes derivation and simplifying provide the Black–Scholes formula.

The general method selected by Black–Scholes is to use a change of variable and scale to transform the fundamental PDE for the European call into a variation of the heat equation (e.g., Berg and McGregor, 1966). This permits the Fourier series results to be applied. In particular, Black and Scholes reference the solutions to the heat equation from Churchill (1963, p. 155). This approach requires a complicated substitution to transform the Black–Scholes PDE into a form of the heat equation for which accessible solutions are available. Once this substitution is available, it is still not easy to derive a solution from the results in Churchill, and it is not immediately obvious that the form of the solution will involve density functions. Substantial effort is required to proceed from the solution derived from Churchill, given in terms of y, to the Black–Scholes call option pricing formula, which is given in terms of the call price w. It is the objective of this section to provide that solution.

Churchill (1963, p. 155) offers a solution, derived using Fourier series methods, for the heat equation subject to a boundary condition of the kind applicable to Black–Scholes. The notation in Churchill differs from that used in Black and Scholes. Remembering that Black–Scholes did a change of variable transform from $w(S,t)$ to $y(u,s)$, Churchill provides:

The solution to:

$$\frac{\partial g(x,t)}{\partial x} = k\frac{\partial^2 g(x,t)}{\partial t^2}$$

subject to $g(x,0) = f(x)$ is given by:

$$g(x,t) = \frac{1}{\sqrt{\pi}} \int_{-\infty}^{\infty} f\left(x + 2\eta\sqrt{kt}\right)e^{-\eta^2} d\eta$$

To match up this notation, change the dummy variable of integration to q'. Also observe that $k = 1$ in Black–Scholes and $g(x,t)$ is written as $y(u,s)$. These substitutions produce:

$$y(u,s) = \frac{1}{\sqrt{\pi}} \int_{-\infty}^{\infty} y(u + 2q'\sqrt{s}, 0)e^{\{-q'\}^2} dq'$$

It is now possible to exploit the properties of the boundary condition provided by the max [·] function to restrict the region of integration.

To do this, observe that $y(u,0) = 0$ for $u < 0$ and $y(u + 2q'\sqrt{s}, 0) = 0$ for $u = -2q'\sqrt{s}$. This can be solved for the dummy variable q' to get: $q' < -u/(2\sqrt{s})$. It follows that the lower limit of integration can be set to produce, in the Black–Scholes notation:

$$y(u,s) = \frac{1}{\sqrt{\pi}} \int_{-\frac{u}{2\sqrt{s}}}^{\infty} X \exp\left[\frac{(u + 2q'\sqrt{s})\left(\frac{v^2}{2}\right)}{r - \frac{v^2}{2}} - 1\right] \exp\left[\{-q'\}^2\right] dq'$$

In effect, the Black–Scholes solution involves a change of variable from w to y to transform the PDE to a form that is comparable to a type for which solutions are more readily derived. This change of variable imposes specific solutions on the boundary condition associated with $y(u,0)$. The properties of $y(u,0)$ are used to restrict the range of integration and provide a solvable problem. Changing the variable of integration q' to be $q/\sqrt{2}$ reproduces the Black–Scholes result.

What remains is to do as Black–Scholes suggests and "substitute back into (9)." The first step is to rewrite $y(u,s)$ to get:

$$y(u,s) = \frac{1}{\sqrt{2\pi}} \int_{-\frac{u}{\sqrt{2s}}}^{\infty} X \exp\left[\frac{(u + q\sqrt{2s})\left(\frac{v^2}{2}\right)}{\left(r - \frac{v^2}{2}\right)}\right] \exp\left[\frac{-q^2}{2}\right] dq - \frac{X}{\sqrt{2\pi}} \int_{-\frac{u}{\sqrt{2s}}}^{\infty} \exp\left[-\frac{q^2}{2}\right] dq$$

Given this, the operation of substituting involves unbundling the change of variable. Observing that the $y(u,s)$ specified by Black–Scholes in their Eq. (9) provides the relevant definitions for u and s, the lower limit of integration can be solved as:

$$\frac{u}{\sqrt{2s}} = \frac{\dfrac{2}{v^2}\left(r - \dfrac{v^2}{2}\right)\left[\ln\left(\dfrac{S}{X}\right) - \left(r - \dfrac{v^2}{2}\right)(t-T)\right]}{\sqrt{\dfrac{4}{v^2}\left(r - \dfrac{v^2}{2}\right)^2(t-T)}}$$

$$= \frac{\ln\left(\dfrac{S}{X}\right) + \left(r - \dfrac{v^2}{2}\right)(t-T)}{v\sqrt{t-T}} = d_2$$

Using this result, the second term in $y(u,s)$ becomes:

$$-\frac{X}{\sqrt{2\pi}}\int_{-d_2}^{\infty} \exp\left[\frac{-q^2}{2}\right]dq = -\frac{X}{\sqrt{2\pi}}\int_{-\infty}^{d_2} \exp\left[\frac{-v^2}{2}\right]dv = -XN\,[d_2]$$

The connection with the Black–Scholes formula is now apparent.

The first term of $y(u,s)$ follows appropriately. Examining the numerator in the exponential, the following terms can be solved:

$$\frac{u - \dfrac{v^2}{2}}{r - \dfrac{v^2}{2}} = \ln\frac{S}{X} + \left(r - \dfrac{v^2}{2}\right)(t-T) = d_2(v\sqrt{t-T}); \quad \frac{\sqrt{2s}\dfrac{v^2}{2}}{r - \dfrac{v^2}{2}} = v\sqrt{(t-T)}$$

Using this the first term can now be written:

$$\frac{X}{\sqrt{2\pi}}\int_{-d_2}^{\infty} \exp\left[d_2 v\sqrt{t-T}\right]\exp\left[qv\sqrt{t-T}\right]\exp\left[\frac{-q^2}{2}\right]dq$$

What follows is a considerable amount of manipulation. Using the following two results:

$$\exp\left[\frac{-q^2}{2}\right]\exp\left[qv\sqrt{t-T}\right] = \exp\left[-\frac{1}{2}\left(q - v\sqrt{t-T}\right)^2\right]\exp\left[\frac{v^2(t-T)}{2}\right]$$

$$d_2 v\sqrt{t-T} + \frac{v^2(t-T)}{2} = \ln\frac{S}{X} + r(t-T)$$

This produces for the first term:

$$\frac{X}{\sqrt{2\pi}}\int_{-d_2}^{\infty} \exp\left[\ln\frac{S}{X} + r(t-T)\right]\exp\left[-\frac{1}{2}\left(q - v\sqrt{t-T}\right)^2\right]dq$$

$$= \frac{S}{\sqrt{\pi}}\exp[r(t-T)]\int_{-d_2}^{\infty} \exp\left[-\frac{1}{2}\left(q - v\sqrt{t-T}\right)^2\right]dq$$

What remains is to change the variable of integration:

$$q' = v\sqrt{t - T} - q$$

which produces:

$$\frac{S}{\sqrt{2\pi}} \exp[r(t - T)] \int_{-\infty}^{d_1} \exp\left[-\frac{1}{2}q'\right] dq' = S \exp[r](t - T)] N[d_1]$$

Substituting the first and second terms into Eq. (9) from Black–Scholes reproduces the famous formula.

C. RISK-NEUTRAL VALUATION

The analytical advantages of the risk neutral valuation approach are apparent upon considering the use of this approach to solving the Black–Scholes formula. For exposition purposes, it is instructive to consider two solutions to the risk-neutral valuation problem: the solution to the Black–Scholes option pricing problem, which assumes geometric Brownian motion for the state variable, and the solution to the Bachelier option pricing problem, which assumes arithmetic Brownian motion for the state variable (Poitras, 1998b). The solution to the risk-neutral Black–Scholes valuation problem for geometric Brownian motion is available in several sources (e.g., Stoll and Whalley, 1993). The general risk-neutral valuation problem, given in Eq. (8.1) starts by considering the valuation problem for a European call option on a non-dividend-paying stock. In words, Eq. (8.1) indicates that the value of the call option depends only on the paths where $S_T \geq X$. The density associated with $S_T < X$, which includes the potentially negative price paths, does not directly enter the valuation. While there is some difference in the shape of the upper portions of the normal and log-normal distributions, this difference provides a basis for contrasting the performance of the Bachelier and Black–Scholes options. Given that neither assumption generally provides a particularly close fit to observed price distributions, it does not follow that lognormality will necessarily provide better pricing accuracy than normality in all situations. This issue must be addressed empirically.

Evaluation of Eq. (8.1) requires the integration of variables that follow the standard normal distribution. Two different specifications are needed to do this, one for the arithmetic Brownian motion and the other for geometric Brownian motion. For the case of arithmetic Brownian motion, over the time interval starting at t and ending at T:

$$S_T = S_t + \alpha t^* + \sigma\sqrt{t^*}\, Z \quad \text{or} \quad Z = \frac{S_T - S_t - \alpha t^*}{\sigma\sqrt{t^*}}$$

where Z is $N[0,1]$ and α is the drift in the SDE (see Section IV). The standard normal specification associated with geometric Brownian motion is stated in Appendix III.

Evaluating Eq. (8.1) for the arithmetic Brownian motion case gives:

$$X \operatorname{Prob}[S_T \geq X] = X \, N\left[\frac{S_t + \alpha t^* - X}{\sigma\sqrt{t^*}}\right]$$

$$E[S_T | S_T \geq X] = \int_{(X-S_t-\alpha t^*)/\sigma\sqrt{t^*}}^{+\infty} \left(S_t + \alpha t^* + \sigma\sqrt{t^*}Z\right) n[Z] \, dZ$$

$$= (S_t + \alpha t^*) \int_{-\infty}^{(S_t+\alpha t^*-X)/\sigma\sqrt{t^*}} n[Z] \, dZ + \sigma\sqrt{t^*} \int_{(X-S_t-\alpha t^*)/\sigma\sqrt{t^*}}^{+\infty} Z \, n[Z] \, dZ$$

$$= (S_t + \alpha t^*) \, N\left[\frac{S_t + \alpha t^* - X}{\sigma\sqrt{t^*}}\right] + \sigma\sqrt{t^*} \, n\left[\frac{S_t + \alpha t^* - X}{\sigma\sqrt{t^*}}\right]$$

Observing that risk neutrality requires that $(S_t + \alpha t^*) = S_t \exp[rt^*]$, substituting these results into Eq. (8.1) gives the closed-form solution for the Bachelier call option pricing formula. To verify that this is the absence-of-arbitrage-consistent solution requires the derivatives of the fundamental PDE for the Bachelier call option formula stated in Proposition 8.1 (see Section IV) to be evaluated and then substituted in the fundamental PDE for the Bachelier option. Determining that the PDE, together with the boundary and terminal conditions, is satisfied ensures that absence-of-arbitrage is satisfied.

The risk-neutral solution for the geometric Brownian motion proceeds much as with the arithmetic Brownian solution:

$$X \operatorname{Prob}[S_T \geq X] = X \, N\left[\frac{\ln\left[\dfrac{S_t}{X}\right] + \mu t^*}{\sigma\sqrt{t^*}}\right]$$

$$E[S_T | S_T \geq X] = \int_{(\ln[X/S_t]-\mu t^*)/\sigma\sqrt{t^*}}^{+\infty} \left(S_t \, e^{\mu t^* + \sigma\sqrt{t^*}Z}\right) n[Z] \, dZ$$

$$= \left[S_t \, e^{\mu t^* + \frac{\sigma^2 t^*}{2}}\right] \int_{-\infty}^{\frac{(\ln[S_t/X]+\mu t^*)}{\sigma\sqrt{t^*}} + \sigma\sqrt{t^*}} n[Z] \, dZ$$

$$= \left(S_t \, e^{\mu t^* + \frac{\sigma^2 t^*}{2}}\right) N\left[\frac{\ln[S_t/X] + \mu t^*}{\sigma\sqrt{t^*}} + \sigma\sqrt{t^*}\right]$$

The risk-neutral valuation approach now permits the result that the risk-free interest rate (r) can be used for continuously compounded rate of return on the stock (α). This produces $r = \alpha = \mu + \sigma^2/2$ to be used to make a substitution for $\mu(= r - \sigma^2/2)$. Collecting all these results into Eq. (8.1) gives:

$$C_t = e^{-rt^*}\{E[S_T|S_T \geq X] - X \, \text{Prob}[S_T \geq X]\} = e^{-rt^*}\{S(t) \, e^{rt^*} N[d_1] - X \, N[d_2]\}$$

Taking the discounting operator $\exp\{- rt^*\}$ through gives the Black–Scholes formula.

V. EXTENDING THE BLACK–SCHOLES MODEL

Since the introduction of the basic Black–Scholes model, various extensions have been developed, including permitting dividends on the stock; allowing early exercise by valuing American options; assuming different diffusion processes for the stock price, such as the CEV process; allowing interest rates or volatility to be stochastic; applying the model to commodities other than stocks, including options that permit delivery of the spot commodity or future contracts; applying the model to warrants instead of exchange-traded options; allowing options to have special features such as "look back" or multiple delivery specifications; introducing transactions and short-selling costs; and developing different analytical methodologies for solving the option pricing problem. This section provides an overview of the work that has been done on some of these topics. However, except in a limited number of cases, relaxing the basic Black–Scholes framework produces significant complications. For example, introducing American options produces *path dependence* in the option price, effectively eliminating the possibility for a closed-form solution to the valuation problem. Similarly, using other (potentially more realistic) diffusion processes than the log-normal again makes it difficult to derive a closed-form solution. For this reason, evaluation of option prices for more complicated situations typically involves application of techniques from numerical analysis, e.g., Tilley (1993).

A. INCORPORATING DIVIDENDS

Various methods are available for incorporating dividends into the Black–Scholes model. When the European assumption is retained and the timing and size of future dividend payments are known, only minor modifications are required to the formula.[24] The most direct method of incorporating dividends without undermining the basic Black–Scholes framework is to assume that the dividend payment is paid continuously, as a constant fraction or proportion (δ) of the value of the stock price, $D = \delta S$. It is also possible to be more general and assume that $\delta = \delta[S,\tau]$, but this complicates derivation of the closed form. In the constant proportional dividend case, the Black–Scholes formula is altered to permit the stock price to be discounted using the dividend payment rate to produce the constant proportional dividend call option pricing formula:

$$C = S\exp\{-\delta t^*\}N[d_1] - X\exp\{-rt^*\}\,N[d_2]$$

where:

$$d_1 = \frac{\ln\{\frac{S}{X}\} + \{(r-\delta) + \frac{1}{2}\sigma^2\}t^*}{\sigma\sqrt{t^*}}$$

$$d_2 = d_1 - \sigma\sqrt{t^*}$$

This formula would be applicable to firms with stated dividend policies given in terms of *yields* as opposed to a fixed dollar payment. While not common, there are firms that follow such policies. More importantly, this formula can be readily extended to options on other types of securities, such as currencies.

To derive the constant proportional dividend call option formula requires modifying the return on the riskless hedge portfolio:

$$dV = \left[S - \frac{C}{C_S}\right]r\,dt - \delta S\,dt = \left\{S(r-\delta) - \frac{C}{C_S}r\right\}dt$$

In other words, the net investment of funds in the riskless hedge portfolio must earn the riskless rate of interest adjusted for the dividend payments received. Because the dividend payment only enters into the return on the riskless hedge portfolio, the relevant partial differential equation becomes:

$$\frac{\partial C}{\partial t} = rC - (r-\delta)S\frac{\partial C}{\partial S} - \frac{1}{2}\frac{\partial^2 C}{\partial S^2}$$

It can be verified by direct differentiation that the constant proportional dividend call option pricing formula satisfies this PDE.

Incorporating known, discrete dividends follows in a similar fashion. Recalling the approach used in Chapter 7, Section II, when payment dates

---

[24]In general, Black–Scholes requires path independence of the hedge portfolio for a closed-form solution to be possible. Hence, in order to keep any modifications "simple" this property cannot be undermined. This happens, for example, where the dividend payments are uncertain or where the options are American puts or American calls on dividend-paying stocks.

and amounts for dividends are known with certainty, all that is required is to adjust the stock position in the riskless hedge portfolio by the *appropriately* discounted value of the dividends occurring between the purchase date and the expiration date. A single dividend payment D_1 paid at time t_1^* $(t^* > t_1^* > 0)$ leads to:[25]

$$C = [S - D_1 \exp\{-rt_1^*\}] \, N[d_1'] - X \exp\{-rt^*\} \, N[d_2']$$

where:

$$d_1' = \ln\left\{\frac{S - D_1 \exp\{-rt_1^*\}}{X \exp\{-rt^*\}}\right\} + \frac{1}{2}\sigma\sqrt{t^*}$$

$$d_2' = d_1' - \sigma\sqrt{t^*}$$

BOX 4

Application of the Black–Scholes Formula with Dividends

Consider the following information observed for a dividend-paying stock on February 8, 1988, with call option expiring on March 25, 1988 (a leap year): $S = \$51.70$, $X = \$52$, $r = 5.61\%$, $t^* = 46/366 = 0.125683$, and $\sigma = 0.1235$. Assume that a quarterly dividend payment of $1.50 is expected on March 15, 1988: $t_1^* = 36/366 = 0.09836$. Substituting this value into the call option pricing formula adjusted for dividends gives $C = \{51.7 - 1.5 \exp\{(-0.0561)(0.09836)\}N[d_1'] - 52 \exp\{(-0.0561)(0.125683)\}N[d_2']$. Evaluating $N[\cdot]$ gives $N[d_1'] = 0.271$ and $N[d_2'] = 0.2546$. This produces $C = \$0.37$. This result can be contrasted with the same parameters, *excluding the dividend payment*. In this case, $C = 51.7N[d_1] - 52 \exp\{(-0.0561)(0.125683)\}N[d_2]$. Observing that $d_1 = 0.290611$ and $d_2 = 0.248026$ and evaluating give $C = \$0.937$. Hence, this example demonstrates that dividends can have a significant impact on option pricing.

---

[25]This presentation uses the equivalent representation for d_1 (i.e., except for the inclusion of the dividend d_1 is unchanged). For further discussion, see footnote 17 associated with the specification of the Black–Scholes formula in Section II. In practice, the discrete dividend-adjusted model is easy to apply; all that is required is that the stock price be adjusted by subtracting the appropriately discounted dividend.

Similarly, incorporating multiple dividend payments occurring at times t_1^*, t_2^*, t_3^* involves taking the discounted value of each dividend payment from the relevant payment dates and subtracting these values from the current stock price. The implication of this result for option prices is that European options on dividend paying stocks will have lower call prices and higher put prices when compared with European options identical in X and t^* except that the stock does not pay a dividend. While seemingly an artificial method of introducing dividends, given the short maturities (9 months and less) for many exchange-traded options, combined with the typically stable dividend payout patterns of many stocks, this approach can often provide reasonable approximations to observed option prices.[26]

Given the formulae for incorporating known dividend payments, an important practical question concerns the extent to which these models capture actual option prices for dividend paying stocks, particularly for longer dated options such as warrants and long term equity anticipation securities (LEAPS). This is an active research area (e.g., Lauterbach and Schultz, 1990). In general, extending the Black–Scholes model to include uncertain dividend streams is not possible because this introduces a path-dependent payoff. While it is possible to introduce a stochastic process for dividends, producing a model with two state variables, the resulting option pricing solutions are complicated, e.g., Rabinovitch (1989) provides a workable solution for the related two-state variable case with stochastic interest rates. In addition, the stochastic process generating dividends is not typically the same as for variables such as interest rates and volatility.

B. Options on Futures and Forward Contracts

The techniques and issues associated with dividends arise naturally when the Black–Scholes framework is extended to options on futures contracts (e.g., Black, 1976; Wolf 1982; Brenner, *et al.*, 1985; Shastri and Tandon, 1986b; Ramaswamy and Sundaresan, 1985). Starting from the Black–Scholes assumptions, the futures option pricing model can be derived most expediently by assuming that the commodity underlying the futures contract does not pay a carry return; this permits the relationship between spot and futures prices to be expressed as $F(t) = S(t) \exp\{rt^*\}$.[27] In general, when a carry return is

---

[26]The example is taken from Gibson (1991, chap. 5).

[27]While not realistic for many commodities to assume this full carry futures pricing model, extending to the case where the cash commodity also pays a continuous carry return is straightforward. The more complicated case where the carry return is stochastic is examined in Gibson and Schwartz (1990).

admitted, $F(t) = S(t) \exp\{bt^*\}$, where b is the *net* carry return, the continuous carry cost rate minus the continuous carry return rate. When the stock or spot commodity price is assumed to follow a log-normal diffusion, $dS = \alpha S\ dt + \sigma S\ dW$ and $dF = (\alpha - b)F\ dt + \sigma F\ dW$.[28] Given this, the riskless hedge portfolio used to derive the PDE for futures options contains one futures contract and $(\partial C/\partial F)^{-1}$ written options positions:

$$V = -\beta_F C \quad \Rightarrow \quad dV = [-\beta_F C]\ r\ dt$$

where:

$$\beta_F = \left[\frac{\partial C}{\partial F}\right]^{-1} = \frac{1}{C_F}$$

Unlike stock (or spot commodity) options, the futures contract can be assumed not to involve a net investment of funds.[29] The only relevant cash flow is the income received on the written options position.

The Black–Scholes formula for futures options can be derived with the fundamental PDE for a call option on futures and forward contracts:

$$\frac{\partial C}{\partial t} = rC - \frac{1}{2}\frac{\partial^2 C}{\partial F^2}\sigma^2 F^2$$

where C is the price of a call option on a futures contract. This PDE differs substantively from that for a call option on the spot. This PDE can be compared with the fundamental PDE for a stock that pays a continuous dividend at rate δ given previously:

$$\frac{\partial C}{\partial t} = rC - (r - \delta)S\frac{\partial C}{\partial S} - \frac{1}{2}\frac{\partial^2 C}{\partial S^2}\sigma^2 S^2$$

Comparing the two PDEs reveals that, when $r = \delta$, there is an approximate equivalence relationship. From this it follows that the formula for pricing options on futures contracts can be inferred from the formula for the constant proportional dividend option pricing formula, under the condition that $r = \delta$:

$$C = \exp\{-rt^*\}\{F(t,T)\ N[d_1] - X\ N[d_2]\}$$

---

[28]This formulation requires that b is, at most, a function of time, but not a function of S or any other stochastic variable.

[29]This is not technically correct because of margin, transactions, and other costs. In addition, over time variation margin will undermine this assumption. However, for present purposes this assumption is not severe.

where:

$$d_1 = \frac{\ln\left\{\dfrac{F(t,T)}{X}\right\} + \left(\dfrac{\sigma^2}{2}\right)t^*}{\sigma\sqrt{t^*}}$$

$$d_2 = d_1 - \sigma\sqrt{t^*}$$

The validity of this formula depends on the noted assumptions about both the relationship between futures and spot prices as well as the constancy of the futures price volatility. Extensions of this model appear in a number of sources (e.g., Ramaswamy and Sundaresan, 1985; Brenner *et al.*, 1985).

C. American Options

The extensions to Black–Scholes considered to this point have permitted closed-form solutions. Unfortunately, for many extensions of practical value, closed-form solutions are not possible. The problem of path dependence has already been encountered in the analysis of introducing dividend payments and the American option feature. Because of the possibility for early exercise, the price of American puts as well as American calls on dividend-paying stocks cannot be precisely determined for a finite expiration date. Whether early exercise actually occurs will depend on the specific path that the stock price follows, hence the problem of path dependence. Given this, Roll (1977), Geske (1979b), and Whaley (1981) show that it is possible to approximate the value of an American call by valuing hypothetical portfolios of European options that capture the American option payoff. Various analytical approximation methods have also been proposed (e.g., Brennan and Schwartz, 1977; Geske and Johnson, 1984; Barone-Adesi and Whaley, 1987). Tilley (1993) is an important recent contribution. Comparison of the American pricing models with the appropriately adjusted Black–Scholes formula (e.g., Shastri and Tandon, 1986c), reveals a significant but not dramatic improvement in pricing accuracy.

Formal analysis of American options begins with McKean (1965), where the American option pricing problem is formulated as a solution to the heat equation subject to a free boundary condition. McKean demonstrated that the American option price can be determined but only by introducing a function that has come to be called the *optimal stopping boundary*. Hence, the American option pricing problem can be formulated as an optimal stopping problem where the stopping boundary is determined by the benefits of early exercise. As a consequence, the price of an American option can be formally decomposed into the value of a European option plus the early exercise premium, producing a functional representation for Property 3 (see Chapter 7). Since

McKean, the optimal stopping representation has been developed considerably, and other solution techniques such as variational inequalities have been introduced. Myneni (1992) provides an overview of these developments. One important implication of formalizing American option pricing as a free boundary problem occurs when the option is a perpetual. In this case, time does not directly enter the PDE problem, and a closed form solution is available. This insight has been used to price other types of perpetuals such as the Russian option (e.g., Gerber and Shiu, 1994a,b; Shepp and Shirayev, 1993).

Recognizing that the American option price can be represented as the sum of the European price and the early exercise premium provides some intuitive insight. When the early exercise premium is zero, then the European option pricing formula can be used to value the American option. Because the right of early exercise combined with non-negative prices prevents the American option price from falling below $\max[0, S(t) - X]$ for a call and $\max[0, X - S(t)]$ for a put, early exercise cannot occur when the European option price is greater than these values, even when the early exercise premium is zero. It will be rational to sell the option instead of exercising. Because the European option achieves these values when $t = T$, it follows that one general factor involved in the early exercise decision is the time to expiration. However, even though the early exercise premium goes to zero as the time to expiration goes to zero, higher values of the time to expiration imply a larger time value for the European option. Recognizing that early exercise involves foregoing the time value on the option, the precise impact of time to expiration is not obvious.

Under what conditions will American options be exercised early? Rationality requires that the option be exercised only when the price received by selling the option is less than the value when exercised. Hence, one limited answer to this question is obvious: Only in-the-money options will be exercised. Another early exercise property that has already been provided is that American calls on non-dividend-paying stocks will *not* be exercised early. This is an implication of Property 10 in Chapter 7. The European option price provides a lower bound on the American price. The arbitrage supporting the European call price prevents that price from falling below $\{S(t) - X\}$. Hence, early exercise for calls has something to do with dividends or, in the case of commodities other than stocks, with carry returns.[30]

In the case of a stock with one dividend payment remaining prior to the expiration date on the option, the arbitrage support for the European call price requires the stock price to be adjusted for the dividend payment (D_1):

$$C_A[S,\tau,X] \geq C[S,\tau,X] \geq \max[0, S(t) - (D_1\, PV[r,\tau_1]) - X\, PV[r,\tau]]$$

---

[30]Early exercise can also be related to exercise price adjustment. Conditions for adjustment of the exercise price, such as stock splits or mergers, are specified in the option contract. Exercise price adjustments are not considered here.

The requirement of adjusting the stock price for the receipt of the dividend payment creates a situation where the lower bound to the American call price provided by the European call price is not necessarily greater than or equal to $S(t) - X$. For a given τ and r, the larger the dividend payment, the farther below $S(t) - X$ the European bound on the American. For a given r and D, the same result applies for smaller τ. The implication is that short-dated American options on stocks expecting a sizable dividend will tend to be exercised early. The case of early exercise for continuous dividend payments is discussed in section IV.

The early exercise incentive for an American call on a dividend-paying stock is even more complicated than the European lower bound indicates. As discussed in Chapter 7, Section I, the European lower bound is derived by comparing the expiration date returns for a European call with a portfolio that combines a long stock position financed by a borrowing with maturity value of X. When there are dividend payments on the stock, the cost of the purchasing the portfolio is reduced by the appropriately discounted value of the dividends received. The American option provides the flexibility to exercise the call just prior to the ex-dividend date, thereby receiving the dividend and avoiding the *expected* fall in the stock price typically occurring on the ex-dividend date. This result can be intuitively seen by comparing the European lower bound on the ex-dividend date, $\max[0, S(t + 1) - X\ PV[r, \tau + 1]]$, with the value on the previous cum-dividend date, $\max[0, S(t) - (D_1\ PV[r, \tau_1]) - X\ PV[r, \tau]]$.

Early exercise for puts on non-dividend-paying stocks is different than the case for calls. Consider the extension of Property 10 (Chapter 7) to puts:

$$P_A[S, \tau, X] \geq P[S, \tau, X] \geq \max[0, X - S(t)] \geq \max[0, X\ PV[r, \tau] - S(t)]$$

Unlike calls, the impact of $PV[\ \cdot\ ]$ acts in the opposite direction on X, making the possibility of early exercise for puts on non-dividend-paying stocks (or commodities where the carry return is less than r) a likely possibility.

Because the conditions developed from Property 10 are only lower bounds, American put prices will typically be higher than the lower bound. The intuition for early exercise follows from recognizing that for the stock price paths going close to zero, the put will be deep in-the-money. This implies that $N[-d] \to 1$ and $P \to (PV[\ \cdot\ ]X - S) \leq X - S$. Instead of selling the put for $(PV[\ \cdot\ ]X - S)$, the American put holder will exercise the put and receive $X - S$. In practice, exercise of a put requires that the stock be delivered in exchange for X. Hence, early exercise will be done by traders holding stock in combination with a put. The essential point to recognize is that Property 10 of Chapter 7 applied to puts provides an arbitrage strategy that bounds the European option price. Because this bound is *below* the exercise value, holders of American options will choose to exercise the put rather than to sell the option at a lower price. Hence, deep in-the-money American puts will tend to be exercised early.

In addition to establishing early exercise of the American put using the distribution-free arbitrage bounds, the optimal stopping boundary for American puts can be used to motivate early exercise activity related to deep in-the-money puts. Puts are in the money because the stock price has fallen below the exercise price. At some point it is no longer profitable to hold the put (plus stock) because the possibility of further profits due to lower stock prices is more than offset by the loss of interest income on the exercise value, together with the interest opportunity cost of holding a non-dividend-paying stock (spot) position. This leads to the simplest optimal stopping boundary: At any time between purchase and expiration, exercise the American put on a non-dividend-paying stock when the loss of interest income on the exercise value plus the opportunity cost of holding the spot position exceeds the difference between the current put price and the exercise value.

The need to adjust for the difference between the put price and the exercise value is the result of selling the put being an alternative to early exercise. Where a stock and a put position are involved, as is required for exercise, transaction costs will impact the exercise decision. Selling the put will incur transaction costs in both option and stock markets, while exercise only involves delivery. When the put is exercised, there is some loss because the time premium is lost. This premium reflects the maximum future gain from the expected drop in stock prices between the current date and the expiration date. When the option goes deep in-the-money or when $\tau \to 0$ and the option is close to expiration, this additional premium will be near zero. This brings out another important feature of early exercise: put options that are in-the-money and close to expiration may get exercised early.

D. Option Valuation with Alternative Diffusion Processes

Empirically, there is little support for the hypothesis that financial prices precisely conform to the log-normal assumption that is essential to deriving the Black–Scholes option pricing formula. However, log normality does have the desirable feature that non-negative values are not admitted, consistent with financial prices, and the deviation from observed prices is not dramatic. There are better distributional fits to the data, but log normality does typically provide a useful first approximation. Unfortunately, making the distributional assumption more realistic also undermines the ability to derive a closed-form option pricing formula. This issue is made even more complicated by a lack of agreement over which distributional assumption has the best goodness of fit with observed prices. In addition, it is not clear how much of an increase in pricing accuracy can be gained over the Black–Scholes solution if more complexity is introduced.

Closed-form solutions are available for a limited number of other distributional assumptions. The simplest solution occurs when it is assumed that prices follow arithmetic Brownian motion: $dS = \alpha\, dt + \sigma\, dW$. Progressively more complicated solutions can be obtained for a stochastic process that is a combination of a diffusion process and a Poisson jump process (Merton, 1976), the constant elasticity of variance process (Cox and Ross, 1976), and the Bessel process (German and Yor, 1993). Solutions for related processes, such as the Brownian bridge (Ball and Torous, 1983) and the inverse gamma (Milevsky, 1998), are also available. Jarrow and Rudd (1983) have collected many relevant results.

In the arithmetic Brownian case, it is the change in prices that follows an arithmetic Brownian motion, not the rate of return as in the log-normal case. Reasons for selecting geometric over arithmetic Brownian motion were advanced at least as early as Samuelson (1965) and some of the studies in Cootner (1964). In reviewing previous objections, Goldenberg (1991) recognizes three of practical importance: (1) a normal process admits the possibility of negative values, a result that is seemingly inappropriate when a security price is the relevant state variable; (2) for a sufficiently large time to expiration, the value of an option based on arithmetic Brownian motion exceeds the underlying security price; and (3) as a risk-neutral process, arithmetic Brownian motion without drift implies a zero interest rate. Taken together, these three objections are relevant only to an unrestricted, risk-neutral "arithmetic Brownian motion" that is defined to have a zero drift. As such, some objections to arithmetic Brownian motion are *semantic*, avoidable if the process is appropriately specified.

Smith (1976) defines arithmetic Brownian motion to be driftless and provides an option pricing formula that is attributed to Bachelier (1900) and is subject to all of the three objections. Smith (p. 48) argues that objection (2) is due to the possibility of negative sample paths, although this objection can also be avoided by imposing an appropriate drift. Goldenberg (1991) reproduces the Smith–Bachelier formula and proceeds to alter the pricing problem by replacing the unrestricted driftless process with an arithmetic Brownian motion that is absorbed at zero. The resulting option pricing formula avoids the first two objections. The third objection is addressed by setting the drift of the arithmetic Brownian process equal to the riskless interest rate times the security price, consistent with an OU process. Using this framework, Goldenberg generalizes an option pricing result in Cox and Ross (1976) to allow for changing variances and interest rates. With the use of appropriate transformations for time and scale, Goldenberg argues that a wide range of European option pricing problems involving diffusion prices can be handled using the absorbed-at-zero arithmetic Brownian motion approach.

The Bachelier option prices derived here use the same perfect market and continuous trading assumptions as in Black and Scholes (1973). Bachelier options for three types of underlying securities are considered: a non-dividend-paying asset, an asset with proportional dividend payments, and a futures contract. For the non-dividend-paying asset, the security price is assumed to follow an unrestricted arithmetic Brownian motion:

$$dS = rS\,dt + \sigma\,dW$$

This SDE is compatible with absence-of-arbitrage. Exploiting the riskless hedge portfolio construction leads to the following PDE associated with the Bachelier option:

$$\frac{\partial C}{\partial t} = rC - \frac{\partial C}{\partial S}rS - \frac{1}{2}\sigma^2\frac{\partial^2 C}{\partial S^2}$$

which is subject to the terminal boundary condition $C[S_T] = \max[0, S_T - X]$. Solving the general valuation problem leads to Proposition 8.1.[31] Wilcox

---

PROPOSITION 8.1

Absence-of-Arbitrage Formula for the Bachelier Option

Assuming perfect markets and continuous trading, if the non-dividend-paying security price follows the unrestricted arithmetic Brownian motion, then the solution to the absence-of-arbitrage valuation problem is given by:

$$C_G(S,t^*; r,\sigma,X) = e^{-rt^*}\left\{\left(S_t e^{rt^*} - X\right)N[g] + \sigma\sqrt{t^*}\,n\,[g]\right\}$$

where:

$$g = \frac{S_t e^{rt^*} - X}{\sigma\sqrt{t^*}}$$

C_G is the price of the general Bachelier call option, and $N[g]$ and $n[g]$ represent the cumulative normal probability function and normal density function, respectively, evaluated at g.

---

[31] All proofs are given in the Poitras (1998b).

(1990) and Poitras (1998b) adapts this form of the Bachelier option to provide a solution to the spread option pricing problem.

It is possible to generalize the analysis to include constant proportional dividend payments (D) of the form $D = \delta S$. Following market convention, the option contract is assumed *not* to be dividend-payout protected. To derive a Bachelier option that both satisfies the PDE associated with the riskless hedge portfolio *and* incorporates proportional dividend payments, it is sufficient to restate the arithmetic Brownian motion as an OU process of the form:

$$dS = (r - \delta)S\,dt + \sigma_V\,dW$$

The associated PDE for the riskless hedge portfolio problem has the form:

$$\frac{\partial C}{\partial t} = rC - (r - \delta)S\frac{\partial C}{\partial S} - \frac{1}{2}\sigma_v^2\frac{\partial^2 C}{\partial S^2}$$

Even though the drift does not enter the PDE directly, it does alter both the variance of the process and, as reflected in Proposition 8.1, the expected future spot price. The proof of Proposition 8.2 involves direct differentiation of the option pricing formula to verify that this solution does satisfy the PDE for the riskless hedge portfolio problem.

PROPOSITION 8.2

Absence-of-Arbitrage Formula for the Bachelier Option with Dividends

Assuming perfect markets and continuous trading, if the proportional dividend-paying security price follows the arithmetic Brownian motion with continuous proportional dividends, then the absence-of-arbitrage solution to the valuation problem is given by:

$$C_R[S,t;\ r,\sigma,X] = \left(S_t e^{-\delta t^*} - X e^{-rt^*}\right)N[h] + V\,n[h]$$

where:

$$h = \frac{S_t e^{-\delta t^*} - X e^{-rt^*}}{V}, \quad V = \sigma_V\sqrt{\left\{\frac{e^{-2\delta t^*} - e^{-2rt^*}}{2(r - \delta)}\right\}}$$

and $N[h]$ and $n[h]$ represent the cumulative normal probability function and normal density function, respectively, evaluated at h.

Despite a certain similarity, there are substantive differences in option prices derived using geometric and arithmetic Brownian motion. For example, the PDE for the riskless hedge portfolio associated with options on futures contracts for arithmetic Brownian motion involves setting $r = \delta$ in the SDE for the OU process:

$$\frac{\partial C}{\partial t} = rC - \frac{1}{2}\sigma^2 \frac{\partial^2 C}{\partial F^2}$$

where F is the price for the relevant futures contract. A similar result holds for the geometric case. However, when it comes to solving for the option price formula, the simplification available for the geometric case (setting $r = \delta$ in the option price formula for stocks with proportional dividends) is not available in the arithmetic case due to a singularity in the Proposition 8.2 solution at $r = \delta$. The appropriate solution is given by Proposition 8.3, which is useful both for pricing options on futures spreads and for comparing the normal and log-normal prices of exchange options (Poitras, 1998b).

The question of whether arithmetic Brownian motion is an appropriate stochastic process for asset pricing is complicated. In any event, conventional wisdom maintains that an important limitation of the OU and arithmetic Brownian processes is that the state variable has a non-zero probability of taking on negative values. Because prices are often the state variables in

---

PROPOSITION 8.3

Absence-of-Arbitrage Formula for the Bachelier Futures Option

Assuming perfect markets and continuous trading, if the futures price follows an arithmetic Brownian motion, then the absence-of-arbitrage solution to the European call option valuation problem is given by:

$$C_F[F,t;\, r,\sigma,X] = e^{-rt^*}\left\{(F_t - X)N[k] + \sigma\sqrt{t^*}\; n[k]\right\}$$

where:

$$k = \frac{F_t - X}{\sigma\sqrt{t^*}}$$

C_F is the price of the Bachelier futures call option, and $N[k]$ and $n[k]$ represent the cumulative normal probability function and normal density function, respectively, evaluated at k.

continuous time models, some method of bounding the variable at zero is needed. The log-normal process, geometric Brownian motion, has a natural boundary at zero. Another possible method of imposing non-negative state-variable values is to impose an *absorbing barrier* at zero. A solution to the option pricing problem using absorbed Brownian motion was initially presented by Cox and Ross (1976) and later extended by Goldenberg (1991).

Converting an unrestricted arithmetic Brownian motion by imposing an absorbing barrier at zero on the process is not as difficult as it might seem.[32] All those paths that hit zero end and, from that point, do not contribute to the ensemble of paths that combine to determine the distribution at any future point in time. The solution to this option pricing problem was given by Cox and Ross (1976, pp. 162–163) and is shown in Proposition 8.4. Extensions of the absorbed arithmetic Brownian motion (e.g., to allow for volatility being a deterministic function of time) can be found in Goldenberg (1991).

PROPOSITION 8.4

Absence-of-Arbitrage Formula for the Absorbed Brownian Option

Assuming perfect markets and continuous trading, if the proportional dividend paying security price follows the arithmetic Brownian motion of Proposition 8.2 subject to an absorbing barrier at zero, then the absence-of-arbitrage solution to the valuation problem is given by:

$$C_{AB}[S,t; r,\sigma,X] = \left(S_t e^{-\delta t^*} - X e^{-rt^*}\right) N[h_1] + \left(S_t e^{-\delta t^*} + X e^{-rt^*}\right) N[h_2]$$
$$+ V(n[h_1] - n[h_2])$$

where:

$$h_1 = \frac{S_t e^{-\delta t^*} - X e^{-rt^*}}{V}, \quad V = \sigma_V \sqrt{\left\{ \frac{e^{-2\delta t^*} - e^{-2rt^*}}{2(r - \delta)} \right\}}, \quad h_2 = \frac{-S_t e^{-\delta t^*} - X e^{-rt^*}}{V}$$

$N[h]$ and $n[h]$ represent the cumulative normal probability function and normal density function, respectively, evaluated at h.

---

[32] The derivation of the transition probability density associated with the absorbed process is greatly facilitated thanks to the reflection principle (e.g., Karlin and Taylor, 1975, v. 1).

In the discussion of implied volatility, it was observed that it was possible to construct pricing results using two stochastic processes, one for the commodity price and another for volatility. Hull and White (1987), Heston (1993), and Scott (1997) have demonstrated that it is possible to obtain closed-form solutions for the case of two random variables. However, analytical solutions are substantively simplified in cases where the two random processes are assumed to be uncorrelated. This approach is not restricted to volatility. For example, in addition to random exchange rates, currency option pricing can also model the randomness in the foreign and domestic interest rates, pricing the option written on three stochastic processes. Other examples would include introducing a stochastic dividend yield to price a stock index option, using a stochastic short interest rate process to price a T-bond option, and using a stochastic convenience yield to price an option on oil futures. In general, it is only possible to achieve closed-form solutions for a very small class of stochastic processes.

Rabinovitch (1989) is an example of a case where the two stochastic processes are chosen carefully enough to permit a closed form solution to be derived. As in Black–Scholes, Rabinovitch assumes that the stock prices follow a log-normal diffusion: $dS = \alpha S\, dt + \sigma S\, dW_S$. In addition, there is a single default-free interest rate r that is also permitted to be stochastic, to follow a mean-reverting OU (Ornstein–Uhlenbeck) process of the form:

$$dr = q(m - r)dt + v\, dW_r$$

where $q(m - r)$ is the instantaneous expected change in the short-term rate, and v is the instantaneous volatility for the interest rate. The parameter m is the unconditional expected interest rate to which the current rate, r, reverts to at speed proportional to q. This type of process is also (descriptively) called a *mean-reverting* process.[33] The presence of the two Wiener processes, dW_r and dW_s requires specification of a contemporaneous covariance, $\{dW_r\, dW_s\} = \rho\, dt$. From the Markov construction, lagged correlations are zero. Within this framework, it is possible to derive a closed-form expression for the call price that is similar in form to Black–Scholes. However, in order to do this, it is necessary to convert the information in the stochastic interest rate into a formula for the discount bond price. The resulting solutions, while expressible in the same form as Black–Scholes, are significantly more complicated.

---

[33]The OU suffers from the defect that there is a positive probability of negative interest rates. While for short time paths such events will be possible, almost surely, only when the process starts close to zero, this does raise difficulties for long time paths. Hence, valuation of long-term options may be problematic with this type of model.

V. FOREIGN CURRENCY OPTIONS

Unlike exchange-traded options for most other commodities, the major U.S. exchange for trading currency options was, for many years, the Philadelphia Stock Exchange (PHLX). This situation was unusual in that the PHLX is not also a major commodity futures exchange, such as the International Money Market (IMM) or Chicago Board of Trade (CBOT). This situation has now changed and comparison of the volume and open interest available for the currency options reveals that the futures options on the IMM division of the Chicago Mercantile Exchange (CME) now is well in excess of the volume and option interest on the Philadelphia Stock Exchange, which was previously the most important exchange trading currency option contracts. This is consistent with the usual result that the futures exchange trading the highest volume of an options contract also trades the highest volume of the futures contracts for that commodity. This is significant for currency options trading on the IMM, the most important currency futures exchange. The PHLX was something of an innovator in options trading practices. In addition to offering American currency futures options, the PHLX also offers European spot currency options. Outside the United States, currency option trading is a global operation with currency option contracts traded on the major foreign futures exchanges (see Chapter 1, Section IV), as well as being traded over the counter (OTC).

A. THE CURRENCY OPTIONS PRICING FORMULA

Derivation of the pricing formula for foreign currency options involves an adaption of the constant proportional dividend version of the Black–Scholes model. It is assumed that the spot exchange rate follows a log-normal diffusion, where the domestic interest rate, r, and the foreign interest rate, r^*, together with the instantaneous standard deviation σ of the spot exchange rate, are all constants. This leads to the following formula for a European currency call option on spot exchange:

$$C = S \exp\{-r^*t^*\}N[d_1] - X \exp\{-rt^*\} N[d_2]$$

where:

$$d_1 = \frac{\ln\left\{\dfrac{S}{X}\right\} + \left(r - r^* + \frac{1}{2}\sigma^2\right)t^*}{\sigma\sqrt{t^*}}$$

$$d_2 = d_1 - \sigma\sqrt{t^*}$$

As with previous call option pricing results, the formula for currency put options is obtained by substitution into the put–call parity condition for currency options:

$$P = X \exp\{- rt^*\} \, N[- d_2] - S \, \exp\{- r^*t^*\} \, N[- d_1]$$

where:

$$-d_1 = \frac{\ln\left\{\dfrac{X}{S}\right\} + \left(r^* - r - \dfrac{1}{2}\sigma^2\right)t^*}{\sigma\sqrt{t^*}}$$

$$-d_2 = -d_1 + \sigma\sqrt{t^*}$$

Close examination of the put and call pricing formulae reveals a fundamental feature of currency options: The right to put currency A for currency B at X is identical to the right to call currency B in exchange for currency A at X. Unlike other commodities that involve the exchange of some commodity for money, currency options involve the exchange of two monies with the numeraire being arbitrary.

While the European currency option pricing formula can be derived by following much the same approach as for the Black–Scholes call option on a stock with a constant proportional dividend, because the single source of randomness is now a spot exchange rate the conceptualization of the hedge portfolio is somewhat different. The riskless hedge portfolio requires an investment in a pure discount (zero coupon) foreign bond that matures to a maturity value of one unit of foreign currency. In foreign currency terms, the continuous time representation for the price of this bond is $\exp\{- r^*t^*\} = PV^*[r^*,\tau]$. The value of this bond is then converted to a domestic currency value by multiplying by the spot exchange rate to get $S(t)\exp\{- r^*t^*\}$. As currency options are typically priced as though the domestic bond is U.S., this implies that the exchange rate is measured in U.S. direct terms. The objective of the riskless hedge portfolio is to protect (hedge) the domestic currency value of the foreign bond position.

The riskless hedge portfolio is now constructed by writing β currency call options to protect the domestic currency value of the foreign bond against changes in the spot exchange rate. However, in this case, β has a slightly different interpretation than for the option on the non-dividend-paying stock:

$$\frac{\partial V}{\partial S} = e^{-r^*t^*} - \frac{\partial C}{\partial S} = 0 \quad \Rightarrow \quad \beta = \frac{e^{-r^*t^*}}{\dfrac{\partial C}{\partial S}} = \{N[d_1]\}^{-1}$$

More precisely, $V(t) = S(t)\exp\{- r^*t^*\} - \beta C$ where $S(t)$ is the spot exchange rate at time t. Much as in the constant proportional dividend case, the riskless return associated with the net investment in the portfolio must now be adjusted to reflect the return earned on the foreign bond:

$$dV = \left\{ S(t)e^{-r^*t^*} - \beta C \right\} r\, dt - \left\{ S(t)e^{-r^*t^*} \right\} r^*\, dt$$

$$= S(t)e^{-r^*t^*}(r - r^*)\, dt - \beta C r\, dt$$

Following the usual procedure of evaluating Ito's lemma:

$$dV = e^{-r^*t^*}\, dS - \frac{e^{-r^*t^*}}{\frac{\partial C}{\partial S}}\, dC = e^{-r^*t^*} \left[dS - \frac{1}{\frac{\partial C}{\partial S}}\, dC \right] = e^{-r^*t^*} \left[dS - \frac{dC}{C_s} \right]$$

where: $dS = \alpha S\, dt + \sigma S\, dW$

$$dC = \left[C_t + C_s \alpha S + \frac{1}{2} C_{SS} \sigma^2 S^2 \right] dt + C_s \sigma S\, dW$$

Equating the two conditions for dV, canceling and manipulating where appropriate, produces:

$$C_t = rC - S(r - r^*)C_S - \frac{1}{2}\sigma^2 S^2 C_{SS}$$

This is the fundamental PDE for a European spot currency call option.

The original presentation of the currency call option formula was by Garman and Kohlhagen (1983), Grabbe (1983), and Biger and Hull (1983). Though the formula presented in each case was the same, the derivations provided in these sources did not follow the constant proportional dividend approach. For example, Grabbe (1983) shows that a one-unit long position in the domestic bond can be hedged with $-\alpha/\beta$ units of the foreign bond combined with $-1/\beta$ written call positions, where α and β are the appropriate partial derivatives. In effect, by creating a self-financing riskless hedge portfolio, Grabbe utilized the concept of an arbitrage portfolio. Grabbe also provides a generalization of the formula to admit deterministic changes in the volatility over time. Garman and Kohlhagen also use a different approach relying on the equality of risk-adjusted excess returns in an arbitrage-free economy. Chiang and Okunev (1993) demonstrate that the formula can be generalized to permit the foreign and domestic bond prices to follow Brownian bridge processes.

The extension to options on currency futures and forwards follows by using the continuous time version of covered interest parity. Recall from Chapter 4, Section II, that:

$$F(t,T) = \frac{1 + r(t,T)}{1 + r^*(t,T)}S(t) = \frac{1 + rt^*}{1 + r^*t^*}S(t)$$

$$\Rightarrow \quad F(t,T) = e^{rt^*}e^{-r^*t^*}S(t) = e^{(r - r^*)t^*}S(t) \Rightarrow S(t) = e^{(r^* - r)t^*}F(t,T)$$

Substituting for S in the spot currency call option formula produces:

$$C = e^{-rt^*}\{F(t,T)\,N[d_1] - X\,N[d_2]\}$$

where:

$$d_1 = \frac{\ln[F(t,T)/X] + \frac{1}{2}\sigma^2 t^*}{\sigma\sqrt{t^*}}$$

$$d_2 = d_1 - \sigma\sqrt{t^*}$$

Comparison of this formula with the general formula for options on futures contracts reveals that the two results are the same, confirming the application of the general model in the specific case of options on currency futures and forward contracts.

B. Put–Call Parity and Early Exercise for Currency Options

Results for currency put options follow from the put–call parity arbitrage condition for European foreign currency options. For spot currencies the condition is

$$P[S,\tau,X] = C[S,\tau,X] - S(t)PV^*[r^*,\tau] + X\,PV[r,\tau]$$

Using the CIP condition and substituting for S, gives the put–call parity condition for futures contracts:

$$P[S,\tau,X] = C[S,\tau,X] + \{(X - F(t,T))PV[r,\tau]\}$$

The put–call parity result for spot currency options can be derived in much the same fashion as put–call parity for non-dividend-paying stocks given in Chapter 7, Section II.

While there are a number of different possible portfolio pairings that could be compared for illustrating the arbitrage, for present purposes the two relevant portfolios are (1) the domestic portfolio, a long (short) foreign currency call with exercise price X and τ days to maturity combined with a long (short) position in a domestic zero-coupon bond with maturity value of X; and (2) the foreign portfolio, a long (short) foreign currency put—with the same terms as the call—combined with long (short) foreign zero-discount bond yielding r^* with maturity value of one unit of foreign currency and term to maturity of τ.[34] When $S(T) \geq X$, the domestic portfolio has a value equal to

[34] The foreign bond position can be illustrated by observing that $PV^*[r^*,\tau]$ is denominated in foreign currency, say F\$. The maturity value of the bond is one F\$. The domestic currency (D\$) cost of acquiring this bond when the portfolio is created at time t is $PV^*S(t)$, where $S(t)$ is measured in domestic direct terms, D\$/F\$. The domestic currency value of the foreign bond at maturity will be $PV^*S(T) = S(T)$.

the maturity value of the bonds X, because the call expires worthless. The foreign portfolio will have maturity value of $S(T)$ plus $(X - S(T))$ that gives a value of X. Similarly, when $S(T) > X$, the domestic portfolio will be worth $S(T)$ because the call will be worth $(S(T) - X)$ and the domestic bonds X. The foreign portfolio will be worth the maturing value of the bonds $S(T)$, with the put expiring worthless.

The put–call parity results have significant practical implications. For example, the notion of covered interest arbitrage discussed in Chapter 4, Section II, required that securities that were identical in all respects except currency of denomination will have the same fully covered returns. In the put–call parity case, another somewhat more complicated equivalence result is provided. More precisely, a foreign bond portfolio that is protected against adverse currency movements by purchasing currency put options will have the same return as a domestic portfolio that combines a long fixed-income secur- ity with purchased currency call options. Chapter 9, Section III demonstrates how the put–call parity condition for currency options can be used to create insured portfolios of foreign bonds.

Early exercise for American currency options depends on the relationship between the foreign and domestic interest rate. To see this, consider the extension of Property 10 of Chapter 7 to the continuous dividend case:

$$C_A[S,\tau,X] \geq C[S,\tau,X] \geq \max[0, S(t)PV^*[r^*,\tau] - X\,PV[r,\tau]]$$

where r^* is the continuous dividend payment, in this case paid in the form of interest on the foreign bond position. If $r^* > r$, then the European bound will be less than $S(t) - X$ and there is an incentive for the American call option to be exercised early. The extension to puts follows from observing that a currency call option giving the right to buy D\$ for F\$ at exchange rate X is also a put option giving the right to sell F\$ for D\$ at X. When the call is in-the-money, the put is out-of-the-money. Hence, if $r > r^*$, then the European bound for the put will be less than $X - S(t)$ and there is an incentive for the American put option to be exercised early.

To see how the extension of Property 10 translates into an early exercise condition, recall that when an option is exercised early the time value remaining in the option is given up. In practice, currency options are often exercised early, sometimes long before the stated expiration date (e.g., Bod- urtha and Courtadon, 1995). The incentives to exercise early follow by examining the European option price when the option is deep in-the-money, $S \gg X$ for the call and $X \gg S$ for the put. For the call, deep in-the-money implies $N[d] \to 1$ and $C \to Se^{-r^*t^*} - Xe^{-rt^*}$ which is less than $S - X$ when $r^* > r$. Similarly, $N[-d] \to 1$ when $X \gg S$, which gives $P \to Xe^{-rt^*} - Se^{-r^*t^*}$, which is less than $X - S$ when $r > r^*$. Hence, in these cases, the European option does not provide an effective lower bound for the American option.

There is no arbitrage support in the market to induce the American option to trade above the exercise boundary, $S(t) - X$.

To see the rationale for exercise in the cases without support from the European boundary, let $r^* > r$ and have $Se^{-r^*t^*} - Xe^{-rt^*} < S - X$ and the call option in-the-money. If the option holder borrows X at r to buy S and invests this one unit of foreign currency in the foreign bond at r^*, then on the maturity date the early exercise strategy will receive a profit of: $S(T) \exp\{r^*t^*\} - X \exp\{rt^*\}$. If the option holder does not exercise then the profit will be max $[0, S(T) - X]$. Comparing these two values reveals that, if the probability of the option of finishing out-of-the-money is ignored, then early exercise will be optimal. Hence, if the option is deep enough in-the-money that the time value has gotten close enough to zero, then it will be optimal to exercise the call option early if $r^* > r$. A similar result holds for in-the-money puts if $r > r^*$.

To compare the early exercise and hold-to-maturity values directly requires two observations. First, the call option on the exercise date is assumed to be sufficiently in-the-money that $N[d] \to 1$ and the value of the American call has been forced to the exercise boundary $S(t) - X$. In practice, there is little or no time value on deep-in-the-money options because there is no demand to buy this type of security, only those wishing to sell. Hence, this condition is often observed in practice. Second, if the option is deep in-the-money on the exercise date, the closer this date is to the exercise date, the smaller the probability that the option will finish out-of-the-money. If the option finishes out-of-the-money, then the hold-to-maturity strategy will be superior. So there is a tradeoff between the time to expiration and the difference between r^* and r required to trigger early exercise. In the jargon of Chapter 9, Section IV, early exercise is, once again, an optimal stopping problem.

C. Empirical Studies of Currency Options

A number of studies have investigated the empirical validity of applying the Black–Scholes-based currency option pricing model as well as competing alternatives. For example, Chesney and Scott (1989) use data on European currency options traded in Geneva to compare the Black–Scholes model with a model that allows for stochastic variance, which is a mean-reverting diffusion. When an updated implied standard deviation is used to compute the Black–Scholes option price, Black–Scholes outperforms the stochastic variance model (Black–Scholes with constant variance performed poorly). Limited evidence is found for significant mispricing. Similar results are reported by Shastri and Tandon (1986a) who compare a number of different methods of calculating the variance. Profit opportunities that were identified were found to be exhausted within one day. Using PHLX options data, Hilliard *et al.* (1991) compare the constant-variance Black–Scholes model with a model that admits stochastic interest rates. While the stochastic rate model is found to be more accurate, it would have been useful if this study had reported results for Black–Scholes using implied standard deviations, as in Shastri and Tandon (1986a) and other sources. Ritchken and Trevor (1999) is a recent effort along this line of research.

Other empirical studies have examined the performance of other option pricing models. For example, Bodurtha and Courtadon (1987) examined the pricing accuracy of the American option pricing model and found that "the standard American option pricing model does not explain the pricing of foreign currency options as well as it explains the pricing of stock options. In particular . . . this model under-prices out-of-the-money options relative to at-the-money options and in-the-money options" (p. 165). As noted previously, Shastri and Tandon (1986a) also report pricing shortcomings when the European model is used to price American options. Finally, along a more analytical line, Hull and White (1987) provide results for various delta, delta + gamma, and delta + vega strategies for hedging risks associated with writing foreign currency options. With reference to the discussion in Chapter 9, Section I, delta + gamma hedging is found to perform relatively better only when the traded option has a relatively constant implied standard deviation and a short time to expiration. Typically, delta + vega hedging is found to produce superior results. Malz (2000) is a recent effort along this line of research.

QUESTIONS

1. In Chapter 8, Section I, a verbal description was provided to describe the geometry of the evolution of the Wiener process. Construct the appropriate geometry.

2. The Black–Scholes solution to the fundamental PDE for a European call on a non-dividend-paying stock requires a change of variables to transform the PDE into the general form of a parabolic PDE. Provide the steps required to specify this change of variable.

3. Extend the discussion of Section IV to derive the solution for the perpetual put option. This requires a different specification of θ associated with the second root of the fundamental quadratic equation (e.g., Dixit and Pindyck, 1994, p. 143).

4. "A call option benefits from increases in the stock price and these increases can be very large. A put option benefits from stock price declines, but the stock price can only fall to zero. Therefore, if we

have a put and a call on the same stock with the same terms, the put must sell for less than the call." Do you agree or disagree? Explain.

5. Given that $S = \$47, X = \$45, i = 0.12$, and $\sigma = 0.40$ (*annual*), calculate the 3-month call option price that is consistent with the Black–Scholes pricing model.

6. Outline the continuous time derivation of the Black–Scholes model. What assumptions are being used to derive the results? What are the limitations of applying the model to actual options prices? Under what conditions will American calls be exercised early? What early exercise conditions apply to puts?

7. Using the two-portfolio approach, develop the trading strategy underlying Property 12 of Chapter 7. How does the argument work when puts are used?

8. Section IV states the following extension of Property 10 to the continuous dividend case: $C_A[S,\tau,X] \geq C[S,\tau,X] \geq$ max $[0, S(t)\ PV^*[r^*,\tau] - X\ PV\ [r,\tau]]$. Using the two-portfolio approach, verify this condition.

6. Extend Property 12 of Chapter 7 to demonstrate that it will not be rational to exercise an American put just prior the stock's ex-dividend date.

7. For currency options, there is a smile relationship between volatility and moneyness. Yet, implied volatilities for equity options exhibit a volatility skew that is downward sloping in moneyness. Discuss the possible reasons for this differing behavior in implied volatility for these two commodities.

CHAPTER 9

Application of Option Valuation Techniques

I. PORTFOLIO MANAGEMENT: DELTA, THETA, AND GAMMA[1]

A. BASIC DEFINITIONS

One of the most useful applications of the Black–Scholes formula involves applying the partial derivatives of the formula to analyze and design portfolios containing derivative securities. The presence of an option pricing formula

---

[1]The material in this section is covered in more detail in Cox and Rubinstein (1985, chap. 6), Hull (2000, chap. 13), and Gibson (1991, chap. 4). The former reference provides an important special case of the calculus chain rule which is required to simplify evaluation of the derivatives:

$$\frac{\partial N[z]}{\partial v} = N'[z] \, \frac{\partial z}{\partial v}$$

where $N'[z]$ is the standard normal density evaluated for the argument z. More precisely:

$$N'[z] = \frac{1}{\sqrt{2\pi}} \, \exp\left\{\frac{-z^2}{2}\right\}$$

permits partial derivatives to be solved directly, instead of having to rely on numerical techniques. Correct evaluation of the partial derivatives permits theoretical portfolios to be precisely constructed to have desirable properties.

Delta, theta, and *gamma* are names used to refer to the most commonly referenced partial derivatives. The partial derivatives are also referred to as *Greeks,* after the symbols used identify the derivatives. Applied to a call option, these three Greeks are defined as:[2]

$$\Delta_C = \frac{\partial C}{\partial S}, \quad \theta_C = -\frac{\partial C}{\partial t^*}, \quad \Gamma_C = \frac{\partial \Delta}{\partial S}$$

While delta, theta, and gamma are typically the most commonly referenced partial derivatives, there are numerous other partial derivatives that could also be of value for certain types of situations. For example:

$$\frac{\partial C}{\partial \sigma}, \quad \frac{\partial \theta}{\partial t}, \quad \frac{\partial^2 C}{\partial \sigma \, \partial S}, \quad \frac{\partial C}{\partial r}$$

This is only a partial list. *From put–call parity,* similar concepts can be derived for puts:

$$\Delta_P = \frac{\partial P}{\partial S} = \frac{\partial C}{\partial S} - 1 = \Delta_C - 1$$

$$\theta_P = -\frac{\partial P}{\partial t^*} = -\left\{ \frac{\partial C}{\partial t^*} - rX \, e^{-rt^*} \right\}$$

$$\Gamma_P = \frac{\partial \Delta_C}{\partial S} = \Gamma_C$$

The other partial derivatives for puts follow appropriately.

To employ the derivative properties of Black–Scholes to design portfolios of securities requires recognizing that the various securities that can be included in a given portfolio, such as stocks, commodities, futures, and options, all possess derivative properties. From linearity, this permits the delta, theta, gamma, and other Greeks of a portfolio to be calculated. More precisely, let V be the dollar value of the portfolio, V_i represent the price of security i, and n_i be the number of units of security i held where $n < 0$ indicates a short

---

[2]In some presentations, the elasticity rather than the derivative is of interest; for example, the call price elasticity with respect to stock price changes is

$$\eta_{C,S} = \frac{S}{C} \frac{\partial C}{\partial S}$$

The advantage of using elasticity is that the elasticity value is normalized and the derivative is not. The elasticity form makes it easier to interpret a calculated value. This approach will not be used here.

(written) position and $n > 0$ represents a long (purchased) position. In general, for portfolios containing a large number of securities:

$$V = n_1 \, V_1 + n_2 \, V_2 + n_3 \, V_3 + \, \ldots$$

Taking partial derivatives of V now permits the derivation of Δ_V, Γ_V, and the other Greeks. For example, in the *two-security case*, the delta of the portfolio can be derived:

$$\Delta_V = \frac{\partial V}{\partial S} = n_1 \, \frac{\partial V_1}{\partial S} + n_2 \, \frac{\partial V_2}{\partial S} = n_1 \, \Delta_1 + n_2 \, \Delta_2$$

Taking the total derivative, dV, provides the mathematical foundation for determining the VaR (see Chapter 2, Section II). (See Crouhy *et al.* 2001 for such extensions.) This section is primarily concerned with stating the exact analytical values for the Greeks applicable to calls and puts. Sections II and III are concerned with demonstrating how these concepts can be used in portfolio design.

The results in this section are derived by evaluating partial derivatives of the Black–Scholes formula. As a consequence, these derivatives apply only to options on *non-dividend-paying* securities or commodities. In cases where the assumptions are similar to the Black–Scholes case (e.g., log-normal state variables and European options), evaluating the Greeks for other types of options, such as European currency options, follows the same procedure and produces similar, though not identical, expressions. In cases where the assumptions are substantively different (e.g., for American options on dividend paying stocks), the Black–Scholes derivatives will be imprecise. In cases where closed-form price formulas are not available, numerical techniques are required to precisely evaluate the derivatives. This highlights another reason why having closed forms for option prices is important. Closed forms can be differentiated to arrive at expressions for the Greeks. Where the option price can only be solved numerically, the further evaluation of derivatives can present nontrivial numerical complications.

B. Delta

One application of Δ_C, the sensitivity of the call price to changes in the stock price, has already been encountered in specification of the riskless hedge portfolio which was the basis of the derivation for the Black–Scholes formula. More precisely, after some effort and manipulation the derivative can be evaluated as (see Appendix III).

$$\Delta_C = \frac{\partial C}{\partial S} = N[d_1] > 0$$

Diagrammatically, the delta of a call measures the slope of $C[\cdot]$ given in Graphs 7.1 and 7.2 of Chapter 7, Section I. In addition to providing a precise mathematical specification of the slope, evaluating the sensitivity of delta as different variables change also provides important information. For example, the relationship between delta and S is depicted in Fig. 9.1. This figure indicates that the price of deep out-of-the-money calls will be unresponsive to stock price changes, while deep in-the-money calls will move one-to-one with stock price. An at-the-money call has a delta of approximately 1/2 when t^* is small. This value for Δ_C can be seen by evaluating d_1 when $S = X$. In this case, $\ln\{S/X\} = \ln\{1\} = \ln\{\exp\{0\}\} = 0$:

$$d_1 = \frac{\ln\{1\} + \left(r + \frac{1}{2}\sigma^2\right)t^*}{\sigma\sqrt{t^*}} = \frac{\left(r + \frac{1}{2}\sigma^2\right)t^*}{\sigma\sqrt{t^*}}$$

Because the remaining part of d_1 is small when t^* is small, an approximation of $N[0] = 0.5$ is evaluated.

The delta for a put, Δ_P, follows from taking the partial derivative of the put option pricing formula:

$$P = S\,(N[d_1] - 1) - X\,e^{-rt^*}(N[d_2] - 1)$$
$$= X\,e^{-rt^*}N[-d_2] - S\,N[-d_1]$$

Because all that has been done is to introduce 1, a constant, into the formula, the delta for a put follows appropriately:

$$\Delta_P = \frac{\partial P}{\partial S} = N[d_1] - 1$$

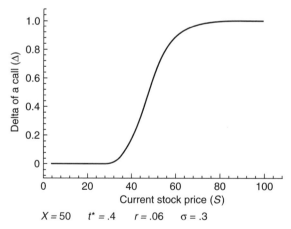

FIGURE 9.1   The delta of a call as a function of the stock price. *Source*: Adapted from Cox and Rubinstein (1985), with permission.

Effectively, the put delta is the negative of the call delta, as illustrated in Fig. 9.2. When Δ_C is 1 then Δ_P is zero and when Δ_C is zero then Δ_P is -1. Deep in-the-money puts increase (decrease) by $1 when the stock price *falls* (rises) by $1. Similarly, deep out-of-the-money puts are not sensitive to changes in the stock price.

As discussed in Chapter 8, Section II, one important practical implication of the delta arises in specification of a riskless hedge portfolio: The inverse of delta gives the number of written (purchased) call options required to hedge a long (short) stock position. Recalling that the properties of both probability densities and call options require that $N[d_1] \leq 1$, the implication of Fig. 9.1 is that, unless the option is deep in the money, call prices will change less than $1 if the stock price changes by $1. When the stock price changes, the delta changes; therefore, the riskless hedge must be *rebalanced* in order to maintain the hedge. A similar comment applies to changes in time to expiration. Consider the number of written *at-the-money* options required to form a riskless hedge for different times to expiration, where $r = .06$, $\sigma = .3$, and $X = S$:

Time to expiration, t^*	d_1	$N[d_1]$	$N[d_1]^{-1} =$ of options
5 years	0.783	0.5283	1.893
1 year	0.350	0.5137	1.947
6 months	0.248	0.5098	1.962
3 months	0.175	0.5069	1.973
1 month	0.101	0.5044	1.983

For at-the-money options, *ceteris paribus*, rebalancing with respect to changes in time is not overly important.

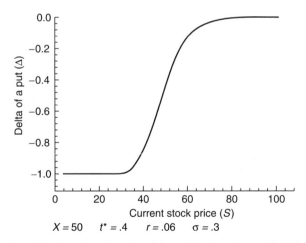

FIGURE 9.2 The delta of a put as a function of the stock prices. *Source*: Adapted from Cox and Rubinstein (1985), with permission.

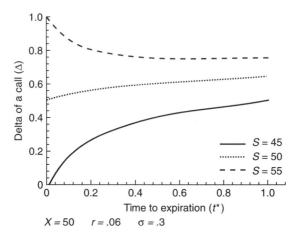

FIGURE 9.3   The delta of a call as a function of the time to expiration. *Source*: Adapted from Cox and Rubinstein (1985), with permission.

Given that the delta for a put is the call delta minus 1 (Fig. 9.2), $\Delta_P < 0$ and a purchased put will fall (rise) in value as the stock increases (decreases). Even though the riskless hedge portfolio was derived with written call options, Δ_P could also be used to establish the number of puts that must be purchased in order to create a riskless hedge portfolio combining puts and stock. Because the resulting hedge ratio for a long stock position will be positive, this implies that puts will be purchased, not written as in the case of calls. As with calls, to maintain the hedge, the position will have to be rebalanced as the stock price changes in order to maintain the delta of the portfolio equal to zero. The relationship between delta and t^* is given in Figs. 9.3 (call) and 9.4 (put). Observing that for $t^* = 0$ the option has expired, it is apparent that the closer the option gets to expiration, the greater the time sensitivity of delta to whether the option is in-, at-, or out-of-the-money. In addition to deltas for puts and calls, the delta for the relevant spot commodity (e.g., a stock), or for a futures contract, can be seen to be 1.[3]

C. GAMMA

The gamma of the position measures the sensitivity of the delta to changes in stock prices:

---

[3]For options written on spot commodities (futures), the stock position can be replaced with the spot (futures) and, as with stocks, the delta is one in this case also.

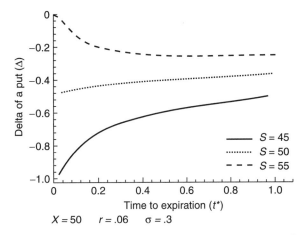

FIGURE 9.4 The delta of a put as a function of the time to expiration. *Source*: Adapted from Cox and Rubinstein (1985), with permission.

$$\Gamma_C = \frac{\partial \Delta_C}{\partial S} = \frac{\partial^2 C}{\partial S^2} = \frac{1}{S\,\sigma\sqrt{t^*}} N'[d_1] = \frac{1}{S\,\sigma\sqrt{t^*}}\, n[d_1]$$

where:

$$N'[d_1] \equiv \frac{1}{\sqrt{2\pi}}\, \exp\left\{\frac{-d_1^2}{2}\right\} \equiv n[d_1]$$

This value is the same for both puts and calls; the stock (futures contract) has a gamma of zero. In effect, gamma reexpresses the information in Figs. 9.1 and 9.2. Much as with delta, gamma can be plotted as a function of the stock price (Fig. 9.5) and time to expiration (Fig. 9.6). Gamma has two important practical features: size and sign. *For cases such as the riskless hedge portfolio that require rebalancing in order to achieve a delta target*, the size of gamma determines how frequently the position has to be adjusted to maintain the hedge portfolio feature. "High" values indicate that frequent adjustments are required; "low" values mean the position delta is relatively immune to stock price changes and rebalancing can be done infrequently. A *gamma-neutral* ($\Gamma = 0$) position is one in which the delta is "locally" protected from changes in the stock price. For example, from Fig. 9.5, long positions for deep in- and out-of-the-money options are found to be gamma neutral.

The size of gamma also has significance for positions that do not have to be rebalanced. Examples would be portfolios insured with purchased puts or option strategy positions such as straddles and vertical spreads. These positions are established with a specific delta and gamma that will provide

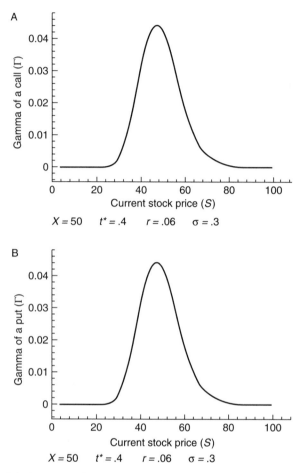

FIGURE 9.5 (A) The gamma of a call as a function of the stock price. (B) The gamma of a put as a function of the stock price. *Source*: Adapted from Cox and Rubinstein (1985), with permission.

information about the speed at which the delta changes as the stock price changes. To see this, consider a stock position insured with an at-the-money put. This position has a positive delta and, given that the put is at-the-money, a sizable gamma. As the stock price increases, the delta on the stock-plus-put position will increase, because the delta of the put will become less negative, to the point where the put delta is zero and the stock-plus-put position delta approaches one and the gamma is zero. Gamma indicates that the delta of the position will change the most when the option is at-the-money. As discussed in

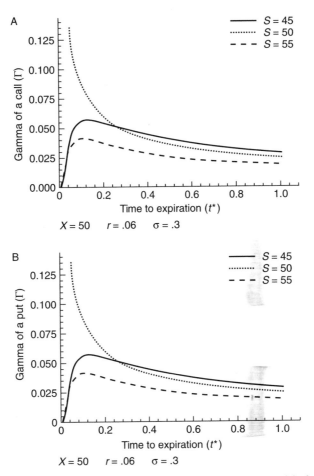

FIGURE 9.6 (A) The gamma of a call as a function of the time to expiration. (B) The gamma of a put as a function of the time to expiration. *Source*: Adapted from Cox and Rubinstein (1985), with permission.

Chapter 8, Section II, positions with equal delta and gamma will experience the same local movement in delta but may have substantively different expiration-date payoffs. In these cases, once the stock price has changed, the delta and gamma of the positions will not typically be equal.

The other important practical feature of gamma is the sign. Basic calculus identifies the sign of the second derivative with the shape of a function, say $f[x]$. If the second derivative, $d^2f/dx^2 > 0$, the function is locally increasing with changes in x; if $d^2f/dx^2 < 0$, the function is locally decreasing with changes in x. Heuristically, the connection to options can be motivated by taking $f[x]$ to be the payoff function given by an expiration-date profit diagram. For example, the purchased straddle has an expiration-date payoff that is increasing away from the exercise price. This implies a positive gamma. Similarly, the written straddle decreases away from the exercise price, which implies a negative gamma. For any strategy, part of the payoff function will be positive and part is negative. It follows that *if the position has $\Gamma < 0$, then stable stock prices are required for position $\pi > 0$.* A $\Gamma > 0$ will require volatile stock price behavior for $\pi > 0$. Combining delta and gamma information incorporates directional preference into the analysis. A basic example is provided by a purchased call: $\Gamma_C > 0$ indicates that volatile stock prices are required for profitability, and the positive relationship between the call and stock prices ($\Delta_C > 0$) indicates that upward price movements are also needed.

Two distinct uses of gamma have been identified. For portfolios designed to achieve a delta target, such as delta neutrality, gamma provides analytical information on the rebalancing frequency. For portfolios aiming to achieve trading profits, such as straddles and vertical spreads, gamma indicates the degree of movement in stock prices required to achieve profitability. Given this, it is possible to combine these two uses for gamma to analyze portfolios where discrete rebalancing is being used to achieve a delta target. In practice, it is not possible to trade continuously. In general, discrete rebalancing will not be able to exactly achieve the delta target. Recognizing there will be some slippage, gamma can provide information about whether the slippage will tend to generate positive or negative profits.

D. THETA

The theta of the position measures the sensitivity of the option price to changes in time. Because "time" in options counts backwards, two different definitions of theta are encountered, depending how the impact of time is evaluated. One approach (e.g., Stoll and Whalley, 1993, p. 228), takes theta to be the sensitivity of the call price with respect to changes in time to expiration. Recalling that $\tau = T - t$ and $t^* = (\tau/365)$, because τ is counting "backward," the alternative approach is to specify theta as the negative value in order for the *intuitive interpretation* of how the value of the position changes as t (not t^*) increases. Given these two alternative definitions of theta, it is also possible to differentiate with respect to either t^* or τ, with these results differing only by a factor of proportionality:

$$\frac{\partial C}{\partial t^*} = \frac{S\sigma}{2\sqrt{t^*}} \, N'[d_1] + X \, \exp\{-rt^*\}r \, N[d_2] > 0 \quad \Rightarrow \quad \theta < 0$$

The intuitive interpretation follows from the sign of θ, colloquially referred to as the "time decay" of the position. As time t passes, the value of a long *call* option position will fall in value. Similarly, this result provides a significant development to Property 5 of Chapter 7, Section I. The sensitivity of the time decay is found to vary as time to expiration approaches (Fig. 9.8). Again, there is a significant divergence between the cases where the call option is at the money and where it is not. This is also reflected in Fig. 9.7, where the sizable

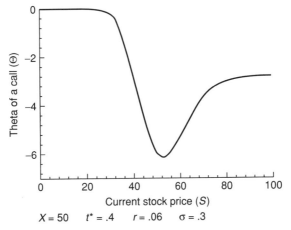

FIGURE 9.7   The theta of a call as a function of the stock price. *Source*: Adapted from Cox and Rubinstein (1985), with permission.

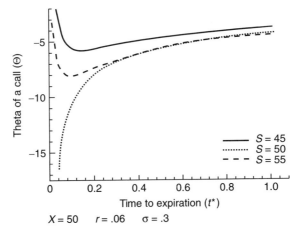

FIGURE 9.8   The theta of a call as a function of the time to expiration. *Source*: Adapted from Cox and Rubinstein (1985), with permission.

discrepancy between deep out-of-the-money and deep in-the-money call options is apparent: The relationship is not symmetric.

A seemingly counterintuitive result applies to the theta of a European put. Recalling that the put values are determined from put-call parity:

$$\frac{\partial P}{\partial t^*} = \frac{\partial C}{\partial t^*} - X \exp\{-rt^*\}r$$

The value of this derivative can be either positive or negative. (This result only holds for European puts; American puts will be always positive.) This result is illustrated in Figs. 9.9 and 9.10, which provide the relationship between the put theta and both stock prices and time to expiration. From Fig. 9.9, the theta of the put being positive tends to occur when the stock price is low, implying that the put is in-the-money. From Fig. 9.10, in-the-money puts are required, though this condition is not restrictive in the case where the stock price approaches zero.

To see why this ambiguous result occurs, reformulate the put–call parity condition in the form: $S(t) + P[S,t^*,X] = C[S,t^*,X] + X \exp\{-rt^*\}$. Differentiating both sides by t^* produces the condition stated for the European put theta. As S approaches zero, the theta of a call gets close to zero, leaving the put theta to be determined by the last term on the righthand side associated with the discounted value of the exercise price. In effect, when the stock price approaches zero, a longer time to maturity will have a negative impact on put price by lowering the cost of acquiring the bond investment needed to replicate the insured stock portfolio which, when the stock price is close to

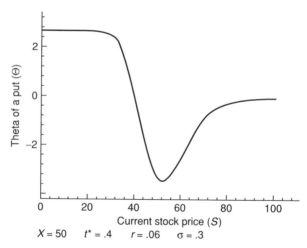

FIGURE 9.9   The theta of a put as a function of the stock price. *Source:* Adapted from Cox and Rubinstein (1985), with permission.

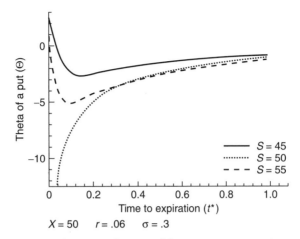

FIGURE 9.10 The theta of a put as a function of the time to expiration. *Source*: Adapted from Cox and Rubinstein (1985), with permission.

zero, is almost completely associated with the intrinsic value of the put. However, on balance, while *positive theta* values are possible, the theta of a put should typically be negative, just as with the call.

This ambiguous result for the European put can be further motivated by considering the theta for an American put. The possibility of a positive theta for European puts is due to the inability to exercise the deep-in-the-money put early. Recalling the discussion of Properties 10 and 11 in Chapter 7, Section I, when the European put goes deep in-the-money, the value of the put is bounded below by max $[0, X \exp\{-rt^*\} - S(t)]$. However, in the case of the American put, the lower bound will be the exercise boundary $X - S(t)$. Hence, as S approaches zero and the put goes deep in-the-money, the associated call is deep out-of-the-money, indicating that the call theta goes to zero. For the American put, the deep in-the-money put price will fall to the exercise boundary $X - S(t)$ and, combined with the result that the call theta is zero in this case, the American put theta is bounded below by zero.

E. RHO AND VEGA

While delta, gamma, and theta are the most commonly considered features, the partial derivatives with respect to both sigma and r also receive attention. The relationship between option prices and volatility was initially referred to as the *lambda* but the convention is now to refer to the *vega*. The partial derivative between option prices and interest rates is referred to as the *rho* of the position. Evaluating the relevant values for calls and puts gives:

$$\upsilon_C = \upsilon_P = \frac{\partial C}{\partial \sigma} = S\sqrt{t^*}\ N'[d_1] > 0$$

$$\rho_C = \frac{\partial C}{\partial r} = t^*X\ \exp\{-rt^*\}\ N[d_2] > 0$$

$$\rho_P = \frac{\partial P}{\partial r} = t^*X\ \exp\{-rt^*\}[N[d_2] - 1] < 0$$

The equivalence of vega for the put and call (with the same terms) is as expected: The more volatile the underlying stock, the higher the option price. As illustrated in Figs. 9.11 and 9.12, the strength of this relationship will depend on both the time to expiration and whether the option is in- or out-of-the-money. Given this, the different signs for each put and call rho require some explanation (see Figs. 9.13 and 9.14). The impact on the call price follows immediately from considering Property 10 of Chapter 7, Section I, which can be interpreted as using a long call plus lending to approximate the return from holding the stock. A higher interest rate will lower the present value of the bond investment (which has an expiration value equal to the exercise price). This frees up funds for investment in the call position, resulting in a higher call price. The impact on the put, which is unambiguous, follows from the same argument where it is recognized that the stock plus a purchased put exactly equal the call plus lending portfolio.

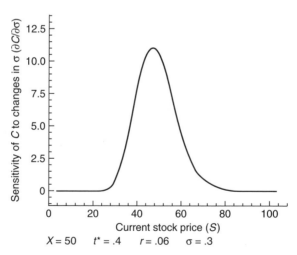

FIGURE 9.11 The sensitivity of C to changes in σ as a function of the stock price. *Source*: Adapted from Cox and Rubinstein (1985), with permission.

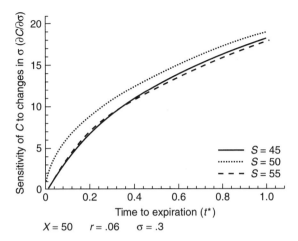

FIGURE 9.12 The sensitivity of C to changes in σ as a function of the time to expiration. *Source*: Adapted from Cox and Rubinstein (1985), with permission.

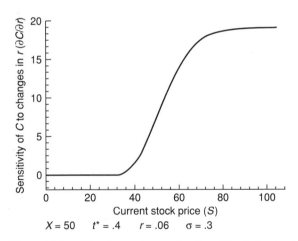

FIGURE 9.13 The sensitivity of C to changes in r as a function of the stock price. *Source*: Adapted from Cox and Rubinstein (1985), with permission.

F. VERIFYING THE BLACK–SCHOLES SOLUTION

Given that the analytical form of the derivatives for the Black–Scholes formula have been specified, it is now possible to demonstrate that the Black–Scholes

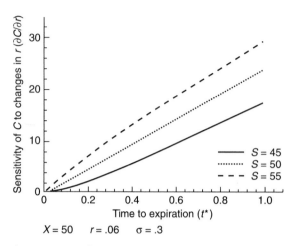

FIGURE 9.14 The sensitivity of C to changes in r as a function of the time to expiration. *Source*: Adapted from Cox and Rubinstein (1985), with permission.

formula is the solution to the fundamental partial differential equation (PDE) given in Chapter 8, Section II. In terms of delta, theta, and gamma:

$$C_t = rC - rS\ C_S - \frac{1}{2}\ \sigma^2\ S^2\ C_{SS} \quad \Rightarrow \quad \theta_C = rC - rS\ \Delta_C - \frac{1}{2}\ \sigma^2 S^2\ \Gamma_C$$

Substituting in the relevant derivatives gives:

$$-\frac{\partial C}{\partial t^*} = -\left[\frac{S\sigma}{2\sqrt{t^*}}\ N'[d_1] + X\ \exp\{-rt^*\}r\ N[d_2]\right]$$

$$= r\{SN[d_1] - X\ \exp\{-rt^*\}\ N[d_2]\} - rS\ N[d_1] - \frac{1}{2}\ \sigma^2 S^2\ \frac{1}{S\sigma\sqrt{t^*}}\ N'[d_1]$$

$$= -rX\ \exp\{-rt^*\}\ N[d_2] - \frac{1}{2}\ \frac{S\sigma}{2\sqrt{t^*}}\ N'[d_1]$$

Hence, the Black–Scholes formula satisfies the fundamental PDE. Verifying that the boundary conditions are satisfied is not difficult: max $[0,S(T) - X]$ follows because, when $S(T) > X$, dividing a positive numerator by $t^* = 0$ in d_1 and d_2 produces $N[\infty] = 1$ and $C = S - X$. When $S(T) < X$, dividing a negative numerator by $t^* = 0$ produces $N[-\infty] = 0$ and $C = 0$. Similarly, when $S = 0$, taking the log of zero in both d_1 and d_2 produces $N[-\infty] = 0$, and $C[0,\tau,X] = 0$ is also satisfied.

II. HEDGE PORTFOLIOS, SPREAD TRADES, AND OTHER STRATEGIES

A. RISKLESS HEDGE PORTFOLIOS

A riskless hedge portfolio is a theoretical construct. In general, it is a portfolio with a value that does not change when a specific random variable changes. While it is usually possible to construct a hedge portfolio in some fashion, the riskless hedge condition may not always be attainable in practice. For example, consider a portfolio containing k securities with prices per unit of $\{X_1, X_2, \ldots, X_k\}$ and number of units held in the portfolio of $\{\alpha_1, \alpha_2, \ldots, \alpha_k\}$. Then, the market value of the portfolio, V, is equal to $V = \alpha_1 X_1 + \alpha_2 X_2 + \ldots + \alpha_k X_k$. If the Xs are functions of a random variable (say, Y), then the riskless hedge portfolio condition is

$$\frac{\partial V}{\partial Y} = \alpha_1 \frac{\partial X_1}{\partial Y} + \alpha_2 \frac{\partial X_2}{\partial Y} + \ldots + \alpha_k \frac{\partial X_k}{\partial Y} = 0$$

The variable Y could be a price of one security (e.g., X_j), or Y could be a non-priced variable, such as the weather. It is also possible for Y to be vector valued.

The statement that a hedge portfolio is *riskless* requires that the αs can be determined such that the value of the position will not change when Y changes. In effect, the position is *delta neutral* with respect to Y. This will depend on the precision with which the coefficients $\{\alpha\}$ can be determined. In turn, there may be considerable reliance on the assumption of continuous trading to achieve the hedge condition. In the Black–Scholes case, there are only two securities: $X_1 = S$ and $X_2 = C$, with $\alpha_1 = 1$, $\alpha_2 = -\{1/\Delta_C\}$ and $Y = X_1$. The role of continuous trading in the call option to achieve the riskless hedge portfolio condition is captured by the restriction on α_2. Insofar as $\alpha_2 = -\{1/\Delta_C\}$ can be achieved, changes in X_1 can be offset by altering the size of the call option position. The problem is not altered by letting $Y = X_3$. Riskless hedging now involves:

$$\frac{\partial V}{\partial X_3} = \alpha_1 \frac{\partial S}{\partial X_3} + \alpha_2 \frac{\partial C}{\partial X_3} = \left\{ 1 - \alpha_2 \frac{\partial C}{\partial S} \right\} \frac{\partial S}{\partial X_3} = 0$$

This produces the same continuous trading restriction on α_2.

As originally conceived by Black and Scholes, the riskless hedge portfolio involved a net investment of funds. This approach requires Black–Scholes to impose the further requirement that the funds invested in a position earn the riskless rate of interest. A more modern approach is to construct the hedge portfolio with no net investment of funds. Yet, *an arbitrage portfolio is a riskless hedge portfolio involving no net investment of funds*. More precisely, the arbitrage portfolio for the Black–Scholes model is

$$V = S - \beta\, C - (S - \beta C) \quad \rightarrow \quad dV = dS - \beta dC - (S - \beta C)\, r\, dt = 0$$

Initial investment in the portfolio $V = 0$ because the difference between the cash outflow of purchasing the stock and the cash inflow from writing the options is made up by borrowing $(S - \beta C)$.

Delta neutrality for a position is one of many possible derivative properties. The usefulness of the derivative properties of Black–Scholes presented in Section I is well illustrated by applying these concepts to the options trading strategies discussed in Chapter 7, Section III. To accomplish this requires recognizing that all securities that can be included in a given portfolio also possess derivative properties. From linearity, this permits the delta, theta, gamma, etc. of a portfolio to be calculated. As discussed in Section I, let V be the dollar value of the portfolio, V_i represent the price of security i, and n_i be the number of units of security i held where $n < 0$ indicates a short (written) position and $n > 0$ a long (purchased) position. In general, for portfolios containing a large number of securities:

$$V = n_1\, V_1 + n_2\, V_2 + n_3\, V_3 + \; \ldots$$

For the applications considered in this section, three types of securities will usually (but not always) be considered: the underlying non-dividend-paying stock as well as European call and put options on that stock. The stock position is generic; with appropriate adjustment, any commodity position could be used.

The delta, theta, and gamma for various combinations follow appropriately. In the two-security case, the delta of the portfolio can be derived:

$$\Delta_V = \frac{\partial V}{\partial S} = n_1\, \frac{\partial V_1}{\partial S} + n_2\, \frac{\partial V_2}{\partial S} = n_1\, \Delta_1 + n_2\, \Delta_2$$

Using this result, it is possible to solve for the n_1 and n_2 which are consistent with $\Delta_V = 0$, creating a portfolio which is delta neutral. The riskless hedge portfolio requires the size of the call option position to be continuously rebalanced in order to maintain the delta neutrality condition. In other cases, such as purchasing an approximately at-the-money straddle, delta neutrality is achieved when the position is initiated but delta neutrality is lost as the stock price moves away from the exercise price.

To see how delta neutrality can be achieved for a portfolio containing a combination of calls and puts, let V_1 be a call and V_2 be a put, and recall that:

$$\Delta_C = \frac{\partial C}{\partial S} = N[d_1] > 0$$

$$\Delta_P = \Delta_C - 1 < 0$$

$$\Delta_S = 1$$

$$\Gamma_S = 0$$

Solving for a $\Delta_V = 0$, delta-neutral position gives:

$$V = n_1 \, C + n_2 \, P$$

$$\Delta_V = 0 \quad \Rightarrow \quad \frac{n_1}{n_2} = \frac{-\Delta_2}{\Delta_1} \quad \Rightarrow \quad n_1 = -n_2 \, \frac{\Delta_2}{\Delta_1}$$

If the options are at-the-money then the put and call deltas will be approximately .5 and the straddle is delta neutral. Another application of delta neutrality occurs where V_1 refers to a long stock position and V_2 is either a put or a call. In this case, delta neutrality is a requirement for a hedge portfolio.[4] However, delta neutrality is only a property at a specific point. When the stock price changes, the portfolio must be adjusted to maintain the hedge, though it is not necessary to do this. The position can be left unadjusted, and gains or losses will occur as the stock price and other variables change. In this case, delta neutrality has a different meaning. A straddle is one example of a *possibly* delta-neutral position which is not rebalanced.

Anticipating the discussion in Section III, a delta-neutral portfolio can be contrasted with portfolio insurance. One possible method of insuring a stock position is to form a portfolio that combines purchased puts with a long stock position. In this case:

$$V = n_1 S + n_2 P \quad \Rightarrow \quad \Delta_V = n_1 + n_2 \Delta_P$$

For full insurance, the number of units of stock underlying the put equals the size of the long stock position, such that $n_1 = n_2$:

$$\Delta_V = n_1 \, \{1 + \Delta_P\} > 0$$

where $\Delta_P > -1$. The implication is that, in opposition to hedge portfolios and other positions that are delta neutral, full portfolio insurance requires the

---

[4]One immediate method of creating a hedge portfolio is to combine a short (long) stock index futures position with a long (short) position in the stock index. When the size of the futures and stock index position are equal, this produces:

$$\Delta_V = 1 - \frac{\partial F}{\partial S}$$

Provided the stock position of interest is the deliverable, this position will be delta neutral. Where cross hedges and other sources of slippage are present, adjustment would have to be made to achieve delta neutrality.

position delta to be greater than zero where the V exhibits a positive response to stock price increases.[5] In addition, the position is not rebalanced over time in order to maintain the starting delta value. As discussed in Section III, the precise degree of delta sensitivity depends on the delta characteristics of the puts selected. Hence, the Greeks can be used to improve the construction of insured portfolios.

As discussed in Chapter 8, Section II, setting a specific position partial derivative equal to a desired value imposes restrictions on the other partial derivatives of the fundamental PDE. To see this, consider the gamma of a delta-neutral position involving two securities. Substituting in the n_2 previously derived for the two security portfolio gives:

$$\Gamma_V = n_1\Gamma_1 + n_2\Gamma_2 \quad \Rightarrow \quad \Gamma_V = n_1\Delta_1 \left\{ \frac{\Gamma_1}{\Delta_1} - \frac{\Gamma_2}{\Delta_2} \right\}$$

In the special case where V_1 refers to a stock position (or some other gamma zero security), the portfolio gamma reduces to $\Gamma_V = -\{\Gamma_2/\Delta_2\}$. Given this, compare the delta-neutral strategies involving hedging a stock position with futures contracts and hedging a stock position using written calls.[6] For hedges involving futures, $\Gamma = 0$. Hence, this form of hedge portfolio is insulated against stock price changes. Now consider the strategy of creating a hedge portfolio by writing options against a long stock position. Setting $n_1 = 1$ and using the delta for a stock, n_2 is the same value as for the Black–Scholes hedge portfolio. However, unlike the futures-based hedge portfolio, the gamma of this hedge portfolio is negative. This follows from the positive gamma and delta values for a call position. Recalling the interpretation of the sign of gamma, stable stock prices are required for the hedge portfolio to be successful. In addition, the size of the position gamma will depend on the relationship between the exercise price of the options and the current stock price.

Another practical example of using delta to create a hedge portfolio occurs with the *ratio spread* of Chapter 7, Section III. This trade involves the creation of a hedged position, where n_1 units of the overpriced (correctly priced) option are sold and n_2 units of the correctly priced (underpriced) option are purchased. More precisely:

$$V = n_1 C_1 + n_2 C_2 \quad \Rightarrow \quad \Delta_V = 0 \quad \Rightarrow \quad \frac{n_1}{n_2} = -\frac{\Delta_2}{\Delta_1}$$

[5]In effect fully insured long positions require the delta of the portfolio to be positive and the gamma to be equal to zero. Over time, this will require rebalancing the derivative positions.

[6]This example is stylized because, in general, it is not possible to hedge a given stock position with a futures contract. This is because futures contracts are only available for stock indices (recently, the Hong Kong and Singapore exchanges have started to offer futures on individual stocks). However, in addition to positions in the stock index, the analysis does apply where a relevant spot position is being hedged.

Because the hedge ratio n_1/n_2, ensures that there will be no change in the value of the position as S changes, the option trader is able to lock in the *positive* difference between the premiums received and premiums paid. Much as with other riskless hedge portfolios, this trade will require rebalancing in order to maintain $\Delta_V = 0$.

B. DELTA PLUS GAMMA HEDGE PORTFOLIOS

An important practical aspect of strategic portfolio design for portfolios containing derivatives involves the achievement of multiple partial derivative targets (e.g., delta *and* gamma neutrality). Typically, the portfolio will contain a long stock position. Because of the relationship between the number of equations and the number of unknown derivative position sizes, achieving delta plus gamma targets will typically require the use of more than one derivative.[7] To see this, consider the strategy of selling call options in order to create a delta-neutral position. The gamma of the stock being zero produces a position that is gamma negative. In order to get position gamma equal to zero, it is necessary to include a derivative with a positive gamma, such as a long put position. *Assuming, for simplicity, that the puts and calls have the same exercise price and time to expiration,* in this case:

$$\Delta_V = n_1\Delta_C + n_2\Delta_P + n_3\Delta_S$$

Observing that the delta of the stock is equal to one, setting $n_3 = 1$ produces the following requirements for position delta neutrality per unit of the long stock position:

$$\Delta_V = 0 = n_2\Delta_P + n_1\Delta_C + 1 = n_2\{\Delta_C - 1\} + n_1\Delta_C + 1$$
$$\Rightarrow \quad [n_1 + n_2]\Delta_C - n_2 = -1$$

In order to solve for the sizes of the put and call positions it is necessary to impose gamma neutrality:

$$n_1\Gamma_P + n_2\Gamma_C = 0 \quad \Rightarrow \quad -\frac{n_2}{n_1} = 1 \quad \rightarrow \quad -n_2 = n_1$$

Substituting this result back into the equation associated with Δ_V, reveals that $n_1 = -1$, $n_2 = 1$, and $n_3 = 1$.

This illustration of the additional use of a gamma restriction in the construction of a riskless hedge portfolio reveals the need to use a written call with a purchased put to hedge the stock position. Because the put and call

---

[7]Derivatives here do not include the possibility of using futures or forward contracts where, in combination with a long stock position, position deltas and gammas are zero.

have been assumed to have the same X and t^* and that an equal number of puts and calls are used in the hedge, it follows that:

$$V = S - n_1\ C + n_2\ P = S - n_1(P - C)$$

$$\Delta_V = 0 = 1 - n_1(\Delta_C - 1 - \Delta_C) \quad \Rightarrow \quad n_1 = 1 \quad \Rightarrow \quad \Gamma_V = \Gamma_C - \Gamma_C = 0$$

This result is an extension of the put–call parity replication strategies derived in Chapter 7, using the expiration-date profit diagram technique. More precisely, for the delta- and gamma-neutral portfolio: $S + P - C = X \exp\{-rt^*\}$. Imposing a combination of delta neutrality and gamma neutrality on the hedge portfolio produces a portfolio with a payout identical to that of the riskless bond.

Another useful application of delta plus gamma targets can be illustrated with the design of the Black–Scholes riskless hedge portfolio. This example is used because it is familiar, and the notions extend naturally to other important cases such as portfolio insurance. In deriving the Black–Scholes formula it was assumed that the riskless hedge portfolio involved a stock being combined with written call options featuring only one specific exercise price. Recalling that gamma can be interpreted as the frequency with which the hedge portfolio has to be rebalanced, it would be more appropriate to write calls at a number of different exercise prices in order to achieve a lower gamma. Writing options that feature only one exercise price may be convenient for purposes of deriving the Black–Scholes formula, but this approach is not to be recommended in practical situations where rebalancing frequency is a concern. To see this, consider hedging the stock position by writing an equal combination of in-the-money and out-of-the-money call options:

$$V = S - n_1\ C_1 - n_2\ C_2 = S - n_1(C_1 + C_2) \quad \Delta_V = 0 \quad \Rightarrow \quad n_1 = \frac{1}{\Delta_1 + \Delta_2}$$

$$\Gamma_V = -n_1\ (\Gamma_1 + \Gamma_2) = -\frac{\Gamma_1 + \Gamma_2}{\Delta_1 + \Delta_2}$$

It follows that the gamma of a hedge portfolio which uses at-the-money options will have the highest gamma and, as a consequence, the greatest need to rebalance.

To understand this result, it is useful to refer back to the delta and gamma diagrams of Section I. Using 0.5 as the delta for the at-the-money option, two at-the-money options have to be written to hedge the stock position. Taking 0.2 and 0.8 as the delta values for the in-the-money and out-of-the-money options, one of each option has to be written. In both portfolios, two options are written. Assuming for simplicity that the sum of the in-the-money and out-of-the-money gammas are approximately equal to the gamma of the at-the-money option, then it follows that the gamma of the hedge portfolio that involves writing options at two different exercise prices will be one half the value of the portfolio using only one exercise price. Of course, this result depends on the "moneyness" of the various options selected. In the extreme case, it would be possible to choose deep in- and out-of-the-money options to produce a gamma that is virtually zero, but this would be difficult to implement in practice. Similarly, it would be possible to use either an in- or out-of-the-money option in the portfolio containing the one exercise price options. If that option was sufficiently in- or out-of-the-money it would be possible to construct a case where the one exercise price option portfolio would have a lower gamma.

C. VERTICAL SPREADS AND BUTTERFLIES

In addition to evaluating insured and hedged portfolios, it is also possible to use delta, theta, and gamma to provide a more precise description of the payouts on the option spread trading strategies discussed in Chapter 7. Consider the general case for a vertical spread involving n_1 calls purchased (written) at exercise price X_1 and n_2 calls written (purchased) at X_2 where $X_1 < X_2$. For the purchased vertical spread using calls, also referred to as a *bull spread*, $n_1 = 1$ and $n_2 = -1$. It is straightforward to verify that the delta for the call with the lower exercise price is highest. This can be shown by considering the analytical values for the deltas on $C_1[S,\tau,X_1]$ and $C_2[S,\tau,X_2]$:

$$\frac{\partial C_1}{\partial S} = N[d_{1,1}] \qquad \frac{\partial C_2}{\partial S} = N[d_{1,2}]$$

where:

$$d_{1,1} = \frac{\ln\left\{\dfrac{S}{X_1}\right\} + \left(r + \frac{1}{2}\sigma^2\right)t^*}{\sigma\sqrt{t^*}}$$

$$d_{1,2} = \frac{\ln\left\{\dfrac{S}{X_2}\right\} + \left(r + \frac{1}{2}\sigma^2\right)t^*}{\sigma\sqrt{t^*}}$$

Evaluation of the $N[\cdot]$ functions verifies the relationship between the deltas. Given this:

$$V = n_1 C_1 + n_2 C_2 \quad \Rightarrow \quad \Delta_V = n_1 \Delta_{C1} + n_2 \Delta_{C2}, \text{ when } n_1 = -n_2 = 1$$
$$\Delta_V = \Delta_{C1} - \Delta_{C2} > 0$$

As illustrated in Figs. 9.15 and 9.16, the delta of the vertical spread will depend on the current stock price as well as the time to expiration. Using this result, it is possible to expand considerably the information provided by

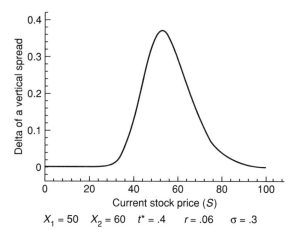

$X_1 = 50 \quad X_2 = 60 \quad t^* = .4 \quad r = .06 \quad \sigma = .3$

FIGURE 9.15   The delta of a vertical spread as a function of the stock price. *Source*: Adapted from Cox and Rubinstein (1985), with permission.

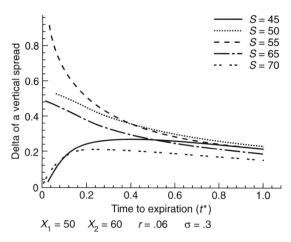

$X_1 = 50 \quad X_2 = 60 \quad r = .06 \quad \sigma = .3$

FIGURE 9.16   The delta of a vertical spread as a function of the time to expiration. *Source*: Adapted from Cox and Rubinstein (1985), with permission.

the expiration-date profit diagram for the vertical spread given in Chapter 7, Section II. Given this, it is straightforward to compute the gamma of the vertical spread. The sensitivity of gamma to both the current stock price and time to expiration is given in Figs. 9.17 and 9.18.

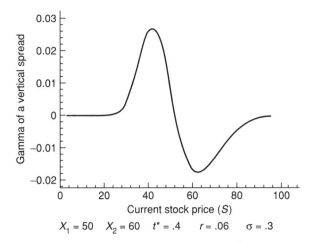

FIGURE 9.17 The gamma of a vertical spread as a function of the stock price. *Source*: Adapted from Cox and Rubinstein (1985), with permission.

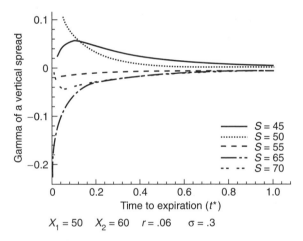

FIGURE 9.18 The gamma of a vertical spread as a function of the time to expiration. *Source*: Adapted from Cox and Rubinstein (1985), with permission.

The butterfly (sandwich) spread provides a useful illustration of gamma. Consider the case where purchased options at X_1 and X_3 are combined with two written options at X_2, with $X_1 < X_2 < X_3$ and $S = X_2$:

$$V = n_1 V_1 + n_2 V_2 + n_3 V_3$$

where $n_1 = 1$, $n_2 = -2$, and $n_3 = 1$. Also,

$$\Delta_V = \Delta_{C1} + \Delta_{C3} - 2\Delta_{C2}$$
$$\Gamma_V = \Gamma_{C1} + \Gamma_{C3} - \Gamma_{C2}$$

Evaluating these derivatives using the results of Section I, if the X_1 option is deep in-the-money its delta will be close to 1. If this position is combined with a deep out-of-the-money option at X_3 which has a delta of close to 0 this produces an approximately delta-neutral position because the two at-the-money options will have a delta of 1/2. This result holds whether the butterfly is being written or purchased. Based on this, it should be apparent that with the appropriate selection of the exercise prices of the options included in the butterfly, it is not necessary for the middle exercise price to be at-the-money in order to produce a delta-neutral position. Given this, differences in gamma have to be recognized. Unlike delta, gamma will be nonzero and will be negative for a purchased butterfly and positive for a written butterfly.[8] The importance of selecting the at-the-money option for the middle two positions is apparent when gamma is considered: In order to get Γ_V as negative (positive) as possible, an at-the-money option is required.

D. STRADDLES, STRAPS, AND STRANGLES

The straddle provides another practical application of the partial derivatives of Black–Scholes. Consider the delta for a straddle:

$$\Delta_V = n_1\Delta_C + n_2\Delta_P, \text{ for } n_1 = n_2 = 1$$
$$\Delta_V = \Delta_C + \{\Delta_C - 1\} = 2\Delta_C - 1$$

In Section I, it was demonstrated that, for short-dated options, d_1 for $S = X$ is small, permitting the approximation of $N[0] = 0.5$. In this case, when the put and call options are at-the-money, both the purchased and written straddles are approximately delta neutral. Examination of delta further reveals that once the stock price moves away from the money, the straddle is no longer delta neutral. Consider the delta when $S > X$, and the C is in-the-money with the put out-of-the-money. In this case, evaluation of Δ_V reveals that the $\Delta_C > .5$, which produces a positive position delta. To see the intuition of the impact of moneyness on delta, consider the case where the call option is deep in-the-money and the put option is deep out-of-the-money. In this case, increases in

---

[8]The terms *written* and *purchased* in this case refer to whether a net cash flow is derived from premiums. Typically, the bulk of the premium income for a butterfly with calls is associated with the option exhibiting the lower exercise price.

the stock price will increase the call price almost one-for-one, without having any impact on the put price. Similarly, for C out-of-the-money and P in-the-money, $\Delta_C < .5$, which produces a negative position delta. Decreases in the stock price will have a much greater positive impact on the put than negative impact on the call price.

Evaluation of gamma reveals different signs for purchased and written straddle positions. The purchased position has a positive gamma, indicating that volatile stock price movements are required for profitability, while the written position has a negative gamma, indicating that a stable stock price is needed for profitability. This much was already known from the expiration-date profit diagram analysis of Chapter 7, Section I. The gamma reveals how sensitive the position profitability will be to changes in stock prices. When $S > X$ or $S < X$, the position gamma will be significantly less than when $S = X$, to the point where gamma approaches zero when deep-in and deep-out options are used to create the straddle. It follows that, while it is possible to tailor a straddle to combine directional (delta not equal zero) and volatility bets by using options which are not at-the-money, there is a tradeoff: The greater the delta of the position, the less sensitive the profitability of the position to the volatility of stock prices. This raises the question of how a straddle, constructed using options that are not at-the-money, compares to straps and strips, which are designed to combine directional and volatility bets.

Consider the strap, which combines two calls and one put, all with the same exercise price and time to expiration. The delta of this position is

$$\Delta_V = n_1 \Delta_C + n_2 \Delta_P, \text{ for } n_1 = 2 \; n_2 = 1$$
$$\Delta_V = 2\Delta_C + \{\Delta_C - 1\} = 3\Delta_C - 1$$

When the options are at-the-money, the strap is delta positive. If the exercise price is selected such that $\Delta_C = .5$, the Δ_V for the strap would be .5. Because of the different costs associated with the straddle and the strap, it is useful to provide specific option prices. For this purpose, assume that $X = 40$, $\sigma^2 = .25$, $r = .05$, and $t^* = .25$. Using these parameter values, the Black–Scholes option prices, consistent with the simplifying assumption that $d_1 = 0$, are $C = \$3.29$ and $P = \$4.51$, making the price of the delta-neutral straddle $\$7.80$ for an initial stock price of $\$38.29$. At these values the strap would cost $\$11.09$.

Recognizing that it is possible to make the strap delta neutral by combining an in-the-money put with two out-of-the-money calls, it follows that this can be done precisely when the call options have a delta of 1/3. For the volatility, interest rate, and time to expiration values given, this occurs with an exercise price of $X = 44.55$ when the stock price is $\$38.29$. The corresponding put price of $7.56 and call price of $1.85 produce a strap that costs $11.26. At 0.11395, the gamma of this position is considerably higher than the gamma of the delta-neutral straddle which is $2(0.4168) = 0.08336$, indicating that greater stock price volatility is required for profitability of the strap. This is reflected in the different expiration-date payoffs. For example, consider the expiration-date values of the strategies, assuming that interest on the premium is ignored. If $S(T) = 40$, the straddle loses the maximum of $7.80, but the strap only loses $(-11.26 + (44.55 - 40)) = -\$6.71$. For $S(T) = 44.55$, the strap loses the maximum of $11.26 and the straddle loses $(-7.80 + (44.55 - 40)) = -\$3.25$. Similarly, at $S(T) = 50$, the straddle provides $(-7.80 + (50 - 40)) = \$2.20$ and the strap $(-11.26 + 2(50 - 44.55))$ $= -\$0.36$ at $S(T) = 55$, the straddle earns $7.70 and the strap $9.64. Hence, a strap that is initiated as delta neutral requires a larger upward increase in the stock price to outperform the straddle but will lose slightly less if the stock price remains unchanged or falls.

A similar comparison can be made between the strangle and the straddle. Recalling that the strangle combines put and call options with different exercise prices and the same time to maturity, the delta for a strangle is

$$\Delta_V = n_1 \Delta_C + n_2 \Delta_P, \text{ for } n_1 = n_2 = 1$$
$$\Delta_V = \Delta_{C1} + \{\Delta_{C2} - 1\} = \{\Delta_{C1} + \Delta_{C2}\} - 1$$

If the stock price lies approximately halfway between the two exercise prices, then the strangle will be delta neutral. It is also possible to create strangles that are delta positive (e.g., using at-the-money calls and out-of-the-money puts) or delta negative (e.g., using at-the-money puts and out-of-the-money calls). In general, if the straddle is delta neutral, even with discrete exercise price intervals it is possible to specify a strangle that is close to being delta neutral. To see this, consider the previous example of the delta-neutral straddle with $X = 40$ and $S(0) = \$38.29$. With $5 exercise intervals, there are three comparable $\{X_1 \text{ for } C, X_2 \text{ for } P\}$ strangle variations: $\{X_1 = 40, X_2 = 35\}$, $\{X_1 = 45, X_2 = 40\}$ and $\{X_1 = 45, X_2 = 35\}$.

Consider the last case, where a call, $C[X_1 = 45]$, with price $= \$1.74$, delta $= .318772$, and gamma $= 0.0373$, is combined with a put, $P[X_2 = 35]$, with price $= 2.06$, delta $= (0.7034 - 1)$, and gamma $= 0.0361$. The cost of the position is $3.80 with a delta approximately equal to the straddle value of zero and a *smaller* gamma of 0.0734. As for the straddle, delta neutral implies that the position profitability is the same whether the stock price goes up or down. The smaller gamma implies that the delta of the position does not (locally) change as much as the delta for a straddle. The delta and gamma results change when different options are used. Consider the case of $C[X_1 = 40]$ and $P[X_2 = 35]$; premiums paid would be $(\$3.29 + \$2.06) = \$5.35$ with

$\Delta_V = 0.5 + (0.7034 - 1) = 0.2034$ and $\Gamma_V = 0.05224 + 0.0361 = 0.08885$. In this case, the positive delta indicates that the position is more profitable when prices rise. The higher gamma, compared to the case where both the call and put are out-of-the-money, indicates the change in the value of this position is more sensitive to stock price changes.

III. PORTFOLIO INSURANCE

Portfolio insurance, in its purest and simplest form, is equivalent to a securities position comprised of an underlying portfolio plus an insurance policy that guarantees the insured portfolio against loss through a specified policy expiration date. Should the underlying portfolio (including any income earned and reinvested in the portfolio but deducting the cost of buying the insurance) experience a loss by the policy expiration date, the insurance policy can be used to refund the amount of the loss. On the other hand, should the underlying portfolio show a profit, all profit net of the cost of insurance is retained.

Rubinstein (1985, p. 42)

A. THE HISTORY OF PORTFOLIO INSURANCE

In relatively recent history, portfolio insurance has had a significant impact in both practical and theoretical areas. Many of these developments have been associated with the emergence of financial engineering. However, heuristic forms of portfolio insurance have been used for decades. For example, a form of portfolio insurance can be achieved with the systematic use of order placement strategies, such as stop-loss and limit orders, which have been acceptable market practice at least since the 19th century. As discussed below, these types of trading-dependent strategies suffer from the defect of being path dependent, an undesirable property of insurance schemes. In addition to trading-related techniques, option replication strategies using stock and bond combinations were also likely to be used, although in the realm of proprietary management practices. These techniques also suffer from the defect of path dependence and, in the absence of Greek information, would probably have been imprecise. The application of option replication to specifying dynamically traded stock and bond portfolios was not of academic interest until much later, after the development of the Black–Scholes formula.

As for the history of insurance-related financial products, some of the insurance schemes of the late 17th and 18th century did offer payouts based on specific outcomes associated with joint stock performance. Being introduced prior to the development of actuarial science, these insurance schemes were more like gambling than insurance. In more recent history, Benninga and Blume (1985) reported the selling of insurance against investment losses in the United Kingdom as early as 1956. In the United States, Gatto et al. (1980) reported on portfolio insurance plans offered to individuals by both the Harleysville Mutual Insurance Company and Prudential Insurance Company of America. Brennan and Schwartz (1987) observed that the Harleysville plan was the first without any element of mortality insurance. Academically, Brennan and Schwartz (1976) were the first to make the connection between the potential for integrating insurance and equity returns. The firm of Leland, O'Brien, Rubinstein, and Associates was an important proponent in the marketing of dynamically traded option replication strategies to institutional clients.

The explosion in the use of the various types of portfolio insurance techniques can be traced to the introduction of exchange trading in options. Liquid options markets made possible the implementation of numerous portfolio insurance strategies. Even more strategies were permitted with the development of futures and options markets for stock indices. Analytical contributions based on Black–Scholes resulted in further portfolio insurance strategies being introduced. Many "alternative paths to portfolio insurance" (Rubinstein, 1985) were proposed and implemented. The widespread use of dynamically traded portfolio insurance techniques has been identified as an important contributing factor in the October 1987 stock market crash (e.g., Tosini, 1988) (see Chapter 1, Section III). Academic understanding of notions associated with portfolio insurance have expanded considerably since the early work by Leland (1980) and Rubinstein and Leland (1981). The 1987 crash provided a textbook illustration of the inadequacies of the academically inspired option replication strategies; sizable unexpected losses were experienced by investors holding what were expected to be "insured" portfolios.

One of the fundamentals driving institutions to use dynamic trading strategies was the absence of risk-management products with maturities and other characteristics that captured the time profile of their particular risk exposures. Since the crash, an array of OTC and exchange-traded risk-management products have been introduced that greatly enhance the ability to implement path-independent strategies. Included in the list of such new products are long-dated exchange-traded option products, such as long term equity anticipation securities (LEAPS) for individual stocks and long-dated index options and equity swaps. Despite these improvements, the bulk of contract liquidity on both the exchanges and over the counter (OTC) market is still concentrated in short-dated contracts. The relative absence of strict mark-to-market rules in OTC contracts provides a strong incentive to use short-dated contracts.

B. PROPERTIES OF INSURED PORTFOLIOS

Before describing the various forms of portfolio insurance, it is useful to introduce two features associated with insured portfolios: *path independence* and *time invariance*. The first concept has already been introduced in Chapter 7, Section I. In effect, true portfolio insurance strategies should be path independent: "A strategy that is not path independent gives an uncertain payoff, and therefore violates the very premise of portfolio insurance: giving a known payoff" (Bookstaber and Langsam, 1988). Time invariance requires that the insurance strategy does not depend on the time remaining in the program (or on the use of a fixed time horizon). The primary practical difficulty arises because of the option price convexity with respect to time; for example, an option with 6 months to expiration will cost less than twice what a 3-month option costs. Until recently, a strong argument in favor of so-called dynamic replication strategies was that the short-dated maturities available for liquid exchange-traded options have insufficient time convexity for typical portfolios with long-term investment horizons. The recent introduction of LEAPs and longer dated futures and options on stock indices has substantively reduced this problem.

Given this background, the basic idea behind portfolio insurance is to provide a rate of return that will not fall below a given floor. As was illustrated in Chapter 7, Section I, trying to do so by purchasing puts in conjunction with a long stock position will replicate the payoff on a purchased call position. However, while this strategy will typically be path independent, it will not be time invariant. Based on application of the *binomial option pricing formula* (e.g., Ritchken, 1987, chap. 9; Rubinstein and Leland, 1981), it is also possible to replicate the payoff on a call option by dynamically adjusting a portfolio of stocks and bonds. While the dynamic replication strategies are path dependent, there are other desirable features that can be achieved by these strategies. The widespread use of these strategies is reflected in Fig. 9.19 where the sizable volume attributed to other strategies is largely due to dynamic replication. Required reporting of such positions to the New York Stock Exchange (NYSE) was introduced following the 1987 crash. Unfortunately, as discovered by market participants involved in the use of these strategies during the crash of October 1987, at times when the market is moving down these strategies involve selling the spot, thereby adding to the downward market pressure.

PROGRAM TRADING

NEW YORK — Program trading in the week ended July 2 accounted for 11.6%, or an average of 23.6 million daily shares, of New York Stock Exchange volume.

Brokerage firms executed an additional 6.8 million daily shares of program trading away from the Big Board, mostly on foreign markets. Program trading is the simultaneous purchase or sale of at least 15 different stocks with a total value of $1 million or more.

Of the program total on the Big Board, 22.5% involved stock-index arbitrage, down from 35.4% the prior week. In this strategy, traders dart between stocks and stock-index options and futures to capture fleeting price differences.

Some 24.6% of program trading reflected firms' trading for their own accounts, or principal trading, while 63.3% involved trading for customers. An additional 12.1% was executed by firms using principal positions to facilitate customer trades.

Of the five most-active firms, all did most or all of their program trading for customers, rather than for their own accounts, except for Nomura Securities Co., which split its trading between customers and itself.

Volume (in millions of shares) for the week ending
July 2, , 1992

Top 15 Firms	Index Arbitrage	Other Strategies	Total
Nomura Securities	8.1	7.4	15.5
Morgan Stanley	0.5	12.9	13.4
Walsh Greenwood	1.9	10.0	11.9
Bear Stearns	.....	6.9	6.9
Merrill Lynch	.....	6.1	6.1
Shearson Lehman	.....	5.4	5.4
Kidder Peabody	1.8	3.6	5.4
PaineWebber	1.0	4.0	5.0
Salomon Bros.	0.3	3.3	3.6
W&D Securities	0.3	2.9	3.2
UBS Securities	2.4	0.8	3.2
First Boston	0.8	1.6	2.4
Miller Tabak	.....	2.3	2.3
Susquehanna	1.6	0.5	2.1
Goldman Sachs	.....	1.6	1.6
OVERALL TOTAL	21.2	73.2	94.4

Source: New York Stock Exchange

FIGURE 9.19   Example of weekly program trading report.

C. Types of Portfolio Insurance

The basic mechanics of portfolio insurance can be isolated from the put–call parity arbitrage condition for a non-dividend paying stock: $S + P = C + X e^{-rt^*}$. For portfolio insurance, instead of an individual stock, S now refers to a portfolio of stocks and dividends have been ignored for simplicity of exposition. As stated, put–call parity provides two path-independent insurance strategies. One strategy is $S + P$, buy puts against the portfolio. If S is an index portfolio, relevant exchange-traded puts may be available. Another strategy is $C + X\,e^{-rt^*}$, buy calls and invest the remainder in appropriately dated bonds. Again, if the portfolio is an index portfolio, exchange-traded calls may be available. One important advantage of this strategy is that transaction costs in bond markets are typically lower than transaction costs for stocks, and the bond portfolio can be actively managed (e.g., by riding the yield curve to earn potentially higher returns than the $S + P$ approach).

While the path-independent strategies have some desirable features, there are some drawbacks. One disadvantage is the inability to accurately replicate insurance for portfolios that do not track an index; the relevant options are not available. Another disadvantage is that the maturity dates for options may not be long enough to match the portfolio's investment horizon (insufficient time invariance). To handle these types of problems, dynamic trading strategies have been developed for actively trading portfolios composed of stocks and bonds in order to replicate the payoff on an insured stock portfolio. These strategies can be illustrated by substituting the Black–Scholes formula into the put–call parity condition:

$$S + P = S\,N[d_1] - X\,e^{-rt^*}N[d_2] + X\,e^{-rt^*}$$
$$= S\,N[d_1] + X\,e^{-rt^*}(1 - N[d_2]) = w_1\,S + w_2\,Xe^{-rt^*}$$

The weights w_1 and w_2 indicate the proportions of the portfolio held in stocks and bonds in order to achieve insurance with an exercise price of X and time to maturity of t^*. Unlike the portfolio optimization models, the weights here will not sum to one, as the relationship is derived to equate values on the right- and lefthand sides. The sum of the weights will be close to one but not equal to one unless the put value is equal to zero.

As illustrated in Table 9.1, there are a number of potential path dependent and path independent portfolio insurance strategies. While the information about portfolio insurance given in this table is not novel, the source and date of the publication *are* novel. This figure was taken from a 1984 Goldman Sachs publication, "The Different Forms of Portfolio Insurance," (D. Zurack, 1984) produced when Fischer Black, the head of investment research at Goldman was actively involved in publishing and marketing portfolio insurance plans in the period up to and including the summer of 1987 as part of Goldman's concentrated effort to capture market share in the lucrative portfolio insurance business. This was not an isolated effort, as evidenced by a range of Goldman Sachs publications, authored by Black and others from the Goldman research group, e.g. Black and Jones (1986).

TABLE 9.1   Different Forms of Equity Portfolio Insurance[a]

Strategy	Advantages	Disadvantages
Buying index puts against a portfolio	Insurance cost determined in advance. Investor captures portfolio nonmarket return.	Listed puts do not trade with expirations greater than 4 months. Must accept the pricing risk of subsequent options purchases.
Buying puts on individual stocks	Portfolio positions protected against decline on a stock-by-stock basis.	Premiums greater than for index puts. Not every stock has a listed put.
Buying index calls and money market securities	Can vary fixed income strategy around the call position; call performance tied to a diversified index.	Cannot capture nonmarket return on a portfolio of stocks. Must accept the pricing risk of subsequent options purchases.
Buying calls on individual stocks and money-market securities	Full participation in all gains from individual stock movement.	Premiums greater than for index calls. Not every stock has a listed call.
Selling stock index futures to create a synthetic put	Can create strike price and expiration date. Will capture portfolio alpha.	Actual cost cannot be predetermined. Must accept pricing risk of the futures contract.
Raising cash by selling stocks to create a synthetic put	No futures pricing risk.	Higher transaction costs and market impact costs in most instances.
Buying stock index futures to own a synthetic call	Can vary fixed income investment. Equity performance tied to a common index such as the S&P 500.	Cost cannot be predetermined. Position is exposed to index futures pricing risk.

[a]In addition to the insurance strategies using listed options and stock index futures, it is possible to create an over-the-counter European or American index option with a longer life than that available in the listed markets.
Source: Zurack, D., "The Many Forms of Portfolio Insurance," Goldman-Sachs Stock Index Research, October 16, 1984.

From a practical perspective, it is important for the potential portfolio insurer to identify why dynamic replication strategies (i.e., strategies dynamically replicating a call option payoff using stock and bond positions) should be used. Related to this are subsidiary issues concerning how to replicate and when to replicate. In this vein, large-fund managers would consider the liquidity needed to establish large enough positions using derivatives and whether there are suitable X and τ available. For example, while a well-diversified fund (e.g., an index fund) could make use of options or futures written on the appropriate index, funds targeted at nonsystematic risk are more likely to be obligated to use dynamic replication strategies. However, even a well-diversified fund may find that available expiration dates on traded derivatives are not long enough; that is, sufficient "time convexity" cannot be achieved. That the dynamic replication strategies can be designed to theoretically achieve almost any desired expiration date and exercise price provides another reason for the use of these strategies.

Examination of Table 9.1 reveals that there are a number of alternative approaches to portfolio insurance. The table makes reference to "synthetic calls" and "synthetic puts." Each of the various approaches can be modelled by taking the appropriate approach to the put-call parity relationship: $S + P = C + X\, PV[\tau]$. For example, the synthetic put is determined by using the Black–Scholes put price to make a substitution for the put price: $S+P=S+S\{N[d_1]-1\}-X\, PV[\tau]\{\ N[d_2]-1\}=S(1+\Delta_p)-X\, PV[\tau]\{N[d_2]-1\}$. This formulation can now be used to answer the following stylized portfolio insurance problem: starting from an initial all-equity position, what fraction of the portfolio has to be sold and invested in the zero coupon bond, in order to achieve an outcome consistent with dynamic portfolio insurance? The solution follows from recognizing that, because the put delta is negative, calculation of the put delta gives the desired fraction of the all-equity portfolio which has to be sold and invested in the zero coupon bond. Alternatively, with minor adjustments and provisos, a short position in stock index futures can be substituted for the actual sale of stock. To illustrate the use of dynamic put replication, consider the creation of a synthetic put option for an index portfolio. Given that the dividend yield on the index is q, Hull (2000, p. 332) shows that the delta of a European put on the index is

$$\Delta_P = \exp\{-qt^*\}\,[N[d_1]-1] = \exp\{-qt^*\}\,(\Delta_c - 1)$$

where:

$$d_1 = \frac{\ln\left\{\dfrac{S}{X}\right\} + \left(r - q + \dfrac{\sigma^2}{2}\right)t^*}{\sigma\sqrt{t^*}}$$

Assuming that $S = 300$, $X = 290$, $r = 0.09$, $q = 0.03$, $\sigma = 0.25$, and $t^* = 0.5$, evaluation of the delta of the put gives $\Delta = -0.322$. It follows that, if dynamic replication of a put is being used, 32.2% of the index fund should be sold and invested in (risk-free) fixed-income securities. From the properties of the put delta discussed in Section I, as the value of the index fund drops, the delta of the put will become more negative, indicating that a larger proportion of the index fund has to be sold; i.e., a larger fraction of the portfolio will be invested in fixed-income securities. A similar result would hold where the value of the index was increasing. In this case, the delta of the put would be less negative, indicating that fixed-income securities should be sold to purchase more units of the index fund. In this case, the proportion of the portfolio invested in the index fund would increase.

Consideration of the strategies outlined in Table 9.1 reveals that there are a number of different methods of approaching the portfolio insurance problem. In addition to the strategies already examined, such as combining stocks with purchased puts or dynamically replicating such positions, a number of other strategies attempt to achieve the same objectives by using derivative positions as surrogates for stock ownership, on the presumption that there are execution advantages (e.g., greater liquidity and lower transactions costs) to using derivatives. For example, instead of owning stock, it is possible to form portfolios composed of purchased call options and fixed-income securities (recall Property 10 of Chapter 7, Section I). Another strategy would be to alter the dynamic replication strategies by substituting short futures positions for the stock sales required when the value of the stock position declines. However, if this approach is used (for example, to insure an index fund), it is important to recognize that the number of stock index futures to be shorted for a given long index fund will be different than in the case where the stock position is being sold directly (and invested in bonds). In addition, there is the mechanical problem of calculating the hedge ratio for the futures and cash positions.

The relevant issues regarding the most appropriate portfolio insurance technique to use in a given situation are addressed in a number of sources (e.g., Bookstaber and Langsam, 1988). For example, in considering whether to short the futures or write an option, both of which will require periodic rebalancing, the following proposition applies: "An option will be more efficient than a futures if the gamma of the hedge program is greater than 1/2 the gamma of the hedging instrument." If the stock position is sufficiently large, there are distinct advantages to combining a number of different approaches to portfolio insurance, in order to exploit the benefits of each approach. Further, in keeping with the discussion in Section II about achieving multiple delta, theta, and gamma targets, the use of more than one type of insurance strategy may be required in order to achieve the desired objectives. As mentioned in Chapter 8, Section IV, for the case of hedging foreign currency options, delta + vega positions may provide better results than delta + gamma positions. This result almost certainly extends to insuring stock positions, though that point will not be developed here.

Stoll and Whalley (1993, p. 361–364) provide a helpful tabular presentation of how various methods of portfolio insurance would perform to insure a stock index across a range of index levels (see Table 9.2). The first table gives

TABLE 9.2   Examples of Portfolio Insurance:
Static Insurance and Continuous Rebalancing

Insured stock portfolio value at alternative stock
index levels, using static portfolio insurance

Index level (S)	Put option (P)	Portfolio value (S + P)
59.87	36.21	96.08
63.02	33.06	96.08
66.34	29.75	96.09
69.83	26.29	96.13
73.51	22.70	96.21
77.38	19.03	96.41
81.45	15.38	96.83
85.74	11.87	97.61
90.25	8.67	98.92
95.00	5.94	100.94
100.00	3.79	103.79
105.00	2.29	107.29
110.25	1.27	111.52
115.76	0.65	116.42
121.55	0.31	121.86
127.63	0.13	127.76
134.01	0.05	134.06
140.71	0.02	140.73
147.75	0.01	147.75
155.13	0.00	155.13
162.89	0.00	162.89

Insured stock portfolio value at alternative index levels, using dynamic
portfolio insurance with continuous rebalancing

Index level (S)	T-bill price (Xe^{-rt^*})	Stock portfolio weight (w_1)	T-bill weight (w_2)	Portfolio value
59.87	96.08	0.001	1.000	96.08
63.02	96.08	0.002	0.999	96.08
66.34	96.08	0.005	0.996	96.09
69.83	96.08	0.014	0.990	96.13
73.51	96.08	0.034	0.975	96.21
77.38	96.08	0.072	0.945	96.41
81.45	96.08	0.136	0.892	96.83
85.74	96.08	0.231	0.809	97.61
90.25	96.08	0.355	0.696	98.92
95.00	96.08	0.496	0.560	100.94
100.00	96.08	0.638	0.416	103.79
105.00	96.08	0.758	0.289	107.29

(continues)

TABLE 9.2 *(continued)*

Index level (S)	T-bill price (Xe^{-rt^*})	Stock portfolio weight (w_1)	T-bill weight (w_2)	Portfolio value
110.25	96.08	0.852	0.183	111.52
115.76	96.08	0.918	0.106	116.42
121.55	96.08	0.959	0.056	121.86
127.63	96.08	0.981	0.026	127.76
134.01	96.08	0.992	0.011	134.06
140.71	96.08	0.997	0.004	140.73
147.75	96.08	0.999	0.001	147.75
155.13	96.08	1.000	0.000	155.13
162.89	96.08	1.000	0.000	162.89

Note: To value the European put, it is assumed that the index pays no dividends, $r = .08$, $\sigma = .2$, $X = 100$, and $t^* = .5$.
Source: Stoll, H., and Whalley, R. (1993). With permission.

the payoff for the path independent strategy $S + P$. Comparing the distribution of S with $S + P$ reveals, in a simple tabular form, what Bookstaber and Clark (1983) have examined in much more detail using distributional plots. The addition of a put transforms the symmetric S distribution to a positively skewed $S + P$ distribution. In terms of the return distribution, the additional cost of the put will result is a lower mean value for the $S + P$ distribution.

Applying the dynamic replication portfolio insurance strategy uses weights derived from $S + P = S\,N[d_1] + X\,e^{-rt^*}(1 - N[d_2])$. In practice, dynamic replication faces substantive implementation issues. Trading cannot be conducted under the perfect markets assumption; continuous trading assumptions are required for the Black–Scholes formula to capture the price of the option. Nevertheless, assuming that the Black–Scholes assumptions apply permits the decomposition of $S + P$ into the exact amounts of stocks and bonds to hold in order to precisely replicate the $S + P$ payoff. As the stock index level falls away from $S = 100$, the stock index position will be continuously reduced to the point where the stock position is nearly zero at $S = 59.87$. Similarly, as the stock index rises, the bond is sold to the point where at $S = 162.89$ there are no funds left in bonds. From this, it is apparent how dynamic portfolio insurance strategies, if applied by a large enough fraction of market traders, would amplify market movements.

In practice, dynamic trading strategies have to deal with the realities of discrete trading. Rules have to be determined about how large a movement in S is required before the rebalancing decision is executed. There are a number of possible methods for specifying a rebalancing trigger value. The Stoll and Whalley example assumes that the trigger value is 5%. From this point, the tabular presentation method can only provide an accurate picture of the distribution of weights and the associated impact on portfolio value. For example, upside movements of S will produce increasing weights for S which lag the continuously rebalanced weights, resulting in a slight reduction in portfolio value. A similar result happens for downside movements of S where the reduction in S weights lags the continuously rebalanced weights, again resulting in a slight reduction in portfolio value. Hence, the simple introduction of discrete rebalancing results in a deterioration of the performance of the dynamic replication strategy.

As it turns out, the discretely rebalanced case has considerably more complications than can be captured in one table. Being *path dependent*, the terminal portfolio value can take a range of values, depending on the particular time path realized by S. For the *path-independent* cases, $S + P$ and continuous rebalancing with no transactions costs the distribution of portfolio value can be determined precisely because the terminal portfolio value does not depend on the particular time path realized by S. This does not happen with discrete rebalancing. For example, a price path that starts at 100 and goes to 95 generates a rebalancing involving a sale of S to produce a weight change of .638 to .495. If the next step is back to 100, the rebalancing involves the weight returning from 0.495 to 0.638. The resulting portfolio value will now be less than a portfolio value along a price path where S was unchanged and no rebalancing happened.

Stoll and Whalley also provide results for the case where a stock and bond portfolio is created using the dynamic portfolio weights, but no rebalancing is done along the time path (see Table 9.3). This is another type of path-independent strategy. Though not immediately apparent from the tabular

TABLE 9.3 Examples of Portfolio Insurance: No Rebalancing and Discrete Rebalancing

Insured stock portfolio value at alternative stock index levels, using dynamic portfolio insurance with no rebalancing

Index level (S)	T-bill price (Xe^{-rt^*})	Stock portfolio weight (w_1)	T-bill weight (w_2)	Portfolio value
59.87	96.08	0.638	0.416	78.18
63.02	96.08	0.638	0.416	80.19
66.34	96.08	0.638	0.416	82.31
69.83	96.08	0.638	0.416	84.53
73.51	96.08	0.638	0.416	86.88
77.38	96.08	0.638	0.416	89.35
81.45	96.08	0.638	0.416	91.95
85.74	96.08	0.638	0.416	94.68
90.25	96.08	0.638	0.416	97.56

(continues)

TABLE 9.3   (continued)

Index level (S)	T-bill price (Xe^{-rt^*})	Stock portfolio weight (w_1)	T-bill weight (w_2)	Portfolio value
95.00	96.08	0.638	0.416	100.59
100.00	96.08	0.638	0.416	103.79
105.00	96.08	0.638	0.416	106.98
110.25	96.08	0.638	0.416	110.33
115.76	96.08	0.638	0.416	113.84
121.55	96.08	0.638	0.416	117.54
127.63	96.08	0.638	0.416	121.42
134.01	96.08	0.638	0.416	125.49
140.71	96.08	0.638	0.416	129.76
147.75	96.08	0.638	0.416	134.25
155.13	96.08	0.638	0.416	138.97
162.89	96.08	0.638	0.416	143.92

Insured stock portfolio value at alternative stock index levels, using dynamic portfolio insurance with discrete rebalancing

Index level (S)	T-bill price (Xe^{-rt^*})	Stock portfolio weight (w_1)	T-bill weight (w_2)	Portfolio value
59.87	96.08	0.001	0.985	94.65
63.02	96.08	0.002	0.984	94.66
66.34	96.08	0.005	0.982	94.67
69.83	96.08	0.014	0.976	94.72
73.51	96.08	0.034	0.961	94.85
77.38	96.08	0.071	0.933	95.12
81.45	96.08	0.135	0.882	95.67
85.74	96.08	0.229	0.802	96.65
90.25	96.08	0.353	0.691	98.24
95.00	96.08	0.495	0.558	100.59
100.00	96.08	0.638	0.416	103.79
105.00	96.08	0.755	0.288	106.98
110.25	96.08	0.847	0.183	110.94
115.76	96.08	0.911	0.105	115.61
121.55	96.08	0.951	0.055	120.89
127.63	96.08	0.973	0.026	126.67
134.01	96.08	0.984	0.011	132.87
140.71	96.08	0.988	0.004	139.46
147.75	96.08	0.990	0.001	146.42
155.13	96.08	0.991	0.000	153.73
162.89	96.08	0.991	0.000	161.41

Note: The discrete rebalancing case assumes a trigger value of 5%.
Source: Stoll, H., and Whalley, R. (1993). With permission.

presentation, the distribution of the portfolio value for the no rebalancing case is not unlike the S distribution. Unlike the dynamically traded portfolio, the no-rebalancing distribution retains the symmetric shape of the S distribution, though there is less dispersion due to the presence of a long investment in the riskless asset.[9] In all of this, the no-rebalancing and static portfolio insurance cases are being unfavorably compared with the discrete-rebalancing case because there are no transaction costs factored into the various calculations.

In practice, there will be a tradeoff between rebalancing frequency, the various transactions and execution changes, and the terminal value of the insured portfolio. Wider rebalancing frequencies will permit greater deviation from the path-independent static portfolio insurance case, but this loss of precision will be balanced out with a savings in transactions costs due to reduced trading frequency. All this leads back to Chapter 5, Section II, and the problem of specifying an optimal trigger value for speculative trading strategies. This connection between speculative trading strategies and dynamically traded portfolio insurance strategies is revealing, providing another illustration of the systemic connection between risk management and speculation in the analysis of derivative security applications.

D. Insuring Portfolios with Foreign Assets

There is nothing unique about a portfolio of domestic stocks. The notions of portfolio insurance can be applied to any commodity. One useful extension involves insuring the domestic currency value of a foreign bond position. Much as with dynamic portfolio insurance for stocks, dynamic portfolio insurance for foreign bonds can be derived using put–call parity for currency options. The objective is to dynamically trade a portfolio composed of domestic bonds and foreign bonds in order to achieve the same payout as a path-independent portfolio composed of a foreign bond plus a currency put option. If the exchange rate increases, the value of the domestic currency rises relative to foreign currency, and the dynamic strategy involves selling foreign bonds and buying domestic bonds. If the exchange rate deteriorates, the domestic bond is sold in favor of buying the foreign bond. As before, the Black–Scholes formula for a call can be substituted into the put–call parity condition to derive the appropriate portfolio weights.

To see this consider the path-independent value of a portfolio that contains a foreign currency bond and has the domestic currency value protected with a currency put option. The associated dynamic replication portfolio can now be derived:

---

[9]This observation provides a window into the various complications that nonlinear payoffs, such as options, can have for mean-variance optimization analysis.

$$V = S \ \exp\{-r^*t^*\} + P = C + X \ \exp\{-rt^*\}$$
$$= S \ \exp\{-r^*t^*\} \ N[d_1] - X \ \exp\{-rt^*\} \ N[d_2] + X \ \exp\{-rt^*\}$$
$$= S \ \exp\{-r^*t^*\}N[d_1] + X \ \exp\{-rt^*\}(1 - N[d_2])$$

In this formulation, $S \ \exp\{-r^*t^*\}$ is the domestic currency value of the foreign bond position and $X \ \exp\{-r^*t^*\}$ is the domestic currency value of the domestic bond. More precisely, $\exp\{-r^*t^*\}$ is the foreign currency value of a continuously compounded zero-coupon bond that matures to one unit of foreign currency; multiplying this foreign bond price by S, the time t spot exchange rate expressed in domestic direct terms, converts the foreign bond price to units of domestic currency. Similarly, $X \ \exp\{-rt^*\}$ is the domestic currency value of a continuously compounded zero-coupon bond that matures to the number of units of domestic currency reflected in the exercise price for the currency option.

As with portfolio insurance for stocks, portfolio insurance for foreign bonds involves dynamic trading of the position. When the value of domestic currency rises relative to foreign currency, S will fall and the dynamic strategy requires selling a portion of the foreign bond and using the funds to purchase domestic bonds. The dynamic replication formulation identifies the precise amount of foreign bonds that have to be sold in order to maintain the same payout as the path-independent portfolio $[S \ \exp \{-r^*t^*\} + P]$. While much the same theoretically, dynamic replication for foreign bonds can differ in practice. Unlike the dynamic strategies for stock portfolios, which can suffer from inaccurate replication due to illiquidity in the underlying stocks, the cash markets involved in the dynamic insurance for foreign bonds are typically quite liquid. The foreign exchange market, as well as the domestic and foreign bond markets, are unlikely to be subject to the types of pricing discontinuities that precipitated the October 1987 stock market break.

IV. OPTIMAL STOPPING AND PERPETUAL OPTIONS[10]

A. PERPETUAL OPTIONS

A perpetual option has two features of interest. There is no stated expiration date and, because of this, the option must be American. A perpetual option is alive until it is exercised. As discussed in Section 7.4, practical applications of

---

[10]Early seminal contributions on this subject are Chow, Robbins and Siegmund (1971) and de Groot (1970). A useful summary of the theory can be found in Karlin and Taylor, v.1 and a treatment oriented to economics in Dixit (1993) and Dixit and Pindyck (1994).

perpetual options have been made to real investment decisions, such as real estate development, e.g., Capozza and Li (1994). The perpetual option is of analytical significance because, as first demonstrated by McKean (1965), it is an American option with a valuation formula. This occurs because the infinite expiration date produces a free boundary condition for the American option valuation problem. This permits the intractable PDE problem to be converted to a tractable ODE problem. A number of extensions of the perpetual option have been proposed, such as the Russian option that has a payoff determined by the difference between the exercise value and the maximum value that the stock price achieves over the life of the option. As discussed by Gerber and Shu (1994a and b) and Gerber (1999), there are a number of possible methods to derive the price formula for the perpetual option.

B. STOPPING RULES

A stopping rule problem is a type of optimal control problem where the decision maker has to decide whether to "stop" or "continue" a particular activity. Stopping rule problems occur in many forms in Finance. The simplest forms occur in simple gambling problems. For example, in a coin-flipping game, the stopping rule problem is concerned with when is the best time to leave the game in order to maximize the expected reward from playing the game. The valuation of contingent claims, such as options, provides a number of stopping rule problems. American options pose an obvious stopping rule problem: When is the best time to exercise an American put or call option? Because the concern is typically with identifying the best time to stop, the theory of *optimal* stopping was developed.

There are a number of possible approaches to motivate optimal stopping problems. One approach is to consider optimal stopping as a type of decision making under uncertainty problem, e.g., Dixit and Pindyck (1994). In this context, optimal stopping can be formulated as a dynamic programming problem involving a binary choice, stop or continue, over all future decision dates. Optimal stopping solutions can then be solved using the appropriate Bellman equation. Another approach considers optimal stopping as an application of martingale methods, e.g., Karlin and Taylor (v.1). This leads to introduction of *Markov time* and application of the *optional sampling theorem* and the related *optional stopping theorem* (Karlin and Taylor, v.1, Sections 6.3 and 6.4) to solve optimal stopping problems. In some cases, solutions can be further refined by assuming diffusions and computing the appropriate derivatives of functionals of Brownian motion.

An important feature of optimal stopping problems typically encountered in Finance is the *smooth pasting condition* (Dixit 1993). In various sources, this condition is also referred to as the *high contact condition* (Samuelson 1965) or *principle of smooth fit* (Shepp and Shirayev 1983). The smooth pasting condition is derived by recognizing that the optimal stopping problem requires the identification of values of the state variable that involve either stopping or continuing. This leads to the derivation of an *optimal exercise boundary* using first order conditions of the value functions associated with the exercise decision. These first order conditions form the smooth pasting conditions that the optimal stopping problem must satisfy. In the case of an American option, the valuation problem that has to be solved is subject to this optimal exercise boundary. Because the applicability of this boundary condition usually depends on time, a so-called *free boundary*, the American option pricing problem is a free boundary value problem. Such problems almost always are not possible to solve in closed form.

C. Pricing Perpetual Options

The perpetual option is an optimal stopping problem that does permit the derivation of a closed form solution for a type of American option. This is because in the perpetual case the optimal exercise boundary does not vary with time. While a number of possible solution procedures have been proposed for the perpetual option, e.g., Ingersoll (1987, p. 375), Kim (1990), Jacka (1991), the martingale approach is both expedient and revealing, e.g., Gerber and Shu (1994b). The solution depends on evaluating the Laplace transform of the first passage time to an appropriate exercise boundary. The smooth pasting condition is then derived by maximizing the conditional expected value of the profit function with respect to the stock price that defines the exercise boundary. It is this derivative that can be evaluated precisely because the exercise boundary for the perpetual is not dependent on time. The solution to this optimization is the perpetual option price.

The optimal stopping problem for the perpetual call starts by specifying a price $S^*(>X)$ where exercise of the perpetual option will occur. The optimal S^* is a value to be determined later. Initially, the value of S^* is only restricted to be $>X$. Let the *first passage time* to the barrier imposed by S^* be specified as $T[S^*]$. In other words, if the process is initially at $S(0)$, then $T[S^*]$ is the time that the process takes to first get to S^*. This first passage time will have a distribution that will depend on $S(0)$, S^* and the stochastic process assumed for $S(t)$. If the underlying stock *price* process (where $dS/S = \mu \, dt + \sigma \, dW$) grows at the per-unit-time rate $\alpha = \mu + 1/2 \, \sigma^2 > 0$, then let $\theta = \lambda \mu + 1/2 \, \lambda^2 \, \sigma^2 > \alpha$.

The parameter θ can be interpreted as the discount rate associated with funds invested in the perpetual option. It is the discount rate that is used to calculate the discounted value of expected profit from exercising the option. The condition $\theta > \alpha$ follows because direct ownership of the stock is preferable to indirect ownership through an option. In particular, direct ownership of the stock entitles the holder to receive dividends. The case where the stock pays no dividends produces a limiting solution where the optimal exercise boundary is at infinity and the perpetual call option is never exercised.

The solution to the optimal stopping problem proceeds by applying the following Laplace transform solution applicable to the first passage of a Brownian motion process with drift $\mu \geq 0$ and variance σ^2. $T[z]$ is the first passage time for the Brownian process, starting from $x \geq 0$ to reach the level $z > x$ (Karlin and Taylor, v. 1, p. 362):

$$E[e^{-\theta\, T[z]}] = e^{-\frac{z-x}{\sigma^2}\left(\sqrt{\mu^2 + 2\sigma^2\, \theta} - \mu\right)}$$

The definition of θ is the same as that given above. To apply this Laplace transform solution to the case of a stock price that follows geometric Brownian motion, make the substitutions $z = \ln[S^*]$ and $x = \ln[S(0)]$ to produce the result:

$$E[e^{-\theta\, T[S^*]}] = \left[\frac{S(0)}{S^*}\right]^{\rho} \quad \text{where:} \quad \rho = \frac{1}{\sigma^2}\left(\sqrt{\mu^2 + 2\sigma^2\, \theta} - \mu\right)$$

This first passage result can now be applied to calculating the discounted expected profit.

The risk-neutral valuation approach to pricing options now has an immediate application:

$$C_{\perp}[S(t), S^*] = E\left[e^{-\theta\, T[S^*]}\, [S^* - X]\right] = [S^* - X]\, E\left[e^{-\theta\, T[S^*]}\right]$$

$$= [S^* - X]\left[\frac{S(0)}{S^*}\right]^{\rho}$$

This valuation is aided considerably by the arbitrary S^*. This condition can now be used to solve for the smooth pasting condition. This is done by differentiating $C[S(t), S^*]$ with respect to S^*:[11]

$$\frac{\partial C}{\partial S^*} = -\rho\,(S^{*+} - X)\left[\frac{S(0)}{S^{*+}}\right]^{\rho+1}\frac{1}{S(0)} + \left[\frac{S(0)}{S^{*+}}\right]^{\rho}$$

where S^{*+} is the optimal price to exercise the option and, as before, $S(0)$ is the current stock price. Solving for S^{*+} and substituting back into the $C[S^{*+}, S(0)]$ gives the desired solutions:

[11]To do this derivative it is helpful to observe that the discounted expected profit can be reformulated as:

$$C[S^*, S(0)] = S(0)^{\rho}\, S^{*(1-\rho)} - X\, (S(0)^{\rho}\, S^{*-\rho})$$

$$S^{*+} = \frac{X\,\rho}{\rho - 1}$$

$$C[S^{*+}, S(0)] = \frac{X}{\rho - 1}\left[\frac{S(0)\,(\rho - 1)}{X\,\rho}\right]^{\rho}$$

This is the solution for the price of the perpetual call.

To see the types of solutions produced by the perpetual call formula consider the following examples:

$S(0) = 50 \quad X = 50 \quad \mu = 0 \quad \sigma = 0.1 \quad \theta = 0.06 \rightarrow S^{*+} = 70.2914$

$\quad C_{perp} = 6.23534$

$S(0) = 50 \quad X = 50 \quad \mu = 0.3 \quad \sigma = 0.1 \quad \theta = 0.06 \rightarrow S^{*+} = 135.826$

$\quad C_{perp} = 17.65$

$S(0) = 50 \quad X = 50 \quad \mu = 0.055 \quad \sigma = 0.1 \quad \theta = 0.06 \rightarrow S^{*+} \Rightarrow$ infinity

$\quad C_{perp} = 50$

It is possible to show cases where $S(0)$ is above the optimal exercise boundary, in which case the option would be exercised immediately and $C = S(0) - X$.

V. QUESTIONS

1. Explain how the Black–Scholes model can be used to structure portfolios containing options. What is meant by the delta, theta, and gamma of a position and how are these concepts used in portfolio design?
2. What is portfolio insurance and what role do stock index derivatives play in insuring portfolios? What role did stock index derivatives play in the October 1987 market break? Identify and explain some factors that restrict the execution of stock index futures and option arbitrages.
3. If the risk of a stock increases, what is likely to happen to the prices of call options on the stock? To the prices of put options? What happens if interest rates change? Explain.
4. Explain how to construct an insured stock portfolio that uses a combination of long in-the-money, at-the-money, and out-of-the-money put options, where $\Delta_V > 0$ and $\Gamma_V = 0$.
5. Calculate the Δ, Γ, and θ for the long/short stock replication strategies discussed in Chapter 7. Consider the cases, $X < S$, $X = S$, and $X > S$.
6. Derive the closed form for theta, the sensitivity of the call option price to changes in time. Evaluate theta for a wide range of values of t.
7. Using the results provided in Appendix III, derive the appropriate formulae for the Greeks relevant to puts.
8. Derive the delta plus gamma conditions for the ratio spread and discuss the advantages of constructing the trade with more than two options.

Basic Mathematics and Statistics

I. NOTATION FOR PRESENT VALUE CALCULATION

At various points, the notation $PV[r,\tau]$ appears. This function is the conventional present value discounting operator for a cash flow of \$1 to be received in $\tau = T - t$ days. In Chapter 7, Section I, this is defined as the present value at time t of \$1 to be received at time T. $PV[\tau]$ means the present value evaluated at $\tau = T - t$. This can be evaluated using either a continuous or discrete formulation. In order to reduce the amount of notation, $PV[\tau]$ is used to represent both continuous and discrete compounding, even though there are slight differences in the two cases. However, with correct specification of the interest rates used in the discounting process, results of the continuous and discrete compounding operations are identical.

In discrete time, the discounting operator takes the linear form, $1/(1 + rt^*)$, when t^* is less than 1, and $1/(1 + r)^{t^*}$ where t^* is an integer greater than zero. The geometric form of the discounting operator, $1/(1 + r)^{t^*}$, is also encountered where t^* can take any value. For both these cases, r is expressed as an annualized interest rate. In continuous time, the discounting operator takes the form, $\exp\{-rt^*\} \equiv e^{-rt^*}$ where r is the continuously compounded interest rate. While the same symbol r is used as the interest rate in each of the discounting operators, equality of the present value determined by the continuous and discrete discounting operations requires the discrete and continuous interest rates to be adjusted to account for the difference between stated and effective interest.

II. TAYLOR SERIES EXPANSION

To make a comparison between the various forms of discounting operators, observe that $\ln[\exp\{-rt^*\}] = -rt^*$. The corresponding $\ln[(1+rt^*)^{-1}]$ for the discrete compounding case does not provide a similar simple solution but can be evaluated by taking a *Taylor series expansion*. For univariate functions this useful expansion technique from mathematical analysis takes the form (e.g., Rudin, 1964):

$$f[x] = f[a] + \frac{df[a]}{dx}\,(x-a) + \frac{1}{2!}\frac{d^2f[a]}{dx^2}\,(x-a)^2 + \frac{1}{3!}\frac{d^3f[a]}{dx^3}\,(x-a)^3 + \dots$$

In other words, any function $f[x]$ which has continuous derivatives over some interval $[b, c]$ can be equivalently expressed as the converging infinite sum provided by the Taylor series. This expression expands the univariate function $f[x]$ about the point fixed point a, where $b \le a \le c$. Each of the derivatives in the expansion is evaluated by setting $x = a$. For this expansion to be valid, the function f must have derivatives of all orders over $[b, c]$ (some of which can be zero).

A Taylor series is a specific form of a more general mathematical concept known as a power series. Other types of power series can also be used to represent an admissible function as an expansion expressed as an infinite converging sum. Examples of such expansions occur frequently, particularly in mathematical statistics. Some of the more important are the Edgeworth expansion, Cornish–Fisher expansion, and the Gram–Charlier expansion. The various types of power series are distinguished primarily in the method used for determining the coefficients for each of the terms in the expansion. The Taylor series uses derivatives of the function $f[x]$ in order to determine the coefficients. An important special case of the Taylor series occurs where zero is used as the fixed point in the expansion. This form of the Taylor series is sometimes referred to as a Maclaurin series.

Applied to the function $y[r] = \ln[(1+rt^*)^{-1}]$ evaluated around the origin $(a = 0)$ gives:

$$\ln\left[\frac{1}{1+rt^*}\right] = -\ln[1+rt^*] = -\left\{\ln[1+(0)t^*] + \frac{t^*}{1+(0)t^*}\,(r-0)\right.$$

$$-\frac{1}{2!}\frac{(t^*)}{(1+((0)t^*)^2}\,(r-0)^2 + \frac{1}{3!}\frac{(t^*)}{2(1+(0)t^*)^3}\,(r-0)^3 - \dots\right\}$$

$$= -\left\{0 + rt^* - \frac{r^2\,t^*}{2!} + \frac{r^3\,t^*}{3!\,2} - \dots\right\}$$

For small r, (say r is 0.1), which covers cases involving most interest rates, the terms involving squares, cubes, and so on will quickly disappear and the expansion reduces to $\ln[1/(1 + rt^*)]$ being approximately equal to $-rt^*$, which is the same as the exact value given when the log of the continuous discounting operator was evaluated. Using this approach, the difference between the continuous and discrete interest rates can be represented by the higher order terms which are being ignored in the Taylor series expansion.

Application of the Taylor series to the geometric discounting operator produces $\ln[(1 + r)^{-t^*}] = -t^* \ln[(1 + r)]$ which is also approximately $-rt^*$. However, unlike the linear form where the approximation to the log was taken for $(1 + rt^*)$, this approximation is $-t^*$ times $\ln[1 + r]$, which will, generally, produce a different error of approximation. The solutions will be the same when t^* is an integer greater than zero.

This discussion can also be used to clarify an approximation commonly used in financial calculation: $\ln[1 + x]$ is approximately equal to x when x is small. The question this operation raises is how small can x be in order to ensure that substitution of x for $\ln[1 + x]$ does not produce sizable errors of approximation? Examining the Taylor series for $\ln[1 + x]$ reveals that the square of x must be small relative to x. For example, if x is .1 then $x^2 = 0.01$, which, for many applications, is sufficiently small to permit the approximation. Similarly, if $x = 0.05$, then $x^2 = 0.0025$, and the approximation is again admissible in many situations. However, for $x = 0.5$, $x^2 = 0.25$, a value quite large relative to x. In practice, the admissibility of the approximation will depend on the specific type of problem in which the approximation is used. It is always possible to improve the approximation by taking account of higher order terms in the expansion.

Another useful application of the Taylor series is to expand the bond price function in terms of yield and time. The conventional textbook explanation for the relationship between duration and convexity (e.g., Fabozzi, 1993, Chap. 4) is to treat the bond price as a univariate function of yield $P_B[y]$. Applying a Taylor series expansion to this function gives:

$$P_B[y] = P_B[y_0] + \frac{dP}{dy}(y - y_0) + \frac{1}{2}\frac{d^2P}{dy^2}(y - y_0)^2 + \ldots$$

$$\frac{P_B[y] - P_B[y_0]}{P_B[y_0]} \cong -DUR\,(y - y_0) + \frac{1}{2}\,CON\,(y - y_0)^2$$

where *DUR* and *CON* are the duration and convexity of the bond. This result can be used to show that for two different fixed-income portfolios, with equal initial yield and duration, that the higher convexity portfolio will have a more favorable percentage change in price, whether yields go up or down.

As demonstrated by Christensen and Sorensen (1994) and others, this analysis is faulty because the bond price function depends on two variables: yield and time. This expansion involves the application of a multivariate Taylor series:

$$P_B[y,t] = \sum_{t=1}^{T} \frac{C}{(1+y)^t} + \frac{M}{(1+y)^T}$$

$$= P_B[y_0,t_0] + \frac{\partial P}{\partial y}\,(y - y_0) + \frac{\partial P}{\partial t}\,(t - t_0)$$

$$+ \frac{1}{2}\left\{\frac{\partial^2 P}{\partial y^2}\,(y - y_0)^2 + \frac{\partial^2 P}{\partial t^2}\,(t - t_0)^2\right\} + \frac{\partial^2 P}{\partial y\,\partial t}\,(y - y_0)\,(t - t_0) + \ldots$$

Dividing through by P_B will produce the familiar expansion in terms of modified duration, convexity, theta, and the cross-product terms (e.g., Chance and Jordan, 1995).

There can be some confusion about the approximation properties of a Taylor series. It is not possible to argue that adding an additional term to a Taylor series expansion will provide a superior approximation to $f[x]$ because convergence of the Taylor series does not ensure that this will provide an analytically more precise approximation. Monotonic convergence is too much to expect from Taylor's theorem (e.g., Rudin, 1964), which is concerned with the limiting properties of a specific polynomial series. A Taylor series will only converge *uniformly*. The Cauchy criterion for uniform convergence of a sequence of functions $\{f_n\}$ requires only that, for x within the interval of convergence of the sequence, there exists some integer N such that $m \geq N$, $n \geq N$ implies $|f_n(x) - f_m(x)| \leq \in$, for every $\in > 0$. For a uniformly convergent series, such as a Taylor series, it is possible that adding another term to the approximation may not improve the accuracy of the approximation. The essential requirement is that the series will eventually converge to the true function.

III. RESTRICTIONS ON THE TAYLOR SERIES COEFFICIENTS OF THE EXPECTED UTILITY FUNCTION

From Chapter 2, Section I, once the sign restrictions have been assumed for the derivatives of the utility function, further restrictions on the coefficients can be derived by evaluating the derivatives in the Taylor series expansion which is truncated at the third derivative term. More precisely, for $U[W]' > 0$, $U[W]'' < 0$, and $U[W]''' > 0$, taking derivatives in $U[W]$ produces:

$$U[W]' = a - 2b\,(W - \Omega) + 3c\,(W - \Omega)^2 > 0$$
$$U[W]'' = -2b + 6c\,(W - \Omega) < 0$$

where:

$$a = U[\Omega]', \quad b = -\frac{U[\Omega]''}{2}, \quad c = \frac{U[\Omega]'''}{3!}$$

Solving the second derivative condition produces the result: $(b/3c)$ $= -U''/U''' > (W - \Omega)$. This condition provides a restriction on the maximum possible value for W compatible with specific values of b and c.

From this it is now possible to derive an essential feature of the third-order Taylor series approximation. Taking expectations of the derivatives gives:

$$E[U'[W]] = a + 3c\,\sigma^2 > U'[\Omega] = a > 0$$
$$E[U''[W]] = U''[\Omega] = -2b$$
$$E[U'''[W]] = U'''[\Omega] = 6c$$

The restriction of the first derivative, that the average slope of the $U[W]$ is greater than the slope at the average, is an implication of Jensen's inequality applied to the first derivative. This result can be contrasted with the restrictions provided by the Taylor series derivatives for a second-order approximation that is relevant to the mean-variance case:

$$U'[W] = a - 2b\,(W - \Omega) > 0 \quad \rightarrow \quad E[U'[W]] = a = U'[\Omega]$$
$$U''[W] = -2b = U''[\Omega] < 0$$

For the mean-variance expected-utility function, the average slope equals the slope at the average, a result that differs from the mean-variance-skewness case. In addition, the restriction on admissible values of W is different: $(a/2b) > (W - \Omega)$.

IV. THE PRAKASH *ET AL.* (1996) CLAIM

Taking $W_0 = \Omega$, Prakash *et al.* (1996) claim that a risk-averse manager with sufficient preference for positive skewness will undertake an unfair gamble. For the weaker case of a fair gamble, this implies that the risky outcome $EU[W_1]$ can be preferred to the sure outcome of not gambling: $EU[W_1] > EU[W_0] = U[\Omega]$. Using the third-order Taylor series expansion and taking expectations it follows that:

$$U[\Omega] < U[\Omega] + a\,(W - \Omega) - b\,(W - \Omega)^2 + c\,(W - \Omega)^3 \quad \rightarrow$$

$$U[\Omega] < U[\Omega] - b\,\mathrm{var}[W] + c\,\mathrm{skew}[W]$$

$$\rightarrow \quad 3(W - \Omega) < \frac{b}{c} = \frac{3\,U''}{U'''} < \frac{\mathrm{skew}[W]}{\mathrm{var}[W]}$$

The last inequality involving $(W - \Omega)$ is developed above.

The novelty of this claim can be demonstrated by considering the weaker case where the gamble is fair (expected return on the gamble is equal to zero). Taking initial wealth to be equal to expected wealth next period, $W_0 = \Omega = E[W_1]$, it follows that $U[\Omega] = E[U[W_0]] < EU[W_1] \le U[E[W_1]] = U[\Omega]$, where the first inequality is the Prakash *et al.* proposition, and the second (weak) inequality follows from Jensen's inequality. Prakash *et al.* developed their seemingly impossible claim by manipulating the Taylor series expansion. Examining the coefficient values for the derivatives of $U[W]$ demonstrates that the Prakash *et al.* claim corresponds to the condition: $b/3c < \mathrm{skew}[W_1]/\mathrm{var}[W_1]$. When this result holds, the Prakash *et al.* claim is correct. One apparently obvious case where this condition could apply would be $b = 0$, $c > 0$, and $\mathrm{skew}[W] > 0$. In general, if the distribution of W is negatively skewed or symmetric, the Prakash *et al.* condition cannot apply.

To see this, observe that the Prakash *et al.* condition produces the third-order differential equation:

$$U'''[\Omega] - \left\{ \frac{3\,\mathrm{var}[W]}{\mathrm{skew}[W]} \right\} U''[\Omega] < 0$$

Taking the inequality to be an equality, this can be solved to produce an exponential utility function, $U = -\exp\{-(3\mathrm{var}[W]/\mathrm{skew}[W])W\}$, which is consistent with the derivative restrictions. Horowitz (1998) makes two observations: This solution is inconsistent with the assumption that U'''' and higher derivatives are zero and the parameter $3\sigma^2/\sigma^3$ is "incompatible" with "the existence of a risk preference function that validates the violations" (e.g., assuming $b = 0$ is incompatible). The last observation is the same as saying that there is no utility function with a convergent Taylor series that is compatible with the type of gamble distribution implied by the Prakash *et al.* condition.[1]

---

[1]The first observation of Horowitz (1998) would be applicable to almost any type of Taylor series expansion of a more general utility function. The second observation makes the important point that var[W] and skew[W] are functions of the optimal values of the risky investment, and that varience and skewness are functionally related. As a consequence, it is not possible to determine optimal values to satisfy the needed restrictions on b and c for the Prakash *et al.* condition to apply.

V. RELATIONSHIP OF CONTINUOUS TIME AND DISCRETE INTEREST RATES

Use the notation that: $r(t,T) = r((T - t)/365) = rt^*$, where r is the interest rate expressed as an annualized rate. In other words, rt^* is the actual interest rate earned over the holding period. For example, if $T - t = 91$ days, then rt^* is the interest rate earned over a 3-month period, approximately $r/4$. When $t = 0$, the formula simplifies to $r(0,T) = r(T/365)$. The future value of an investment of $V(t)$ at $r(t,T)$ can now be expressed as: $V(T) = V(t)(1 + r(t,T))$ and $\Delta V = V(T) - V(t) = r(t,T) V(t) = rt^* V(t)$. Recognizing that $V(t)$ and r are fixed and that $t^* = (T - t)/365$ is a time difference $\Delta t/365 = \Delta t'$ gives: $V(T) = V(t) r \Delta t'$. This can be compared with the same calculations done using continuous interest rates:

$$V(t) = V(0) e^{rt} \quad \Rightarrow \quad \frac{dV(t)}{dt} = r\{V(0) e^{rt}\} \quad \Rightarrow \quad dV(t) = V(t) r \, dt$$

This result is used in Chapter 9 to describe the return on the Black–Scholes riskless hedge portfolio, where $V(t) = S(t) - \beta C(t)$, and in Chapter 8, Section I, in the discussion of Fischer (1975). To solve for the continuous time interest rate r_c, which gives the same terminal return as the discrete interest rate r_d, solve $\exp\{-r_c T\} = \{1/(1 + r_d)\}^T$. Taking logs and manipulating give $r_c = [\ln 1 + r_d]$.

VI. BACKGROUND ON STATISTICAL CONCEPTS

The discussion in this book uses a number of statistical concepts that may be unfamiliar, such as the conditional variance and expected value of a profit function. The use of parameters from conditional distributions is consistent with the type of valuation problems encountered in financial economics, where optimal decisions involve evaluating random variables such as future prices. Conditional expectations are required because the information set upon which the expectation is based increases over time, until the decision horizon (T) is reached. Except in restrictive cases, the parameters of the conditional distribution will differ from the parameters of the unconditional distribution, which is derived from the complete information set, available at T. As a consequence of being determined from a fixed information set, unconditional statistical parameters are constant. This will typically not be the case with the parameters of conditional distributions.

A conditional expectation depends on the information set available on the decision date, t. For $t < T$, the information set will increase over time, changing the information used in forming the expectation. When the conditional parameters are constant over time, then the conditional and unconditional parameters are identical. However, conditional statistical parameters will only be constant under restrictive conditions. Given these caveats, if the conditioning information set is ignored, the mathematical operations required to derive the mean and variance of the profit function are identical for both the unconditional and conditional cases. Bearing in mind that the parameters being determined are from conditional distributions, it is conventional to drop notation involving the conditioning information set.

Given this, from Chapter 2, Section I, the mathematical *conditional expectation* of the mean of the *speculative profit* function conditional on information available at the decision date $t = 0$ can be stated:

$$E[\pi(1)] = Q \{E[F(1,T)] - F(0,T)\}$$

This result uses two properties of conditional expectations: linearity of the expectation and $E[F(0,T)] = F(0,T)$. This follows because the information available on the decision date contains $F(0,T)$. The associated *conditional variance* for the *speculative profit* function follows appropriately:

$$\begin{aligned}
\text{var}[\pi(1)] &= E[(\pi(1) - E[\pi(1)])^2] \\
&= E[(Q\{F(1,T) - F(0,T)\} - Q\{E[F(1,T)] - F(0,T)\})^2] \\
&= E[(Q\{F(1,T) - E[F(1,T)]\})^2] = Q^2 \, E[(F(1,T) - E[F(1,T)])^2] \\
&= Q^2 \, \text{var}[F(1,T)] = Q^2 \, \sigma_f^2
\end{aligned}$$

The *conditional expectation* of the stylized *hedger profit* function from Chapter 2, Section I, follows appropriately:

$$\begin{aligned}
E[\pi(1)] &= E[Q_s \{S(1) - S(0)\} + Q_H \{F(0,T) - F(1,T)\}] \\
&= Q_s \{E[S(1)] - S(0)]\} + Q_H \{F(0,T) - E[F(1,T)]\}
\end{aligned}$$

The associated *conditional variance* for the *hedger profit* function follows:

$$\text{var}[\pi(1)] = E[(\pi(1) - E[\pi(1)])^2]$$

$$= E[(Q_s\{S(1) - S(0)\} + Q_H\{F(0,T) - F(1,T)\} - Q_s\{E[S(1)] - S(0)\}$$

$$-Q_H\{F(0,T) - E[F(1,T)]\})^2]$$

$$= E[(Q_s\{S(1) - E[S(1)]\} - Q_H\{F(1,T) - E[F(1,T)]\})^2]$$

$$= Q_s^2 E[(S(1) - E[S(1)])^2] - 2Q_s Q_H \, E[(S(1) - E[S(1)])(F(1,T) - E[F(1,T)])]$$

$$+ Q_H^2 \, E[(F(1,T) - E[F(1,T)])^2]$$
$$= Q_s^2 \, \sigma_s^2 - 2Q_s Q_H \, \sigma_{sf} + Q_H^2 \, \sigma_f^2$$

The mean and variance for other profit functions used in various parts of the book can also be derived using this approach.

Money Market Calculations

Some basic background is required to interpret the interest rate futures quotes provided in the financial press. In order to understand the quoting mechanism, recall the profit functions for the short and long futures speculators: Short positions benefit from falling futures prices while long positions benefit from futures price rises. However, for money market securities, the use of prices would be at variance with cash market practices, which quote in yields. Because yields move inversely to prices, a method was devised for quoting money market futures that retained the notion that longs (shorts) benefit when the futures quote rises (falls) and was still consistent with cash market practices. The futures contract is quoted as $100 - $ Quote $=$ (discount rate, expressed with the first digit starting as a whole number). For example, the June 16, 1992, T-bill for September 1992 delivery closed at 96.21. This converts to $100 - 96.21 = 3.79$. The 3-month U.S. T-bill for September 1992 delivery is being offered at a discount rate of 3.79%. A similar quoting convention is also used for Eurodollar futures contracts.

When comparing interest rates derived from money market futures quotes, it has to be recognized that most U.S. money market securities, T-bills, BAs, commercial paper (CP), and term repos are quoted on a *discount rate* and *not* a true yield (bond equivalent yield) basis. In addition to using a different pricing formula, the discount rate calculation also involves calculating the year as though it has 360 days. To see this, consider the U.S. method for determining the purchase price of a 1-year, $1 million par value T-bill sold at a discount rate of 8%:

$$Discount = (\$1,000,000)(0.08)(364/360) = \$80,888.89$$

As a result, the price paid for this T-bill maturing in 1 year is the maturity (par) value minus the discount or $919,111.11. The general formula for arriving at the discount is

$$D = d \ F \ (tsm/360)$$

where D is the discount, d is the discount rate, F is the maturity value, and tsm is the time from settlement to maturity. Similarly, for a T-bill with 3 days to maturity, par value of $1 million, and discount rate of 9%:

$$D = (0.09) \ (\$1,000,000) \ (3/360) = \$750$$

The bill is purchased for $999,250 and matures in 3 days for $1 million, returning $750 in interest.

The method for valuing an 01 or one basis point (0.0001 expressed as a decimal) for the 3-month $1 million par value T-bill futures contracts should now be apparent:

$$D = (0.0001)(\$1,000,000)(90/360) = \$25$$

In the discussion of dollar value hedge ratios in Chapter 6, reference was made to the value of an 01 for a $1 million, 6-month T-bill. In this case:

$$D = (0.0001)(\$1,000,000)(180/360) = \$50$$

Hence, it is necessary to use two T-bill futures contracts to provide a dollar value equivalent movement for a 6-month, $1 million dollar T-bill position.

It should be recognized that the discount rate understates the simple interest, true yield, or bond equivalent yield formula used in Canada and other countries for money market securities. The formula for calculating the annualized true yield (r) is the familiar:

$$r = \frac{F-P}{P} \ \frac{365}{tsm} \quad \text{or} \quad P = \frac{F}{1 + \left(r \ \dfrac{tsm}{365} \right)}$$

where P is the price paid, or $D = F - P$. Substituting this result gives:

$$r = (D/(F-D)) \ (365/tsm)$$

This can be solved in terms of the discount rate by substituting the method for calculating D for discount securities to give:

$$r = \frac{(365)d}{360 - d \ (tsm)}$$

This is the formula for converting a discount rate into a true or simple interest yield.

To see how this works, consider the covered interest arbitrage example of Chapter 5, Section II. The discount rate for the U.S. BA was quoted at 0.0477 or 4.77%. Using the conversion formula:

$$r = [365 \ (0.0477)]/[360 - \{(0.0477)90\}] = 0.0489462$$

Similarly for the CP rate:

$$r = [365 \ (0.0480)]/[360 - \{(0.0480)90\}] = 0.0492577$$

The general formula can also be used to show that the quoted discount rate will always be below the true yield, $r > d$, as well as showing that the discrepancy between r and d will be greater the higher the rate of discount and the longer the term to maturity. Some manipulation gives the discount rate associated with a given true yield:

$$d = \frac{360 \ r}{365 + r(tsm)}$$

Currently, the relationship between d and r is reported in the financial press, as reflected in the August 8, 1994 U.S. Treasury bill rates reported in Table II.1.

To verify the formula for deriving the discount rate associated with an observed yield, consider the November 3, 1994, bill in Table II.1. This bill is indicated in bold because it is the most recently issued 3-month bill and, due to the focus of market trading on the most recently issued maturities, this bill will tend to be the most liquid. The *tsm* for this bill is 12 weeks plus 3 days or 87 days with a reported ask yield of 4.56. Evaluating for d gives:

$$d = [360 \ (.0456)]/[365 + \{(.0456)(87)\}] = .0445$$

This is the ask value reported in Table II.1.

I. FIXED-INCOME CALCULATIONS

The pricing conventions for T-bond and T-note interest rate futures contracts do not follow the same quoting conventions as for money market securities. Long-term interest rate futures prices are quoted much as in the cash market, with the proviso that the underlying bond or note being quoted is a theoretical instrument. For example, for many years the U.S. T-bond contract traded a theoretical 8% coupon—since 2000, the T-bond contract has featured a 6% theoretical coupon—with 15 years to the call date. The method of quoting prices for these contracts (and the T-note contracts) is in keeping with market convention for trading non-money-market, fixed-income securities on the basis of a $100 par value. In addition, the market convention of quoting prices in 1/8, 1/4, 1/2, and so on is also retained. For the T-bond and T-note quotes, the fractional part of the quote refers to 32nds. Hence, the T-bond quote on May 2, 1984 of 73–20 for June 1984 delivery is offering to provide "equivalent" cash T-bonds at 73–20/32 for the 8%, 15-year (to call) theoretical bond.

In the case of delivery, the short can deliver *any* available cash U.S. T-bond or T-note that meets the maturity restriction. Because the prices of available

TABLE II.1   Treasury Bill Rates

Maturity	Days to mat.	Bid	Asked	Chg.	Ask yld.
Aug. 11 '94	1	4.11	4.01	+0.08	4.07
Aug. 18 '94	8	4.11	4.01	+0.06	4.07
Aug. 25 '94	15	4.13	4.03	+0.04	4.09
Sep. 01 '94	22	4.16	4.06	+0.04	4.13
Sep. 08 '94	29	4.17	4.07	+0.04	4.14
Sep. 15 '94	36	4.16	4.12	+0.04	4.19
Sep. 22 '94	43	4.34	4.30	+0.05	4.38
Sep. 29 '94	50	4.17	4.13	+0.04	4.21
Oct. 06 '94	57	4.27	4.23	+0.03	4.32
Oct. 13 '94	64	4.32	4.30	—	4.39
Oct. 20 '94	71	4.39	4.37	+0.02	4.47
Oct. 27 '94	78	4.41	4.39	+0.01	4.49
Nov. 03 '94	85	4.47	4.45	+0.01	4.56
Nov. 10 '94	92	4.50	4.48	+0.02	4.59
Nov. 17 '94	99	4.52	4.50	—	4.62
Nov. 25 '94	107	4.56	4.54	—	4.67
Dec. 01 '94	113	4.60	4.58	—	4.71
Dec. 08 '94	120	4.65	4.63	—	4.77
Dec. 15 '94	127	4.66	4.64	+0.01	4.78
Dec. 22 '94	134	4.68	4.66	+0.01	4.81
Dec. 29 '94	141	4.65	4.63	+0.01	4.78
Jan. 05 '95	148	4.76	4.74	+0.02	4.90
Jan. 12 '95	155	4.83	4.81	+0.02	4.98
Jan. 19 '95	162	4.86	4.84	+0.01	5.02
Jan. 26 '95	169	4.88	4.86	+0.01	5.04
Feb. 02 '95	176	4.91	4.89	+0.01	5.08
Feb. 09 '95	183	4.93	4.91	—	5.11
Mar. 09 '95	211	4.99	4.97	+0.01	5.17
Apr. 06 '95	239	5.06	5.04	−0.01	5.25
May 04 '95	267	5.17	5.15	—	5.38
Jun. 01 '95	295	5.20	5.18	−0.02	5.43
Jun. 29 '95	323	5.26	5.24	+0.01	5.51
Jul. 27 '95	351	5.29	5.27	+0.01	5.56

Source: *The Wall Street Journal*, August 8. 1994. With permission.

T-bonds and notes differ according to coupon and maturity date, the delivery process requires a pricing procedure for determining the value of any specific T-bond relative to the theoretical 8% (now 6%) bond (otherwise, the lowest coupon bond would typically be delivered). For this purpose, the Chicago Board of Trade (CBOT) devised a method of determining *conversion factors* for assessing the invoice value of potentially deliverable bonds. The conversion factors for the T-bond contract can be obtained from the CBOT exchange website In practice, the conversion factors are not exact, giving rise to the presence of a "cheapest deliverable" T-bond or T-note. In addition to multiple delivery grades associated with the wide range of deliverable cash instruments differing with respect to maturity and coupon, the quotes for note and bond futures are further complicated by other considerations associated with specifics of contract design. These additional factors also need to be taken into account in determining the cheapest deliverable bond or note.

The translation of a quoted futures price to a yield follows the standard conventions for bond pricing applied to semiannual coupon Treasury securities. Consider the problem of translating the 73–20 bond futures price to a yield for the old-style 8% theoretical coupon T-bond contract:

$$P_B = \sum_{t=1}^{2T} \frac{C/2}{\left[1+\frac{r}{2}\right]^t} + \frac{B}{\left[1+\frac{r}{2}\right]^{2T}}$$

$$73.625 = \sum_{t=1}^{40} \frac{4}{\left[1+\frac{r}{2}\right]^t} + \frac{100}{\left[1+\frac{r}{2}\right]^{2T}}$$

Solving the last equation for the yield (r) gives: $r = 0.11352$, or 11.352% Because T-bonds and T-notes are quoted in terms of prices, correspondence with the long/short profitability conventions will automatically be observed.

The above methodology can be used to solve for the conversion factor used in delivery of T-bonds. For example, a 20-year, 14% coupon T-bond would have a conversion factor (CF) determined as though yields were 8%:

$$CF = \sum_{t=1}^{40} \frac{7}{[1.04]^t} + \frac{100}{[1.04]^T} = 159.38$$

The actual conversion factor used is derived by dividing CF by 100. Given this, the deliverable amount of a given bond is determined by taking the par value of the contracts involved and multiplying by the futures settlement price to get the market value in terms of the theoretical 8% deliverable. This value is then multiplied by the conversion factor provided by the exchange, using the formula described. While for most traders the complications of bond delivery are typically of little importance, significant movements in T-bond futures prices can occur when the cheapest deliverable bond changes. Given that the formula tends to favor certain features such as longer maturities, this can occur following a Treasury auction of 30-year T-bonds. As a final note, to get the value of a "tick," in this case 1/32, point movement in the price of the T-bond all that is required is $(1/32)\$100,000 = \$31.25$.

Analysis of the cheapest deliverable bond has received considerable attention in the academic literature (e.g, Livingston, 1984, 1987; references cited in Duffie, 1989, pp. 324–332). The CBOT exchange website (www.cbot.com) has an illustration of the cheapest delivery problem selection process. Some of the interesting issues arising in this area involve the various options embedded in the T-bond delivery process: quality to deliver option, the option to deliver the cheapest bond; accrued interest option arising from the option to make delivery on an arbitrary trading day during the delivery period; end-of-month option, which involves delivering in the 1-week period after futures have finished trading the delivery contract; and the wild-card option, which involves substituting bonds on the delivery day. The issue of deliverable specification has had implications for a number of contract failures (e.g., the Government National Mortgage Association futures contract) (see Duffie, 1989, pp. 339–342).

Mathematics for Option Valuation

This appendix contains derivations of the partial derivatives stated in Chapter 9, Section I. In addition, a number of useful results applicable to probability densities are also derived. These results, which are provided here for ease of reference, are available in a variety other sources (e.g., Cox and Rubinstein, 1985, chap. 5; Stoll and Whalley, 1993, chap. 11). In the following, $N[x,y]$ refers to a normal density with mean x and variance y. $N[x]$ refers to a cumulative normal distribution function evaluated at x, and $n[x] \equiv N'[x]$ is the normal density function evaluated at X.

I. RESULTS FOR PROBABILITY DISTRIBUTIONS AND DENSITIES

1. Chapter 8 makes use of a result concerning the standard deviation of a sum of standard normal random variables. More precisely, the discrete random walk was given the form:

$$X(t + 1) = X(t) + Z(t), \quad \text{for } X(0) = 0 \text{ and } t \in \{1, 2, 3, \ldots\}$$

where $Z(1)$, $Z(2)$, $Z(3)$, ... form a stochastic process of *independent* random variables with the standard normal probability distribution: $Z(t) \sim N[0,1]$. This requires the $Z(t)$ to be identically, independently distributed (iid) random variables. Over any time interval 0 to T, the variance of $\Delta X(t)$ can be evaluated by determining the variance:

$$\text{var}\left\{ \sum_{t=1}^{T} Z(t) \right\} = E\left[\sum_{t=1}^{T} Z(t) \right]^2 = \sum_{t=1}^{T} \sigma_Z^2 = T\,\sigma_Z^2 = T$$

Hence, when $\Delta t = T$, the Z is $N[0,T]$. Now, consider what happens when the time interval Δt shrinks. Because $Z(t)$ is $N[0,\Delta t]$ over any arbitrary time interval, the random walk now has the form:

$$X(t + \Delta t) = X(t) + Z(t)\,\sqrt{\Delta t}$$

Which is the result given in Chapter 9.

2. In the derivation of the Black-Scholes put option formula the following result is needed:

$$N[d] = 1 - N[-d] \rightarrow N[-d] = 1 - N[d]$$

$$N[d] = \frac{1}{\sqrt{2\pi}} \int_{-\infty}^{d} e^{-z^2/2}\, dz - \frac{1}{\sqrt{2\pi}} \int_{-d}^{\infty} e^{-z^2/2}\, dz \quad (symmetry\ of\ N)$$

$$= \frac{1}{\sqrt{2\pi}} \{ \int_{-\infty}^{\infty} e^{-z^2/2}\, dz - \int_{-\infty}^{-d} e^{-z^2/2}\, dz \} = 1 - N[-d]$$

3. Another important property is the chain rule for partial differentiation of the cumulative distribution:

$$\frac{\partial N[d]}{\partial x} = \frac{\partial N[d]}{\partial d}\frac{\partial d}{\partial x} = N'[d]\frac{\partial d}{\partial x} \qquad (for\ d = d[x])$$

where $N'[d]$ is the standard normal probability density evaluated at d (see note 1 of Chapter 9).

4a. Application of the chain rule to the cumulative normal distribution function leads to results involving the normal probability density function evaluated at d_2 and d_1. Simplification of the derivatives requires the relationship between $N'[d_1]$ and $N'[d_2]$ to be identified. Observing that $d_2 = d_1 - \sigma\sqrt{t^*}$ produces:

$$d_2^2 = \{d_1 - \sigma\,\sqrt{t^*}\}^2 = d_1^2 - 2\,d_1\,\sigma\,\sqrt{t^*} + \sigma^2\,t^*$$
$$= d_1^2 - 2\{\ln\{S/X\} + (r + .5\sigma^2)\,t^*\} + \sigma^2\,t^* = d_1^2 - 2\,\ln\{S/(X\,e^{-rt})\}$$

Direct substitution into the formula for the normal probability density function now produces:

$$N'[d_2] = \frac{1}{\sqrt{2\pi}}\,e^{-\frac{d_2^2}{2}} = \frac{1}{\sqrt{2\pi}}\,e^{-\frac{d_1^2}{2}+\ln\{S\,/\,\{Xe^{-rt^*}\}\}}$$

$$= \frac{1}{2\pi}\,e^{-\frac{d_1^2}{2}}\,e^{\ln\{S/Xe^{-rt^*}\}} = N'[d_1]\,\frac{S}{Xe^{-rt^*}} \quad\Rightarrow\quad N'[d_1] = N'[d_2]\,\frac{Xe^{-rt^*}}{S}$$

4b. When the commodity involved has a carry return, as in the case of currency options, it is necessary to adjust $N'[d_1]$ to be

$$N'[d_1] = N'[d_2] \; \frac{X\,e^{-rt^*}}{S\,e^{-r^*t^*}}$$

where r^* is the return on the riskless foreign security.

5. The derivations of the Greeks for the Bachelier options require the following result for differentiating a normal probability density where $n[g] = N'[g]$ is the standard normal density function evaluated at g.

$$\frac{\partial n[g]}{\partial x} = \frac{\partial}{\partial x}\frac{1}{\sqrt{2\pi}}\,e^{-\frac{g^2}{2}} = n[g]\;\frac{\partial\{-g^2/2\}}{\partial g}\;\frac{\partial g}{\partial x} = n[g]\;(-g)\;\frac{\partial g}{\partial x}$$

II. GREEKS FOR BLACK-SCHOLES CALL OPTIONS

For a Black-Scholes call option on a non-dividend paying security, the delta, gamma, theta, and vega are:

A. DELTA

$$\frac{\partial C}{\partial S} = N[d_1] + S\;\frac{\partial N[d_1]}{\partial S} - Xe^{-rt^*}\frac{\partial N[d_2]}{\partial S} = N[d_1]$$

$$+ SN'[d_1]\frac{\partial d_1}{\partial S} - Xe^{-rt^*}N'[d_2]\;\frac{\partial d_2}{\partial S}$$

$$= N[d_1] + S\,N'[d_1]\;\frac{\partial d_1}{\partial S} - Xe^{-rt^*}\,N'[d_1]\frac{S}{Xe^{-rt^*}}\;\frac{\partial d_1}{\partial S} = N[d_1]$$

The last line follows from (4a) in Section I above and observing that $\partial d_1/\partial S = \partial d_2/\partial S$.

B. GAMMA

$$\frac{\partial^2 C}{\partial S^2} = \frac{\partial N[d_1]}{\partial S} = N'[d_1]\;\frac{\partial d_1}{\partial S} = \frac{1}{S\,\sigma\,\sqrt{t^*}}\;N'[d_1]$$

C. THETA

$$-\frac{\partial C}{\partial t} = \frac{\partial C}{\partial t^*} = S\;\frac{\partial N[d_1]}{\partial t^*} + rXe^{-rt^*}\,N[d_2] - Xe^{-rt^*}\;\frac{\partial N[d_2]}{\partial t^*}$$

$$= S\, N'[d_1]\,\frac{\partial d_1}{\partial t^*} + rXe^{-rt^*}\, N[d_2] - Xe^{-rt^*}\, N'[d_2]\,\frac{\partial d_2}{\partial t^*}$$

$$= S\, N'[d_1]\,\frac{\partial d_1}{\partial t^*} - Xe^{-rt^*}\, N'[d_1]\,\frac{S}{Xe^{-rt^*}}\left\{\frac{\partial d_1}{\partial t^*} - \sigma\,\frac{\partial\sqrt{t^*}}{\partial t^*}\right\} + rXe^{-rt^*}\, N[d_2]$$

$$= \frac{S\sigma}{2\sqrt{t^*}}\, N'[d_1] + rXe^{-rt^*}\, N[d_2]$$

D. VEGA

$$\frac{\partial C}{\partial\sigma} = S\,\frac{\partial N[d_1]}{\partial\sigma} - Xe^{-rt^*}\,\frac{\partial N[d_2]}{\partial\sigma} = S\, N'[d_1]\,\frac{\partial d_1}{\partial\sigma}$$

$$- Xe^{-rt^*}\, N'[d_1]\,\frac{S}{Xe^{-rt^*}}\,\frac{\partial d_2}{\partial\sigma} = S\, N'[d_1]\left\{\frac{\partial d_1}{\partial\sigma} - \frac{\partial d_2}{\partial\sigma}\right\}$$

$$= S\, N'[d_1]\,\sqrt{t^*}$$

III. GREEKS FOR THE BACHELIER CALL OPTION

For the Bachelier call option for a dividend paying security given in Chapter 8, the delta, theta, and gamma are

A. DELTA

$$\Delta_{BC} = \frac{\partial C}{\partial S} = e^{-\delta t^*}\, N[h] + \left(Se^{-\delta t^*} - Xe^{-rt^*}\right)\frac{\partial N}{\partial S} + V\,\frac{\partial n}{\partial S} = e^{-\delta t^*}\, N[h]$$

B. GAMMA

$$\Gamma_{BC} = \frac{\partial^2 C}{\partial S^2} = e^{-\delta t^*}\,\frac{\partial N}{\partial S} = e^{-\delta t^*}\, n[h]\,\frac{\partial h}{\partial S} = \frac{e^{-2\delta t^*}}{V}\, n[h]$$

C. THETA

$$-\theta_{BC} = \frac{\partial C}{\partial t^*} = \left(-\delta Se^{-\delta t^*} + rXe^{-rt^*}\right) N[h] + \left(Se^{-\delta t^*} - Xe^{-rt^*}\right)\frac{\partial N}{\partial t^*} + \frac{\partial V}{\partial t^*}$$

$$n[h] + V\,\frac{\partial n}{\partial t^*}$$

$$= -\frac{\partial C}{\partial t} = \left(-\delta Se^{-\delta t^*} + rXe^{-rt^*}\right) N[h] + \frac{\partial V}{\partial t^*}\, n[h]$$

REFERENCES

I. GENERAL BACKGROUND AND INTRODUCTORY TEXTS ON DERIVATIVE SECURITIES

Blank, S., Carter, C., and Schmiesing, B. (1991), *Futures and Options Markets*, Toronto: Prentice Hall.

Briys, E., Bellalah, M., Mai, H., and de Varenne, F. (1998), *Options, Futures and Exotic Derivatives: Theory, Application and Practice*, New York: Wiley.

Chance, D. (2001), *An Introduction to Derivatives and Risk Management* (5th ed.), New York: Dryden.

Chance, D. (1998), *An Introduction to Derivative Securities* (4th ed.), New York: Dryden.

Chance, D. (1989), *An Introduction to Options and Futures*, New York: Dryden.

Cox, J., and Rubinstein, M. (1985), *Options Markets*, Englewood Cliffs, NJ: Prentice-Hall.

Culp, C. (2001), *The Risk Management Process*, New York: Wiley.

Chicago Board of Trade (1989, 1998), *Commodity Trading Manual*, Chicago: Chicago Board of Trade.

Duffie, D. (1989), *Futures Markets*, Englewood Cliffs, NJ: Prentice Hall.

Hieronymous, T. (1977), *The Economics of Futures Trading* (2nd ed.), New York: Commodity Research Bureau.

Hore, J. (1989), *Trading on Canadian Futures Markets* (4th ed.), Toronto: Canadian Securities Institute.

Hull, J. (1998), *Introduction to Futures and Options Markets* (3rd ed.), Englewood Cliffs, NJ: Prentice-Hall.

Hull, J. (2000), *Options, Futures and Other Derivative Securities*, (4th ed.), Toronto: Prentice Hall.

Jarrow, R., and Turnbull, S. (1999), *Derivative Securities* (2nd ed.), Cincinatti, Ohio: South-Western.

Johnson, R., and Giacotto, C. (1995), *Options and Futures*, New York: West Publishing.

Kolb, R. (2000), *Futures, Options and Swaps* (3rd ed.), Malden, Mass.: Blackwell.

Kolb, R. (1988), *Understanding Futures Markets* (2nd ed.), Glenview, IL.: Scott Foresman.

Leuthold, R., Junkus, J., and Cordier, J. (1989), *The Theory and Practice of Futures Markets*, Lexington, Mass.: Lexington Books.

Marshall, J. (1989), *Futures and Option Contracting*, Cincinnati: Southwestern.

Mason, S., Merton, R., Perold, A., and Tufano, P. (1995), *Cases in Financial Engineering*, Englewood Cliffs, NJ: Prentice-Hall.

Siegel, D., and Siegel, D. (1990), *Futures Markets*, New York: Dryden.

Stoll, H., and Whalley, R. (1993), *Futures and Options* Cincinnati: Southwestern.

Wilmott, P. (1998), *Derivatives, The Theory and Practice of Financial Engineering* New York: Wiley.

II. GENERAL BOOKS ON FINANCIAL FUTURES

Britten-Jones, M. (1998), *Fixed Income and Interest Rate Derivative Analysis*, Oxford: Butterworth-Heinemann.

Dubofsky, D. (1992), *Options and Financial Futures* New York: McGraw-Hill.

Livingston, M. (1999), *Bonds and Bond Derivatives*, Oxford: Blackwell.

Rothstein, N. (1984), *The Handbook of Financial Futures*, New York: McGraw-Hill.

Schwarz, E., Hill, J., and Schneeweis, T. (1986), *Financial Futures: Fundamentals, Strategies and Applications*, Homewood, IL: Irwin.

Sundaresan, S. (1997), *Fixed Income Markets and Their Derivatives*, Cincinatti: Southwestern.

Tucker, A. (1991), *Financial Futures, Options and Swaps*, New York: West Publishing.

Winstone, D. (1995), *Financial Derivatives: Hedging with Futures, Forwards, Options and Swaps*, New York: Chapman & Hall.

III. GENERAL BOOKS ON INTERNATIONAL FINANCIAL MANAGEMENT

Eng, M., Lees, F., and Mauer, L. (1995), *Global Finance*, New York: HarperCollins.

Eun, C., and Resnick, G. (2001), *International Financial Management* (2nd ed.), New York: Irwin McGraw-Hill.

Grabbe, O. (1996), *International Financial Markets* (3rd ed.), Englewood Cliffs, NJ: Prentice-Hall.

Madura, J. (2000), *International Financial Management* (6th ed.), New York: Southwestern.

Uppal, R., and Sercu, P. (1995), *International Financial Markets and the Firm*, London: Chapman & Hall.

Shapiro, A. (1999), *Multinational Financial Management* (6th ed.), Saddle River, NJ: Prentice-Hall.

Solnik, B. (1999), *International Investments* (4th ed.), New York: Addison-Wesley.

IV. GENERAL BOOKS ON INVESTMENTS

Alexander, G., and Sharpe, W. (1990), *Investments* (4th ed.), Englewood Cliffs, NJ: Prentice-Hall.
Bodie, Z., Kane, A., and Marcus, A. (1993), *Investments* (2nd ed.), Boston: Irwin.
Elton, E., and Gruber, M. (1995), *Modern Portfolio Theory and Investment Analysis* (5th ed.), New York: Wiley.
Luenberger, D. (1998), *Investment Science*, Oxford, UK: Oxford University Press.

V. JOURNALS AND MAGAZINES

A. JOURNALS DEDICATED TO DERIVATIVES

Journal of Futures Markets (Wiley)
Journal of Derivatives (Institutional Investor)
Derivatives Quarterly
Review of Futures Markets (Chicago Board of Trade, discontinued)
Advances in Futures and Options Research (JMI Press)
Review of Derivatives Research

B. JOURNALS WITH DERIVATIVES CONTENT

American Economic Review
Applied Financial Economics
Applied Mathematical Finance
Canadian Journal of Economics
Econometrica
Financial Analysts Journal
Financial Management
Journal of Applied Corporate Finance
Insurance: Mathematics and Economics
Journal of Banking and Finance
Journal of Econometrics
Journal of Finance (American Finance Association)
Journal of Financial and Quantitative Analysis (Western Finance Association)
Journal of Financial Economics
Journal of Financial Research
Journal of Fixed Income
Journal of International Money and Finance

Journal of Portfolio Management
Management Science
Mathematical Finance
Review of Financial Studies
Transactions of the Society of Actuaries

C. Important Magazines and Newspapers

Risk magazine is an important source of information on developments in financial
   engineering. This source also contains short articles by important academics.
Euromoney sometimes has useful information on market developments.
Commodities
Futures: The Magazine of Commodities and Options
Futures and Options Week (FOW)
Euromoney
Barron's, Wall Street Journal, Globe and Mail (Toronto), *New York Times.*
Northern Miner (newspaper)

VI. REFERENCES

Abken, P. (1991), "Beyond Plain Vanilla: A Taxonomy of Swaps," Federal Reserve Bank
   of Atlanta *Economic Review* (Mar/Apr): 12–29.
Abken, P. (1994), "Over-the-Counter Financial Derivatives: Risky Business?," Federal
   Reserve Bank of Atlanta *Economic Review* (Mar/Apr): 1–22.
Ackerman, C., McNally, R., and Ravenscraft, D. (1999), "The Performance of Hedge
   Funds: Risk, Return and Incentive," *Journal of Finance* 54: 833–74.
Adler, M. (1983), "Designing Spreads in Forward Foreign Exchange Contracts and
   Foreign Exchange Futures," *Journal of Futures Markets* 3: 355–68.
Adler, M., and Dumas, B. (1984), "Exposure to Currency Risk: Definition and Meas-
   urement," *Financial Management* 13: 41–50.
Adler, M., and Dumas B. (1983), "International Portfolio Choice and Corporation
   Finance: A Synthesis," *Journal of Finance* 38: 925–84.
Adler, M., and Jorion, P. (1992), "Universal Currency Hedges for Global Portfolios,"
   Journal of Portfolio Management 18 (Summer): 28–35.
Adler, M., and Lehman, B. (1983), "Deviations from PPP in the Long Run," *Journal of
   Finance* 38: 1471–1478.
Ahn, M., and Falloon, W. (1991), *Strategic Risk Management* Chicago: Probus.
Aizenman, J. (1984), "Modelling Deviations from PPP," *International Economic Review*
   25: 175–91.
Alexander, C., and Leigh, C. (1997), "On the Covariance Matrices Used in Value at Risk
   Models," *Journal of Derivatives* 5: 50–62.
Alexander, G., and Sharpe, W. (1990), *Investments* (4th ed.), Englewood Cliffs, NJ:
   Prentice-Hall.

Allen, L., and Thurston, T. (1988), "Cash-Futures Arbitrage and Forward-Futures Spreads in the Treasury Bill Markets," *Journal of Futures Markets* 8: 563–73.

Ankli, R. (1982), "The Decline of the Winnipeg Futures Market," *Agricultural History* 56: 272–286.

Antl, B. (ed.) (1986), *Swap Finance* (vol.1 and 2), London: Euromoney.

Arthur Anderson and Company (1998), "Financial Risk Management" (mimeo), Boston: Arthur Anderson.

Archer, S., and Francis, J. (1979), *Portfolio Analysis*, Englewood Cliffs, NJ: Prentice-Hall.

Arnold, L. (1974), *Stochastic Differential Equations*, New York: Wiley.

Avellandea, M., Friedman, C., Holmes, R., and Samperi, D. (1997), "Calibrating vol surfaces via relative-entropy minimization," *Applied Mathematical Finance* 4: 37–64.

Bachelier, L. (1900), "Theorie de la Speculation," translated in P. Cootner, *The Random Character of Stock Prices* Cambridge, Mass: MIT Press, 1964.

Bae, S. and Levy, H. (1994), "The Valuation of Stock Purchase Rights as Call Options," *The Financial Review* 29: 419–440.

Baer, H., France, V., and Moser, J. (1995), "What Does a Clearinghouse Do?" *Derivatives Quarterly* 1: 39–46.

Bahmani-Oskooee, M., and Das, S. (1985), "Transactions Costs and the Interest Parity Theorem," *Journal of Political Economy* 93: 794–9.

Baillie, R., and Myers, R. (1991), "Bivariate GARCH Estimation of the Optimal Commodity Futures Hedge," *Journal of Applied Econometrics* 6: 109–24.

Bakken, H. (1984), "Futures Trading—Origin, Development and Present Economic Status," Futures Trading Seminar.

Ball, C., and Roma, R. (1994), "Stochastic Volatility Option Pricing," *Journal of Financial and Quantitative Analysis* 29: 589–608.

Ball, C., and Torous, W. (1983), "Bond Price Dynamics and Options," *Journal of Financial and Quantitative Analysis* 18: 517–31.

Bank of International Settlements, Basle Committee on Banking Supervision (1996), *Amendment to the Capital Accord to Incorporate Market Risks*, Basle, Switzerland: BIS.

Barbour, V. (1950), *Capitalism in Amsterdam in the 17th Century*, Ann Arbor, MI: University of Michigan Press.

Barone-Adesi, G., and Whaley, R. (1987), "Efficient Analytic Approximation of American Option Values," *Journal of Finance* 42: 301–320.

Baskin, J. (1988), "The Development of Corporate Financial Markets in Britain and the United States, 1600–1914: Overcoming Asymmetric Information," *Business History Review* (Summer): 199–237.

Bates, D. (1996), "Dollar jump fears, 1984–1992: Distributional abnormalities implicit in currency futures options," *Journal of International Money and Finance* 15: 65–103.

Bates, D., and Craine, R. (1999), "Valuing the Futures Market Clearinghouse's Default Exposure During the 1987 Crash." *Journal of Money Credit and Banking* 31: 248–272.

Batten, J., Mellor, R., and Wan, V. (1993), "Foreign exchange risk management practices and products used by Australian firms," *Journal of International Business Studies* (3rd Quarter): 557–73.

Bauman, J., Saratore, S., and Liddle, W., William (1994), "A Practical Framework for Corporate Exposure Management," *Journal of Applied Corporate Finance* 7: 66–72.

Bawa, V., Brown, S., and Klein, R. (1979), *Estimation Risk and Optimal Portfolio Choice*, Amsterdam: North Holland.

Beaver, W., and Parker, G. (1995), *Risk Management*, New York: McGraw-Hill.

Beckers, S. (1981), "Standard Deviations Implied in Option Prices as Predictors of Future Stock Price Variability," *Journal of Banking and Finance* 5: 363–82.

Beidleman, C. (ed.) (1992), *Cross Currency Swaps* New York: Irwin.

Bell, D. (1995), "Risk, Return and Utility," *Management Science* 41 (Jan): 23–30.

Bell, D., and Krasker, W. (1986), "Estimating Hedge Ratios," *Financial Management* 15: 34–9.

Benari, Y. (1991), "When is Hedging Foreign Assets Effective," *Journal of Portfolio Management* 18: 66–71.

Benninga, S., and Blume, M. (1985), "On the Optimality of Portfolio Insurance," *Journal of Finance* 40: 1341–52.

Benninga, S., Eldor, R., and Zilcha, I. (1984), "The Optimal Hedge Ratio in Unbiased Futures Markets," *Journal of Futures Markets* 4: 155–59.

Berg, P., and McGregor, J. (1966), *Elementary Partial Differential Equations*, San Francisco: Holden-Day.

Berkman, H., and Bradbury, M. (1996), "Empirical Evidence on the Corporate Use of Derivatives," *Financial Management* 25: 5–13.

Berkman, H. (1997), "An International Comparison of Derivatives Use," *Financial Management* 26: 69–73.

Bernstein, P. (1992), *Capital Ideas: The Origins of Modern Wall Street*, New York: Free Press.

Bhattacharya, M. (1980), "Empirical Properties of the Black-Scholes Formula Under Ideal Conditions," *Journal of Financial and Quantitative Analysis* 15: 1081–95.

Bierwag, G. (1987), *Duration Analysis: Managing Interest Rate Risk*, Cambridge, MA: Ballinger.

Biger, N., and Hull, J. (1983), "The Valuation of Currency Options," *Financial Management* 12: 24–28.

Billingsley, R., and Chance, D. (1985), "Options Market Efficiency and the Box Spread Strategy," *Financial Review* 20: 287–301.

Bilson, J. (1981), "The Speculative Efficiency Hypothesis," *Journal of Business* 54: 435–451.

Bjerksund, P., and Stensland, G. (1994), "An American Call on the Difference of Two Assets," *International Review of Economics and Finance* 3: 1–26.

Black, F. (1976), "The Pricing of Commodity Contracts," *Journal of Financial Economics* 3: 167–79.

Black, F. (1989), "Universal Hedging: Optimizing Currency Risk and Reward in International Equity Portfolios," *Financial Analysts Journal*, (July/Aug): 16–22.

Black, F. (1989a), "How We Came Up with the Option Formula," *Journal of Portfolio Management* 15: 4–8.

Black, F., and Jones, R. (1986), "Portfolio Insurance for Pension Plans," mimeo (October), Goldman-Sachs Research.

Black, F., and Scholes, M. (1973), "The Pricing of Options and Corporate Liabilities," *Journal of Political Economy* 81: 637–59.

Blaug, M. (1978), *Economic Theory in Retrospect* (2nd ed.), Cambridge, UK: Cambridge University Press.

Bodnar, G. M., Hayt, G. S., Marston, R. C., and Smithson, C. W. (1995), "Wharton Survey of Derivatives Usage by U.S. Non-Financial Firms," *Financial Management* 24: 104–114.

Bodnar, G. M., Hayt, G. S., Marston, R. C., and Smithson, C. W. (1996), "Wharton Survey of Derivatives Usage by U.S. Non-Financial Firms," *Financial Management* 25: 113–133.

Bodnar, G. M., Hayt, G. S., and Marston, R. C. (1998), "1998 Wharton Survey of Derivatives Usage by U.S. Non-Financial Firms," *Financial Management* 27: 70–91.

Bodurtha, J., and Courtadon, G. (1987), "Tests of an American Option Pricing Model on the Foreign Currency Options Market," *Journal of Financial and Quantitative Analysis* 22: 153–67.

Bodurtha, J., and Courtadon, G. (1995), "Probabilities and Values of Early Exercise: Spot and Futures Foreign Currency Options," *Journal of Derivatives* 3: 57–75.

Bollerslev, T., Chou, R., and Kroner, K. (1992), "ARCH Modelling in Finance: A Review of Theory and Empirical Evidence," *Journal of Econometrics* 52: 5–59.

Bond, G., and Thompson, S. (1986), "Optimal Commodity Hedging within the Capital Asset Pricing Model," *Journal of Futures Markets* 6: 421–31.

Bookstaber, R. (1997). "Global Risk Management: Are We Missing the Point," *Journal of Portfolio Management* 23 (Spring): 102–7.

Bookstaber, R. (1986), *Option Pricing and Strategies in Investing* New York: Addison-Wesley.

Bookstaber, R., and Clarke, R. (1983), *Option Strategies for Institutional Investment Management*, London: Addison-Wesley.

Bookstaber, R., and Langsam, R. (1988), "Portfolio Insurance Trading Rules," *Journal of Futures Markets* 8: 15–31.

Boothe, P., and Longworth, D. (1986) "Foreign Exchange Market Efficiency Tests: Implications of Recent Empirical Findings," *Journal of International Money and Finance* 5: 135–52.

Branson, W. (1969), "The Minimum Covered Differential Needed for International Arbitrage Activity," *Journal of Political Economy* 77: 1028–35.

Brealey, R., and Myers, S. (1992). *Principles of Corporate Finance*, New York: McGraw-Hill.

Breeden, D., and Viswanathan, S. (1996), "Why Do Firms Hedge: An Asymmetric Information Model," Unpublished working paper.

Brennan, M., and Trigeorgis, L. (2000), *Project Flexibility, Agency, and Competition: New Developments in the Theory and Application of Real Options* New York: Oxford University Press.

Brennan, M., and Schwartz, E. (1987), "Time Invariant Portfolio Insurance Strategies," UCLA Working Paper, (September).

Brennan, M., and Schwartz, E. (1980), "Analyzing Convertible Bonds," *Journal of Financial and Quantitative Analysis* 15: 907–29.

Brennan, M., and Schwartz, E. (1979), "A Continuous Time Approach to the Pricing of Bonds," *Journal of Banking and Finance* 3: 133–55.

Brennan, M., and Schwartz, E. (1977), "The Valuation of American Put Options," *Journal of Finance* 32 (May): 449–62.

Brennan, M., and Schwartz, E. (1976), "The Pricing of Equity-Linked Life Insurance Policies with an Asset Value Guarantee," *Journal of Financial Economics* 3: 195–213.

Brennan, M. (1958), "The Supply of Storage," *American Economic Review* 47: 50–72.

Brenner, M., Courtadon, G., and Subrahmanyam, M. (1985), "Options on the Spot and Options on Futures," *Journal of Finance* 40: 1303–17.

Brinkman, W. (1984), "The Role and Operation of Clearing Houses," Chap. 3, in Ed., Rothstein, N., *The Handbook of Financial Futures*, New York: McGraw Hill.

British Columbia Securities Commission, "Local Policy Statement 4–1 Commodity Contract Act Registration Requirements".

Brys, E. and Solnick, B. (1992), "Optimal Currency Hedge Ratios and Interest Rate Risk," *Journal of International Money and Finance* 11: 431–446.

Brys, E., Crouhy, M., and Schobel, R. (1991), "The Pricing of Default-Free Interest Rate Cap, Floor, and Collar Agreements," *Journal of Finance* 46: 1879–1893.

Brockett, P., and Kahane, Y. (1992), "Risk, Return, Skewness and Preference," *Management Science* 38 (June): 851–66.

Broehl, W. (1992), *Cargill: Trading the World's Grain*, Hanover, NH: University of New England Press.

Brown, K. (1986), "A Reexamination of the Covered Call Option Strategy for Corporate Cash Management," *Financial Management* 15: 13–17.

Brown, S., Goetzmann, W., and Ibbotson, R. (1999), "Offshore Hedge Funds: Survival and Performance 1989–95," *Journal of Business* 72: 91–117.

Burik, P., and Ennis, R. (1990), "Foreign Bonds in Diversified Portfolios: A Limited Advantage," *Financial Analysts Journal* (Mar./Apr.): 31–40.

Buser, S. (1986), "Laplace Transforms as Present Value Rules: A Note," *Journal of Finance* 41: 243–47.

Caldwell, T. (1995), "Introduction: The Model for Superior Performance," Chap. 1 in Lederman and Klein (Eds.), (1995).

Canina, L., and Figlewski, S. (1993), "The Informational Content of Implied Volatility," *Review of Financial Studies* 6: 659–81.

Capozza, D., and Cornell, B. (1978) "Treasury Bill Pricing in the Spot and Futures Markets," *Review of Economics and Statistics* 60: 513–20.

Capozza, D., and Li, Y. (1994), "The Intensity and Timing of Investment: The Case of Land," *American Economic Review* 79: 125–37.

Carlton, D. (1984), "Futures Markets: Their Purpose, Their History, Their Growth, Their Successes and Failures," *Journal of Futures Markets* 4: 237–71.

Carpenter, J. (1998), "The Exercise and Valuation of Executive Stock Options," *Journal of Financial Economics* 48: 127–58.

Carr, P. (1988), "The Valuation of Sequential Exchange Opportunities," *Journal of Finance* 43: 1235–56.

Castelli, C. (1877), *The Theory of Options in Stocks and Shares* London: Matheison.

Cecchetti, S., Cumby, R., and Figlewsk, S. (1988), "Estimation of the Optimal Futures Hedge," *Review of Economics and Statistics* 70: 623–630.

Chance, D. (1998), *An Introduction to Derivative Securities* (4th ed.), New York: Dryden.

Chance, D. (1988), "Boundary Condition Tests Of Bid And Ask Prices Of Index Calls," *Journal of Financial Research* 11: 21–31.

Chance, D., and Hemler, M. (1993), "The Impact of Delivery Options on Futures Prices: A Survey," *Journal of Futures Markets* 13: 127–156.

Chance, D., and Jordan, J. (1995), "Duration, Convexity and Time as Components of Bond Returns," *Journal of Fixed Income* (September): 88–96.

Cheng, S. (1991), "On the Feasibility of Arbitrage-Based Option Pricing when Stochastic Bond Price Processes are Involved," *Journal of Economic Theory* 53: 185–98.

Chesney, M., and Scott, L. (1989), "Pricing European Currency Options: A Comparison of the Modified Black-Scholes and a Random Variance Model," *Journal of Financial and Quantitative Analysis* 24: 267–84.

Chiang, R., and Okunev, J. (1993), "An Alternative Formulation on the Pricing of Foreign Currency Options," *Journal of Futures Markets* 13: 903–7.

Chiarella, C., El-Hassan, N., and Kucera, A. (1999), "Evaluation of American Option Prices in a Path Integral Framework Using Fourier-Hermite Series Expansions," *Journal of Banking and Finance* 23: 1387–1424.

Chicago Board of Trade (1989), *Commodity Trading Manual* Chicago: Chicago Board of Trade.

Chicago Board of Trade (1981), *Research on Speculation Seminar Report* Chicago: CBT.

Chow, Y., Robbins, H., and Siegmund, D. (1971), *Great Expectations: The Theory of Optimal Stopping*, Boston: Houghton Mifflin.

Christensen, P., and Sorensen, B. (1994), "Duration, Convexity and Time Value," *Journal of Portfolio Management* 20 (Winter): 51–60.

Churchill, R. (1963), *Fourier Series and Boundary Value Problems* New York: McGraw-Hill.

Cita, J., and Lien, D. (1992), "Constructing Accurate Cash Settlement Indices: The Role of Index Specifications," *Journal of Futures Markets* 12: 339–360.

Clinton, K. (1988) "Transactions Costs and Covered Interest Parity," *Journal of Political Economy* 96: 358–70.

Clough, S., and Rapp, R. (1975), *European Economic History* New York: McGraw-Hill.

Conlon, S., and Aquilino, V. (1999), *Principles of Financial Derivatives: U.S. and International Taxation* Boston, MA: Warren, Gorham & Lamont.

Cootner, P. (1964), *The Random Character of Stock Market Prices* Cambridge, Mass.: MIT Press.

Cootner, P. (1960), "Returns to Speculators: Telser vs. Keynes," *Journal of Political Economy* 68: 396–404.

Copeland, T., and Copeland, M. (1999), "Managing Corporate FX Risk: A Value-Maximizing Approach," *Financial Management* 28: 68–75.

Copeland, T., and Weston, J. F. (1988), *Financial Theory and Corporate Policy*, New York: Addison-Wesley.

Corbae, D., and Ouliaris, S. (1988), "Conintegration and Tests of PPP," *Review of Economics and Statistics* 70: 508–11.

Cornell, B. (1979), "Relative Price Changes and Deviations from PPP," *Journal of Banking and Finance* 3: 263–80.

Cornell, B. (1997), "Cash Settlement when the Underlying Securities are Thinly Traded: A Case Study," *Journal of Futures Markets* 17: 855–871.

Cornew, R. (1988), "Commodity Pool Operators and Their Pools: Expenses and Profitability," *Journal of Futures Markets* 8: 617–637.

Corrado, C., and Su, T. (1996), "Skewness and Kurtosis in S&P 500 Index Returns Implied by Option Prices," *Journal of Financial Research* 19 (Summer): 175–92.

Courtault, J., Kabanov, Y., Bru, B., Crépel, P., Lebon, I., and le Marchand, A. (2000), "Louis Bachelier on the Centenary of Théorie de la Spéculation," *Mathematical Finance* 10: 341–53.

Coval, J., and Moskowitz, T. (1999), "Home Bias at Home: Local Equity Preference," *Journal of Finance* 54: 2045–2073.

Cowing, C. (1895), *Populists, plungers, and progressives : a social history of stock and commodity speculation, 1890–1936*, Princeton, N.J.: Princeton University Press, 1965 reprint.

Cox, D., and Miller, H. (1965), *The Theory of Stochastic Processes* London: Chapman & Hall.

Cox, J., Ingersoll, J. and Ross, S. (1981), "The Relationship between Forward Prices and Futures Prices," *Journal of Financial Economics* 9: 321–46.

Cox, J., Ingersoll, J., and Ross, S. (1985), "A Theory of the Term Structure of Interest Rates," *Econometrica* 53 (March): 385–407.

Cox, J., and Ross, S. (1976), "The Valuation of Options for Alternative Stochastic Processes," *Journal of Financial Economics* 3: 145–66.

Cox, J., and Rubinstein, M. (1985), *Option Markets*, Englewood Cliffs, NJ: Prentice-Hall.

Crouhy, M., Galai, D., and Mark, R. (2001), *Risk Management*, New York: McGraw-Hill.

Culp, C. (2001), *The Risk Management Process*, New York: Wiley.

Culp, C., and Miller, M. (1994), "Hedging a Flow of Commodity Deliveries with Futures: Lessons from Metallgesellschaft," *Derivatives Quarterly* (Fall): 7–15.

Culp, C., and Miller, M. (1995a), "Metallgesellschaft and the Economics of Synthetic Storage," *Journal of Applied Corporate Finance* 8: 62–76.

Culp, C., and Miller, M. (1995b), "Hedging the the Theory of Corporate Finance: A Reply to Our Critics," *Journal of Applied Corporate Finance* 8: 121–127.

Culp, C., and Miller, M. (1995c), "Basis Risk and Hedging Strategies: Reply to Mello and Parsons," *Derivatives Quarterly* (Summer): 20–26.

Culp, C., Miller, M., and Neves, A. (1998), "Value at Risk: Uses and Abuses," *Journal of Applied Corporate Finance* 11: 26–38.

Culp, C., and Miller, M. (eds.) (1999), *Corporate Hedging in Theory and Practice: Lessons from Metallgesellschaft* London: Risk Publications.

Cummins, D. (1988), "Risk-Based Premiums for Insurance Guaranty Funds," *Journal of Finance* 43: 823–39.

Cummins, D., Phillips, R., and Smith, S. (1998), "The Rise of Risk Management," Federal Reserve Bank of Atlanta *Economic Review* 30–40.

Cuny, C., and Jorion, P. (1995), "Valuing executive stock options with endogenous departure," *Journal of Accounting and Economics* 20: 193–205.

Danielson, J., Jorgenson, B., and deVries, C. (1998), "The Value of Value-at-Risk: Statistical, Financial and Regulatory Considerations," Federal Reserve Bank of New York *Economic Policy Review*: 1–23.

Danthine, J. (1978), "Information, Futures Prices and Stabilizing Speculation," *Journal of Economic Theory* 17 (Dec.), 418–43.

Das, S. (1994), *Swap Financing* London: IFR Publishing.

Das, S., and Sundaram, R. (1997), "Taming the Skew: Higher Order Moments in Modelling Asset Price Processes in Finance," mimeo, Harvard Business School, (May).

Daves, P., and Ehrhardt, M. (1993), "Liquidity, Reconstitution and the Value of US Treasury Strips," *Journal of Finance* 48: 315–329.

Davutyan, N., and Pippenger, J. (1990), "Testing PPP: Some Evidence on the Effects of Transactions Costs," *Econometric Reviews* 9: 211–40.

Davutyan, N., and Pippenger, J. (1985), "PPP did not Collapse during the 1970's," *American Economic Review* 70: 1151–58.

De Groot, M. (1970), *Optimal Statistical Decisions*, New York: McGraw-Hill.

de la Vega, J. (1688). *Confusion de Confusiones* reprinted in M. Fridson (Ed.) (1996).

De Roon, F., and Veld, C. (1996), "Put-Call Parity and the Value of Early Exercise for Put Options on a Performance Index," *Journal of Futures Markets* 16: 71–80.

De Roon, F., Nijman, T., and Veld, C. (1998), "Pricing term structure risk in futures markets," *Journal of Financial and Quantitative Analysis* 33: 139–57.

de Roover, R. (1944), "What is Dry Exchange? A Contribution to the Study of English Mercantilism," *Journal of Political Economy* 52: 250–66; reprinted in J. Kirshner (ed.) (1974, ch. 4).

de Roover, R. (1948), *Banking and Credit in Medieval Bruges*, Cambridge, Mass.: Harvard University Press.

de Roover, R. (1949), *Gresham on Foreign Exchange*, London: Harvard University Press.

Deardorff, A. (1979), "One-Way Arbitrage and Its Implications for the Foreign Exchange Market," *Journal of Political Economy* 87: 351–64.

DeMarzo, P., and Duffie, D. (1995), "Corporate Incentives for Hedging and Hedge Accounting," *Review of Financial Studies* 8: 743–772.

Derman, E., and Kani, I. (1994), "Riding the Smile," *Risk* 7: 32–9.

Dhrymes, P. (1974), *Econometrics, Statistical Foundations and Applications* New York: Springer-Verlag.

Diacogiannis, G. (1994), "Three-parameter Asset Pricing," *Managerial and Decision Economics* 15: 149–58.

Dickson, P. (1967), *The Financial Revolution in England*, New York: St. Martin's Press.

Dixit, A. (1993), *The Art of Smooth Pasting*, New York: Harwood.

Dixit, A., and Pindyck, R. (1994), *Investment Under Uncertainty*, Princeton: Princeton UP.

Dolde, W. (1993), "The Trajectory of Corporate Financial Risk Management," *Journal of Applied Corporate Finance*, 6: 33–41.

Doherty, N. (1985), *Corporate Risk Management* New York: McGraw-Hill.

Doherty, N., and Garven, J. (1986), "Price Regulation in Property-Liability Insurance," *Journal of Finance* 41: 1031–50.

Dooley, M., and Isard, P. (1980), "Capital Controls, Political Risk and Deviations From Interest-Rate Parity," *Journal of Political Economy* 88: 370–84.

Dowd, K. (1998), *Beyond Value at Risk, The New Science of Risk Management*, New York: Wiley.

Duan, S. (1995), "The GARCH Option Pricing Model," *Mathematical Finance* 5: 13–32.

Dubofsky, D. (1992), *Options and Financial Futures: Valuation and Uses*, New York: McGraw-Hill.

Dubofsky, D. and Miller, T. (2002), *Derivatives: Valuation and Risk Management*, (in press), New York: Oxford University Press.

Dufey, G., and Srinivasulu, S. (1983), "The Case for Corporate Management of Foreign Exchange Risk," *Financial Management* 12: 54–62.

Duffey and Giddy, I. (1979), *The International Money Market* Englewood Cliffs, NJ: Prentice Hall.

Duffie, D. (1989), *Futures Markets*, Englewood Cliffs, NJ: Prentice Hall.

Duffie, D., and Pan, J. (1997), "An Overview of Value at Risk," *Journal of Derivatives* 5: 7–49.

Dufresne, D. (2000), "Laguerre Series for Asian and Other Options," *Mathematical Finance* 10: 407–28.

Duguid, C. (1901), *The Story of the Stock Exchange*, London: Grant and Richards.

Dumas, B., Fleming, J., Whalley, R. (1998), "Implied Volatility Functions: Empirical Tests," *Journal of Finance* 53: 2059–2106.

Dumitru, M. (1999), "Implied Volatility in Currency Futures Options," MBA Thesis, Simon Fraser University.

Dunbar, N. (2000), *Inventing Money, The Story of Long-Term Capital Management and the Legends Behind It*, New York: Wiley.

Dym, S. (1988), "Money Market Cash-Futures Relationships," Salomon Bros. CSFI Working Paper, n.454.

Dym, S. (1992), "Global and Local Components of Foreign Bond Risk," *Financial Analysts Journal*: 83–91.

Eades, K., Hess, P., Kim, E., and Han, E. (1984), "On Interpreting Security Returns During the Ex-Dividend Period," *Journal of Financial Economics*, 13: 3–34

Eaker, M., et.al. (1991), "Investment in Foreign Equities: Diversification, Hedging and Risk," *Journal of Multinational Financial Management* 1: 1–21.

Eaker, M., Grant, D., and Woodard, N. (1993), "A Multinational Examination of International Equity and Bond Investment with Currency Hedging," *Journal of Futures Markets* 13: 313–24.

Easterwood, J., and Senchack, A. (Fall 1986), "Arbitrage Opportunities with TBill/ TBond Futures Combinations," *Journal of Futures Markets* 6: 433–42.

Ederington, L. (1979), "The Hedging Performance of the New Futures Markets," *Journal of Finance* 34: 157–70.

Edwards, F. (1983), "The Clearing Association in Futures Markets: Guarantor and Regulator," *Journal of Futures Markets* 3: 369–92.

Edwards, F. (1995), "Derivatives can be Hazardous to Your Health: The Case of Metallgesellschaft," *Derivatives Quarterly* 1: 8–17.

Edwards, F., and Caglayan, M. (2001), "Hedge Fund and Commodity Fund Investments in Bull and Bear Markets," *Journal of Portfolio Management* 27: 97–108.

Edwards, F., and Canter, M. (1995), "The Collapse of Metallgesellschaft: Unhedgable Risks, Poor Hedging Strategy, or Just Bad Luck," *Journal of Applied Corporate Finance* 8: 86–105.

Edwards, F., and Liew, J. (1999), "Hedge Funds versus Managed Futures as Asset Classes," *Journal of Derivatives* 7: 45–64.

Edwards, F., and Ma, C. (1988), "Commodity Pool Performance: Is the Information Contained in Pool Prosepectuses Useful?" *Journal of Futures Markets* 8: 589–616.

Einzig, P. (1970), *The History of Foreign Exchange* London: Macmillan.

Einzig, P. (1937), *The Theory of Forward Exchange* London: Macmillan.

Elton, E., and Gruber, M. (1995), *Modern Portfolio Theory and Investment Analysis* (5th ed.), New York: Wiley.

Elton, E., Gruber, M., and Rentzler, J. (1987), "Professionally Managed. Publicly Traded Commodity Funds," *Journal of Business* 60: 175–200.

Elton, E., and Gruber, M. (1995), *Modern Portfolio Theory and Investment Analysis* (5th ed.), New York: John Wiley.

Emery, H. (1896), *Speculation on the Stock and Produce Exchanges of the United States* New York: AMS Press reprint (1968).

Engle, R. (1982), "Autoregressive Conditional Heterskedasticity, with Estimates of the Variance of United Kingdom Inflation," *Econometrica* 50: 987–1007.

Esty, B., Tufano, P., and Headley, J. (1994), "Banc One Corporation: Asset and Liability Management," *Journal of Applied Corporate Finance* 7: 33–65.

Eun, C., and Resnick, B. (1994), "International Diversification of Investment Portfolios: U.S. and Japanese Perspectives," *Management Science* 40: 140–161.

Eun, C., and Resnick, B. (1988), "Exchange Rate Uncertainty, Forward Contracts and International Portfolio Selection," *Journal of Finance* 43: 197–215.

Eytan, T., and Harpaz, G. (1986), "The Pricing of Futures and Options Contracts on the Value Line Index," *Journal of Finance* 41: 843–855.

Fabozzi, F. (1993), *Bond Markets: Analysis and Strategies*, Englewood Cliffs, NJ: Prentice-Hall.

Fabozzi, B., and Zarb, F. (1984), *Handbook of Financial Markets: Securities, Options and Futures* Chicago: Probus.

Falloon, W. (1998), *Market Maker: A Sesquicentennial Look at the Chicago Board of Trade*, Chicago: CBT.

Fay, S. (1982), *Beyond Greed*, New York: The Viking Press.

Feder, G., Just, R., and Schmitz, A. (1980), "Futures Markets and the Theory of the Firm Under Price Uncertainty," *Quarterly Journal of Economics* 94: (March): 317–28.

Feller, W. (1968), *An Introduction to Probability Theory and Its Applications* Vol.1, New York: John Wiley.

Ferri, M., Goldstein, S., and Oberhelman, H. (1985) "The Performance of the When-Issued Market for T-bills," *Journal of Portfolio Management* 11: 57–61.

Filatov, V., and Rappoport, P. (1992), "Is Complete Hedging Optimal for International Bond Portfolios?," *Financial Analysts Journal* (July/August): 37–47.

Financial Accounting Standards Board (2000), "Accounting For Certain Derivative Instruments and Certain Hedging Activities – an Amendment of FASB Statement No. 133," Statement of Financial Accounting Standard No. 138 (June), Stamford, Conn.: FASB.

Financial Accounting Standards Board (1998), "Accounting For Derivatives and Hedging Activities," Statement of Financial Accounting Standards No. 133 (June), Stamford, Conn.: FASB.

Financial Accounting Standards Board (1995), "Accounting for Stock Based Compensation," Statement of Financial Accounting Standard No. 123, Stamford, Conn.: FASB.

Finucane, T. (1991), "Put-Call Parity and Expected Returns," *Journal of Financial and Quantitative Analysis* 26: 445–57.

Fischer, S. (1975), "The Demand for Index Bonds," *Journal of Political Economy* 83: 509–534.

Fite, D., and Pfleiderer, P. (1995), "Should Firms Use Derivatives to Manage Risk?," in *Risk Management: Problems and Solutions*, edited by William H. Beaver and George Parker. New York: McGraw Hill.

Flood, E., and Lessard, D. (1986), "On the Measurement of Operating Exposure to Exchange Rates: A Conceptual Approach," *Financial Management* 15: 25–36.

Fosburg, R., and Madura, J. (1991), "Risk Reduction Benefits from International Diversification: A Reassessment," *Journal of Multinational Financial Management* 1: 35–42.

Fowke, V. C. (1957), *The National Policy and the Wheat Economy*, Toronto: University of Toronto Press.

Franklin, C., and Colberg, M. (1958), "Puts and Calls: A Factual Survey," *Journal of Finance* 13: 21–34.

Frenkel, J. (1978), "PPP: Doctrinal Perspective from the 1920's," *Journal of International Economics* 8 (May): 161–91.

Frenkel, J. (1981), "The Collapse of Purchasing Power Parities during the 1970's," *European Economic Review* 12: 145–65.

Frenkel, J., and Levich, R. (1975), "Covered Interest Arbitrage: Unexploited Profits," *Journal of Political Economy* 83: 325–38.

Frenkel, J., and Levich, R. (1977), "Transactions Costs and Interest Arbitrage: Tranquil versus Turbulent Periods," *Journal of Political Economy* 85: 1209–66.

Frenkel, J., and Levich, R. (1981), "Covered Interest Arbitrage in the 1970's," *Economic Letters* 8: 267–74.

Fridson, M (ed.) (1996), *Extraordinary Popular Delusions . . . and Confusion des Confusions*, New York: Wiley.

Friesen, G. (1984), *The Canadian Prairies: A History*, Toronto: University of Toronto Press.

Froot, K., and Stein, J. (1998), "Risk Management, Capital Budgeting, and Capital Structure for Financial Institutions: An Integrated Approach," *Journal of Financial Economics* 47: 55–82.

Froot, K., Scharfstein, D., and Stein, J. (1994) "A Framework for Risk Management," *Journal of Applied Corporate Finance* 7: 22–32.

Froot, K., Scharfstein, D., and Stein, J. (1993), "Risk Management: Coordinating Corporate Investment and Financing Policies," *Journal of Finance* 48: 1629–1658.

Fung, W., and Hsieh, D. (2000), "Performance Characteristics of Hedge Funds and Commodity Funds: Natural vs. Spurious Biases," *Journal of Financial and Quantitative Analysis* 35: 291–307.

Fung, W., and Hsieh, D. (1997), "Empirical Characteristics of Dynamic Trading Strategies," *Review of Financial Studies* 10: 275–302.

Futures Industry Association (1984), *An Introduction to Futures Markets* Washington, D.C.

Gagnon, L. (1994), "Empirical Investigation of the Canadian Government Bond Option Market," *Canadian Journal of Administrative Sciences* 11.

Galai, D. (1977), "Tests of Market Efficiency and the Chicago Board Options Exchange," *Journal of Business* 50: 167–97.

Garber, P. (1989), "Tulipmania," *Journal of Political Economy* 97: 535–560.

Garber, P. (1989), "Who Put the Mania in Tulipmania?," *Journal of Portfolio Management* 60: 53–60.

Garman, M., and Kohlhagen, S. (December 1983), "Foreign Currency Option Values," *Journal of International Money and Finance* 2: 231–37.

Gastineau, G. (1995), "Some Derivatives Accounting Issues," *Journal of Derivatives* 3: 73–78.

Gatto, M., Geske, R., Litzenberger, R., and Sosin, H. (1980), "Mutual Fund Insurance," *Journal of Financial Economics* 8: 283–317.

Gay, G. D., and Nam, J. (1998), "The Underinvestment Problem and Corporate Derivatives Use," *Financial Management* 27: 53–69.

Géczy, C., Minton, B., and Shrand, C. (1997), "Why Firms Use Currency Derivatives," *Journal of Finance* 52: 1323–54.

Gehr, A., and T. Martell (1994), "Derivative Usage in the Gold Market and its Impact on Spot Gold," *Journal of Derivatives* 1: 68–79.

Geman, H., and Yor, M. (1993), "Bessel Processes, Asian Options and Perpetuities," *Mathematical Finance* 3 (Oct.): 349–75.

Gemmill, G. (1985), "Optimal Hedging on Futures Markets for Commodity-Exporting Nations," *European Economic Review* 27: 243–61.

Gendreau, B. (1985) "Carrying Costs and Treasury Bill Futures," *Journal of Portfolio Management* 12: 58–64.

Gerber, H. (1999), "From Ruin Theory to Pricing Reset Guarantees and Perpetual Put Options," *Insurance, Mathematics & Economics* 24: 3–15.

Gerber, H. (1996), "Acturarial Bridges to Dynamic Hedging and Option Pricing," *Insurance, Mathematics & Economics* 18: 183–219.

Gerber, H., and Shiu, E. (1994a), "From perpetual strangles to Russian options"; *Insurance, Mathematics & Economics* 15: 121–7.

Gerber, H., and Shiu, E. (1994b), "Martingale Approach to Pricing Perpetual American Options," *ASTIN Bulletin*: 195–220.

Geske, R. (1979a), "The Valuation of Compound Options," *Journal of Financial Economics* 7: 63–81.

Geske, R. (1979b), "A Note on an Analytical Valuation Formula for Unprotected American Call Options on Stocks with Known Dividends," *Journal of Financial Economics* 7: 375–80.

Geske, R., and Johnson, H. (1984), "The American Put Valued Analytically," *Journal of Finance* 39: 1511–24.

Geske, R., and Roll, R. (1984), "On Valuing American Call Options with the Black-Scholes Formula," *Journal of Finance* 39: 443–55.

Geske, R., and Shastri, K. (1985), "The Early Exercise of American Puts," *Journal of Banking and Finance* 9: 207–220.

Gibson, R. (1991), *Option Valuation*, New York: McGraw-Hill.

Gibson, R., and Schwartz, E. (1990), "Stochastic Convenience Yield and the Pricing of Oil Contingent Claims," *Journal of Finance* 45: 959–976.

Gidlow, R. (1983), "Hedging Policies of the South African Gold Mining Industry," *South African Journal of Economics* 5: 270–82.

Gihman, I., and Skorohod, A. (1975), *The Theory of Stochastic Processes* Vol. 1, New York: Springer-Verlag.

Gihman, I., and Skorohod, A. (1979), *The Theory of Stochastic Processes* Vol. 2, New York: Springer-Verlag.

Glen, J., and Jorion, P. (1993), "Currency Hedging for International Portfolios," *Journal of Finance* 48: 1865–1886.

Godfrey, S., and Espinosa, R. (1998), "Value-at-Risk and Corporate Valuation," *Journal of Applied Corporate Finance* 11: 108–115.

Gold, G. (1975), *Modern Commodity Futures Trading*, New York: Commodity Research Bureau.

Gold Fields Mineral Services (1991), *Gold 1991*, London.

Goldenberg, D. (1991), "A Unified Method for Pricing Options on Diffusion Processes," *Journal of Financial Economics* 29: 3–34.

Goldberg, Lawrence C., and Hachey, G. A. (1992), "Price Volatility and Margin Requirements in Foreign Exchange Futures," *Journal of International Money and Finance* 11: 328–339.

Goldberger, A. (1964), *Econometric Theory*, New York: Wiley.

Goldman, M., Sosin, H., and Gatto, M. (1979), "Path Dependent Options: Buy at the Low, Sell at the High," *Journal of Finance* 34: 1111–28.

Gombola, M., Roenfeldt, R., and Cooley, P. (1978), "Spreading Strategies in CBOE Options: Evidence on Market Performance," *Journal of Financial Research* 1: 35–44.

Grabbe, J. O. (1996), *International Financial Markets* (3rd ed.), Englewood Cliffs, NJ: Prentice-Hall.

Grabbe, J. O. (1983), "The Pricing of Put and Call Options on Foreign Exchange," *Journal of International Money and Finance* 2: 239–54.

Grauer, R., and Hakansson, N. (1987), "Gains from International Diversification: 1968–85," *Journal of Finance* 42: 721–39.

Grauer, R., and Hakansson, N. (1992), "Stein and CAPM Estimators of the Means in Asset Allocation: A Case of Mixed Success," SFU Working Paper, (January).

Greenspan, A. (1996), "Remarks at the Federation of Bankers Associations of Japan," Tokyo, Japan.

Gray, R. (1981), "Economic Evidence in Manipulation Cases," *Research on Speculation Seminar Report*, Chicago Board of Trade: 108–114.

Gregory, A., and McCurdy, T. (1984) "Testing the Unbiasedness Hypothesis in the Forward Foreign Exchange Market: A Specification Analysis," *Journal of International Money and Finance* 3: 357–68.

Gregory, D., and Livingston, M. (1992), "Development of the Market for US Treasury STRIPS," *Financial Analysts Journal* (March/April): 68–74.

Grossman, S. (1988), "An Analysis of the Implications for Stock and Futures Price Volatility of Program Trading and Dynamic Hedging Strategies," *Journal of Business* 61: 275–298.

Grubel, H. (1966), *Forward Exchange, Speculation and the International Flow of Capital* Stanford, CA: Stanford University Press.

Grubel, H. (1968), "Internationally Diversified Portfolios: Welfare Gains and Capital Flows," *American Economic Review* 58: 1299–1314.

Hakkio, C. (1984), "A reexamination of PPP," *Journal of International Economics* 17: 265–78.

Haley, C., and Schall, L. (1979), *The Theory of Financial Decisions*, New York: McGraw-Hill.

Hansen, L., and Hodrick, R. (1980), "Forward Exchanges Rates as Optimal Predictors of Futures Spot Exchange Rates," *Journal of Political Economy* 88: 829–53.

Harris, L., Sofianos, G., and Shapiro, J. (1994), "Program Trading and Intraday Volatility," *Review of Financial Studies* 7: 653–686.

Hassett, M., Sears, S., and Trennepohl, G. (1985), "Asset Preference, Skewness and the Measurement of Expected Utility," *Journal of Economics and Business* 37: 35–47.

Hazell, P., Pomareda, C., and Valdes, A. (1986), *Crop Insurance for Agricultural Development*, Baltimore: Johns Hopkins.

Heaney, J., and Poitras, G. (1994), "Securities Markets, Diffusion State Spaces and the Implicit Preference Function," *Journal of Financial and Quantitative Analysis* 29: 223–239.

Heaney, J., and Poitras, G. (1991), "Estimation of the Optimal Hedge Ratio, Expected Utility, and Ordinary Least Squares Regression," *Journal of Futures Markets* 11: 603–612.

Hegde, S., and Branch, B. (1985) "An Empirical Analysis of Arbitrage Opportunities in the Treasury Bill Futures Market," *Journal of Futures Markets* 3: 407–24.

Hegde, S., and Macdonald, B. (1986) "On the Informational Role of Treasury Bill Futures." *Journal of Futures Markets* 6: 629–43.

Hemler, M. (1997), "Box Spread Arbitrage Profits Following the 1987 Market Crash: Real or Illusory?," *Journal of Financial and Quantitative Analysis* 32: 71–90.

Hemler. M. (1990), "The Quality Delivery Option In Treasury Bond Futures Contracts," *Journal of Finance* 45: 1565–1586.

Hemmer, T., Matsunaga, S., and Shevlin, T. (1994), "Estimating the 'fair value' of employee stock options with expected early exercise," *Accounting Horizons* 8: 23–42.

Henderson, J., and Quandt, R. (1980), *Microeconomic Theory*, New York: McGraw-Hill.

Hendricks, D., and Hirtle, B. (1997), "Bank Capital Requirements for Market Risks: The Internal Models Approach," Federal Reserve Bank of New York *Economic Policy Review* (December): 1–12.

Herbst, A., Kare, D., and Caples, S. (1989), "Hedging Effectiveness and Minimum Risk Hedge Ratios in the Presence of Autocorrelation," *Journal of Futures Markets* 9: 185–97.

Heston, S. (1993), "A Closed Form Solution for Options with Stochastic Volatility with Application to Bond and Currency Options," *Review of Financial Studies* 6: 327–43.

Hexton, R. (1989), *Dealing in Traded Options*, Toronto: Prentice Hall.

Heynen, R. (1994), "An Empirical Investigation of Observed Smile Patterns," *Review of Futures Markets* 13: 317–354.

Heynen, R., Kemna, A., and Vorst, T. (1994), "Analysis of the Term Structure of Implied Volatilities," *Journal of Financial and Quantitative Analysis* 29: 31–56.

Hicks, J. D. (1961), *The Populist Revolt: A History of the Farmers' Alliance and the People's Party*, Lincoln, Neb.: University of Nebraska Press.

Hicks, Sir J. (1946), *Value and Capital*, Oxford, UK: Clarendon Press.

Hieronymous, T. (1977), *The Economics of Futures Trading* (2nd ed.), New York: Commodity Research Bureau.

Hietala, R. (1994), "The Efficiency of the Finnish Market for Rights Issues," *Journal of Banking and Finance* 18: 895–920.

Hill, J., and Schneeweis, T. (1982), "The Hedging Effectiveness of Foreign Currency Futures," *Journal of Financial Research* 6: 95–104.

Hill, J., and Jones, F. (1988), "Equity Trading, Program Trading, Portfolio Insurance, Computer Trading, and All That," *Financial Analysts Journal* 44: 29–38.

Hilliard, J., Madura, J., and Tucker, A. (1991), "Currency Option Pricing with Stochastic Domestic and Foreign Interest Rates," *Journal of Financial and Quantitative Analysis* 26: 139–151.

Horowitz, I. (1998), "Will a risk-averse decision maker ever really prefer an unfair gamble," *Decision Sciences* 29: 517–20.

Houghton, J. (1692–1703), *A Collection for Improvement of Husbandry and Trade*, London: Taylor, Hindmarsh, Clavell, Rogers and Brown; reprinted by Gregg International Publishers (1969).

Houthakker, H. (1968), "Normal Backwardation," in J. N. Wolfe (Ed.), *Value, Capital and Growth*, Edinburgh: Edinburgh University Press.

Houthakker, H. (1957), "Can Speculators Forecast Prices?," *Review of Economics and Statistics* 39: 156–66.

Howard, C. (1982), "Are T-bill Futures Good Forecasters of Interest Rates," *Journal of Futures Markets* 1: 305–15.

Howtan, S., and Perfect, S. (1998), "Currency and Interest-Rate Derivatives Use in US Firms," *Financial Management* 27: 111–121.

Hsieh, D. (1988), "Comments on 'Hedging Canadian Treasury Bills with US Money Market Futures'," *Review of Futures Markets* 7: 192–195.

Huddart, S., and Lang, M. (1996), "Employee stock option exercises: An empirical analysis," *Journal of Accounting and Economics* 21: 5–43.

Hull, J. (2000), *Options, Futures and Other Derivatives* (4th ed.), Prentice-Hall.

Hull, J. (1989), "Assessing Credit Risk in a Financial Institution's Off-Balance Sheet Commitments," *Journal of Financial and Quantitative Analysis* 24: 489–502.

Hull, J., and White, A. (1998), "Value at Risk when Daily Changes in Market Variables are not Normally Distributed," *Journal of Derivatives* 6: 9–18.

Hull, J., and White, A. (1988a), "An Analysis of the Bias in Option Pricing Caused by Stochastic Volatility," *Advances in Futures and Options Research* 3: 27–61.

Hull, J., and White, A. (1988b), "The Use of the Control Variate Technique in Option Pricing," *Journal of Financial and Quantitative Analysis* 23: 237–51.

Hull, J., and White, A. (1987), "Hedging the Risks from Writing Foreign Currency Options," *Journal of International Money and Finance* 6: 131–52.

Hurt, H. (1981), *Texas Rich*, New York: Norton.

Husted, S., and Kitchen, J. (1985), "Some Evidence of the International Transmission of US Money Supply Announcements," *Journal of Money, Credit and Banking* 17: 456–66.

Ibbotson, R., et al. (1982), "International Equity and Bond Returns," *Financial Analysts Journal* (July/August): 61–83.

Iben, B. (1992), "The Role of Covered Interest Arbitrage in the Pricing of Cross Currency Swaps," in Beidleman, *Cross Currency Swaps*, Homewood, Ill., Irwin: 400–16.

Ingersoll, J. (1987), *The Theory of Financial Decision Making*, Totawa, NJ: Rowan and Littlefield.

International Financing Corporation (1997), *Emerging Markets Factbook*, Washington, D.C.: International Financing Corporation.

Irwin, H. (1954), *Evolution of Futures Trading*, Madison, Wis.: Mimir Publishing.

Irwin, S., and Brorsen, W. (1985), "Public Futures Funds," *Journal of Futures Markets* 5: 149–172.

Irwin, S., Krukemyer, T., and Zulauf, C. (1993), "Investment Performance of Public Commodity Pools: 1979–1990," *Journal of Futures Markets* 13: 799–820.

Jacka, S. (1991), "Optimal Stopping and the American Put," *Mathematical Finance* 1: 1–14.

Jackson, P., Maude, D., and Perraudin, W. (1997), "Bank Capital and Value at Risk," *Journal of Derivatives* 5: 73–111.

Jackwerth, J., and Rubinstein, M. (1996), "Recovering Probability Distributions from Option Prices," *Journal of Finance* 51: 1611–31.

Jacobs, R., and Jones, R. (1980), "The Treasury-Bill Futures Market," *Journal of Political Economy* 88: 699–721.

Jarrow, R., and Rudd, A. (1983), *Option Pricing*, Homewood, Ill.: Irwin.

Jarrow, R., and Rudd, A. (1982), "Approximate Option Valuation for Arbitrary Stochastic Processes," *Journal of Financial Economics* 10: 347–69.

Jarrow, R., and Turnbull, S. (2000), *Derivative Securities* (2nd ed.), Cincinnati: Southwestern.

Jarrow, R., and Turnbull, S. (1996), *Derivative Securities*, Cincinnati: Southwestern.

Jarrow, R., and Oldfield, G. (1981), "Forward Contracts and Futures Contracts," *Journal of Financial Economics* 9: 373–382.

Jarrow, R., and Wiggins, J. (1989), "Option Pricing and Implicit Volatilities: A Review and a New Perspective," *Journal of Economic Surveys* 3: 59–81.

Johnson, L. (1960), "The Theory of Hedging and Speculation in Commodity Futures," *Review of Economic Studies* 27: 139–51.

Johnson, P. (1981), "Commodity Market Manipulation," reprinted in R. Gray (Ed.), *Research on Speculation*, Chicago: Chicago Board of Trade.

Johnson, R., Zulauf, C., Irwin, S., and Gerlow, M. (1991), "The Soybean Complex Spread: An Examination of Market Efficiency from the Viewpoint of the Production Process," *Journal of Futures Markets* 11: 25–37.

Jones, F. (1981), "Spreads: Tails, Turtles and All That," *Journal of Futures Markets* 1: 565–96.

Jorion, P. (2001), *Value at Risk* (2nd ed.), New York: McGraw-Hill.

Jorion, P. (1997), "Lessons from the Orange County Bankruptcy," *Journal of Derivatives* 5: 61–66.

Jorion, P. (1995), *Big Bets Gone Bad, Derivatives and Bankruptcy in Orange County*, New York: Academic Press.

Jorion, P. (1991), "Bayesian and CAPM Estimators of the Means: Implications for Portfolio Selection," *Journal of Banking and Finance* 15: 717–27.

Jorion, P. (1989), "Asset Allocation with Hedged and Unhedged Foreign Stocks and Bonds," *Journal of Portfolio Management* 15 (Summer): 49–54.

Jorion, P. (1985), "International Portfolio Diversification with Estimation Risk," *Journal of Business* 58: 259–78.

Jorion, P., and Goetzmann, W. (1999), "Global Stock Markets in the Twentieth Century," *Journal of Finance* 54: 953–80.

Jorion, P., and Stoughton, N. (1989), "An Empirical Investigation of the Early Exercise Premium in Foreign Currency Options," *Journal of Futures Markets* 5: 365–75.

J. P. Morgan (1996), *Riskmetrics Technical Model*, New York: J.P. Morgan.

Ju, X., and Pearson, N. (1999), "Using Value-at-Risk to Control Risk Taking: How Wrong Can You Be?" *Journal of Risk* 1: 5–36.

Kairys, J., and Varerio, N. (1997), "The Market for Equity Options in the 1870s," *Journal of Finance* 52: 1707–1723.

Kamara, A., and Siegel, A. (1987), "Optimal Hedging in Futures Markets with Multiple Delivery Specifications," *Journal of Finance* 42: 1007–1021.

Kamara, A., Miller, T., and Siegel, A. (1992). "The Effect of Futures Trading on the Stability of Standard and Poor 500 Returns," *Journal of Futures Markets* 12: 645–658.

Karatzas, I., and Shreve, S. (1988), *Brownian Motion and Stochastic Calculus*, New York: Springer-Verlag.

Karlin, S., and Taylor, H. (1975), *A First Course in Stochastic Processes* (2nd ed.), New York: Academic Press.

Karlin, S., and Taylor, H. (1981), *A Second Course in Stochastic Processes*, New York: Academic Press.

Kawaller, I., and Koch, T. (1984), "Cash-and-Carry Trading and the Pricing of Treasury Bill Futures," *Journal of Futures Markets* 4: 115–23.

Kawaller, I., and Koch, T. (1992), "A Tactical Substitution Rule for Interest Rate Hedging," *Financial Analysts Journal*, (Sept./Oct.): 44–48.

Kemna, A., and Vorst, A. (1990), "A Price Method for Options Based Upon Average Asset Values," *Journal of Banking and Finance* 14: 113–29.

Keynes, J.M. (1923), *Tract on Monetary Reform*, London: Macmillan.

Keynes, J.M. (1936), *The General Theory of Employment, Interest and Money*, London: Macmillan.

Kilcollin, T. (1982), "Tandem T-Bill and CD Spreads," *Journal of Futures Markets* 2: 51–61.

Kim, I. (1990), "The Analytic Valuation of American Options," *Review of Financial Studies* 3: 545–72.

Klemkosky, R., and Resnick, B. (1992), "A Note on the No Premature Exercise Condition of Dividend Payout Unprotected American Call Options: A Clarification," *Journal of Banking & Finance* 16 (April): 373–379.

Klemkosky, R., and Resnick, B. (1980), "An Ex-Ante Analysis of Put-Call Parity," *Journal of Financial Economics* 8: 363–78.

Klemkosky, R., and Resnick, B. (1979), "Put-Call Parity and Market Efficiency," *Journal of Finance* 34: 1141–55.

Klein, R., and Lederman, J. (1995), *Hedge Funds: Investment and Portfolio Strategies for the Institutional Investor*, New York: McGraw-Hill.

Knight, F. (1921), *Risk, Uncertainty and Profit*, New York: Houghton Mifflin.

Kolb, F. R. (1988), *Futures Markets* Chicago, Scott-Foresman.

Koppenhaver, G. (1987), "Futures Market Regulation," *Economic Perspectives* 11 (Jan./Feb.): 3–15.

Koski, J., and Pontiff, J. (1999), "How are Derivatives Used? Evidence from the Mutual Fund Industry," *Journal of Finance* 54: 791–816.

Kramer, A. (1987), *Taxation of Securities, Commodities and Options*, New York: Wiley.

Kraus, A., and Litzenberger, R. (1976), "Skewness Preference and the Valuation of Risk Assets," *Journal of Finance* 31: 1085–1100.

Kreicher, L. (1982), "Eurodollar Arbitrage," *Federal Reserve Bank of New York Quarterly Review*, (Summer): 10–21.

Kroll, Y., Levy, H., and Markowitz, H. (1984), "Mean-Variance versus Direct Utility Maximization," *Journal of Finance* 39: 47–61.

Kroner, K., and Sultan (1993), "Time Varying Distributions and Dynamic Hedging with Foreign Currency Futures." *Journal of Financial and Quantitative Analysis* 28: 535–552.

Kupiec, P. (1995), "Techniques for Verifying the Accuracy of Risk Measurement Models," *Journal of Derivatives* 3: 73–84.

Kupiec, P. (1998), "Stress Testing in a Value at Risk Framework," *Journal of Derivatives* 6: 7–24.

Kuprianov, A. (1995), "Derivatives Debacles," *Federal Reserve Bank of Richmond Economic Quarterly* (Fall): 1–38.

Lamoureux, C., and Lastrapes, W. (1993), "Forecasting Stock-Return Variance: Towards an Understanding of Stochastic Implied Volatilities," *Review of Financial Studies* 6: 293–326.

Landau, M., and Wolkowitz, B. (1987), "Spread Trading with Interest Rate Futures," chap. 46 in F. Fabozzi and I. Pollack (Eds.), *Handbook of Fixed Income Securities*, (Homewood, Ill.: Dow-Jones Irwin).

Latane, H., and Rendleman, R. (1976), "Standard Deviations of Stock Price Ratios Implied in Option Prices," *Journal of Finance* 31: 369–381.

Lauterbach, B., and Schultz, P. (1990), "Pricing Warrants: An Empirical Study of the Black-Scholes Model and its Alternatives," *Journal of Finance* 45: 1181–1209.

Layard and Walters (1979), *Microeconomic Theory*, New York: McGraw-Hill.

Lederman, J., and Klein, R. (Eds.) (1995), *Hedge, Funds* New York: McGraw-Hill.

Leitch, G., and Tanner, J. (1991), "Economic Forecast Evaluation: Profits Versus the Conventional Error Measures," *American Economic Review* 81: 580–61.

Leland, H. (1980), "Who Should Buy Portfolio Insurance," *Journal of Finance* 35: 581–96.

Lessard, D. (1976), "World, Country and Industry Relationships in Equity Returns: Implications for Risk Reduction through International Diversification," *Financial Analysts Journal* (Jan./Feb.): 32–38.

Leuthold, R., Junkus, J., and Cordier, J. (1989), *The Theory and Practice of Futures Markets*, Lexington, Mass.: Lexington Books.

Levi, M., and Sercu, P. (1991), "Erroneous and Valid Reasons for Hedging Foreign Exchange Rate Exposure," *Journal of Multinational Financial Management* 1: 25–37.

Levine, A. (1987), "Open Market or 'Orderly Marketing': The Winnipeg Grain Exchange and the Wheat Pools, 1923–29," *Agricultural History* 61: 50–69.

Levine, A. (1985), "The Voice of the Canadian Grain Trade: A History of the Winnipeg Grain Exchange to 1943," Ph.D. dissertation, University of Toronto.

Levy, H., and Lerman, Z. (1988), "The Benefits of International Diversification in Bonds," *Financial Analysts Journal* (Sept./Oct.): 56–64.

Levy, H., and Markowitz, H. (1979), "Approximating Expected Utility by a Function of Mean and Variance," *American Economic Review* 69: 308–17.

Levy, H., and Sarnat, M. (1970), "International Diversification of Investment Portfolios," *American Economic Review* 60: 668–75.

Lewis, M. (1989), *Liar's Poker: Rising Through the Wreckage on Wall Street*, New York: Norton.

Liang, B. (2000), "Hedge Funds: The Living and the Dead," *Journal of Financial and Quantitative Analysis* 35: 309–26.

Lien, D. (1989a), "Cash Settlement Provisions on Futures Contracts," *Journal of Futures Markets* 9: 263–270.

Lien, D. (1989b), "Sampled Data as a Basis of Cash Settlement Price," *Journal of Futures Markets* 9: 583–588.

Lim. K-G. (1989), "A New Test of the Three Moment Capital Asset Pricing Model," *Journal of Financial and Quantitative Analysis* 24: 205–16.

Lindblom, C. (1968), *The Policy-Making Process*, Englewood Cliffs, NJ: Prentice-Hall.

Livingston, M. (1984), "The Cheapest Deliverable Bond for the CBT Treasury Bond Futures Contract," *Journal of Futures Markets* 4: 161–92.

Livingston, M. (1987), "The Effect of Coupon Level on Treasury Bond Futures Delivery," *Journal of Futures Markets* 7: 303–309.

Loistl, O. (1976), "The Erroneous Approximation of Expected Utility by Means of a Taylor's Series Expansion: Analytic and Computational Results," *American Economic Review* 66: 904–10.

London, A. (1981), "The Stability of the Interest Parity Relationship between Canada and the United States," *Review of Economics and Statistics* 63: 625–6.

Lopez, J. (1999), "Methods for Evaluating Value-at-Risk Estimates," Federal Reserve Bank of San Francisco *Economic Review* (2): 3–17.

Luehrman, T. (1990), "The Exchange Rate Exposure of a Global Competitor," *Journal of International Business Studies*: 225–242.

Luenberger, D. (1998), *Investment Science*, New York: Oxford UP.

Ma, C. (1985), "Spreading Between the Gold and Silver Markets: Is there a Parity?," *Journal of Futures Markets* 5: 579–94.

Macbeth, J., and Merville, L. (1979), "An Empirical Examination of the Black-Scholes Call Option Pricing Model," *Journal of Finance* 34: 1173–86.

MacDonald, S., and Hein, S. (1989), "Futures Rates and Forward Rates as Predictors of Near-Term Treasury Bill Rates," *Journal of Futures Markets* 9: 242–62.

Mackay, C. (1852), *Extraordinary Popular Delusions and the Madness of Crowds* (2nd ed.); reprinted by New York: Bonanza Books (1980); first edition (1841).

MacPherson, I. (1979), *Each for All: A History of the Co-operative Movement in English Canada 1900–1945*, Toronto: University of Toronto Press.

Madura, J., and Reiff, W. (1985), "A Hedge Strategy for International Portfolios," *Journal of Portfolio Management* 12 (Fall): 70–74.

Madura, J., and Tucker, A. (1992), "Hedging International Stock Portfolios: Lessons from the 1987 Crash," *Journal of Portfolio Management* 18 (Spring): 69–73.

Maldonado, R., and Saunders, A. (1981), "International Portfolio Diversification and the Inter-Temporal Stability of International Stock Market Relationships, 1957–78," *Financial Management* 10: 54–63.

Malliaris, A., and Brock, W. (1982), *Stochastic Methods in Economics and Finance*, Amsterdam: North Holland.

Malz, A. (1997), "Estimating the Probability Distribution of the Future Exchange Rate from Option Prices," *Journal of Derivatives* 5: 18–36.

Malz, A. (2000), "Vega Risk and the Smile," RiskMetrics Group Working Paper #99–06, February.

Mandron, A. (1988), "Some Empirical Evidence about Canadian Stock Options, Parts I: Valuation and Part II: Market Structure," *Canadian Journal of Administrative Science* (June).

Margrabe, W. (1978), "The Value of an Option to Exchange One Asset for Another," *Journal of Finance* 33: 177–186.

Markham, J (1987), *The History of Commodity Futures Tading and Its Regulation*, Praeger.

Markowitz, H. (1999), "The Early History of Portfolio Theory," *Financial Analysts Journal* (July/August): 5–16.

Marshall, C., and Siegel, M. (1996), "Value at Risk: Implementing a Risk Measurement Standard," Wharton Financial Institutions Center, Working Paper #96–47.

Marshall, J. (1989), *Futures and Option Contracting*, Cincinnati: Southwestern.

Marston, R. (1976), "Interest Arbitrage in the Euro-Currency Markets," *European Economic Review* 7: 1–13.

Mason, S., Merton, R., Perold, A., and Tufano, P. (1995), *Cases in Financial Engineering*, Englewood Cliffs, NJ: Prentice Hall.

McCalla, A., and Schmitz, A. (1979), "Grain Marketing Systems: The Case of the United States versus Canada," *American Journal of Agricultural Economics* 61 (May): 199–212.

McCarthy, E. (2000), "Derivatives Revisited," *Journal of Accountancy* (May): 35–43.

McCurdy, T., and Morgan, J. (1988) "Testing the Martingale Hypothesis in Deutsche Mark Futures with Models Specifying the Form of Heteroskedasticity." *Journal of Applied Econometrics* 3: 187–202.

McDermott, E. (1979), "Defining Manipulation in Commodity Futures Trading: The Futures 'Squeeze'," *Northwestern University Law Review* 74: 202–25.

McKean, H. (1965), "Appendix: A Free Boundary Problem for the Heat Equation Arising from a Problem in Mathematical Economics," *Industrial Management Review* 6: 32–39.

Mello, A., and Parsons, J. (1995a), "Maturity Structure of the Hedge Matters: Lessons from the Metallgesellschaft Debacle," *Journal of Applied Corporate Finance* 8: 106–120.

Mello, A., and Parsons, J. (1995b), "Hedging a Flow of Commodity Deliveries with Futures: Problems with a Rolling Stack Hedge," *Derivatives Quarterly* (Summer): 16–19.

Merton, R. (1993), "Operation and Regulation in Financial Intermediation: A Functional Perspective," in Peter England (Ed.), *Operation and Regulation of Financial Markets* Stockholm: Ekonomiska Radet.

Merton, R. (1977), "An Analytic Derivation of the Cost of Deposit Insurance and Loan Guarantees: An Application of Modern Option Pricing Theory," *Journal of Banking and Finance* 1: 3–11.

Merton, R. (1976), "Option Pricing when the Underlying Stock Returns are Discontinuous," *Journal of Financial Economics*, 3: 125–44.

Merton, R. (1973), "The Theory of Rational Option Pricing," *Bell Journal of Economics and Management Science*, 4: 141–83.

Meyer, J (1987), "Two-Moment Decision Models and Expected Utility Maximization," *American Economic Review* 77: 421–30.

Meyer, P. (1976), *Un Cours sur les Integrales Stochastiques*, Lecture Notes in Mathematics, no. 511, New York: Springer-Verlag.

Mian, S. (1996), "Evidence on Corporate Hedging Policy," *Journal of Financial and Quantitative Analysis* 31: 419–439

Milevsky, M. (1998), "Asian Options, the Sum of Lognormals, and the Reciprocal Gamma Distribution," *Journal of Financial and Quantitative Analysis* 33: 409–23.

Miller, K. (1992), "A Framework for Integrated Risk Management in International Business," *Journal of International Business Studies*: 311–31.

Miller, M., and Ross, D. (1997), "The Orange County Bankruptcy and its Aftermath: Some New Evidence," *Journal of Derivatives* 5: 51–60.

Modest, D., and Sundaresan, S. (1982), "The Relationship Between Spot and Futures Prices in the Stock Index Futures Markets," mimeo, Columbia University.

Monroe, M. (1992), "Volatility Spreads," *Journal of Futures Markets* 12: 1–9.

Monroe, M., and Cohn, R. (1986), "The Relative Efficiency of the Gold and Treasury Bill Futures Markets," *Journal of Futures Markets* 6: 477–94.

Morgan, V., and Thomas, W. (1962), *The Stock Exchange*, New York: St. Martins.

Mortimer, T. (1761), *Everyman his Own Broker; or a Guide to Exchange Alley* (2nd ed.), London: S. Hooper; with the 13th ed. published (1801).

Mueller, P. (1981), "Covered Call Options: An Alternative Investment Strategy," *Financial Management* 10: 64–71.

Muth, J. (1961), "Rational Expectations and the Theory of Price Movements," *Econometrica* 29 (July): 315–335.

Myers, R., and Thompson, S. (1989), "Generalized Optimal Hedge Ratio Estimation," *American Journal of Agricultural Economics* 71: 858–68.

Myneni, R. (1992), "The Pricing of the American Option," *Annals of Applied Probability* 2: 1–23.

Nance, D., Smith, C., and Smithson, C. (1993), "On the Determinants of Corporate Hedging," *Journal of Finance* 48: 267–284.

Natenberg, S. (1988), *Option Volatility and Pricing Strategies*, Chicago: Probus.

Neal, L. (1990), *The Rise of Financial Capitalism, International Capital Markets in the Age of Reason*, Cambridge: Cambridge University Press.

Neal, R. (1996), "Direct Tests of Index Arbitrage Models," *Journal of Financial and Quantitative Analysis* 31: 541–562.

Nelson, D. (1990), "ARCH Models as Diffusion Approximations," *Journal of Econometrics* 45: 7–38.

Nisbet, M. (1992), "Put-Call Parity Theory and an Empirical Test of the Efficiency of the London Traded Options Market," *Journal of Banking & Finance* 16: 381–403.

O'Brien, T. (1997), "Accounting versus Economic Exposure to Currency Risk," *Journal of Financial Statement Analysis* (Summer): 21–29.

Officer, L. (1976), "The Purchasing-Power-Parity Theory of Exchange Rates," *IMF Staff Papers* 23: 1–60.

Ormiston, M., and Quiggin, J. (1994), "Two-Parameter Decision Models and Rank-Dependent Expected Utility," *Journal of Risk and Uncertainty* 8: 273–82.

Otani, I., and Tiwari, S. (1981), "Capital Controls and the Interest Parity Rate: The Japanese Experience, 1978–81," *I.M.F. Staff Papers* 28 (Dec.): 793–815.

Overdahl, J., and Schachter, B. (1997). "Derivatives Regulation and Financial Management: Lessons from Gibson Greetings," *Financial Management* 24: 68–78.

Overturf, S. (1986), "Interest Rate Expectations and Interest Parity," *Journal of International Money and Finance* 5: 91–98.

Oxelheim, L., and Wihlborg, C. (1997), *Managing in the Turbulent World Economy: Corporate Performance and Risk Exposure*, New York: Wiley.

Papoulis, A. (1965), *Probability, Random Variables, and Stochastic Processes*, New York: McGraw Hill.

Paul, A. (1982), "The Past and Future of the Commodities Exchanges," *Agricultural History* 56: 287–305.

Pearson, N. (1995), "An Efficient Approach for Pricing Spread Options," *Journal of Derivatives* 3: 76–91.

Pennings, J., and Leuthold, R. (2000), "The Motivations for Hedging Revisited," *Journal of Futures Markets* 20: 865–85.

Perold, A., and Schulman, E. (1988), "The Free Lunch in Currency Hedging: Implications for Investment Policy and Performance Standards," *Financial Analysts Journal* (May/June): 45–50.

Perry, R. (Ed.) (1997), *Accounting for Derivatives*, New York: Irwin Professional.

Peterson, R. (1977), "Investor Preferences for Futures Straddles," *Journal of Financial and Quantitative Analysis* 12: 105–120.

Phillips, A. (1995). "Derivatives Practices and Instruments Survey," *Financial Management* 24: 115–125.

Phillips, R., Cummins, D., and Allen, F. (1998), "Financial Pricing of Insurance in the Multiple-Line Insurance Company," *Journal of Risk and Insurance* 65: 597–636.

Pippinger, J. (1982), "PPP: An Analysis of Predictive Error," *Canadian Journal of Economics* 15: 335–46.

Poitras, G. (2001a), "Short Sales Restrictions, Dilution and Rights Issues on the Stock Exchange of Singapore," *Pacific Basin Journal of Finance* (forthcoming).

Poitras, G. (2001b), "The Crack Spread," SFU Working Paper.

Poitras, G. (2000), *The Early History of Financial Economics, 1478–1776*, Aldershot, UK: Edward Elgar.

Poitras, G. (1999), "Fully Hedged Borrowings, Currency Swaps and Covered Interest Arbitrage," paper presented to the 1999 Meetings of the Canadian Economics Association, Vancouver BC.

Poitras, G. (1998a), "TED Tandems: Arbitrage Restrictions and the Eurodollar/Treasury Bill Futures Spread," *International Review of Economics and Finance* 7: 255–78.

Poitras, G. (1998b), "Spread Options, Exchange Options and Arithmetic Brownian Motion," *Journal of Futures Markets* 18: 487–517.

Poitras, G. (1997), "Tails, Turtles and Stereos: Arbitrage and the Design of Futures Spread Trading Strategies," *Journal of Derivatives* 5: 71–87.

Poitras, G. (1994a), "Shareholder Wealth Maximization, Business Ethics and Social Responsibility," *Journal of Business Ethics* 13: 125–34.

Poitras, G. (1994b), *Derivative Security Analysis*, Vancouver: TK Books.

Poitras, G. (1993), "Crop Insurance and Hedging," *Journal of Futures Markets* 13: 373–88.

Poitras, G. (1992), "Long Term Covered Interest Parity and the International Swap Market," *Asia Pacific Journal of Management* 9: 39–49.

Poitras, G. (1991), "The When-Issued Market for Government of Canada Treasury Bills," *Canadian Journal of Economics* 24: 604–23.

Poitras, G. (1989a), "Optimal Futures Spread Positions," *Journal of Futures Markets* 9: 397–412.

Poitras, G. (1989b), "TED's and Triggers: Fundamentals of Trading the Eurodollar/US Treasury Bill Futures Spread," in *Selected Papers of the Fourth International Futures Conference and Research Seminar*, Lloyd Besant, Ed., Toronto: Canadian Securities Institute.

Poitras, G. (1988a) "Hedging Canadian Treasury Bill Positions with US Money Market Futures." *Review of Futures Markets* 7: 176–191.

Poitras, G. (1988b) "Arbitrage Boundaries, Treasury Bills, and Covered Interest Parity." *Journal of International Money and Finance* 7: 429–445.

Poitras, G. (1987), "Golden Turtle Tracks: In Search of Unexploited Profits in Gold Spreads," *Journal of Futures Markets* 7: 397–412.

Poitras, G., and Heaney, J. (1999), "Skewness Preference, Mean-Variance and the Optimal Demand for Put Options," *Managerial and Decision Economics* 20: 327–42.

Popper, H., (1993), "Long-Term Covered Interest Parity: Evidence from Currency Swaps," *Journal of International Money and Finance* 12: 439–48.

Posthumus, N. (1929), "The Tulip Mania in Holland in the Years 1636 and 1637," *Journal of Economic and Business History* 1 (May): 434–91.

Powers, M., and Vogel, R. (1983), *Inside the Financial Futures Markets* New York: Wiley.

Prachowny, M. (1970), "A Note on Interest Parity and the Supply of Arbitrage Funds," *Journal of Political Economy* 78: 540–45.

Prakash, A., Chang, C., Hamid, S., and Smyser, M. (1996), "Why a Decision Maker May Prefer a Seemingly Unfair Gamble," *Decision Sciences* 27: 239–53.

President's Working Group on Financial Markets (1999), *Report:* "Hedge Funds, Leverage and the Lessons of Long-Term Capital Management," Washington, D.C.: US Government Printing Office.

Price, J., and Henderson, S. (1988), *Currency and Interest Rate Swaps* (2nd ed.), London: Butterworths.

Pring, M. J. (1991). *Technical Analysis Explained*, (3rd ed.), New York: McGraw-Hill.

Rabinovitch, R. (1989), "Pricing Stock and Bond Options When the Default-Free Rate Is Stochastic," *Journal of Financial and Quantitative Analysis* 24: 447–57.

Ramaswamy, K., and Sundaresan, S. (1985), "The Valuation of Options on Futures Contracts," *Journal of Finance* 39: 1319–40.

Rance, B. (1995), "The Commodity Futures Trading Commission Order of Settlement with MG Refining and Marketing, Inc. and MF Futures, Inc.," *Derivatives Quarterly* (Winter): 13–17.

Rechner, D. (1990), "Putting on the Crush: Market Structure and the Soybean Complex," unpublished M.A. thesis, Simon Fraser University.

Rechner, D., and Poitras, G., (1993), "Putting on the Crush: Day Trading the Soybean Complex Spread," *Journal of Futures Markets* 13: 61–75.

Rees, G. L. (1972), *Britain's Commodity Markets*, London: Paul Elek.

Reilly, F. (1989), *Investment Analysis and Portfolio Analysis*, Chicago: Dryden.

Reinach, A. (1961), *The Nature of Puts and Calls*, New York: Bookmailer.

Reitano, R. (1991), "Multivariate Duration Analysis," *Transactions of the Society of Actuaries* 43: 335–91.

Reitano, R. (1992), "Non-Parallel Yield Curve Shifts and Immunization," *Journal of Portfolio Management* 18 (Spring): 36–43.

Reitano, R. (1996), "Non-Parallel Yield Curve Shifts and Stochastic Immunization," *Journal of Portfolio Management* 22: 71–78.

Rendleman, R., and Carabini, C. (1979) "The Efficiency of the Treasury Bill Futures Market." *Journal of Finance* 34: 895–914.

Rentzler, J. (1986), "Trading Treasury Bond Spreads against Treasury Bill Futures—A Model and Test of the Turtle Trade," *Journal of Futures Markets* 6: 41–62.

Rich, D. (1994), "The Mathematical Foundations of Barrier Option-Pricing Theory," *Advances in Futures and Options Research* 7: 267–311.

Richard, F., and Sundaresan, S. (1981). "A Continuous Time Equilibrium Model of Forward Prices and Futures Prices in a Multigood Economy," *Journal of Financial Economics* 9: 347–372.

RiskMetrics, see J. P. Morgan reference.

Ritchken, P. (1987), *Options: Theory, Strategy and Applications*, Glenview, Ill.: Scott, Foresman.

Ritchken, P., and Salkin, H. (1981), "Safety First Selection Techniques for Option Spreads," *Journal of Portfolio Management* 9: 61–67.

Ritchken, P., and Trevor, R. (1999), "Pricing Options under Generalized GARCH and Stochastic Volatility Processes," *Journal of Finance* 54: 377–402.

Rogers, L., and Williams, D. (1987), *Diffusions, Markov Processes and Martingales* V.2 *Ito Calculus*, New York: Wiley.

Roll, R. (1979), "Violations of the Law of One Price and their Implications for Differentially-Denominated Assets," in Sarnat and Szego, *International Trade and Finance*.

Roll, R. (1978), "Ambiguity When Performance is Measured by the Security Market Line," *Journal of Finance* 33: 1051–69.

Roll, R. (1977), "An Analytical Formula for Unprotected American Call Options on Stocks with Known Dividends," *Journal of Financial Economics* 5: 251–58.

Rubinstein, M. (1991a), "Exotic Options," University of California at Berkeley Finance Working Paper #220, December.

Rubinstein, M. (1991b), "Somewhere Over the Rainbow," *Risk* (November): 63–66.

Rubinstein, M. (1976), "The Valuation of Uncertain Income Streams and the Pricing of Options," *Bell Journal of Economics* 7: 407–25.

Rubinstein, M. (1985), "Alternative Paths to Portfolio Insurance," *Financial Analysts Journal* (July/August): 42–51.

Rubinstein, R., and Leland, H. (1981), "Replicating Options with Positions in Stock and Cash," *Financial Analysts Journal* (July/August): 63–72.

Rudin, W. (1964), *Principles of Mathematical Analysis*, New York, McGraw-Hill.

Sabatini, M., and Linton, M. (1998), "A GARCH Model of the Implied Volatility of the Swiss Market Index from Option Prices," *International Journal of Forecasting* 14: 199–214.

Samuelson, P. (1969), "Lifetime Portfolio Selection by Dynamic Stochastic Programming," *Review of Economics and Statistics* 51: 239–46.

Samuelson, P. (1965), "Rational Theory of Warrant Pricing," *Industrial Management Review* 6: 13–31.

Sansom, G. (1964), *A History of Japan: 1615–1867* London: Cresset Press.

Sarnoff, P. (1980), *The Silver Bulls*, Westport, CN: Arlington House,

Sawiak, G. (1986), *The Toronto Stock Exchange*, Toronto: Butterworths.

SBC Warburg Dillon Read (1998), *The Practice of Risk Management*, London: Euromoney Books.

Schaede, U. (1989), "Forwards and Futures in Tokugawa-Period Japan," *Journal of Banking and Finance* 13: 487–513.

Schap, K. (1991), "Refining the Trading Mechanism to Improve Refinery Profits," *Futures: The Magazine of Commodities & Options* 20 (October): 34–36.

Schap, K. (1992), "Trading Techniques: Feeding Cattle on Paper," *Futures: The Magazine of Commodities & Options* 21 (October): 46–48.

Schap, K. (1993), "Energy Omens Signal Bullish Prospects," *Futures: The Magazine of Commodities & Options* 22 (February): 26–28.

Schneeweis, T., and Spurgin, R. (1998), "Multifactor Analysis of Hedge Funds, Managed Futures, and Mutual Fund Return and Risk Characteristics," *Journal of Alternative Investments* 1: 1–24.

Scholes, M. (2001), "Risk Management," paper presented to the annual meeting of the Asia-Pacific Finance Association, Bangkok, Thailand.

Schrand, C., and Unal, H. (1998), "Hedging and Coordinated Risk Management: Evidence from Thrift Conversions," *Journal of Finance* 53: 979–1013.

Schwager, J. (1984), *A Complete Guide to Futures Markets*, New York: Wiley.

Schwager, J. D. (1995), *Schwager on Futures: Fundamental Analysis*, New York: John Wiley and Sons

Schwartz, E. (1982), "The Pricing of Commodity-Linked Bonds," *Journal of Finance* 37: 525–39.

Scott, L. (1997), "Pricing Stock Options in a Jump-Diffusion Model with Stochastic Volatility and Interest Rates: Applications of Fourier Inversion Methods," *Mathematical Finance* 7: 413–26.

Scott, L. (1989), "Estimating the Marginal Rate of Substitution in Intertemporal Capital Asset Pricing Models," *Review of Economics and Statistics* 71: 365–75.

Scott, L. (1987), "Option Pricing when the Variance Changes Rapidly: Theory, Estimation and an Application," *Journal of Financial and Quantitative Analysis* 22: 419–38.

Sears, R., and Trennepohl, G. (1983), "Diversification and Skewness in Option Portfolios," *Journal of Financial Research* 6 (Fall): 199–212.

Sephton, P. (1992), "Optimal Hedge Ratios for the Winnipeg Commodity Exchange," *Canadian Journal of Economics* 25: 156–71.

Sercu, P. (1980), "A Generalization of the International Asset Pricing Model," *Revue de l'Association Francaise de Finance* 1 (June): 91–135.

Shaeffer, H. (2000), *Credit Risk Management* New York: Wiley.

Shapiro, A. (1999), *Multinational Financial Management* (6th ed.), Saddle River, NJ: Prentice-Hall.

Shapiro, A. (1992), *Multinational Financial Management*, Boston: Allyn and Bacon.

Shapiro, A. (1984), "Currency Risk and Relative Price Risk," *Journal of Financial and Quantitative Analysis* 19: 365–373.

Shapiro, A. (1983), "What Does Purchasing Power Parity Mean?" *Journal of International Money and Finance* 2: 295–318.

Shapiro, A. (May 1975), "Exchange Rate Changes, Inflation and the Value of the Multinational Corporation," *Journal of Finance* 30: 485–502.

Sharpe, I. (1985), "Interest Parity, Monetary Policy and the Volatility of Australian Short-Term Interest Rates: 1978–82," *Economic Record* 61: 436–44.

Shastri, K., and Tandon, K. (1986a) "Valuation of Foreign Currency Options: Some Empirical Tests," *Journal of Financial and Quantitative Analysis* 21: 145–60.

Shastri, K., and Tandon, K. (1986b), "An Empirical Test of a Valuation Model for American Options on Futures Contracts," *Journal of Financial and Quantitative Analysis* 21: 377–392.

Shastri, K., and Tandon, K. (1986c), "On the Use of European Models to Price American Options on Foreign Currency," *Journal of Futures Markets* 6: 83–108.

Shepp, L., and Shirayev, N. (1993), "The Russian Option: Reduced Regret," *Annals of Applied Probability* 3: 631–40.

Shimko, D. (1992), "The Valuation of Multiple Claim Insurance Contracts," *Journal of Financial and Quantitative Analysis* 27: 229–246.

Shimko, D. (1994), "Options on Futures Spreads: Hedging, Speculation and Valuation," *Journal of Futures Markets* 14: 183–213.

Siegel, D., and Siegel, D. (1990), *Futures Markets*, Chicago: Dryden Press.

Silber, W. (1984), "Marketmaker Behavior in an Auction Market: An Analysis of Scalpers in Futures Markets," *Journal of Finance* 39: 937–954.

Simaan, V. (1993), "Portfolio Selection and Asset Pricing—Three Parameter Framework," *Management Science* 39: 568–77.

Simon, D. (1999), "The Soybean Crush Spread: Empirical Evidence and Trading Strategies," *Journal of Futures Markets* 3: 271–89.

Smith, A. (1986), *Trading Financial Options*, London: Butterworths.

Smith, C. (1995), "Corporate Risk Management: Theory and Practice," *Journal of Derivatives* 3: 21–30.

Smith, C. (1979), "Applications of Option Pricing Analysis," Chap. 4 in J. Bicksler, (Ed.), *Handbook of Financial Economics*, Amsterdam: North Holland.

Smith, C. (1976), "Option Pricing: A Review," *Journal of Financial Economics* 3: 3–51.

Smith, C., and Stulz, R. (1985), "The Determinants of Firms' Hedging Policies," *Journal of Financial and Quantitative Analysis* 20: 391–405.

Smith, D. (1991), "A Simple Method for Pricing Interest Rate Swaptions," *Financial Analysts Journal*, (May/June): 72–6.

Smith, D. (1997), "Aggressive Corporate Finance: A Close Look at the Procter & Gamble-Bankers Trust Leveraged Swap," *Journal of Derivatives* 5: 67–79.

Smithson, C., Smith, C., and Wilford, D. (1995), *Managing Financial Risk*, New York: Irwin.

Soffer, L. (2000), "SFAS No. 123 Disclosures and Discounted Cash Flow Valuation," *Accounting Horizons* 14: 169–89.

Solnik, B. (1974), "Why not Diversify Internationally Rather than Nationally?," *Financial Analysts Journal* (July/August): 48–54.

Solnik, B. (1991), *International Investments* (2nd ed.), New York: Addison-Wesley.

Stassen, H. (1984), "Regulatory Considerations," chapter 20 in N. Rothstein (ed.), *The Handbook of Financial Futures*, New York: McGraw-Hill.

Stein, J. (1989), "Overreactions in the Options Market," *Journal of Finance* 44: 1011–1023.

Sterk, W. (1983), "Comparative Performance of the Black-Scholes and Roll-Geske-Whalley Option Pricing Models," *Journal of Financial and Quantitative Analysis* 18: 345–54.

Stigum, M. (1990), *The Money Market* (2nd ed.), Homewood, Ill.: Dow Jones-Irwin.

Stigum, M. (1983) *The Money Market*, Homewood, Ill.: Dow-Jones/Irwin.

Stockman, A. (1978), "Risk, Information and Foreign Exchange Rates," in J. Frenkel and H. Johnson (Eds.), *The Economics of Exchange Rates*, Reading, Mass.: Addison-Wesley, Chap. 9.

Stoll, H. (1969), "The Relationship Between Put and Call Options Prices," *Journal of Finance* 24: 802–24.

Stoll, H., and Whalley, R. (1993), *Futures and Options*, New York: Wiley.

Stulz, R. (1984), "Optimal Hedging Policies," *Journal of Financial and Quantitative Analysis* 19: 127–40.

Sundaresan, S. (1997), *Fixed Income Markets and Their Derivatives*, Cincinatti: Southwestern.

Sundaresan, S. (1991), "Futures Prices on Yields, Forward Prices and Implied Forward Prices from the Term Structure," *Journal of Financial and Quantitative Analysis* 26: 409–24.

Takezawa, N. (1995), "Three Empirical Essays in International Financial Economics," unpublished Ph.D. thesis, Simon Fraser University.

Taylor, C. H. (1917), *History of the Board of Trade of the City of Chicago*, Chicago: Robert O. Law Co.

Telser, L. (1958), "Futures Trading and the Storage of Cotton and Wheat," *Journal of Political Economy* 68: 235–53.

Telser, L. G. (1981), "Margins and Futures Contracts," *Journal of Futures Markets* 1: 225–253.

Telser, L., and Higinbotham, H. (1977), "Organized Futures Markets: Costs and Benefits," *Journal of Political Economy* 85: 969–1000.

Teweles, J., and Bradley, E. (1982), *The Stock Market* (4th ed.), New York: Wiley.

Tilley, J. (1993), "Valuing American Options in a Path Simulation Model," *Transactions of the Society of Actuaries* 45: 499–549.

Toevs, A., and Jacob, D. (1986), "Futures and Alternative Hedge Ratio Methodologies," *Journal of Portfolio Management* 12: 60–70.

Tomek, W., and Peterson, H. (2001), "Risk Management in Agricultural Markets: A Review," *Journal of Futures Markets* 21: 955–985.

Tosini, P. (1988), "Stock Index Futures and Stock Market Activity in October 1987," *Financial Analysts Journal* (Jan./Feb): 28–37.

Trigeorgis, L. (1996), *Real Options: Managerial Flexibility and Strategy in Resource Allocation*, Cambridge, Mass.: MIT Press.

Tufano, P. (1996). "Who Manages Risk? An Empirical Examination of Risk Management Practices in the Gold Mining Industry," *Journal of Finance* 51: 1097–1138

Tufano, P. (1998), "The Determinants of Stock Price Exposure: Financial Engineering and the Gold Mining Industry," *Journal of Finance* 53: 1015–1052.

Turnbull, S. (1987), *Option Valuation*, Dryden Press.

Turnovsky, S. (1983), "The Determination of Spot and Futures Prices with Storable Commodities," *Econometrica* 51: 1363–88.

Turvey, C., and Baker, T. (1989), "Optimal Hedging Under Alternative Capital Structures," *Canadian Journal of Agricultural Economics* 37: 135–43.

Tzang, D., and Leuthold, R. (1990), "Hedge Ratios Under Inherent Risk Reduction in a Commodity Complex," *Journal of Futures Markets* 10: 497–504.

Ulen, T. (1982), "The Regulation of Grain Warehousing and its Economic Effects: The Competitive Position of Chicago in the 1870's and 1880's," *Agricultural History* 56: 94–210.

Uppal, R., and Sercu, P. (1995), *International Financial Markets and the Firm*, London: Chapman & Hall.

van der Wee, H. (1977), "Monetary, Credit and Banking Systems," in Rich and Wilson (Eds), *The Cambridge Economic History of Europe* vol. 5, London: Cambridge University Press.

van Dillen, J. (1935), "Issac le Maire et le commerce des actions de la Compaigne de Indes Orientales," *Revue d'Histoire Moderne*: 5–21, 121–37.

van Dillen, J. (1930), "Issac Le Maire en de handel in actien der Oost-Indische Compagnie," *Economisch-Historisch Jaarboek*: 1–165.

Vaughan, E. (1982), *Fundamentals of Risk and Insurance*, New York: Wiley.

Vignola, A., and Baker, C. (1979), "Market Liquidity, Security Trading and the Estimation of Empirical Yield Curves." *Review of Economics and Statistics* 61: 131–35.

von Neumann, J., and Morgenstern, O. *Theory of Games and Economic Behavior* (2nd ed.), Princeton, NJ: Princeton University Press.

Wagner, D., Ellis, D., and Dubofsky, D. (1996), "The Factors Behind Put-Call Parity Violations of S&P 100 Index Options," *The Financial Review* 31: 535–552.

Wall, L., and Pringle, J. (1989), "Alternative Explanations of Interest Rate Swaps: An Empirical Analysis," *Financial Management* 18: 119–49.

Wentzel, (1981), *A Course in the Theory of Stochastic Processes*, New York: McGraw Hill.

Weymar, H. (1968), *Dynamics of the World Cocoa Market*, Cambridge, Mass.: MIT Press.

Whaley, R. (1981), "On the Valuation of American Options on Stocks with Known Dividends," *Journal of Financial Economics* 9 (June): 207–11.

Wiggins, J. (1987), "Option Values under Stochastic Volatility: Theory and Empirical Estimates," *Journal of Financial Economics* 19: 351–72.

Wilcox, D. (1990), "Energy Futures and Options: Spread Options in Energy Markets," Goldman Sachs and Co., New York.

Wilcox, J. (2000), "Better Risk Management," *Journal of Portfolio Management* 26 (Summer): 53–64.

Williams, J. (1982), "The Origin of Futures Markets," *Agricultural History* 56: 306–325.

Williams, J. (1995), *Manipulation on Trial: Economic Analysis and the Hunt Silver Case*, Cambridge, UK: Cambridge University Press.

Wilmott, P. (1998), *Derivatives*, New York: Wiley.

Wilson, C. (1941), *Anglo-Dutch Commerce and Finance in the Eighteenth Century* London: Cambridge University Press.

Witt, H., Schroeder, T., and Hayenga, M. (1987), "Comparison of Analytical Approaches for Estimating Hedge Ratios for Agricultural Commodities," *Journal of Futures Markets* 7: 135–46.

Wolf, A. (1982), "Fundamentals of Commodity Options on Futures," *Journal of Futures Markets* 2: 391–408.

Working, H. (1977), *Selected Writings of Holbrook Working*, Chicago: Chicago Board of Trade.

Working, H. (1962), "New Concepts Concerning Futures Markets and Prices," *American Economic Review* 52: 432–59.

Working, H. (1963), "Futures Markets Under Renewed Attack," *Food Research Institute Studies* 4: 13–24.

Working, H. (1949), "The Theory of Price of Storage," *American Economic Review* 39: 1254–1262.

Xu, X., and Taylor, S. (1995), "Conditional Volatility and the Informational Efficiency of the PHLX Currency Options Market," *Journal of Banking and Finance* 19: 803–21.

Xu, X., and Taylor, S. (1994), "The Term Structure of Volatility Implied by Foreign Exchange Options," *Journal of Financial and Quantitative Analysis* 29: 57–74.

Yano, A. (1989), "Configurations for Arbitrage Using Financial Futures," *Journal of Futures Markets* 9: 439–48.

Yates, J., and Kopprasch, R. (1980), "Writing Covered Call Options: Profits and Risks," *Journal of Portfolio Management* 6: 74–80.

Zhang, P. (1998), *Exotic Options*, London: World Scientific.

Zivney, T. (1991), "The Value of Early Exercise in Option Prices: An Empirical Investigation," *Journal of Financial and Quantitative Analysis* 26: 129–38.

Zurack, D. (1984), "The Many Forms of Portfolio Insurance," Oct. 16, 1984, Goldman-Sachs Stock Index Research.

INDEX